# FOR STUDENTS

**Over the past four years we have spent time in classrooms across Canada, speaking to students just like you.**

We've asked what you want to see in a textbook, how you learn, how many hours a week you spend online, and what you find most valuable when preparing for a test. Based on your feedback, we've developed a new hybrid learning solution—**ORGB**. Your textbook, the Chapter Review cards, and our online resources present a new, exciting, and fresh approach to learning. Check out the website at **www.icanorgb.com** for an unrivalled set of learning tools.

- Interactive quizzing
- Interactive eBook
- Key Term Flashcards
- Interactive Games
- Audio chapter summaries
- Cases and Exercises
- PowerPoint slides
- Videos
- **And more!**

Purestock/Getty Images

# NELSON / EDUCATION

**ORGB, Canadian Edition**

by Debra L. Nelson, James Campbell Quick,
Ann Armstrong, and Joan Condie

**Vice President,
Editorial Director:**
Evelyn Veitch

**Editor-in-Chief,
Higher Education:**
Anne Williams

**Acquisitions Editor:**
Amie Plourde

**Marketing Manager:**
Kathaleen McCormick

**Developmental Editor:**
Toula Di Leo

**Photo Researcher:**
Indu Arora

**Permissions Coordinator:**
Indu Arora

**Content Production Manager:**
Jennifer Hare

**Production Service:**
MPS Limited, a Macmillan Company

**Copy Editor:**
Karen Rolfe

**Proofreader:**
Barbara Storey

**Indexer:**
Maura Brown

**Manufacturing Manager:**
Joanne McNeil

**Design Director:**
Ken Phipps

**Managing Designer:**
Franca Amore

**Interior Design Revisions:**
Peter Papayanakis

**Cover Design:**
Dianna Little

**Cover Image:**
Ben Blankenburg/Corbis

**Compositor:**
MPS Limited, a Macmillan Company

**Printer:**
RR Donnelley

**Library and Archives Canada
Cataloguing in Publication Data**

ORGB / Debra L. Nelson ... [et al.].
— 1st Canadian ed.

Includes bibliographical references
and index.
ISBN: 978-0-17-650283-6

1. Organizational behavior—
Textbooks. I. Nelson, Debra L.,
1956–

HD58.7.O76 2011          302.3'5
C2010-907810-1

ISBN-13: 978-0-17-650283-6
ISBN-10: 0-17-650283-1

# Brief Contents

## Part 1
### Introduction

## Part 2
### Individual Processes and Behaviour

## Part 3
### Interpersonal Processes and Behaviour

## Part 4
### Organizational Processes and Structure

# Contents

## Chapter 3
## Personality, Perception, and Attribution   36

## Chapter 4
## Attitudes, Emotions, and Ethics   56

## Chapter 5
## Motivation at Work   74

## Chapter 6
## Learning and Performance Management  90

## Chapter 7
## Stress and Well-Being at Work  104

## Part 3
## Interpersonal Processes and Behaviour  122

## Chapter 8
## Communication  122

## Chapter 9
## Work Teams and Groups 138

## Chapter 10
## Decision Making by Individuals and Groups 154

## Chapter 14
## Jobs and the Design of Work  228

## Chapter 15
## Organizational Design and Structure  244

## Chapter 16
## Organizational Culture  262

**Chapter 17**
Managing Change  280

**Chapter 18**
Career Management  298

# Organizational Behaviour and Opportunity

> **"** *Organizations have been described as clockworks, but they often seem like snake pits.* **"**

# Human Behaviour in Organizations

Human behaviour in organizations is complex and often difficult to understand. Organizations have been described as clockworks in which human behaviour is logical and rational, but they often seem like snake pits to those who work in them.[1] The clockwork metaphor reflects an orderly, idealized view of organizational behaviour devoid of conflict or dilemma because all the working parts (the people) are believed to mesh smoothly. The snake pit metaphor conveys the daily conflicts, distress, and struggle in organizations. Each metaphor reflects reality from a different perspective—the organization's versus the individual's point of view. These metaphors reflect the complexity of human behaviour, the dark side of which is seen in cases of road rage and workplace violence. On the positive side, the Gallup Organization's Marcus Buckingham suggests that people's psychological makeup is at the heart of the emotional economy.[2]

This chapter introduces organizational behaviour. The first section provides an overview of human behaviour in organizations, its interdisciplinary origins, and behaviour in times of change. The second section presents an organizational context within which behaviour occurs. The third section highlights the **opportunities** that exist in times of **change** and **challenge** for people at work.[3]

**opportunities**
Favourable times or chances for progress and advancement.

**change**
The transformation or modification of an organization and/or its stakeholders.

**challenge**
The call to competition, contest, or battle.

## LEARNING OUTCOMES

After reading this chapter, you should be able to do the following:

**1** Define *organizational behaviour*.

**2** Identify four action steps for responding positively in times of change.

**3** Identify the important system components of an organization.

**4** Describe the formal and informal elements of an organization.

**5** Understand the diversity of organizations in the economy.

**6** Evaluate the opportunities that change creates for organizational behaviour.

**7** Demonstrate the value of objective knowledge and skill development in the study of organizational behaviour.

**8** Explain the process of organizational design thinking.

The fourth section addresses the ways people learn about organizational behaviour and explains how the text's pedagogical features relate to the various learning styles. The final section presents the plan for the book.

**Organizational behaviour** is individual behaviour and group dynamics in organizations. The study of organizational behaviour is primarily concerned with the psychosocial, interpersonal, and behavioural dynamics in organizations. However, organizational variables that affect human behaviour at work are also relevant to the study of organizational behaviour. These organizational variables include jobs, the design of work, communication, performance appraisal, organizational design, and organizational structure.

## Understanding Human Behaviour

The vast majority of theories and models of human behaviour fall into two basic categories. One category has an internal perspective, and the other an external perspective. The internal perspective looks at individuals' minds to understand their behaviour. It is psychodynamically oriented and its proponents understand human behaviour in terms of the thoughts, feelings, past experiences, and needs of the individual. The internal perspective explains people's actions and behaviour in terms of their history and personal value systems. The internal processes of thinking, feeling, perceiving, and judging lead people to act in specific ways. The internal perspective has given rise to a wide range of motivational and leadership theories. It implies that people are best understood from the inside and that people's behaviour is best interpreted alongside their thoughts and feelings.

The external perspective, on the other hand, focuses on factors outside the person to understand behaviour. People who subscribe to this view understand human behaviour in terms of the external events, consequences, and environmental forces to which a person is subject. From the external perspective, a person's history, feelings, thoughts, and personal value systems cannot help interpret actions and behaviour. This perspective has given rise to an alternative set of motivational and leadership theories, which are covered in Chapters 5 and 12. The external perspective implies that examining the surrounding external events and environmental forces is the best way to understand behaviour.

The internal and external perspectives offer alternative explanations for human behaviour. For example, the

©Amanda Rohde/iStockPhoto

internal perspective might say Mary is an outstanding employee because she has a high need for achievement, whereas the external perspective might say it is because she is extremely well-paid for her work. Kurt Lewin combined both perspectives with his claim that behaviour is a function of the person and the environment.[4]

## Interdisciplinary Influences

Organizational behaviour is a blended discipline that has grown out of contributions from numerous earlier fields of study. The sciences of psychology, sociology, engineering, anthropology, management, and medicine have each contributed to our understanding of human behaviour in organizations. These interdisciplinary influences have evolved into the independent discipline of organizational behaviour.

**Psychology**, the science of human behaviour, developed during the closing decades of the nineteenth century. Psychology traces its own origins to philosophy and the science of physiology. One of the most prominent early psychologists, William James, held a degree in medicine (M.D.). Since its origin, psychology has branched into a number of specialized fields, including clinical, experimental, organizational, and social psychology. Organizational psychology frequently overlaps with organizational behaviour; for instance, both investigate work motivation.[5] Johnson & Johnson and Chaparral Steel used World War I era psychological research for the U.S. military to develop their personnel selection methods.[6]

**Sociology**, the science of society, has contributed greatly to our knowledge of group and intergroup dynamics. Because sociology takes society rather than the individual as its point of departure, sociologists focus on the variety of roles within a society or culture, the

**organizational behaviour**
The study of individual behaviour and group dynamics in organizations.

**psychology**
The science of human behaviour.

**sociology**
The science of society.

norms and standards of behaviour in groups, and the consequences of compliant and deviant behaviour. For example, a team of Harvard educators used the concept of *role set*, i.e., "that complement of role-relationships in which persons are involved by virtue of occupying a particular social status,"[7] a key contribution of Robert Merton's 1957 role theory, to study the school superintendent role in Massachusetts.[8] More recently, the role set concept has helped explain the effects of codes of ethics in organizations.[9]

**Engineering** is the applied science of energy and matter. It enhances our understanding of the design of work. Frederick Taylor took basic engineering ideas and applied them to human behaviour at work, influencing the early study of organizational behaviour.[10] With his engineering background, Taylor placed special emphasis on human productivity and efficiency in work behaviour. His notions of performance standards and differential piece-rate systems still shape organizational goal-setting programs, such as those at Black & Decker, IBM, and Weyerhaeuser.[11]

**Anthropology**, the science of human learned behaviour, is especially important to our understanding of organizational culture. Cultural anthropology focuses on the origins of culture and the patterns of behaviour that develop with symbolic communication. Anthropological research has examined the effects of efficient cultures on organizational performance[12] and the ways pathological personalities may lead to dysfunctional organizational cultures.[13] Schwartz used a psychodynamic, anthropological mode of inquiry to explore corporate decay at General Motors and NASA.[14]

**Management**, originally called administrative science, is the study of overseeing activities and supervising people in organizations. It emphasizes the design, implementation, and management of various administrative and organizational systems. March and Simon, in their important work, started with the human organization as their point of departure and investigated administrative practices that enhance the effectiveness of the system.[15] Management is the first discipline to take the modern corporation as the unit of analysis, a viewpoint that distinguishes its contribution to the study of organizational behaviour.

**Medicine** is the applied science of healing or treating diseases to enhance an individual's health and well-being. Medicine concerns itself with both physical and psychological health, as well as occupational mental health.[16] As modern care defeats acute diseases, medical attention has shifted to more chronic diseases, such as hypertension, and to occupational health and well-being.[17] These trends have contributed to the growth of organizational

wellness programs, such as Johnson & Johnson's "Live for Life Program" or Hershey Canada's "Fit for Life."[18] Skyrocketing health care costs continue to contribute to increased organizational concern with wellness and health care in the workplace.[19]

# Behaviour in Times of Change

Early research with individuals and organizations in the midst of environmental change found that people often experience change as a threat and respond by relying on well-learned and dominant forms of behaviour.[20] That is, in the midst of change, people often become rigid and reactive, rather than open and responsive. This behaviour works well in the face of gradual, incremental change. However, rigid and well-learned behaviour may be a counterproductive response to significant change. Outsourcing is a significant change in North American industry that has been forced by dramatic advances in the Internet and networking technology.[21] Big changes disrupt people's habitual behaviour and force them to learn new skills. Eric Brown, Alberto Culver's VP of Global Business Development, offers some sage words of advice to see the opportunity in change.[22] He recommends adapting to change by seeing it as positive, and challenge

**engineering**
The applied science of energy and matter.

**anthropology**
The science of the learned behaviour of human beings.

**management**
The study of overseeing activities and supervising people in organizations.

**medicine**
The applied science of healing or treatment of diseases to enhance an individual's health and well-being.

as good rather than bad. His action steps for doing this are to (1) have a positive attitude, (2) ask questions, (3) listen to the answers, and (4) be committed to success.

However, success is never guaranteed, and change often results in failure. If this happens, do not despair. Some of the world's greatest leaders, such as Winston Churchill, experienced dramatic failures before they achieved lasting success. Their capacity to learn from the failure and to respond positively to new opportunities helped them overcome early setbacks. One venture capitalist with whom the authors have worked likes to ask those seeking to build a business to tell him about their greatest failure. He wants to hear how the executive responded to the failure and what he or she learned from the experience. Change carries both the risk of failure and the opportunity for success; our behaviour often determines the outcome. Success can come through enlightened opportunism, the accumulation of small wins, and the use of microprocesses, as has been found with middle managers engaged in institutional change.[23]

# The Organizational Context

A complete understanding of organizational behaviour requires both an understanding of human behaviour and an understanding of the organizational context—that is, the specific setting—within which human behaviour is acted out.

## Organizations as Open Systems

Just as two different perspectives offer complementary explanations for human behaviour, two views shape complementary explanations of organizations. Organizations are open systems of interacting components: people, tasks, technology, and structure. These internal components also interact with components in the organization's task environment. Open system organizations consist of people, technology, structure, and purpose, all interacting with elements in the organization's environment.

What, exactly, is an organization? Today, the corporation is the dominant organizational form for much of the Western world, but other organizational forms have dominated other societies. Religious organizations, such as the temple corporations of ancient Mesopotamia and the Catholic Church in 19th–century Quebec, can often dominate society.[24] So can military organizations, like the clans of the Scottish Highlands and the regional armies of the People's Republic of China.[25, 26] All of these societies are woven together by family organizations, which themselves may vary from nuclear and extended families to small, collective communities.[27, 28] The purpose and structure of the religious, military, and family organizational forms vary, but people within different organizations often behave alike. In fact, early discoveries about power and leadership in work organizations were remarkably similar to findings about power and leadership within families.[29]

Organizations may manufacture products, such as aircraft components or steel, or deliver services such as managing money or providing insurance protection. We must first understand the open system components of an organization and the components of its task environment in order to see how the organization functions.

Katz and Kahn and Leavitt established open system frameworks for understanding organizations.[30] The four major internal components are structure, technology, people, and task. These four components, along with the organization's inputs, outputs, and key elements in the task environment, are depicted in Figure 1.1. The **structure** is the systems of communication, systems of authority, and the systems of workflow.

The **technology** is the wide range of tools, knowledge, processes, and/or techniques used to transform the inputs into outputs. The **people** are the human resources of the organization. The **task** of the organization is its mission, purpose, or goal for existing. In addition to these major internal components, the organization, as a system, also has an external task environment. The task environment is composed of different

**structure**

The systems of communication, authority, and workflow.

**technology**

The tools, knowledge, and/or techniques used to transform inputs into outputs.

**people**

The human resources of the organization.

**task**

An organization's mission, purpose, or goal for existing.

## FIGURE 1.1

### AN OPEN-SYSTEMS VIEW OF AN ORGANIZATION

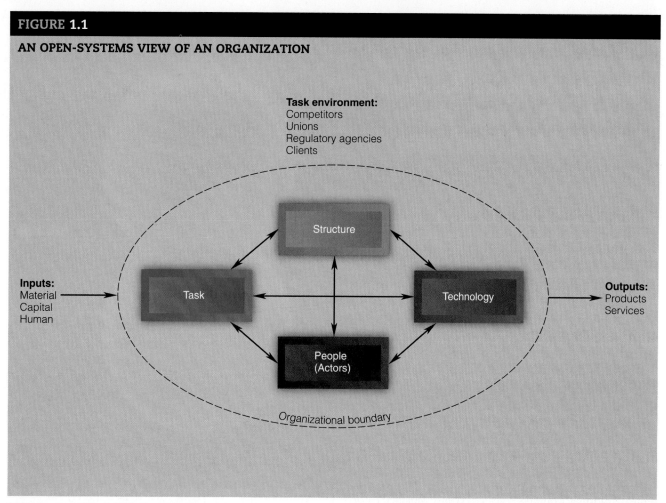

**Task environment:**
Competitors
Unions
Regulatory agencies
Clients

Structure

**Inputs:**
Material
Capital
Human

Task

Technology

People
(Actors)

**Outputs:**
Products
Services

Organizational boundary

SOURCE: Based on Harold Levitt, "Applied Organizational Change in Industry: Structural, Technological, and Humanistic Approaches." in J.G. March, ed., *Handbook of Organizations* (Chicago: Rand McNally, 1965), p. 1145. Reprinted by permission of James G. March.

constituents, such as suppliers, customers, and federal regulators. Thompson describes the task environment as that element of the environment related to the organization's degree of goal attainment; that is, the task environment is composed of those elements of the environment related to the organization's basic task.[31] For example, Tim Horton's is the chief competitor for Starbucks Canada and therefore a key element in Starbuck's task environment. Therefore, Starbucks Canada must develop a business strategy and approach that considers the actions and activities of Tim Horton's.

The organization works by taking inputs, converting them into throughputs, and delivering outputs to its task environment. Inputs are the human, informational, material, and financial resources used by the organization. Throughputs are the materials and resources as they are transformed by the organization's technology component. Once the transformation is complete, they become outputs for customers, consumers, and clients.

The actions of suppliers, customers, regulators, and other elements of the task environment affect the organization and the behaviour of people at work. For

example, Onsite Engineering and Management's survival was threatened by its total dependence on one large utility for its outputs during the mid-1980s. By broadening its client base and improving the quality of its services (that is, its outputs) over the next several years, Onsite grew healthier and more successful. Transforming inputs into high-quality outputs is critical to every organization's success.

### LEARNING OUTCOME 4

# The Formal and Informal Organization

The open systems view of organization suggests that organizations are designed like clockwork with a neat, precise, interrelated functioning. The **formal organization** is the official, legitimate, and most visible part that enables people

**formal organization**

The official, legitimate, and most visible part of the system.

> **The open systems view of organization suggests that they are designed like clockwork with a neat, precise, interrelated functioning.**

FIGURE 1.2

**FORMAL AND INFORMAL ORGANIZATION**

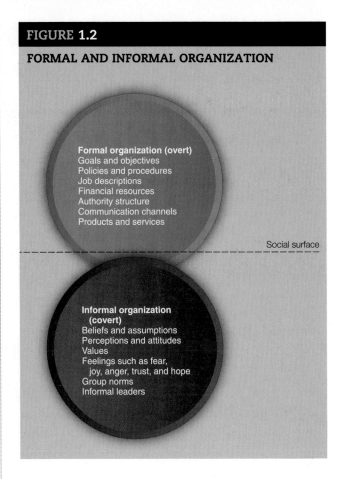

**Formal organization (overt)**
Goals and objectives
Policies and procedures
Job descriptions
Financial resources
Authority structure
Communication channels
Products and services

Social surface

**Informal organization (covert)**
Beliefs and assumptions
Perceptions and attitudes
Values
Feelings such as fear,
    joy, anger, trust, and hope
Group norms
Informal leaders

to think of organizations in logical and rational ways. The snake-pit metaphor mentioned earlier originates from the study of the **informal organization**, which is unofficial and less visible. The **Hawthorne studies**, conducted during the 1920s and 1930s, first suggested the importance of the informal elements. During the interview study, the third of the four Hawthorne studies, the researchers began to fully appreciate the informal elements of the Hawthorne Works as an organization.[32] The formal and informal elements of the organization are depicted in Figure 1.2.

Since the formal and informal elements of an organization can sometimes conflict, we must understand both. Conflicts erupted in many organizations during the early years of the 20th century and were embodied in the union–management strife of that era. Sometimes formal–informal conflicts escalated into violence. For example, during the 1920s, supervisors at the Homestead Works of U.S. Steel were issued pistols "just in case" they felt it necessary to shoot unruly, dangerous steelworkers. Not all organizations are characterized by such potential formal–informal, management–labour conflict. During the same era, the progressive Eastman Kodak company helped with financial backing for employees' neighbourhood communities, such as Meadowbrook in Rochester, New York. Kodak's apparent concern for employees and attention to informal issues made unions unnecessary within the company.

The informal elements of the organization are often points of diagnostic and intervention activities in organization development, though the formal elements must always be considered since they provide the context for the informal.[33] Informal elements are important because people's feelings, thoughts, and attitudes about their work affect their behaviour and performance. Individual behaviour plays out in the context of the formal and informal elements of the

**informal organization**
The unofficial and less visible part of the system.

**Hawthorne studies**
Studies conducted during the 1920s and 1930s that discovered the existence of the informal organization.

system, becoming organizational behaviour. Employees' moods, emotions, and dispositions all influence critical organizational outcomes, such as job performance, decision making, creativity, turnover, teamwork, negotiation, and leadership.[34]

# Diversity of Organizations

Organizational behaviour always occurs in the context of a specific organizational setting. Most attempts at explaining or predicting organizational behaviour rely heavily on factors within the organization and give less weight to external environmental considerations.[35] Students can benefit from being sensitive to the industrial and sectoral context of organizations and from developing an appreciation for each organization as a whole.[36]

Large and small organizations operate in each sector of the economy. The private sectors play an important role in the economy. The manufacturing sector includes the production of basic materials, such as steel, and the production of finished products, such as automobiles

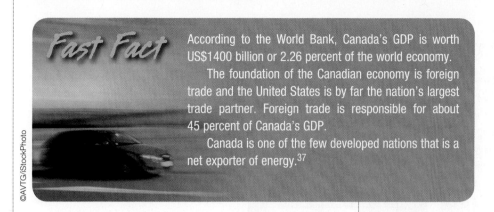

*Fast Fact* According to the World Bank, Canada's GDP is worth US$1400 billion or 2.26 percent of the world economy.

The foundation of the Canadian economy is foreign trade and the United States is by far the nation's largest trade partner. Foreign trade is responsible for about 45 percent of Canada's GDP.

Canada is one of the few developed nations that is a net exporter of energy.[37]

and electronic equipment. The service sector includes transportation, financial services, insurance, and retail sales. The government sectors, which provide essential infrastructure, and nonprofit organizations are also important to our collective well-being because they meet needs that aren't addressed by other sectors. The non-profit sector, for example, accounts for approximately 10 percent of Canada's gross domestic product (GDP).

Hundreds of small, medium, and large organizations contribute to Canada's economic health and human welfare. Throughout this book, we provide examples from a variety of organizations to help you develop a greater appreciation for your own organization and for others in the diverse world of business enterprises and nonprofit organizations.

# Change Creates Opportunities

Change creates opportunities and risks. Global competition is a leading force driving change at work. Competition in the Canadian and world economies has increased significantly during the past few decades, especially in industries such as banking, finance, and air transportation. Competition creates performance and cost pressures, which have a ripple effect on people and their behaviour at work. While one risk for employees is the marginalization of part-time professionals, good management practice can ensure their integration.[38] Competition may lead to downsizing and restructuring, but it can provide the opportunity for revitalization.[39] Further, small companies don't necessarily lose in this competitive environment. Scientech Inc., a small power and energy company, in the laboratory and analytical markets for 40 years, needed to enhance its managerial talent and service quality to meet the challenges of growth and

big-company competitors. Product and service quality helps companies win in a competitive environment. Organizations as different as IBM, WestJet Airlines, and Vancity all use problem-solving skills to achieve high-quality products and services.

Too much change leads to chaos; too little change leads to stagnation. Change in the coffee industry is a key stimulus for both Tim Horton's and Starbucks as they innovate and improve. Winning in a competitive industry can be a transient victory however; staying ahead of the competition requires constant change.

## Four Challenges for Managers Related to Change

Chapter 2 develops four challenges for managers related to change in contemporary organizations: globalization, workforce diversity, ethics and character, and technological innovation. These four driving forces create and shape changes at work. Further, success in global competition requires organizations to respond to cultural, religious, and gender diversity and to personal integrity in the workforce, in addition to responding positively to the competition in the international marketplace. Workforce demographic change and diversity are critical challenges in themselves for the study and management of organizational behaviour.[40] The theories of motivation, leadership, and group behaviour based on research in a workforce of one composition may not be applicable in a workforce of a very different composition.[41] This may be especially problematic if cultural, gender, and/or religious differences lead to conflict between leaders and followers in organizations. For example, the Russian military establishment has found cultural and religious conflicts between the officers and enlisted corps a real impediment to unit cohesion and performance.

## Global Competition in Business

Managers and executives in North America face radical change in response to increased global competition. According to noted economist Lester Thurow, this competition is characterized by intense rivalry between the United States, Japan, and Europe in core industries.[42] Economic competition places pressure on all categories of employees to be productive and to add value to the firm.

## [ Nintendo Wins with Wii ]

In the 1980s, Nintendo ushered in the modern age of video games and dominated the market. By 2000, however, the company saw its market share of hardware sales decline by 50 percent as competitors like Sony and Microsoft introduced incredibly powerful systems and games saturated with increasingly lifelike graphics. Spending billions of dollars on game development became a standard in the industry, and Nintendo needed to rethink how it was competing. Top managers decided to build something simple, economically priced, and enjoyable for the whole family. The result was Wii, a game console controlled by a motion-sensitive wireless handheld. Although the decision was risky when it was made, thinking in a new way about the controller and the console has paid off handsomely for Nintendo, and demand for Wii well outstripped supply during 2006. Wii is reversing 20 years of declining Nintendo console sales.

SOURCE: J. Gaudiosi, "Why Wii Won," *Business 2.0* 8 (May 2007): 35–37.

Daniel Karmann/dpa/Landov

Corporate warfare and competition make employment uncertain for people in companies or industries that pursue cost-cutting strategies to achieve economic success. The global competition in the fragile automotive industry among the Japanese, North American and European car companies embodies the intensity that other industries can expect in the future.

Some people feel that the future must be the focus in coming to grips with this international competition, whereas others believe we can deal with the future only by studying the past.[43] Global, economic, and organizational changes have dramatic effects on the study and management of organizational behaviour.

## Customer Focused for High Quality

Global competition has challenged organizations to become more customer focused, to meet changing product and service demands, and to exceed customers' expectations of high quality. Quality has the potential to give organizations

**Economic competition places pressure on all categories of employees to be productive and to add value to the firm.**

inviable industries a competitive edge against international competition.

*Quality* became a rubric for products and services of high status. Total quality is defined in many ways.[44] Total quality management (TQM) is the total dedication to continuous improvement and to customers so that the customers' needs are met and their expectations exceeded. Quality is a customer-oriented philosophy of management with important implications for virtually all aspects of organizational behaviour. Quality cannot be optimized, because customer needs and expectations are always changing, but it is embedded in highly successful organizations. Part of what has catapulted Toyota to the top of the auto industry is its attention to quality and detail throughout the organization. However, when Toyota decided to expand rapidly, it lost its quality focus. In 2010, the President of Toyota, Akio Toyoda, testified,

I would like to point out here that Toyota's priority has traditionally been the following: First; Safety, Second; Quality, and Third; Volume. These two priorities became confused and we were not able to stop, think, and make improvements as much as we were able to before, and our basic stance to listen to customers' voices to make better products has weakened somewhat.[45]

Even though TQM management consulting has experienced a boom-to-bust cycle, the main concepts underlying its initial rise in popularity are here to stay.

## Diversicare

### Our CQI motto is "I Can Do It Better!"

Quality improvement enhances the probability of organizational success in increasingly competitive industries. One study of 193 general medical hospitals examined seven TQM practices and found them positively related to the financial performance of the hospital.[46] Quality improvement is an enduring feature of an organization's culture and of the economic competition we face today. It leads to competitive advantage through customer responsiveness, results acceleration, and resource effectiveness.[47] The three key questions in evaluating quality-improvement ideas for people at work are (1) Does the idea improve customer response? (2) Does the idea accelerate results? (3) Does the idea increase the effectiveness of resources? A "yes" answer means the idea should be implemented to improve quality. Organizations as diverse as Diversicare Canada Management Services Co. Inc.; City of St. George, BC; ARSC Energy Services, Tri Ocean Engineering Ltd.; and Manulife Financial—Individual Wealth Management Operations received the 2009 Canada Awards for Excellence in Quality from the National Quality Institute.[48]

**TABLE 1.1** Contrasting Six Sigma and Total Quality Management

| SIX SIGMA | TOTAL QUALITY MANAGEMENT |
|---|---|
| Executive ownership | Self-directed work teams |
| Business strategy execution system | Quality initiative |
| Truly cross-functional | Largely within a single function |
| Focused training with verifiable return on investment | No mass training in statistics and quality Return on investment |
| Business results oriented | Quality oriented |

SOURCE: M. Barney, "Motorola's Second Generation." *Six Sigma Forum Magazine* (May 2002), 13.

Taguchi's methods and the Shainin system) and found it to be the most complete strategy of the three, with a strong emphasis on exploiting statistical modelling techniques.[50]

## Behaviour and Quality at Work

Whereas total quality may draw on reliability engineering or just-in-time management, total quality improvement can succeed only when employees have the skills and authority to respond to customer needs.[51] Total

> ( Total quality isn't a panacea for all organizations and it doesn't guarantee unqualified success )

*Six Sigma* is a philosophy for company-wide quality improvement developed by Motorola and popularized by General Electric. The Six Sigma program is characterized by its customer-driven approach, its emphasis on using quantitative data to make decisions, and its priority on saving money.[49] It has evolved into a high-performance system to execute business strategy. Part of its quality program is a 12-step problem-solving method specifically designed to lead a Six Sigma "Black Belt" to significant improvement within a defined process. Six Sigma tackles problems in four phases: (1) measure, (2) analyze, (3) improve, and (4) control. In addition, it forces executives to align the right objective and targets and quality improvement teams to mobilize for action in order to accelerate and monitor sustained improvement. Six Sigma is set up so that that it can be applied to a range of situations, from manufacturing settings to service work environments. Table 1.1 contrasts Six Sigma and TQM. One study compared Six Sigma to two other methods for quality improvement (specifically,

quality has important direct effects on the behaviour of employees at all levels in the organization, not just on employees working directly with customers. Chief executives can advance total quality by engaging in participative management, being willing to change everything, focusing quality efforts on customer service (not cost cutting), including quality as a criterion in reward systems, improving the flow of information regarding quality-improvement successes or failures, and being actively and personally involved in quality efforts. While serving as chairman of Motorola, George Fisher emphasized the behavioural attributes of leadership, cooperation, communication, and participation as important elements in the company's Six Sigma program.

Quality improvement is crucial to competitive success. The National Quality Institute, whose mission is "Helping Canada Live and Work Better" has an awards program to honour and to inspire a commitment to quality excellence broadly. The award categories are Quality Award

## Hot Trend: Six Sigma

Developed by and for the manufacturing industry, Six Sigma is a quality and management trend with staying power. The fundamental goal of Six Sigma is to increase quality by reducing the variation between manufactured parts. To achieve Six Sigma, an organization must incur only 3.4 defective or nonstandard parts per million. It's easy to see why organizations across a wide range of industries are implementing Six Sigma techniques: the goal of stratospheric perfection is motivating and actually measurable.

luchschen/Shutterstock

(Business and Public Sector), *Healthy Workplace®*, Education, *Healthy Workplace®* for Small Organizations, Customer Service for Small Business, Quality and *Healthy Workplace®* (Integrated), Community Building, and Order of Excellence.[52]

*Quality* is one watchword for competitive success. Organizations that do not respond to customer needs find their customers choosing alternative product and service suppliers who are willing to exceed customer expectations. Keep in mind, however, that total quality isn't a panacea for all organizations and it doesn't guarantee unqualified success.

## Managing Organizational Behaviour in Changing Times

Over and above the challenge of quality improvement to meet international competition, managing organizational behaviour during changing times is challenging for at least four reasons: (1) the increasing globalization of organizations' operating territory, (2) the increasing diversity of organizational workforces, (3) the continuing demand for higher levels of moral and ethical behaviour at work, and (4) continuing technological innovation with its companion need for skill enhancement.

Each of these four issues is explored in detail in Chapter 2 and highlighted throughout the text as they appear intertwined with contemporary organizational practices. For example, the issue of women in the workplace concerns workforce diversity and at the same time overlaps with the globalization issue. Gender roles are often defined differently in various cultures, and sexual harassment often plagues organizations in North America and elsewhere.

**objective knowledge**

Knowledge that results from research and scientific activities.

**skill development**

The mastery of abilities essential to successful functioning in organizations.

# Learning about Organizational Behaviour

Organizational behaviour is based on scientific knowledge and applied practice. It involves the study of abstract ideas, such as valence and expectancy in motivation, as well as the study of concrete matters, such as observable behaviours and physical and emotional symptoms of distress at work. Therefore, learning about organizational behaviour includes at least three activities, as shown in Figure 1.3. First, the science of organizational behaviour requires the mastery of a certain body of **objective knowledge**. Objective knowledge results from research and scientific activities. Second, the practice of organizational behaviour requires **skill development** based on knowledge and an understanding of yourself in order to master the abilities essential to success. Third, both objective knowledge and skill development must be applied in real-world settings.

Learning is challenging and fun because we are all different. Within learning environments, student diversity is best addressed in the learning process when students have more options and can take greater responsibility as coproducers in the effort and fun of learning.[53] For those with learning exceptionalities, learning can be a special challenge. Teaching and learning styles should be aligned carefully and educators should be aware that teaching is no longer merely verbal and visual, it has now become virtual.[54] If you are a visual learner, use charts, maps, PowerPoint slides, videos, the Internet, notes, or flash cards, and write things out for visual review. If you are an auditory learner, listen, take notes during lectures, and consider taping them so you can fill in gaps later; review your notes frequently; and recite key concepts out loud. If you are a tactile learner, trace words as you are saying them, write down facts several times, and make study sheets.

## Objective Knowledge

Objective knowledge, in any field of study, is developed through basic and applied research. Research in organizational behaviour has continued since early research on scientific management. Acquiring objective knowledge requires the cognitive mastery of theories, conceptual models, and research findings. In this book, the objective knowledge in each chapter is reflected in the supporting

should evolve into a critical consumer of knowledge related to organizational behaviour—one who is able to intelligently question the latest research results and distinguish plausible, sound new approaches from fads that lack substance or adequate foundation. Ideally, the student of organizational behaviour develops into a scientific professional manager who is knowledgeable in the art and science of organizational behaviour.

notes. Mastering the concepts and ideas that come from these notes enables you to intelligently discuss topics such as motivation, performance, leadership,[55] and executive stress.[56]

We encourage instructors and students of organizational behaviour to think critically about the objective knowledge in organizational behaviour. Only by engaging in critical thinking can you question or challenge the results of specific research and responsibly consider how to apply research results in a particular work setting. Rote memorization does not prepare students to appreciate the complexity of specific theories or the intricacies of interrelated concepts, ideas, and topics. Good critical thinking, however, enables the student to identify inconsistencies and limitations in the current body of objective knowledge.

Critical thinking, based on knowledge and understanding of basic ideas, leads to inquisitive exploration and is a key to accepting the responsibility of coproducer in the learning process. A questioning, probing attitude is at the core of critical thinking. The student of organizational behaviour

### FIGURE 1.3

**LEARNING ABOUT ORGANIZATIONAL BEHAVIOUR**

**Learning activity**

Mastery of basic objective knowledge

↓

Development of specific skills and abilities

↓

Application of knowledge and skills

## Skill Development

Learning about organizational behaviour requires doing as well as knowing. The development of skills and abilities requires that students be challenged by the instructor and by themselves. The What about You? features on the Chapter Review Cards give you a chance to learn about yourself, challenge yourself, and developmentally apply what you are learning.

Human Resources and Skills Development Canada has identified nine "essential skills" for work, learning, and life. The nine were identified through research and are needed to be successful in most types of work and life. The nine are (1) reading text, (2) document use, (3) numeracy, (4) writing, (5) oral communication, (6) working with others, (7) continuous learning, (8) thinking skills, and (9) computer use. While the skills are used in different degrees and at different levels of complexity in different types of work, they are all needed.[57] All these skills are used in the study of organizational behaviour.

> ❝ A group cannot learn for its members.

Developing skills is different from acquiring objective knowledge because it requires structured practice and feedback. A key function of experiential learning is engaging the student in individual or group activities that are systematically reviewed, leading to new skills and understandings. Objective knowledge acquisition and skill development are interrelated. The process for learning from structured or experiential activities is depicted in Figure 1.4 on page 14. The student engages in an individual or group-structured activity and systematically reviews that activity, gaining new or modified knowledge and skills.

## FIGURE 1.4

### LEARNING FROM STRUCTURED ACTIVITY

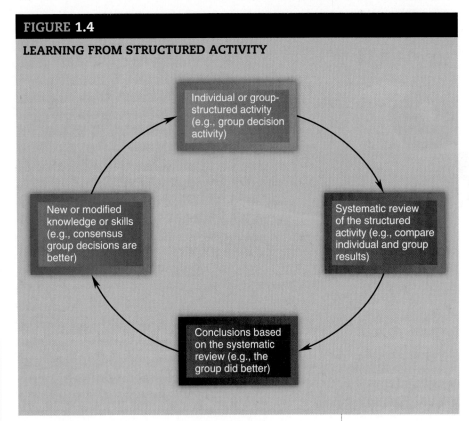

If skill development and structured learning occur in this way, there should be an inherently self-correcting element to learning because of the modification of the student's knowledge and skills over time.[58] To ensure that skill development does occur and that the learning is self-correcting as it occurs, three basic assumptions must be followed.

First, each student must accept responsibility for his or her own behaviour, actions, and learning. This is a key to the coproducer role in the learning process. A group cannot learn for its members. Each member must accept responsibility for what he or she does and learns. Denial of responsibility helps no one, least of all the learner.

Second, each student must actively participate in the individual or group-structured learning activity. Structured learning is not passive; it is active. In group activities, everyone suffers if just one person adopts a passive attitude. Therefore, everyone must actively participate.

Third, each student must be open to new information, new skills, new ideas, and experimentation. This does not mean that students need to be confessional. It does mean that students should have a nondefensive, open attitude so that they can learn and adjust to new ideas.

## Application of Knowledge and Skills

Understanding organizational behaviour includes an appreciation and understanding of working realities, as well as of science and of yourself. One of the advantages of structured, experiential learning is that a person can explore new behaviours and skills in a comparatively safe environment. Losing your temper in a classroom activity and learning about the potentially adverse impact on other people will probably have dramatically different consequences from losing your temper with an important customer in a tense work situation. Learning spaces that offer the interface of student learning styles with institutional learning environments give learners safe spaces to engage their brains to form abstract hypotheses, to actively test these hypotheses through concrete experience, and to reflectively observe the outcomes in behaviour and experience.[59] The ultimate objective of skill application and experiential learning is that the student transfers the process employed in learning from structured activities in the classroom and

# By The Numbers

**1920** supervisors at U.S. Steel issued pistols

**3** activities involved in learning organizational behaviour

**9** number of "essential skills"

**10%** of Canada's GDP comes from the nonprofit sector

**12** steps in the GE Six Sigma problem-solving method

©Andresr/Shutterstock

learning spaces to learning from unstructured opportunities in the workplace.

Although organizational behaviour is an applied discipline, students are not "trained" in organizational behaviour. Rather, they are "educated" in organizational behaviour and are coproducers in learning. The distinction between these two modes of learning is found in the degree of direct and immediate applicability of either knowledge or skills. As an activity, training more nearly ties direct objective knowledge or skill development to specific applications. By contrast, education enhances a person's residual pool of objective knowledge and skills that may then be selectively applied later—sometimes significantly later—when the opportunity presents itself. Hence, education is highly consistent with the concept of lifelong learning. Especially in a growing area of knowledge such as organizational behaviour, the student can think of the first course as the outset of lifelong learning about the topics and subject.

An exciting new idea is starting to shape managerial thinking and practice. It helps to bring together all the various elements of organizational behaviour. Design thinking is gaining traction among thoughtful organizational leaders. Roger Martin, a leading management guru, argues that "[in] a global economy, elegant design is becoming a competitive advantage. Trouble is most business folks don't think like designers."[60] In his view, the design economy will replace the information economy. Managers will need to think like designers when they face a problem—they will accept the mystery of the problem, take on the abstract challenge, and design a solution rather than rely on past approaches and tools. Such managers will demonstrate "abductive" reasoning, i.e., they will suggest something that could be and then explore it.[61] Apple is a fine example of an organization that understands design thinking in its work of creating "insanely great" products. Martin goes on to argue that businesspeople need to shift to becoming masters of heuristics from being the masters of algorithms.[62]

Such a shift is considerable and will require a new approach to managing people and organizations. Fusenet Inc., a Toronto-based firm that develops products and brands for the creation, storage, and delivery of digital media, allows its staff to spend a day a week to work on their own projects in a lab. It is an in-house business incubator. According to Fusenet's founder and CEO, Sanjay Singhal, "The lab gives them a safe environment in which they can tell us about [their project] and they'll know we won't steal the idea. Nothing changes other than we can invest in it and we know we won't lose the person a year down the road when it becomes commercial."[63]

# Visit **icanorgb.com** to find the resources you need today!

*Located at the back of the textbook are rip-out Chapter Review Cards. Make sure you also go online to check out other tools that ORGB offers to help you successfully pass your course.*

- Interactive Quizzing
- Key Term Flashcards
- PowerPoint Slides
- Audio Chapter Summaries

- Cases and Exercises
- Interactive Games
- Self-Assessments
- "On the Job" and "Bizflix" Videos

# Challenges for Individuals

## "What major challenges must managers overcome in order to remain competitive?"

Most North American executives believe that organizations are encountering unprecedented global competition.[1] Globalization is being driven on the one hand by the spread of economic logic centred on freeing, opening, deregulating, and privatizing economies to attract investment and, on the other hand, by the technological digitization that is revolutionizing communication.[2] The challenges for managers in this context are manifest in both opportunities and threats.

What major challenges must Canadian managers overcome in order to remain competitive? According to the Canadian Council of Chief Executives, Canadian organizations face many significant challenges: (1) Canada remains an export-dependent economy that is highly dependent on the United States, its largest trading partner; (2) organizations in every sector face the challenge of a strong currency combined with a weak demand for products and services from our largest trading partner, (3) Canada has low labour productivity growth, which averages about 0.7 percent a year. However, Canada weathered the 2008–2009 recession relatively unscathed and in the first quarter of 2010, Canada's GDP grew by an estimated 6.2 percent.[3]

### LEARNING OUTCOME 1

# Competing in the Global Economy

Only a few years ago, business conducted across national borders was referred to as "international" activity. The word *international* implies that the individual's or the organization's nationality is held strongly in consciousness.[4] *Globalization*, by contrast, suggests that the world is free from national boundaries and is borderless.[5] North American workers now compete with workers in other countries. Organizations from other countries are locating subsidiaries in North America, such as the Canadian manufacturing locations of Honda, Toyota, 3M, and Black & Decker Manufacturing, to name a few.

## LEARNING OUTCOMES

After reading this chapter, you should be able to do the following:

1 Describe the factors that affect organizations competing in the global economy.

2 Explain how cultural differences form the basis of

4 Discuss the role of ethics, character, and personal integrity in the organization.

5 Explain five issues that pose ethical dilemmas for managers and employees.

6 Describe the effects of technological advances on

Similarly, what were once called *multinational organizations* (organizations that did business in several countries) are now referred to as transnational organizations. In **transnational organizations**, the global viewpoint supersedes national issues.[6] Transnational organizations operate across long distances and employ a multicultural mix of workers. While there are few transnational organizations in Canada,[7] Magna International is well known and operates worldwide and locally with diverse populations of employees.

## Social and Political Changes

Social and political upheavals have led organizations to change the way they conduct business and encouraged their members to think globally. For example, Toyota is learning to speak to the 60-million-strong Generation Y, or millennials.[8] In the Soviet Union, *perestroika* led to liberation and created opportunities for North American businesses, as witnessed by the long waiting lines at Moscow's first McDonald's restaurant.

Business ventures in China have become increasingly attractive to North American companies. One challenge managers have tackled is understanding the Chinese way of doing business. Chinese managers' business practices were shaped by the Communist Party, socialism, feudalistic values, and *guanxi* (building networks for social

agreements in order to interact effectively with Chinese managers. Using the foreign government as the local franchisee may be effective in China. For example, KFC Corporation's operation in China is a joint venture between KFC (60 percent) and two Chinese government bodies (40 percent).[10]

In 1993, the European Union integrated 15 nations into a single market by removing trade barriers. At that time, the member nations of the European Union were Austria, Belgium, Denmark, Finland, France, Germany, Greece, Ireland, Italy, Luxembourg, the Netherlands, Portugal, Spain, Sweden, and the United Kingdom. By 2007, Bulgaria, Cyprus, the Czech Republic, Estonia, Hungary, Latvia, Lithuania, Malta, Poland, Slovakia, and Slovenia had also joined. Europe's integration provides many opportunities for North American organizations, with half a billion potential customers. Companies such as Ford Motor Company and IBM, which entered the market early with wholly owned subsidiaries, were able to capitalize on their much-anticipated head start.[11] Competition within the European Union will intensify, however, as will competition from Japan and the nations of the former Soviet Union.

Canada, the United States, and Mexico dramatically reduced trade barriers with the North American Free Trade Agreement (NAFTA), which took effect in 1994. Organizations found promising new markets for their products, and many companies located plants in

> **Start thinking about yourself as a global manager. Do the activity What about You? on the Chapter 2 Review Card.**

exchange). Once *guanxi* is established, individuals can ask favours of each other with the expectation that the favour will be returned. For example, many Chinese use *guanxi,* or personal connections, to conduct business or obtain jobs.

The concept of *guanxi* is not unique to China. There are similar concepts in many other countries, including Russia and Haiti. It is a broad term that can mean anything from strongly loyal relationships to ceremonial gift-giving, sometimes seen as bribery. *Guanxi* is more common in societies with underdeveloped legal support for private businesses.[9] North Americans can learn to build their own guanxi; understand the Chinese chain of command and negotiate slow, general

**transnational organization**
An organization in which the global viewpoint supersedes national issues.

**guanxi**
The Chinese practice of building networks for social exchange.

Mexico to take advantage of low labour costs. Prior to NAFTA, Mexico placed heavy tariffs on exports. The agreement immediately eliminated many of these tariffs and provided that the remaining tariffs be phased out over time.

Given these changes, managers must think globally and adopt a long-term view. Entering global markets requires long-term strategies and cultural fluency.

## Cultural Differences

One key for any organization competing in the global marketplace is to understand diverse cultures. Whether managing culturally diverse individuals within a single location or managing individuals at remote locations around the globe, organizations must appreciate the differences between cultures. Edgar Schein suggests that to understand an organization's culture, or more broadly any culture, it is important to dig below the surface of visible artifacts and uncover the basic underlying assumptions at the core of the culture.[12]

Microcultural differences (i.e., differences within cultures) are key to our understanding of the global work environment.[13] Differences in symbols are extremely important. The thumbs-up sign, for example, means approval in North America, whereas in Australia, it is an obscene gesture. Many European countries don't use manila file folders and, therefore do not recognize the icons used in Microsoft Office applications.[14] Do cultural differences translate into differences in work-related attitudes? Pioneering Dutch researcher Geert Hofstede investigated this question.[15] He and his colleagues surveyed 160,000 managers and employees of IBM working in 60 different countries[16] to study individuals from the same company in the same jobs, but living in different countries. Hofstede's studies showed that national culture explains more differences in work-related attitudes than do age, gender, profession, or position within the organization. Hofstede found five dimensions of cultural differences that formed the basis for work-related attitudes. These dimensions are shown in Figure 2.1.

Management careers have taken on a global dimension. Working in transnational organizations may give managers the opportunity to work in other countries. **Expatriate managers**, those who work in a country other than their home country, benefit greatly from knowledge of cultural differences.

International executives are executives whose jobs have international scope, whether in an expatriate assignment or in dealing with international issues. What kind of competencies should such executives have? There are several attributes that individuals should develop in order to prepare for an international career. Some of the key competencies are integrity, insightfulness, risk taking, courage to take a stand, and ability to bring out the best

> ## " Understanding cultural differences becomes especially important for organizations that are considering opening global offices.

in people. Learning-oriented attributes of international executives include cultural adventurousness, flexibility, openness to criticism, desire to seek learning opportunities, and sensitivity to cultural differences.[17] Further, strong human capital generally has a positive effect on internationalization.[18]

Because workplace customs vary widely, understanding cultural differences becomes especially important for organizations that are considering opening global offices. Carefully researching this information in advance helps organizations manage foreign operations. Consulate offices and companies operating within the foreign country provide excellent information about national customs and legal requirements. Table 2.1 (on page 20) presents a business guide to cultural differences in three countries: Japan, Mexico, and Saudi Arabia.

Another reality affecting global business practices is the cost of layoffs in other countries. Downsizing presents challenges worldwide. Dismissing a 45-year-old middle manager with 20 years of service and a $50,000 annual salary varies in cost from a low of $13,000 in Ireland to a high of $130,000 in Italy.[19] The wide variability in costs stems from the various legal protections that certain countries give workers. In Italy, laid-off employees must receive a "notice period" payment (one year's pay if they have nine years or more of service) plus a severance payment (based on pay and years of service). North American companies operating overseas often adopt the European tradition of training and retraining workers to avoid overstaffing and potential layoffs. Appreciating the customs and rules for doing business in another country is essential to global success.

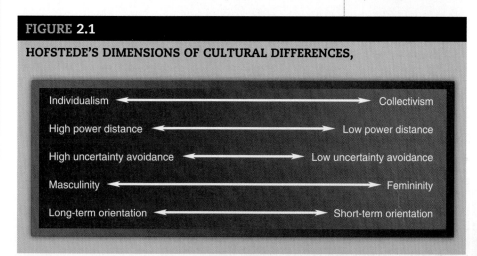

### FIGURE 2.1

#### HOFSTEDE'S DIMENSIONS OF CULTURAL DIFFERENCES,

| | |
|---|---|
| Individualism | Collectivism |
| High power distance | Low power distance |
| High uncertainty avoidance | Low uncertainty avoidance |
| Masculinity | Femininity |
| Long-term orientation | Short-term orientation |

SOURCE: Reprinted with permission of Academy of Management, PO Box 3020, Briarcliff Manor, NY 10510-8020. *Cultural Constraints in Management Theories* (Figure). G. Hofstede; *Academy of Management Executive* 7 (1993). Reproduced by permission of the publisher via Copyright Clearance Center, Inc.

**expatriate manager**

A manager who works in a country other than his/her home country.

**TABLE 2.1** Business Guide to Cultural Differences

| COUNTRY | APPOINTMENTS | DRESS | GIFTS | NEGOTIATIONS |
|---|---|---|---|---|
| Japan | Punctuality is necessary when doing business here. It is considered rude to be late. | Conservative for men and women in large to medium companies, though pastel shirts are common. May be expected to remove shoes in temples and homes, as well as in some *ryokan* (inn) style restaurants. In that case, slip-on shoes should be worn. | Important part of Japanese business protocol. Gifts are typically exchanged among colleagues on July 15 and January 1 to commemorate mid-year and the year's end, respectively. | Business cards (*meishi*) are an important part of doing business in Japan and key for establishing credentials. One side of your card should be in English and the reverse in Japanese. It is an asset to include information such as membership in professional associations. |
| Mexico | Punctuality is not always as much of a priority in Mexican business culture. Nonetheless, Mexicans are accustomed to North Americans arriving on time, and most Mexicans in business, if not government, will try to return the favour. | Dark, conservative suits and ties are the norm for most men. Standard office attire for women includes dresses, skirted suits, or skirts and blouses. Femininity is strongly encouraged in women's dress. Women business travellers will want to bring hosiery and high heels. | Not usually a requirement in business dealings though presenting a small gift will generally be appreciated as a gesture of goodwill. If giving a gift, be aware that inquiring about what the receiver would like to receive can be offensive. | Mexicans avoid directly saying "no." A "no" is often disguised in responses such as "maybe" or "we'll see." You should also use this indirect approach in your dealings. Otherwise, your Mexican counterparts may perceive you as being rude and pushy. |
| Saudi Arabia | Customary to make appointments for times of day rather than precise hours. The importance Saudis attach to courtesy and hospitality can cause delays that prevent keeping to a strict schedule. | Only absolute requirement of dress code in the Kingdom is modesty. For men, this means covering everything from navel to knee. Females are required to cover everything except the face, hands and feet in public; they can wear literally anything they want providing they cover it with an *abaya* (standard black cloak) and headscarf when they go out. | Should be given only to the most intimate of friends. For a Saudi to receive a present from a lesser acquaintance is so embarrassing that it is considered offensive. | Business cards are common but not essential. If used, the common practice is to have both English and Arabic printed, one on each side so that neither language is perceived as less important by being on the reverse of the same card. |

SOURCE: Adapted from information obtained from Business culture guides accessed online at http://www.executiveplanet.com.

# Cultural Differences and Work-Related Attitudes

Hofstede's work has implications for work-related attitudes. However, it is worth noting that

> *Hofstede's analysis is done by country. While this is valid for many countries, it does not hold in the countries where there are strong subcultures that are based on ethnicity of origin or geography. In Canada, for instance, there is a distinct French Canadian culture that has quite a different set of norms compared to English-speaking Canada. And in Italy, masculinity scores would differ between North and South.*[20]

We'll now take a closer look at how Hofstede's five dimensions of cultural differences are manifested in a variety of countries.

## Individualism versus Collectivism—IDV

In cultures where **individualism** predominates, employees put loyalty to themselves first, and loyalty to their company and work group second. Cultures characterized by **collectivism** are tightly knit social frameworks in which individual members depend strongly on extended families or clans. Group decisions are valued and accepted.

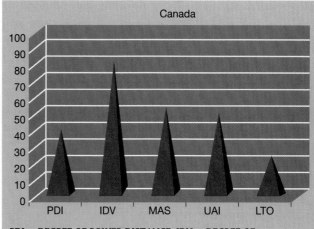

PDI = DEGREE OF POWER DISTANCE, IDV = DEGREE OF INDIVIDUALISM, MAS = DEGREE OF MASCULINITY, UAI = DEGREE OF UNCERTAINTY AVOIDANCE, AND LTO = DEGREE OF LONG-TERM ORIENTATION

SOURCE: From *Culture's Consequences: Comparing Values, Behaviors, Institutions and Organizations Across Nations* (2ⁿᵈ ed.) by G.H. Hofstede, 2001. p. 500. Copyright © 2001 by Geert Hofstede. Reproduced by permission of the publisher via Copyright Clearance Center, Inc.

The North American culture is individualistic in orientation. Individualistic managers, as found in Great Britain and the Netherlands, emphasize and encourage individual achievement. In collectivist cultures, such as Israeli kibbutzim and the Japanese culture, people view group loyalty and unity as paramount. Collectivistic managers seek to fit harmoniously within the group. Managers also encourage these behaviours among their employees. The world's regions are patterned with varying degrees of cultural difference.

Because these dimensions vary widely, management practices should be adjusted to account for cultural differences. Managers in transnational organizations must learn as much as they can about other cultures in order to lead their culturally diverse organizations effectively.

## Power Distance— PDI

Power distance relates to the acceptance of unequal distribution of power. In countries with a high **power distance**, bosses are afforded more power,

**individualism**
A cultural orientation in which people belong to loose social frameworks, and their primary concern is for themselves and their families.

**collectivism**
A cultural orientation in which individuals belong to tightly knit social frameworks, and they depend strongly on large extended families or clans.

**power distance**
The degree to which a culture accepts unequal distribution of power.

titles are used, formality is the rule, and authority is seldom bypassed. Managers and employees see one another as fundamentally different kinds of people. India, Venezuela, and Mexico all demonstrate high power distance.

In societies with low power distance, people believe in minimizing inequality. People at various power levels are less threatened by, and more willing to trust, one another. Managers and employees judge each other equally. Managers are given power only if they have expertise. Employees frequently bypass the boss in order to get work done in countries with a low power distance, such as Denmark and Australia.

## Uncertainty Avoidance—UAI

Cultures with high uncertainty avoidance are concerned with security and tend to avoid conflict. People need consensus and struggle constantly against the threat of life's inherent uncertainty. Cultures with low uncertainty avoidance tolerate ambiguity better. People are more willing to take risks and more comfortable with individual differences. Conflict is seen as constructive, and people accept dissenting viewpoints. Norwegians and Australians value job mobility because they have low uncertainty avoidance; Japan and Italy are characterized by high uncertainty avoidance, and not surprisingly, their cultures emphasize career stability.

## Masculinity versus Femininity—MAS

In cultures characterized by masculinity, assertiveness and materialism are valued. Men should be assertive, tough, and decisive, whereas women are expected to be nurturing, modest, and tender.[21] Money and possessions are important, and performance is what counts. Achievement is admired. Cultures characterized by femininity emphasize relationships and concern for others. Men and women are expected to assume both assertive and nurturing roles. Quality of life is important, and people and the environment are emphasized.

**uncertainty avoidance**
The degree to which a culture tolerates ambiguity and uncertainty.

**masculinity**
The cultural orientation in which assertiveness and materialism are valued.

**femininity**
The cultural orientation in which relationships and concern for others are valued.

**time orientation**
Whether a culture's values are oriented toward the future (long-term orientation) or toward the past and present (short-term orientation).

## Time Orientation—LTO

Cultures also differ in time orientation; that is, whether the culture's values are oriented toward the future (long-term orientation) or toward the past and present (short-term orientation).[22] In China, which has a long-term orientation, values such as thrift and persistence, which look toward the future, are emphasized. Russians generally have a short-term orientation and value respect for tradition (past) and meeting social obligations (present).

## Developing Cross-cultural Sensitivity

In today's multicultural environment, it is imperative that organizations help their employees recognize and appreciate cultural differences. One way companies do this is through cultural sensitivity training. Another way to develop sensitivity is by using cross-cultural task forces or teams. GE Medical Systems Group (GEMS) has 19,000 employees working worldwide. GEMS has developed a vehicle for bringing managers from each of its three regions (the Americas, Europe, and Asia) together to work on a variety of business projects. The Global Leadership Program forms several work groups made up of managers from various regions and has them work on important projects, such as worldwide employee integration, to increase employees' sense of belonging throughout the GEMS international organization.[23]

The globalization of business affects all parts of the organization, particularly human resource management. Human resource managers must adopt a global view of human resource planning, recruitment and selection, compensation, and training and development. They must possess a working knowledge of the legal systems in various countries, as well as of global economics, culture, and customs. HR managers must not only prepare employees to live outside their native country but also help global employees interact with local culture. Employees need to become culturally fluent, i.e., they need to develop "the ability to internalize and respond to a range of different worldviews or perspectives . . . to understand a range of starting points and cultural currencies, and to be able to respond to [them] in related contexts."[24] Global human resource management is complex, but critical to organizations' success in the global marketplace.

## The Diverse Workforce

Canada is a very diverse country. In addition to our many different Aboriginal peoples, and the Anglophone and Francophone communities, we have attracted people from the world over.

## Fast Facts

Canada's Aboriginal population is younger and faster-growing than its non-Aboriginal one. In 2006, the median age for Aboriginal people was 27 years, compared with 40 years for non-Aboriginal people.

In 2006, 1,172,790 people identified themselves as an Aboriginal person, either as North American Indian (or First Nations people), Métis, or Inuit.

Aboriginal people own over 30,000 businesses in Canada.

SOURCE: Reproduced from Statistics Canada, Canadian Demographics at a Glance, Catalogue no.: 91-003-XWE.

## Cultural Diversity

The globalization of business is promoting cultural diversity in the workplace. In addition, changing domestic demographics affect organizations' cultural diversity. In 2017, more than one Canadian in five will be foreign-born. According to data from StatsCan,

Cultural differences contribute a great deal to the diversity of the workforce, but there are other forms of diversity that are important as well. Diversity encompasses all forms of differences among individuals, including culture, gender, age, ability, religion, personality, social status, and sexual orientation. Diversity has garnered increasing attention in recent years, largely because of demographic changes in the working population. Many managers believe that dealing with diversity is a paramount concern for two reasons. First, managers need to motivate diverse work groups. Second, managers must communicate with employees who have different values and language skills.

Several demographic trends are affecting organizations. By the year 2020, the workforce will be more culturally diverse, more female, and older than ever. Recent legislation and new technologies have helped more individuals with disabilities enter the workforce. Hence, learning to work together is an increasingly important skill, as is working with an open mind.[25] Alcon Laboratories, the Swiss-owned international company whose mission is to improve and preserve eyesight and hearing, offers diversity training to help employees learn to work together.[26] Calgary-based Agrium Inc. received an award in 2010 as one of Canada's best diversity employers. It provides mentoring, networking, and career development opportunities to women employees through formal women's leadership groups, mentoring dinners, and seminars on work–life balance and stress management and, based on the success of the women employees' leadership group, the company is launching a long-term, formal diversity and inclusiveness strategy with wider scope; the program is being led by the CEO and supported by an in-house diversity council.[27]

*Strong immigration to Canada in recent decades has led to a rise in the number of foreign-born persons and the portion of the population that they represent. Thus, from 1986 to 2006, the immigrant population went from 3.9 million to 6.2 million, accounting for respectively 15.6% and 19.8% of the Canadian population.*

*If current immigration trends were to continue in the coming years, the proportion of immigrants in Canada could reach slightly over 22% by 2017. This would be equal to the highest level observed since the beginning of the last century, namely the 22% recorded between 1911 and 1931.*

*Few countries have a larger proportion of foreign-born than Canada. In the United States, for example, the proportion of foreign-born was 12.5% in 2006. However, Australia stands out, with immigrants comprising 22.2% of its population.[28]*

Strong shifts in the demographic makeup of society have important implications for organizations. Table 2.2 (on page 24) highlights the degree of multiculturalism across Canada.

**diversity**
All forms of individual differences, including culture, gender, age, ability, religion, personality, social status, and sexual orientation.

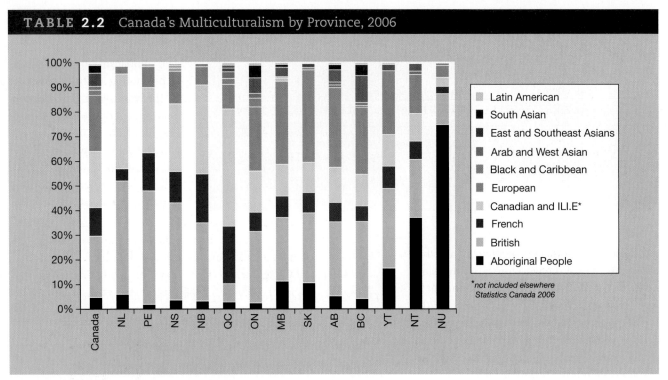

**TABLE 2.2** Canada's Multiculturalism by Province, 2006

Legend:
- Latin American
- South Asian
- East and Southeast Asians
- Arab and West Asian
- Black and Caribbean
- European
- Canadian and ILI.E*
- French
- British
- Aboriginal People

*not included elsewhere
Statistics Canada 2006

SOURCE: Reproduced with the permission of the Minister of Public Works and Government Services, 2010.

Organizations need to be open to hiring individuals from many different countries so that the organizations become as diverse as the communities in which they operate. However, Canada's organizations are not as diverse as they can and should be. A recent study of the labour market experience of racialized, i.e., subjected to racism, Ontarians found that

> Racialized Ontarians are far more likely to live in poverty, to face barriers to Ontario's workplaces, and, even when they get a job, are more likely to earn less than the rest of Ontarians

> While a larger share of racialized workers in Ontario were looking for work, fewer of them found jobs compared to the rest of Ontarians

> Racialized women in Ontario made 53.4 cents for every dollar nonracialized men made in 2005

> Controlling for age, immigration status, and education did not eliminate the gap.[29]

It need not be this way. For example, Coca-Cola has made substantial progress on diversity by monitoring its human resource systems.[30] Similarly, RBC has made diversity central to its strategy. RBC, which has 52,500 employees, has set up cross-cultural training, mentorship programs, and employee

Vince Talotta/GetStock.com

resource groups. It works with nonprofit agencies to hire newcomers to Canada.[31] The globalization of business and changing demographic trends present organizations with a culturally diverse workforce, creating both challenge and risk. The challenge is to harness the wealth of differences provided by cultural diversity. The risk is that prejudices and stereotypes may prevent managers and employees from having cooperative interactions to benefit the organization.

## Gender Diversity

The workforce has feminized substantially. In 2009, there were more women than men in our workforce. Women outnumbered men in both the under-25 and 25-and over groups. However, according to Laurel Ritchie of the Canadian Auto Workers, "[nobody] should break out the champagne here," as she believes the numbers speak more about the layoffs that men experienced than substantive gains made by women.[32]

Women's share of authority and compensation is not increasing commensurately with their participation in the workforce. Women hold only 16.4 percent of corporate officer positions in the Fortune 500 companies.[33] In 2005, only eight Fortune 500 companies had women CEOs.[34] Xerox CEO Anne Mulcahy is a very positive example yet still the exception, not the rule. Median weekly earnings for women persist at a level of 81 percent of their male counterparts' earnings.[35] Furthermore, because benefits are tied to compensation, women also receive fewer benefits.

In addition to lower earnings, women face obstacles at work. The **glass ceiling** is a transparent barrier that keeps women from rising above a certain level in organizations. In Canada, it is still quite unusual to find women in positions above middle management.[36] The ultimate glass ceiling may well be the corporate boardroom and the professional partnership. Women in 2006 represented 52 percent of graduates of Canada's top 10 law schools.[37] However, there are still few women who are partners in Canadian firms.

On a global basis, the leadership picture for women is improving somewhat. For example, the number of female political leaders has grown dramatically worldwide in recent decades. In the 1970s there were only five such leaders. In the 1990s, 21 female leaders came into power, and women around the world are leading major global companies. These global female business leaders do not come predominantly from North America or Europe. For example, Chanda Kochhar took over as managing director and CEO of ICICI Bank in 2009.[38] In addition, a large number of women have founded entrepreneurial businesses. For example, former chief of ICICI Venture Renuka Ramnath launched the Multiples Alternate Asset Management in 2009.[39]

Removing obstacles to women's success continues to be a challenge for organizations. Organizations must develop policies that promote equity in pay and benefits, encourage benefit programs of special interest to women, and provide equal starting salaries for jobs of equal value. Organizations that shatter the glass ceiling share several practices. Upper managers demonstrate support for the advancement of women through mentoring programs. Leaders incorporate practices into their diversity management programs to ensure that women perceive the organization as attractive.[40] Women are represented on standing committees addressing key strategic business issues, and are targeted for participation in executive education programs. Systems are in place for identifying women with high potential for advancement.[41] Companies such as Motorola, Deloitte & Touche, and the Bank of Montreal offer excellent programs

for advancing and developing women executives.[42]

Typically, women have adopted the caregiving role. Women are still largely responsible for home management, childcare, and often, elder care. Because of their multiple roles, women frequently experience conflicts between work and home. In response, organizations can offer incentives such as flexible work schedules, childcare, elder care, and work site health promotion programs to assist working women in managing the stress of their lives.[43]

Organizations must help their increasing numbers of female employees achieve their potential, or risk underutilizing the talents of more than half of the Canadian workforce.

## Age Diversity

The graying of the workforce is another source of workplace diversity. Aging baby boomers (those individuals born between 1946 and 1964) contribute to the rise of the median age and the number of middle-aged Canadians is rising dramatically. The numbers of younger workers and older workers (over age 65) are declining. According to data from StatsCan, "[in] 2006, 13.7% of Canadians were 65 or older, up from 7.7% in 1956. It is projected that by 2056 seniors will comprise between 25% and 30% of the Canadian population. While the proportion of seniors is increasing, children and young people comprise a decreasing portion of the Canadian population. . . . It is projected that the proportion of youth in Canada will continue to decline."[44]

This change in worker profile has profound implications for organizations. The job crunch among middle-aged workers will intensify as companies seek flatter organizations and eliminate middle management jobs. Older workers are often higher paid, and companies that employ large numbers of aging baby boomers may find these pay scales a handicap to competitiveness.[45] Conversely, a more experienced, stable, reliable, and healthier workforce can pay dividends to companies. The baby boomers are well trained and educated, and their knowledge is a definite asset to organizations.

The aging workforce is increasing intergenerational contact at work.[46] As organizations flatten, workers traditionally segregated by old corporate hierarchies find themselves working together. Four generations are cooperating: *the silent generation* (people born from 1930 through 1945), a

**glass ceiling**

A transparent barrier that keeps women from rising above a certain level in organizations.

small group that includes most organizations' top managers; *the baby boomers,* whose substantial numbers give them a strong influence; *the baby bust generation, popularly known as Generation X* (those born from 1965 through 1976); and the subsequent generation, tentatively called *Generation Y, millenials,* or *the baby boomlet.*[47] The millenials bring new challenges to the workplace because of their early access to technology and their continuing connection to parents.[48]

The differences in attitudes and values among these four generations can be substantial, and managers struggle to integrate their workers into a cohesive group. Currently, most leadership positions are held by members of the silent generation. Baby boomers regard the silent generation as complacent, strive for moral rights in the workplace, and take a more activist position regarding employee rights. The baby busters, newer to the workplace, are impatient, want short-term gratification, and value family over work. They scorn the achievement orientation and materialism of the baby boomers. Younger workers may have false impressions of older workers, viewing them as resistant to change, unable to learn new work methods, less physically capable, and less creative than younger employees. Research indicates, however, that older employees are more satisfied with their jobs, more committed to the organization, and more internally motivated than their younger cohorts.[49] Research also indicates that direct experience with older workers reduces younger workers' negative beliefs.[50] Motivating aging workers and helping them maintain high levels of contribution to the organization is a key task for managers.

## Ability Diversity

Employees with different abilities present yet another form of diversity. Individuals with disabilities are an underutilized human resource. About 4.4 million Canadians (14.3 percent) reported having a disability in 2006. The percentage of Canadians with disabilities increased with age, ranging from 3.7 percent for children 14 years and under to 56.3 percent for those 75 years and over.[51] While individuals with disabilities have entered the workforce in greater numbers, the progress is still slow.

Some companies have recognized the value of employing workers with disabilities. McDonald's created McJOBS, a corporate

[ **Ability or Disability?** ]

Brian McKeever, who is legally blind, wanted to compete in both the Vancouver 2010 Paralympics and the Olympics in cross-country skiing.[52] Although he did not make the cut for the Olympic team, and was devastated, he competed in the Paralympics and won gold for Canada.

plan to recruit, train, and retain individuals with disabilities that has hired more than 9,000 mentally and physically challenged individuals since 1981.[53] Its participants include workers with visual, hearing, or orthopedic impairments; learning disabilities; and mental impairments. McJOBS holds sensitivity training sessions with managers and crew members before workers go onsite to help workers without disabilities understand what it means to be a worker with a disabling condition. Most McJOBS workers start part-time and advance according to their own abilities and the opportunities available.

## Valuing Diversity

Diversity involves more than culture, gender, age, ability, and personality. It also encompasses religion, social status, and sexual orientation. These diversity types bring heterogeneity to the workforce.

Managers must combat prejudice and discrimination to manage diversity. Prejudice is an attitude, and discrimination describes behaviour; both diminish organizational productivity. Organizations benefit when they ensure that good workers are promoted and compensated fairly, but

as the workforce becomes increasingly diverse, the potential for unfair treatment also increases as some individuals may discriminate more.

Diversity helps organizations in many ways. Some organizations recognize the potential benefits of aggressively working to increase the diversity of their workforces. Yum! Brands' Kentucky Fried Chicken (KFC) tries to attract and retain diverse group executives. A president of KFC's U.S. operations said, "We want to bring in the best people. If there are two equally qualified people, we'd clearly like to have diversity."[54]

In an effort to understand and appreciate diversity, Alcon Laboratories developed a diversity training class called Working Together. The course takes advantage of two key ideas. First, people work best when they are valued and when diversity is taken into account. Second, when people feel valued, they build relationships and work together as a team.[55] Even majority group managers may be more supportive of diversity training if they learn to appreciate their own ethnic identity. It is important to frame diversity training as part of a larger, more general, human resource development. One evaluation of diversity training found that participants preferred training that was described as focusing on human relations, rather than on diversity per se, and had a broad focus.[56] Further, women react more positively to diversity training than men.[57] Organizations should measure the effects of training so they can monitor its positive payoffs.

Managing diversity helps companies become more competitive, as discussed next. But managing diversity takes more than simply being a good organizational citizen or complying with employment equity.[58] Managing diversity requires a painful examination of employees' hidden assumptions. Biases and prejudices about people's differences must be uncovered through structured self-reflection and addressed so that differences can be celebrated and used to their full advantage.

## Diversity's Benefits and Problems

Diversity enhances organizational performance. Table 2.3 summarizes the main benefits, as well as problems, with diversity at work. Organizations reap five main benefits from diversity. First, diversity management helps firms attract and retain the best available human talent. The companies topping the "Best Places to Work" lists are usually excellent at managing diversity. Second, diversity aids marketing efforts. Just as workforces are diversifying, so

**TABLE 2.3**  Diversity's Benefits and Problems

| BENEFITS | PROBLEMS |
| --- | --- |
| • Attracts and retains the best human talent | • Resistance to change |
| • Improves marketing efforts | • Lack of cohesiveness |
| • Promotes creativity and innovation | • Communication problems |
| • Results in better problem solving | • Interpersonal conflicts |
| • Enhances organizational flexibility | • Slowed decision making |

are markets. A diverse workforce can improve a company's marketing plans by drawing on insights from various employees' cultural backgrounds. Third, diversity promotes creativity and innovation. The most innovative companies, such as Hewlett-Packard, deliberately build diverse teams to foster creativity. Fourth, diversity improves problem solving. Diverse groups bring more expertise and experience to bear on problems and decisions and they encourage higher levels of critical thinking. Fifth, diversity enhances organizational flexibility. Diversity makes an organization challenge old assumptions and become more adaptable. These five benefits add up to competitive advantage for companies with well-managed diversity.

We must also recognize diversity's potential problems. Five problems are particularly important: resistance to change, lack of cohesiveness, communication problems, conflicts, and decision making. People are attracted to, and more comfortable with, others like themselves. It stands to reason that workers may resist diversity efforts when they are forced to interact with others unlike themselves. Managers should be prepared for this resistance rather than naively assuming that everybody supports diversity. Another difficulty with diversity is the issue of cohesiveness, that invisible "glue" that holds a group together. Cohesive groups have higher morale and better communication, but diverse groups take longer to achieve cohesiveness, so they may also take longer to develop high morale.

Another obstacle to performance in diverse groups is communication. Culturally diverse groups may encounter special communication barriers. Misunderstandings can lower work group effectiveness by creating conflict and hampering decision making.[59]

[ To the Point ]

Diversity has several advantages that can improve productivity and competitive advantage. Diverse groups, however, may sometimes have trouble functioning. Managers must maximize diversity's benefits, while preventing or resolving potential problems.

Organizations that manage diversity reap the rewards of increased productivity and improved organizational health. A healthy organization has employees of good character, ethical behaviour, and personal integrity.

# Ethics, Character, and Personal Integrity

Managers and employees frequently face ethical dilemmas and tradeoffs. Some organizations display good character and have executives known for their personal integrity. Merck & Company manages ethical issues well and its emphasis on ethical behaviour has earned it recognition as one of the most admired companies in *Fortune*'s polls of CEOs.[60]

Despite many organizations' careful handling of ethical issues, unethical conduct sometimes occurs. The toughest problems for managers to resolve include employee theft, environmental issues, comparable worth of employees, conflicts of interest, and sexual harassment.[61]

Ethical theories help us understand, evaluate, and classify moral arguments; make decisions; and then defend conclusions about what is right and wrong. Ethical theories can be classified as consequential, rule-based, or character.

## Consequential Theories of Ethics

**Consequential theories** of ethics emphasize the consequences or results of behaviour. John Stuart Mill's utilitarianism, a well-known consequential theory, suggests the consequences of an action determine whether it is right or wrong.[62] "Good" is the ultimate moral value, and we should maximize good effects for the greatest number of people. But do good ethics make for good business?[63] Right actions do not always produce good consequences, and good consequences do not always follow right actions. And how do we determine the greatest good—in short-term or long-term consequences? Using the "greatest number" criterion implies that minorities (less than 50 percent) might be excluded in evaluating the morality of actions. An issue that matters to a minority but not to the majority might be ignored. These are but a few of the dilemmas raised by utilitarianism.

Corporations often subscribe to consequential ethics, partly due to the persuasive arguments of the Scottish political economist and moral philosopher Adam Smith.[64] He believed that the self-interest of human beings is God's providence, not the government's. Smith set forth a doctrine of natural liberty, presenting the classical argument for open market competition and free trade. Within this framework, people should be allowed to pursue what is in their economic self-interest, and the natural efficiency of the marketplace would serve the well-being of society. However, virtue ethics offer an alternative rule-based theory.

## Rule-based Theories of Ethics

**Rule-based theories** of ethics emphasize the character of the act itself, not its effects, in arriving at universal moral rights and wrongs.[65] Moral rights, the basis for legal rights, are associated with such theories. In a theological context, the Bible, the Talmud, and the Koran are rule-based guides to ethical behaviour. Immanuel Kant worked toward the ultimate moral principle in formulating his categorical imperative, a universal standard of behaviour.[66] Kant argued that individuals should be treated with respect and dignity and that they should not be used as a means to an end. He argued that we should put ourselves in the other person's position and ask if we would make the same decision if we were in that person's situation.

**consequential theory**
An ethical theory that emphasizes the consequences or results of behaviour.

**rule-based theory**
An ethical theory that emphasizes the character of the act itself rather than its effects.

ARISTOTLE

Panos Karapanagiotis/Shutterstock

# Character Theories of Ethics

**Character theories** of ethics emphasize the character of the individual and the intent of the actor, instead of the character of the act itself or its consequences. These theories emphasize virtues and are based on an Aristotelean approach to character. Robert Solomon is the best known advocate of this Aristotelean approach to business ethics.[67] He advocates a business ethics theory centred on the individual within the corporation, thus emphasizing both corporate roles and personal virtues. Aristotle shaped his vision around an individual's inner character and virtuousness, not the person's behaviour. Thus, the "good" person who acted out of virtuous and "right" intentions was one with integrity and ultimately good ethical standards. Solomon's six dimensions of virtue ethics are community, excellence, role identity, integrity, judgment (phronesis), and holism. The "virtues" summarize the ideals defining good character. These include honesty, loyalty, sincerity, courage, reliability, trustworthiness, benevolence, sensitivity, helpfulness, cooperativeness, civility, decency, modesty, openness, gracefulness, and many others.

Cultural relativism contends that there are no universal ethical principles and that people should not impose their own ethical standards on others; local standards guide ethical behaviour. Cultural relativism encourages individuals to operate under the old adage "When in Rome, do as the Romans do." Unfortunately, people who adhere strictly to cultural relativism may avoid or ignore difficult ethical dilemmas by denying their own accountability.

# Ethical Dilemmas Facing the Organization Today

People need ethical theories to guide them through confusing, complex moral choices and ethical decisions. Contemporary organizations experience a wide variety of ethical and moral dilemmas. Here we address employee rights, sexual harassment, organizational justice, and whistle-blowing. We conclude with a discussion of social responsibility and codes of ethics.

## Employee Rights

Managing the rights of employees at work creates many ethical dilemmas in organizations. These dilemmas include privacy issues related to technology. Many believe that the monitoring of computer use, for example, to see what websites employees are visiting constitutes an invasion of privacy. Using employee data from computerized information systems presents many ethical concerns. Safeguarding the employee's right to privacy while preserving access to the data for those who need it forces managers to balance competing interests.

Drug testing, free speech, downsizing and layoffs, and due process are but a few of the employee rights issues managers face. For example, the reality of AIDS in the workplace illustrates the difficulties managers face in balancing the interests of their employees and their organizations. Managers may face a conflict between the rights of HIV-infected workers and the rights of their coworkers who feel threatened. Employers are not required to make concessions to coworkers, but employers do have obligations to educate, reassure, and provide emotional support to coworkers.

Confidentiality may also present challenges. Some employees with HIV or AIDS fear stigmatization or reprisals and do not want to reveal their condition to their coworkers. Management should discuss the ramifications of trying to maintain confidentiality and should assure the affected employee that every effort will be made to prevent negative consequences for him/her in the workplace.[68]

Laws protect HIV–infected workers. How does a manager protect the dignity of the HIV–infected employee and preserve the morale and productivity of the work group when so much prejudice and ignorance surround this disease? Many organizations believe the answer is education.[69] The Global Business Coalition on HIV/AIDS, Tuberculosis and Malaria comprises many organizations in different industries that bring health and opportunity to those afflicted with the three diseases. MTV Networks International, Bayer AG, Booz & Company, and MAC Cosmetics, to name only a few, are members of the Coalition.[70]

> **character theory**
>
> An ethical theory that emphasizes the character, personal virtues, and integrity of the individual.

## Sexual Harassment

Sexual harassment is unwelcome verbal or physical sexual attention that affects an employee's job conditions or creates a hostile working environment.[71] Sexual harassment is more likely to occur in male-dominated workplaces.[72] Managers can defend themselves by demonstrating that they took action to eliminate workplace harassment and that the complaining employee did not take advantage of company procedures to deal with harassment. Even the best sexual harassment policy, however, will not absolve a company when harassment leads to firing, demotions, or undesirable working assignments.[73] The Canadian Human Rights Commission recommends three critical steps to create a healthy workplace, free of harassment: (1) begin to change a culture of fear by discussing harassment, sharing information and involving employees in the development of an anti-harassment policy, (2) illustrate what constitutes harassing behaviour and provide clear directions for filing complaints, and (3) monitor progress and engage in ongoing training.[74]

> ❝ Sexual harassment costs the typical Fortune 500 company $6.7 million per year in absenteeism, turn-over, and lost productivity.

There are three types of sexual harassment. *Gender harassment* includes crude comments or behaviours that convey hostility toward a particular gender. *Unwanted sexual attention* involves unwanted touching or repeated pressures for dates. *Sexual coercion* consists of implicit or explicit demands for sexual favours by threatening negative job-related consequences or promising job-related rewards.[75] Recent theory has focused attention on the aggressive behaviour of sexual harassers.[76]

Sexual harassment costs the typical *Fortune* 500 company $6.7 million per year in absenteeism, turn-over, and lost productivity. Valeant Pharmaceuticals International paid out millions to settle several sexual harassment complaints against former CEO Milan Panic.[77] These sorts of costs do not take into account the negative publicity sexual harassment cases may attract. Sexual harassment victims are less satisfied with their work, supervisors, and coworkers and may psychologically withdraw at work. They may suffer poorer mental health, and even exhibit symptoms of post-traumatic stress disorder in conjunction with the harassment experience. Some victims report alcohol abuse, depression, headaches, and nausea.[78]

Several companies have created comprehensive sexual harassment programs. Atlantic Richfield (ARCO), owned by British Petroleum, now infamous for the world's largest oil spill and ecological disaster, and a player in the male-dominated energy industry, has a handbook on preventing sexual harassment that includes phone numbers of agencies where employees can file complaints. The openness seems to work. Lawsuits rarely happen at ARCO. When employees make sexual harassment complaints, the company investigates thoroughly. ARCO fired the captain of an oil tanker for sexually harassing coworkers.

## Organizational Justice

Organizational justice also generates moral and ethical dilemmas at work. **Distributive justice** concerns the fairness of outcomes individuals receive. For example, Japanese CEOs, in the past, have questioned the distributive justice of keeping North American CEOs' salaries so high while many companies were struggling and laying off workers.

**Procedural justice** concerns the fairness of the process by which outcomes are allocated. The ethical questions in procedural justice examine the process by which an organization distributes its resources. Has the organization used the correct procedures in allocating resources? Have the right considerations, such as competence and skill, been brought to bear in the decision process? And have the wrong considerations, such as race and gender, been excluded from the decision process? One study of work scheduling found voluntary turnover negatively related to advance notice and consistency, two dimensions of procedural justice.[79] Some research suggests cultural differences in the effects of distributive and procedural justice.[80]

## Whistle-Blowing

**Whistle-blowers** are employees who inform authorities of wrongdoings by their companies or coworkers. Whistle-blowers can be perceived as either heroes or "vile wretches" depending on their situations. Those seen as heroes generally report serious and high-magnitude ethical breaches widely perceived as abhorrent.[81] Others may see the whistle-blower as a vile wretch if they feel the act of whistle-blowing is more offensive than the situation reported.

---

**distributive justice**
The fairness of the outcomes that individuals receive in an organization.

**procedural justice**
The fairness of the process by which outcomes are allocated in an organization.

**whistle-blower**
An employee who informs authorities of the wrongdoings of his/her company or coworkers.

terekhov.igor/Shutterstock

Whistle-blowing can be a powerful influence on corporate North America because committed organizational members sometimes engage in unethical behaviour in an intense desire to succeed. Organizations can manage whistle-blowing by explaining the conditions that are appropriate for disclosing wrongdoing. Clearly delineating wrongful behaviour and the appropriate ways to respond are important organizational actions.

## Social Responsibility

Corporate **social responsibility** is an organization's obligation to behave ethically in its social environment. Ethical conduct at the individual level can translate into social responsibility at the organizational level. Socially responsible actions are expected of organizations. Current concerns include protecting the environment, promoting worker safety, supporting social issues, and investing in the community, among others. Some organizations, such as IBM, loan executives to inner-city schools to teach science and math. Firms that are seen as socially responsible have a competitive advantage in attracting applicants.[82]

## Codes of Ethics

Most mature professions guide their practitioners' actions and behaviour with codes of ethics. For example, the Hippocratic oath guides doctors. A profession's code of ethics becomes a standard against which members can measure themselves in the absence of internalized standards.

No universal code of ethics or oath exists for business as it does for medicine. However, Paul Harris and four business colleagues, who founded Rotary International in 1905, addressed ethical and moral behaviour early. They developed the four-way test, shown in Figure 2.2, which is now used in more than 166 nations by 1.2 million Rotarians. The four-way test focuses the questioner on key ethical and moral questions. Beyond the individual and professional level, corporate culture is another excellent starting point

Reprinted by permission of The University of Western Ontario

### FIGURE 2.3

**IVEY PLEDGE**

**IVEY** | Alumni Association
Richard Ivey School of Business
The University of Western Ontario

*Ivey Pledge*

I, _____, Ring number _____, standing before my mentors and my peers, commit myself to venerate the traditions, reputation and integrity of the practice of business.

I accept entry into an exclusive network of Ivey Business School Alumni. I acknowledge the responsibilities and value the benefits of being a member of such an association.

I will, to the best of my ability, act honourably and ethically in all my dealings, in the belief and knowledge that doing so will lead to a greater good.

I will express my ideas and opinions openly and without reservation, so long as they do not impinge on the rights and freedoms of others, whoever they may be.

I will endeavour to act with moral clarity, grace and nobility.

I understand that I am now a member of a distinguished community. I will strive to uphold the standing of the community, with special obligation placed on encouraging and championing the pursuits of my fellow members.

I will acknowledge my limitations and my mistakes so that I may learn from them.

I will continue to seek new knowledge, never resting on past wisdom or successes.

Above all, I will aspire to make a positive contribution to my society.

I promise to uphold the traditions, integrity and high standards set by those Alumni that came before me. I promise this to myself, my family, my fellow Alumni and my School.

I accept this Ivey Pledge freely and upon my honour.

SIGNATURE: _____   WITNESS: _____

DATE: _____   DATE: _____

for addressing ethics and morality. Sometimes codes articulate a corporation's ethics. Johnson & Johnson's credo helped hundreds of employees ethically address criminal tampering with Tylenol products. Students in business schools have developed graduation codes of ethics to guide them in their work. Graduates of the Richard Ivey School Business at the University of Western Ontario can take the Ivey Pledge, shown in Figure 2.3, to act honourably and ethically in their dealings.[83]

Individual codes of ethics, professional oaths, and organizational credos must all be anchored in a moral, ethical framework. We must continue using ethical theories to question and improve our individual current standards. Although a universal right and wrong may exist, it would be hard to agree upon a single code of ethics to which all individuals, professions, and organizations can subscribe.

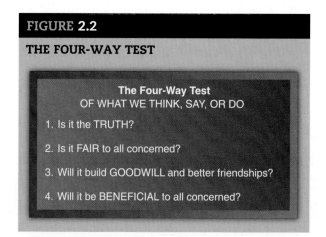

### FIGURE 2.2

**THE FOUR-WAY TEST**

**The Four-Way Test**
OF WHAT WE THINK, SAY, OR DO

1. Is it the TRUTH?

2. Is it FAIR to all concerned?

3. Will it build GOODWILL and better friendships?

4. Will it be BENEFICIAL to all concerned?

**social responsibility**

The obligation of an organization to behave in ethical ways.

# Technological Innovation and Today's Workforce

Another challenge that managers face is managing technological innovation. **Technology** can incorporate the intellectual and mechanical processes an organization uses to transform inputs into products or services that meet its goals. Managers must adapt to rapidly changing technology and ensure its optimum use in their organizations. Managers' inability to incorporate new technologies into their organizations limits economic growth in North America.[84] Although North America still leads the way in developing new technologies, it lags behind in using them productively in workplace settings.[85] Great organizations avoid technology fads and bandwagons, instead pioneering the application of carefully selected technologies.[86]

The Internet has radically changed organizations' communication and work performance. By integrating computer, cable, and telecommunications technologies, businesses have learned new ways to compete. For example, Amazon.ca uses the Internet exclusively, thereby drastically reducing its investments in inventories. Networked organizations conduct business anytime and anywhere, which is essential in the global marketplace.

The Internet and electronic innovation have made surveillance of employees more widespread. However, companies need to balance the use of spyware, monitoring of employee e-mails and websites, and video monitoring systems with respect for employee rights to privacy. Managers with excellent interpersonal skills do more to ensure high productivity, commitment, and appropriate behaviour on the part of employees than intense employee performance monitoring systems. Organizations with clearly written policies spelling out their approach to monitoring employees walk the fine line between respecting employees' privacy and protecting the interests of the organization.

©Jupiter Images

One fascinating technological change is the development of **expert systems**, computer-based applications that use a representation of human expertise in a specialized field of knowledge to solve problems. Expert systems can be used in many ways, including providing advice to nonexperts, providing assistance to experts, replacing experts, and serving as a training and development tool in organizations.[87] They are used in medical decision making, diagnosis, and medical informatics.[88] Anheuser-Busch has used an expert system to assist managers in ensuring that personnel decisions comply with anti-discrimination laws.[89]

Japan leads the world in the use of **robotics** in organizations; while organizations in North America have fewer total robots than Japan, the gap is narrowing. As well, the growth in the use of robots is expected to come from the 'BRIC countries', i.e., Brazil, Russia, India and China.[90] Whereas Japanese workers are happy to let robots take over repetitive or dangerous work, North American employees and unions worry that they will be replaced by labour-saving robots.[91] However, the main reason for the reluctance of North American organizations to use robots is their slow payout. Robotics represents a big investment that does not pay off in the short term. Japanese managers are more willing to evaluate the effectiveness of robotics technology along a long-term horizon.

It is tempting to view technology from only the positive side; however, some realism is in order. Some firms that have been disappointed with costly technologies are electing to *de*-engineer: 42 percent of information

**technology**

The intellectual and mechanical processes used by an organization to transform inputs into products or services that meet organizational goals.

**expert system**

A computer-based application that uses a representation of human expertise in a specialized field of knowledge to solve problems.

**robotics**

The use of robots in organizations.

[ *42 percent of information technology projects are abandoned before completion, and half of all technology projects fail to meet managers' expectations* ]

technology projects are abandoned before completion, and half of all technology projects fail to meet managers' expectations. Pacific Gas and Electric (part of PG&E Corporation) spent tens of millions of dollars on a new IBM–based system. Then deregulation hit the utility industry, allowing customers to choose among utility companies. Keeping up with multiple suppliers and fast-changing prices was too much for the massive new system; it was scrapped in favour of a new project using the old first-generation computer system, which is still being updated and gradually replaced. Because some innovations fail to live up to expectations, managers have to handle both revolutionary and evolutionary approaches to technological transitions.[92]

## Alternative Work Arrangements

Technological advances have prompted the advent of alternative work arrangements, the nontraditional work practices, settings, and locations that are now supplementing traditional workplaces. One alternative work arrangement is **telecommuting**, electronically transmitting work from a home computer to the office. IBM was one of the first companies to experiment with the notion of installing computer terminals at employees' homes and having employees work at home. By telecommuting, employees gain flexibility, save the commute to work, and enjoy the comforts of being at home. Telecommuting also has disadvantages, however, including distractions and lack of opportunities to socialize with other workers. Despite these disadvantages, telecommuters still feel "plugged in" to the communication system at the office. Studies show that telecommuters often report higher satisfaction with office communication than do workers in traditional office environments.[93]

Telus Corp. sees telecommuting as part of its green strategy. Hundred of Telus employees work from home offices and the results have included significant cost savings in office space, increased employee productivity, and savings of many tonnes in greenhouse gases.[94] Telecommuting lets companies access workers with key skills regardless of their locations. Alternative workplaces also give organizations an advantage in hiring and keeping talented employees, who find the flexibility of working at home very attractive.

*Satellite offices* comprise another alternative work arrangement. In such offices, large facilities are broken into a network of smaller workplaces located near employees' homes. Satellites are often located in comparatively inexpensive cities and suburban areas. They usually have simpler furnishings than the more centrally located offices. Satellites can save a company as much as 50 percent in real estate costs and can attract employees who do not want to work in a large urban area, thus broadening the pool of potential employees.[95]

These alternative work arrangements signal a trend toward *virtual offices*, in which people work anytime, anywhere, and with anyone. The concept suggests work occurring where people are, rather than people coming to work. Information technologies make connectivity, collaboration, and communication easy. Critical voicemails and messages can be delivered to and from the central office, a client's office, the airport, the car, or home. Wireless Internet access and online meeting software such as WebEx allow employees to participate in meetings anywhere at any time.

## Impact of Technology on Management

Technological innovation affects the very nature of the management job. Managers who once had to coax workers back to their desks from coffee breaks now find that they need to encourage workers mesmerized by new technology to take more frequent breaks.[96] Working with a computer can be stressful, both physically and psychologically. Long hours at computer terminals can cause eye, neck, and back strain, and headaches. In addition, workers accustomed to the fast response time of the computer come to expect the same from their coworkers and scold coworkers when they fail to match the computer's speed and accuracy. New technology, combined with globalization and intensified business pressures, has created extreme workers, pushing up the ranks of workaholics.[97] These extreme workers pay a price in relationships; other dimensions of a full, rich life; and increased stress.

Computerized monitoring provides managers with a wealth of information about employee performance, and it holds great potential for misuse. The telecommunications, airline, and mail-order merchandise industries make wide use of systems that secretly monitor employees' interactions with customers. Employers praise such systems for improving customer service. Workers, however, react to secret scrutiny with higher levels of depression, anxiety, and exhaustion. Bell Canada evaluated operators using a system that tabulated average working time with customers. Operators found the practice highly stressful, and they sabotaged the system by giving callers wrong directory assistance numbers rather than taking the time to look up the correct

**telecommuting**
Electronically transmitting work from a home computer to the office.

ones. Bell Canada now uses average working time scores for entire offices rather than for individuals.[98]

New technologies and rapid innovation place a premium on a manager's technical skills. Managers must develop technical competence in order to gain workers' respect. Computer-integrated manufacturing systems, for example, require managers to use participative management styles, open communication, and greater technical expertise to be effective.[99]

In a world of rapid technological innovation, managers must focus on helping workers manage the stress of their work. They must take advantage of the wealth of information available to motivate, coach, and counsel workers rather than to stringently control or police them.

## DID YOU KNOW?

>> Braille was invented in 1821 by Frenchman Louis Braille. Braille characters are called *cells* and each comprises six dots in various positions arranged in a rectangular format of two columns of three dots each.

## Helping Employees Adjust to Technological Change

Most workers understand the benefits of modern technologies. Innovation has improved working conditions and increased the availability of skilled jobs. Technology is also bringing disadvantaged individuals into the workforce. Microchips have dramatically increased opportunities for workers with visual impairments. Information can be decoded into speech using a speech synthesizer, into braille using a hard-copy printer, or into enlarged print visible on a computer monitor.[100] Engineers at Carnegie Mellon University have developed PizzaBot, a robot that individuals with disabilities can operate using a voice-recognition system, to fill a pizza order from the crust to the toppings. Despite these and other benefits of new technology in the workplace, however, employees may still resist change.

Technological innovations change employees' work environments, generating stress. Many workers react negatively to change that they feel threatens their work situation. Many of their fears centre around loss—of freedom, of control, of the things they like about their jobs.[101] Employees may fear diminished quality of work life and increased pressure. Further, employees may fear being replaced by technology or being displaced into jobs of lower skill levels.

Managers can take several actions to help employees adjust to changing technology. Encouraging workers' participation in early phases of decisions regarding technological changes is important. Individuals who participate in planning for the implementation of new technology learn about the potential changes in their jobs; therefore, they are less resistant to the change. Workers' input in early stages can smooth the transition into the new ways of performing work.

Managers should also keep in mind the effects that new technology has on the skill requirements of workers. Many employees support changes that increase the skill requirements of their jobs. Increased skill requirements often lead to increased job autonomy, responsibility, and (potentially) pay. Whenever possible, managers should select technology that increases workers' skill requirements.

Providing effective training is essential. Training helps employees perceive that they control the technology rather than being controlled by it. The training should be designed to match workers' needs, and it should increase the workers' sense of mastery of the new technology.

A related challenge is to encourage workers to invent new uses for existing technology. **Reinvention** is the term for creatively applying new technology.[102] Individuals

**reinvention**
The creative application of new technology.

luchschen/Shutterstock

*Hot Trend: Intangible Assets*

Roughly 75 percent of the Fortune 100's total market capitalization is in intangible assets, such as patents, copyrights, and trademarks. That means that managing intellectual property cannot be left to technology managers or corporate lawyers. Managers and companies with well-conceived strategies and policies for their intellectual property can use it for competitive advantage in the global marketplace.

SOURCE: M. Reitzig, "Strategic Management of Intellectual Property," *MIT Sloan Management Review* 45 (Spring 2004): 35–40.

who explore the boundaries of a new technology can personalize the technology and adapt it to their own job needs, and share this information with others in their work group.

Managers must lead organizations to adopt new technologies more humanely and effectively. Technological changes are essential for earnings growth and for expanded employment opportunities. The adoption of new technologies is a critical determinant of North American competitiveness in the global marketplace.

# Visit **icanorgb.com** to find the resources you need today!

*Located at the back of the textbook are rip-out Chapter Review Cards. Make sure you also go online to check out other tools that ORGB offers to help you successfully pass your course.*

- Interactive Quizzing
- Key Term Flashcards
- PowerPoint Slides
- Audio Chapter Summaries
- Cases and Exercises
- Interactive Games
- Self-Assessments
- "On the Job" and "Bizflix" Videos

# Personality, Perception, and Attribution

# Individual Differences and Organizational Behaviour

Over the next two chapters, we'll explore the concept of **individual differences**. Individuals are unique in terms of their skills, abilities, personalities, perceptions, attitudes, emotions, and ethics. Individual differences represent the essence of the challenge of management. The more managers understand individual differences, the better they can work with others. Figure 3.1 (on page 38) illustrates how individual differences affect human behaviour.

The basis for understanding individual differences stems from Lewin's early contention that behaviour is a function of the person and the environment.[1] Lewin expressed this idea in an equation: $B = f(P, E)$, where $B$ = behaviour, $P$ = person, and $E$ = environment. This idea has been developed by the **interactional psychology** approach.[2] Basically, this approach says that in order to understand human behaviour, we must know something about the person and something about the situation. There are four basic propositions of interactional psychology:

1. Behaviour is a function of a continuous, multi-directional interaction between the person and the situation.

2. The person is active in this process and is both changed by situations and changes situations.

**individual differences**
The way in which factors such as skills, abilities, personalities, perceptions, attitudes, values, and ethics differ from one individual to another.

**interactional psychology**
The psychological approach that emphasizes that in order to understand human behaviour, we must know something about the person and about the situation.

## LEARNING OUTCOMES

After reading this chapter, you should be able to do the following:

**1** Describe individual differences and their importance in understanding organizational behaviour.

**2** Explain how personality influences behaviour in organizations.

**4** Define *social perception* and explain the factors that affect it.

**5** Identify seven common barriers to social perception.

**6** Explain the attribution process and how attributions affect managerial behaviour.

## FIGURE 3.1

### VARIABLES INFLUENCING INDIVIDUAL BEHAVIOUR

**The person**
Skills and abilities
Personality
Perception
Attribution
Attitudes
Values
Ethics

**The environment**
Organization
Work group
Job
Personal life

Behaviour

## Skills and Abilities

Many skills and abilities influence work outcomes. This is why so many selection procedures include an assessment of specific job-related skills. General mental ability has also been shown to be strongly correlated with work performance.[4,5] However, few employers use intelligence tests to screen employees, relying instead on education as an indication of general mental ability.

LEARNING OUTCOME **2**

# Personality and Organizations

What makes an individual behave consistently in a variety of situations? Personality is an individual difference that lends consistency to a person's behaviour. **Personality** is the relatively stable set of characteristics that influence an individual's behaviour. Although researchers debate the determinants of personality, we conclude that it has several origins. One determinant is heredity. Researchers have found that identical twins who were separated at birth and raised in very different situations share personality traits and job preferences. For example, about half of the variation in traits like extraversion, impulsiveness, and flexibility is genetically determined; that is, identical twins who grew up in different environments share these traits and hold similar jobs.[6] Thus, genetics appear to influence personality.

3. People vary in many characteristics, including cognitive, affective, motivational, and ability factors.

4. Two interpretations of situations are important: the objective situation and the person's subjective view of the situation.[3]

The interactional psychology approach points out the need to study both persons and situations. We will focus on personal and situational factors throughout the text. The person consists of individual differences such as personality, perception, attribution, attitudes, emotions, and ethics. The situation consists of the environment the person operates in, including the organization, work group, personal life situation, job characteristics, and other environmental influences.

**personality**

A relatively stable set of characteristics that influence an individual's behaviour.

Jupiter Images

## TABLE 3.1 The "Big Five" Personality Traits

| Extraversion | The person is gregarious, assertive, and sociable (as opposed to reserved, timid, and quiet). |
| --- | --- |
| Agreeableness | The person is cooperative, warm, and agreeable (rather than cold, disagreeable, and antagonistic). |
| Conscientiousness | The person is hardworking, organized, and dependable (as opposed to lazy, disorganized, and unreliable). |
| Emotional stability | The person is calm, self-confident, and cool (as opposed to insecure, anxious, and depressed). |
| Openness to experience | The person is creative, curious, and cultured (rather than practical with narrow interests). |

SOURCES: P.T. Costa and R.R. McCrae, *The NEO-PI Personality Inventory* (Odessa, Fla.: Psychological Assessment Resources, 1992); J.F. Salgado, "The Five Factor Model of Personality and Job Performance in the European Community," *Journal of Applied Psychology* 82 (1997): 30–43.

Environment is also a personality determinant, shaping personality through family influences, cultural influences, educational influences, and other environmental factors. Personality traits are not fixed, continuing to develop and change to some degree through adulthood.[7]

## Big Five Personality Model

Personality theorists have long argued that to understand individual behaviour, we must break behavioural patterns down into a series of observable traits. One popular personality classification is the Big Five. The "Big Five" traits (described in Table 3.1) include extraversion, agreeableness, conscientiousness, emotional stability, and openness to experience.[8] The Big Five are broad, global traits associated with behaviours at work.

From preliminary research, we know that introverted and conscientious employees are less likely to be absent from work.[9] Individuals with high agreeableness tend to rate others more leniently on peer evaluations, while those with high conscientiousness tend to be tougher raters.[10] Extraverts tend to have higher salaries, receive more promotions, and be more satisfied with their careers.[11] Across many occupations, conscientious people are more motivated and are high performers.[12] When you examine specific occupations, however, different patterns of the Big Five factors are related to high performance. For customer service jobs, individuals

high in emotional stability, agreeableness, and openness to experience perform best. Managers with emotional stability and extraversion are top performers.[13] Recent research results indicate that in work teams, the minimum level of agreeableness in a team and the mean levels of conscientiousness and openness to experience have a strong effect on overall team performance.[14] The Big Five framework has shown to be a valid framework for studying personality in multinational studies.[15]

The trait approach has many critics. Some theorists argue that simply identifying traits is not enough, since personality is dynamic and never completely stable. Further, early trait theorists tended to ignore the influence of situations.[16] Also, the trait theory tends to ignore process—that is, how we get from a trait to a particular outcome.

## Integrative Approach

Recently, researchers have taken a broader, more **integrative approach** to the study of personality.[17] To capture its influence on behaviour, personality is described as a composite of the individual's psychological processes. Personality dispositions include emotions, cognitions, attitudes, expectancies, and fantasies.[18]

**integrative approach**
The broad theory that describes personality as a composite of an individual's psychological processes.

## Hot Trend

Does your personality affect life outcomes? In a recent comprehensive review of research on the Big Five personality model, researchers found that the answer seems to be a resounding yes. Extraverts, for example, are happier, more satisfied with romantic relationships, and less likely to be depressed. Agreeable individuals are less likely to have heart disease, and more likely to have a positive leadership style. Conscientious people are healthier and enjoy greater occupational success, and they are less likely to engage in criminal or antisocial behaviours. Emotionally stable individuals experience greater job satisfaction, commitment, and occupational success. Those who are open to new experiences tend to choose occupations that involve creative and artistic skills, but they are also more likely to engage in substance abuse.

SOURCE: D. J. Ozer and V. Benet-Martinez, "Personality and the Prediction of Consequential Outcomes," *Annual Review of Psychology* 57 (2006): 401–421.

luchschen/Shutterstock

> *People with low general self-efficacy often feel ineffective at work and may express doubts about performing a new task well.*

*Dispositions* are simply individuals' tendencies to respond to situations in consistent ways. Influenced by both genetics and experiences, dispositions can be modified. The integrative approach focuses on both person (dispositions) and situational variables as combined predictors of behaviour.

## Personality Characteristics in Organizations

Managers should learn as much as possible about personality in order to understand their employees. While researchers have identified hundreds of personality characteristics, we have selected three with particularly strong influences on individual behaviour in organizations: Core Self-Evaluations (CSE), self-monitoring, and positive/negative affect.

### Core Self-Evaluations (CSE)

Core self-evaluation (CSE) is a broad set of personality traits that refers to the positiveness of one's self-concept.[19] It comprises locus of control, self-esteem, generalized self-efficacy, and emotional stability. Research suggests that people with high CSE are more popular[20], make more money, have higher prestige jobs, and higher job satisfaction. Their more successful career paths are based partly on the fact that they are more likely to pursue further education and maintain better health.[21] Transformational leadership is linked to leaders with high CSE.[22]

### Locus of Control

An individual's generalized belief about internal (self) versus external (situation or others) control is called **locus of control**. People who believe they control what happens to them have an internal locus of control, whereas people who believe that circumstances or other people control their fate have an external locus of control.[23] Internals (those with an internal locus of control) have higher job satisfaction, health, organizational commitment, job involvement, motivation, and career success. Their stress levels are lower, as are their levels of role ambiguity, role conflict, and work–family conflict.[24] It appears that internals' beliefs change their behaviour in such a way as to promote positive outcomes. The externals' perception of their passive role means they are less likely to deal directly with problems or initiate constructive actions.

Knowing about locus of control can prove valuable to managers. Because internals believe they control what happens to them, they will want to exercise control in their work environment. Internals don't react well to close supervision, so managers should give them considerable voice in how work is performed. Externals, in contrast, may appreciate a more structured work setting and greater management support and prefer not to participate in decision making.

### Self-Efficacy

General self-efficacy is a person's overall view of himself/herself as being able to perform effectively in a wide variety of situations.[25] Employees with high general self-efficacy have more confidence in their job-related abilities and other personal resources (i.e., energy, influence over others, etc.) that help them function effectively on the job. People with low general self-efficacy often feel ineffective at work and may express doubts about performing a new task well. Previous success or performance is one of the most important determinants of self-efficacy. People who trust their own efficacy tend to attempt difficult tasks, to persist in overcoming obstacles, and to experience less anxiety when faced with adversity.[26] Because they are confident in their capability to provide meaningful input, they value the opportunity to participate in decision making.[27] High self-efficacy has also been related to higher job satisfaction and performance.[28]

Another form of self-efficacy, called *task-specific self-efficacy*, describes a person's belief that he or she can perform a specific task ("I believe I can do this sales presentation today."). In contrast, general self-efficacy is broader ("I believe I can perform well in just about any part of the job.").

Managers can support self-efficacy by providing clear, prompt feedback, particularly evidence of success.

**core self-evaluation**

The positiveness of one's self-concept; comprises locus of control, self-esteem, self-efficacy and emotional stability.

**locus of control**

An individual's generalized belief about internal control (self-control) versus external control (control by the situation or by others).

**general self-efficacy**

An individual's general belief that he or she is capable of meeting job demands in a wide variety of situations.

**Self-Esteem** Self-esteem is an individual's general feeling of self-worth. Individuals with high self-esteem have positive feelings about themselves, perceive themselves to have strengths as well as weaknesses, and believe their strengths are more important than their weaknesses.[29] Individuals with low self-esteem view themselves negatively. They are more strongly affected by what other people think of them, and they compliment individuals who give them positive feedback while cutting down people who give them negative feedback.[30]

Evaluations from others affect our self-esteem. You might be liked for who you are or you might be liked for your achievements. Being liked for who you are is more stable, and people with this type of self-esteem are less defensive and more honest with themselves. Being liked for your achievements is more unstable; it waxes and wanes depending on the magnitude of your achievements.[31]

A person's self-esteem affects attitudes and behaviour in organizations. People with high self-esteem perform better and are more satisfied with their jobs.[32] They tend to seek out higher status jobs.[33] A work team made up of individuals with high self-esteem is more likely to succeed than a team with low or average self-esteem.[34]

Very high self-esteem can be too much of a good thing. People with high self-esteem may brag inappropriately when they find themselves in stressful situations.[35] Very high self-esteem may also lead to overconfidence and to relationship conflicts.[36] A study of CEOs in major league baseball showed that the more narcissistic the leader was, the less likely he was to offer recognition and rewards to others when objectives were met.[37]

Self-esteem may be strongly affected by situations. Success tends to raise self-esteem, while failure lowers it. Managers should encourage employees to raise their self-esteem by giving them appropriate challenges and opportunities for success.

Stephen Coburn/Shutterstock

Locus of control, self-efficacy, self-esteem, and the effects of emotional stability together constitute the core self-evaluations. CSE is a strong predictor of both job satisfaction and job performance, next only to general mental ability.[38]

**Self-Monitoring** Self-monitoring—the extent to which people base their behaviour on cues from other people and situations—has a huge impact on behaviour in organizations.[39] High self-monitors pay attention to what is appropriate in particular situations and to the behaviour of other people, and they behave accordingly. Low self-monitors, in contrast, pay less attention to situational cues and act from internal states instead. As a result, low self-monitors behave consistently across situations. High self-monitors, because their behaviour varies with the situation, appear more unpredictable. One study of managers at a recruitment firm found that high self-monitors were more likely to offer emotional help to people dealing with work-related anxiety. Low self-monitors, on the other hand, were unlikely to offer such emotional support.[40] Another study demonstrated that high self-monitors may be better suited to jobs requiring emotional regulation than low self-monitors. The high scorers were better able to provide effective emotional performances, expressing the expected

*Fast Fact*

A recent study of 288 R&D engineers from four organizations found that self-esteem predicted supervisor ratings of job performance. This research suggests that high self-esteem might improve performance in knowledge-based occupations (or that self-judgments convince others' judgments in subjective situations).

SOURCE: R. T Keller. "Predicting Job Performance from Individual Characteristics among R&D Engineers," *The Business Review, 8*(1) (2007): 12–18.

©AVTG/iStockPhoto

**self-esteem**
An individual's general feeling of self-worth.

**self-monitoring**
The extent to which people base their behaviour on cues from other people and situations.

professional approach (e.g., acting angry in order to collect rent) without experiencing a high degree of stress.[41] Use What about You? on the Chapter 3 Review Card to assess your own self-monitoring tendencies.

According to research, high self-monitors get promoted because they accomplish tasks by meeting the expectations of others and because they seek out central positions in social networks.[42] They are also more likely to use self-promotion to make others aware of their skills and accomplishments.[43] However, the high self-monitor's flexibility may not be suited for every job, and the tendency to move may not fit every organization.[44] The high self-monitoring person also runs the risk of being seen as hypocritical or two-faced by those who perceive a change in behaviour to indicate insincerity. Because high self-monitors base their behaviour on cues from others and from the situation, they demonstrate higher levels of managerial self-awareness. This means that, as managers, they assess their own workplace behaviour accurately.[45] Managers who are high self-monitors are also good at reading their employees' needs and changing the way they interact with employees.[46]

We can further speculate that high self-monitors respond more readily to work group norms, organizational culture, and supervisory feedback than do low self-monitors, who adhere more to internal guidelines for behaviour ("I am who I am"). In addition, high self-monitors may support the trend toward work teams because they can easily assume flexible roles.

### Positive/Negative Affect

Individuals who focus on the positive aspects of themselves, other people, and the world in general are said to have **positive affect**.[47] In contrast, those who accentuate the negative in themselves, others, and the world are said to possess **negative affect** (also called *negative affectivity*).[48] Individuals with positive affect are more satisfied with their jobs.[49] They are also more likely to help others at work and engage in more organizational citizenship behaviours (OCBs).[50] Employees with positive affect have fewer absentee days.[51] Positive affect has

---

**positive affect**

An individual's tendency to accentuate the positive aspects of himself or herself, other people, and the world in general.

**negative affect**

An individual's tendency to accentuate the negative aspects of himself or herself, other people, and the world in general.

**strong situation**

A situation that overwhelms the effects of individual personalities by providing strong cues for appropriate behaviour.

---

also been linked to more life satisfaction and better performance across a variety of life and work domains.[52] Individual affect also influences the work group. Positive individual affect produces positive team affect, which promotes cooperation and reduces conflict.[53] Leader affectivity influences subordinate outcomes.

## DID YOU KNOW?

>> Negative attitudes are contagious. A study of leaders and subordinates found that leaders' negative affectivity has a negative effect on subordinate attitudinal outcomes like organizational commitment, job satisfaction, and anxiety.

SOURCE: J. Schaubroeck., F. O. Walumbwa, D. C. Ganster, and S. Kepes. "Destructive Leader Traits and the Neutralizing Influence of an 'Enriched' Job," *Leadership Quarterly* 18(3) (2007): 236–251.

Positive affect is a definite asset in work settings. Managers can encourage it by allowing participative decision making and providing pleasant working conditions.

Can managers predict the behaviour of their employees from their personalities? Not completely. Recall that the interactional psychology model (Figure 3.1 on page 38) requires both person and situation variables to predict behaviour. Also, situations vary in strength. **Strong situations** overwhelm the effects of individual personalities because they exert clear pressure on all to act in a specific way. For example, at performance appraisal sessions, employees know to listen to their boss and to contribute when asked to do so.

Weak situations are open to many interpretations. They provide few cues to appropriate behaviour and no obvious rewards for any particular behaviour. Thus, individual personalities have a stronger influence in weak situations than in strong situations. An informal meeting without an agenda might be a weak situation.

Since organizations present combinations of strong and weak situations, personality affects behaviour more in some situations than in others.[54] Managers must recognize this interaction between personality and situation. For example, a study of salespeople showed that situational opportunities (in the form of referrals provided by headquarters) had much more impact on actual sales than did the personalities of the individual salespeople, but the more conscientious the salesperson, the more likely that person effectively turned the referrals into sales.[55]

# Application of Personality Theory in Organizations

An understanding of employee personality can assist a manager in many ways: combining compatible individuals in a team, matching jobs to individuals, choosing a management approach to which an individual is likely to respond well, and understanding what circumstances a person may find stressful.

An area that remains controversial is the use of personality tests in personnel selection. Generally, the validity is low for predicting performance, accounting for only 15 percent of the variation in performance.[56] This may be partially due to the fact that most tests are self-reports. But it also lies in the fact that the profile of an excellent performer is influenced by an organization's culture, the work group, and the specific tasks assigned.

It is simplistic to expect that there is a single set of characteristics defining the ideal applicant. Different jobs have

©Gina Sanders—Fotolia.com

different demands. For example, although conscientiousness generally predicts stronger performance,[57] it has been shown to be a potential liability in jobs requiring innovation and creativity and in jobs requiring expedient completion of many tasks (because individuals may be overly concerned with detail and not accomplish as much as needed).[58] Before attempting to use a personality measure as a screening device, a manager must have a clear idea of what truly characterizes successful employees in that particular position in the organization and then select a measure that avoids the typical self-report pitfalls.

Given that managers may have limited control over who is hired anyway, it may be more useful for managers to focus on how they can manage the work environment to get the most out of the employees they have. For example, conscientious, extraverted and emotionally stable employees all work more effectively in a work environment with a strong goal orientation than one without.[59]

## Carl Jung and the Myers-Briggs Type Indicator® Instrument

Another approach to applying personality theory in organizations is the Jungian approach and its measurement tool, the MBTI® instrument. The **Myers-Briggs Type Indicator® instrument** was developed to measure Jung's ideas about individual differences. Many organizations use the MBTI instrument, and we will focus on it as an example of how some organizations use personality concepts to help employees appreciate diversity.

Swiss psychiatrist Carl Jung built his work on the notion that people are fundamentally different, but also fundamentally alike. His classic treatise *Psychological Types* proposed that the population was made up of two basic types—Extraverted types and Introverted types.[60] He also identified how people differ in their styles when gathering information and making decisions.

Jung suggested that human similarities and differences could be understood by combining preferences. We prefer and choose one way of doing things over another. We are not exclusively one way or another; rather, we have a preference for Extraversion or Introversion, just as we have a preference for right-handedness or left-handedness. Jung's type theory argues that no preferences are better than others. Differences are to be understood, celebrated, and appreciated.

**Myers-Briggs Type Indicator (MBTI)® instrument**

An instrument developed to measure Carl Jung's theory of individual differences.

During the 1940s, a mother–daughter team became fascinated with individual differences among people and with the work of Carl Jung. Katharine Briggs and her daughter, Isabel Briggs Myers, developed the **Myers-Briggs Type Indicator**® instrument to put Jung's type theory into practical use. The MBTI instrument is used extensively in organizations as a basis for understanding individual differences. Millions of people have completed the instrument.[61] The MBTI instrument has been used in career counselling, team building, conflict management, and understanding management styles.[62] Note that the MBTI is not appropriate for selection decisions.

**The Preferences**  There are four scale dichotomies in type theory with two possible choices for each scale. Table 3.2 shows these preferences. The combination of these preferences makes up an individual's psychological type.

**Extraversion/Introversion**  The **Extraversion/Introversion** preference represents where you find energy. The Extraverted type (E) is energized by interaction with other people. The Introverted type (I) is energized by time alone. Extraverted types typically have a wide social network, whereas Introverted types have a more narrow range of relationships. As articulated by Jung, this preference has nothing to do with social skills. Many introverts have excellent social skills but prefer the internal world of ideas, thoughts, and concepts. Jung's theory holds that the Extraversion/Introversion preference reflects the most important distinction between individuals. In work settings, extraverts prefer variety, and do not mind being interrupted by phone calls or visits. They communicate freely but may say things that they regret later.

Introverts prefer to concentrate quietly and think things through privately. They are detail oriented and do not mind working on a project for a long time; but they dislike interruptions. Note that some research with managers and with university students suggests that Canadians are more introverted than Americans.[63,64]

**Sensing/Intuition**  The **Sensing/Intuition** preference represents perception or information gathering. The Sensing type (S) pays attention to information gathered through the five senses and to what actually exists. The Intuitive type (N) pays attention to a "sixth sense" and to what could be rather than to what actually exists.[65]

At work, Sensing types prefer specific answers to questions and can be frustrated by vague instructions. They like jobs yielding tangible results, and would rather use established skills than learn new ones. Intuitive types like solving new problems and are impatient with routine details. They enjoy learning new skills more than actually using them. They tend to think about several things at once and may appear absent-minded. They like figuring out how things work just for the fun of it.

**Research suggests that Canadians are more introverted than Americans.**

**extraversion**

A preference indicating that an individual is energized by interaction with other people.

**introversion**

A preference indicating that an individual is energized by time alone.

**sensing**

Gathering information through the five senses.

**intuition**

Gathering information through a "sixth sense" and focusing on what could be rather than what actually exists.

**TABLE 3.2** Type Theory Preferences and Descriptions

| EXTRAVERSION | SENSING | THINKING | JUDGING |
|---|---|---|---|
| Outgoing | Practical | Analytical | Structured |
| Publicly expressive | Specific | Clarity | Time oriented |
| Interacting | Feet on the ground | Head | Decisive |
| Speaks, then thinks | Details | Justice | Makes lists/uses them |
| Gregarious | Concrete | Rules | Organized |
| **INTROVERSION** | **INTUITION** | **FEELING** | **PERCEIVING** |
| Quiet | General | Subjective | Flexible |
| Reserved | Abstract | Harmony | Open ended |
| Concentrating | Head in the clouds | Heart | Exploring |
| Thinks, then speaks | Possibilities | Mercy | Makes lists/loses them |
| Reflective | Theoretical | Circumstance | Spontaneous |

## [ From Street Performer to Billionaire ]

Guy Laliberté, the founder of Cirque du Soleil, recently gained international attention via his space tourism on board the international space station. He brought his jokes and clown nose with him, which is not surprising for an extraverted personality who started his career as a folk musician and fire-breathing busker. Laliberté's talent for organizing shows and festivals ultimately led to the creation of an innovative circus with no ring or animals. What MBTI type preferences do you think complemented his extraversion, aiding his success in creating a half-billion-dollar global company?

SOURCES: L. Tischler, "Join the Circus," *Fast Company* (December 19, 2007); I. Halperin, "Guy Laliberté: The First Clown in Space?" *The Independent* (September 22, 2009); J. K. Nestruck, "Guy Laliberté," *The Globe and Mail* (December 18, 2009)

emotional expression. They respond more readily to other people's thoughts. They tend to be firm minded and like putting things into a logical framework. Feeling types, in contrast, are comfortable with emotion in the workplace. They enjoy pleasing people and receiving frequent praise and encouragement.

### Judging/Perceiving

The **Judging/Perceiving** dichotomy reflects one's orientation to the outer world. The Judging type (J) loves closure. They prefer to lead planned, organized lives and like making decisions. On the other hand, Perceiving types (P) prefer flexible and spontaneous lives and like to keep options open. Imagine two people, one with a preference for Judging and the other for Perceiving, going out for dinner. J asks P to choose a restaurant, and P suggests ten alternatives. J just wants to decide and get on with it, whereas P wants to explore all the options.

Judging types love getting things accomplished and delight in checking off completed tasks on their calendars. Perceiving types generally adopt a wait-and-see attitude, collecting new information instead of drawing conclusions. Perceiving types are curious and welcome new information. They may start many projects without finishing them.

> " In work settings, thinking types tend to show less emotion.

**Thinking/Feeling** The **Thinking/Feeling** preference describes the way we prefer to make decisions. The Thinking type (T) makes decisions in a logical, objective fashion, whereas the Feeling type (F) makes decisions in a personal, value-oriented way. Thinking/feeling type preference is the only one to show a consistent sex difference, with males somewhat more likely to show a Thinking preference and females a Feeling preference. Thinking types tend to analyze decisions, while Feeling types sympathize. Thinking types try to be impersonal, whereas Feeling types base their decisions on how the outcome will affect the people involved.

In work settings, Thinking types tend to show less emotion and be less comfortable with should be others'

**The Sixteen Types** The preferences combine to form sixteen distinct types, as shown in Table 3.3 on pages 46–47.

The MBTI instrument has been found to have good reliability and validity as a measurement instrument for identifying type.[66] There are no good and bad types; each has its own strengths and

**thinking**
Making decisions in a logical, objective fashion.

**feeling**
Making decisions in a personal, value-oriented way.

**judging**
Preferring closure and completion in making decisions.

**perceiving**
Preferring to explore many alternatives and flexibility.

### [ MBTI Research at the University of Western Ontario showed engineering students significantly more ISTJ than science/humanities students. ]

TABLE 3.3 Characteristics Frequently Associated with Each Type

| SENSING TYPES | | INTUITIVE TYPES | |
|---|---|---|---|
| **ISTJ** | **ISFJ** | **INFJ** | **INTJ** |
| Quiet, serious, earn success by thoroughness and dependability. Practical, matter-of-fact, realistic, and responsible. Decide logically what should be done and work toward it steadily, regardless of distractions. Take pleasure in making everything orderly and organized—their work, their home, their life. Value traditions and loyalty. | Quiet, friendly, responsible, and conscientious. Committed and steady in meeting their obligations. Thorough, painstaking, and accurate. Loyal, considerate, notice and remember specifics about people who are important to them, concerned with how others feel. Strive to create an orderly and harmonious environment at work and at home. | Seek meaning and connection in ideas, relationships, and material possessions. Want to understand what motivates people and are insightful about others. Conscientious and committed to their firm values. Develop a clear vision about how best to serve the common good. Organized and decisive in implementing their vision. | Have original minds and great drive for implementing their ideas and achieving their goals. Quickly see patterns in external events and develop long-range explanatory perspectives. When committed, organize a job and carry it through. Skeptical and independent, have high standards of competence and performance for themselves and others. |
| **ISTP** | **ISFP** | **INFP** | **INTP** |
| Tolerant and flexible, quiet observers until a problem appears, then act quickly to find workable solutions. Analyze what makes things work and readily get through large amounts of data to isolate the core of practical problems. Interested in cause and effect, organize facts using logical principles, value efficiency. | Quiet, friendly, sensitive, and kind. Enjoy the present moment, what's going on around them. Like to have their own space and to work within their own time frame. Loyal and committed to their values and to people who are important to them. Dislike disagreements and conflicts, do not force their opinions or values on others. | Idealistic, loyal to their values and to people who are important to them. Want an external life that is congruent with their values. Curious, quick to see possibilities, can be catalysts for implementing ideas. Seek to understand people and to help them fulfill their potential. Adaptable, flexible, and accepting unless a value is threatened. | Seek to develop logical explanations for everything that interests them. Theoretical and abstract, interested more in ideas than in social interaction. Quiet, contained, flexible, and adaptable. Have unusual ability to focus in depth to solve problems in their area of interest. Skeptical, sometimes critical, always analytical. |

*Introverted Types*

weaknesses. Type influences learning style, teaching style, and choice of occupation. A study of the MBTI types of engineering students at the University of Western Ontario showed that the engineering students were significantly more ISTJ than science/humanities students, those who graduate the fastest show more of the ISTJ type, and those who drop out are likely to be more SFP.[67]

## How Companies Use MBTI

Recent studies have focused on the relationship between type and specific managerial behaviours. The Introverted type (I) and the Feeling type (F), for example, appear to be more effective at participative management than their counterparts, the Extraverted type and the Thinking type.[68] Companies like AT&T, ExxonMobil, and Honeywell use the MBTI instrument in their management development programs to help employees understand the different viewpoints of others in the organization. The MBTI instrument can also be used for team building. The Vancouver Organizing Committee for the 2010 Olympic Winter Games used the MBTI for developing team effectiveness.

Managers value type theory for its simplicity and accuracy. Type theory helps managers develop interpersonal skills. They also use it to build teams that capitalize on individuals' strengths and to help individual team members appreciate differences.

Information from the MBTI instrument can be misused in organizational settings.[69] Some inappropriate uses include labelling one's coworkers, claiming results as a convenient excuse that one simply can't work with someone, and avoiding responsibility for learning to work flexibly with others. Type is not an excuse for inappropriate behaviour.

**TABLE 3.3** Concluded

| | SENSING TYPES | | INTUITIVE TYPES | |
|---|---|---|---|---|
| | **ESTP** | **ESFP** | **ENFP** | **ENTP** |
| **Extraverted Types** | Flexible and tolerant, they take a pragmatic approach focused on immediate results. Theories and conceptual explanations bore them—they want to act energetically to solve the problem. Focus on the here-and-now, spontaneous, enjoy each moment that they can be active with others. Enjoy material comforts and style. Learn best through doing. | Outgoing, friendly, and accepting. Exuberant lovers of life, people, and material comforts. Enjoy working with others to make things happen. Bring common sense and a realistic approach to their work and make work fun. Flexible and spontaneous, adapt readily to new people and environments. Learn best by trying a new skill with other people. | Warmly enthusiastic and imaginative. See life as full of possibilities. Make connections between events and information very quickly, and confidently proceed based on the patterns they see. Want a lot of affirmation from others, and readily give appreciation and support. Spontaneous and flexible, often rely on their ability to improvise and their verbal fluency. | Quick, ingenious, stimulating, alert, and outspoken. Resourceful in solving new and challenging problems. Adept at generating conceptual possibilities and then analyzing them strategically. Good at reading other people. Bored by routine, will seldom do the same thing the same way, apt to turn to one new interest after another. |
| | **ESTJ** | **ESFJ** | **ENFJ** | **ENTJ** |
| | Practical, realistic, matter-of-fact. Decisive, quickly move to implement decisions. Organize projects and people to get things done, focus on getting results in the most efficient way possible. Take care of routine details. Have a clear set of logical standards, systematically follow them, and want others to also. Forceful in implementing their plans. | Warmhearted, conscientious, and cooperative. Want harmony in their environment, work with determination to establish it. Like to work with others to complete tasks accurately and on time. Loyal, follow through even in small matters. Notice what others need in their day-by-day lives and try to provide it. Want to be appreciated for who they are and for what they contribute. | Warm, empathetic, responsive, and responsible. Highly attuned to the emotions, needs, and motivations of others. Find potential in everyone, want to help others fulfill their potential. May act as catalysts for individual and group growth. Loyal, responsive to praise and criticism. Sociable, facilitate others in a group, and provide inspiring leadership. | Frank, decisive, assume leadership readily. Quickly see logical and inefficient procedures and policies, develop and implement comprehensive systems to solve organizational problems. Enjoy long-term planning and goal setting. Usually well informed, well read, enjoy expanding their knowledge and passing it on to others. Forceful in presenting their ideas. |

NOTE: I = Introversion; E = Extraversion; S = Sensing; N = Intuition; T = Thinking; F = Feeling; J = Judging; and P = Perceiving.

SOURCE: Modified and reproduced by special permission of the Publisher, CPP, Inc., Mountain View, CA 94043 from *Introduction to Type®* by Isable Briggs Myers as revised by Linda K. Kirby and Katharine D. Myers. Copyright 1998 by CPP, Inc. All rights reserved. Further reproduction is prohibited without the Publisher's written consent.

LEARNING OUTCOME **4**

# Social Perception

Perception is another psychological process that creates individual differences. Our perception is our understanding of the world around us. The primary vehicle through which we come to understand ourselves and our world, perception adds meaning to information gathered via the five senses of touch, smell, hearing, vision, and taste. Here, we focus specifically on **social perception**, the process of interpreting information about another person. Virtually all management activities rely on perception.

The selection interview highlights the importance of perception. The consequences of a bad match between an individual and the organization are devastating for both parties, so accurate data must be gathered. Typically first interviews are brief, and the candidate is usually one of many seen by an interviewer during a day. How long does it take for the interviewer to reach a decision about a candidate? In the first four to five minutes, the interviewer often makes an accept or reject decision based on his or her perception of the candidate.[70]

One study found that perceptions of dissimilarity in values between CEOs and top management teams led to increased conflict. Even if, in reality, there wasn't any difference in values, just the perception of it increased conflict.[71]

**social perception**
The process of interpreting information about another person.

Another study indicated that the perception of how closely organizational values match an individual's values has a powerful effect on trust in the organization.[72] These studies highlight the importance of perception in organizations by recommending that managers pay attention to how their employees perceive organizational decisions, since this perception will influence their behaviour.

Perception is also culturally determined. For example, long hours and a heavy workload are perceived as conflicting with the family much more in individualistic societies like ours (where work is seen more as a personal achievement) than in collectivistic societies (where work is seen as serving the family).[73]

A fascinating set of experiments demonstrated that males from an "honour" culture are much more likely to perceive threats in the behaviour of others and react accordingly.[74] The white male participants, students from either the U.S. North or South, were each insulted by a peer who bumped into him and called him an "asshole." Those from the U.S. North were relatively unaffected by the insult and tended to ignore it. The southerners were more likely to think their masculine reputation was threatened, and reacted with a rise in testosterone, and more aggressive and dominant behaviour (e.g., swearing, yelling). A variation of this study with male Dutch train travellers showed that adherence to honour norms was linked to insult perceptions and emotional reactions.[75]

Awareness of how others perceive things is important to understanding why they think and act the way they do. But, being human, people will tend to assume that others see things the way they do (projection as a perceptual error is discussed later). This is why conflicting perceptions are often an underlying source of conflict and why

so many conflict resolution techniques are focused on communication, so people can share their perceptions and gain an understanding of the other's true intentions.

Three major categories of factors influence our perception of others: characteristics of ourselves, as perceivers; characteristics of the target person we are perceiving; and characteristics of the situation in which the interaction takes place. Figure 3.2 models social perception.

## Characteristics of the Perceiver

Several characteristics of the perceiver can affect social perception. One such characteristic is *familiarity* with the target (the person being perceived). When we are familiar with someone, we have multiple observations on which to base our impression of him or her. Familiarity does not always mean accuracy, however. Sometimes, when we know a person well, we tend to screen out information that is inconsistent with our beliefs about that person. This

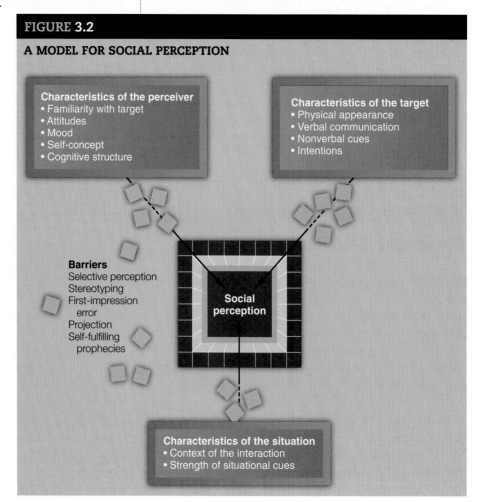

**FIGURE 3.2**

**A MODEL FOR SOCIAL PERCEPTION**

Characteristics of the perceiver
• Familiarity with target
• Attitudes
• Mood
• Self-concept
• Cognitive structure

Characteristics of the target
• Physical appearance
• Verbal communication
• Nonverbal cues
• Intentions

**Barriers**
Selective perception
Stereotyping
First-impression error
Projection
Self-fulfilling prophecies

Social perception

Characteristics of the situation
• Context of the interaction
• Strength of situational cues

is a particular danger in performance appraisals where the rater is familiar with the person being rated.

The perceiver's *attitudes* also affect social perception. Suppose you are interviewing candidates for a very important position in your organization—a position that requires negotiating contracts with suppliers, most of whom are older. You may feel that young people are not capable of holding their own in tough negotiations. This attitude will doubtlessly affect your perceptions of the young candidates you interview.

*Mood* can have a strong influence on the way we perceive someone.[76] We think differently when we are happy than we do when we are depressed. When in a positive mood, we form more positive impressions of others. When in a negative mood, we tend to evaluate others unfavourably.

Another factor that can affect social perception is the perceiver's *self-concept.* An individual with a positive self-concept tends to notice positive attributes in another person. In contrast, a negative self-concept can lead a perceiver to pick out negative traits in another person. The better we understand ourselves, the more accurate our perceptions of others.

*Cognitive structure*, an individual's pattern of thinking, also affects social perception. Some people tend to perceive physical traits, such as height, weight, and appearance, more readily. Others focus on central traits, or personality dispositions. Cognitive complexity allows a person to perceive multiple characteristics of another person rather than attending to just a few traits.

## Characteristics of the Target

Characteristics of the target, the person being perceived, influence social perception. *Physical appearance* plays a big role in our perception of others. The perceiver will notice physical features like height, weight, estimated age, race, and gender. Perceivers tend to notice physical appearance characteristics that contrast with the norm, those that are intense, new, or unusual.[77] A loud person, one who dresses outlandishly, a very tall person, or a hyperactive child will be noticed because he or she contrasts with what is commonly encountered. Novel individuals, like newcomers or minorities, also attract attention.

Physical attractiveness often colours our entire impression of another person. Interviewers rate attractive candidates more favourably and award them higher starting salaries.[78] Whether male or female, attractive people are judged more positively in terms of their occupational, academic, and interpersonal competence.[79]

*Verbal communication* from targets also affects our perception of them. We listen to the topics they discuss, their voice tone, and their accent and make judgments based on this input.

*Nonverbal communication* conveys a great deal of information about the target. Eye contact, facial expressions, body movements, and posture all are deciphered by the perceiver in an attempt to form an impression of the target. Some nonverbal signals mean very different things in different cultures. The "okay" sign in Canada (forming a circle with the thumb and forefinger) is an insult in South America. Facial expressions, however, seem to have universal meanings. Individuals from different cultures can recognize and decipher expressions the same way.[80]

The *intentions* of the target are inferred by the perceiver, who observes the target's behaviour. We may see our boss appear in our office doorway and think, "Oh no! She's going to give me more work to do." Or we may perceive that her intention is to congratulate us on a recent success. In any case, the perceiver's interpretation of the target's intentions affects the way the perceiver views the target.

## Characteristics of the Situation

The situation in which the interaction between the perceiver and the target takes place also influences perception. The *social context* of the interaction is a major influence. Meeting a professor in his or her office affects your impression differently than meeting your professor in a local restaurant would. In Japan, social context is very important. Business conversations after working hours or at lunch are taboo. If you try to talk business during these times, you may be perceived as rude.[81]

South American
Not okay

Canada
okay

Other Places
Better check first

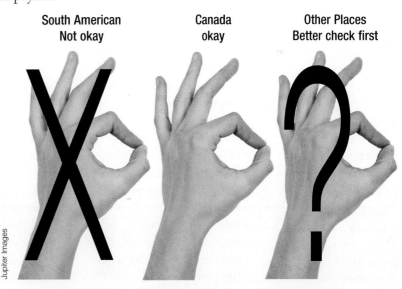

Jupiter Images

The *strength of situational cues* also affects social perception. As we discussed earlier in the chapter, some situations provide strong cues as to appropriate behaviour. In these situations, we assume that the individual's behaviour can be accounted for by the situation, and that it may not reflect the individual's disposition. This is the **discounting principle** in social perception.[82] For example, you may encounter an automobile salesperson who has a warm and personable manner, asks about your work and hobbies, and seems genuinely interested in your taste in cars. You probably cannot assume that this behaviour reflects his or her personality, because of the influence of the situation. This person is trying to sell you a car, and he or she probably treats all customers in this manner.

## Stereotypes reduce information about other people to a workable level, so that it can be compiled efficiently.

A **stereotype** is a generalization about a group of people. Stereotypes reduce information about other people to a workable level, so that it can be compiled efficiently. Stereotypes become even stronger when they are shared with and validated by others.[83] Stereotypes can be accurate and serve as useful perceptual guidelines. Inaccurate stereotypes are harmful, however, because they generate false impressions that may never be tested or changed.[84] Stereotyping pervades work life.

In multicultural work teams, members often stereotype foreign coworkers rather than getting to know them before forming an impression. Team members from less-developed countries are often assumed to know less simply because their homeland is economically or technologically less developed.[85] Stereotypes like these can deflate the productivity of the work team and lower morale.

Attractiveness is a powerful stereotype. We assume that attractive individuals are also warm, kind, sensitive, poised, sociable, outgoing, independent, and strong. However, a study of romantic relationships showed that most attractive individuals do not fit the stereotype, except for possessing good social skills and being popular.[86]

Some individuals may seem to us to fit the stereotype of attractiveness because our behaviour elicits from them behaviour that confirms the stereotype. Consider, for example, a situation in which you meet an attractive fellow student. Chances are that you respond positively to this person, because you assume he or she is warm, sociable, and so on. Even though the person may not possess these traits, your positive response may bring out these behaviours in the person. Thus, your interaction may be channelled to confirm the stereotype.[87] In fact, research shows that we treat attractive people better than unattractive people, giving them more attention, rewards, cooperation, and help, and this is true of not only attractive strangers but also people with whom we are familiar. Is it a surprise that attractive people are healthier, more confident, and have better social skills?[88]

First impressions are lasting impressions, so the saying goes. We tend to remember what we perceive first about a person, and sometimes we are quite reluctant to change our initial impressions.[89] **First-impression error** occurs when we observe a very brief bit of a person's behaviour in our first encounter and infer that this behaviour reflects what the person is really like. Primacy effects can be particularly dangerous in interviews, given that we form first impressions quickly and that these impressions may be the basis for long-term employment relationships.

# Barriers to Social Perception

It would be wonderful if all of us had accurate social perception skills. Unfortunately, barriers often prevent us from perceiving others accurately. Seven barriers to social perception are selective perception, stereotyping, first-impression error, recency effect, contrast effect, projection, and self-fulfilling prophecies.

**Selective perception** is our tendency to prefer information that supports our viewpoints. Individuals often ignore information that threatens their viewpoints. Suppose, for example, that a sales manager is evaluating the performance of his employees. One employee does not get along well with colleagues and rarely completes sales reports on time. This employee, however, generates the most new sales contracts in the office. The sales manager may ignore the negative information, choosing to evaluate the salesperson only on contracts generated. The manager is exercising selective perception.

**discounting principle**
The assumption that an individual's behaviour is accounted for by the situation.

**selective perception**
The process of selecting information that supports our individual viewpoints while discounting information that threatens our viewpoints.

**stereotype**
A generalization about a group of people.

**first-impression error**
The tendency to form lasting opinions about an individual based on initial perceptions.

What factors do interviewers rely on when forming first impressions? Perceptions of the candidate, such as whether the person is likeable, trustworthy, or credible, all influence the interviewer's decision.

Something seemingly as unimportant as a handshake can leave a lasting impression. Despite all the relevant information that emerges in an interview following the initial handshake, the firmness of that handshake is significantly related to interview ratings. The correlation is stronger for female job candidates than male candidates.[90]

The **recency effect** is the opposite of a first impression error in that it describes the tendency to weigh recent events more heavily than earlier events. Many employees take advantage of the recency effect by increasing their effort right before their annual appraisal, guessing correctly that the supervisor is more likely to be influenced by this vivid recent performance than the errors made months ago.

In addressing the **contrast effect**, consider the following: you are waiting for a job interview with the other applicants, all delayed because of a traffic jam holding up the recruiter. Through chatting with the other applicants, you have formed the impression that one of them is the "perfect" candidate, articulate and experienced, whereas another is a "loser," obviously unqualified for the position. Who would you rather follow when it comes time for your interview? Yes, the loser, because comparison between the two of you will likely enhance the impression you make whereas immediate comparison between you and the "ideal" candidate may diminish the impression you make.

**Projection**, also known as the false-consensus effect, causes inaccurate perceptions of others. It is the misperception of the commonness of our own beliefs, values, and behaviours that leads us to overestimate the number of others who share them. We assume that others are similar to us, and that our own values and beliefs are appropriate. People who are different are viewed as unusual and even deviant. Projection occurs most often when you surround yourself with others similar to you. You may overlook important information about others when you assume we are all alike and in agreement.[91]

**Self-fulfilling prophecies** (also

called the Pygmalion effect) interfere with social perception. Sometimes our expectations affect the way we interact with others such that we get what we wish for.

Early studies of self-fulfilling prophecy were conducted in elementary school classrooms. Teachers were given bogus information that some of their pupils had high intellectual potential. These pupils were chosen randomly; there were really no differences among the students. Eight months later, the "gifted" pupils scored significantly higher on an IQ test. The teachers' expectations had elicited growth from these students, and the teachers had given them tougher assignments and more feedback on their performance.[92]

A manager's expectations of an individual affect both the manager's behaviour toward the individual and the individual's response. For example, suppose your initial impression is that an employee has the potential to move up within the organization. Chances are, you will spend a great deal of time coaching and counselling the employee, providing challenging assignments, and grooming the individual for success.

Managers can harness the power of the Pygmalion effect to improve productivity in the organization simply by expecting positive results from a group of employees.[93]

## Impression Management

Most people want to make favourable impressions on others. This is particularly true in organizations, where individuals compete for jobs, favourable performance evaluations, and salary increases. The process by which individuals try to control the impressions others have of them is called **impression management**. Individuals use several techniques to control others' impressions of them.[94]

Some impression management techniques are self-enhancing, for example, name-dropping, manipulating "face time" at work to appear to be putting in long hours and extra work even when not doing so, ensuring others know of personal accomplishments, and using dress to "look the part."

Another group of impression management

**recency effect**
The tendency to weigh recent events more than earlier events.

**contrast effect**
The tendency to diminish or enhance the measure of one target through comparison with another recently observed target.

**projection**
Overestimating the number of people who share our own beliefs, values, and behaviours.

**self-fulfilling prophecy**
The situation in which our expectations about people affect our interaction with them in such a way that our expectations are fulfilled.

**impression management**
The process by which individuals try to control the impressions others have of them.

Kurhan/Shutterstock

CHAPTER 3 Personality, Perception, and Attribution **51**

techniques are *other-enhancing*. They focus on the individual on whom one is trying to make an impression rather than on one's self. People often use flattery and favours to win approval. Agreeing with someone's opinion can create a positive impression. People with disabilities, for example, often use other-enhancing techniques. They may feel that they must take it upon themselves to make others comfortable interacting with them. Impression management techniques help them prevent potential avoidance by others.[95]

Research results indicate that job candidates who engage in impression management techniques perform better in interviews, are more likely to be hired and are rated more favourably in performance appraisals than those who do not.[96,97] However, research also shows that what you see may not be what you get in that there is no link between the use of those impression management techniques and actual performance on the job.[98]

No wonder coworkers have ugly names for those who engage in impression management techniques. For managers to accurately assess current and potential future performance, it is important that they use clear criteria to focus the assessment on valid measures and away from contaminants. For example, unstructured employment interviews are much more vulnerable to the influence of impression management techniques than structured interviews.

# Attribution in Organizations

Human beings are innately curious. We want to know *why* people behave the way they do. We also seek to understand and explain our own behaviour. **Attribution theory** explains how we pinpoint the causes of our own behaviour (and therefore our performance) and that of other people.[99]

**attribution theory**
A theory that explains how individuals pinpoint the causes of their own behaviour and that of others.

**fundamental attribution error**
The tendency to make attributions to internal causes when focusing on someone else's behaviour.

**self-serving bias**
The tendency to attribute one's own successes to internal causes and one's failures to external causes.

## Internal and External Attributions

We can attribute events to an internal source of responsibility (something within the individual's control) or an external source (something outside the individual's control). Suppose you perform well on an exam. You might say you aced the test because you are smart or because you studied hard; this internal attribution credits your ability or effort. Alternatively, you might make an external attribution for your performance by saying it was an easy test or that you had good luck.

Attribution patterns differ among individuals.[100] Achievement-oriented individuals attribute their success to ability and their failures to lack of effort, both internal causes. Failure-oriented individuals attribute their failures to lack of ability, and they may develop feelings of incompetence (or even depression) as a result.[101] Women managers are less likely to attribute their success to their own ability. This may be because they are adhering to social norms that compel women to be modest or because they believe that success has more do to with hard work than ability.[102]

Attribution theory has many applications in the workplace. The way you explain your own behaviour affects your motivation. If you believe careful preparation and rehearsal led to your successful presentation, you're likely to take credit for the performance and to have a sense of self-efficacy about future presentations. If, however, you believe that you were just lucky, you may not be motivated to repeat the performance because you believe you had little influence on the outcome.

> " The way you explain your own behaviour affects your motivation.

## Attributional Biases

The attribution process may be affected by two very common errors: the fundamental attribution error and the self-serving bias. The tendency to make attributions to internal causes when focusing on someone else's behaviour is known as the **fundamental attribution error**.[103] For example, if you see someone fall on the stairs ahead of you, you are likely to assume that the person is clumsy or was not watching carefully (an internal attribution), whereas when the same thing happens to you, you may look for something on the stair that tripped you like a puddle or loose tread, an external attribution. Looking for external reasons for others' behaviours is complex and difficult because of limited information so it is much faster and easier to assume internal causation. This means that we tend to blame people for their problems, even when the situation is the actual culprit, and we may credit people for their successes even when they did nothing to truly deserve it. The other error, **self-serving bias**, occurs when focusing on one's own behaviour. Individuals tend to make internal attributions for their own successes and external attributions for their own failures.[104] In other

Phil Date/Shutterstock

*Luck or skill?*

words, when we succeed, we take credit for it; when we fail, we blame the situation on other people.

Both biases were illustrated in a study of health care managers asked to cite the causes of their employees' poor performance.[105] The managers claimed that internal causes (their employees' lack of effort or lack of ability) explained their employees' poor performance. When the employees were asked to pinpoint the cause of their own performance problems, they blamed a lack of support from the managers (an external cause), which illustrates self-serving bias.

There are cultural differences in these two attribution errors. In fatalistic cultures, such as India's, people tend to believe that fate is responsible for much that happens. People in such cultures tend to emphasize external causes of behaviour.[106]

In China, people are taught that hard work is the route to accomplishment. When faced with either a success or a failure, Chinese individuals first introspect about whether they tried hard enough or whether their attitude was correct. In analyzing a cause, they first look to their own effort.[107]

The way individuals interpret the events around them has a strong influence on their behaviour. People try to understand the causes of behaviour so they can predict

and control future behaviour. Managers use attributions in all aspects of their jobs. In evaluating performance and rewarding employees, managers must determine the causes of behaviour and a perceived source of responsibility.

## Performance and Kelley's Attribution Theory

According to attribution theory, managers make attributions (inferences) concerning employees' behaviour and performance.[108] The attributions may not always be accurate. Supervisors and employees who share perceptions and attitudes tend to evaluate each other highly.[109] Supervisors and employees who do not share perceptions and attitudes are more likely to blame each other for performance problems.

Harold Kelley's attribution theory aims to help us explain the behaviour of other people. He also extended attribution theory by trying to identify the antecedents of internal and external attributions. Kelley proposed that individuals make attributions based on information gathered in the form of three informational cues: consensus, distinctiveness, and consistency.[110]

Consensus is the extent to which peers in the same situation behave the same way. **Distinctiveness** is the degree to which the person behaves the same way in other situations. **Consistency** refers to the frequency of a particular behaviour over time.

We form attributions based on whether these cues are low or high. Figure 3.3 shows how the combination of these cues fosters internal or external attributions. Suppose you have received several complaints from customers regarding one of your customer service representatives, John. You have not received complaints about your other service representatives (low consensus). Reviewing John's records, you find that he also received customer complaints during his previous job as a sales clerk (low distinctiveness). The complaints have been coming in steadily for three months (high consistency). In this case, you would most likely make an internal attribution and conclude that the complaints must stem from John's behaviour. The combination of low consensus, low distinctiveness, and high consistency suggests internal attributions.

FIGURE **3.3**

**INFORMATIONAL CUES AND ATTRIBUTIONS**

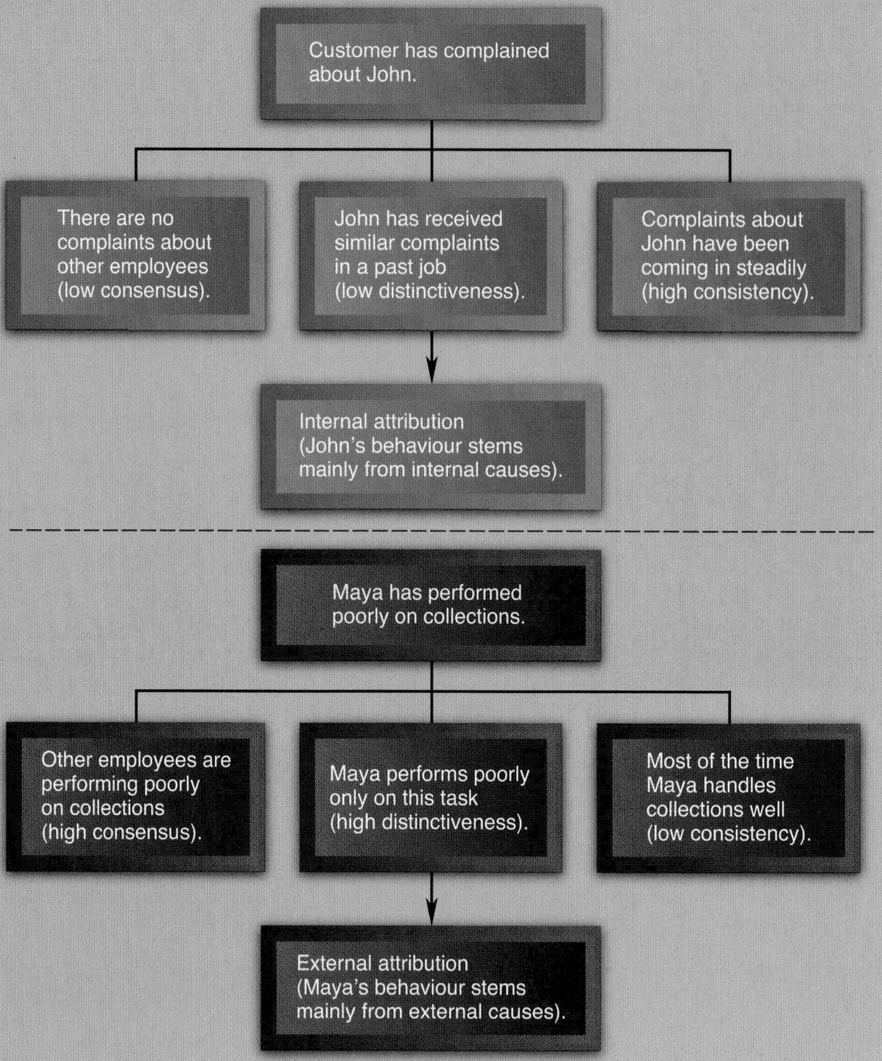

Other combinations of these cues, however, produce external attributions. High consensus, high distinctiveness, and low consistency, for example, produce external attributions. Suppose one of your employees, Maya is performing poorly on collecting overdue accounts. You find that the behaviour is widespread within your work team (high consensus) and that Maya is performing poorly only on this aspect of the job (high distinctiveness), and that most of the time she handles this aspect of the job well (low consistency). You will probably decide that something about the work situation caused the poor performance.

The process of determining the cause of a behaviour is not always so simple and clear-cut, however, because some biases sometimes interfere.

Figure 3.4 presents an attribution model of supervisors' responses to poor performance.

On the basis of this information, the supervisor makes either an internal (personal) attribution or an external (situational) attribution. Internal attributions might include low effort, lack of commitment, or lack of ability. External attributions are outside the employee's control and might include equipment failure or unrealistic goals.

Supervisors may choose from a wide range of responses. They can, for example, express personal concern, reprimand the employee, or provide training. Supervisors who attribute the cause of poor performance to a person (an internal cause) will respond more harshly than supervisors who

**consensus**

An informational cue indicating the extent to which peers in the same situation behave in a similar fashion.

**distinctiveness**

An informational cue indicating the degree to which an individual behaves the same way in other situations.

**consistency**

An informational cue indicating the frequency of behaviour over time.

FIGURE **3.4**

**ATTRIBUTION MODEL**

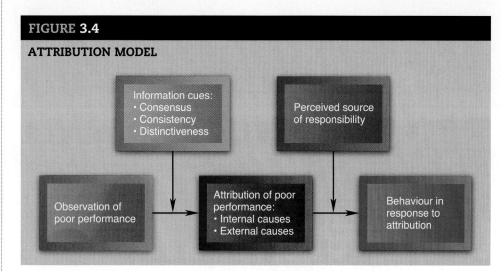

blame the work situation (an external cause). Supervisors should avoid both common attribution errors: the fundamental attribution error and the self-serving bias.

## Influencing Perceptions

Perceptual issues underlie many organizational issues. Perceptions of fairness are a critical influence on motivation—an impression that one is getting a bad deal compared to others, even if untrue, is demotivating. Employees who perceive that management does not trust them show lower performance because they do not accept personal responsibility for organizational outcomes.[111] Minority and female job applicants are harder to recruit if they perceive the

**The process of determining the cause of a behaviour is not always so simple and clear-cut.**

organization does not value diversity.[112] If employees see management practices as self-serving rather than reflecting true concern for employee well-being, employee commitment and satisfaction and organizational citizenship behaviours suffer.[113] How employees perceive change has a huge impact on their resistance to it.

Management perceptions are also important. For example, when managers see employees engage in prosocial, proactive behaviour, they give credit only to the employees whom they perceive to be doing it for selfless reasons. They ignore the same behaviour in employees whose motives are seen to be questionable (thereby discouraging the latter from engaging in further proactive behaviour).[114] Management's attributions are assumptions, rather than fact, however.

We want and need to understand others' perceptions. This means observing and communicating rather than jumping to conclusions. We also want others to perceive our own actions favourably. This means thinking through potential misinterpretations and reactions before we act and communicating the "whys" clearly when we do act.

# Visit **icanorgb.com** to find the resources you need today!

*Located at the back of the textbook are rip-out Chapter Review Cards. Make sure you also go online to check out other tools that ORGB offers to help you successfully pass your course.*

- Interactive Quizzing
- Key Term Flashcards
- PowerPoint Slides
- Audio Chapter Summaries

- Cases and Exercises
- Interactive Games
- Self-Assessments
- "On the Job" and "Bizflix" Videos

# Attitudes, Emotions, and Ethics

# Attitudes

An **attitude** is a psychological tendency expressed when we evaluate a particular entity with some degree of favour or disfavour.[1] We respond favourably or unfavourably toward many things: animals, coworkers, our own appearance, and politics.

Attitudes are closely linked to behaviour and an integral part of the world of work. Managers complain about workers with "bad attitudes" and conduct "attitude adjustment" talks. Often, poor performance attributed to bad attitudes really stems from lack of motivation, minimal feedback, lack of trust in management, or other problems.

Managers should understand the antecedents to attitudes as well as their consequences. Managers also need to understand the different components of attitudes, how attitudes are formed, the major attitudes that affect work behaviour, and how to use persuasion to change attitudes.

## The ABC Model

Three components—affect, behavioural intentions, and cognition—compose what we call the ABC model of an attitude.[2] **Affect** is the emotional component of an attitude. It refers to an individual's feeling about something or someone. Statements such as "I like this" or "I prefer that" reflect the affective component of an attitude. Affect is measured by physiological indicators, such as blood pressure, which show emotional changes by measuring physiological arousal.

The second component is the intention to behave in a certain way toward an object or person. Our

**attitude**
A psychological tendency expressed by evaluating an entity with some degree of favour or disfavour.

**affect**
The emotional component of an attitude.

## LEARNING OUTCOMES

After reading this chapter, you should be able to do the following:

**1** Explain the ABC model of an attitude.

**2** Describe how attitudes are formed.

**3** Identify the sources and consequences of job satisfaction.

**4** Distinguish between organizational citizenship and workplace deviance behaviours.

**5** Identify the characteristics of the source, target, and message that affect persuasion.

**6** Discuss the definition and importance of emotions at work.

**7** Describe the consequences of individual and organizational ethical behaviour.

**8** Identify the factors that affect ethical behaviour.

attitudes toward management, for example, may be inferred from observing the way we treat a supervisor. We may be supportive, passive, or hostile, depending on our attitude. The behavioural component of an attitude is measured by observing behaviour or by asking a person about behaviour or intentions.

The third component of an attitude, cognition (thought), reflects a person's perceptions or beliefs. Cognitive elements are evaluative beliefs measured by attitude scales or by asking about thoughts. The statement "I believe Japanese workers are industrious" reflects the cognitive component of an attitude.

The ABC model (see Table 4.1) shows we must consider all three components to understand an attitude.

## Cognitive Dissonance

As rational beings, people prefer consistency (consonance) between their attitudes and behaviour. Anything that disrupts this consistency causes tension (dissonance), which motivates individuals to change either their attitudes or their behaviour to maintain consistency. The tension produced by a conflict between attitudes and behaviour is **cognitive dissonance.**[3]

Suppose, for example, a salesperson is required to sell damaged televisions for the full retail price, without revealing the damage to customers. She believes, however, that this is unethical. This creates a conflict between her attitude (concealing information from customers is unethical) and her behaviour (selling defective TVs to uninformed customers).

The salesperson, uncomfortable with the dissonance, will try to resolve the conflict. She

**cognitive dissonance**

A state of tension that is produced when an individual experiences conflict between attitudes and behaviour.

**TABLE 4.1** The ABC Model of an Attitude

| | COMPONENT | MEASURED BY | EXAMPLE |
|---|---|---|---|
| A | Affect | Physiological indicators Verbal statements about feelings | I don't like my boss. |
| B | Behavioural intentions | Observed behaviour Verbal statements about intentions | I want to transfer to another department. |
| C | Cognition | Attitude scales Verbal statements about beliefs | I believe my boss plays favourites at work. |

SOURCE: Adapted from M. J. Rosenberg and C. I. Hovland, "Cognitive, Affective, and Behavioral Components of Attitude," in M. J. Rosenberg, C. I. Hovland, W. J. McGuire, R. P. Abelson, and J. H. Brehm, *Attitude Organization and Change* (New Haven, Conn.: Yale University Press, 1960). Copyright 1960 Yale University Press. Used with permission.

might change her behaviour by refusing to sell the defective TV sets. Alternatively, she might rationalize that the defects are minor and that the customers won't be harmed by not knowing about them. These are attempts by the salesperson to restore equilibrium between her attitudes and behaviour, thereby eliminating the tension from cognitive dissonance.

Managers need to understand cognitive dissonance because employees often find themselves in situations in which their attitudes conflict with their behaviour. Employees who display sudden shifts in behaviour may be attempting to reduce dissonance. Some employees find the conflicts between strongly held attitudes and required work behaviour so uncomfortable that they leave the organization to escape the dissonance.

A manager can sometimes use dissonance deliberately to change an employee's attitude. This is done by involving the employee in a task that contradicts the underlying attitude. For example, a manager who wants an employee to take safety more seriously may ask the person to join the health and safety committee, emphasizing the importance of the role, how this employee is well suited to it, and allocating time for the commitment. It would be difficult for the employee to refuse. The employee would then be involved in audits of the workplace and meetings to discuss needed changes. This involvement contradicts an attitude that health and safety is a trivial concern, creating dissonance. But the involvement is public and cannot be retracted, leading the employee to resolve the dissonance by changing the attitude. Health and safety is now judged to be a more important concern, in line with the employee's observable behaviour.

corepics/Shutterstock

# Attitude Formation

Attitudes are learned. Our responses to people and issues evolve over time. Two major influences on attitudes are direct experience and social learning.

Direct experience with something strongly influences attitudes towards it. How do you know that you like biology or dislike math? You have probably formed these attitudes from experience in studying the subjects. Research has shown that attitudes derived from direct experience are stronger, held more confidently, and more resistant to change than attitudes formed through indirect experience.[4] These attitudes are powerful because of their availability; they are easily accessed and active in our cognitive processes.[5]

In **social learning**, the family, peer groups, and culture shape an individual's attitudes indirectly.[6] Children adopt certain attitudes when their parents reinforce attitudes they approve. Peer pressure moulds attitudes through group acceptance of individuals who express popular attitudes and through sanctions, such as exclusion from the group, placed on individuals who espouse unpopular attitudes.

Substantial social learning occurs through modelling, in which individuals acquire attitudes by observing others. For example, research indicates that the example set by an ethical manager is more effective in altering employee attitudes than is formal ethical training.[7]

## LEARNING FROM OBSERVING A MODEL

>> For an individual to learn from observing a model, four processes must take place:

1. The learner must focus attention on the model.

2. The learner must retain what was observed from the model. Retention is accomplished in two basic ways. In one, the learner "stamps in" what was observed by forming a verbal code for it. The other way is through symbolic rehearsal, by which the learner forms a mental image of himself or herself behaving like the model.

3. Behavioural reproduction must occur; that is, the learner must practise the behaviour.

4. The learner must be motivated to learn from the model.

Employers may rely on modelling in training approaches such as job shadowing. However, the effectiveness of learning from a model depends on attention, motivation, and practice (see Learning from Observing a Model).

Culture also plays a role in attitude development. Consider, for example, the contrast in the American and European attitudes toward vacation and leisure. The typical vacation in the United States is two weeks. In Europe, longer vacations are the norm; and in some countries, *holiday* means everyone taking a month off. The European attitude is that an investment in longer vacations is important to health and performance.

## Attitudes and Behaviour

The correspondence between attitude and behaviour has concerned organizational behaviourists and social psychologists for quite some time. Can attitudes predict behaviours like being absent from work or quitting your job? Some studies suggested that attitudes and behaviour are closely linked, while others found no relationship at all. Researchers then focused on when attitudes predict behaviour and when they do not. Attitude–behaviour correspondence depends on five things: attitude specificity, attitude relevance, timing of measurement, personality factors, and social constraints.

Individuals possess both general and specific attitudes. You may be a health and fitness proponent who works out regularly. Yet you may still take the elevator at work to go up two floors, and accept the cake offered by a colleague. These actions appear to weaken the link between attitudes and behaviours, but the fact is all actions are influenced by a variety of elements (e.g., you are helping a friend carry some equipment; it is your colleague's birthday and you do not want to offend). Given a choice of company benefits between a free gym membership or a parking space close to the building, you will probably choose the gym membership. Your attitude is predictive of your behaviour in this case because it is much more specific.[8]

Another factor that affects the attitude–behaviour link is relevance.[9] Attitudes that address an issue in which we have some self-interest are more relevant for us, and our subsequent behaviour is consistent with our expressed attitude. Consider a proposal to raise income taxes for those earning $150,000 or more. If you are a student, you may not find the issue of great personal relevance. Individuals in that income bracket, however, might find it highly relevant; their attitude toward the issue would be strongly predictive of whether they would vote for the tax increase.

**social learning**

The process of deriving attitudes from family, peer groups, and culture.

The timing of the measurement also affects attitude–behaviour correspondence. The shorter the time between the attitude measurement and the observed behaviour, the stronger the relationship. For example, voter preference polls taken close to an election are more accurate than earlier polls.

Personality factors also influence the attitude–behaviour link. One personality disposition that affects the consistency between attitudes and behaviour is self-monitoring. Recall from Chapter 3 that low self-monitors rely on their internal states when making decisions about behaviour, while high self-monitors are more responsive to situational cues. Low self-monitors therefore display greater correspondence between their attitudes and behaviours.[10] High self-monitors may display little correspondence between their attitudes and behaviour because they behave according to signals from others and from the environment.

Finally, social constraints affect the relationship between attitudes and behaviour.[11] The social context provides information about acceptable attitudes and behaviours.[12,13] New employees in an organization are exposed to the attitudes of their work group. A newcomer from Afghanistan may hold a negative attitude toward women in management because this attitude prevails in his country. He sees, however, that his work group members respond positively to their female supervisor. His own behaviour may therefore be compliant because of social constraints. This behaviour is inconsistent with his attitude and cultural belief system.

## Work Attitudes

Attitudes at work are important because, directly or indirectly, they affect work behaviour. Employee work attitudes correlate with performance, absenteeism, turnover, unionization, grievances, and drug abuse.[14] Studies have shown employee attitudes to be predictive of financial performance measures such as market share,[15] and to be related to customer satisfaction. Chief among the things that

negatively affect employees' work attitudes are demanding jobs over which they have little control.[16] A positive climate, on the other hand, can generate positive attitudes and good performance.[17] A field experiment demonstrated that hotel customers developed a more positive attitude toward the hotel when offered helpful, concerned service by employees. Customers responded to employee warmth by increasing loyalty and a willingness to pay more for the service.[18] Because of the power of attitudes, it is important to know how employees feel about their work, and what influences lie behind those attitudes so action can be taken to guide attitudes in a constructive way where possible.

# Job Satisfaction

**Job satisfaction** is a pleasurable or positive emotional state resulting from the appraisal of one's job or job experiences.[19] It has been treated both as a general attitude and as satisfaction with specific dimensions of the job such as pay, the work itself, promotion opportunities, supervision, and coworkers.[20]

Many organizations formally survey job satisfaction in their employees. The two most extensively validated measures of job satisfaction are the Job Descriptive Index (JDI) and Minnesota Satisfaction Questionnaire (MSQ). Figure 4.1 presents sample items from each questionnaire. These tools have been of value to practitioners because they examine how employees are

**job satisfaction**

A pleasurable or positive emotional state resulting from the appraisal of one's job or job experiences.

## [ Yahoo: Down and Out? ]

When several industry analysts started to speculate that Yahoo! would be at risk of a takeover if the company didn't cut costs or divest assets, employee morale plummeted. Low morale precipitated a mass exodus of experienced managers—including top executives and engineers—taking with them years of knowledge and know-how. To make matters worse, an entrenched bureaucratic organizational structure was slowing down decision making, and employees complained about the lack of passion from their CEO, Terry Semel, who ultimately lost his job because of the severity of morale problems at Yahoo!

SOURCES: R. D. Hof, "Even Yahoo! Gets the Blues." *BusinessWeek* (2007): 37; M. Helft, "Can She Turn Yahoo into, Well, Google?" *The New York Times*, 07/01/2007; http://news.com.com/Can+she+turn+Yahoo+into%2C+well%2C+Google/2100-1024_3-6194437.html?tag=st.num

Assess your own job satisfaction by completing What about You? on the Chapter 4 Review Card.

reacting to specific aspects of the job and circumstances. Global measures of job satisfaction (e.g., simply asking "Overall, how satisfied are you with your job?") are highly correlated with faceted measures like the JDI and MSQ, and a lot easier, cheaper, and quicker to administer. However, if job satisfaction is not high, the global mea-

sure does not allow exploration of the underlying issues. If employees are not satisfied, what needs to be changed?

What does tend to make employees more satisfied? Studies have shown the importance of good relations with management and interesting work,[21] coworker support,[22] good pay, and security.[23] Factors important for job satisfaction will vary with the individual. For example, more educated workers are more likely to emphasize the intrinsic job content (interesting job, meets one's abilities, opportunity to use initiative, useful for society) and less educated workers are more likely to endorse extrinsic factors such as pay, good hours, and generous holidays.[24] Personality research shows that those with high core self-evaluation will tend to be more satisfied with their work, no matter what they are doing, than people with low core self-evaluation.[25] Employees with negative affectivity (who tend towards being distressed, pessimistic and generally dissatisfied) will tend to be less satisfied with any job they have than those with positive affectivity.[26,27] One study showed that affective disposition measured when the participants were 15 to 18 years of age correlated significantly with their job satisfaction measured 40 years later.[28]

Managers and employees believe that happy or "satisfied" employees are more productive at work. The satisfaction–performance link is actually more complex than that. There is a correlation between the two (r = .3)[29] so that individuals who are satisfied do tend to be better performers, but job satisfaction only explains a modest amount of the variation in performance. Many factors influence an individual's performance, and there are many exceptions to the satisfaction–performance link, where satisfied workers do not perform well and dissatisfied workers do work effectively. Even in those cases where satisfaction and performance are closely linked, it is unclear whether satisfaction leads to performance, or strong performance leads to personal satisfaction, or another variable mediates both, or if all are true. We do know that job satisfaction is a better predictor of performance in complex professional jobs. Rewards may act as a link between satisfaction and performance. Employees who receive valued rewards are more satisfied. In addition,

---

## FIGURE 4.1

### SAMPLE ITEMS FROM SATISFACTION QUESTIONNAIRES

**Job Descriptive Index**

Think of the work you do at present. How well does each of the following words or phrases describe your work? In the blank beside each word given below, write

   Y    for "Yes" if it describes your work
   N    for "No" if it does NOT describe it
   ?    if you cannot decide

WORK ON YOUR PRESENT JOB:

_____ Routine
_____ Satisfying
_____ Good

Think of the majority of the people that you work with now or the people you meet in connection with your work. How well does each of the following words or phrases describe these people? In the blank beside each word, write

   Y    for "Yes" if it describes the people you work with
   N    for "No" if it does NOT describe them
   ?    if you cannot decide

COWORKERS (PEOPLE):

_____ Boring
_____ Responsible
_____ Intelligent

---

**Minnesota Satisfaction Questionnaire**

1 = Very dissatisfied
2 = Dissatisfied
3 = I can't decide whether I am satisfied or not
4 = Satisfied
5 = Very satisfied

On my present job, this is how I feel about:

_____ The chance to work alone on the job (independence)
_____ My chances for advancement on this job (advancement)
_____ The chance to tell people what to do (authority)
_____ The praise I get for a good job (recognition)
_____ My pay and the amount of work I do (compensation)

SOURCES: Minnesota Satisfaction Questionnaire from D. J. Weiss, R. V. Davis, G. W. England, and L. H. Lofquist, *Manual for the Minnesota Satisfaction Questionnaire* (University of Minnesota Vocational Psychology Research, 1967). The Job Descriptive Index is copyrighted by Bowling Green State University. The complete forms, scoring key, instructions, and norms can be obtained from Dr. Patricia C. Smith, Department of Psychology, Bowling Green State University, Bowling Green, OH 43403.

employees who receive rewards that are contingent on performance (the higher the performance, the larger the reward) tend to perform better. Rewards thus influence both satisfaction and performance. The key to influencing both satisfaction and performance through rewards is that the rewards are valued by employees and are tied directly to performance.

Although job satisfaction does not predict individual performance reliably, researchers have found a strong link between job satisfaction and organizational performance. Companies with satisfied workers have better performance than companies with dissatisfied workers.[30] This may be due to the more intangible elements of performance, like organizational citizenship behaviour, that contribute to organizational effectiveness but aren't necessarily captured by measuring individual job performance.

Job satisfaction connects to other important outcomes. Dissatisfied workers are more likely to skip work and quit their jobs, driving up the cost of turnover. Dissatisfied workers also report more psychological and medical problems than do satisfied employees.[31]

One factor that leads to dissatisfaction at work is a misfit between an individual's values and the organization's values, which is called a lack of person–organization fit. People who feel that their values don't mesh with the organization's values experience job dissatisfaction and eventually leave the organization.[32]

**LEARNING OUTCOME 4**

# Organizational Citizenship versus Workplace Deviance

Job satisfaction encourages **organizational citizenship behaviour**—behaviour that is above and beyond the call of duty. Satisfied employees are more likely to help their coworkers, make positive comments about the company, and refrain from complaining when things at work go poorly.[33] Going beyond the call of duty is especially important to organizations using teams. Employees depend on extra help from each other to get things accomplished.

Satisfied workers are more likely to want to give something back to the organization because they want

**organizational citizenship behaviour**

Behaviour that is above and beyond the call of duty.

> " Dissatisfied workers are more likely to skip work and quit their jobs.

to reciprocate their positive experiences.[34] Often, employees may feel that citizenship behaviours are not recognized because they occur outside the confines of normal job responsibilities. Organizational citizenship behaviours (OCBs) do, however, influence performance evaluations. Employees who help others, suggest innovations, and develop their skills receive higher performance ratings[35] and are recognized through reward allocations.

Individuals who identify strongly with the organization are more likely to perform OCBs.[36] High self-monitors, who base their behaviour on cues from the situation, are also more likely to perform OCBs.[37] One study found that individual workers were more likely to offer OCBs when doing so was the norm among other team members. The impact of one worker's OCBs can spread throughout an entire department.[38]

The impact of OCBs is not simply on team interaction; OCB's influence "bottom-line" effectiveness in the organization. OCBs have been shown to relate to productivity, efficiency, reduced costs, customer satisfaction, and unit-level turnover.[39] Given the value of OCBs, how can an organization motivate employees to engage in these behaviours? To start with, managers can focus on selecting employees likely to engage in OCBs, using structured interviews designed to assess this propensity[40] and looking for evidence of conscientiousness. Managers can also take steps to ensure work decisions are fair and perceived to be fair; consider using a transformational leadership style where possible (to be discussed further in Chapter 12); and address issues that detract from employee attitudes such as job satisfaction and commitment.[41]

In direct contrast to the desirability of OCBs is the existence of workplace deviance. When employees

©Angel Herrero de Frutos/iStockPhoto

are dissatisfied with their jobs, they are more likely to engage in workplace deviance. Workplace deviance is defined as any voluntary counterproductive behaviour that violates organizational norms and causes some degree of harm to organizational functioning. *Workplace deviance behaviour (WDB)*, then, is a result of negative attitudes and consists of counterproductive behaviour that violates organizational norms and harms others or the organization.[42] Negative events in the business world, such as downsizing and technological insecurities, are generally considered responsible for spikes in workplace deviance. Layoffs, for example, may inspire employees to develop negative attitudes, to feel anger and hostility toward the organization, and to retaliate. Even when an employee keeps his or her job but believes the procedure used to determine the layoff is unfair, he or she may still take revenge against the manager.[43] Unfairness at work is a major cause of deviance, sabotage, and retaliation. Positive attitudes decrease deviance. Managers must prevent and manage WDB to keep it from harming performance.

## Organizational Commitment and Job Satisfaction

The strength of an individual's identification with an organization is known as **organizational commitment**. There are three kinds of organizational commitment: affective, continuance, and normative. **Affective commitment** is an employee's intention to remain in an organization because of a strong desire to do so. Affective commitment encompasses loyalty and a deep concern for the organization's welfare.

Affective commitment consists of three factors:

> A belief in the goals and values of the organization
> A willingness to put forth effort on behalf of the organization
> A desire to remain a member of the organization.[44]

**Continuance commitment** is an employee's tendency to remain in an organization because the person cannot afford to leave.[45] Sometimes, employees believe that if they leave, they will lose a great deal of their investments in time, effort, and benefits.

**Normative commitment** is a perceived obligation to remain with the organization. Individuals who experience normative commitment stay with the organization because they feel that they should.[46]

All three types of commitment are related to lower turnover. Looking at outcomes aside from turnover, research shows that employees with affective commitment show higher attendance, better performance, higher OCB and, on a personal level, less stress and less

**A source who is perceived as an expert is particularly persuasive.**

work–family conflict.[47] Normative commitment is also associated with desirable outcomes but not as strongly. Continuance commitment is not associated with any desirable outcomes other than lower turnover.

Managers can increase affective commitment by communicating their appreciation of employees' contributions, and their concern for employees' well-being.[48] Affective commitment also increases when the organization and employees share the same values, and when the organization emphasizes values such as moral integrity, fairness, creativity, and openness.[49] Negative experiences at work, such as perceived age discrimination, diminish affective commitment.[50]

# Persuasion and Attitude Change

To change attitudes, managers need to understand the process of persuasion. The days of command-and-control management, in which executives simply told employees what do to, are over. Modern managers must be skilled in the art of persuasion.[51] Through persuasion, one individual (the source) tries to change the attitude of another person (the target). Certain characteristics of the source, target, and message affect the persuasion process. There are two cognitive routes to persuasion.

## Source Characteristics

Three major characteristics of the source affect persuasion: expertise, trustworthiness, and attractiveness.[52]

You may feel there is nothing you can do about the last characteristic but, in fact, you can influence people's perception of your attractiveness through your behaviour: others' liking for you, respect for you, their familiarity with you, and their perception that

**organizational commitment**
The strength of an individual's identification with an organization.

**affective commitment**
The type of organizational commitment that is based on an individual's desire to remain in an organization.

**continuance commitment**
The type of organizational commitment that is based on the fact that an individual cannot afford to leave.

**normative commitment**
The type of organizational commitment that is based on an individual's perceived obligation to remain with an organization.

you are contributing to shared goals will all enhance how they judge your physical attractiveness. Research by Kniffen and Wilson demonstrated that the perceived attractiveness of a team member can go down significantly if that person proves to be lazy and uncooperative, or up significantly when the person is hard working and well liked.[53]

Trustworthiness is earned through employees observing five dimensions of a manager's actions: consistency, integrity, sharing and delegation of control, communication, and demonstration of concern.[54] Expertise is a judgment—others can see someone as expert only if he/she has relevant information, for example, regarding credentials, experience, and specific outcomes earned.

Canadian Sergio Marchionne, now CEO of Chrysler, is attempting to turn around Chrysler's fortunes and will have to be persuasive (with investors, employees, management, and industry partners) to be effective. What will help him is his perceived expertise and trustworthiness (he is both a lawyer and accountant, has decades of pertinent experience, and turned around Fiat's fortunes as CEO in the mid-2000s).

©Rebecca Cook/Reuters/Landov

Sergio Marchionne

## Target Characteristics

Individuals with low self-esteem are more likely to change their attitudes in response to persuasion than are individuals with high self-esteem. Individuals who hold very extreme attitudes are more resistant to persuasion, and people who are in a good mood are easier to persuade.[55] Undoubtedly, individuals differ widely in their susceptibility to persuasion. Managers must recognize these differences and realize that their attempts to change attitudes may not be universally accepted.

## Message Characteristics

Suppose you want to persuade your employees that an unpopular policy is a positive change. Should you present one side of the issue or both sides? Given that your employees are already negatively inclined toward the policy, you will have more success in changing their attitudes if you present both sides. This shows support for one side of the issue while acknowledging that another side does exist. Moreover, refuting the other side makes it harder for the targets to hang on to their negative attitudes.

Undisguised deliberate attempts at changing attitudes may drive employees' attitudes in the opposite direction! This is most likely to occur when the target of the persuasive communication feels his or her freedom is threatened.[56] Less threatening approaches are less likely to elicit negative reactions. The emotional tone of the message is also important. Messages framed with the same emotion as that felt by the receiver are more persuasive.[57]

## Cognitive Routes to Persuasion

When are message characteristics more important, and when are other characteristics more important in persuasion? The elaboration likelihood model of persuasion, presented in Figure 4.2, proposes that persuasion occurs through two routes: the central route and the peripheral route.[58] The routes are differentiated by the amount of elaboration, or scrutiny, the target is motivated to give the message.

The *central route* to persuasion involves direct cognitive processing of the message's content. Individuals think carefully about issues that are personally relevant. The listener may nod his or her head at strong arguments and shake his/her head at weak ones.[59] Logical and convincing arguments will change attitudes

In the *peripheral route* to persuasion, the individual is not motivated to pay much attention to the message's content because he or she is distracted or perceives the message as personally irrelevant. Instead, the individual is persuaded by characteristics of the persuader—for example, expertise, trustworthiness, and attractiveness. In addition, the individual may be persuaded by statistics, the number of arguments presented, or the method of presentation—all of which are nonsubstantial aspects of the message.

The elaboration likelihood model shows that the target's level of involvement with the issue is important. That involvement also determines which route to persuasion will be more effective. In some cases, attitude change comes about through both the central and the peripheral routes. To cover all of the bases, managers should structure the content of their messages carefully, develop their own effective persuasive attributes, and choose a method of presentation that will appeal to the audience.[60]

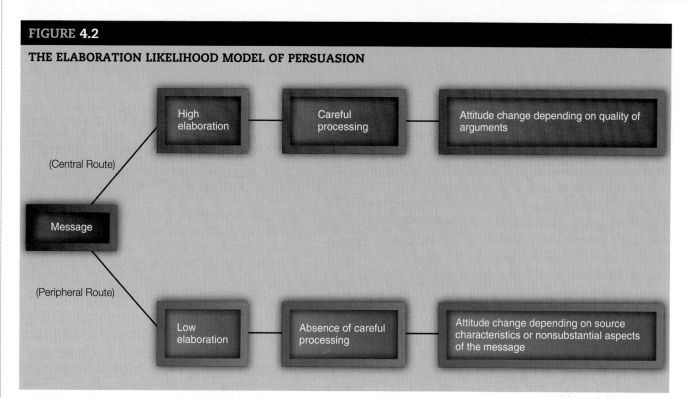

## FIGURE 4.2

### THE ELABORATION LIKELIHOOD MODEL OF PERSUASION

(Central Route)

High elaboration → Careful processing → Attitude change depending on quality of arguments

Message

(Peripheral Route)

Low elaboration → Absence of careful processing → Attitude change depending on source characteristics or nonsubstantial aspects of the message

SOURCE: Adapted from R. E. Petty and J. T. Cacioppo, "The Elaboration Likelihood Model of Persuasion," in L. Berkowitz, ed., *Advances in Experimental Social Psychology*, vol. 19 (New York: Academic Press, 1986), 123–205.

LEARNING OUTCOME 6

# Emotions at Work

Traditional management theories held that emotions were "bad" for rational decision making. Ideas about management centred around the stereotypic ideal employee who kept his or her emotions in check and behaved in a totally rational, nonemotional manner. Recent research has proven that emotions and cognitions are intertwined and that both are normal parts of human functioning and decision making.

**Emotions** are mental states including feelings, physiological changes, and the inclination to act.[61] They (e.g., anger, joy, pride, hostility) are short-lived, intense reactions to an event and affect work behaviours. Individuals differ in their capacity to experience both positive emotions (e.g. happiness, pride) and negative emotions (e.g. anger, fear, guilt).[62] When events at work are positive and goals are being met, employees experience positive emotions and are inspired to perform more OCBs.[63] Events that threaten or thwart the achievement of goals cause negative emotions, endangering employees' job satisfaction and commitment.[64] Negative emotions can get in the way of good decisions; for example, anger reactions can lead negotiators to reject offers that are in their best interests.[65]

Negative emotions generate workplace deviance. The use of power and influence in organizations, even if it is routine, can spark several forms of deviance. Such deviance could be targeted at both the organization and other individuals in the work environment.[66]

Positive emotions improve cognitive functioning, physical and psychological health, and coping mechanisms.[67] People who experience positive emotions tend to do so repeatedly and to be more creative.[68] Overall, people who experience positive emotions are more successful across a variety of life domains and report higher life satisfaction. Negative emotions, on the other hand, lead to

**emotions**
Mental states that typically include feelings, physiological changes, and the inclination to act.

©Wavebreak MediaMicro—Fotolia.com

unhealthy coping behaviours and diminish cardiovascular function and physical health.[69]

# Emotional Labour

You have likely worked in a customer service role of some kind and know that maintaining your composure while dealing with rude or frustrating customers is stressful. This describes **emotional labour**, the effort needed to manage your emotions in order to perform your job effectively. The emotional labour involved in many jobs can be demanding. Consider police expected to hide their anxiety in a dangerous situation, or health professionals expected to provide support to critically injured people when they themselves may be feeling sad or helpless in the situation.

People vary in their ability to handle emotional labour and employers can do much to help them. First, if the demands of the job are made clear before hiring, candidates themselves can choose whether to pursue the opportunity, knowing what will be involved. Upon hiring, employers can train employees in techniques both for managing their own emotions and for dealing with the emotions of others, for example, through role plays. Then, understanding the inevitable stresses of dealing with emotional labour on an ongoing basis, employers can offer support and stress release through, for example, regular breaks, timeout rooms to get away, appreciation for handling tough situations well, supportive coaching, and opportunities to socialize and share stories.

The degree of an individual's emotional labour is related both to the degree of **emotional dissonance** felt (contradiction between emotions experienced and expressed), and the way the contradiction is handled. Although we tend to see the emotional labour as "acting a part," it is important whether the employee is using surface acting or deep acting. In surface acting, the employee is trying to mask his or her true feelings but has not changed his or her beliefs about the situation. As a result, employees feel more stressed[70] and are more likely to appear insincere to customers because their true feelings "leak out." In deep acting, employees deal with the situation by changing their thoughts about the situation to better match the desired emotions. As a result, they feel less stress and are more effective in handling the situation. For example, some airlines have trained their service staff to handle difficult flyers by approaching them from the assumption that the customer's inappropriate behaviour is related to a fear of flying rather than an abusive personality.[71]

# Emotional Intelligence

The limited success of IQ in predicting many indicators of life success led to a search for other factors. There has been a long-held understanding that "people skills" or "soft" skills can make a significant difference and this has been formally recognized by the research on emotional intelligence. **Emotional intelligence** refers to a set of abilities related to understanding and managing one's own emotions, and recognizing and influencing the emotions of others in order to enhance social functioning. Emotional intelligence has been shown to influence job performance above and beyond general mental ability and personality factors, particularly in jobs requiring high emotional labour.[72]

Because emotional intelligence affects performance, it is appropriate to look for evidence of emotional intelligence when hiring, for example, in interview questions ("Tell me about a time when you were under intense pressure at work"), in checking references ("How would you say this person handles pressure?") and in selection testing (set up a role play where the candidate must deal with an unpleasant customer). Emotional intelligence is not fixed, however, and can be enhanced through training, feedback, and coaching.

# Emotional Display Rules

Part of emotional intelligence is awareness of others' emotions. Skill in recognizing others' emotions is complicated by the fact that others' emotions are not always visible and that different groups of people have different **emotional display rules**, their expectations about what emotions are appropriate to express in specific situations. Emotional recognition accuracy means recognizing "hidden" emotions that are disguised by people playing along with their display rules. If you are unfamiliar with the display rules, you may mistakenly take the communicated emotion to be the actual emotion.

Display rules vary widely with culture. For example, individualistic cultures are more expressive than collectivistic cultures overall.[73] A study comparing Canadian, American, and Japanese students[74] showed that Japanese display rules suppress displays of powerful negative emotion (anger, disgust, contempt) significantly more than North Americans and the Japanese were less

**emotional labour**
The need to manage emotions in order to perform one's job effectively.

**emotional dissonance**
Conflict between what one feels and what one is expected to express.

**emotional intelligence**
A set of abilities related to the understanding and management of emotions in oneself and others.

**emotional display rules**
Expectations regarding what emotions are appropriate to express in specific situations.

likely to endorse the display of positive emotions than were Canadians. The only difference between the Canadians and Americans was that Canadians believed contempt should be expressed less than did the Americans. It would be easy for a Canadian unaware of Japanese display rules to assume that a Japanese colleague is not pleased with something when his or her reaction appears too muted according to Canadian expectations, or to assume that the Japanese colleague accepts something that really is quite upsetting. For a manager dealing with a multicultural staff or for a businessperson interacting with customers, suppliers, and bankers from a different culture, we can see how easy it would be to misinterpret another's emotional reaction. This mistaken perception could have a large negative ripple effect. Consider the challenges for employees and management in a firm like i3DVR, a Toronto-based electronics manufacturing company, where 50 percent of staff are skilled immigrants, including the entire R&D department.

CPimages.ca PHOTO/The Home Depot Canada

Home Depot employees work with Habitat for Humanity

## Emotional Contagion

The influence of emotion at work is extended by **emotional contagion**, which is the dynamic process through which the emotions are transferred from one person to another, either consciously or unconsciously, through nonverbal channels.

Emotions need to be managed at work because they spread easily. Emotional contagion occurs primarily through nonverbal cues and the basic human tendency of mimicry. We tend to mimic each other's facial expressions, body language, speech patterns, vocal tones, and even emotions. Contagion affects any job involving interpersonal interaction. Positive emotions that travel through a work group through emotional contagion produce cooperation and task performance.[75] The opposite also occurs when negative emotions destroy morale and performance.

When organizations and their employees experience change and/or huge losses, they can struggle to recover. Good leaders use compassion to heal and rebuild employee morale.[76] Organizations need to give employees a comfortable place to share their mutual grief and trauma. These issues can be resolved by caring leaders willing to share their emotions with employees.

LEARNING OUTCOME **7**

# Ethical Behaviour

*Ethics* is the study of moral values and moral behaviour. **Ethical behaviour** is acting in ways consistent with one's personal values and the commonly held values of the organization and society.[77]

Paying attention to ethical behaviour is important in many ways for an organization. Consumers shy away from products and services if a company has an unethical reputation. Of course, illegal actions lead to liability and financial risk. Unethical behaviour also has an impact on employees via stress, lower job satisfaction, and turnover.[78]

On the positive side, firms with ethical reputations attract more applicants, creating a larger hiring pool, and evidence suggests that respected firms can choose higher quality applicants.[79]

Failure to handle situations ethically can hurt companies. Employees who are laid off or terminated are very concerned about the quality of treatment they receive. Honestly explaining the reasons for the dismissal and preserving the dignity

**emotional contagion**

A dynamic process through which the emotions of one person are transferred to another, either consciously or unconsciously, through nonverbal channels.

**ethical behaviour**

Acting in ways consistent with one's personal values and the commonly held values of the organization and society.

**TABLE 4.2** Ethical Issues from One Week in *The Wall Street Journal*

| | |
|---|---|
| 1. Stealing | Taking things that don't belong to you |
| 2. Lying | Saying things you know aren't true |
| 3. Fraud and deceit | Creating or perpetuating false impressions |
| 4. Conflict of interest and influence buying | Bribes, payoffs, and kickbacks |
| 5. Hiding versus divulging information | Concealing information that another party has a right to know or failing to protect personal or proprietary information |
| 6. Cheating | Taking unfair advantage of a situation |
| 7. Personal decadence | Aiming below excellence in terms of work performance (e.g., careless or sloppy work) |
| 8. Interpersonal abuse | Behaviours that are abusive of others (e.g., sexism, racism, emotional abuse) |
| 9. Organizational abuse | Organizational practices that abuse members (e.g., inequitable compensation, misuses of power) |
| 10. Rule violations | Breaking organizational rules |
| 11. Accessory to unethical acts | Knowing about unethical behaviour and failing to report it |
| 12. Ethical dilemmas | Choosing between two equally desirable or undesirable options |

SOURCE: Kluwer Academic Publishers, by J. O. Cherrington and D. J. Cherrington, "A Menu of Moral Issues: One Week in the Life of *The Wall Street Journal*," *Journal of Business Ethics* 11 (1992): 255–265. Reprinted with kind permission of Springer Science and Business Media.

of the employee will reduce the likelihood of employees initiating a claim against the company. One study showed that less than 1 percent of employees who felt the company was being honest filed a claim; more than 17 percent of those who felt the company was being less than honest filed claims.[80]

Unethical behaviour by employees can affect individuals, work teams, and even the organization. Organizations thus depend on individuals to act ethically. For this reason, more and more firms are starting to monitor their employees' Internet usage. Although some employees complain that this monitoring violates their privacy, the courts tend to disagree, arguing that companies have the right to monitor employees' use of company-owned hardware and software.

Individuals face complex ethical issues at work. A review of articles in one week of *The Wall Street Journal* revealed over 60 articles dealing with ethical issues in business.[81] As Table 4.2 suggests, few of these issues are clear-cut. They depend on the specifics of the situation, and their interpretation depends on the characteristics of the individuals examining them. Consider lying, for instance. Many business people tell "white lies." Is this

acceptable? The perception of what constitutes ethical versus unethical behaviour in organizations varies among people.

## Corporate Social Responsibility

If one considers ethical behaviour to be "values in action," one of the ways in which many Canadian organizations are demonstrating those values is through their corporate social responsibility (CSR). Roots Canada is engaging employees in work with the Jane Goodall Institute of Canada's Roots and Shoots program. Tim Hortons Children's Foundation sends over 11,000 children to camp each year. Home Depot's volunteer program, Team Depot, has seen thousands of employees build homes with Habitat for Humanity and build or improve community playgrounds through its partnership with KaBOOM!. Ericsson Response, the emergency telecommunications service team, has been active in many disaster zones, including Haiti after the earthquake and South Asia after the tsunami.[82] In Canada, 18 percent of Canadian organizations encourage employees to do volunteer work during work hours, paying for that time.[83] For example, at KPMG during its annual Volunteers Week, KPMG staff volunteer one workday each to make a difference to a worthy cause in their local community. CSR initiatives like these can be instrumental in team building, in enhancing corporate pride and identity, and in reinforcing an ethical climate within the organization.

LEARNING OUTCOME **8**

# Factors that Affect Ethical Behaviour

Two sets of factors—individual characteristics and organizational factors—influence ethical behaviour.[84] Here, we'll look at the individual influences on ethical behaviour. We examine organizational influences throughout

## FIGURE 4.3

### INDIVIDUAL/ORGANIZATIONAL MODEL OF ETHICAL BEHAVIOUR

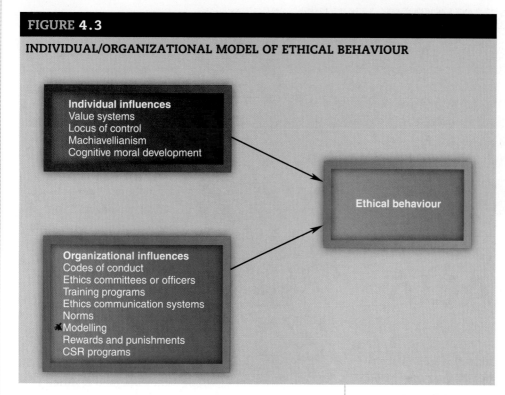

**Individual influences**
Value systems
Locus of control
Machiavellianism
Cognitive moral development

**Ethical behaviour**

**Organizational influences**
Codes of conduct
Ethics committees or officers
Training programs
Ethics communication systems
Norms
Modelling
Rewards and punishments
CSR programs

3. Toughmindedness—the willingness to make decisions when all that needs to be known cannot be known and when the ethical issue has no established, unambiguous solution.

Which individual characteristics influence these qualities? According to our model, they are value systems, locus of control, Machiavellianism, and cognitive moral development.

## Values

Different values generate different ethical behaviours. Though values vary widely among individuals, we use them to evaluate our own behaviour and that of others. **Values** are enduring beliefs that a specific mode of conduct or end state of existence is personally or socially preferable to an opposite or converse mode of conduct or end state of existence.[86] As individuals grow and mature, they learn values, which may change as an individual develops a sense of self. Cultures, societies, and organizations shape values. Parents and other respected role models influence value development by providing guidance about what is right and wrong. As general beliefs about right and wrong, values form the basis for ethical behaviour. Values are deeply held and quite stable, meaning that employers need to understand employee values and their impact but should not try to change those values.

the remainder of the book. Figure 4.3 will guide our discussion of individual influences on ethical behaviour. It shows both individual and organizational influences.

Ethical decision making requires three qualities of individuals:[85]

1. The competence to identify ethical issues and evaluate the consequences of alternative courses of action

2. The self-confidence to seek out different opinions about the issue and decide what is right in terms of a particular situation

## Age and Culture in Values

Although relatively fixed, values do change over time. Baby boomers' values contrast with those of the baby busters, who are beginning to enter the workforce. The baby busters value

**values**

Enduring beliefs that a specific mode of conduct or end state of existence is personally or socially preferable to an opposite or converse mode of conduct or end state of existence.

A new "name and shame" report published in Australia by RepuTex embarrasses companies that behave unethically. Nineteen groups graded each of Australia's top companies on corporate governance policies, environmental friendliness, and workplace practices and published the grades in a 500-page report.

SOURCE: Tony Jones, "Survey Finds Big Business Lacking in Social Responsibility," Australian Broadcasting Corporation (October 13, 2003), http://www.abc.net.au/lateline/content/2003/s966137.htm; RepuTex, http://www.reputex.com.au.

# AUSTRALIA

family life and time off from work and want to balance work and home life. This contrasts with the more driven, work-oriented value system of the boomers. The baby boomers placed a huge emphasis on achievement values. Their successors, the Generation X and Generation Y, though, are markedly different in what they value at work. Generation X values self-reliance, individualism, and balance between family and work life. Generation Y values freedom in scheduling and embraces a work-to-live mindset rather than the live-to-work adage of the baby boomers.[87]

Organizations facing the challenges of an increasingly diverse workforce and a global marketplace must understand culture's influence on values. Doing business in a global marketplace often means encountering a clash of values among different cultures. Consider loyalty, for example. In Japan, loyalty means "compassionate overtime." Even when you have no work yourself, you should stay late to provide moral support for your peers who are working late.[88] In contrast, Koreans value loyalty to the person for whom one works.[89] In Canada, family and other personal loyalties are held above loyalty to the company or one's supervisor.

Cultures differ in the individual contributions they value at work. Collectivist cultures such as China and Mexico value a person's contributions to relationships in the work team. In contrast, individualist cultures (Canada, the Netherlands) value a person's contribution to task accomplishment. Both collectivist and individualist cultures value rewards based on individual performance.[90] Iran's collectivist managers demonstrate little tolerance for ambiguity, high need for structure, and willingness to sacrifice for the good of society—all values they derive from Islam, which promotes belonging, harmony, humility, and simplicity.[91]

Values also affect individuals' views of what constitutes authority. French managers value authority as a right of office and rank. Their behaviour reflects this value, as they tend to exercise power based on their position in the organization. In contrast, managers from the Netherlands value group inputs to decisions and expect employees to challenge and discuss their decisions.[92]

We may be prone to judging the value systems of others, but we should resist this tendency. Tolerating diverse values can help us understand other cultures. Value systems of other nations are not necessarily right or wrong—they are merely different.

**Work Values** Work values influence individual perceptions of right and wrong on the job.[93] All may say they value fairness, honesty, achievement, and concern for others, but the relative weight they put on each value will influence their decisions. For example, should I look in my colleague's office files after hours without her permission to get some information? It will help me do my job better, but she will likely look on it as an invasion of privacy. Should I spend my weekend finishing this project? It will please the customer and my boss, but my colleague will say it is unfair he is excluded from the supposed "team" work, and my child really needs my company because she is feeling ill. Sharing values with work colleagues means less stress and easier relationships. Employees who share their supervisors' values are more satisfied with their jobs and more committed to the organization.[94]

Values have a profound effect on job choice. All organizations will say they value diversity. But do they show that in their recruiting and promotions? Minority candidates will judge the sincerity of diversity claims and this judgment will affect their interest in working for the company.[95] If they discover that the recruiting sales job on diversity was misleading, they are likely to leave.[96]

## Locus of Control

Another individual influence on ethical behaviour is locus of control. Recall from Chapter 3 that individuals with an internal locus of control believe that they control events in their lives and that they are responsible for their own experiences. Those with an external locus of control believe that outside forces such as fate, chance, or other people control what happens to them.[97]

Internals are more likely than externals to take personal responsibility for the consequences of their ethical or unethical behaviour. Externals are more apt to believe that external forces caused their ethical or unethical behaviour. Research has shown that internals make more ethical decisions than do externals.[98] Internals also are more resistant to social pressure and are less willing to hurt another person, even if ordered to do so by an authority figure.[99]

## Machiavellianism

Machiavellianism also influences ethical behaviour. Niccolò Machiavelli was a 16th-century Italian statesman. He wrote *The Prince,* a guide for acquiring and using power.[100] He suggested that manipulating others was the best way to achieve power. **Machiavellianism**, then, is a personality characteristic indicating one's willingness to do whatever it takes to get one's own way.

A high-Mach individual operates from the notion that it is better to be feared than loved. High-Machs tend to be deceitful, have a cynical view of human nature, and care little for conventional notions of right and wrong.[101] They are skilled manipulators, relying on their persuasive abilities. Low-Machs, in contrast, value loyalty and relationships. They are less willing to manipulate others for personal gain and are concerned with others' opinions.

High-Machs believe that the desired ends justify any means; therefore, they feel it's fine to manipulate others in order to achieve a goal.[102] They are emotionally detached from other people and focus on the objective aspects of situations. And high-Machs are more likely to engage in ethically questionable behaviour.[103] Employees can counter Machiavellian individuals by focusing on teamwork instead of on one-on-one relationships, where high-Machs have the upper hand. Making interpersonal agreements public reduces their susceptibility to Machiavellian manipulation.

## Cognitive Moral Development

An individual's level of **cognitive moral development** also affects ethical behaviour. Psychologist Lawrence Kohlberg proposed that as individuals mature, they move through a series of six stages of moral development.[104] (See Table 4.3) With each successive stage, they become less dependent on other people's opinions of right and wrong and less self-centred (focusing less on their own interests). At higher levels of moral development, individuals are concerned with broad principles of justice and with their

| **TABLE 4.3** Kohlberg's Levels of Moral Development | |
|---|---|
| **Level I: Premoral**<br>**Ethical behaviour based on self-interest** | |
| Stage 1 | Obey rules to avoid punishment |
| Stage 2 | Follow rules if in own best interest, if rewards follow |
| **Level II: Conventional**<br>**Ethical behaviour based on others' expectations** | |
| Stage 3 | Live up to expectations of others close to oneself |
| Stage 4 | Live up to expectations of society |
| **Level III: Principled**<br>**Ethical behaviour based on universal values** | |
| Stage 5 | Act on principles of justice and rights |
| Stage 6 | Act on own self-selected principles |

©Author created

**Machiavellianism**
A personality characteristic indicating one's willingness to do whatever it takes to get one's own way.

**cognitive moral development**
The process of moving through stages of maturity in terms of making ethical decisions.

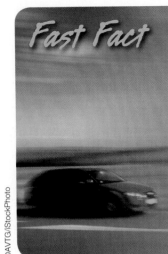
self-chosen ethical principles. Kohlberg's model focuses on the decision-making process and on how individuals justify ethical decisions. His cognitive developmental theory explains how people decide what is right and wrong and how the decision-making process changes through interaction with peers and the environment.

In the premoral first stage typical of children, the focus is on doing what's best for oneself. Think of the child who tells a bald-faced lie to avoid punishment. At level II, typical of most adults and therefore suitably labelled "conventional," people focus on the expectations of others. At the final, principled level, what is "right" is determined by universal values. The person sees beyond laws, rules, and the expectations of others.

Since it was proposed, more than 30 years ago, Kohlberg's model of cognitive moral development has been supported by a great deal of research.

Individuals at higher stages of development are less likely to cheat,[105] more likely to engage in whistle-blowing,[106] and more likely to make ethical business decisions.[107]

Individual differences in values, locus of control, Machiavellianism, and cognitive moral development all influence ethical behaviour in organizations. Organizations might use this knowledge to promote ethical behaviour by hiring and promoting individuals who share the organization's values or hiring and promoting only internals, low-Machs, and individuals at higher stages of cognitive moral development. This strategy obviously presents practical and legal problems.

As values, locus of control and cognitive moral development are fairly stable in adults; an organization is unlikely to change them through training. The best way to use the knowledge of individual differences may be to recognize that they help explain why ethical behaviour differs among individuals and to focus managerial efforts on creating a work situation supporting ethical behaviour.

Most workers are susceptible to external influences and look to their organization for guidance. Managers can offer such guidance by encouraging ethical behaviour through codes of conduct, ethics committees, ethics communication systems, training, norms, modelling, CSR programs and rewards and punishments, as shown in Figure 4.3 (on page 69). We discuss these areas further in Chapter 16.

## By The Numbers

**3** levels of moral development

**3** elements of affective commitment

**18%** of Canadian organizations encourage volunteer work during work hours

**11,000** Children at camp each year due to Tim Hortons Children's Foundation

**1/3** of employees surveyed witnessed ethical misconduct in past year

One of the challenges of encouraging ethical behaviour is the "better-than-average" phenomenon. People tend to see their own behaviour as more ethical than the behaviour of others, including their friends.[108] If they already think they are highly ethical, will they listen to guidance on ethical matters?

# Visit **icanorgb.com** to find the resources you need today!

*Located at the back of the textbook are rip-out Chapter Review Cards. Make sure you also go online to check out other tools that ORGB offers to help you successfully pass your course.*

- Interactive Quizzing
- Key Term Flashcards
- PowerPoint Slides
- Audio Chapter Summaries
- Cases and Exercises
- Interactive Games
- Self-Assessments
- "On the Job" and "Bizflix" Videos

# Motivation
# at Work

# Motivation and Work Behaviour

All employers want motivated employees. Skill alone is not enough, and motivational levels play a significant role in typical performance.[1] This is why so many theories have tackled the issue of work **motivation**, trying to explain why employees are motivated or not, and to suggest what employers can do to enhance worker motivation. The irony is that, although employers want to be told how to motivate their employees, employee motivation is not under their control. An employee has limited time and resources and chooses how to use them. The most an employer can do is create the right circumstances to provide what the employee is looking for so both can meet their needs. However, the better the employer understands employee motivation, the more likely those "right" circumstances can be created.

Managers often make assumptions about what motivates employee behaviour and those assumptions influence how managers behave toward employees. For example, Douglas McGregor proposed two sets of opposite assumptions that managers may follow, Theory X and Theory Y[2] (see Table 5.1 on page 76). Managers who abide by **Theory X** assumptions view workers as basically lazy and self-centred. As a result, the manager will tend to use a command and control style of leadership, motivating through threats. On the other hand, managers abiding by **Theory Y** that views workers as liking work and seeking responsibility are more likely to motivate in a positive way

**motivation**
The energizing forces that influence the direction, intensity, and persistence of effort.

**Theory X**
A set of assumptions that workers are lazy and dislike responsibility.

**Theory Y**
A set of assumptions that workers like work and will seek responsibility.

## LEARNING OUTCOMES

After reading this chapter, you should be able to do the following:

**1** Define *motivation*.

**2** Discuss the needs for achievement, power, and affiliation.

**4** Describe the role of inequity in motivation.

**5** Describe the expectancy theory of motivation.

**6** Explain how goal setting can motivate performance.

**7** Describe the cultural differences in motivation.

## TABLE 5.1 McGregor's Assumptions about People

| THEORY X | THEORY Y |
|---|---|
| > People are by nature indolent. That is, they work as little as possible.<br>> People lack ambition, dislike responsibility, and prefer to be led.<br>> People are inherently self-centred and indifferent to organizational needs.<br>> People are by nature resistant to change.<br>> People are gullible and not very bright, the ready dupes of the charlatan and the demagogue. | > People are not by nature passive or resistant to organizational needs. They have become so as a result of experience in organizations.<br>> The motivation, the potential for development, the capacity for assuming responsibility, and the readiness to direct behaviour toward organizational goals are all present in people. Management does not put them there. It is a responsibility of management to make it possible for people to recognize and develop these human characteristics for themselves.<br>> The essential task of management is to arrange conditions and methods of operation so that people can achieve their own goals best by directing their own efforts toward organizational objectives. |

SOURCE: From "The Human Side of Enterprise" by Douglas M. McGregor; reprinted from Management Review, November 1957. Copyright 1957 American Management Association International. Reprinted by permission of American Management Association International, New York, NY. All rights reserved. http://www.amanet.org.

by offering autonomy and opportunities to workers. Neither approach works with all individuals or in all situations with any particular individual. Motivation is a more complex interaction between the individual and the environment.

Motivation refers to the energizing forces that influence the direction, intensity, and persistence of a person's efforts. What motivates a student to take one course rather than another? Once in the course, what motivates one student to work hard while another slacks off? When a course gets really tough, what motivates one student to persist while another drops out? It would be impossible to create a course that all students would willingly choose to take, work hard at, and persist at when there are significant difficulties. There are no magical motivation formulas. But there are general principles about motivation that will apply to most students, and to most employees. Students in general are more likely to take a course that meets their personal needs, and to work hard and persist through difficulties if they see potential benefit and believe their efforts are likely to mean successful completion of the course. This approach of needs interacting with the work environment provides the framework for the chapter. We will examine various needs theories that help

us understand why a person must act. These **needs theories** identify internal factors, typically deficiencies, that influence motivation. We then look at process theories that try to explain why a person chooses to act in a specific way in a specific situation. **Process theories** identify how internal factors interact with the environment to influence motivation.

## Internal Needs

Philosophers and scholars have theorized for centuries about human needs and motives. During the past century, researchers have focused on motivation in a business context.[3] Max Weber, an early German organizational scholar, argued that the meaning of work lies not in the work itself but in its deeper potential for contributing to a person's ultimate salvation.[4] From this Calvinistic perspective, the Protestant work ethic was the fuel for human industriousness. The Protestant work ethic encouraged hard work on the grounds that prosperous workers were more likely to find a place in heaven. Although Weber, and later Blood, both used the term *Protestant ethic*, its value elements stem from a broader Judeo-Christian tradition. What about You? on the Chapter 5 Review Card helps you evaluate your own work ethic.

Sigmund Freud proposed a more complex motivational theory,

Fuat Kose/iStockPhoto

**needs theories**
Identify internal factors, typically deficiencies, that influence motivation.

**process theories**
Identify how internal factors interact with the environment to influence motivation.

[ *What about You? on the Chapter 5 Review Card helps you evaluate your own work ethic.* ]

suggesting that a person's organizational life was founded on the compulsion to work and the power of love.[5] He emphasized the unconscious mind's influence on human motivation. **Psychoanalysis** is Freud's method for delving into the unconscious mind to better understand a person's motives and needs. Freud's psychodynamic theory offers explanations for irrational and self-destructive behaviours, such as suicide or workplace violence. Analyzing a person's unconscious needs and motives can help us understand such traumatic work events. The psychoanalytic approach also helps explain workplace deviant behaviour.[6] Freud's theorizing served as the basis for subsequent need theories of motivation.

According to the needs theories regarding work motivation, we are a perpetually needy species. We are driven to get what we don't have enough of. And we cannot make a need go away by fulfilling it once; it will emerge again. The various theories emphasize different needs but they agree that understanding needs can help us take the next step of providing people with a means to meet their needs.

## Maslow's Need Hierarchy

Abraham Maslow's famous hierarchy of needs has spawned a great deal of attention since it emerged in 1943. As shown in Figure 5.1,

**TABLE 5.2** Ways in which Employers Can Address Needs Identified by Maslow

| Physiological Needs | | |
|---|---|---|
| | | Meals |
| | | Access to cafeteria, vending machines, drinking fountains |
| | | Working conditions: temperature, cleanliness, space, noise, lighting, ventilation |
| | | Rest periods |
| **Safety and Security Needs** | | |
| | Economic | Wages and salaries<br>Benefits (medical, retirement, etc.) |
| | Psychological | Job descriptions<br>Thorough training<br>Managerial availability<br>Avoid abrupt changes<br>Clear communication |
| | Physical | Prevent hazards<br>Training in safety practices |
| **Love/Social Needs** | | Opportunities to work in teams<br>Social interaction<br>Social activities |
| **Esteem Needs** | | Opportunities for responsibility<br>Recognition<br>Participation in decisions<br>Challenging goals |
| **Self-actualization Needs** | | Opportunities for creative and challenging tasks/jobs<br>Autonomy to pursue own interests<br>Training |

### FIGURE 5.1

**MASLOW'S NEED HIERARCHY**

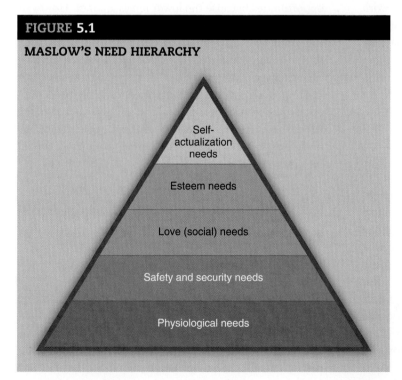

Maslow created a visual pyramid to represent the relative importance of five basic needs he believed true of all humans.[7] According to Maslow, our physiological needs are of prime importance and we will do anything to ensure we have the means (food, water, air) for survival. Safety and security needs are a close second, followed by love or social needs, and esteem needs (the need to feel important or recognized). Self-actualization at the tip of the pyramid represents the need to discover oneself, to realize one's potential. Maslow claimed that an unsatisfied need is a motivating need, and when more than one need is unsatisfied, the one closer to the base of the pyramid takes precedence. His progression hypothesis says that we progress up the pyramid as the lower

**psychoanalysis**
Sigmund Freud's method for delving into the unconscious mind to better understand a person's motives and needs.

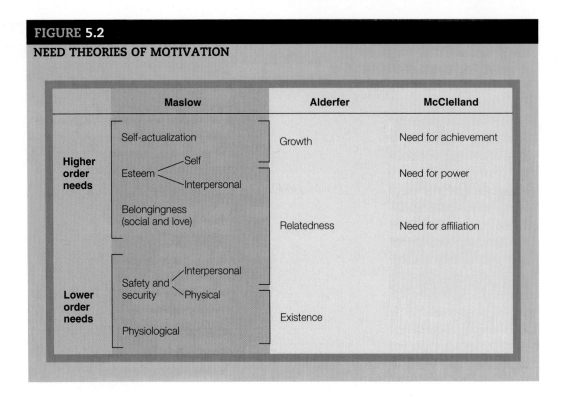

**FIGURE 5.2**

**NEED THEORIES OF MOTIVATION**

level needs are met. Our actions are directed to fulfill the lowest level of unmet need. A single action can meet more than one need, however; for example, a meal fulfills physiological needs but often social needs (e.g., a family gathering when you keep eating to avoid hurting your grandmother's feelings) and esteem needs (you cooked a gourmet meal). Maslow's model has not been useful for predicting individual needs. There are simply too many exceptions. However, Maslow's work was important in prompting people to consider that the upper-level needs are important, that for the majority of employees whose basic needs are met, keeping them motivated means offering opportunities to meet social, esteem, and self-actualization needs. Figure 5.2 presents some examples of how employer actions can meet the various need levels.

## ERG Theory

Clayton Alderfer recognized Maslow's contribution to understanding motivation, yet believed that the original need hierarchy didn't accurately identify and categorize human needs.[8] He proposed the ERG theory of motivation, which grouped human needs into only three basic categories: existence, relatedness, and growth.[9] Alderfer classified Maslow's physiological and physical safety needs in an existence need category; Maslow's interpersonal safety, love, and interpersonal esteem needs in a relatedness need category; and Maslow's self-actualization and self-esteem needs in a growth need category.

ERG theory also added a regression hypothesis to Maslow's original progression hypothesis. Alderfer's regression hypothesis suggests that when people are frustrated by their inability to meet needs at the next higher level in the hierarchy, they regress to the next lower category of needs and intensify their desire to gratify these needs.

For example, an employee may be looking for growth opportunities because the lower levels are met. However, the employee's job does not offer those opportunities and the employee is not about to quit and seek another job due to tough economic times and the need for ongoing financial security. So, rather than bemoaning the lack of stimulating growth opportunities, the employee refocuses on social opportunities available at work through friendships. He trades jokes with his buddies, joins the hockey pool, and gets together with coworkers for a beer on Fridays.

## McClelland's Need Theory

A second major need theory of motivation focuses on personality and learned needs. David McClelland identified three learned needs, acquired through a person's upbringing.[10] These were the needs for achievement, for power, and for affiliation. Some individuals have a high need for achievement, whereas others have a moderate or low need for achievement. The same is true for the other two needs. A manager may have a strong need for power, a moderate need for achievement, and a weak need for affiliation. Different needs are dominant in different people. Because McClelland believed these needs were subconscious, he could not simply ask people how important each of the three needs was to them—they would not know. Instead he used a projective test to measure their needs. He asked them to create stories about a standard set of pictures (the Thematic Apperception Test[11]) and analyzed those stories for their motivational themes. Although McClelland believed people's own needs were subconscious or below their own awareness, those needs are "manifest" or easily perceived by others. A manager who knows her staff well can pinpoint reasonably well who would like power, who cherishes affiliation opportunities, and who particularly values achievement.

**People with a need for affiliation like to maintain and establish warm relationships with other people.**

©oliveromg/Shutterstock

## Need for Achievement

The **need for achievement** encompasses excellence, competition, challenging goals, persistence, and overcoming difficulties.[12] People with a high need for achievement seek performance excellence, enjoy difficult and challenging goals, and are persevering and competitive.

McClelland found that people with a high need for achievement perform best. Individuals with a high need for achievement have three unique characteristics. First, they set goals that are moderately difficult, yet achievable. Second, they like to receive feedback on their progress toward these goals. Third, they do not like having external events or other people interfere with their progress toward the goals.

High achievers often hope and plan for success. They may be quite content to work alone or with other people—whichever is more appropriate to their task. High achievers like being very good at what they do, and they develop expertise and competence in their chosen endeavours. The need for achievement generalizes well across countries with adults who are employed full-time, but researchers

have found international differences in the tendency for achievement.[13] Achievement tendencies are highest in individualistic cultures and lowest in collectivistic societies.[14]

## Need for Power

The **need for power** includes the desire to influence others, the urge to change people or events, and the wish to make a difference in life. The need for power is interpersonal, because it involves influence over other people. McClelland distinguishes between socialized power, which is used for the benefit of many, and personalized power, which is used for individual gain. The former is a constructive force, whereas the latter may be a very disruptive, destructive force.

Specifically, the best managers (according to McClelland's research) have a very high need for socialized power, as opposed to personalized power.[15] They are concerned for others; have an interest in organizational goals; and want to be useful to the larger group, organization, and society.

A study of 555 nurses in specialized units found that intrinsic motivation increased with supportive relationships on the job.

SOURCE: N. W. van Yperen and M. Hagedoorn, "Do High Job Demands Increase Intrinsic Motivation or Fatigue or Both? The Role of Job Control and Job Social Support," *Academy of Management Journal* 46 (2003): 339–348.

**need for achievement**
A need that concerns individuals' desire for excellence, competition, challenging goals, persistence, and overcoming difficulties.

**need for power**
A need that concerns an individual's need to make an impact on others, influence others, change people or events, and make a difference in life.

Stephen Coburn/Shutterstock

## Need for Affiliation

The **need for affiliation** means an urge to establish and maintain warm, close, intimate relationships with others.[16] People with a high need for affiliation are motivated to express their emotions to others and expect them to do the same in return. They find conflicts disturbing and are strongly motivated to work through any such barriers to closeness.

A need that is not addressed directly in any of the above models but has emerged in research is the need for autonomy. This is the desire for independence and freedom from constraints. People with a high need for autonomy prefer to work alone and to control the pace of their work. They dislike bureaucratic rules, regulations, and procedures. Although it will certainly vary with individuals, the need for autonomy is common in many cultures. A study comparing employee need patterns in eight foreign subsidiaries of a multinational company (Belgium, Spain, Germany, Italy, Venezuela, Mexico, Columbia, and Japan) found that the need to control one's environment was strong in all.[17] Relevant to this autonomy issue is the reaction people have to surveillance. Being watched by an observer with a controlling purpose (e.g., evaluation) lowers employee intrinsic interest in their task as compared to when watched by a non-controlling observer (e.g., personal interest). And if there is no explanation for an observer's monitoring, the reaction is one of distrust and lowered intrinsic motivation, assuming a controlling intention.[18] The importance of autonomy will arise in Chapter 9 as we discuss empowerment and self-managed teams and in Chapter 14 as we discuss the design of work.

Note that all the needs theorists believe we need to work with the motivational needs people have, providing opportunities for them to meet their needs. We cannot change their needs or motivations. For example, as a manager you may recognize the exceptional ability of one of your staff and want to promote this person. However, the employee, who has a high need for affiliation and only moderate need for achievement and power, resists this opportunity. Getting promoted would mean being pulled away from working with friends or being put in charge of them, which would be even worse. You may feel frustrated at the employee giving up what you feel is a wonderful chance to make more money and pursue interesting work. It would not have been your choice. But we cannot project our own needs onto others.

Figure 5.2 (on page 78) shows the parallel structures of Maslow's, Alderfer's, and McClelland's theories of motivation.

LEARNING OUTCOME 3

# Herzberg's Two-Factor Theory

In developing his two-factor theory, Frederick Herzberg departed from the need theories of motivation and examined the experiences that satisfied or dissatisfied people at work.[19] Herzberg's original study included 200 engineers and accountants in western Pennsylvania during the 1950s. He asked them to describe two important incidents at their jobs: one that was very satisfying and made them feel exceptionally good at work, and another that was very dissatisfying and made them feel exceptionally bad at work.

As a result of this research, Herzberg came to believe that people had two sets of needs—one based upon avoiding pain and one stemming from the desire for psychological growth. Conditions in the work environment would affect one or the other of these two needs. Work conditions related to satisfaction of the need for psychological growth were labelled **motivation factors**. Work conditions related to dissatisfaction caused by discomfort or pain were labelled **hygiene factors**. Motivation factors relate to job satisfaction, and hygiene factors relate to job dissatisfaction,[20] as shown in Figure 5.3.

## Motivation Factors

According to Herzberg, job enrichment—or building motivation factors into a job—creates job satisfaction. In the original research, the motivation factors were identified as responsibility, achievement, recognition, advancement, and the work itself. When these intrinsic factors are present, they improve performance and effort on the part of job incumbents. Figure 5.3 also shows that salary is a motivational factor in some studies. Many organizational reward systems now include other financial benefits, such as stock options, as part of an employee's compensation package.

Motivation factors lead to positive mental health; they challenge people to grow, contribute to the work environment, and invest themselves in the organization. The absence of these factors does not lead to dissatisfaction, but rather to the lack of satisfaction.

---

**need for affiliation**

A need that concerns an individual's need to establish and maintain warm, close, intimate relationships with other people.

**motivation factor**

A work condition related to satisfaction of the need for psychological growth.

**hygiene factor**

A work condition related to dissatisfaction caused by discomfort or pain.

FIGURE 5.3

## THE MOTIVATION–HYGIENE THEORY OF MOTIVATION

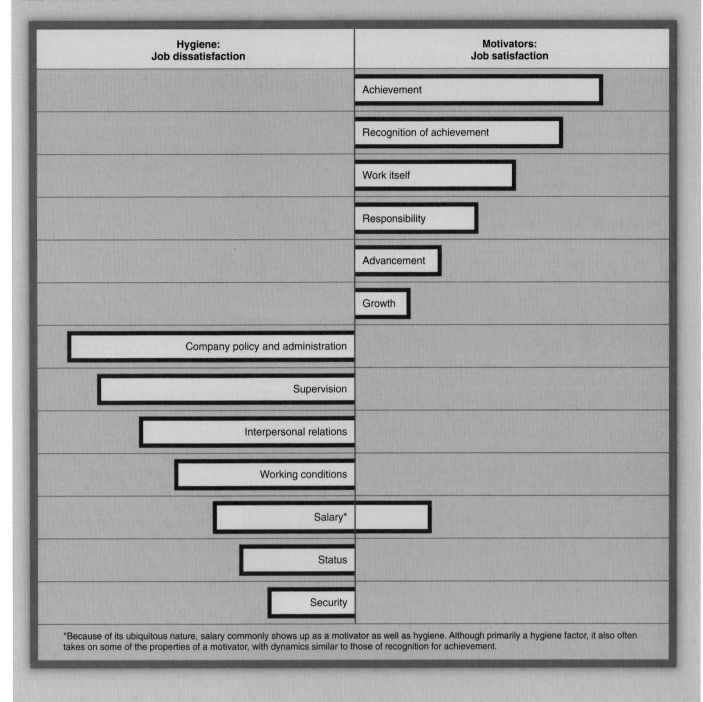

| Hygiene: Job dissatisfaction | Motivators: Job satisfaction |
| --- | --- |
| | Achievement |
| | Recognition of achievement |
| | Work itself |
| | Responsibility |
| | Advancement |
| | Growth |
| Company policy and administration | |
| Supervision | |
| Interpersonal relations | |
| Working conditions | |
| Salary* | |
| Status | |
| Security | |

*Because of its ubiquitous nature, salary commonly shows up as a motivator as well as hygiene. Although primarily a hygiene factor, it also often takes on some of the properties of a motivator, with dynamics similar to those of recognition for achievement.

SOURCE: Reprinted from Frederick Herzberg, *The Managerial Choice: To Be Efficient or to Be Human* (Salt Lake City: Olympus, 1982). Reprinted by permission.

The motivation factors are the more important of the two sets of factors, because they directly affect a person's motivational drive to do a good job. When they are absent, the person is demotivated to perform well and achieve excellence. The hygiene factors are a completely distinct set of factors unrelated to the motivation to achieve and do excellent work.

## Hygiene Factors

Job dissatisfaction occurs when the hygiene factors are either absent or insufficient. In the original research, the hygiene factors were company policy and administration, technical supervision, interpersonal relations with one's supervisor, working conditions, salary, and status. They cannot stimulate psychological growth

## [ The Effects of Motivational Factors ]

A recent study of nonacademic staff at a Pakistani university supported Herzberg's theory, showing a significant relationship between intrinsic motivational factors and employee job satisfaction, but no relationship between hygiene (extrinsic) factors and satisfaction. Interestingly, it also showed that female employees had higher satisfaction than male employees, even in identical positions. Found in U.K. research as well, the sex differential has been attributed to different expectations, with women happier because they had lower expectations. The difference disappears in the young, the higher educated, professionals, and those in male-dominated workplaces, for all of whom there is less likely to be a gender difference in job expectations.

SOURCES: I. Ahmed, M. M. Nawaz, N. Iqbal, I. Ali, Z. Shaukat, and Ahmad Usman, "Effects of Motivational Factors on Employees' Job Satisfaction: A Case Study of University of the Punjab, Pakistan," *International Journal of Business Management*, 5 (2010): 70–80; A. Clark, "Job Satisfaction and Gender: Why Are women So Happy at Work?" *Labour Economics*, 4 (1997): 341–372.

*Jupiter Images*

Many companies have initiated formal flextime policies to reduce dissatisfaction and persuade women leaders to come back to work.[21] Even in the absence of good hygiene factors, employees may still be very motivated to perform their jobs well if the motivation factors are present.

Two conclusions can be drawn. First, hygiene factors are important up to a threshold level, but unimportant beyond the threshold. Second, the presence of motivation factors is essential to enhancing employee motivation to excel at work.

or human development but act as maintenance factors influencing the extent of a person's discontent. Excellent hygiene factors result in employees being not dissatisfied.

When these hygiene factors are poor or absent, the dissatisfied employee complains about "poor supervision," "poor pay," or whatever hygiene factor is poor.

## Critique of the Two-Factor Theory

One criticism of Herzberg's theory concerns the classification of the two factors. Data have not shown a clear dichotomization of incidents into hygiene and motivator factors. For example, employees generally classify pay as both a hygiene factor and a motivation factor. A second criticism is the absence of individual differences in the theory. Differences in age, sex, social status, education, or occupational level may influence the classification of factors. A third criticism is that intrinsic job factors, like the work flow process, may be more important in determining satisfaction or dissatisfaction on the job. Finally, almost all of the supporting data for the theory come from Herzberg and his students, using his peculiar critical-incident technique. These criticisms challenge and qualify, yet do not invalidate, the theory. Independent research found his theory valid in a government research and development environment.[22] Herzberg's two-factor theory has important implications for the design of work, as discussed in Chapter 14.

## Hot Trend

Adam Grant's research shows that motivation is not always characterized by self-interest. He has shown that, given the chance for respectful contact with the beneficiaries of their work, workers show substantial increases in effort and performance. For example, in a longitudinal field experiment with fundraising callers, the intervention group was given ten minutes of direct contact with a student whose scholarship had been funded partly through their fundraising efforts. The controls had either indirect contact (a letter from a beneficiary) or no exposure. One month later, the intervention group showed significantly greater persistence (142 percent more phone time) and job performance (171 percent more money raised) whereas the control groups did not. The contact with beneficiaries makes the work seem more important; doing it seems more meaningful and purposeful. It makes the worker feel better about doing it. Is this self-interest or altruism? In the end, that does not matter because both individual and organization gain.

SOURCES: A.M. Grant, "Relational Job Design and the Motivation to Make a Prosocial Difference," *Academy of Management Review* 32(2007): 393–417; A.M. Grant, E.M. Campbell, G. Chen, K. Cottone, D. Lapedis, and K. Lee, "Impact and the Art of Motivation Maintenance: The Effects of Contact with Beneficiaries on Persistence Behaviour," *Organizational Behaviour and Human Decision Processes* 103 (2007) 53–67.

©luchschen/Shutterstock

# Adams's Theory of Inequity

Imran was just given a $10,000 year-end bonus on top of his regular salary. Imran feels demotivated. Is he crazy? Equity theory would suggest Imran's reaction is understandable if he feels the amount is unfair. For example, perhaps he feels he worked twice as hard as a colleague yet the colleague received a larger bonus.

Equity theory says that motivation is a function of perceived fairness (equity) in a social exchange and that inequity (unfairness) is an important motivator. **Inequity** creates tension, which motivates a person to take action to resolve the inequity.[23] Employees perceive themselves as contributing inputs (e.g., time, experience, creativity) to the organization and receiving outcomes (e.g., pay, recognition) from that organization. They weigh their outcome/input ratio against that of a comparison other. The comparison is seen as fair if the ratios are the same, so it is acceptable for a colleague to receive greater outcomes if his or her inputs were also greater; it is acceptable for a colleague to receive a lot less if his or her input was commensurately smaller. If the ratios are not matched, there is inequity. Tension is created and the employee is motivated to reduce the tension. Figure 5.4 shows one equity situation and two inequity situations, one negative and one positive. For example, inequity in (b) could occur if the comparison other earned a higher salary, and inequity in (c) could occur if the person had more vacation time, in both cases all else being equal. Although not illustrated in the example, nontangible inputs, such as emotional investment, and nontangible outcomes, such as job satisfaction, may well enter into a person's equity equation.

Pay inequity has been a thorny issue for women in some companies and has led to the application of "equal pay for work of equal value" concepts in determining fairness in pay for female- versus male-dominated jobs within an organization (in some Canadian jurisdictions).[24] As organizations grow internationally, they may have trouble determining pay and benefit equity/inequity across national borders.

Adams would consider the inequity in Figure 5.4(b) to be a first level of inequity. A more severe, second level of inequity would occur if the comparison other's inputs were lower than the person's inputs. Inequalities in one (inputs or outcomes) coupled with equality in the other (inputs or outcomes) are experienced as a less severe inequity than inequalities in both inputs and outcomes. Adams's theory, however, does not provide a way of determining if some inputs or some outcomes are more important than others.

## The Resolution of Inequity

Once a person establishes the existence of an inequity, he or she might use a number of strategies to restore equity. Adams's theory provides seven basic strategies for restoring equity: (1) alter the person's outcomes, (2) alter the person's inputs, (3) alter the comparison other's outcomes, (4) alter the comparison other's inputs, (5) change who is used as a comparison other, (6) rationalize the inequity, and (7) leave the organizational situation.

So Imran could try to convince his supervisor to increase his bonus or recognize his work in another way; he could work a lot less to bring his efforts in line with the bonus; he could try to get the colleague's

### FIGURE **5.4**

#### EQUITY AND INEQUITY AT WORK

| | Person | Comparison other |
|---|---|---|
| (a) Equity | $\dfrac{\text{Outcomes}}{\text{Inputs}}$ = | $\dfrac{\text{Outcomes}}{\text{Inputs}}$ |
| (b) Negative Inequity | $\dfrac{\text{Outcomes}}{\text{Inputs}}$ < | $\dfrac{\text{Outcomes}}{\text{Inputs}}$ |
| (c) Positive Inequity | $\dfrac{\text{Outcomes}}{\text{Inputs}}$ > | $\dfrac{\text{Outcomes}}{\text{Inputs}}$ |

**inequity**
The situation in which a person perceives he or she is receiving less than he or she is giving, or is giving less than he or she is receiving.

Jupiter Images

## New Perspectives on Equity Theory

Equity theory has been revised in light of new theories and research. One important theoretical revision proposes three types of individuals based on preferences for equity.[28] **Equity sensitives** prefer equity based on the originally formed theory. Equity sensitivity contributes significantly to variation in free time spent working.[29] **Benevolents** are comfortable with an equity ratio less than that of their comparison other.[30] These people may be thought of as givers. **Entitleds** are comfortable with an equity ratio greater than that of their comparison other.[31] These people may be thought of as takers.

Benevolents show less distress in inequitable situations and are more likely to engage in OCBs in a team environment.[32] They also differ from Entitleds in that Benevolents seem to put more emphasis on intrinsic outcomes at work whereas Entitleds place a higher emphasis on external tangible organizational outcomes such as pay.[33] Interestingly, there may be cultural differences in equity sensitivity. One study found that Chinese employees had more of a benevolent orientation, whereas British and French employees were more entitlement oriented.[34]

Adams' equity theory has been supplemented by research on other issues of organizational justice. Whereas equity theory focused on distributive justice (fairness in who gets what), it appears that people are also sensitive to **procedural justice** (fairness in how things are done) and **interactional justice** (fairness in how they are treated). People who feel fairly treated are more likely to engage in OCBs, giving back to the people and organization that have been good to them. People who feel unfairly treated are not only less likely to help others but also more likely to engage in theft,[35] sabotage,[36] and retaliation.[37]

Treating employees fairly is critical. However, it is also a challenge, particularly when one considers the advice of other motivational theories to customize rewards in order to provide those valued by the individual. How do you treat people differently but ensure they feel the differences are fair? Managers may find themselves in a situation parallel to parents at gift-giving time, wanting to offer gifts that are special to each child yet not be seen as favouring one over the other. What managers can do is make processes as transparent as possible and explain the criteria underlying decisions.

bonus cut or insist that person take on a bigger part of the workload; he could realize that in fact he is lucky to get such a bonus because his brother works longer hours at his job, earns less, and got no bonus at all; he could decide that perhaps he was overestimating his own contributions and not giving enough credit to his colleague; or he could quit. Equity theory does not suggest which strategy he is likely to choose.

Evidence strongly supports equity theory's contention that undercompensated workers react with negative attitudes[25] and lowered performance.[26]. However, research less clearly supports the contention equity theory makes that employees who feel overcompensated will be motivated to restore equity by, for example, increasing their own inputs or decreasing their outcomes. People seem to be able to rationalize inequity in their own favour quite easily.

The selection of a strategy and a set of tactics is a sensitive issue with possible long-term consequences. In this example, a strategy aimed at reducing the comparison other's outcomes may have the desired short-term effect of restoring equity but reduce morale and productivity in the long-term. The equity theory does not include a hierarchy predicting which inequity reduction strategy a person will or should choose, but it is nevertheless a reminder of the importance of fairness. One study found that workers who perceived compensation decisions as equitable displayed greater job satisfaction and organizational commitment.[27]

**equity sensitive**

An individual who prefers an equity ratio equal to that of his or her comparison other.

**benevolent**

An individual who is comfortable with an equity ratio less than that of his or her comparison other.

**entitled**

An individual who is comfortable with an equity ratio greater than that of his or her comparison other.

**procedural justice**

Fairness in how things are done.

**interactional justice**

Fairness in how people are treated.

# Expectancy Theory of Motivation

Whereas equity theory focuses on a social exchange process, Vroom's expectancy theory of motivation focuses on personal perceptions of the performance process. This cognitive process theory is founded on the basic notions that people desire certain outcomes of behaviour and performance, which may be thought of as rewards or consequences of behaviour, and that they believe there are relationships between the effort they put forth, the performance they achieve, and the outcomes they receive. Expectancy theory has been used in a wide variety of contexts, including test-taking motivation among students.[38]

The key constructs in the expectancy theory of motivation are the **valence** of an outcome, **expectancy**, and **instrumentality**.[39] Valence is the value or importance one places on a particular reward. Expectancy is the belief that effort leads to performance (for example, "If I try harder, I can do better"). Instrumentality is the belief that performance is related to rewards (for example, "If I perform better, I will get more pay"). Figure 5.5 models the expectancy theory notions of effort, performance, and rewards.

Valence, expectancy, and instrumentality all influence a person's motivation. Expectancy and instrumentality concern a person's beliefs about how effort, performance, and rewards are related. One person might believe that an increase in effort has a direct, positive effect on performance. Another person might have a very different set of beliefs about the effort–performance link. The perceived relationship between effort and performance varies from person to person and from activity to activity.

In a similar fashion, people's beliefs about the performance–reward link vary. From a motivation perspective, it is the person's belief about the relationships between these constructs that is important, not the actual nature of the relationship.

The practical implications of expectancy theory are that it is important for employees to see a strong link between their efforts and results, for them to see that differential results lead to different outcomes, and for those outcomes to be relevant to employees. Managers can take steps to enhance these links.[40] To enhance expectancy, managers can match people to jobs and tasks and provide training, resources, and support so employees will believe they can be successful.

Fotolia XIII—Fotolia.com

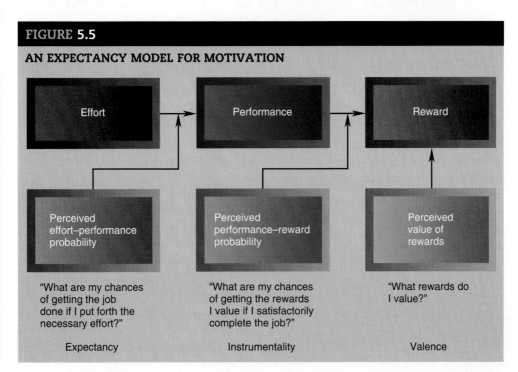

## FIGURE 5.5

### AN EXPECTANCY MODEL FOR MOTIVATION

| Effort | → | Performance | → | Reward |
|---|---|---|---|---|

| Perceived effort–performance probability | Perceived performance–reward probability | Perceived value of rewards |
|---|---|---|
| "What are my chances of getting the job done if I put forth the necessary effort?" | "What are my chances of getting the rewards I value if I satisfactorily complete the job?" | "What rewards do I value?" |
| Expectancy | Instrumentality | Valence |

**valence**

The value or importance one places on a particular reward.

**expectancy**

The belief that effort leads to performance.

**instrumentality**

The belief that performance is related to rewards.

Instrumentality is enhanced when a manager observes and responds to varying performance levels. Managers can respond to strong, moderate, and weak performances differently. The last step is for the manager to be sensitive to the valence of various rewards to individuals and do whatever is possible to attach valued rewards to strong performance. This means the manager must be willing to treat people differently, e.g., rewarding one with time off and another with a bonus, keeping in mind the need to be seen as fair at the same time.

> **"Expectancy theory cannot explain altruistic behaviour for the benefit of others.**

Research results on expectancy theory have been mixed.[41] The theory predicts job satisfaction accurately, but its complexity makes it difficult to test the full model, and the measures of instrumentality, valence, and expectancy have only weak validity.[42] In addition, measuring the expectancy constructs is time consuming, and the values for each construct change over time for an individual. Finally, the theory assumes the individual is totally rational and acts as a minicomputer, calculating probabilities and values. In reality, the theory may be more complex than people as they typically function.

## Motivation and Moral Maturity

Expectancy theory predicts that people will work to maximize their personal outcomes. Expectancy theory cannot explain altruistic behaviour for the benefit of others. Therefore, it may be necessary to consider an individual's **moral maturity** in order to understand altruistic, fair, and equitable behaviour. Moral maturity is the measure of a person's cognitive moral development, which was discussed in Chapter 4. Morally mature people act and behave based on universal ethical principles, whereas morally immature people act and behave based on egocentric motivations.[43]

**moral maturity**
The measure of a person's cognitive moral development.

**goal setting**
The process of establishing desired results that guide and direct behaviour.

# Goal-setting Theory

**Goal setting** is the process of establishing desired results that guide and direct behaviour. Locke and Latham's goal-setting theory is one of the most robust theories of motivation, with research strongly supporting its basic principles. According to this theory, people with specific, challenging goals will outperform those with general, "do your best goals" or no goals at all. The higher the goal, the better the performance; that is, people work harder to reach difficult goals, as long as they are committed to the goal and have the skills to achieve it. Goal setting is most effective when there is feedback regarding progress.

As illustration, research showed that negotiators with specific, challenging goals consistently achieved more profits than those with no goals, and negotiators with higher goals earned more than those with lower goals.[44] Loggers cut more trees[45] and unionized truckers increased the logs loaded on their trucks from 60 percent to 90 percent of the legal allowable weight as a result of assigned goals.[46]

How do goals make such a difference? They seem to affect performance in several ways.[47] First, goals serve a directive function, focusing attention on relevant activities and away from irrelevant activities. If you create "to do" lists for yourself, you'll recognize that you are creating a set of goals that focus your energies on what is important. If you have had the experience of attending meetings both with agendas and without agendas, you know that meetings with agendas are more efficient. The set of goals represented by an agenda has a focusing effect on everyone at the meeting. Second, goals have an energizing function, with high goals leading to greater effort than low goals. Third, goals affect persistence. Those with hard goals choose to spend more time on the task.

The only exception in the research supporting the value of specific, challenging goal setting is when people are confronted with highly complex tasks. In this case a "do your best" goal can lead to better performance than setting a specific high performance goal.[48] However, performance is even stronger when the performance goal is replaced by a learning goal, in terms of discovering a specific number of ways to solve the complex task.[49]

For best results, managers who use goal-setting need to get employee commitment to the goals. This can be achieved in a variety of ways: getting the employee to make a public commitment to the goal[50]; the leader providing an inspiring vision and behaving supportively[51]; having subordinates participate in setting the goals so they feel ownership; providing a clear rationale when assigning goals; and offering incentives. A large and difficult goal can be broken down into smaller, more immediate, and achievable goals. Providing ongoing feedback on progress is important in all cases. Many use the SMART acronym to remind them of effective goal characteristics: specific, measurable, achievable, realistic, and time-bound.

Since people with high self-efficacy are more likely to commit to goals, managers can take steps to raise the self-efficacy of their subordinates by ensuring appropriate training, by providing role models with whom the employee can identify, and through expressing confidence in the employee. Interestingly, the mere fact of assigning a difficult goal in itself tends to raise self-efficacy because it is a sign that the manager believes in the employee.[52]

# Cultural Differences in Motivation

Most motivation theories in use today have been developed by and about Americans.[53] When researchers have examined the universality of these theories, they have found cultural differences in the way people are motivated. For example, while self-actualization is the pinnacle need for Americans in Maslow's need hierarchy, security may be the most important need for people in cultures with a high need to avoid uncertainty.[54] Although achievement is an important need for Americans, research suggests that other cultures do not value achievement as much as Americans do.

The two-factor theory has been tested in other countries as well. Results in New Zealand did not replicate the results found in the United States; supervision and interpersonal relationships were important motivators in New Zealand rather than hygienic factors, as in America.[55] Researchers examining equity theory

©Dmitriy Shironosov/Shutterstock

Jessica L. Archibald/Shutterstock

**Despite cultural differences in motivation, many countries attempt to motivate their Olympic athletes in the same way—by offering cash awards. Countries as varied as China, Russia, South Korea, Canada, and the United States all reward medals with money.**

in cross-cultural contexts have suggested reexamining equity preferences, selection of referent others, and reactions to inequity.[56]

American-developed motivational theories and practices are mainly guided by the merit idea that rewards should differ for different people, depending on their performance.[57] This is true of the expectancy model, the equity model, and in merit-based individual incentive plans (to be discussed in the next chapter). All suggest a close match between performance and consequences so that the better the individual's performance, the greater the rewards should be. This may not be as easily accepted in other countries, especially collectivistic cultures and those with low power distance, where the rule of equality (all should be treated the same) or the rule of need (people should be treated according to their needs) may prevail. For example, the greater level of collectivism (compared to Americans) in North European countries helps us understand why only 19 percent of the Netherlands workforce and only 4 percent of the German workforce receive "payment by results."[58] Swedes, who have low power distance, express preference for allocation rules favouring equality, followed by needs and by merit, whereas Americans favour the merit rule and negatively view the needs rule.[59] On the other hand, a comparison between the United States and India of the three allocation rules shows Indians' order of preference was need, equality, and merit across situations.[60] Attempts to implement individual-based incentive plans that use individual performance appraisal as the criterion are often rejected in collectivistic, low power distance cultures.[61]

Even the goal-setting model of motivation is subject to cultural influences. Although Americans respond well both to participatively set goals and to assigned goals (as long as they accept the reasonableness of those goals), a study comparing Israel and the United States showed that the performance of Israelis was significantly lower when goals were assigned to them than when they participated in setting the goals, but equal to the Americans when goals were participatively set. The Israelis are a more collectivistic and lower power distance culture and reacted much more negatively to goal assignment than the more individualistic, higher power distance Americans.[62]

No research has been carried out to show how well the motivation theories apply specifically to Canadians. You have read about the values of Canadians compared to Americans. And, in learning about motivational theories, you got a sense of how well the theories described your own experiences. So what would you say about motivation in Canadians?

# Learning and Performance Management

## Models of Learning in Organizations

**Learning** is a change in behaviour acquired through experience. Learning helps guide and direct motivated behaviour. Learning may begin with the cognitive activity of developing knowledge about a subject, which then leads to a change in behaviour. We will examine cognitive and social theories of learning. Alternatively, another approach to learning assumes that observable behaviour is a function of its consequences. This is where we begin our discussion of models of learning.

LEARNING OUTCOME **1**

## Reinforcement Theory

Reinforcement theory focuses on the power of consequences to influence behaviour. Recall the concepts of instrumentality and valence from expectancy theory, discussed in Chapter 5, and expectancy theory's contention that we are motivated if we see a connection between our actions and valued outcomes. Reinforcement theory focuses on the power of those outcomes and can be applied to the motivation to learn new tasks as well as perform known ones. Reinforcement theory emerged from Skinner's work on **operant conditioning** with animals. Skinner's animal subjects learned to "operate" on their environment in response to the consequences Skinner provided. For example, rats learned to press levers a specific number of times to release food pellets, not a natural way for them to get food. Skinner and others extended

**learning**
A change in behaviour acquired through experience.

**operant conditioning**
Modifying behaviour through the use of positive or negative consequences following specific behaviours.

### LEARNING OUTCOMES

After reading this chapter, you should be able to do the following:

**1** Describe reinforcement theory's approach to learning.

**2** Describe Bandura's social learning theory.

**3** Describe evidence showing that thinking about

**4** Explain the aspects of performance management.

**5** Explain the importance of performance feedback and how it can be delivered effectively.

**6** Identify ways managers can reward performance.

**7** Describe how to correct poor performance.

the work to humans, providing reinforcements in response to specific behaviour and watching the results. Humans have used consequences in the form of rewards and punishments to try to modify others' behaviour for a long time (e.g., gold stars for schoolwork, imprisonment for committing crimes). Reinforcement theory and its research systematically examine the motivational effect of consequences on all aspects of human behaviour. Many of the findings from Skinner's animal research also apply to people: timing of consequences is important (the closer an outcome is to the behaviour, the more impact it has); the consistency of reinforcement affects how fast something is learned and how quickly it is "unlearned" once reinforcement stops; performers will learn behaviours in order to avoid unpleasant consequences as well as achieve desirable consequences; learning is faster when the reinforcement is more valued (when the person is "hungrier" for it); learning can be accidental and unintended when outcomes just happen to coincide with behaviours (the origin of many superstitions); people will work at less desirable activities in order to get the opportunity of working on highly desirable activities; and people can learn complex tasks by a shaping process of reinforcing first only crude attempts and then requiring performance closer and closer to the ideal before reinforcement is given.[1,2,3]

Reinforcement theory is central to the design and implementation of organizational reward systems (e.g., paying sales commissions), and many aspects of performance management, like disciplinary approaches. The underlying premise is that people develop or strengthen behaviours that are followed by positive consequences and weaken or eliminate behaviours that are not.

Organizations applying reinforcement theory can use four basic strategies: positive reinforcement, negative reinforcement (both of which serve to encourage more of the behaviour), punishment and extinction (both of which discourage the repetition of the behaviour). Figure 6.1 shows these approaches.

**Reinforcement** Reinforcement is the attempt to develop or strengthen desirable behaviour by either bestowing positive consequences or withholding negative consequences. **Positive**

**reinforcement** occurs when a positive consequence (like a bonus) follows a desirable behaviour (like a successful business year).

The Pressure Pipe Inspection Company based in Mississauga, Ontario has instituted a "going to the moon" philosophy as their theme, aiming to double their revenues over the next year and quintuple it over the next five. To motivate staff to work toward this common goal, employees who best represent the company and pull their weight are rewarded with an all-expenses-paid trip to Cape Canaveral.

**Negative reinforcement** occurs when there is an attempt to strengthen desirable behaviour by withholding a negative consequence. For example, if a teacher says to students that an 80 percent or higher on all term work before the final will mean they do not need to write the final exam, the teacher is using negative reinforcement to motivate student effort and learning. The same approach is being used by a manager who promises an employee that, if she figures out how to resolve a tough debugging problem, he will take her place at the committee meeting this week, the one she dislikes attending so much. In a less deliberate example of negative reinforcement, an employee might learn to come in early each day to avoid the manager's critical look when she arrives after him.

Managers can use either continuous or intermittent schedules of positive reinforcement. Table 6.1 describes both. When managers design organizational reward systems, they consider not only the type of reinforcement but also how often to provide it. Research results indicate that ratio schedules of reinforcement that link reinforcement to specific responses are more effective than interval ones based on time passed.[4] Unsurprisingly, this suggests pay for performance schemes will motivate greater effort than fixed salaries. Research also suggests that variable, unpredictable schedules of reinforcement motivate a steadier high rate of response than fixed schedules. Not knowing the likely outcome of the next

**positive reinforcement**
Attempting to strengthen desirable behaviour by bestowing positive consequences.

**negative reinforcement**
Attempting to strengthen desirable behaviour by withholding negative consequences.

**FIGURE 6.1** Using Consequences to Change Behaviour

| Increase behaviour via… | **Positive reinforcement**<br>e.g., top salesperson earns car |
| | **Negative reinforcement**<br>e.g., top salesperson's paperwork is completed by other person for next month |
| Decrease behaviour via… | **Punishment**<br>e.g., poorest salesperson gets moved to less promising sales territory and has to go for (disliked) sales training |
| | **Extinction**<br>e.g., ignore the salesperson when he whines and complains |

## TABLE 6.1 Schedules of Reinforcement

| SCHEDULE | DESCRIPTION | EFFECTS ON RESPONDING |
|---|---|---|
| **Continuous** | Reinforcer follows every response. | 1. Steady high rate of performance as long as reinforcement follows every response<br>2. High frequency of reinforcement may lead to early satiation<br>3. Behaviour weakens rapidly (undergoes extinction) when reinforcers are withheld<br>4. Appropriate for newly emitted, unstable, low-frequency responses |
| **Intermittent** | Reinforcer does not follow every response. | 1. Capable of producing high frequencies of responding<br>2. Low frequency of reinforcement precludes early satiation<br>3. Appropriate for stable or high-frequency responses |
| **Fixed Ratio** | A fixed number of responses must be emitted before reinforcement occurs. Example: bonus for every 50 trees planted | 1. A fixed ratio of 1:1 (reinforcement occurs after every response) is the same as a continuous schedule<br>2. Tends to produce a high rate of response that is vigorous and steady |
| **Variable Ratio** | A varying or random number of responses must be emitted before reinforcement occurs. Example: salesperson rewarded with sale after unpredictable number of calls | Capable of producing a high rate of response that is vigorous, steady, and resistant to extinction |
| **Fixed Interval** | The first response after a specific period of time has elapsed is reinforced. Example: salary given every two weeks for continued performance | Produces an uneven response pattern varying from a very slow, unenergetic response immediately following reinforcement to a very fast, vigorous response immediately preceding reinforcement |
| **Variable Interval** | The first response after varying or random periods of time have elapsed is reinforced. Example: promotion based on seniority occurs when space becomes available | Tends to produce a high rate of response that is vigorous, steady, and resistant to extinction |

SOURCE: Table adapted from *Organizational Behavior Modification* by Fred Luthans and Robert Kreitner. Copyright © 1985, p. 58, by Scott Foresmand and Company and the authors. Reprinted by permisison of the authors.

move and knowing it could be important will trigger a more motivated employee than knowing exactly when and how one will be reinforced. Of course, all reinforcement schedules have to be created within the constraints of what is fair and reasonable in the organizational context.

©bikeriderlondon/Shutterstock

**Punishment** Punishment is the attempt to eliminate or weaken undesirable behaviour. One way to punish a person is to follow an undesirable behaviour with a negative consequence. For example, a professional athlete who is excessively offensive to an official (undesirable behaviour) may be ejected from a game (negative consequence). The other way to punish a person is to withhold a positive consequence following an undesirable behaviour. For example, a salesperson who makes few visits to potential clients (undesirable behaviour) will likely receive a very small commission cheque (positive consequence).

**punishment**
Attempting to eliminate or weaken undesirable behaviour by bestowing negative consequences or withholding positive consequences.

Punishment sometimes has unintended results. Because punishment is discomforting to the individual being punished, it can bring about negative psychological, emotional, performance, or behavioural consequences (such as workplace deviance). Some managers use the threat of punishment to scare workers into greater effort.[5]

**Extinction** An alternative to punishing undesirable behaviour is extinction—the attempt to weaken a behaviour by attaching no consequences (either positive or negative) to it. Extinction may require time and patience, but the absence of consequences eventually weakens a behaviour.

Extinction may be most effective when used in conjunction with the positive reinforcement of desirable behaviours. For example, by complimenting a colleague for constructive comments (reinforcing desirable behaviour) while ignoring sarcastic comments (extinguishing undesirable behaviour).

Extinction is not always the best strategy, however. In cases of dangerous, or seriously undesirable, behaviour, punishment might better deliver a swift, clear lesson.

Note that extinction can happen unintentionally, with unwanted results. Imagine you are a keen new employee who works hard yet gets no praise and attention. Eventually you stop trying so hard. Your manager believes she has been showing her faith in you by leaving you alone. She has no idea that her lack of response has extinguished your eagerness.

---

LEARNING OUTCOME **2**

# Social and Cognitive Theories of Learning

Reinforcement theory is not the only model of learning. Albert Bandura's social learning theory offers an alternative and complement to Skinner's behaviourist approaches.[6] Cognitive theory draws on the theories of Carl Jung discussed in Chapter 3. Recent research has emphasized the importance of learners thinking about what and how they are learning.

## Bandura's Social Learning Theory

**extinction**
Attempting to eliminate or weaken undesirable behaviour by attaching no consequences to it.

**task-specific self-efficacy**
An individual's beliefs and expectancies about his or her ability to perform a specific task effectively.

Albert Bandura believes learning occurs when we observe other people and model their behaviour. Since employees look to their supervisors for acceptable norms of behaviour, they are likely to pattern their own actions after the supervisor's.

Central to Bandura's social learning theory is the notion of **task-specific self-efficacy**, an individual's beliefs and expectancies about his or her ability to perform a specific task effectively. Individuals with high self-efficacy believe that they have the ability to get things done. Self-efficacy is higher in a learning context than in a performance context, especially for individuals with a high learning orientation.[7] There are four sources of task-specific self-efficacy: prior experiences, behaviour models (witnessing the success of others), persuasion from other people, and assessment of current physical and emotional capabilities.[8] Evidence suggests that self-efficacy leads to high performance on a wide variety of physical and mental tasks.[9] Conversely, success can enhance one's self-efficacy. For example, women who trained in physical self-defence increased their self-efficacy in self-defence and new tasks.[10]

Bandura saw the power of social reinforcement, recognizing that financial and material rewards often occur following or in conjunction with the approval of others, whereas punishments often follow social disapproval. Thus, self-efficacy and social reinforcement influence behaviour and performance at work.

Managers can empower employees and help them develop self-efficacy by providing job challenges, coaching and counselling for improved performance, and rewarding employees' achievements. Given the increasing diversity of the workforce, managers may want to target their efforts toward women and minorities, who tend to have lower than average self-efficacy.[11]

> " Managers can help employees develop self-efficacy.

## Cognitive Theories of Learning

The cognitive approach to learning is based on the *Gestalt* school of thought and draws on Jung's theory of personality differences (discussed in Chapter 3).

Recall the distinction between introverts (who need to study, concentrate, and reflect) and extraverts (who need to interact with other people). Introverts learn best alone, and extraverts learn best by exchanging ideas with others.

The personality functions of intuition, sensing, thinking, and feeling all have learning implications, which are listed in Table 6.2 on page 95. Each person has a preferred mode of gathering information and a preferred mode of evaluating and making decisions about that information. For example, an intuitive thinker may want to skim research reports about implementing total

**TABLE 6.2** Personality Functions and Learning

| PERSONALITY PREFERENCE | IMPLICATIONS FOR LEARNING BY INDIVIDUALS |
|---|---|
| **Information Gathering** | |
| Intuitors | Prefer theoretical frameworks. Look for the meaning in material. Attempt to understand the grand scheme. Look for possibilities and interrelations. |
| Sensors | Prefer specific, empirical data. Look for practical applications. Attempt to master details of a subject. Look for what is realistic and doable. |
| **Decision Making** | |
| Thinkers | Prefer analysis of data and information. Work to be fairminded and evenhanded. Seek logical, just conclusions. Do not like to be too personally involved. |
| Feelers | Prefer interpersonal involvement. Work to be tenderhearted and harmonious. Seek subjective, merciful results. Do not like objective, factual analysis. |

SOURCE: O. Kroeger and J.M. Thuesen, *Type Talk: The 16 Personality Types That Determine How We Live, Love, and Work* (New York: Dell Publishing Co., 1989). Reprinted with permission.

Jupiter Images

an eye on how the learner is doing. Self-regulation prompting puts the learner into the role of monitoring his or her own learning. In this technique, learners are prompted at regular intervals to reflect on their learning through questions interspersed in the online delivery of material, e.g., am I concentrating on learning the training material? Are the study tactics I have been using effective for learning the training material? Which main points haven't I understood yet? Do I need to continue to review before taking the final exam?[12] Research shows that the prompting not only increases learning (compared to participants not given the prompts) but learners are less likely to disengage after failures

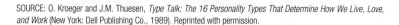

[ *When it comes to learning, the more errors you make, the better* ]

quality programs and then, based on hunches, decide how to apply the research findings to the organization. A sensing feeler may prefer viewing videotaped interviews with people in companies that implemented total quality programs and then identify people in the organization most likely to be receptive to the approaches presented.

LEARNING OUTCOME **3**

# The Value of Thinking about Learning

Regardless of an individual's personality, the success of several learning approaches emphasizes the value of getting learners to reflect on what and how they are learning. These approaches are self-regulation prompts in online training, error management training, and after-events reviews.

**Self-regulation prompting** is a technique that was developed for online training, an increasingly popular approach for organizational training because it can be cost-effective and convenient. Online training means the learning is essentially self-controlled and no teacher can easily keep

and are less likely to drop out of the course. The prompts to self-regulate lead to more time spent on task and may create more internal attributions and a sense of personal control so learners are less likely to give up.[13]

**Error management training** suggests that when it comes to learning, the more errors you make, the better. In error management training, the learner is immersed in a safe training environment where errors are likely to occur, given minimum guidance, and encouraged to explore and make mistakes. The errors are positively framed as learning experiences. Research shows that not only is learning more effective than in a proceduralized approach, but also after the training the learners are more likely to transfer their learning to new situations.[14] This seems to be because they have had so much feedback and had a chance to develop rich mental models of their actions and the consequences. Error management training also seems to

**self-regulation prompting**
Questions that encourage the learner to reflect on what and how they are learning.

**error management training**
Immersion in a safe training environment where learners are encouraged to deliberately make mistakes and see what happens.

# SEVEN KEYS FOR TALENT MANAGEMENT AT GE

>> General Electric's legendary reputation for talent management owes much to one man, William J. Conaty, who retired in 2007 after thirteen years as head of human resources and forty years at GE. Conaty had seven keys to nurture leaders so they could achieve great performance.

1. Dare to differentiate the best from the rest by constantly judging, ranking, rewarding, and punishing employees for their performance.
2. Constantly raise the bar to improve performance, which leaders do both among their own team members and for themselves.
3. Do not be friends with the boss but establish your own trustworthiness and integrity as a confidant to all.
4. Become easy to replace by developing great succession plans, especially when you do not need them, and mentoring the next generation.
5. Be inclusive and do not favour people that you know because it can undermine your success.
6. Free up others to do their jobs, especially by taking things off your boss's desk that are better done by you or others.
7. Keep it simple by being consistent and straightforward because most organizations require simple, focused, and disciplined communications.

SOURCE: D. Brady, "Secrets of an HR Superstar," *BusinessWeek* 4029 (9 April 2007): 66.

help participants learn to deal less emotionally with errors and setbacks in general and to plan, monitor, and evaluate their progress during task completion.[15]

The **after-events review** (AER, also known as after-action review, post-event review, or incident review) is a training procedure that gives the individual the chance to systematically analyze his or her decisions and behaviours after a learning activity or real performance. For example, after his first project management experience, an employee may be asked to reconstruct his actions in the project and suggest which of his behaviours supported the project's success and which hindered the project's progress, trying to figure out his mistakes and why they occurred, and determine his successful decisions or actions, and what he can learn from his mistakes to improve future performance.[16] There is no sense of blame and there is no reward offered; the focus is on the task and analyzing what worked and what did not. AERs advance learning from experience because they direct learners to analyze their experience, create rich mental models of the events[17] and produce more internal and specific attributions. After successful events, the most effective way to gain lessons is from reviewing wrong actions. After failed experience, any kind of review (correct or wrong actions) is effective, though focusing on correct actions is slightly less effective in improving later performance.[18] Interestingly, watching an AER of another person whose performance is relevant can be just as effective as a personal AER if the film models a thorough, systematic analysis, because watching still triggers self-reflection.[19] AERs seem to enhance learning not only through increased information but also through increased self-efficacy. Because learners have a deeper understanding of the reasons for their success or failure, there is a greater sense of mastery. AERs have been successfully used in organizations as different as Chrysler, British Petroleum, and the United States Army.[20]

## LEARNING OUTCOME 4

# Performance Management

Ultimately an organization is concerned with the performance, or task accomplishments, of the individuals and teams within it. The organization's success and survival depend on that performance. Research has shown that the more people know what to do, why and how, and care about it, the more likely their performance will be successful. This is the underlying premise of performance management.

**Performance management** is a process of defining, measuring, appraising, providing feedback on, and responding to performance.[21] Defining performance in behavioural terms is an essential first step in the process. Once defined, performance can be measured and assessed so that workers can receive feedback and managers can set goals to improve performance. Positive performance behaviours should be rewarded, and poor performance behaviours should be corrected.

## Defining Performance

Managers must clearly define performance if their employees are to perform well at work. Most work performance is multidimensional. For example, a sales executive's performance will require administrative, financial, and interpersonal skills. Defining performance (listing the skills and behaviours needed to perform) is a prerequisite to measuring and evaluating job performance.

**after-events review**

Procedure where, following an experience, the learner systematically analyzes how his/her actions and decisions contributed to the success and failure of the performance.

**performance management**

A process of defining, measuring, appraising, providing feedback on, and responding to performance.

One of the reasons goal setting (Chapter 5) can be effective is that it clarifies task–role expectations for employees. Goal setting typically involves a discussion between supervisor and employee about what goals are relevant, what levels and deadlines are reasonable, and how varying goals compare in importance. The process of goal setting therefore improves communication between managers and employees[22] and reduces the role stress associated with confusing and conflicting expectations. A fourteen-month evaluation found that goal setting reduced conflict, confusion, and absenteeism.[23]

## Goals Improve Performance Evaluation

Goal setting (see Chapter 5) is effective not only for motivational purposes but also improves the accuracy and validity of performance evaluation. One of the best

> **Goal setting is applicable to all employees, even lower-level organizational members and professional staff.**

methods for this is **management by objectives (MBO)**—a goal-setting program based on interaction and negotiation between employees and managers.

According to Peter Drucker, who developed the concept of MBO over 50 years ago, the objectives-setting process begins with the employee writing an "employee's letter" to the manager. The letter explains the employee's general understanding of the scope of the manager's job, as well as the scope of the employee's own job, and lays out a set of specific objectives to be pursued over the next six to twelve months. After some discussion and negotiation, the manager and the employee finalize these items into a performance plan.

Drucker considers MBO a participative and interactive process. This does not mean that goal setting begins at the bottom of the organization. It means that goal setting is applicable to all employees; even lower-level organizational members and professional staff having influence in the goal-setting process.[24] Most goal-setting programs are designed to enhance performance, especially when incentives are associated with goal achievement.[25]

The two central ingredients in goal-setting programs are planning and evaluation. The planning component consists of organizational and individual goal setting, two essential and interdependent processes.[26]

In planning, individuals and departments usually have discretionary control to develop operational and tactical plans to support the corporate objectives. The idea is to formulate a clear, consistent, measurable, and ordered set of goals to articulate *what* to do. Operational support planning then determines *how* to do it. The concept of intention encompasses both the goal (*what*) and the set of pathways that lead to goal attainment (*how*).[27]

---

## [ Set Work Goals and Manage Yourself ]

A large organization like the federal government can provide a great career, but if it is to be a productive one, you'll need to manage yourself, set your own work goals, reward yourself when you do well, and penalize yourself when you do a poor job. This is especially true for mid-level managers, one of the most challenging positions in any organization and one that often gets overlooked. Underperformance often triggers immediate negative feedback and punishment, but good performance is overlooked. Setting your own goals lets you set up measures and feedback systems to tell you if you are making positive progress toward these goals. Don't worry about being overly self-critical concerning performance problems; think more about rewarding yourself. Praise breeds confidence, leading to better performance.

SOURCE: B. Friel, "Manage Yourself," *Government Executive* (1 May 2007): http://www.govexec.com/features/0507-01/0507-01admm.htm.

**management by objectives (MBO)**

A goal-setting program based on interaction and negotiation between employees and managers.

The evaluation component consists of interim reviews of goal progress (conducted by managers and employees) and formal performance evaluation. The reviews are mid-term assessments designed to help employees take self-corrective action. The formal performance evaluation occurs at the close of a reporting period, usually once a year. Effective performance reviews must be tailored to the business, capture what goes on in the business, and be easily adapted to business changes.[28]

Because goal-setting programs are somewhat mechanical by nature, they are most easily implemented in stable, predictable industrial settings and less useful at unpredictable organizations. Finally, individual, gender, and cultural differences do not appear to threaten the success of goal-setting programs, making them useful tools for a diverse workforce.[29]

## Measuring Performance

Ideally, actual performance matches measured performance. Practically, this is seldom the case. Since operational performance generates more quantifiable data, it is easier to measure than managerial performance.

Because quantifiable data is easier to discuss and respond to, there is a temptation to focus only on it. That means that other behaviour, equally important but harder to measure, gets ignored in performance measurement. For example, an employee may have high productivity numbers and a low reject rate but at the same time not follow safety practices, refuse to assist others in the team environment when there are difficulties, and not maintain his or her equipment. As a result, the company has to pay for new equipment that wears out prematurely, there is enhanced safety risk for all, and morale in the team is damaged. Yet, if only the employee's production rate and reject rate are measured, the problems will not be flagged or addressed. What gets measured is what gets done, so it is important that all important behaviours are addressed in performance measurement.

Performance appraisal systems should improve the accuracy of measured performance and increase its agreement with actual performance. The extent of agreement is called the *true assessment,* as Figure 6.2 shows. The performance measurement problems, including deficiency, unreliability, and invalidity, contribute to inaccuracy. Deficiency occurs when important aspects of a person's actual performance are overlooked. Unreliability results from poor-quality performance measures. Invalidity stems from inaccurate definition of the expected job performance.

Many performance-monitoring systems use modern electronic technology to measure the performance of vehicle operators, computer technicians, and customer service representatives. For example, such systems might record the rate of keystrokes or the total number of keystrokes for a computer technician, or how long the employee was at the work station.[30]

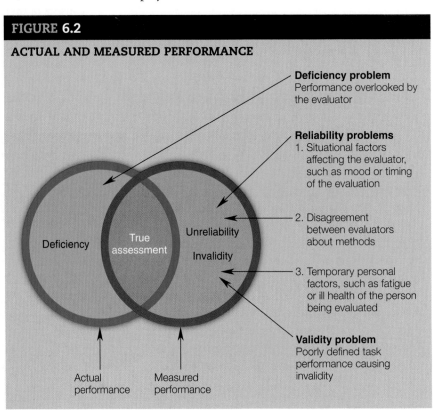

### FIGURE 6.2

**ACTUAL AND MEASURED PERFORMANCE**

**Deficiency problem**
Performance overlooked by the evaluator

**Reliability problems**
1. Situational factors affecting the evaluator, such as mood or timing of the evaluation

2. Disagreement between evaluators about methods

3. Temporary personal factors, such as fatigue or ill health of the person being evaluated

**Validity problem**
Poorly defined task performance causing invalidity

Deficiency — True assessment — Unreliability — Invalidity

Actual performance — Measured performance

When is electronic monitoring spying and when is it acceptable to employees? Employees who show strong commitment and identification with the organization are more likely to accept electronic monitoring and surveillance and those with low commitment are most likely to find innovative ways to circumvent the monitoring system. This creates an interesting paradox in that committed individuals are unlikely to need monitoring anyway because their goals align with the organization's goals, whereas the uncommitted employees may need monitoring yet are more likely to undermine its success. Monitoring seems to be more accepted where employees know what is being monitored and the rationale behind it (enhancing procedural justice), and how the information will be used (and not abused). If the company has an ethical culture that clearly practices and rewards ethical behaviour, electronic monitoring is more accepted.[31]

Measuring the performance is one step and sharing the performance appraisal with the employee is another step, also fraught with potential difficulties. The value and challenges of giving performance feedback are addressed next.

# Performance Feedback

Feedback sessions create stress for both supervisors and employees. Early research at General Electric found employees responded constructively to positive feedback but often responded defensively to critical or negative feedback, by shifting responsibility for the problem, denying it outright, or providing a wide range of excuses for it.[32] However, although it is easier to give and accept positive feedback, negative feedback is typically more effective in improving subsequent performance.[33] Sometimes performance actually decreases after feedback, particularly positive feedback, because people feel they have achieved their aim and do not need to continue to work so hard.[34] The earlier discussion of AERs emphasized the value of discussing errors even within the context of success.

Both supervisor and employee should try to make performance feedback a constructive learning experience, since feedback has long-term implications for the employee's performance and for his or her working relationship. The following three guidelines are useful for providing evaluative feedback.[35] First, refer to specific, verbatim statements and specific, observable behaviours displayed by the employee. This enhances the acceptance of the feedback while discouraging denial. Second, focus on changeable behaviours, not intrinsic or personality-based attributes. Third, plan the session ahead of time, notifying the person who will receive the feedback so that both parties can be ready.

Supervisors should start coaching and counselling sessions with something positive. Once the session is under way and rapport is established, then the evaluator can introduce more difficult and negative material. No one is perfect, so everyone can learn and grow through performance feedback sessions. Critical feedback is the basis for improvement. It is especially challenging to give feedback in times of stress because employees are less likely to make good use of the feedback, reacting emotionally rather than focusing on systematically determining what happened.[36] Because evaluation itself can be stressful, it is advisable to let employees know beforehand when it will happen but not to emphasize it, to avoid comparisons with others and focus strictly on the tasks, and not to emphasize the negative consequences, especially for employees who are high in trait anxiety to start with.[37]

## 360-Degree Feedback

Many organizations use **360-degree feedback**, which is based on multiple sources of information, to improve the accuracy of performance appraisals. Evidence suggests that including self-evaluations in this process makes evaluation interviews more satisfying, more constructive, and

> **360-degree feedback**
>
> A process of self-evaluation and evaluations by a manager, peers, direct reports, and possibly customers.

> ## No one is perfect, so everyone can learn and grow through performance feedback sessions.

less defensive.[38] Some dislike the fact that self-evaluations often disagree with supervisory evaluations.[39] However, these disagreements are part of the full picture of the person's performance. The 360-degree feedback method provides a well-rounded view of performance from superiors, peers, followers, and customers.[40] It has high reliability and validity, and individuals usually improve after receiving the feedback, although not by a large amount. Interestingly, the ones who improve the most are the ones who originally overrate their performance, and receive negative feedback indicating they are out of line with how others see them.[41]

360-degree feedback can be improved by adding a systematic coaching component.[42] By focusing on enhanced self-awareness and behavioural management, feedback-coaching improves performance, satisfaction, and commitment, and reduces intent to turnover.

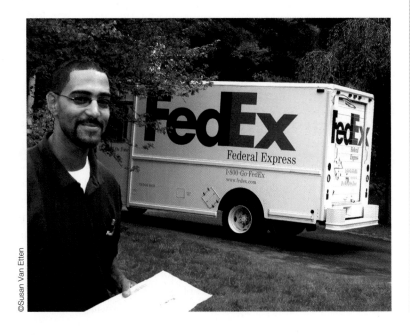

©Stockbyte/Getty Images

Separating the performance feedback component from the management development component also improves the 360-degree method.[43] The feedback component contains quantitative feedback and performance measures, while the management development component emphasizes qualitative feedback and competencies for development.

## Developing People and Enhancing Careers

Good performance appraisal systems develop people and enhance careers. Developmentally, performance appraisals should explore individual growth needs and future performance. The supervisor must establish mutual trust to coach and develop employees. The supervisor must be vulnerable and open to challenge from the subordinate while maintaining responsibility for the subordinate's best interests.[44] Good supervisors are skilled, empathetic listeners who encourage employees to discuss their aspirations.[45]

Employees must also take active responsibility for future development and growth. This might mean challenging the supervisor's ideas about future development and expressing their own goals. Passive, compliant employees cannot accept responsibility for themselves or achieve full emotional development.

FedEx has incorporated a novel and challenging approach to evaluation in its blueprint for service quality. All managers at FedEx are evaluated by their employees through a survey-feedback-action system. Employees evaluate their managers using a five-point scale on twenty-nine standard statements and ten local option ones. Low ratings suggest problem areas requiring management attention. One year the survey revealed that employees thought upper management was not paying attention to ideas and suggestions from people at their level. CEO Fred Smith developed a biweekly employee newsletter to correct the problem.

©Susan Van Etten

Jupiter Images

## Key Characteristics of an Effective Appraisal System

Effective performance appraisal systems have five key characteristics: validity, reliability, responsiveness, flexibility, and equitability. Validity means capturing multiple dimensions of a person's job performance. Reliability means collecting evaluations from multiple sources and at different times throughout the evaluation period. Responsiveness means allowing the person being evaluated some input. Flexibility means staying open to modification based on new information, such as situational demands. Equitability means evaluating fairly against established criteria, regardless of individual differences.

LEARNING OUTCOME 6

# Rewarding Performance

Performance appraisals can provide input for reward decisions. If companies celebrate "teamwork," "values," and "customer focus," then they must reward behaviours demonstrating these ideas. Despite their importance, reward decisions are among the most difficult and complicated decisions managers make. While pay and rewards for performance have value, so, too, do trust, fun, and meaningful work.

Reward and punishment decisions affect entire organizations, not just the individuals receiving the consequence. Reward allocation involves sequential decisions about which people to reward, how to reward them, and when to reward them. These decisions shape all employees' behaviour, either directly or through vicarious learning especially when new programs are implemented. People watch what happens to peers who succeed and who make mistakes; then they adjust their own behaviour accordingly.

## Individual versus Team Reward Systems

Although some say it is a myth that people work for money,[46] evidence shows that money is a powerful reward that can trigger dramatic improvements. Meta-analytic reviews comparing different motivational approaches showed individual pay incentives increased productivity on average by 30 percent, far beyond any other approaches (e.g., job enrichment achieves gains of 9–17 percent; enhanced employee participation less than 1 percent).[47,48] This is because money is not simply an extrinsic motivator but also a form of recognition, providing information on competence. Besides an incentive effect, pay-for-performance plans can have a sorting effect, influencing who applies to a job and who stays with the organization.[49] Less productive workers may quit when switched from salary to an incentive system[50] whereas incentive plans are attractive to those higher in need for achievement[51] and self-efficacy.[52] Individual incentive plans may create problems by undermining cooperative behaviour and encouraging dysfunctional competition. They may also be seen as unfair when factors out of the control of the employee affect performance (e.g., employees assigned to "bad" shifts selling less because there are simply fewer customers walking through the door).

Team reward systems solve the problems caused by individual competitive behaviour by encouraging joint effort, cooperation, and the sharing of information and expertise. For example, incentives or merit pay can be based on group performance rather than individual performance. Gainsharing plans emphasize collective cost reduction by allowing workers to share in the gains achieved by reducing production costs. Profit sharing encourages everyone in the organization to support each other as they all play a role in contributing to the organization's ultimate success and their pay-offs. However, group-based plans also have their drawbacks. One is the fact that, in an individualistic society like Canada, many prefer their pay to be based on individual performance,[53] and this preference is strongest among the most productive and achievement-oriented employees who may feel frustrated at "carrying" weaker workers. Group size is a moderator of any group plan effectiveness. Expectancy effects weaken as the employee sees less impact of his or her own effort on group output. For example, doubling the number of employees involved in a gainsharing plan can cut the productivity gain in half.[54]

A third option is to use a hybrid approach to rewarding employees. With interdependent teams, higher performance can result from the use of both individual and shared rewards, recognizing individual contributions while also encouraging cooperation. Hybrid reward systems lead

to increased sharing of information and reduced social loafing.[55]

## The Power of Earning

Both individual and team reward systems shape productive behaviour. Effective performance management boosts

**Organizations get the performance they reward, not the performance they say they want**

# Correcting Poor Performance

Often a challenge for supervisors, correcting poor performance is a three-step process. First, they must identify the cause or primary responsibility for the poor performance. Second, if the primary responsibility is a person's, they must determine the source of the personal problem. Third, they must develop a plan for correcting the poor performance. What about You? on the Chapter 6 Review Card helps you examine one of your own poor performances.

A number of problems trigger poor performance. These include poorly designed work systems, poor selection processes, inadequate training and skills development, lack of personal motivation, and personal problems intruding on the work environment. Not all poor performance is self-motivated; some is induced by the work system. Therefore, a good diagnosis should precede corrective action. For example, it may be that an employee is subject to a work design or resources issue that keeps the employee from exhibiting good performance.

> *What about You? on the Chapter 6 Review Card helps you examine one of your own poor performances.*

individual and team achievements in an organization. Performance management and reward systems assume a demonstrable connection between performance and rewards. Organizations get the performance they reward, not the performance they say they want.[56] Further, when there is no apparent link between performance and rewards, people may begin to believe they are entitled to rewards regardless of their performance.

The notion of entitlement at work is counterproductive when it counteracts the power of earning.[57] People who believe they are entitled to rewards are not motivated to behave constructively. Merit raises in some organizations, for example, have come to be viewed as entitlements, thus reducing their positive value in the organizational reward system. Entitlement engenders passive, irresponsible behaviour, whereas earning engenders active, responsible, adult behaviour. The power of earning rests on a direct link between performance and rewards.

If the poor performance can't be attributed to work design or organizational process problems, then supervisors should examine the employee. The problem may lie in (1) some aspect of the person's relationship to the organization or supervisor, (2) some area of the employee's personal life, or (3) a training or developmental deficiency. In the latter two cases, poor performance may be treated as a symptom rather than a motivated consequence. In such cases, identifying financial problems, family difficulties, or health disorders may help the employee solve problems before they become too extensive.

Poor performance may also stem from an employee's displaced anger or conflict with the organization or supervisor. In such cases, the employee may be unaware of the internal reactions causing the problem. Such angry motivations can generate sabotage, work slowdowns, and work stoppages. The supervisor may attribute the cause of the problem to the employee, while the employee attributes it to the supervisor or organization. Supervisors must treat the poor performance as a symptom with a deeper cause and resolve the underlying anger or conflict.

Recalling the fundamental attribution bias from Chapter 3, there is a danger that supervisors will tend to leap prematurely to the conclusion that performance problems are to be blamed on the employee. It is important for a supervisor to think through the consensus, consistency, and distinctiveness aspects of the situation: how have others done in a similar situation? How has this employee performed in similar situations in the past? How is this employee performing in very different tasks?

## Coaching, Counselling, and Mentoring

Supervisors have important coaching, counselling, and mentoring responsibilities to their subordinates. Supervisors and coworkers are often more effective guides than formally assigned mentors from higher up in the organizational hierarchy.[58] Success in the mentoring relationship depends on openness and trust.[59] This relationship may help address performance-based deficiencies or personal problems.[60] In either case, the supervisors can play a helpful role in employee problem-solving activities without accepting responsibility for the employees' problems. They may also refer the employee to trained professionals.

Coaching and counselling are among the career and psychosocial functions of a mentoring relationship.[61] **Mentoring** is a work relationship that encourages development and career enhancement. Mentor relationships typically go through four phases: initiation, cultivation, separation, and redefinition. Mentoring offers protégés many career benefits.[62] The relationship can significantly

Nicole waring/iStockPhoto

enhance the early development of a newcomer and the mid-career development of an experienced employee. One study found that good performance by newcomers increased delegation from leaders.[63] Peer relationships can also enhance career development.[64] Executive coaching is increasingly used to outsource the business mentoring functions.[65] Informational, collegial, and special peers aid the individual's development by sharing information, career strategizing, job-related feedback, emotional support, and friendship.

**mentoring**

A work relationship that encourages development and career enhancement for people moving through the career cycle.

# Visit **icanorgb.com** to find the resources you need today!

*Located at the back of the textbook are rip-out Chapter Review Cards. Make sure you also go online to check out other tools that ORGB offers to help you successfully pass your course.*

- Interactive Quizzing
- Key Term Flashcards
- PowerPoint Slides
- Audio Chapter Summaries

- Cases and Exercises
- Interactive Games
- Self-Assessments
- "On the Job" and "Bizflix" Videos

# Stress and Well-Being at Work

# What Is Stress?

Stress is an important topic in organizational behaviour. It affects every worker and every organization on a regular basis. It influences each person's quality of life and a wide variety of behaviours significant to an organization's success including productivity, turnover, employee satisfaction, and absenteeism.

**Stress** has many interpretations and is one of the most ambiguous words in the English language. Even stress experts do not agree on its definition. Stress carries a negative connotation for some people, as though it were to be avoided. This is unfortunate, because stress is a great asset in managing legitimate emergencies and achieving peak performance. We will define _stress_, or the stress response, as the unconscious preparation to fight or flee that a person experiences when faced with any demand.[1] A **stressor**, or demand, is the person or event that triggers the stress response. **Distress** or **strain** refers to the adverse psychological, physical, behavioural, and organizational consequences that _may_ occur as a result of stressful events.

## Stress—A Worldwide Issue

Stress is a common work phenomenon and a costly one. One third of Canadians report feeling quite a bit or extremely stressed at work most days.[2] In 1991, one in 10 Canadian workers worked

**stress**
The unconscious preparation to fight or flee that a person experiences when faced with any demand.

**stressor**
The person or event that triggers the stress response.

**distress**
The adverse psychological, physical, behavioural, and organizational consequences that may arise as a result of stressful events.

**strain**
Distress.

## LEARNING OUTCOMES

After reading this chapter, you should be able to do the following:

**1** Define _stress_, _stressor_, and _distress_.

**2** Compare four different approaches to stress.

**3** Explain the psychophysiology of the stress response.

**4** Identify work and nonwork causes of stress.

**5** Explain the JDCS and ERI models that link stress to negative consequences.

**6** Describe the consequences of stress.

**7** Discuss individual factors that influence a person's response to stress and strain.

**8** Identify the stages of preventive stress management.

over 50 hours a week. By 2001 that had changed to one in four.[3] It is unlikely that the 2011 statistics will show any improvement. Stress-related absences cost Canadian employers billions of dollars each year.[4] Stress affects all sectors, as shown in Canadian research focused on workers as varied as sawmill workers,[5] hospital staff,[6] and financial services workers.[7]

Increasing levels of work stress seem to be a global concern. European studies show that stress is the second most common work-related health problem (affecting 28 percent of workers and second only to backache).[8] The majority of European employees report working at high speeds or under tight deadlines more than 50 percent of the time and this percentage has increased significantly since the 90s.[9] In Australia, compensation claims due to work stress increased 62 percent from 1996 to 2003.[10] Stress has become an increasing concern in Chinese[11] and South African[12] workplaces. In 2004 the European Union level social partners (participating countries) signed a voluntary agreement on workplace stress, recognizing the importance of the problem and creating a framework to combat stress at work. This agreement was a catalyst for action and awareness in a broad spectrum of countries, each of which took their own approach.[13] The United Kingdom's Health and Safety Executive created an extensive management education system called the Management Standards approach, creating and distributing training materials to enhance the awareness of stress issues and the understanding of suitable organizational actions for preventing and dealing with stress.[14] Some of those standards are illustrated later in the chapter.

An important advancement in the thinking on stress is the increasing realization that individual interventions are not sufficient, and stress is something that can and should be tackled by organizations. For example, the World Health Organization has said that "Most of the causes of work stress concern the way work is designed and the way in which organizations are managed."[15]

---

LEARNING OUTCOME **2**

# Four Approaches to Stress

One of the pioneers of stress research was Canadian Hans Selye, who is noted as one of the most prolific scientists of all time.[16,17] It was Selye who popularized the now common understanding that chronic stress increases vulnerability to health problems. According to Selye, stress is the nonspecific response of

**homeostasis**

A steady state of bodily functioning and equilibrium.

[ *Evaluate your stress level. Complete the questionnaire What about You? on the Chapter 7 Review Card* ]

the body to demands put on it,[18] whether those are pleasant demands (such as preparing for a birth) or unpleasant ones (such as awaiting a critical performance review). Later researchers defined stress differently than Selye, however, so we will review four different approaches to defining stress: the homeostatic/medical, cognitive appraisal, person–environment fit, and psychoanalytic approaches.

## The Homeostatic/ Medical Approach

Walter Cannon was the first to describe the "emergency response" as an animal's response to threat. This is the basis of our current concept of the fight-or-flight response. According to Cannon, stress results when an external, environmental demand upsets the person's natural steady-state balance.[19] He referred to this steady-state balance, or equilibrium, as **homeostasis**. Cannon believed the body was designed with natural defence mechanisms to keep it in homeostasis. He was especially interested in the role of the sympathetic nervous system in activating a person under stressful conditions.[20]

## The Cognitive Appraisal Approach

Richard Lazarus was more concerned with the psychology of stress, emphasizing instead the psychological and cognitive aspects of the response.[21] Like Cannon, Lazarus saw stress as a result of a person–environment interaction, yet he emphasized the person's cognitive appraisal in classifying persons or events as stressful or not. Individuals differ in their appraisal of events and people. Perception and cognitive appraisal are important processes in determining what is stressful. For example, people who are higher in neuroticism (or lower in emotional stability, as described in Chapter 3), seem to have a propensity to perceive threat. Given the same situation, those who make a threat appraisal and those who make a challenge appraisal react with different physiological patterns to the stressor and experience different emotions.[22] In addition to cognitive appraisal, Lazarus introduced the concepts of problem-focused and emotion-focused coping. Problem-focused coping emphasizes managing the stressor, and emotion-focused coping emphasizes managing individual response.

## The Person–Environment Fit Approach

Robert Kahn was concerned with the social psychology of stress, so his approach emphasized how confusing and conflicting expectations of a person in a social role create stress for the person.[23] He extended the approach to examine a person's fit in the environment. A good person–environment fit occurs when a person's skills and abilities match a clearly defined, consistent set of role expectations. Stress occurs when the role expectations are confusing and/or conflict with a person's skills and abilities. After a period of this stress, the person can expect to experience strain, for example, depression.

## The Psychoanalytic Approach

Harry Levinson defined stress based on Freudian psychoanalytic theory.[24] Levinson believed that two elements of the personality interact to cause stress. The first element is the **ego-ideal**—the embodiment of a person's perfect self. The second element is the **self-image**—how the person really sees him- or herself, both positively and negatively. Although not sharply defined, the ego-ideal encompasses admirable attributes of parental personalities, desired and/or imaginable qualities, and the absence of any negative or distasteful qualities. Stress results from the discrepancy between the idealized self (ego-ideal) and the real self-image; the greater the discrepancy, the more stress a person experiences. More generally, psychoanalytic theory helps us understand the role of unconscious personality factors as causes of stress within a person.

In preparing to fight—or flee—the body:

1. Redirects blood to the brain and large-muscle groups
2. Increases alertness through improved vision, hearing, and other sensory processes
3. Releases glucose (blood sugar) and fatty acids into the bloodstream to sustain the body during the stressful event
4. Suppresses the immune system as well as restorative and emergent processes (such as digestion)

### LEARNING OUTCOME 3

# The Stress Response

Whether activated by an ego-ideal/self-image discrepancy, a poorly defined social role, cognitive appraisal suggesting threat, or a lack of balance, the resulting stress response is characterized by a predictable sequence of mind and body events as first observed by Selye. The stress response begins with the release of chemical messengers, primarily adrenaline, into the bloodstream. These messengers activate the sympathetic nervous system and the endocrine (hormone) system. These two systems work together and trigger mind–body changes to prepare the person for fight or flight.

As the body responds, the person shifts from a neutral posture to an offensive posture. The stress response can be very functional in preparing a person to handle legitimate emergencies through peak performance. It is neither inherently bad nor necessarily destructive.

Prolonged stress is dangerous, however. For example, research now shows that stress plays a role in triggering or worsening depression and cardiovascular disease and in speeding the progression of HIV/AIDS.[25]

### LEARNING OUTCOME 4

# Sources of Work Stress

Work stress is caused both by factors in the work environment and by nonwork (external) pressures that "spill over" into the workplace. An example of an external pressure is when a working mother or father is called at work to come pick up a sick child from daycare. Therefore, the two major categories of sources of work stress are the work demands and nonwork demands shown in Table 7.1.

**ego-ideal**
The embodiment of a person's perfect self.

**self-image**
How a person sees himself or herself, both positively and negatively.

**TABLE 7.1** Work and Nonwork Demands

**WORK DEMANDS**

| Task Demands | Role Demands |
| --- | --- |
| Change | Role conflict: |
| Lack of control | Interrole |
| Career progress | Intrarole |
| New technologies | Person-role |
| Time pressure | Role ambiguity |

| Interpersonal Demands | Physical Demands |
| --- | --- |
| Emotional toxins | Extreme environments |
| Sexual harassment | Strenuous activities |
| Poor leadership | Hazardous substances |
| | Global travel |

**NONWORK DEMANDS**

| Home Demands | Personal Demands |
| --- | --- |
| Family expectations | Workaholism |
| Child-rearing/daycare arrangements | Civic and volunteer work |
| Parental care | Traumatic events |

Firefighters have to overcome the anatomical response that pushes them to flee and make running into the burning building a conditioned response.

©Lauri Wiberg/iStockPhoto

## Work Demands

Work demands become stressful when there is a mismatch with the skills and resources of the workers, whether this is time, equipment, or knowledge.

**Task Demands** We have already seen that an intensification of work seems to have occurred for many, whether this is in workload, responsibilities, or time pressures. Globalization is creating dramatic changes at work, causing on-the-job pressure and stress.[26] Change leads to uncertainty in a person's daily tasks and activities, and may be caused by job insecurity related to difficult economic times.

Technological innovation creates change and uncertainty for many employees, requiring additional training, education, and skill development. Additionally, new technologies create both career stress and "technostress" for people at work who wonder if "smart" machines will replace them.[27] Although they enhance the organization's productive capacity, new technologies may be viewed as the enemy by workers who must ultimately learn to use them. This creates a real dilemma for management.

Intended to make work easier and more convenient, information technology may have a paradoxical effect and incur stress rather than relieve it, especially if it blurs the line between work and private life, for example, leading people to think they need to respond to those late-evening e-mails from work.

Lack of control is a second major task-related source of stress, especially in work environments that are difficult and psychologically demanding. The lack of control may be caused by the inability to:

> Influence the timing of tasks and activities

> Select tools or methods for accomplishing the work

> Make decisions that influence work outcomes

> Exercise direct action to affect the work outcomes.

Concerns over career progress and time pressures (or work overload) are two additional task demands triggering stress for the person at work. Career stress has occurred in many organizations as the middle-manager ranks have been thinned due to mergers, acquisitions, and downsizing during the past two decades.[28] Leaner organizations, unfortunately, mean overload for the employees who are retained. Fewer people doing the same amount (or more) of work creates time pressure, a leading cause of stress often associated with work overload. It may also result from poor time management skills.

Not all task demands are negative. Challenge stressors that promote personal growth and achievement are positively related to job satisfaction and organizational commitment.[29]

**Role Demands** The social–psychological demands of the work environment may be every bit as stressful as task demands at work. People encounter two major categories of role stress at work: role conflict and role ambiguity.[30] Role conflict results from inconsistent or incompatible expectations communicated to a person. The conflict may be an interrole, intrarole, or person–role conflict.

Interrole conflict is caused by conflicting expectations related to two separate roles, such as employee and parent. For example, the employee with a major sales presentation on Monday and a sick child at home Sunday night is likely to experience interrole conflict. Work–family conflicts like these can lead individuals to withdrawal behaviours.[31]

Intrarole conflict is caused by conflicting expectations related to a single role, such as employee. For example, the manager who presses employees for both very fast work *and* high-quality work may be viewed at some point as creating a conflict for employees.

Ethics violations are likely to cause person–role conflicts. Employees expected to behave in ways that violate personal values, beliefs, or principles experience conflict. Person–role conflicts and ethics violations create a sense of divided loyalty for an employee.

The second major cause of role stress is role ambiguity. Role ambiguity is the confusion a person experiences related to the expectations of others. Role ambiguity may be caused by not understanding what is expected, not knowing how to do it, or not knowing the result of failure to do it. For example, a new magazine employee asked to copyedit a manuscript for the next issue may experience confusion because of lack of familiarity with copyediting procedures and conventions for the specific magazine.

The case of *Zorn-Smith versus the Bank of Montreal* exemplifies the stress caused by task and role demands, the impact on the employee, and the trouble it can lead

**The stress related to switching from worker role to parent role can be intense.**

to for the employer. It is a sad story of a hard-working, committed long-term employee who ended up depressed and jobless. Zorn-Smith was originally pressured to take a promotion although she was not provided with the necessary training, then required to perform at a high level and supervise others despite the lack of training. Asking for a demotion due to the stress, she then had to cover for her replacement, who went on leave.[32] Zorn-Smith took sick leave and then was terminated when she refused to do part-time work. The court hearing the case ordered BMO to pay wrongful dismissal damages but also to pay damages for creating the work environment that led to her stress, stating, "This callous disregard for the health of an employee was flagrant and outrageous. That Susanne Zorn-Smith would suffer a further burnout was predictable—the only question was when it would come . . . I find that the Bank's conduct was the primary cause of Susanne Zorn-Smith's adjustment disorder with depressed and anxious mood."[33]

**Interpersonal Demands** Emotional toxins, such as sexual harassment and poor leadership in the organization, are interpersonal demands for people at work. Emotional

toxins are often generated at work by abrasive personalities.[34] These emotional toxins can spread through a work environment and cause a range of disturbances. Even emotional dissonance can be a cause of work stress.[35] Organizations are increasingly less tolerant of sexual harassment, a gender-related interpersonal demand that creates a stressful working environment both for the person being harassed and for others. The vast majority of sexual harassment is directed at women in the workplace and is a chronic yet preventable workplace problem.[36] Poor leadership in organizations or excessive, demanding management styles or leadership styles mismatched to employees are leading causes of work stress for employees. Employees who feel secure with strong, directive leadership may be anxious with an open management style. Those comfortable with participative leaders may feel restrained by a directive style. Trust is an important characteristic of the leader–follower interpersonal relationship, so a threat to a worker's reputation with his or her supervisor may be especially stressful.[37] Functional diversity in project groups also causes difficulty in the establishment of trusting relationships, thus increasing job stress, which leads to lower cohesiveness within the group.[38]

## [ It May Not Kill You ... But the Wear and Tear? ]

The World Health Organization's (WHO) Special Programme on Health and Environment has identified noise and occupational health and air quality as major health concerns across all nations. According to WHO, one of the most disturbing aspects of noise is chronic exposure. The chronic din of construction sites, airports, and even leaf blowers triggers the stress response with all of its associated "fight-or-flight" hormones. Urban, occupational, and everyday noise is often under the radar yet it has a constant wear and tear effect on a person's mind and body. While the chronic exposure to noise is unlikely to be lethal, it does lead to fatigue, irritability, and poor concentration along with sleep disturbance.

SOURCE: R. Weiss, "Health," *The Washington Post* (5 June 2007): F-1.

Canadian law is increasingly recognizing the link between interpersonal treatment at work and stress. Nancy Sulz was awarded nearly $1 million in damages when her mental health was damaged by her RCMP superiors' treatment of her.[39] Workers exposed to harassment and bullying are now protected by provincial anti-harassment legislation in Quebec (2002), Saskatchewan (2007), and Ontario (2010).

**Physical Demands** Extreme environments, strenuous activities, hazardous substances, and global travel create physical demands for people at work. One cross-cultural study that examined the effects of national culture and ambient temperature on role stress concluded that ambient temperature does affect human well-being, leading to the term *sweat shop* for inhumane working conditions.[40] The unique physical demands of work are often occupation-specific, such as the risk of gravitationally induced loss of consciousness for military pilots flying high-performance fighters[41] or jet lag and loss of sleep for globe-trotting CEOs. Despite the fact that there are many positive aspects to business travel, the associated demands are increasingly recognized as sources of stress.[42]

Office work has its physical hazards as well. Noisy, crowded offices, such as those of some stock brokerages, can prove stressful as well as harmful. Working with a computer can also be stressful, especially if the ergonomic fit between the person and machine is not correct. Eyestrain, neck stiffness, and arm and wrist problems may result. Office designs that use partitions rather than full walls may create stress, by offering little privacy for the occupant and little protection from interruptions.

## Nonwork Demands

Nonwork demands also create stress for people, which may carry over into the work environment, or vice versa.[43] Nonwork demands may broadly be identified as home demands from an individual's personal life environment and personal demands that are self-imposed.

### Home Demands
The wide range of home and family arrangements in contemporary Canadian society has created great diversity in the home demand arena. Traditional families may experience demands that create role conflicts or overloads that are difficult to manage. For example, the loss of good daycare for children may be especially stressful for dual-career and single-parent families.[44] The tension between work and family may lead to a real struggle to achieve balance in life. As a result of the maturing of the Canadian population, an increasing number of people face the added demand of parental care. Even when a person works to achieve an integrative social identity, integrating many social roles into a "whole" identity for a more stress-free balance in work and nonwork identities, the process of integration is not an easy one.[45]

**Personal Demands** Self-imposed, personal demands are the second major category of nonwork demands identified in Table 7.1 on page 107. Although self-imposed and personal, these demands contribute to work stress on the job. Workaholism may be the most notable of these demands that causes stress for people at work and has been identified as a form of addiction.[46] Some of the early warning signs of workaholism include overcommitment to work, inability to enjoy vacations and respites from work, preoccupation with work problems when away from the workplace, and constantly taking work home on the weekend. Another type of personal demand comes from civic activities, volunteer work, and nonwork organizational commitments, such as in religious and public service organizations. These demands become more or less stressful depending on their compatibility with the person's work and family life and their capacity to provide alternative satisfactions for the person.

LEARNING OUTCOME 5

# Two Models Linking Stress Sources to Negative Consequences

The many sources of stress described above have been pulled together by two comprehensive models: the **job demand-control-support model** and the **effort-reward imbalance model**.

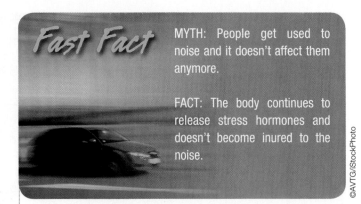

*Fast Fact*

MYTH: People get used to noise and it doesn't affect them anymore.

FACT: The body continues to release stress hormones and doesn't become inured to the noise.

**workaholism**
An imbalanced preoccupation with work at the expense of home and personal life satisfaction.

**job demand-control-support model (JDCS)**
This stress model asserts that high demands, low control, and low support all contribute to strain.

**effort-reward imbalance model (ERI)**
This stress model attributes strain to a combination of high effort and low reward.

## Job Demand-Control-Support Model

Karasek's job demand-control-support model (JDCS) asserts that high demands (work or nonwork), low control, and low support all contribute to strain, and strain can be modified or prevented by altering these factors. In its original form, the model focused only on the stress related to job demands and level of control a worker has over the job. If a worker has a heavy workload, the work is complex, and there are deadlines to meet, that job is high in demands. If the worker has a lot of decision latitude—able to decide how, when and what to do—Karasek believed that control would make the high demands more bearable. Job strain is created when the high demands are intensified by low control, having to meet expectations but unable to control the situation.[47] Research supports this claim, showing that high demands combined with low control increases the risk of physical and mental health conditions. Chronic job strain is a predictor for initial[48] and recurrent[49] heart attacks.[50] A study of BC sawmill workers showed that high psychological demands were associated with a higher risk of neurotic disorders.[51] Data from a Canadian mental health survey showed that those who reported high demand and low control in the workplace were more likely to have had depression or anxiety disorders.[52] A longitudinal study of Finnish dentists found that job demands predicted burnout and depression.[53]

The importance of the control aspect of the model is clear in the finding that voluntary overtime is not seen as stressful (even when there is no reward) whereas mandated overtime is associated with fatigue and low satisfaction.[54] A study with the leaders of several hundred addiction treatment centres found that the emotional exhaustion associated with the high demands in their job was decreased if their centres engaged in long-term planning, which gave a greater sense of control.[55] New York firefighters all face stressful critical events on a regular basis. The likelihood of their turning to alcohol as a stress release turns out to be strongly associated with the resources provided to their particular unit. Those units with good resources (e.g., quality and availability of apparatus, tools, support services, and information) have a significantly lower level of drinking, likely because the greater resources give the firefighters a greater sense of control.[56]

The support dimension of the Karasek model was added later when it became clear that low support at work can magnify the strain in a high demand/low control job but also that low support on its own can be very stressful. A study of 14,000 Belgian men over three years showed that those with low social support at work experienced a higher risk of coronary heart disease.[57] Nurses given support from their coworkers and supervisors experience less fatigue and higher intrinsic motivation when job demands increase.[58] Research with Canadian prison employees showed that if people feel supported by coworkers, they were less likely to suffer psychological stress when exposed to injustice.[59]

## Effort-Reward Imbalance Model

Siegrist's model attributes job strain to a combination of high effort and low reward.[60] Like the inequity model of motivation discussed in Chapter 5, the effort-reward imbalance (ERI) model is a reciprocity model that says people look for a balance between what they put out and what they receive in return. In the ERI model, if a person expends high effort and receives little reward in return, strain is created and adverse health conditions may follow. The ERI model explains that the effort may arise from external sources (time pressure, workload, interruptions, responsibilities) but may also be generated internally (by a worker's need to surpass his- or herself, need for approval, and satisfaction from tackling challenging situations). Low rewards can arise from low wages, being treated with a lack of respect or esteem for the work, job insecurity, and lack of career opportunities. Reducing or preventing strain can be achieved if the organization modifies the efforts required and improves the rewards offered, thereby righting the balance.

The ERI model helps explain the high stress level in many service jobs because of the high effort involved and the fact that many interactions are not rewarding. The self-control involved in service jobs requires significant effort that is often not matched by appreciation from customers. This imbalance can be associated with emotional exhaustion and anxiety.[61,62]

The ERI model has strong research support, demonstrating that a high effort-reward imbalance is associated with higher risk for depression, anxiety and psychotropic drug consumption[63]; cardiovascular disease[64]; and neck and back injuries.[65]

The ERI and JDCS models are not mutually exclusive and, in fact, can complement each other. A Canadian study showed that the two models together were a better predictor of self-reported health status in a group of BC workers than either model alone.[66] An interesting addition to the recent research literature is the evidence that perceived unfairness can be a significant contributor to experienced stress.[67] Injustice could be interpreted as a lack of control, a lack of support, or a lack of reward so it fits into either model.

Figure 7.1 (on page 112) is a summary from Health Canada of the link between negative effects from constant exposure to high demands and low control, or high effort and low rewards in the workplace.[68]

## FIGURE 7.1

### THE COSTS OF AN UNHEALTHY WORKPLACE

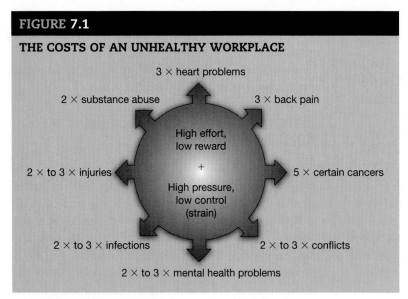

3 × heart problems

2 × substance abuse

3 × back pain

High effort, low reward

+

High pressure, low control (strain)

2 × to 3 × injuries

5 × certain cancers

2 × to 3 × infections

2 × to 3 × conflicts

2 × to 3 × mental health problems

SOURCE: http://www.hc-sc.gc.ca/ewh-semt/alt_formats/pdf/pubs/occup-travail/stress-part-2/stress-part-2-eng.pdf

law, shown in Figure 7.2, indicates that stress leads to improved performance up to an optimum point.[71] Beyond the optimum point, further stress and arousal have a detrimental effect on performance. Therefore, healthy amounts of eustress are desirable to improve performance by arousing a person to action. It is in the mid-range of the curve that the greatest performance benefits from stress are achieved. You can likely recall instances where you have produced some of your best work or come up with a great idea when "under the gun." Adrenaline can be a great motivator. The stress response does provide momentary strength and physical force for brief periods of exertion, thus providing a basis for peak performance in athletic competition or other events.

LEARNING OUTCOME **6**

# The Positive Consequences of Stress

So far our discussion has focused on the link between stress and negative consequences, e.g., medical, performance, and behavioural problems. Stress may be positive, however, creating a healthy, thriving work environment.

Some managers and executives thrive under pressure because they practise what world-class athletes already know,[69] that bringing mind, body, and spirit to peak condition requires recovering energy, which is as important as expending energy. Hence, world-class athletes and managers get high marks on any "stress test" because they use stress-induced energy in positive, healthy, and productive ways. The consequences of healthy, normal stress (called *eustress*, for "euphoria + stress") include a number of performance and health benefits to be balanced against the more commonly known costs of individual and organizational distress.[70] An organization striving for high-quality products and services needs a healthy workforce to support the effort. Eustress is a characteristic of healthy people; distress is not.

Positive stress can bring performance and health benefits. The Yerkes-Dodson

LEARNING OUTCOME **7**

# Individual Differences in the Stress-Strain Relationship

Individual differences play a central role in the stress–strain relationship. The weak organ hypothesis in medicine, also known as the Achilles' heel phenomenon, suggests that a person breaks down at his or her weakest

## FIGURE 7.2

### YERKES-DODSON LAW

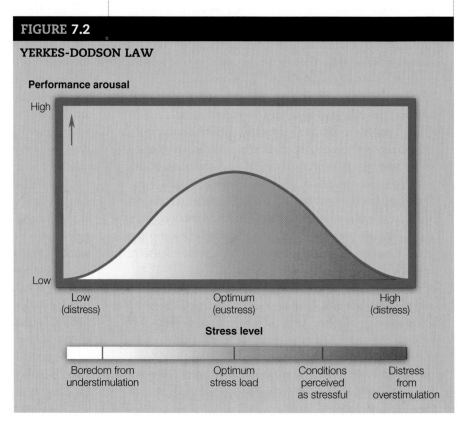

Performance arousal

High

Low

Low (distress)

Optimum (eustress)

High (distress)

**Stress level**

Boredom from understimulation

Optimum stress load

Conditions perceived as stressful

Distress from overstimulation

point. Individual differences, such as negative affectivity and Type A behaviour pattern, enhance vulnerability to strain under stressful conditions. Other individual differences, such as personality hardiness, self-esteem, self-efficacy, and self-reliance, reduce vulnerability to strain under stressful conditions.

## Self-Esteem, Self-Efficacy and Negative Affectivity

Several personality characteristics discussed in Chapter 3 are linked to stress vulnerability. Self-esteem (feelings of personal worth) and self-efficacy (belief in personal capability to meet demands) seem to buffer people from stress whereas negative affectivity seems to make stress more likely.

Those with high self-esteem react differently to stressors and are ultimately less harmed[72] than those with low self-esteem because they appraise the situation differently and use more effective coping strategies. For example, in a study that experimentally induced rejection from an online "date," those with low self-esteem showed greater cortisol reactivity (a physiological measure), appraised themselves more negatively, made more self-blaming attributions, and were more likely to derogate the rejecter.[73]

The fact that self-efficacy is associated with lower levels of stress is not surprising since it suggests a greater sense of personal control. Research in China showed that primary and secondary school teachers with high self-efficacy were less stressed and were more likely to use active coping and positive thinking strategies whereas those with low self-efficacy were more likely to use emotion-focused coping.[74] When those with high self-efficacy are given greater job control, it reduces their stress level, whereas greater job control can actually be stressful for those with low self-efficacy.[75]

People with negative affectivity (tendency to accentuate the negative aspects of the world around them) seem to be sensitized to experience threat and respond strongly to it. Physiological measures show that those with high negative affectivity show greater muscle tension during stress and are slower to recover normal muscle tension and skin temperature after the stress is over than those low on negative affectivity.[76] Those with high negative affectivity are also more likely to react to stress with counterproductive work behaviours (harming the organization or its members) because they anger more easily and tend to be impulsive.[77] Not surprisingly, the other personality characteristic that predicts counterproductive work behaviours in response to stress is low conscientiousness.[78]

# TYPE A BEHAVIOUR PATTERN COMPONENTS

>> 1. Sense of time urgency (a kind of "hurry sickness").

2. The quest for numbers (success is measured by the number of achievements).

3. Status insecurity (feeling unsure of oneself deep down inside).

4. Aggression and hostility expressed in response to frustration and conflict.

## Type A Behaviour Pattern

Type A behaviour pattern is also labelled *coronary-prone behaviour*.[79] **Type A behaviour pattern** is a combination of personality and behavioural characteristics, including competitiveness, time urgency, social status insecurity, aggression, hostility, and a quest for achievements. There are two primary hypotheses concerning the lethal part of the Type A behaviour pattern. One hypothesis suggests that the problem is time urgency, whereas the other hypothesis suggests that it is hostility and aggression. The weight of evidence suggests that hostility and aggression, not time urgency, are the lethal agents.[80]

> **Type A behaviour pattern**
> A complex of personality and behavioural characteristics, including competitiveness, time urgency, social status insecurity, aggression, hostility, and a quest for achievements.

How workers handle stress can depend in large measure on their personalities.

©Tim McClean Photography/iStockPhoto

The alternative to the Type A behaviour pattern is the Type B behaviour pattern. People with Type B personalities are relatively free of the Type A behaviours and characteristics. Type B people are less coronary prone, but if they do have a heart attack, they do not appear to recover as well as those with Type A personalities. Organizations can also be characterized as Type A or Type B.[81] Type A individuals in Type B organizations and Type B individuals in Type A organizations experience stress related to a misfit between their personality type and the predominant type of the organization.

Type A behaviour can be modified. The first step is recognizing that an individual is prone to the Type A pattern and, possibly, spending time with Type B individuals. Type B people often recognize Type A behaviour and can help Type A individuals judge situations realistically. Type A individuals can also learn to pace themselves, manage their time well, and try not to do multiple things at once. Focusing only on the task at hand and its completion, rather than worrying about other tasks, can help Type A individuals cope more effectively.

## Personality Hardiness

People who have personality hardiness resist strain reactions when subjected to stressful events more effectively than do people who are not hardy.[82] The components of personality hardiness are commitment, control, and challenge. Commitment is an engagement with one's environment that leads to the experience of activities as interesting and enjoyable. Control is an ability to influence the process and outcomes of events that leads to the experience of activities as personal choices. Challenge is the viewing of change as a stimulus to personal development, which leads to the experience of activities with openness.

The hardy personality appears to use these three components actively to engage in transformational coping when faced with stressful events.[83] **Transformational coping** is the act of actively changing an event into something less subjectively stressful by viewing it in a broader life perspective, by altering the course and outcome of the event through action, and/or by achieving greater understanding of the process. The alternative to transformational coping is regressive coping, characterized by a passive avoidance of events and decreased interaction with the environment. Regressive coping may lead to short-term stress reduction at the cost of long-term healthy life adjustment.

| Hardy | Not Hardy |
|---|---|
| Commitment | Alienation |
| Control | Powerlessness |
| Challenge | Threat |

## Self-Reliance

There is increasing evidence that social relationships have an important impact on health and life expectancy.[84] **Self-reliance** is a personality attribute related to how people form and maintain supportive attachments with others. Self-reliance was originally based in attachment theory, a theory about normal human development.[85] The theory identifies three distinct patterns of attachment, and research suggests that these patterns extend into behavioural strategies during adulthood, in professional as well as personal relationships.[86] Self-reliance results in a secure pattern of attachment and interdependent behaviour. Interpersonal attachment is emotional and psychological connectedness to another person. The two insecure patterns of attachment are counterdependence and overdependence.

Self-reliance is a healthy, secure, *interdependent* pattern of behaviour. It may appear paradoxical, because a person appears independent while maintaining a host of supportive attachments.[87] Self-reliant people respond to stressful, threatening situations by reaching out to others appropriately. Self-reliance is a flexible, responsive strategy of forming and maintaining multiple, diverse relationships. Self-reliant people are confident, enthusiastic, and persistent in facing challenges.

**Counterdependence** is an unhealthy, insecure pattern of behaviour that leads to separation in relationships with other people. When faced with stressful and threatening situations, counterdependent people withdraw. Counterdependence may be characterized as a rigid, dismissing denial of the need for other people in difficult and stressful times. Counterdependent people exhibit a fearless, aggressive, and actively powerful response to challenges.

**Overdependence** is also an unhealthy, insecure pattern of behaviour. Overdependent people respond to stressful and threatening situations by clinging to other people in any way possible. Overdependence may be characterized as a desperate, preoccupied attempt to achieve a sense of security through relationships.

**personality hardiness**
A personality resistant to distress and characterized by commitment, control, and challenge.

**transformational coping**
A way of managing stressful events by changing them into less subjectively stressful events.

**self-reliance**
A healthy, secure, *interdependent* pattern of behaviour related to how people form and maintain supportive attachments with others.

**counterdependence**
An unhealthy, insecure pattern of behaviour that leads to separation in relationships with other people.

**overdependence**
An unhealthy, insecure pattern of behaviour that leads to preoccupied attempts to achieve security through relationships.

Overdependent people exhibit an active but disorganized and anxious response to challenges. Overdependence prevents a person from being able to organize and maintain healthy relationships and thus creates much distress. It is interesting to note that both counterdependence and overdependence are exhibited by some military personnel who are experiencing adjustment difficulties during the first thirty days of basic training.[88] In particular, basic military trainees who have the most difficulty have overdependence problems and find it difficult to function on their own during the rigours of training.

## LEARNING OUTCOME 8

# Preventive Stress Management

Stress is an inevitable feature of work and personal life. **Preventive stress management** is an organizational philosophy about people and organizations taking joint responsibility for promoting health and preventing distress and strain. Preventive stress management is rooted in the public health notions of prevention, which were first used in preventive medicine. The three stages of prevention are primary, secondary, and tertiary prevention. A framework for understanding preventive stress management is presented in Figure 7.3.

**Primary prevention** is intended to reduce, modify, or eliminate the demand or stressor causing stress. The idea behind primary prevention is to eliminate or alleviate the source of a problem. True organizational stress prevention is largely primary in nature, because it changes and shapes the demands the organization places on people at work. **Secondary prevention** is intended to alter or modify the individual's or the organization's response

**preventive stress management**
An organizational philosophy that holds that people and organizations should take joint responsibility for promoting health and preventing distress and strain.

**primary prevention**
The stage in preventive stress management designed to reduce, modify, or eliminate the demand or stressor causing stress.

**secondary prevention**
The stage in preventive stress management designed to alter or modify the response to a demand or stressor.

## FIGURE 7.3

### A FRAMEWORK FOR PREVENTIVE STRESS MANAGEMENT

| Focus | Level | Aim |
|---|---|---|
| Organizational stressors | Primary prevention: stressor directed | **Prevent the stress:** Reduce work demands / Increase control / Flexibility / Appropriate selection and training / Fairness / Provide support / Management development / Clear structure and practices / Clear expectations / Strong communication / Healthy change processes / Culture |
| Stress responses | Secondary prevention: response directed | **Influence the reaction to stressful events:** Encourage challenge appraisal rather than threat appraisal / Give employees more control / Give employees support |
| Distress | Tertiary prevention: symptom directed | **Help employees deal with stress symptoms:** Debriefing/defusing sessions / EAP / Time off / Adjust work demands / Work with employee to plan changes that will reduce stress |

SOURCE: Adapted from J. D. Quick, R. S. Horn, and J. C. Quick, "Health Consequences of Stress," *Journal of Organizational Behavior Management* 8, No. 2, figure 1 (Fall 1986): 21. Reprinted with permission of Haworth Press, Inc., 10 Alice Street, Binghamton, NY 13904. Copyright 1986.

**People must learn to manage inevitable work stressors.**

Diego Cervo/Shutterstock

to a demand or stressor. People must learn to manage the inevitable, inalterable work stressors and demands to avert distress and strain while promoting health and well-being. **Tertiary prevention** is intended to heal individual or organizational symptoms of distress and strain. The symptoms may range from early warning signs (such as headaches or absenteeism) to more severe forms of distress (such as hypertension, work stoppages, and strikes). We discuss the stages of prevention in the context of organizational prevention and individual prevention.

## Organizational Stress Prevention

**Primary Prevention** As seen in the research emerging from the JDCS model, a natural starting point for preventing stress is to remove or reduce high job demands, give workers more control over their circumstances, and offer support. Physical demands can be reduced through better ergonomics, job rotation (see Chapter 14), and better planning that distributes work over time and employees. Task demands can be modified through improved work systems, increased staffing levels, and having more realistic expectations. Organizations can enhance employee control by inviting their participation in organizational decisions that affect them, and by giving workers more flexibility in how they do their job, when, and where (e.g., permitting flexible work schedules and telecommuting).

**tertiary prevention**
The stage in preventive stress management designed to heal symptoms of distress and strain.

If workers have been well matched to their position through appropriate selection, training, and promotion, they will have a stronger sense of self-efficacy. A focus on fairness in all organizational processes and decisions will also enhance employees' sense of control and predictability. Support comes in two forms: socioemotional and instrumental. Socioemotional support makes the person feel accepted, trusted, and appreciated, and comes from positive social interactions with management and coworkers, responsibilities entrusted, and recognition offered. Instrumental support lies in a worker knowing they will get assistance when it is needed. These all point to the critical role of management. Research by Duxbury, Higgins, and Coghill[89] on stress in thousands of Canadians leads them to suggest more support from managers will come from giving them the skills for people management (e.g., training in project planning and giving feedback), the tools to manage people (e.g., appropriate policies, training on implementing alternative work arrangements), the time they need to manage people, and the incentives to focus on the people part of their job (e.g., measurement and accountability, 360-feedback, and rewards recognizing good people skills).

A great deal of stress can be prevented by having clear structure, policies, and practices, and clearly communicating expectations. If workers know exactly what they are expected to do, why and how, what they are accountable for achieving, what the rules are, what to do when things do not go as expected, and what resources they have, it helps tremendously by reducing role ambiguity and role conflict and giving them a sense of security. Job descriptions, regular team meetings, manager availability, and the use of goal setting have all been shown to be important contributors to clear expectations.

When organizational change is underway, demands seem to inevitably increase, but research in Norway[90] and the United States[91] shows that a healthy change process (see Chapter 18) can greatly reduce the stress. Good practice includes communicating what the change involves, why it is happening, and exactly where the employee fits in; providing ongoing support (accepting resistance as natural); and enhancing control through active participation by employees.

Organizational culture can also play a role in preventing or creating stress. In some companies, the culture

## FIGURE 7.4

### SELECTED MANAGEMENT COMPETENCIES FOR PREVENTING AND REDUCING STRESS AT WORK FROM UNITED KINGDOM HEALTH AND SAFETY EXECUTIVE'S MANAGEMENT STANDARDS, 2007

| Management Standard | Competency | Examples of Positive Manager Behaviour | Examples of Negative Manager Behaviour |
|---|---|---|---|
| Demands | Managing workload and resources | • Bringing in additional resources to handle workload<br>• Awareness of team members' abilities<br>• Monitoring team workload<br>• Refusing to take on additional work when team is under pressure | • Delegating work unequally to team members<br>• Creating unrealistic deadlines<br>• Showing lack of awareness of how much pressure team is under<br>• Asking for tasks without checking workload first |
| Control | Participative approach | • Providing opportunities to express opinions<br>• Regular team meetings<br>• Knowing when to consult employees and when to make decisions | • Not listening when employee asks for help<br>• Presenting a final solution<br>• Making decisions without consultations |
| Support | Accessible/visible | • Communicating that employees can talk to them any time<br>• Having an open-door policy<br>• Making time to talk to employees at their desks or work stations | • Being constantly at meetings away from office<br>• Saying "don't bother me now"<br>• Not attending lunches or social events |
| Support | Individual consideration | • Provides regular one-on-ones<br>• Flexible when employee needs time off<br>• Provides info on additional sources of support<br>• Regularly asks "how are you?" | • Assuming everyone is OK<br>• Badgering employees to tell them what is wrong<br>• Not giving enough notice of shift changes<br>• No consideration of work-life balance |

SOURCE: Contains public sector information published by the Health and Safety Executive and licensed under the Open Government Licence v1.0

encourages long hours and putting work over family. People feel guilty if they leave work on time or if they say no to a request that means overload. Promotions are limited to those who put in significant unpaid overtime.[92] Ironically, in many organizations where the workers deal with stressful critical incidents on a regular basis (e.g., ambulance workers, police) and one would expect support, the culture stigmatizes vulnerability so workers are reluctant to admit they need help.[93] A culture that values employees and work–life balance is more likely to make reasonable demands in the first place, offer support and employee control, and be proactive in dealing with the stresses that inevitably occur.

Figure 7.4 shows a selection of the Management Standards created by the UK's Health and Safety Executive as part of its stress management educational program.[94] Its recommendations fit closely with the suggestions above.

**Secondary Prevention** One of the ways in which organizations can help employees deal with stress is to influence their interpretation of the stressful events so they perceive the event in a positive way (recall Lazarus's cognitive appraisal approach to stress). Positive appraisals are linked to more effective active coping strategies whereas negative appraisals are associated with less effective escapist strategies.[95] Stressors seen as a challenge tend to increase performance. They are motivating, associated with positive emotions, and seen as under the employee's control.[96] When stressors are seen as a hindrance, they tend to decrease performance and are associated with negative emotions. For example, if an employer knows the organization must undergo a change and must communicate that to his/her staff, the way in which he/she presents the change will shape their reaction. If employees see it as an opportunity that, although demanding, is within their ability to handle, they will be less stressed than if they see it as a threat. An intriguing study demonstrated the importance of a task's description. Glynn[97] gave experimental subjects the same puzzle to do but introduced the task differently. Those in the work condition were told they were production managers

Graduate work is demanding and stressful in itself, but many students choose to add to this stress by studying in a foreign country and language. A study by Fan and Wanous demonstrated that a stress-coping orientation can significantly reduce the stress. Working with Asian graduate students doing graduate work at American universities, they gave some a traditional orientation and others the experimental approach. The stress-coping orientation identified major stressors (e.g., language difficulties, social interaction difficulties), provided realistic information on future tasks and the environment in which they would be living and studying, and taught coping skills to handle the stressors. Nine months later, those given the stress-coping orientation felt less stressed and reported higher levels of adjustment in academic performance and social interactions. Why was the orientation helpful? It gave them clearer information and roles that were delineated so they had more sense of control and felt ready to cope.

Supri Suharjoto/Shutterstock

SOURCE: J. Fan and J. P. Wanous, "Organizational and Cultural Entry: A New Type of Orientation Program for Multiple Boundary Crossings," *Journal of Applied Psychology* 93 (2008): 1390–1400.

performing the activity and those in the play condition were told they were starship captains playing a game. This small manipulation affected information processing and behaviours in the activity itself, with "play" subjects focusing more on performance quality and "work" subjects focusing on quantity.

When employees face stressful events, the employer may also be in a position to assist them by giving them greater control through which they can tackle the challenge[98,99] and giving them support, both emotionally and in practical, instrumental ways. A team from Laval University worked with several Quebec health units to mitigate the high levels of stress in their workplaces. A range of staff participated in identifying constraints, proposing interventions, disseminating information, and monitoring the implementation of the changes. Comparison to control units before and after the intervention showed that in the units with the participatory intervention, there was a lowering of psychological demands and burnout rates, sleep problems were lessened, and there were fewer issues with quality of work.[100]

**Tertiary Prevention** The first step in dealing with the symptoms of stress is detecting their existence. Employees may be visibly upset, irritable, or aggressive but frequently the signs are more subtle and the employer needs to be alert for changes in absenteeism, performance level, accidents, mistakes, and client complaints.[101] If work conditions are such that the employer or manager suspects stress may be an issue, it is important to ask the employee how he or she is doing, asking if there are any problems.

When critical incidents happen, some organizations are formally set up to offer debriefing and defusing sessions in which employees can talk through the stressful incident with knowledgeable and supportive people.[102] More commonly, though, employees must cope on their own with stressful events. A sensitive manager can help by steering the employee to support through the organization's Employee Assistance Program (EAP) or through referral to other supportive services. Time off may help ease the stress reaction. The manager can also work collaboratively with the employee to adjust demands underlying the stress.

## Individual Prevention

Clinical research shows that individuals may use a number of self-directed interventions to help prevent distress and enhance positive well-being.[103]

**Positive Thinking** The power of positive thinking is found as an optimistic, nonnegative thinking style used by people to explain the good and bad events in their lives to themselves.[104] A positive, optimistic explanatory style is a habit of thinking learned over time, though some people are predisposed to positive thinking. Pessimism is an alternative explanatory style leading to depression, physical health problems, and low levels of achievement. In contrast, positive thinking and optimism enhance physical health and achievement and avert susceptibility to depression. Positive thinking does not mean ignoring real stress and challenge, though.

Optimistic people avoid distress by viewing the bad events and difficult times in their lives as temporary, limited, and caused by an external event. Optimistic people face difficult times and adversity with hope, and take more credit for the good events in their lives, which they see as more pervasive and generalized. Learned optimism

clean the house or mow the lawn. These activities are fine, as long as the individual gets the stress-reducing benefit of pleasure from them. Some say our work ethic is a cultural barrier to pleasure. We work longer hours, and two-income families are the norm. Leisure is increasingly a luxury among working people. The key to the effective use of leisure time is enjoyment. Leisure time can be used for spontaneity, joy, and connection with others in our lives. Although vacations can be a relief from job burnout, they may suffer fade-out effects.[106] Hence, leisure time and vacations must be periodic, recurring activities.

**Physical Exercise** Different types of physical exercise are important stress prevention activities for individuals. Aerobic exercise improves a person's responsiveness to stressful activities. Research has found that aerobically fit people (1) have lower levels of adrenaline in their blood at rest; (2) have a slower, stronger heart functioning; and (3) recover from stressful events more quickly.[107]

begins with identifying pessimistic thoughts and then distracting oneself from these thoughts or disputing them with evidence and alternative thoughts. Learned optimism is nonnegative thinking.

**Time Management** Time pressure is one of the major sources of stress for people both at work and in school. The leading symptoms of poor time management include constant rushing, missed deadlines, work overload and the sense of being overwhelmed, insufficient rest time, and indecision. Effective time managers are "macro" time managers who use a $GP^3$ method of time management.[105] The $GP^3$ method includes (1) *setting* goals that are challenging yet attainable; (2) *prioritizing* these goals in terms of their relative importance; (3) *planning* for goal attainment through specific tasks, activities, scheduling, and even delegation; and (4) *praising* oneself for specific achievements along the way. Setting concrete goals and prioritizing these goals are the most important first steps in time management skills, ensuring that the most important work and study activities receive enough time and attention. This system of time management enables a person to track his/her success over time and goes a long way toward reducing unnecessary stress and confusion.

**Leisure Time Activities** Unremitted striving characterizes many people with a high need for achievement. Leisure time activities provide employees an opportunity for rest and recovery from strenuous activities either at home or at work. When asked what they do with their leisure time, many individuals say that they

luchschen/Shutterstock

# Hot Trend: Say No to the Borderless Workday

Technology is blurring the borders of the workday, inviting people to take their work with them whenever and wherever they are. Does this make us more productive? Research now shows that a clear separation between work and non-work time is important to well-being and to performance at work. Studies with German and Swiss employees showed that those thinking about or actively working on "work" in the evening were more fatigued the next day at work, and more likely to be tense and distressed. Those who engaged in relaxing activities were more at ease the next day. Those who engaged in mastery activities (e.g., playing a sport or music) felt stronger and more active at work the next day. Interestingly, the need for psychological detachment is especially strong for those employees who are intensely involved in their jobs. What is the role of the employer in ensuring this separation? The CEO of Cisco Systems told all employees to take vacation from December 23 to January 4 and not to send text messages or e-mails to colleagues during that time. It is interesting that he needed to encourage people to take true holiday time and that he recognized the importance of doing it.

SOURCES: S. Sonnentag, C. Binnewies, E.J. Mojza, "Did You Have a Nice Evening?" A Day-level Study on Recovery Experiences, Sleep and Affect," *Journal of Applied Psychology* 93 (2008): 674–684; S. Sonnentag, E. J. Mojza, C. Binnewies, and A. Scholl, "Being Engaged at Work and Detached at Home: A Week-level Study of Work Engagement, Psychological Detachment and Affect," *Work & Stress* 22 (2008): 257–276; W. Immen, "Surviving the January Grind," *The Globe and Mail*, January 9, 2010, B15.

Flexibility training is an important type of exercise because of the muscular contractions associated with the stress response. One component of the stress response is the contraction of the flexor muscles, which prepares a person to fight or flee. Flexibility training enables a person to stretch and relax these muscles to prevent the accumulation of unnecessary muscular tension.[108] Flexibility exercises help maintain joint mobility, increase strength, and play an important role in the prevention of injury.

## Relaxation Training

Herbert Benson was one of the first people to identify the relaxation response as the natural counter-response to the stress response.[109] In studying Western and Eastern peoples, Benson found that Judeo-Christian people have elicited this response through their time-honoured tradition of prayer, whereas Eastern people have elicited it through meditation. The relaxation response does not require a theological or religious component. If you have a practice of regular prayer or meditation, you may already elicit the relaxation response regularly.

**Diet** Diet may play an indirect role in stress and stress management. High sugar content in the diet can stimulate the stress response, and foods high in cholesterol can adversely affect blood chemistry. Good dietary practices contribute to a person's overall health, making the person less vulnerable to distress.

Jupiter Images

**High sugar, high-fat diets stimulate the stress response.**

**Opening Up** Everyone experiences a traumatic, stressful, or painful event in life at one time or another. One of the most therapeutic, curative responses to such an event is to confide in another person.[110] Discussing difficult experiences with another person is not always easy, yet health benefits, immune system improvement, and healing accrue through self-disclosure. In one study comparing those who wrote once a week about traumatic events with those who wrote about non-traumatic events, significant health benefits and reduced absenteeism were found in the first group.[111] Confession need not be through a personal relationship with friends. It may occur through a private diary. The process of opening up and confessing appears to counter the detrimental effects of stress.

**Professional Help** Confession and opening up may occur through professional helping relationships. People who need healing have psychological counselling, career counselling, physical therapy, medical treatment, surgical intervention, and other therapeutic techniques available. Employee assistance programs (EAPs) may be very helpful in referring employees to the appropriate caregivers. Even combat soldiers who experience battle stress reactions severe enough to take them out of action can heal and be ready for subsequent combat duty.[112] The early detection of distress and strain reactions, coupled with prompt professional treatment, can be instrumental in averting permanent physical and psychological damage.

# Visit **icanorgb.com** to find the resources you need today!

*Located at the back of the textbook are rip-out Chapter Review Cards. Make sure you also go online to check out other tools that ORGB offers to help you successfully pass your course.*

- Interactive Quizzing
- Key Term Flashcards
- PowerPoint Slides
- Audio Chapter Summaries

- Cases and Exercises
- Interactive Games
- Self-Assessments
- "On the Job" and "Bizflix" Videos

# Communication

# Interpersonal Communication

**Communication** evokes a shared or common meaning in another person. **Interpersonal communication** occurs between two or more people in an organization. Reading, listening, managing and interpreting information, and serving clients are among the interpersonal communication skills often identified as being necessary for successful functioning in the workplace.[1] In Chapter 7, we noted that interpersonal communication is the key to social support for preventive stress management.[2] Interpersonal communication is central to health and well-being.

Interpersonal communication is also important in building and sustaining human relationships at work. Advances in information technology and data management that have taken place during the past several decades cannot replace interpersonal communication. The interpersonal communication model in Figure 8.1 (on page 124) illustrates the key elements of interpersonal communication: the communicator, the receiver, the perceptual screens, and the message.

**communication**
The evoking of a shared or common meaning in another person.

**interpersonal communication**
Communication between two or more people in an organization.

**communicator**
The person originating a message.

**receiver**
The person receiving a message.

## An Interpersonal Communication Model

The **communicator** is the person originating the message. The **receiver** is the person receiving the message.

## LEARNING OUTCOMES

After reading this chapter, you should be able to do the following:

**1** Describe the interpersonal communication process and the role of listening in the process.

**2** Describe the five communication skills of effective supervisors.

**3** Explain five communication barriers and gateways through them.

**4** Distinguish between defensive and nondefensive communication.

**5** Explain the impact of nonverbal communication.

**6** Explain positive, healthy communication.

**7** Identify communication technologies and how they affect the communication process.

## FIGURE 8.1

### A BASIC INTERPERSONAL COMMUNICATION MODEL

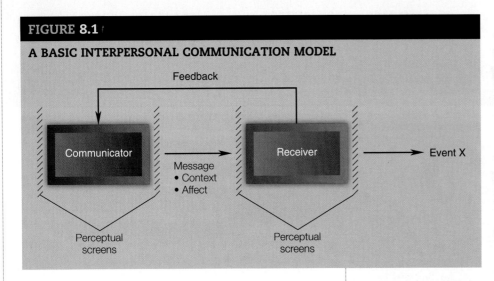

**Perceptual screens** are the windows through which we interact with people in the world. The communicator's and the receiver's perceptual screens influence the quality, accuracy, and clarity of the message. The screens influence whether the message sent and the message received are the same or whether noise or distortion occurs in transmission. Perceptual screens are composed of the sender's and receiver's individual traits, including age, gender, values, beliefs, past experiences, cultural influences, and individual needs. The extent to which these screens are open or closed significantly influences both the sent and received messages.

The **message** contains the thoughts and feelings that the sender (communicator) intends to evoke in the receiver. The message has two primary components. The thought or conceptual component of the message (its content) is contained in the words, ideas, symbols, and concepts chosen to relay the message. The feeling or emotional component of the message (its affect) is contained in the demeanour, intensity, force, and sometimes the gestures of the communicator. The emotional component of the message adds the overtones of joy, anger, fear, or pain, to the conceptual component. This addition often enriches and clarifies the message. The emotional component completes the message.

**Feedback** may or may not be activated in the model. Feedback occurs when the receiver provides the communicator with a response to the message. More broadly, feedback occurs when information is fed back to the sender that completes two-way communication.

The **language** of the message is important because of the multilingualism and multiculturalism of many organizations. Language is the words, their pronunciation, and the methods of combining them used by a community of people.

**Data** are the uninterpreted, unanalyzed elements of a message. **Information** is data with meaning to a person who has interpreted or analyzed them. Messages are conveyed through a medium, such as a telephone or face-to-face discussion. Messages differ in **richness**, the ability of the medium to convey the meaning.[3] Table 8.1 compares different media with regard to data capacity

**perceptual screen**

A window through which we interact with people that influences the quality, accuracy, and clarity of the communication.

**message**

The thoughts and feelings that the communicator is attempting to elicit in the receiver.

**feedback**

Information fed back that completes two-way communication.

**language**

The words, their pronunciation, and the methods of combining them used and understood by a group of people.

**data**

Uninterpreted and unanalyzed facts.

**information**

Data that have been interpreted, analyzed, and have meaning to some user.

**richness**

The ability of a medium or channel to elicit or evoke meaning in the receiver.

**TABLE 8.1** Data Capacity and Richness of Various Media

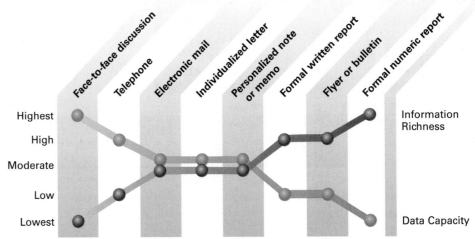

SOURCE: E. A. Gerloff, "Information Richness: A New Approach to Managerial Behavior and Organizational Design," in R. L. Daft and R. H. Lengel, eds., *Research in Organizational Behavior* 6 (JAI Press, 1984) 191–233. Reprinted by permission of JAI Press Inc.

and information richness. Attributes of communication media affect how influence-seeking behaviour is generated and perceived in organizations.[4]

## Reflective Listening

Even though listening isn't explicitly called out in the communication model, good listening is vital for effective communication. **Reflective listening** is the skill of carefully listening to another person and repeating back to the speaker the heard message to correct any inaccuracies or misunderstandings. Reflecting back the message helps the communicator clarify and sharpen the intended meaning. This kind of listening emphasizes the role of the receiver or audience in interpersonal communication. Managers use it to understand other people and help them solve problems at work.[5] Reflective listening enables the listener to understand the communicator's meaning, reduce perceptual distortions, and overcome interpersonal barriers that lead to communication failures. Especially useful in problem solving, reflective listening can be learned in a short time with positive effects on behaviours and emotions in organizational situations.[6]

Reflective listening can be characterized as personal, feeling oriented, and responsive.[7] First, reflective listening emphasizes the personal elements of the communication process. The reflective listener demonstrates empathy and concern for the communicator as a person, not an inanimate object. Second, reflective listening emphasizes the feelings communicated in the message. The receiver should pay special attention to the feeling component of the message. Third, reflective listening emphasizes responding to the communicator, not leading the communicator. Receivers should distinguish their own feelings and thoughts from those of the speaker. The focus must be on the speaker's feelings and thoughts in order to respond to them. A good reflective listener does not lead the speaker according to the listener's own thoughts and feelings.

Four levels of oral response by the receiver are part of active reflective listening: affirming contact, paraphrasing expressed thoughts and feelings, clarifying implicit

thoughts and feelings, and reflecting "core" feelings not fully expressed. Nonverbal behaviours also are useful in reflective listening. Specifically, silence and eye contact are responses that enhance reflective listening.

Each reflective response is illustrated through the case of a software engineer and her supervisor. The engineer has just discovered a major problem, which is not yet fully defined, in a large information system she is building for a very difficult customer.

**Affirming Contact** The receiver affirms contact with the communicator by using simple statements such as "I see," "Uh-huh," and "Yes, I understand." The purpose of an affirmation response is to communicate attentiveness, not necessarily agreement. In the case of the software engineer, the supervisor might most appropriately use several affirming statements as the engineer begins to talk through the problem. Affirming contact is especially reassuring to a speaker in the early stages of expressing thoughts and feelings about a problem, especially when there may be some associated anxiety or discomfort. As the problem is more fully explored and expressed, it is increasingly useful for the receiver to use additional reflective responses.

**Paraphrasing the Expressed** After an appropriate time, the receiver might paraphrase the expressed thoughts and feelings of the speaker. Paraphrasing is useful because it reflects back to the speaker the thoughts and feelings as the receiver heard them. This oral response enables the receiver to build greater empathy, openness, and acceptance into the relationship while ensuring the accuracy of the communication process.

In the case of the software engineer, the supervisor may find paraphrasing the engineer's expressed thoughts and feelings particularly useful for both of them in developing a clearer understanding of the system problem. For example, the supervisor might say, "I hear you saying that you are very upset about this problem and that you are not

*The purpose of an affirmation response is to communicate attentiveness, not necessarily agreement.*

**reflective listening**
A skill intended to help the receiver and communicator clearly and fully understand the message sent.

Andresr/Shutterstock

yet clear about what is causing it." It is difficult to solve a problem until it is clearly understood.

**Clarifying the Implicit** People often communicate implicit thoughts and feelings about a problem in addition to their explicitly expressed thoughts and feelings. Implicit thoughts and feelings are not clearly or fully expressed. The receiver may or may not assume that the implicit thoughts and feelings are within the awareness of the speaker. For example, the software engineer may be anxious about how to talk with a difficult customer concerning the system problem. This may be implicit in her discussion with her supervisor because of the previous discussions about this customer. If her anxiety feelings are not expressed, the supervisor may want to clarify them. For example, the supervisor might say, "I hear that you are feeling very upset about the problem and may be worried about the customer's reaction when you inform him." This would help the engineer shift the focus of her attention from the main problem, which is in the software, to the important and related issue of discussing the matter with the customer.

**Reflecting "Core" Feelings** Next, the receiver should go beyond the explicit or implicit thoughts and feelings that the speaker is expressing. The receiver, in reflecting the core feelings that the speaker may be experiencing, is reaching beyond the immediate awareness level of the speaker. "Core" feelings are the deepest and most important ones from the speaker's perspective. For example, if the software engineer had not been aware of any anxiety in her relationship with the difficult customer, her supervisor's ability to sense the tension and bring it to the engineer's awareness would exemplify reflecting core feelings.

The receiver runs a risk of overreaching in reflecting core feelings if a secure, empathetic relationship with the speaker does not already exist or if strongly repressed feelings are reflected back. Even if the receiver is correct, the speaker may not want those feelings brought to awareness. Therefore, it is important to exercise caution and care in reflecting core feelings to a speaker.

**Silence** Long, extended periods of silence may cause discomfort and be a sign or source of embarrassment, but silence can help both speaker and listener in reflective listening. From the speaker's perspective, silence may be useful in moments of thought or confusion

about how to express difficult ideas or feelings. The software engineer may need some patient, silent response as she thinks through what to say next. Listeners can use brief periods of silence to sort out their own thoughts and feelings from those of the speaker. Reflective listening focuses only on the latter. In the case of the software engineer's supervisor, any personal, angry feelings toward the difficult customer should not intrude on the engineer's immediate problem. Silence provides time to identify and isolate the listener's personal responses and exclude them from the dialogue.

**Eye Contact** Eye contact is a nonverbal behaviour that may help open up a relationship and improve communication between two people. The absence of any direct eye contact during an exchange tends to close communication. Cultural and individual differences influence what constitutes appropriate eye contact. For example, some cultures, such as in India, place restrictions on direct eye contact initiated by women or children. Too much direct eye contact, regardless of the individual or culture, has an intimidating effect.

Moderate direct eye contact, therefore, communicates openness and affirmation without causing either speaker or listener to feel intimidated. Periodic aversion of the eyes allows for a sense of privacy and control, even in intense interpersonal communication.

**One-Way versus Two-Way Communication** Reflective listening encourages two-way communication. **Two-way communication** is an interactive form of communication in which there is an exchange of thoughts, feelings, or both and through which shared meaning often occurs. Problem solving and decision making are often examples of two-way communication.

Two-way communication involves exchange.

©Irina Zolina/iStockPhoto

**One-way communication** occurs when a person sends a message to another person and no feedback, questions, or interaction follow. Giving instructions or giving directions are examples of one-way communication. One-way communication occurs whenever a person sends a one-directional message to a receiver with no reflective listening or feedback in the communication.

One-way communication is faster, although how much faster depends on the amount and complexity of information communicated and the medium chosen. Even though it is faster, one-way communication is often less accurate than two-way communication. This is especially true for complex tasks where clarifications and iterations may be required for task completion. Where time and accuracy are both important to the successful completion of a task, such as in combat or emergency situations, extensive training prior to execution enhances accuracy and efficiency of execution without two-way communication.[8] Firefighters and military combat personnel engage extensively in such training to minimize the need for communication during emergencies. These highly trained professionals rely on fast, abbreviated, one-way communication as a shorthand for more complex information. However, this communication works only within the range of situations for which the professionals are specifically trained.

It is difficult to draw general conclusions about people's satisfaction with one-way versus two-way communication. For example, communicators with a stronger need for feedback or who are not uncomfortable with conflicting or confusing questions may find two-way communication more satisfying. In contrast, receivers who believe that

a message is very straightforward may be satisfied with one-way communication and dissatisfied with two-way communication because of its lengthy, drawn-out nature.

It is important to recognize the role of the **organizational grapevine** in communication. The grapevine is an informal, uncensored communication network. "If you want to know about the kind of insurance coverage your employer offers, look in the company handbook. But if you want to know who to avoid, who the boss loathes or loves, who to go to when you need help, what it really takes to get a promotion or raise, and how much you can safely slack off, you're better off paying attention to the [organizational] grapevine."[11] In other words, the grapevine provides rich and revealing information about organizational reality.

# Communication Skills for Effective Managers

Interpersonal communication, especially between managers and employees, is a critical foundation for effective performance in organizations, as well as for health and well-being. Language and power are intertwined in the communication that occurs between managers and their employees.[12] This is especially critical when leaders are articulating vision and achieving buy-in from employees.[13] One large study of managers in a variety of jobs and industries found that managers with the most effective work units engaged in routine communication within their units, whereas the managers with the highest promotion rates engaged in networking activities with superiors.[14] Another study of male and female banking managers suggested that higher-performing managers were better and less apprehensive communicators than lower-performing

## [ Communications in Crisis ]

In 2008, Maple Leaf Foods faced a crisis—one of its plants was the source of a serious food-borne illness, listeriosis. In response, it recalled all its products and shut down the plant. Since the crisis began, Michael McCain, CEO of Maple Leaf Foods, was visible in the media by posting an apology on the company website and by taking out full-page advertisements and holding press conferences. Communication experts praised the company for its communication strategy of having the CEO front and centre in responding to the crisis.[9] A year after the crisis, McCain took out a full-page advertisement and said, "It was a year ago that some of our products were linked to a listeriosis outbreak that caused the death of 22 Canadians.... The friends and family of these people will never forget and neither will we."[10]

The Canadian Press/Ryan Remiorz

**one-way communication**
Communication in which a person sends a message to another person and no feedback, questions, or interaction follows.

**organizational grapevine**
Informal, uncensored communication network.

managers.[15] Oral communication (voice) and cooperative behaviours are important contextual performance skills that have positive effects on the psychosocial quality of the work environment.[16]

A review of the research on manager–employee communication identified five communication skills that distinguish "good" from "bad" supervisors.[17] These skills include being expressive speakers, empathetic listeners, persuasive leaders, sensitive people, and informative managers. Some supervisors are good and effective without possessing all of these skills, and some organizations value one or another skill over the others. Thus, dyadic relationships are often at the core of much organization-based communication.[18]

## Expressiveness

Better supervisors express their thoughts, ideas, and feelings and speak up in meetings. They tend toward extroversion. Supervisors who are not talkative or who tend toward introversion may at times leave their employees wondering what their supervisors are thinking or feeling about certain issues. Supervisors who speak out let the people they work with know where they stand, what they believe, and how they feel and why.

## Empathy and Sensitivity

In addition to being expressive speakers, the better supervisors are willing, empathetic listeners who use reflective listening skills. Empathetic listeners are able to hear the feelings and emotional dimensions of the messages people send them, as well as the content of the ideas and issues. Better supervisors are approachable and willing to listen to suggestions and complaints. In the case of physicians, those with high perceived control were more open in their communication and patients found them more empathetic.[19]

Better supervisors are also sensitive to the feelings, self-image, and psychological defences of their employees. Public settings are reserved for the praise of employees' accomplishments, honours, and achievements; criticism is delivered confidentially, in private. In this manner, the better supervisors are sensitive to the self-esteem of others.

**barriers to communication**
Aspects of the communication content and context that can impair effective communication in a workplace.

**gateways to communication**
Pathways through barriers to communication and antidotes to communication problems.

## Persuasion

All supervisors and managers must exercise power and influence in organizations if they are to ensure performance and achieve results. More effective supervisors are persuasive leaders, distinguished by their use of persuasive communication when influencing others. They are not directive or autocratic. Specifically, they encourage results instead of manipulating others.

The exceptions to this pattern of communication occur in emergency or high-risk situations, such as life-threatening traumas in medical emergency rooms or in oil rig firefighting. In these cases, the supervisor must be directive and assertive.

## Informative

Finally, better supervisors keep their employees well informed, while appropriately and selectively disseminating information. The failure to filter and disseminate information selectively may lead to either information overload for the employees or a lack of sufficient information for performance and task accomplishment. Better supervisors favour giving advance notice of organizational changes and explaining the rationale for organizational policies.

A person may become a good supervisor even in the absence of one of these communication skills. For example, a person with special talents in planning, organizing, or decision making may compensate for a shortcoming in expressiveness or sensitivity. Further, when supervisors and employees engage in overt behaviours of communication and forward planning, they have a greater number of agreements about the employee's performance and behaviour.[20]

# Barriers and Gateways to Communication

Barriers to communication are factors that block or significantly distort successful communication. About 20 percent of communication problems that cause organizational problems and drain profitability can be prevented or solved by communication policy guidelines.[21] Gateways to communication are pathways through these barriers and subsequently serve as antidotes. Communication barriers may be temporary and easily resolved. Awareness and recognition are the first steps in formulating ways to overcome the

**What about You?, found on the Chapter 8 Review Card, gives you an opportunity to evaluate how active a listener you are.**

barriers. Obvious barriers to communication in the workplace are physical separation (employees in different geographic locations or buildings) and status differences (related to the organizational hierarchy). Not so obvious—but no less important—are the barriers caused by gender differences, cultural diversity, and language.

## Gender Differences

Communication barriers can be explained in part by differences in conversational styles.[22] When people of different ethnic or class backgrounds converse, the receiver's understanding may not be the same as the speaker's meaning. In a similar way, men and women have different conversational styles. For example, women prefer to converse face to face, whereas men are comfortable sitting side by side and concentrating on some focal point in front of them. Hence, conversation style differences may result in a failure to communicate between men and women. Male–female conversation is really cross-cultural communication. In a work context, one study found that female employees sent less information to their supervisors and experienced less information overload than did male employees.[23]

An important gateway through the gender barrier to communication is developing an awareness of gender-specific differences in conversational style. These differences can enrich organizational communication and empower professional relationships.[24] A second gateway is to actively seek clarification of the person's meaning rather than freely interpreting meaning from your own frame of reference.

## Cultural Diversity

Cultural values and patterns of behaviour can be very confusing barriers to communication. Important international differences in work-related values exist among people in Canada, Germany, the United Kingdom, Japan, and other nations.[25] These value differences impact motivation, leadership, and teamwork in work organizations.[26] Habitual patterns of interaction within a culture often substitute for communication. For example, the German culture places greater value on authority and hierarchical differences. It is therefore more difficult for German workers to engage in direct, open communication with their supervisors than it is for North American workers.[27]

When people from one culture view those in another culture through the lens of stereotypes, they are in effect

Culture provides the context for consensually derived metaphors that facilitate understanding.

toomas/Stock.Xchng

discounting the individual differences within the other culture. For example, an Asian stereotype of North Americans may be that they are aggressive and arrogant and, thus, insensitive and unapproachable. Or, a North American stereotype of Chinese and Japanese may be that they are mild and subservient, unable to be appropriately strong and assertive. Individuals who depend on the accuracy of these forms of cultural stereotypes will be badly misled in communicating with those in other cultures.

One gateway through cultural diversity as a communication barrier is increasing awareness and sensitivity. In addition, organizations can provide seminars for expatriate managers as part of their training for overseas assignments. Bernard Isautier, chairman, president, and CEO of PetroKazakstan, believes that understanding and communication are two keys to success with workplace diversity, which is an essential ingredient for success in international markets.[28] A second gateway is developing or acquiring a guide, map, or beacon for understanding and interacting with members of other cultures. One approach is to describe a nation in terms of a suitable and complex metaphor.[29] For example, Irish conversations, the Spanish bullfight, and American football are consensually derived metaphors that can enable those outside the culture to understand members within the culture.

Cultural differences in communication can be examined through four lenses: (1) time and space, (2) fate and personal responsibility, (3) face and face saving, and (4) nonverbal communication.[30] In North America, time is seen as a limited linear resource. In contrast, the Indian conception of time highlights its cyclical nature. North American culture tends to emphasize personal responsibility but others, whose history is marked by oppression, tend to emphasize more fatalism. Cultures that value community tend to place greater emphasis on face saving so that individuals do not become alienated from the community. In cultures that value individualism, face saving is not a significant concern. Lastly, there are notable cultural differences in ascribing the importance of nonverbal cues. In North America, they are seen as less important than in Japan and Colombia, where the intended meaning is conveyed both verbally and nonverbally. It is therefore vital to understand these four cultural differences to enhance communication and to reduce conflict. "Careful observation, ongoing study from a variety of sources, and cultivating relationships across cultures will all help develop the cultural fluency to work effectively …"[31]

Right to Play, headquartered in Canada, uses sport to foster cross-cultural communication. Its mission is "to improve the lives of children in some of the most disadvantaged areas of the world by using the power of sport and play for development, health and peace."[32] Sport is a particularly effective way to enhance communication as it "[brings] individuals and communities together, highlighting commonalties and bridging cultural or ethnic divides."[33]

## Language

Although English is the international language of aviation, it is not the international language of business. Although increasing numbers of individuals are bilingual or multilingual, less obvious barriers are subtle distinctions in dialects within the same language. For example, the word *lift* means an elevator in Great Britain and a ride in Canada. In a different vein, language barriers are created across disciplines and professional boundaries by technical terminology. Acronyms may be very useful to those on the inside of a profession or discipline as a means of shorthand communication. Technical terms can convey precise meaning between professionals. However, acronyms and technical

**defensive communication**
Communication that can be aggressive, attacking, and angry, or passive and withdrawing.

**nondefensive communication**
Communication that is assertive, direct, and powerful.

# WHAT'S KEEPING YOU FROM COMMUNICATING EFFECTIVELY? MAYBE IT'S

> Physical separation     > Cultural diversity
> Status differences      > Language
> Gender differences

# DEALING WITH DEFENSIVE PEOPLE

>> Catherine Crier had extensive experience as a trial lawyer and judge in dealing with defensive people. She carried this knowledge over into her position as a news anchor for CNN, ABC, Fox News, and Court TV. Her four basic rules are

1. Define the situation
2. Clarify the person's position
3. Acknowledge the person's feelings
4. Bring the focus back to the facts.

terms may serve only to confuse, alienate, and derail any attempt at clear understanding for people unfamiliar with their meaning and usage. Use simple, direct, declarative language. Speak in brief sentences and use terms or words you have heard from your audience. As much as possible, speak in the language of the listener. Do not use jargon or technical language except with those who clearly understand it.

LEARNING OUTCOME **4**

# Defensive and Nondefensive Communication

Defensive communication in organizations also creates barriers between people, whereas nondefensive communication helps open up relationships.[34] **Defensive communication** includes aggressive and angry communication as well as passive, withdrawing communication. **Nondefensive communication** is an assertive, direct, powerful form of communication. Although aggressiveness and passiveness are both forms of defensive communication, assertiveness is nondefensive communication. Organizations are increasingly engaged in courtroom battles and media exchanges, which are especially fertile settings for defensive communication.

Defensive communication in organizations leads to a wide range of problems, including injured feelings, communication breakdowns, alienation in working relationships, destructive and retaliatory behaviours, nonproductive efforts, and problem-solving failures. When such problems arise in organizations, everyone is prone to blame everyone else for what is not working.[35] The defensive responses of counterattack or sheepish withdrawal derail communication. Such responses tend to lend heat, not light, to the communication. An examination of some defensive tactics follows the discussion of the two basic patterns of defensiveness in the next section.

Nondefensive communication, in contrast, provides a basis for asserting and defending yourself when attacked, without being defensive. There are appropriate ways to defend against aggression, attack, or abuse. An assertive, nondefensive style restores order, balance, and effectiveness in working relationships. A discussion of nondefensive communication follows the discussion of defensive communication.

## Defensive Communication at Work

Defensive communication often elicits defensive communication in response. The two basic patterns of defensiveness are subordinate defensiveness and dominant defensiveness.

Subordinate defensiveness is characterized by passive or submissive behaviour. The psychological attitude of the subordinately defensive person is "You are right, and I am wrong." People with low self-esteem may be prone to this form of defensive behaviour, as well as people at lower organizational levels. People who are subordinately defensive do not adequately assert their thoughts and feelings, so their input is likely to be lost even if it is critical to organizational performance.[36] Passive-aggressive behaviour is a form of defensiveness that begins as subordinate defensiveness and ends up as dominant defensiveness. It is behaviour that appears very passive but, in fact, masks underlying aggression and hostility.

By contrast, dominant defensiveness is characterized by active, aggressive, attacking behaviour. It is offensive in nature: "The best defence is a good offence." The psychological attitude of the dominantly defensive person is "I am right, and you are wrong." People who compensate for low self-esteem may exhibit this pattern of behaviour, as well as people who are in higher-level positions within the organizational hierarchy.

## [ The Finger ]

Junior officers in a regional banking organization nicknamed the bank chairman "The Finger." When giving orders or admonishing someone, he would point his index finger in a domineering, intimidating, emphatic manner that caused defensiveness on the part of the recipient.

## Defensive Tactics

©Lev Dolgatsjov—Fotolia.com

Defensive tactics are how defensive communication is acted out. Unfortunately, defensive tactics are all too common in organizations. Until defensiveness and defensive tactics are recognized for what they are, it is difficult either to change them or to respond to them in nondefensive ways. In many cases, such tactics raise difficult ethical dilemmas and issues. For example, is it ethical to raise doubts about another person's values, beliefs, or sexuality? At what point does simple defensiveness become unethical behaviour?

Power plays are used by people to control and manipulate others through the use of choice definition (defining the choice another person is allowed to make), either/or conditions, and overt aggression. The underlying dynamic in power plays is that of domination and control. Another tactic is the insult or put-down in which the speaker tries to gain the upper hand in the relationship. Intentionally ignoring another person or pointing out his or her mistakes in a meeting are kinds of put-downs.

Labelling is often used to portray another person as abnormal or deficient. Psychological labels are often used out of context for this purpose, such as calling a person "paranoid," a word that has a specific, clinical meaning. Similar to labelling is raising doubts about a person's abilities, values, preferential orientations, or other aspects of his or her life, which creates confusion and uncertainty. This tactic tends to lack the specificity and clarity present in labelling.

Giving misleading information, a form of deception, is the selective presentation of information designed to leave a false and inaccurate impression in the listener's mind. Scapegoating and its companion, buck passing, are methods of shifting responsibility to the wrong person. Blaming other people is another form of scapegoating or buck passing. Finally, hostile jokes should not be confused with good humour, which is both therapeutic and nondefensive. Jokes created at the expense of others are destructive and hostile.

## Nondefensive Communication

Nondefensive communication is a constructive, healthy alternative to defensive communication in working relationships. The person who communicates nondefensively may be characterized as centred, assertive, controlled, informative, realistic, and honest. Nondefensive communication is powerful because the speaker is exhibiting self-control and self-possession without rejecting the listener. Nondefensive communication should be self-affirming without being self-aggrandizing, however.

Converting defensive patterns of communication to nondefensive ones enhances relationship building at work. Relationship-building behaviours and communication help reduce adverse responses, such as blame and anger, following negative events at work.[37]

The subordinately defensive person needs to learn to be more assertive. One way to do so, instead of asking for permission to do something, is to report what you intend to do and invite confirmation. Another way is to stop using self-deprecating words, such as "I'm just following orders." Drop the *just*, and convert the message into a self-assertive, declarative statement.

The person prone to be domineering and dominantly defensive needs to learn to be less aggressive. This may be especially difficult because it requires overcoming the person's sense of "I am right." People who are working to overcome dominant defensiveness should be particularly sensitive to feedback from others about their behaviour. To change this behaviour, stop giving and denying permission. Instead, give people free rein except in situations where permission is essential as a means of clearing approval or ensuring the security of the task. Alternatively, instead of becoming inappropriately angry, provide information about the adverse consequences of a particular course of action.

# Nonverbal Communication

Defensive and nondefensive communication focus on the language used in the communication. However, most of the meaning in a message (an estimated 65 to 90 percent) is conveyed through nonverbal communication.[38] Nonverbal communication includes all elements of communication, such as gestures and the use of space, that do not involve words or do not involve language.[39] The four basic kinds of nonverbal communication that managers need to

**nonverbal communication**

All elements of communication that do not involve words.

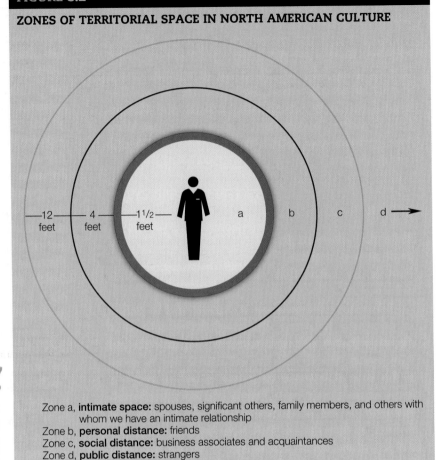

## FIGURE 8.2

### ZONES OF TERRITORIAL SPACE IN NORTH AMERICAN CULTURE

12 feet — 4 feet — 1 1/2 feet — a — b — c — d →

Zone a, **intimate space:** spouses, significant others, family members, and others with whom we have an intimate relationship
Zone b, **personal distance:** friends
Zone c, **social distance:** business associates and acquaintances
Zone d, **public distance:** strangers

understand and decipher are proxemics, kinesics, facial and eye behaviour, and paralanguage. Managers also need to understand that nonverbal communication is influenced by both psychological and physiological processes.[40]

The interpretation of nonverbal communication is specific to the context of the interaction and the actors. In other words, nonverbal cues give meaning only in the context of the situation and the interaction of the actors. For example, some judges attempt to curb nonverbal communication in the courtroom. The judges' primary concern is that nonverbal behaviour may unfairly influence jurors' decisions. It is also important to note that nonverbal behaviour is culturally bound. (Recall from Chapter 2 the difference in meaning the "thumbs-up" hand gesture has in different countries.)

## Proxemics

The study of an individual's perception and use of space, including territorial space, is called *proxemics*.[41] *Territorial space* refers to bands of space extending outward from the body. These bands constitute comfort zones. Figure 8.2 presents four zones of territorial space based on North American culture.

Territorial space varies greatly across cultures. In each comfort zone, different cultures prefer different types of interaction with others. People often become uncomfortable when operating in territorial spaces different from those in which they are familiar.

Edward Hall, a leading proxemics researcher, says North Americans working in the Middle East tend to back away to a comfortable conversation distance when interacting with Arabs. Because Arabs' comfortable conversation distance is closer than that of North Americans, Arabs perceive North Americans as cold and aloof. One Arab wondered, "What's the matter? Does he find me somehow offensive?"[42] Personal space tends to be larger in cultures with cool climates, such as Canada, Great Britain, and northern Europe, and smaller in cultures with warm climates, such as southern Europe, the Caribbean, India, or South America.[43]

Our relationships shape our use of territorial space. For example, we hold hands with, or put an arm around, significant others to pull them into intimate space. Conversely, the use of territorial space can shape people's interactions. A 1.5-metre-wide business desk pushes business interactions into the social distance zone. An exception occurred for one manager who met with her seven first-line supervisors around her desk. Being elbow to elbow placed the supervisors in one another's intimate and personal space. They appeared to act more like friends and frequently talked about their children, favourite television shows, and other personal concerns. When the manager moved the staff meeting to a larger room and the spaces around each supervisor were in the social distance zone, the personal exchanges ceased, and they acted more like business associates again.

Seating dynamics, another aspect of proxemics, is the art of seating people in certain positions according

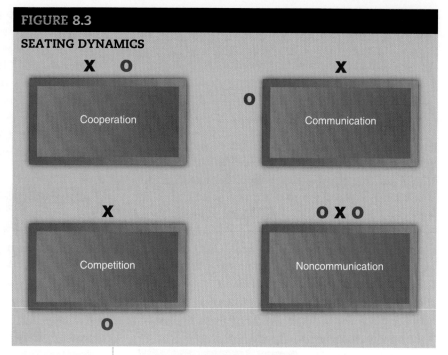

**FIGURE 8.3**

**SEATING DYNAMICS**

X O    X
        O
Cooperation    Communication

X        O X O
Competition    Noncommunication
O

to the person's purpose in communication. Figure 8.3 depicts some common seating dynamics. To encourage cooperation, you should seat the other party beside you, facing the same direction. To facilitate direct and open communication, seat the other party across a corner of your desk from you or in another place where you will be at right angles. This allows for more honest disclosure. To take a competitive stand with someone, position the person directly across from you. Suppose you hold a meeting around a conference table, and two of the attendees are disrupting your meeting. Where should you seat them? If you place one on each side of yourself, it should stifle the disruptions (unless one is so bold as to lean in front of you to keep chatting).

## Kinesics

*Kinesics* is the study of body movements, including posture.[44] Like proxemics, kinesics is culturally bound. With this in mind, we can interpret some common North American gestures. Rubbing your hands together or exhibiting a sharp intake of breath indicates anticipation. Stress is indicated by a closed hand position (that is, tight fists), hand wringing, or rubbing the temples. Nervousness may be exhibited through drumming fingers, pacing, or jingling coins in the pocket. Kinesics also includes insulting gestures like giving someone "the finger."

## Facial and Eye Behaviour

The face is a rich source of nonverbal communication. Facial expression and eye behaviour are used to add cues for the receiver and may give unintended clues to emotions the sender is trying to hide. Dynamic facial actions

Competitive stands require face-to-face seating.

gjfoto/Shutterstock

and expressions in a person's appearance are key clues of truthfulness, especially in deception situations.[45]

Smiles, frowns, raised eyebrows, and wrinkled foreheads must all be interpreted in conjunction with the actors, the situation, and the culture. One study of Japanese and U.S. students illustrates the point. The students were shown a stress-inducing film, and their facial expressions were videotaped. When alone, the students had almost identical expressions. However, the Japanese students masked their facial expressions of unpleasant feelings much better than did the American students when another person was present.[46]

As mentioned earlier, eye contact can enhance reflective listening and, along with smiling, is one good way of displaying positive emotion.[47] However, eye contact must be understood in a cultural context. A direct gaze indicates honesty, truthfulness, and forthrightness in North America. This may not be true in other cultures. For example, Barbara Walters was uncomfortable interviewing Muammar al-Qaddafi in Libya because he did not look directly at her. However, in Libya, it is a serious offence to look directly at a woman.[48] In Asian cultures it is considered good behaviour to bow the head in deference to a superior rather than to look in the supervisor's eyes.

**communicative disease**

The absence of heartfelt communication in human relationships leading to loneliness and social isolation.

## Paralanguage

Paralanguage consists of variations in speech, such as pitch, loudness, tempo, tone, duration, laughing, and crying.[49] People make assumptions about the sender by deciphering paralanguage cues. A high-pitched, breathy voice in a female may contribute to the stereotype of the "dumb blonde." Rapid, loud speech may be taken as a sign of nervousness or anger. Interruptions such as "mmm" and "ah-hah" may be used to speed up the speaker so that the receiver can get in a few words. Clucking of the tongue or the "tsk-tsk" sound is used to shame someone. All these cues relate to how something is said.

### LEARNING OUTCOME 6

# Positive, Healthy Communication

The absence of heartfelt communication in human relationships leads to loneliness and social isolation and has been labelled communicative disease by James Lynch.[50] Communicative disease has adverse effects on the heart and cardiovascular system and can ultimately lead to premature death. According to Lynch, heartfelt communication is a healing dialogue and central antidote for communicative disease. Lynch suggests that the heart may be equally as important or more important than cognition in the communications process.

Positive, healthy communication is one important aspect of working together when the term "working together" is taken for its intrapersonal meaning as well as its interpersonal meaning.[51] The balance between head and heart is achieved when a person displays positive emotional competence and is able to have a healthy internal conversation between his or her thoughts and feelings, ideas, and emotions. In addition, working together occurs when there are cooperative work behaviours between people based upon positive, healthy, and open communication that is based on trust and truthfulness. Honest competition within the workplace is consistent with this notion of working together; forthright, well-managed, honest competition can bring out the best in all those involved.

Positive, healthy communication is at the core of personal integrity as displayed by healthy executives.[52] Former Prime Minister Pierre Trudeau was a great communicator who displayed strong ethical character, personal integrity, and directness in his communication. He exemplified heartfelt communication because his messages derived from his core

Fast Fact

Crossing your arms has been shown to increase persistence, which in turn leads to better performance. Two studies used anagrams to demonstrate this relationship. Participants who crossed their arms when presented with an unsolvable anagram persisted longer in trying to decode the impossible. In another study with solvable anagrams, participants who crossed their arms not only were more persistent, their performance was also better (they solved the anagram more frequently). So if you think body posture and position don't inform subjective experience and influence behaviour, you might want to reconsider.

SOURCE: R. Friedman and A. J. Elliott, "The Effect of Arm Crossing on Persistence and Performance," *European Journal of Social Psychology* (In press).

Pierre Trudeau, a great communicator.

©Reuters/CORBIS

# Communicating through New Technologies

Nonverbal behaviours can be important in establishing trust in working relationships, but modern technologies may challenge our ability to maintain trust in relationships. Managers in today's business world have access to more communication tools than ever before. All of these new technologies, surprisingly, have relatively little impact on work culture but they do influence effective, successful communication and affect behaviour. Finally, information technology can encourage or discourage moral dialogue, and moral conversations are central to addressing ethical issues at work.[55]

## Written Communication

Even though many organizations are working toward paperless offices and paperless interfaces with their customers, that does not mean written communication is dead. Quite the opposite! There are many types of written communication. Manuals and reports are generally the longest forms of written communication. Policy manuals are important in organizations because they set out guidelines for decision making and rules of actions for organizational members. Operations and procedures manuals explain how to perform various tasks and resolve problems that may occur at work. Reports, such as annual reports, may summarize the results of a committee's or department's work or provide information on progress toward certain objectives.

Letters and memoranda (memos) are briefer than manuals and reports and are more frequently used categories of written communication in organizations. Letters are used to communicate formally with people outside

values, beliefs, and aspirations for himself and others. Communication from core values and beliefs is communication anchored in personal integrity and ethical character.

Personal integrity in positive, healthy communication is achieved through emotional competence and the head-to-heart dialogue mentioned earlier. In addition to the public self, as is familiar in the case of Pierre Trudeau, all executives have a private self. Karol Wasylyshyn has shown that one dimension of coaching star executives is to enhance their emotional competence and capacity to talk through challenging issues, both personally and professionally.[53] Quick and Macik-Frey focus on the private-self aspect of positive, healthy communication in developing their model of executive coaching through deep interpersonal communication.[54] Their executive coaching model relies on what might be called a healing dialogue between executive and coach. However, their model of deep interpersonal communication is one that can enhance positive, healthy communication in a wider range of human relationships.

## Hot Trend: Supplanting E-mail

luchschen/Shutterstock

Several corporations are working to minimize the waste of resources associated with huge amounts of junk e-mail. The Capital One model for addressing the e-mail problem is to teach employees, who receive an average of 40 or 50 messages per day, how to write better messages and subject lines. Over 3,000 employees have gone through a specially designed workshop for writing better e-mail messages and the company estimates an 11-day per year savings per employee as a result. Another financial institution has used a different model for managing the e-mail glut. Rather than carpet-bombing all 10,000 employees with all kinds of informational e-mails, the bank has developed a targeting strategy called KnowNow that employs RSS Web feeds. The new system feeds information only to the employees in jobs and locations that need it, resulting in annual savings of over $750,000 (conservatively).

SOURCE: D. Beizer, "Email Is Dead," *Fast Company* 117 (July/August 2007): 46.

> *[Interpersonal skills such as tact and graciousness diminish, and managers are more blunt when using electronic media.]*

the organization and may vary substantially in length. Memos are also used to communicate formally, but with constituencies within the organization. Memos are sometimes used to create a historical record of a specific event or occurrence to which people in the organization may want to refer at some future date.

The shortest kind of written communication is the form, which may be used to collect information from constituencies inside or outside the organization.

## Communication Technologies

Computer-mediated communication influences virtually all managers' behaviour in the work environment. E-mail, voice mail, and facsimile (fax) machines have been common in the business world for over a decade, and now informational databases are becoming commonplace. These databases provide a tremendous amount of information with the push of a button. An example of an informational database is the type of system used in many university libraries, in which books and journals are available through an electronic card catalogue.

The newest technology to enter the work environment is the cell phone, which is nearly as ubiquitous in the work environment as in our personal lives, particularly for sales jobs involving travel. Not all reactions to cell phones are positive. For example, one oil producer did not want his thinking time while driving disturbed by a cell phone. Some estimates suggest that using a cell phone while driving is as risky as driving while under the influence of alcohol. For this reason, some provinces have outlawed the use of cell phones while driving a motor vehicle.

### How Do Communication Technologies Affect Behaviour?

Information communication technology (ICT) provides faster, more immediate access to information than was available in the past. It provides instant exchange of information in minutes or seconds across geographic boundaries and time zones. Schedules and office hours become irrelevant. The normal

considerations of time and distance become less important in the exchange. Hence, these technologies have important influences on people's behaviour.

Because computer-mediated communication is impersonal in nature, technology shields the sender from personal interaction. As mentioned earlier, studies show that using these technologies results in an increase in flaming, or making rude or obscene outbursts by computer.[56] Interpersonal skills such as tact and graciousness diminish, and managers are more blunt when using electronic media. People who participate in discussions quietly and politely when face to face may become impolite, more intimate, and uninhibited when they communicate using computer conferencing or electronic mail.[57]

Another effect of the new technologies is that the nonverbal cues we rely on to decipher a message are absent. Gesturing, touching, facial expressions, and eye contact are not available, so the emotional element of the message is difficult to access. In addition, clues to power, such as organizational position and departmental membership, may not be available, so the social context of the exchange is altered.

Communication via technologies also changes group interaction by equalizing participation. As a result, charismatic or higher-status members may have less power.[58] Studies of groups that make decisions via computer interaction (computer-mediated groups) have shown that the computer-mediated groups took longer to reach consensus than face-to-face groups. In addition, they were more uninhibited, and there was less influence from any one dominant person. Groups that communicate

**information communication technology (ICT)**

The various new technologies, such as e-mail, voice mail, teleconferencing, and wireless access, which are used for interpersonal communication.

## 6 WAYS TO USE COMMUNICATION TECHNOLOGY MORE EFFECTIVELY

1. Striving for completeness in your message.
2. Building in opportunities for feedback.
3. Not assuming you will get an immediate response.
4. Asking yourself if the communication is really necessary.
5. "Disconnecting" yourself from the technology at regular intervals.
6. Providing opportunities for social interaction at work.

by computer seem to experience a breakdown of social norms and organizational barriers.

The potential for overload is particularly great with the new communication technologies. Not only is information available more quickly, but also the sheer volume of information at the manager's fingertips is staggering. An individual can easily become overwhelmed by information and must learn to be selective about the information accessed.

A paradox created by the new, modern communication technology lies in the danger it may pose for managers. The danger is that managers cannot get away from the office as much as in the past, because they are more accessible to coworkers, subordinates, and the boss through telecommunications. Interactions are no longer confined to the 9:00 to 5:00 work hours.

In addition, the use of new technologies encourages polyphasic, or multitasking activity (that is, doing more than one thing at a time). Managers can simultaneously make phone calls, send computer messages, and work on memos. Polyphasic activity has its advantages in terms of getting more done—but only up to a point. Paying attention to more than one task at a time splits a person's attention and reduces effectiveness at individual tasks. Constantly focusing on multiple tasks can become a habit, making it psychologically difficult for a person to let go of work.

Finally, the new technologies may make people less patient with face-to-face communication. The speed advantage of the electronic media may translate into an expectation of greater speed in all forms of communication. However, individuals may miss the social interaction with others and may find their social needs unmet. Communicating by computer means an absence of small talk; people tend to get to the point right away.

# Visit **icanorgb.com** to find the resources you need today!

*Located at the back of the textbook are rip-out Chapter Review Cards. Make sure you also go online to check out other tools that ORGB offers to help you successfully pass your course.*

- Interactive Quizzing
- Key Term Flashcards
- PowerPoint Slides
- Audio Chapter Summaries

- Cases and Exercises
- Interactive Games
- Self-Assessments
- "On the Job" and "Bizflix" Videos

# Work Teams and Groups

Fishman, C. (2007) Total Team Work, December 19

> **" Teamwork is a harder way of doing the work. But when it clicks, the result is a seamless experience. "**
> **Charles Fishman, Fast Company**

# Groups and Work Teams

A **group** is two or more people having common interests, objectives, and continuing interaction. A **work team** is a group of people with complementary skills who are committed to a common mission, performance goals, and approach for which they hold themselves mutually accountable.[1] All work teams are groups, but not all groups are work teams. Groups emphasize individual leadership, individual accountability, and individual work products. Work teams emphasize shared leadership, mutual accountability, and collective work products.

Work teams are task-oriented groups, though in some organizations the term *team* has a negative connotation for some unions and union members. Work teams make important and valuable contributions to the organization and are important to member need satisfaction.

Several kinds of work teams exist. One classification scheme uses a sports analogy. Some teams work like baseball teams with set responsibilities, other teams work like football teams through coordinated action, and still other teams work like doubles tennis teams with primary yet flexible responsibilities. In addition, crews are a distinct type of work teams that can be studied using the concept of "crewness."[2] Although each type of team may have a useful role in the organization, the individual expert should not be overlooked.[3] That is, at the right time and in the right context, individual members must be allowed

---

**group**

Two or more people with common interests, objectives, and continuing interaction.

**work team**

A group of people with complementary skills who are committed to a common mission, performance goals, and approach for which they hold themselves mutually accountable.

---

## LEARNING OUTCOMES

After reading this chapter, you should be able to do the following:

**1** Define *group* and *work team*.

**2** Explain the benefits organizations and individuals derive from working in teams.

**3** Identify the factors that influence group behaviour.

**4** Describe how groups form and develop.

**5** Explain how task and maintenance functions influence group performance.

**6** Discuss the factors that influence group effectiveness.

**7** Describe how empowerment relates to self-managed teams.

**8** Explain the importance of upper echelons and top management teams.

to shine. In particular, virtuoso teams—teams designed to effect large-scale change—need to put the spotlight on the individuals in the teams.[4]

For example, the Ontario Provincial Police's Behavioural Science Analysis Services, which has earned a stellar reputation, comprises highly specialized cerebral investigators who regard teamwork as critical to their recent successes.[5]

Not all teams and groups work face to face. In today's information age, advanced computer and telecommunications technologies enable organizations to be more flexible through the use of virtual teams.[6] Organizations use virtual teams to access expertise and the best employees located anywhere in the world. Whether a traditional group or a virtual team, groups and teams continue to play a vital role in organizational behaviour and performance at work.

©Lise Gagne/iStockPhoto

LEARNING OUTCOME 2

# Why Work Teams?

Teams are very useful in performing work that is complicated, complex, interrelated, and/or more voluminous than one person can handle. Obviously, people working in organizations cannot do everything because of the limitations of arms, legs, time, expertise, knowledge, and other resources. Individual limitations are overcome and problems are solved through teamwork and collaboration. World-class North American corporations, such as Motorola Inc., are increasingly deploying work teams in their global affiliates to meet the competition and gain an advantage.[7] Motorola's "Be Cool" team in the Philippines has a family atmosphere and may even begin a meeting with a prayer, yet is committed to improving individual and team performance.

**teamwork**

Joint action by a team of people in which individual interests are subordinated to team unity.

## Benefits to Organizations

Teams make important contributions to organizations in work areas that lend themselves to teamwork. Teamwork is a core value at Hewlett-Packard. Complex, interdependent work tasks and activities that require collaboration particularly lend themselves to teamwork. Teams are appropriate where knowledge, talent, skills, and abilities are dispersed across organizational members and require integrated effort for task accomplishment. The recent emphasis on team-oriented work environments is based on empowerment with collaboration, not on power and competition. Teams with experience working together may produce valuable innovations, and individual contributions are valuable as well.[8] Larry Hirschhorn labels this "the new team environment" founded on a significantly more empowered workforce in the industrial sectors of the North American economy. (See Table 9.1 for a comparison of new and old environments.)

| TABLE 9.1 New Team Environment versus Old Work Environment | |
|---|---|
| **NEW TEAM ENVIRONMENT** | **OLD WORK ENVIRONMENT** |
| Person comes up with initiatives. Team has considerable authority to chart its own steps. | Person follows orders. Team depends on the manager to chart its course. |
| Members form a team because people learn to collaborate in the face of their emerging right to think for themselves. People both rock the boat and work together. | Members were a team because people conformed to direction set by the manager. No one rocks the boat. |
| People cooperate by using their thoughts and feelings. They link up through direct talk. | People cooperated by suppressing their thoughts and feelings. They wanted to get along. |

SOURCE: *Managing in the New Team Environment,* by Hirschhorn, © 1991. Reprinted by permission of Pearson Education, Inc., Upper Saddle River, N.J.

## Social Benefits to Individuals

On an individual level, team or group members also derive benefits from the collective experience of teamwork. These individual benefits are best organized into two categories of social benefits. One set of social benefits accrues from achieving psychological intimacy; the other comes from achieving integrated involvement.[9]

**Psychological intimacy** is emotional and psychological closeness to other team or group members. It results in feelings of affection and warmth, unconditional positive regard, opportunity for emotional expression, openness, security and emotional support, and giving and receiving nurturance. Failure to achieve psychological intimacy results in feelings of emotional isolation and loneliness. This may be especially problematic for chief executives who experience loneliness at the top. Although psychological intimacy is valuable for emotional health and well-being, it need not necessarily be achieved in the work setting.

**Integrated involvement** is closeness achieved through tasks and activities. It results in enjoyable and involving activities, social identity and self-definition, being valued for your skills and abilities, opportunity for power and influence, conditional positive regard, and support for your beliefs and values. Failure to achieve integrated involvement results in social isolation. Whereas psychological intimacy is more emotion based, integrated involvement is more behaviour and activity based. Integrated involvement contributes to social psychological health and well-being.

# Group Behaviour

Group behaviour has been a subject of interest in social psychology for a long time, and many different aspects of group behaviour have been studied. We now look at four topics relevant to groups functioning in organizations: norms of behaviour, group cohesion, social loafing, and loss of individuality. Group behaviour topics related to decision making, such as polarization and groupthink, are addressed in Chapter 10.

## Norms of Behaviour

The standards that a work group uses to evaluate the behaviour of its members are its **norms of behaviour**. These norms may be written or unwritten, expressed or not, implicit or explicit. As long as individual members of the group understand the norms, the norms can be effective in influencing behaviour. Norms may specify what members of a group should do (such as a specified dress code for men and for women), or they may specify what members of a group should not do (such as executives not behaving arrogantly with employees).

Norms may exist in any aspect of work group life. They may evolve informally or unconsciously, or they may arise in response to challenges, such as the norm of firefighters' disciplined behaviour in responding to a three-alarm fire to protect the group.[10] Performance norms are among the most important group norms from the organization's perspective. Even when group members work in isolation on creative projects, they display conformity to group norms.[11] Group norms of cooperative behaviour within a team can lead to members working for mutual benefit, which in

# Characteristics of a Well-Functioning, Effective Group

- The atmosphere tends to be relaxed, comfortable, and informal.
- The group's task is well understood and accepted by the members.
- The members listen well to one another; most members participate in a good deal of task-relevant discussion.
- People express both their feelings and their ideas.
- Conflict and disagreement are present and centred around ideas or methods, not personalities or people.
- The group is aware and conscious of its own operation and function.
- Decisions are usually based on consensus, not majority vote.
- When actions are decided, clear assignments are made and accepted by members of the group.

SOURCE: D. M. McGregor, *The Human Side of Enterprise* (New York: McGraw-Hill, 1960).

Ilker canikigil/Shutterstock

**psychological intimacy**
Emotional and psychological closeness to other team or group members.

**integrated involvement**
Closeness achieved through tasks and activities.

**norms of behaviour**
The standards that a work group uses to evaluate the behaviour of its members.

turn facilitates team performance.[12] Organizational culture and corporate codes of ethics, such as Johnson & Johnson's credo, reflect behavioural norms expected within work groups. Finally, norms that create awareness of emotions and help regulate emotions are critical to groups' effectiveness.[13]

## Group Cohesion

The "interpersonal glue" that makes the members of a group stick together is **group cohesion**. Group cohesion can enhance job satisfaction for members and improve organizational productivity.[14] Highly cohesive groups are able to control and manage their membership better than work groups low in cohesion. In one study of 381 banking teams in Hong Kong and the United States, increased job complexity and task autonomy led to increased group cohesiveness, which translated into better performance.[15] In addition to performance, highly cohesive groups are strongly motivated to maintain good, close relationships among the members. We examine group cohesion in further detail, along with factors leading to high levels of group cohesion, when discussing the common characteristics of well-developed groups.

## Social Loafing

**Social loafing** occurs when one or more group members rely on the efforts of other group members and fail to contribute their own time, effort, thoughts, or other resources to a group.[16] This may create a real drag on the group's efforts and achievements. Some scholars argue that, from the individual's standpoint, social loafing, or free riding, is rational behaviour in response to an experience of inequity or when individual efforts are hard to observe. However, it shortchanges the group, which loses potentially valuable resources possessed by individual members.[17]

A number of methods for countering social loafing exist, such as identifying individual contributions to the group product and member self-evaluation systems. For example, if each group member is responsible for a specific input to the group, a member's failure to contribute will be noticed by everyone. If members must formally evaluate their contributions to the group, they are less likely to loaf.

*Jupiter Images*

## Loss of Individuality

*"mob mentality"*

Social loafing may be detrimental to group achievement, but it does not have the potentially explosive effects of **loss of individuality**. Loss of individuality is a social process in which individual group members lose self-awareness and its accompanying sense of accountability, inhibition, and responsibility for individual behaviour.[18]

People may engage in morally reprehensible acts and even violent behaviour as committed members of their group or organization when their individuality is lost. Loss of individuality was one of several contributing factors in the violent and aggressive acts that resulted in one of the darkest events in Canada's recent military history—the torture of a Somali teenager by Canadian peacekeepers.[19] Loss of individuality is not always negative or destructive, however. The loosening of normal ego control mechanisms in the individual may lead to prosocial behaviour and heroic acts in dangerous situations.[20]

## Group Formation and Development

After its formation, a group goes through predictable stages of development. If each of the stages is successfully negotiated, it emerges as a mature group. One logical group development model proposed by Bennis and Shepard delineates four stages following the group's formation.[21] These stages are mutual acceptance, decision making, motivation and commitment, and control and sanctions.

According to this group development model, a group addresses three issues: interpersonal issues, task issues, and authority issues.[22] The interpersonal issues include matters

---

**group cohesion**

The "interpersonal glue" that makes members of a group stick together.

**social loafing**

The failure of a group member to contribute personal time, effort, thoughts, or other resources to the group.

**loss of individuality**

A social process in which individual group members lose self-awareness and its accompanying sense of accountability, inhibition, and responsibility for individual behaviour.

of trust, personal comfort, and security. Trust is a key issue for any organization in its working relationships. The task issues include the mission or purpose of the group, the methods the group employs, and the outcomes expected of the group. The authority issues include decisions about who is in charge, how power and influence are managed, and who has the right to tell whom to do what. This section addresses group formation, each stage of group development, and the characteristics of a mature group.

## Group Formation

Formal and informal groups develop in organizations for different reasons. Formal groups are sometimes called official or assigned groups, and informal groups may be called unofficial or emergent groups. Formal groups gather to perform various tasks and include an executive and staff, standing committees of the board of directors, project task forces, and temporary committees. An example of a formal group was the task force, created by the Ontario government, to address English and French instruction of reading between kindergarten and grade 3. A panel of experts in early reading strategies was formed to develop recommendations for teachers throughout the province. The panel included teachers, consultants, principals, school board administrators, academics, and researchers from English, French, and Aboriginal communities. The panel itself noted that "[when] passions for the outcome run high, and opinions are diverse, working together to find solutions that will make a meaningful difference for all children can be a huge challenge. We know what it's like: we members of the Early Reading Panel came from diverse backgrounds and brought to the table the perspectives of years of experience in our own milieus."[23]

Diversity is an important consideration in the formation of groups and can enhance group performance. One study of gender diversity among U.S. workers found that men and women in gender-balanced groups had higher job satisfaction than those in homogeneous groups.[24] Ethnic diversity has characterized industrial work groups in North America since the 1800s. This was especially true during the early years of the 1900s, when waves of immigrant workers arrived from European and Scandinavian nations. Organizations were challenged to blend these culturally and linguistically diverse peoples into effective work groups.

In addition to ethnic, gender, and cultural diversity, there is interpersonal diversity, which may be indicated by different needs for inclusion, control of people and events,

and affirmation from others. Successful interpersonal relationships are the basis of group effort, a key foundation for organizational success.

Informal groups evolve in the work setting to gratify a variety of member needs not met by formal groups. For example, organizational members' inclusion and affirmation needs might be satisfied through interest groups. Increasingly lesbian, gay, bisexual, and transgender (LGBT)—specific resource groups are forming in organizations; IBM Canada, TD, Ernst & Young, and KPMG are working to create LGBT—positive environments. Similarly, Richard Cote of Hewitt Associates has created a Canadian chapter of Pride Alliance.[25]

## Stages of Group Development

As stated earlier, all groups, formal and informal, go through stages of development, some more successfully than others. Groups emerging successfully become a mature and productive unit. Mature groups are able ✳ to work through the necessary interpersonal, task, and authority issues to achieve at high levels. Demographic diversity and group fault lines (i.e., potential breaking points in a group) are two potential predictors of the sense-making process, subgroup formation patterns, and nature of group conflict at various stages of group development.[26] Hence, group development through these stages is seldom smooth.

**Immigrants arriving at Pier 21 in Halifax.**

Photo courtesy of Pier 21, Canada's Immigration Museum.

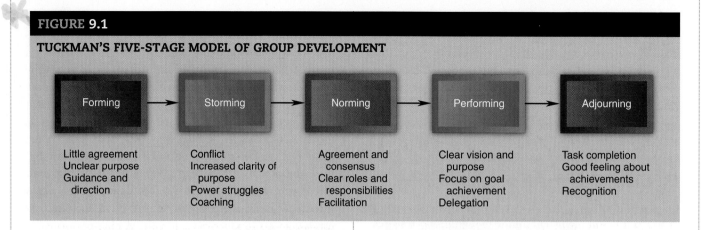

## FIGURE 9.1

### TUCKMAN'S FIVE-STAGE MODEL OF GROUP DEVELOPMENT

| Forming | Storming | Norming | Performing | Adjourning |
|---|---|---|---|---|
| Little agreement<br>Unclear purpose<br>Guidance and direction | Conflict<br>Increased clarity of purpose<br>Power struggles<br>Coaching | Agreement and consensus<br>Clear roles and responsibilities<br>Facilitation | Clear vision and purpose<br>Focus on goal achievement<br>Delegation | Task completion<br>Good feeling about achievements<br>Recognition |

In addition to the Bennis and Shepard group development model, we will discuss two other group development models. Tuckman's Group Development model focuses on leadership and evolution of behaviour in teams. Gersick's group model also looks at the evolution of behaviour in teams.

**The Five-Stage Model** Bruce Tuckman's five-stage model of group development proposes that team behaviour progresses through five stages: forming, storming, norming, performing, and adjourning.[27] These stages and the emphasis on relationships and leadership styles in each are shown in Figure 9.1. It is important to note the process is not necessarily sequential. There are feedback loops at the different stages and some teams may get stuck in one stage or may cycle between two stages and therefore are not able to move to the performing stage.

Dependence on guidance and direction is the defining characteristic in the *forming* stage. Team members are unclear about individual roles and responsibilities and tend to rely heavily on the leader to answer questions about the team's purpose, objectives, and external relationships. Moving from this stage requires that team members feel they are part of the team.

Team members compete for position in the *storming* stage. As the name suggests, this is a stage of considerable conflict as power struggles, cliques, and factions within the group begin to form. Clarity of purpose increases, but uncertainties still exist. This is also the stage when members assess one another about their trustworthiness, emotional comfort, and evaluative acceptance. For the Valuing Diversity task force at Monsanto, trust was one of the early issues to be worked through. A coaching style by the leader is key during this stage of group development as team members may challenge him or her.

Agreement and consensus are characteristic of team members in the *norming* stage. It is in this stage that roles and responsibilities become clear and accepted, with major decisions being made by group agreement.

The focus turns from interpersonal relations to decision-making activities related to the group's task accomplishment. Small decisions may be delegated to individuals or small teams within the group. The group addresses authority questions such as: Who is responsible for what aspects of the group's work? Does the group need one primary leader and spokesperson? Wallace Supply Company, an industrial distributor of pipes, valves, and fittings, has found employee teams particularly valuable in this aspect of work life.[28] Leadership is facilitative, with some leadership responsibilities being shared by the team.

As a team moves into the *performing* stage, it becomes more strategically aware and clear about its mission and purpose. In this stage of development, the group has successfully worked through the necessary interpersonal, task, and authority issues and can stand on its own two feet with little interference from the leader. Primarily, the team makes decisions, and disagreements are resolved positively with necessary changes to structure and processes attended to by the team. A mature group is able to control its members through the judicious application of specific positive and negative sanctions based on the evaluation of specific member behaviours. Recent research shows that evaluation biases stemming from liking someone operate in face-to-face groups but not in electronic groups, such as virtual teams.[29] Members at this stage do not need to be instructed but may ask for assistance from the leader with personal or interpersonal development. The team requires a leader who delegates and oversees.

The final stage of group development is the *adjourning* stage. When the task is completed, everyone on the team can move on to new and different things. Team members have a sense of accomplishment and feel good knowing that their purpose is fulfilled. The leader's role is primarily one of recognition of the group's achievements. Unless the group is a task force or other informal team, most groups in organizations remain at the performing stage and do not disband as the adjourning stage suggests.

> ## It is in these periods of energy where the majority of a group's work is accomplished.

## Punctuated Equilibrium Model

Though it is still highly cited in team and group research, Tuckman's "forming–norming–storming–performing–adjourning" model may be unrealistic from an organizational perspective. Research has shown that many teams experience relational conflicts at different times and in different contexts. Connie Gersick proposes that groups do not necessarily progress linearly from one step to another in a predetermined sequence but alternate between periods of inertia with little visible progress toward goal achievement *punctuated* by bursts of energy as work groups develop. It is in these periods of energy where the majority of a group's work is accomplished.[30] For example, a task force given nine months to complete a task may use the first four months to choose its norms, explore contextual issues, and determine how it will communicate. The final five months would then be dedicated to executing the task itself.

## Characteristics of a Mature Group

A mature group has four characteristics: a clear purpose and mission, well-understood norms and standards of conduct, a high level of group cohesion, and a flexible status structure.

**Purpose and Mission** The purpose and mission may be assigned to a group (as in the previous example of the Early Reading Panel) or emerge from within the group (as in the case of the LGBT–specific resource groups). In the case of an assigned mission, the group may embrace the mission as stated or reexamine, modify, revise, or question the mission. The importance of mission is exemplified in IBM's Process Quality Management, which requires that a process team of not more than 12 people develop a clear understanding of mission as the first step in the process.[31] The IBM approach demands that all members agree to go in the same direction. The mission statement is converted into a specific agenda, clear goals, and a set of critical success factors. Stating the purpose and mission in the form of specific goals enhances productivity over and above any performance benefits achieved through individual goal setting.[32]

**Behavioural Norms** Behavioural norms, which evolve over a period of time, are well-understood standards of behaviour within a group.[33] They are benchmarks against which team members are evaluated and judged by other team members. Some behavioural norms become written rules, such as an attendance policy or an ethical code for a team. Other norms remain informal. Dress codes and norms about after-hours socializing may fall into this category. Behavioural norms also evolve around performance and productivity.[34] Productivity norms even influence the performance of sports teams.[35] The group's productivity norm may or may not be consistent with the organization's productivity standards. A high-performance team sets productivity standards above organizational expectations with the intent to excel. Average teams set productivity standards based on, and consistent with, organizational expectations. Noncompliant or counterproductive teams may set productivity standards below organizational expectations with the intent of damaging the organization or creating change. On the positive side, behavioural norms can permeate an entire organizational culture for the benefit of all.

**Group Cohesion** Group cohesion enables a group to exercise effective control over its members in relation to its behavioural norms and standards. Goal conflict, unpleasant experiences, and domination of a subgroup are among the threats to a group's cohesion. Groups with low levels of cohesion have greater difficulty exercising control over their members and enforcing their standards of behaviour. Specifically, work-related tension and anxiety are lower in highly cohesive teams. Conversely, these traits are higher in teams low in cohesion, as depicted in Figure 9.2 on page 146. This relationship suggests that cohesion has a calming effect on team members, concerning work-related tension and anxiety. In addition, actual productivity was found to vary significantly less in highly cohesive teams, making them much more predictable. The actual productivity levels were primarily determined by the productivity norms within each work group. That is, highly cohesive groups with high production standards are very productive. Similarly, highly cohesive groups with

**Cohesion has a calming effect on team members.**

## FIGURE 9.2

### COHESIVENESS AND WORK-RELATED TENSION*

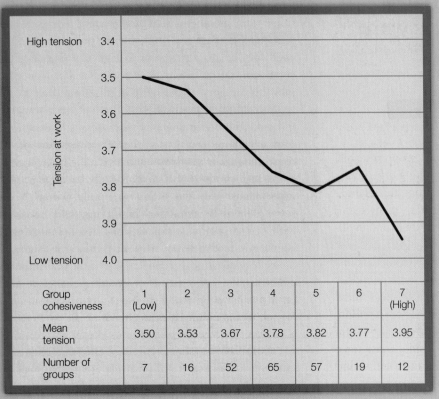

| Group cohesiveness | 1 (Low) | 2 | 3 | 4 | 5 | 6 | 7 (High) |
|---|---|---|---|---|---|---|---|
| Mean tension | 3.50 | 3.53 | 3.67 | 3.78 | 3.82 | 3.77 | 3.95 |
| Number of groups | 7 | 16 | 52 | 65 | 57 | 19 | 12 |

Note: Product–moment correlation is 0.28, and critical ratio is 4.20; the group cohesion–tension relationship is highly significant at the .001 level.

*The measure of tension at work is based on group mean response to the question "Does your work ever make you feel 'jumpy' or nervous?" A low numerical score represents relatively high tension.

SOURCE: From S. E. Seashore, *Group Cohesiveness in the Industrial Work Group*, 1954. Research conducted by Stanley E. Seashore at the Institute for Social Research, University of Michigan. Reprinted by permission

low productivity standards are unproductive. Conversely, member satisfaction, commitment, and communication are better in highly cohesive groups.

Group cohesion is influenced by a number of factors, most notably time, size, the prestige of the team, external pressure, and internal competition. Group cohesion evolves gradually over time through a group's normal development. Smaller groups—those of 5 or 7 members, for example—are more cohesive than those of more than 25, although cohesion does not decline much with size after 40 or more members. Prestige or social status may also enhance a group's cohesion. More prestigious groups, such as the Candian Snowbirds acrobatic team, are highly cohesive. However, even groups of very low prestige may be highly cohesive in how they stick together. Finally, external pressure and internal competition influence

**status structure**

The set of authority and task relations among a group's members.

group cohesion. In 2008, for example, the federal NDP and the Liberals, supported by the Bloc Québécois, set aside their political differences to sign a deal on a proposed coalition. They signed a six-point accord that specified the roles of the NDP and Liberal caucuses. The leader of the Liberal Party informed the Governor-General that he had the confidence of the House of Commons to form a government and that the Conservative minority government would be defeated.[36] Whereas external pressures tend to enhance cohesion, internal competition usually decreases cohesion within a team. One study found that company-imposed work pressure disrupted group cohesion by increasing internal competition and reducing cooperative interpersonal activity.[37]

**Status Structure** Status structure is the set of authority and task relations among a group's members. The status structure may be hierarchical or egalitarian (i.e., democratic), depending on the group. Successful resolution of the authority issue within a team results in a well-understood status structure of leader–follower relationships. Where leadership problems arise, it is important to find solutions and build team leader effectiveness.[38] Whereas groups tend to have one leader, teams tend to share leadership. For example, one person may be the team's task master who sets the agenda, initiates much of the work activity, and ensures that

Merrill Dyck/Shutterstock

>> What about You? on the Chapter 9 Review Card includes the three group cohesion questions from this research project. Use it to determine the level of cohesion in a group of which you are a member.

the team meets its deadlines. Another team member may take a leadership role in maintaining effective interpersonal relationships in the group. Hence, shared leadership is very feasible in teams. An effective status structure results in role interrelatedness among group members,[39] such as that displayed by Jim Balsillie and Mike Lazaridis, whose tag-team style of cooperation in leading Research in Motion has served the company well.

## LEARNING OUTCOME 5

# Task and Maintenance Functions

An effective group or team carries out various task functions to perform its work successfully and various maintenance functions to ensure member satisfaction and a sense of team spirit.[40] Teams that successfully fulfill these functions afford their members the potential for the social benefits of psychological intimacy and integrated involvement we discussed at the beginning of the chapter as a rationale for teams. Table 9.2 presents nine task and nine maintenance functions in teams or groups.

**Task functions** are those activities directly related to the effective completion of the team's work. For example, the task of initiating activity involves suggesting ideas, defining problems, and proposing approaches and/or solutions to problems. The task of seeking information involves asking for ideas, suggestions, information, or facts. Effective teams have members who fulfill various task functions as they are required.

Different task functions vary in importance throughout the life cycle of a group. For example, during the engineering test periods for new technologies, the engineering team needs members who focus on testing the practical applications of suggestions and those who diagnose problems and suggest solutions.

The effective use of task functions leads to the success of the group. The successful initiation and coordination of an emergency room (ER) team's activities by the senior resident saved the life of a knife-wound victim.[41] The victim was stabbed one-quarter inch below the heart, and the ER team acted quickly to stem the bleeding, begin intravenous fluids, and monitor the victim's vital signs.

**Maintenance functions** are those activities essential to the effective, satisfying interpersonal relationships within a group or team. Following another group member's lead may be as important as being a leader. Communication gatekeepers within a group ensure balanced contributions from all members. Because task activities build tension into teams and groups working together, tension-reduction activities are important to drain off negative or destructive feelings. In a study of 25 work groups over a five-year period, humour and joking behaviour were found to enhance the social relationships in the groups.[42] The researchers concluded that performance improvements in the 25 groups indirectly resulted from improved relationships attributable to the humour and joking behaviours. Maintenance functions enhance togetherness, cooperation, and teamwork, enabling members to achieve psychological intimacy while furthering the success of the team. General Rick Hillier's leadership style and his demonstrated commitment to rejuvenating Canada's military have had a significant impact on the legitimacy of the Canadian Forces. Hillier earned support not only from the civilian and military employees of the Canadian Forces but also

| TABLE 9.2 Task and Maintenance Functions in Teams or Groups | |
| --- | --- |
| **TASK FUNCTIONS** | **MAINTENANCE FUNCTIONS** |
| Initiating activities | Supporting others |
| Seeking information | Following others' leads |
| Giving information | Gatekeeping communication |
| Elaborating concepts | Setting standards |
| Coordinating activities | Expressing member feelings |
| Summarizing ideas | Testing group decisions |
| Testing ideas | Consensus testing |
| Evaluating effectiveness | Harmonizing conflict |
| Diagnosing problems | Reducing tension |

**task function**
An activity directly related to the effective completion of a team's work.

**maintenance function**
An activity essential to effective, satisfying interpersonal relationships within a team or group.

from the public. He was determined to confront and overcome the damage of the Somali Affair (described earlier in the chapter). Both task and maintenance functions are important for successful groups and teams.

## LEARNING OUTCOME 6

# Factors that Influence Group Effectiveness

Work team effectiveness in the new team environment requires management's attention to both work team structure and work team process.[43] In addition to how the team is structured and what the team does, diversity and creativity are two areas with significant impact on team performance.

## Work Team Structure

Work team structure issues include goals and objectives, operating guidelines, performance measures, and role specification. A work team's goals and objectives specify what must be achieved, while the operating guidelines set the organizational boundaries and decision-making limits within which the team must function. The goal-setting process discussed in Chapter 6 applies to work teams, too. In addition to these two structural elements, the work team needs to know what performance measures are being used to assess its task accomplishment. For example, a medical emergency team's performance measures might include the success rate in saving critically injured patients and the average number of hours a patient is in the emergency room before being transferred to a hospital bed. Finally, work team structure requires a clearly specified set of roles for the executives and managers who oversee the work of the team, for the work team leaders who exercise influence over team members, and for team members. These role specifications should include information about required role behaviours, such as decision making and task performance, as well as restrictions or limits on role behaviours, such as the limitations on managerial interventions in work team activities and decision making. Expectations, as well as experience, may be especially important for newcomer role performance in work teams.[44]

## Work Team Process

Work team process is the second important dimension of effectiveness. Two of the important process issues in work teams are the managing of cooperative behaviours and the managing of competitive behaviours. Both sets of behaviours are helpful in task accomplishment, and they should be viewed as complementary. Cooperative teamwork skills include open communication, trust, personal integrity, positive interdependence, and mutual support. On the other hand, positive competitive teamwork skills include the ability to enjoy competition, play fair, and be a good winner or loser; to have access to information for monitoring where the team and members are in the competition; and not to overgeneralize or exaggerate the results of any specific competition. In a study of reward structures in 75 four-member teams, competitive rewards enhanced speed of performance, while cooperative rewards enhanced accuracy of performance.[45]

Work team process issues have become more complex in the global workplace with teams composed of members from many cultures and backgrounds. This is enhanced by the presence of virtual work teams operating in the global landscape. In addition to the process issues of cooperation, competition, and diversity, three other process issues are related to topics we discuss elsewhere in the text. These are empowerment, discussed in the next major section of this chapter; team decision making, which is discussed in Chapter 10; and conflict management and resolution, which are discussed in Chapter 13.

## Diversity

Diversity also plays a large role in how effective groups and work teams are. Diversity in a group is healthy, and members may contribute to the collective effort through one of four basic styles.[46] These are the contributor, the collaborator, the communicator, and the challenger. The contributor is data driven, supplies necessary information, and adheres to high performance standards. The collaborator sees the big picture and is able to keep a constant focus on the mission and urge other members to join efforts for mission accomplishment. The communicator listens well, facilitates the group's process, and humanizes the collective effort. The challenger is the devil's advocate who questions everything from the group's mission, purpose, and methods to its ethics. Members may exhibit one or more of these four basic styles over a period of time. In addition, an effective group must have an integrator.[47] This can be especially important in cross-functional teams, where different perspectives carry the seeds of conflict. However, cross-functional teams are not necessarily a problem. Effectively managing cross-functional teams of artists, designers, printers, and financial experts enabled Hallmark Cards to cut its new-product development time in half.[48]

**Dissimilarity** Recent research in diversity has focused on the issue and effect of dissimilarity within the team itself. This is often studied based on social identity theory and self-categorization theory. Creativity concerns new and/or dissimilar ideas or ways of doing things within teams. Novelty and innovation are creativity's companions. While creativity is developed in some detail in Chapter 10, we treat it briefly here in the context of teams.

We defined diversity in Chapter 1 in terms of individual differences. Recent relational demography research

**148**    **PART 3**    Interpersonal Processes and Behaviour                    NEL

# THE (10) GOLDEN RULES

In-depth case studies of successful virtual teams at Ogilvy & Mather, BP, and Nokia have led to 10 golden rules to enhance effectiveness of virtual teams.

1. Invest in an online resource where members can learn quickly about one another.
2. Choose a few team members who already know each other.
3. Identify "boundary spanners" and ensure that they make up at least 15 percent of the team.
4. Cultivate boundary spanners as a regular part of organizational practices and processes.
5. Break the team's work into modules so that progress in one location is not overly dependent on progress in another.
6. Create an online site where a team can collaborate, exchange ideas, and inspire one another.
7. Encourage frequent communication.
8. Assign only tasks that are challenging and interesting.
9. Ensure the task is meaningful to the team and the organization.
10. When building a virtual team, solicit volunteers as much as possible. These rules come from successful experience, and any organization implementing virtual teams should monitor the success and problems within its own work context.

SOURCE: L. Gratton, "Working Together… When Apart," *The Wall Street Journal* (16 June 2007): R4.

finds that demographic dissimilarity influences employees' absenteeism, commitment, turnover intentions, beliefs, workgroup relationships, self-esteem, and organizational citizenship behaviour (OCB).[49] Thus, dissimilarity may have positive or negative effects in teams and on team members. While value dissimilarity may be positively related to task and relationship conflict, it is negatively related to team involvement.[50] This highlights the importance of managing dissimilarity in teams, being open to diversity, and turning conflicts over ideas into positive outcomes.

Functional background is one way to look at dissimilarity in teams. One study of 262 professionals in 37 cross-functional teams found that promoting functional background social identification helped individuals perform better as team members.[51] Another study of multifunctional management teams in a Fortune 100 company found that functional background predicted team involvement.[52] Finally, in a slightly different study of 129 members on 20 multidisciplinary project teams, informational dissimilarity had no adverse effects when there was member task and goal congruence.[53]

**Structural Diversity** Structural diversity concerns the number of structural holes within a work team. A structural hole in a team is a disconnection between two members of that team. Is the disconnection of team members good or bad for the team? What are the consequences of having more or fewer structural holes between team members?

One research study examined diversity and performance of 19 teams in a wood products company. The investigators were interested in demographic diversity among team members as well as the structural diversity of the team. Neither race nor gender was a demographic factor that influenced the proportion of structural holes within a work team. However, age diversity significantly reduced the extent of structural holeyness within the teams. Hence, greater variance in age within a team leads to more member-to-member connections and fewer member-to-member disconnections.

Teams with few structural holes may have problems with creativity while teams with a high proportion of structural holes may have difficulty coordinating. These observations led the researchers to conclude that there is a curvilinear relationship between structural diversity, or structural holeyness, and team performance. The teams with moderate structural diversity achieve the best performance. This research is important because it points out that managers should look at the overall structure and network of relationships within their work teams in addition to the individual characteristics of team members in attempting to achieve the best performance from these teams.[54]

## [ Gender, Status, and Leadership ]

Emergent leadership in groups was studied among 62 men and 62 women. Groups performed tasks not classified as either masculine or feminine, that is, "sex neutral" tasks. Men and women both emerged as leaders, and neither gender had significantly more emergent leaders. However, group members who described themselves in masculine terms were significantly more likely to emerge as leaders than group members who described themselves in feminine, androgynous (both masculine and feminine), or undifferentiated (neither masculine nor feminine) terms. Hence, gender stereotypes may play a role in emergent leadership.

SOURCE: J. R. Goktepe and C. E. Schneier, "Role of Sex, Gender Roles, and Attraction in Predicting Emergent Leaders," *Journal of Applied Psychology* 74 (1989): 165–167.

## Creativity

Creativity is often thought of in an individual context rather than a team context. However, there is such a thing as team creativity. In a study of 54 research and development teams, one study found that team creativity scores would be explained by aggregation processes across both people and time.[55] The investigators concluded that it is important to consider aggregation across time and individuals when you are attempting to understand team creativity. In another study of creative behaviour, a Korean electronics company found that individual dissimilarity in age and performance, as well as functional diversity within the team, positively affected individual employees' creative behaviour.

Some think that the deck is stacked against teams as agents of creativity. Leigh Thompson thinks differently and suggests that team creativity and divergent thinking can be enhanced through greater diversity in teams, electronic brainwriting, training facilitators, membership change in teams, electronic brainstorming, and building a playground.[56] These practices can overcome social loafing, conformity, and downward norm setting in teams and organizations. Team members might exercise care in timing the insertion of their novel ideas into the team process so as to maximize the positive impact and benefits.[57]

---

### LEARNING OUTCOME 7

# Empowerment and Self-Managed Teams

To be successful, teams require a culture of empowerment in the organization in which they are implemented. This is especially true of **self-managed teams**, which are designed to take on responsibilities and address issues traditionally reserved for management.

Empowerment may be thought of as an attribute of a person or an organization's culture.[58] As an organizational culture attribute, empowerment encourages participation, an essential ingredient for teamwork.[59] Quality action teams (QATs) at FedEx are the primary quality improvement process (QIP) technique used by the company to engage management and hourly employees in four-to-ten-member problem-solving teams.[60] The teams are empowered to act and

**self-managed team**

A team that makes decisions that were once reserved for managers.

solve problems as specific as charting the best route from the Vancouver airport to the local distribution centre or as global as making major software enhancements to the online package-tracking system.

Empowerment may give employees the power of a lightning strike, but empowered employees must be properly focused through careful planning and preparation before they strike.[61]

## Empowerment Skills

Empowerment through employee self-management is an alternative to empowerment through teamwork.[62] Whether through self-management or teamwork, empowerment requires the development of certain skills if it is to be enacted effectively.

Competence skills are the first set of skills required for empowerment. Mastery and experience in your chosen discipline and profession provide an essential foundation for empowerment. New employees and trainees should experience only limited empowerment until they demonstrate the capacity to accept more responsibility.

Empowerment also requires certain process skills. The most critical process skills include negotiating skills, especially with allies, opponents, and adversaries.[63] Allies are the easiest people to negotiate with because they agree with you about the team's mission and you can trust their actions and behaviour. Opponents require a different negotiating strategy; although you can predict their actions and behaviour, they do not agree with your concept of the team's mission. Adversaries are dangerous, difficult people to negotiate with because you cannot predict their actions or behaviours and they do not agree with your concept of the team's mission.

A third set of empowerment skills involves the development of cooperative and helping behaviours.[64] Cooperative people engage in encouraging, helpful behaviour to maximize the gains for everyone on the team. The alternative orientations to cooperation are competitive, individualistic, and egalitarian. Competitive people are motivated to maximize their personal gains regardless of the expense to other people. This motivation can be very counterproductive to the team. Individualistic people are motivated to act autonomously, though not necessarily to maximize their personal gains. They are less prone to contribute to the efforts of the team. Egalitarian people are motivated to equalize the outcomes for each team member, which may or may not be beneficial to the team's well-being. Actually, the team members who need the most help often get the least help because helping behaviours are often targeted to the most "expert" team members, a dynamic that actually compromises overall team performance.[65]

Communication skills are a final set of essential empowerment skills.[66] These skills include self-expression skills

> ## " Individualistic people are less prone to contribute to the efforts of the team.

and skills in reflective listening. Empowerment cannot occur in a team unless members are able to express themselves effectively as well as listen carefully to one another.

## Self-Managed Teams

Self-managed teams, also called *self-directed teams* or *autonomous work groups*, are teams that make decisions that were once reserved for managers. Self-managed teams are one way to implement empowerment in organizations. Even though self-managed teams are self-directed, that does not negate the influence of managers. In fact, managers have an important role in providing leadership and influence.[67] There is strong support for the use of soft influence tactics in managers' communication with self-directed teams, which yields more positive results.[68] A one-year study of self-managed teams suggests that they have a positive impact on employee attitudes but not on absenteeism or turnover.[69] Evaluative research is helpful in achieving a better understanding of this relatively new way of approaching teamwork and the design of work. Research helps establish expectations for self-managed teams. Nevertheless, there are risks, such as groupthink in self-managing teams, that must be prevented or managed if the team is to achieve full development and function.[70] Finally, one evaluation of empowerment, teams, and TQM programs found that companies that used these popular management techniques did not have higher economic performance.[71]

Other evaluations of self-managed teams are more positive. Southwest Industries, a high-technology aerospace manufacturing firm, embarked on a major internal reorganization in the early 1990s that included the creation of self-managed teams to fit its high-technology production

> **Self-directed teams generally have the resources and expertise to know what they need to do and how they need to do it.**
>
> ©Fotolia XXII—Fotolia.com

process. Southwest's team approach resulted in a 30 percent increase in shipments, a 30 percent decrease in lead time, a 40 percent decrease in total inventory, a decrease in machinery downtime, and almost a one-third decrease in production costs.[72] An overall positive history has resulted in North American multinational corporations increasingly using self-managed teams in their global operations.

---

LEARNING OUTCOME **8**

## Upper Echelons: Teams at the Top

*\* not too much from LO8*

Self-managed teams at the top of the organization—top-level executive teams—are referred to as **upper echelons**. Organizations are often a reflection of these upper echelons.[73] Upper echelon theory argues that the background characteristics of the top management team can predict organizational characteristics, and set standards for values, competence, ethics, and unique characteristics throughout the organization. Furthermore, upper echelons are one key to the strategic success of the organization.[74] The ability to exert power and influence throughout the entire organization makes the top management team a key to the organization's success. This ability may be compromised if the top team sends mixed signals about teamwork and if executive pay systems foster competition, politics, and individualism.[75]

For example, when Lee Iacocca became CEO at the Chrysler Corporation, his top management team was assembled to bring about strategic realignment within the corporation by building on Chrysler's historical engineering strength. The dramatic success of Chrysler during the early 1980s was followed by struggle and accommodation during the late 1980s. This raises the question of how long a CEO and the top management team can sustain organizational success.

Hambrick and Fukutomi addressed this question by examining the dynamic relationship between a CEO's tenure and the success of the organization.[76] They found five seasons in a CEO's tenure: (1) response to a mandate, (2) experimentation, (3) selection of an enduring theme, (4) convergence, and (5) dysfunction. A summary of each season is shown in Table 9.3 on page 152. All else being equal, this seasonal model has significant implications for organizational performance. Specifically, organizational performance increases during a CEO's tenure to a peak, after which performance declines. This relationship is depicted in Figure 9.3 on page 152. The peak has been found to come at about seven years—somewhere in the middle of the executive's seasons. As indicated by the dotted lines in the

> **upper echelon**
>
> A top-level executive team in an organization.

---

**TABLE 9.3** The Five Seasons of a CEO's Tenure

| CRITICAL CEO CHARACTERISTICS | 1 RESPONSE TO MANDATE | 2 EXPERIMENTATION | 3 SELECTION OF AN ENDURING THEME | 4 CONVERGENCE | 5 DYSFUNCTION |
|---|---|---|---|---|---|
| COMMITMENT TO A PARADIGM | Moderately strong | Could be strong or weak | Moderately strong | Strong; increasing | Very strong |
| TASK KNOWLEDGE | Low but rapidly increasing | Moderate; somewhat increasing | High; slightly increasing | High; slightly increasing | High; slightly increasing |
| INFORMATION DIVERSITY | Many sources; unfiltered | Many sources but increasingly unfiltered | Fewer sources; moderately filtered | Few sources; highly filtered | Very few sources; highly filtered |
| TASK INTEREST | High | High | Moderately high | Moderately high but diminishing | Moderately low and diminishing |
| POWER | Low; increasing | Moderate; increasing | Moderate; increasing | Strong; increasing | Very strong; increasing |

SOURCE: D. Hambrick and G. D. S. Fukutomi, "The Seasons of a CEO's Tenure," *Academy of Management Review*, 1991, p. 729. Permission conveyed through Copyright Clearance Center, Inc.

figure, the peak may be extended, depending on several factors, such as diversity in the executive's support team.

## Diversity at the Top

From an organizational health standpoint, diversity and depth in the top management team enhance the CEO's well-being.[77] From a performance standpoint, the CEO's top management team can influence the timing of the performance peak, the degree of dysfunction during the closing season of the CEO's tenure, and the rate of decline in organizational performance. Diversity and heterogeneity in the top management team help sustain high levels of organizational performance at the peak and help maintain the CEO's vitality. The presence of a "wild turkey" in the top management team can be a particularly positive

force. The wild turkey is a devil's advocate who challenges the thinking of the CEO and other top executives and provides a counterpoint during debates. If not shouted down or inhibited, the wild turkey helps the CEO and the team sustain peak performance and retards the CEO's dysfunction and decline. For example, Nelson Mandela, first Prime Minister of post-apartheid South Africa, now serves as the moral conscience of the world's leaders.

Leaders must develop communication strategies to bring together a team that is functionally, intellectually, demographically, and temperamentally diverse in order to complement one another. It is out of dissimilarity that strength is developed, and it is out of similarity that connections are built.

We conclude that the leadership, composition, and dynamics of the top management team have an important influence on the organization's performance, leading, in some cases, to the elimination of a single CEO. Research has shown a dramatic increase in the number of co-CEO arrangements in both public and private corporations.[78] While more common in Europe than in North America, the RIM example, noted earlier in the chapter, is one of the most successful. At Southwest Airlines, the new top management team is emerging from the long shadow of legendary founder Herb Kelleher. This new top team led Southwest successfully through the terrorist crisis of September 2001.

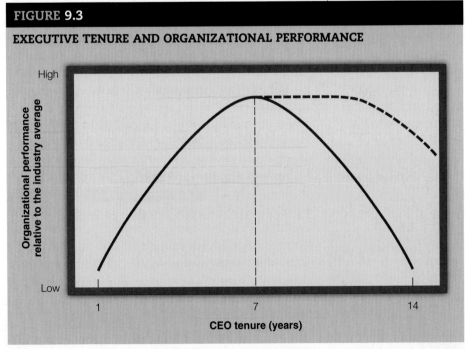

**FIGURE 9.3**

**EXECUTIVE TENURE AND ORGANIZATIONAL PERFORMANCE**

Organizational performance relative to the industry average (High / Low)

CEO tenure (years): 1, 7, 14

SOURCE: D. Hambrick, The Seasons of an Executive's Tenure, keynote address, the Sixth Annual Texas Conference on Organization, Lago Vista, Texas, April 1991.

A "wild turkey" is a devil's advocate who keeps top management on track by challenging conventional thinking.

©malerapaso/iStockPhoto

> *The ability to exert power and influence throughout the entire organization makes the top management team a key to the organization's success.*

## Multicultural Top Teams

Homogeneous groups in which all members share similar backgrounds are giving way to token groups in which all but one member come from the same background, bicultural groups in which two or more members represent each of two distinct cultures, and multicultural groups in which members represent three or more ethnic backgrounds.[79] Diversity within a group may increase the uncertainty, complexity, and inherent confusion in group processes, making it more difficult for the group to achieve its full, potential productivity.[80] On the positive side, Merck, for example, attributes its long-term success to its leadership model that promotes and develops the leadership skills of all Merck employees. Chairman, President, and CEO Ray Gilmartin values diversity in Merck's top management team because he believes that diversity sparks innovation when employees with different perspectives work together to offer solutions. The advantages of culturally diverse groups include the generation of more and better ideas while limiting the risk of groupthink, to be discussed in Chapter 10.

**It is out of dissimilarity that strength is developed, and it is out of similarity that connections are built.**

## [ Organizational Success Factors ]

To have effective teams, you need to understand organizational success factors. Five have been identified.[81] First, it is particularly important that there is strong demonstrated support for teams from the senior managers in the organization. Without such support, teams may be treated as a fad that employees will wait out. Second, teams need to serve the key purposes of the organization. Third, role clarity is very important. "The best team-based organizations determine a "how far/how fast" plan that specifies which responsibilities will be assumed by teams and at what pace."[82] Fourth, a commitment to continuous learning and reflection helps teams to learn and evolve from their practices. Last, teams need to be supported by systems that reinforce team behaviours and processes. For example, the reward systems need to promote team-based behaviour rather than individual behaviour.

## Visit **icanorgb.com** to find the resources you need today!

*Located at the back of the textbook are rip-out Chapter Review Cards. Make sure you also go online to check out other tools that ORGB offers to help you successfully pass your course.*

- Interactive Quizzing
- Key Term Flashcards
- PowerPoint Slides
- Audio Chapter Summaries

- Cases and Exercises
- Interactive Games
- Self-Assessments
- "Workplace" and "Biz Flix" Videos

# Decision Making by Individuals and Groups

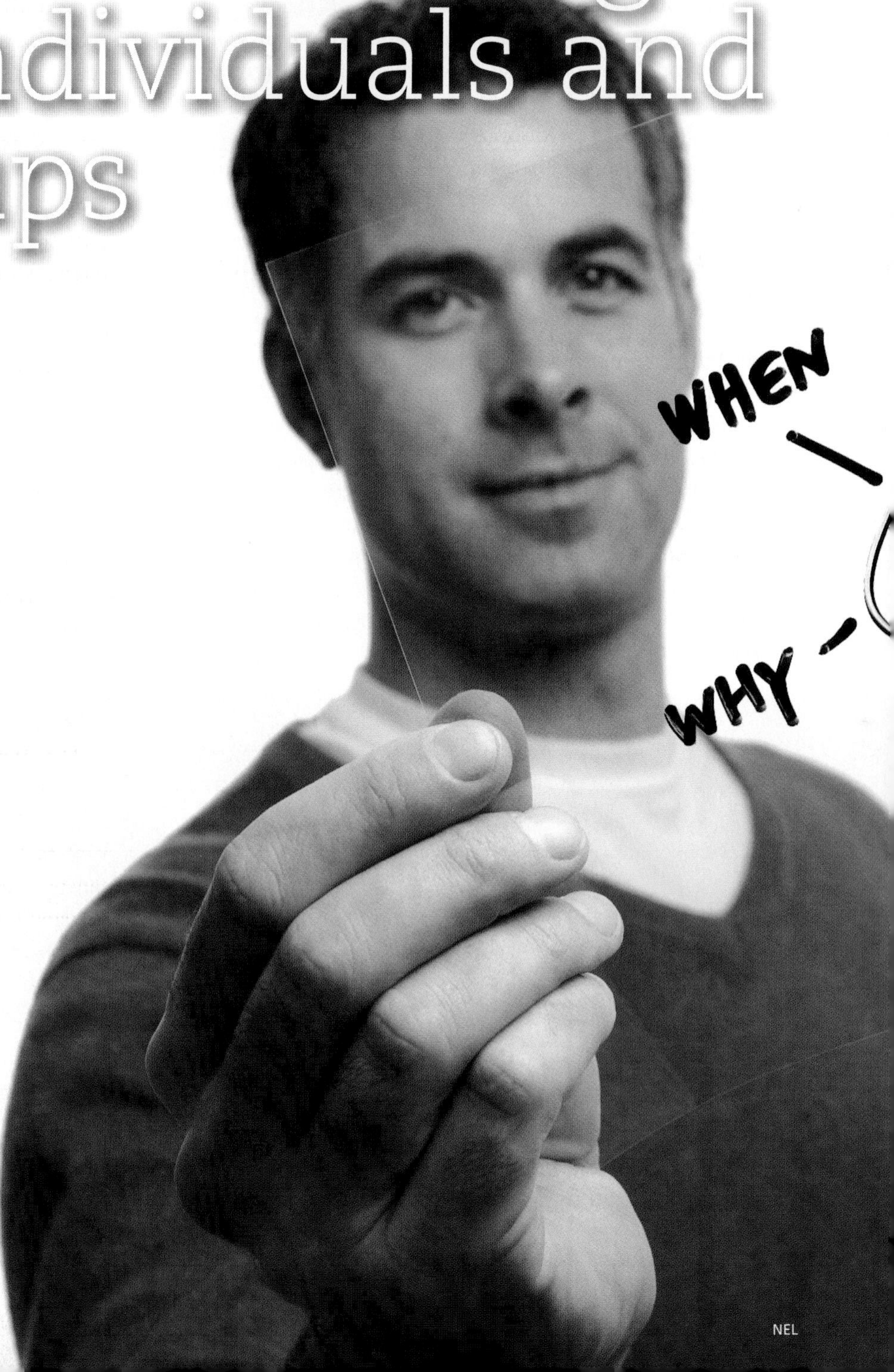

WHEN

WHY

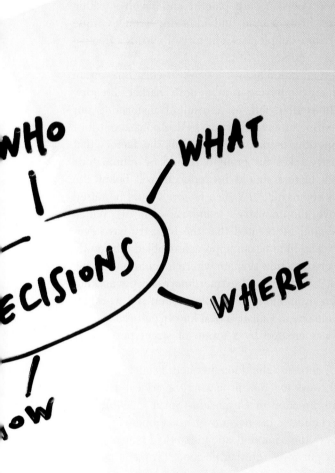

# The Decision-Making Process

Decision making is a critical activity in the lives of managers. The decisions a manager faces can range from very simple, routine matters for which the manager has an established decision rule (**programmed decisions**) to new and complex decisions that require creative solutions (**nonprogrammed decisions**).[1] Scheduling lunch hours for a work group is a programmed decision. The manager performs the decision activity on a daily basis, using an established procedure with the same clear goal in mind. In contrast, decisions such as buying out another company are nonprogrammed. The decision to acquire a company is another unique, unstructured situation and requires considerable judgment. Regardless of the type of decision made, it is helpful to understand as much as possible about how individuals and groups make decisions.

Decision making is a process involving a series of steps, as shown in Figure 10.1 (page 156). The first step is recognizing the problem; that is, the manager realizes that a decision must be made. Identifying the real problem is important; otherwise, the manager may be reacting to symptoms rather than dealing with the root cause of the problem. Next, a manager must identify the objective of the decision. In other words, the manager must determine what is to be accomplished by the decision.

The third step in the decision-making process is gathering information relevant to the problem. The manager must accumulate sufficient information about why the problem occurred. This involves conducting a

**programmed decision**
A simple, routine matter for which a manager has an established decision rule.

**nonprogrammed decision**
A new, complex decision that requires a creative solution.

FIGURE **10.1**

**THE DECISION-MAKING PROCESS**

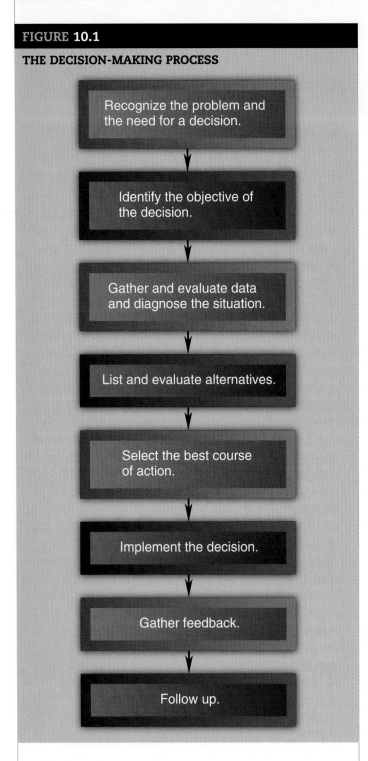

Recognize the problem and the need for a decision.

Identify the objective of the decision.

Gather and evaluate data and diagnose the situation.

List and evaluate alternatives.

Select the best course of action.

Implement the decision.

Gather feedback.

Follow up.

Next, the manager selects the alternative that best meets the decision objective. If the problem has been diagnosed correctly and sufficient alternatives have been identified, this step is much easier.

Finally, the solution is implemented. The situation must then be monitored to see whether the decision met its objective. Consistent monitoring and periodic feedback are essential parts of the follow-up process.

Decision making can be stressful. Managers must make decisions with significant risk and uncertainty, and often without full information. They must trust and rely on others in their decision-making process, but they are ultimately responsible for the final decision. Sometimes decisions are painful and involve exiting businesses, firing people, and admitting wrong. Cirque du Soleil, for example, has a history of making effective decisions.

The organization has successfully used a "blue ocean approach" by entering into a new market, creating a true innovation and, as a result, transforming our understanding of a circus. It made decisions about four key competitive issues: (1) Which of the factors that the industry takes for granted should be eliminated? (2) Which factors should be reduced well below the industry's standard? (3) Which factors should be raised well above the industry's standard? and (4) Which factors should be created that the industry has never offered?[2] The blue ocean approach enabled Cirque du Soleil to create a new domain where it could set its own direction. It has enjoyed extraordinary success and has been seen by millions of people around the world. It has become one of Canada's best known cultural exports since it was created by a group of street performers in 1984.

Guy Laliberté, the founder, and Daniel Lamarre, the CEO, work together in making the critical decisions about the direction of Cirque du-Soleil. According to Lamarre, Laliberté has never overturned one of his decisions as ". . . the communication is so fluid between us, I will never put myself in that position. I've been good in reading him."[3]

thorough diagnosis of the situation and going on a fact-finding mission.

The fourth step is listing and evaluating alternative courses of action. During this step, a thorough "what-if" analysis should also be conducted to determine the various factors that could influence the outcome. It is important to generate a wide range of options and creative solutions in order to be able to move on to the next step.

**effective decision**

A timely decision that meets a desired objective and is acceptable to those individuals affected by it.

LEARNING OUTCOME **2**

# Models and Limits of Decision Making

The success of any organization depends on managers' abilities to make **effective decisions**. An effective decision is timely, is acceptable to the individuals affected by it, and meets the desired objective.[4] This section describes five models of decision making: the rational

model, the bounded rationality model, the Vroom-Yetton-Jago model, the Z model, and the garbage can model. The section will conclude with a discussion of the limits of decision making techniques.

## Rational Model

**Rationality** refers to a logical, step-by-step approach to decision making, with a thorough analysis of alternatives and their consequences. The rational model of decision making comes from classic economic theory and contends that the decision maker is completely rational in his or her approach. The rational model assumes the following:

1. The outcome will be completely rational.
2. The decision maker has a consistent system of preferences, which is used to choose the best alternative.
3. The decision maker is aware of all the possible alternatives.
4. The decision maker can calculate the probability of success for each alternative.[5]

In the rational model, the decision maker strives to optimize, that is, to select the best possible alternative.

Given the assumptions of the rational model, it is unrealistic. There are time constraints and limits to human knowledge and information-processing capabilities. In addition, a manager's preferences and needs change often. The rational model is thus an ideal that managers strive for in making decisions. It captures the way a decision should be made but does not reflect the reality of managerial decision making.[6]

## Bounded Rationality Model

Recognizing the deficiencies of the rational model, Herbert Simon suggested that there are limits on how rational a decision maker can actually be. His decision theory, the bounded rationality model, earned a Nobel Prize in 1978.

Simon's model, also referred to as the "administrative man" theory, rests on the idea that there are constraints that force a decision maker to be less than completely rational. The bounded rationality model has four assumptions:

1. Managers select the first alternative that is satisfactory.
2. Managers recognize that their conception of the world is simple.
3. Managers are comfortable making decisions without determining all the alternatives.
4. Managers make decisions by rules of thumb or heuristics.

**Bounded rationality** assumes that managers **satisfice**; that is, they select the first alternative that is "good enough," because the costs of optimizing in terms of time and effort are too great.[7] Further, the theory assumes that managers develop shortcuts, called **heuristics**, to make decisions in order to save mental activity. Heuristics are rules of thumb that allow managers to make decisions based on what has worked in past experiences.

Does the bounded rationality model more realistically portray the managerial decision process? Research indicates that it does.[8] One of the reasons managers face limits to their rationality is that they must make decisions under risk and time pressure. The situation they find themselves in is highly uncertain, and the probability of success is not known.

## Vroom-Yetton-Jago Normative Decision Model

Victor Vroom, Phillip Yetton, and Arthur Jago developed and refined the normative decision model, which helps leaders and managers determine the appropriate level of employee participation in decision making. The model recognizes the benefits of authoritative, democratic, and consultive styles of

**rationality**
A logical, step-by-step approach to decision making, with a thorough analysis of alternatives and their consequences.

**bounded rationality**
A theory that suggests that there are limits to how rational a decision maker can actually be.

**satisfice**
To select the first alternative that is "good enough," because the costs in time and effort are too great to optimize.

**heuristics**
Shortcuts in decision making that save mental activity.

leader behaviour.[9] Five forms of decision making are described in the model:

> *Decide.* The manager makes the decision alone and either announces it or "sells" it to the group.

> *Consult individually.* The manager presents the problem to the group members individually, gets their input, and then makes the decision.

> *Consult group.* The manager presents the problem to the group members in a meeting, gets their inputs, and then makes the decision.

> *Facilitate.* The manager presents the problem to the group in a meeting and acts as a facilitator, defining the problem and the boundaries that surround the decision. The manager's ideas are not given more weight than any other group member's ideas. The objective is to get concurrence.

> *Delegate.* The manager permits the group to make the decision within the prescribed limits, providing needed resources and encouragement.[10]

The key to the normative decision model is that a manager should use the decision method most appropriate for a given decision situation. The manager arrives at the proper method by working through model. Factors such as decision significance, commitment, and leader expertise are the situational factors in the normative decision model. Although the model offers very explicit predictions as well as prescriptions for leaders, its utility is limited to the leader decision-making tasks.

## Z Model

Isabel Briggs Myers, creator of the MBTI described in Chapter 3, also developed the Z problem-solving model, which capitalizes on the strengths of the four separate preferences (sensing, intuiting, thinking, and feeling). By using the Z problem-solving model, managers can use both their preferences and nonpreferences to make decisions more effectively. The Z model is presented in Figure 10.2.

According to this model, good problem solving has four steps:

1. *Examine the facts and details.* Use sensing to gather information about the problem.

2. *Generate alternatives.* Use intuiting to develop possibilities.

3. *Analyze the alternatives objectively.* Use thinking to logically determine the effects of each alternative.

4. *Weigh the impact.* Use feeling to determine how the people involved will be affected.

Using the Z model can help an individual develop his or her nonpreferences. Another way to use the Z model is to rely on others to perform the nonpreferred activities. For example, an individual who is an NF might want to turn to a trusted NT for help in analyzing alternatives objectively.

## Garbage Can Model

The **garbage can model** of decision making emerged as a critique of Simon's model. The garbage can model asserts that decision making is fundamentally a process characterized by organizational anarchy.[11] Organizations function like garbage cans into which go problems, solutions, participants with different preferences, and choice opportunities. As Figure 10.3 illustrates, they can come

**garbage can model**

Decision making is a process of organizational anarchy.

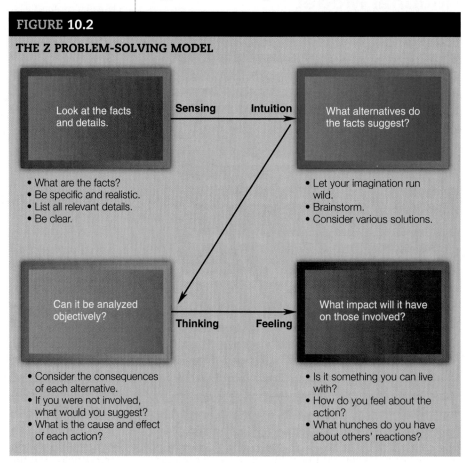

### FIGURE 10.2

**THE Z PROBLEM-SOLVING MODEL**

Look at the facts and details.
- What are the facts?
- Be specific and realistic.
- List all relevant details.
- Be clear.

*Sensing* → *Intuition*

What alternatives do the facts suggest?
- Let your imagination run wild.
- Brainstorm.
- Consider various solutions.

Can it be analyzed objectively?
- Consider the consequences of each alternative.
- If you were not involved, what would you suggest?
- What is the cause and effect of each action?

*Thinking* → *Feeling*

What impact will it have on those involved?
- Is it something you can live with?
- How do you feel about the action?
- What hunches do you have about others' reactions?

SOURCE: Excerpted from *Type Talk at Work* by Otto Kroeger and Janet M. Thuesen, 1992, Delacorte Press. Reprinted by permission of Otto Kroeger Associates.

## FIGURE 10.3

### GARBAGE CAN MODEL OF DECISION MAKING

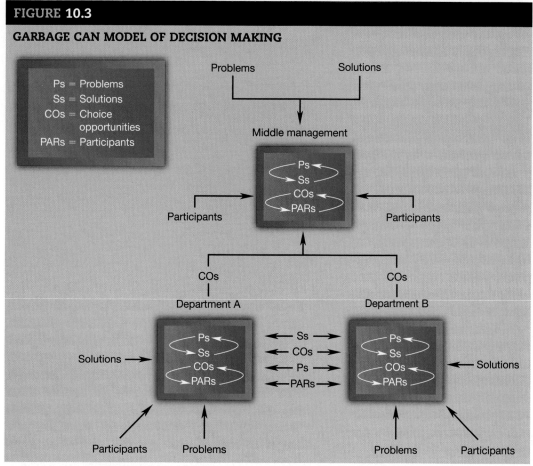

Ps = Problems
Ss = Solutions
COs = Choice opportunities
PARs = Participants

Problems     Solutions

Middle management

Ps
Ss
COs
PARs

Participants                    Participants

COs                    COs

Department A          Department B

Ps                          Ss              Ps
Ss                          COs             Ss
COs                         Ps              COs
PARs                        PARs            PARs

Solutions                                           Solutions

Participants  Problems              Problems  Participants

SOURCE: From *Richard Daft. Organization Theory and Design.* (7th edition). © 2001 South-Western Publishing, a part of Cengage Learning, Inc. Reproduced by permission, www.cengage.com/permissions.

together in different ways in different organizational subunits. The garbage can model can help us understand why sometimes solutions drive problems, and why individuals with power can control the outcomes of decisions. It gives us further insight into the nonrational processes in decision making. The theory has been used notably in the study of public-sector budget decision making.[12]

The model also has been used to understand UN peacekeeping. "The UN is particularly amenable to models focusing on agenda setting and decision making in organized anarchies or settings characterized by uncertain preferences, unclear organizational processes, and fluid participation in decision making, since these features accurately describe the UN."[13]

## Escalation of Commitment

Each decision-making model carries its own limits. This is, however, one limitation that they all share: the decision maker's unwillingness to abandon a bad decision. Continuing to support a failing course of action is known as **escalation of commitment.**[14] In situations characterized by escalation of commitment, individuals who make decisions that turn out to be poor choices tend to hold fast to those choices, even when substantial costs are incurred.[15] An example of

escalation is the price wars that often occur between airlines. The airlines reduce their prices in response to competitors until at a certain stage, both airlines are in a "no-win" situation. They continue to compete despite the heavy losses they are incurring. The desire to win is a motivation to continue to escalate, and each airline continues to reduce prices (lose money) based on the belief that the other airline will pull out of the price war. Another example of escalation of commitment is NASA's enormous International Space Station. Originally estimated to cost $8 billion, the Space Station has been redesigned five times and remains unfinished. As of 2003, its estimated cost topped $30 billion, and some pundits speculate that the total bill may reach $100 billion for what physicist Robert Park describes as "the biggest technological blunder in history."[16]

Why does escalation of commitment occur? One explanation is offered by cognitive dissonance theory, as we discussed in Chapter 4. This theory assumes that humans dislike inconsistency and that when inconsistency exists among their attitudes or between their attitudes and behaviour, they strive to reduce the dissonance.[17]

Other reasons people may hang on to a losing course of action are optimism and control. Some people are overly optimistic and overestimate the likelihood that positive things will happen to them. Other people operate under an illusion of control—that they have special skills to control the future that other people don't have.[18] The closer a project is to completion, the more likely escalation is to occur.[19]

Hanging on to a poor decision can be costly to organizations. While most American airlines originally placed orders for the prestigious Mach 2 Concorde airliner during the 1960s, their orders for the plane were eventually cancelled,

**escalation of commitment**

The tendency to continue to support a failing course of action.

leaving only British Airways and Air France as customers. While these two firms doggedly held on to their marginally profitable Concorde operations for almost three decades, a crash in 2000 led to closer scrutiny of the aging fleet, which was eventually retired in 2003. Industry insiders estimate that every customer who took the Concorde rather than a 747 cost British Airways more than $1,200 in profits.[20]

Organizations can deal with escalation of commitment in several ways. One is to split the responsibility for project decisions, by allowing different individuals to make decisions at different project stages. Organizations have also tried to eliminate escalation of commitment by closely monitoring decision makers.[21] Another suggestion is to provide individuals with a graceful exit from poor decisions so that their images are not threatened. One way of accomplishing this is to reward people who admit to poor decisions before escalating their commitment to them, or having groups make an initial investment decision. Participants in group decision making may experience a diffusion of responsibility for the failed decision rather than feeling personally responsible; thus, they can pull out of a bad decision without threatening their image.[22]

We have seen that there are limits to how rational a manager can be in making decisions. Most managerial decisions involve considerable uncertainty and risk, and individuals react differently to risk situations.

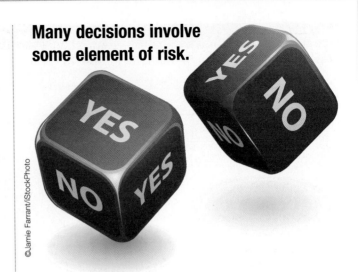

**Many decisions involve some element of risk.**

©Jamie Farrant/iStockPhoto

# Individual Influences on Decision Making

No decision is made in a vacuum. In many ways, decisions reflect the people who make them, so it is appropriate to examine the individual influences on decision making: comfort for risk, cognitive style, personality, intuition, and creativity.

## Risk and the Manager

Many decisions involve some element of risk. For managers, hiring decisions, promotions, delegation, acquisitions and mergers, overseas expansions, new product development, and other decisions make risk a part of the job.

Individuals differ in terms of their willingness to take risks. Some people experience **risk aversion**. They choose options that entail fewer risks, preferring familiarity and certainty. Other individuals are risk takers; that is, they accept greater potential for loss in decisions, tolerate greater uncertainty, and in general are more likely to make risky decisions. Risk takers are also more likely to take the lead in group discussions.[23]

Research indicates that women are more averse to risk taking than men and that older, more experienced managers are more risk averse than younger managers. There is also some evidence that successful managers take more risks than unsuccessful managers.[24] However, the tendency to take risks or avoid them is only part of behaviour toward risk. Risk taking is influenced not only by an individual's tendency but also by organizational factors. In commercial banks, loan decisions that require the assessment of risk are made every day.

Upper-level managers face a tough task in managing risk-taking behaviour. By discouraging lower-level managers from taking risks, they may stifle creativity and innovation. If upper-level managers are going to encourage risk taking, however, they must allow employees to fail without fear of punishment. One way to accomplish this is to consider failure "enlightened trial and error."[25] The key is establishing a consistent attitude toward risk within the organization.

When individuals take risks, losses may occur. Suppose an oil producer thinks there is an opportunity to uncover oil by reentering an old drilling site. She gathers a group of investors and shows them the logs, and they chip in to finance the venture. The reentry is drilled to a certain depth, and nothing is found. Convinced they did not drill deep enough, the producer goes back to the investors and requests additional financial backing to continue drilling. The investors consent, and she drills deeper, only to find nothing. She approaches the investors, and after lengthy discussion, they agree to provide more money to drill deeper. Why do decision makers sometimes throw good money after bad?

**cognitive style**

An individual's preference for gathering information and evaluating alternatives.

**risk aversion**

The tendency to choose options that entail fewer risks and less uncertainty.

# Personality, Attitudes, and Values

In addition to all of the individual differences variables (discussed in Chapters 3 and 4), personality characteristics, attitudes, and values, managers must use both their logic and their creativity to make effective decisions. Most of us are more comfortable using either logic or creativity, and we show that preference in everyday decision making.

Our brains have two lateral halves (Figure 10.4). The right side is the centre for creative functions, while the left side is the centre for logic, detail, and planning. There are advantages to both kinds of thinking, so the ideal situation is to be "brain-lateralized" or to be able to use either logic or creativity or both, depending on the situation. There are ways to develop the side of the brain you are not accustomed to using. To develop your right side, or creative side, you can ask "what-if" questions, engage in play, and follow your intuition. To develop the left side, you can set goals for completing tasks and work to attain these goals. For managers, it is important to see the big picture, craft a vision, and plan strategically—all of which require right-brain skills. It is equally important to be able to understand day-to-day operations and flow chart work processes, which are left-brain skills.

Two particular individual influences that can enhance decision-making effectiveness will be highlighted next: intuition and creativity.

## Intuition

There is evidence that managers use their **intuition** to make decisions.[26] Henry Mintzberg, in his work on managerial roles, found that in many cases managers do not appear to use a systematic, step-by-step approach to decision making. Rather, Mintzberg argued, managers make judgments based on "hunches."[27] Daniel Isenberg studied the way senior managers make decisions and found that intuition was used extensively, especially as a mechanism to evaluate decisions made more rationally.[28] Robert Beck studied the way managers at BankAmerica (now Bank of America) made decisions about the future direction of the company following the deregulation of the banking industry. Beck described their use of intuition as an antidote to "analysis paralysis," or the tendency to analyze decisions rather than developing innovative solutions.[29]

FIGURE 10.4

**FUNCTIONS OF THE LEFT AND RIGHT BRAIN HEMISPHERES**

**Two Brains, Two Cognitive Styles**

**Left hemisphere**    **Right hemisphere**

| Left hemisphere | Right hemisphere |
| --- | --- |
| Verbal | Nonverbal, visuospatial |
| Sequential, temporal, digital | Simultaneous, spatial, analogical |
| Logical, analytic | Gestalt, synthetic |
| Rational | Intuitive |
| Western thought | Eastern thought |

SOURCE: Created based on ideas from *Left Brain, Right Brain* by Springer and Deutsch, p. 272. © 1993 by Sally P. Springer and Georg Deutsch (New York: W. H. Freeman and Company, 1993).

## DID YOU KNOW?

>> Brain hemispheric dominance is related to students' postsecondary education choices. Left-brained students gravitate toward business, engineering, and sciences, whereas right-brained students are attracted to education, nursing, communication, and literature.[30]

Gary Klein and colleagues insist that skilled decision makers rely on patterns of learned information in making quick and efficient decisions. In a series of studies conducted with the U.S. Navy, U.S. Army, and firefighters, they found that decision makers normally relied on intuition in unfamiliar, challenging situations. These decisions were superior to those made after careful evaluation of information and potential alternatives.[31]

Just what is intuition? In Jungian theory, intuiting (N) is one preference used to gather data. This is only one way that the concept of intuition has been applied to managerial decision

**intuition**

A fast, positive force in decision making that is utilized at a level below consciousness and involves learned patterns of information.

making, and it is perhaps the most widely researched form of the concept of intuition. There are, however, many definitions of *intuition* in the managerial literature. Chester Barnard, one of the early influential management researchers, argued that intuition's main attributes were speed and the inability of the decision maker to determine how the decision was made.[32] Other researchers have contended that intuition occurs at an unconscious level and that this is why the decision maker cannot verbalize how the decision was made.[33]

Intuition has been variously described as follows:

> > The ability to know or recognize quickly and readily the possibilities of a situation.[34]
>
> > Smooth automatic performance of learned behaviour sequences.[35]
>
> > Simple analyses frozen into habit and into the capacity for rapid response through recognition.[36]

These definitions share some common assumptions. First, there seems to be a notion that intuition is fast. Second, intuition is used at a level below consciousness. Third, there seems to be agreement that intuition involves learned patterns of information. Fourth, intuition appears to be a positive force in decision making.

The use of intuition may lead to more ethical decisions. Intuition allows an individual to take on another's role with ease, and role taking is a fundamental part of developing moral reasoning. You will recall from Chapter 4 the role of cognitive moral development in ethical decision making. One study found a strong link between cognitive moral development and intuition. The development of new perspectives through intuition leads to higher moral growth, and thus to more ethical decisions.[37]

One question that arises is whether managers can be taught to use their intuition. Weston Agor, who has conducted workshops on developing intuitive skills in managers, has attained positive results in various types of organizations. After giving intuition tests to more than 10,000 executives, he has concluded that in most cases, higher management positions are held by individuals with higher levels of intuition. Just as the brain needs both hemispheres to work, Agor cautions that organizations need both analytical and intuitive minds to function at their peak. Agor suggests relaxation techniques, using images to guide the mind, and taking creative pauses before making a decision.[38] Lee Iacocca, in his autobiography, spends pages extolling intuition: "To a certain extent, I've always operated by gut feeling."[39] A review of the research on intuition suggests that although intuition itself cannot be taught, managers can be trained to rely more fully on the promptings of their intuition.[40]

Intuition, with many definitions, is an elusive concept. Some researchers view "rational" methods as preferable to intuition, yet satisfaction with a rational decision is usually determined by how the decision feels intuitively.[41] Intuition appears to have a positive effect on managerial decision making, but it is not without controversy. Some writers argue that intuition has its place and that instincts should be trusted, but not as a substitute for reason. With new technologies, managers can analyze a lot more information in a lot less time, making the rational method less time consuming than it once was.[42]

## Creativity

In some ways, creativity is as elusive a concept as intuition. (We know it when we encounter it and feel its absence.) Even though creativity is also highly individual, it is also collective. Personal creativity plays a role in the decisions made in organizations every day. **Creativity** is a process influenced by individual and organizational factors that results in the production of novel and useful ideas, products, or both.[43]

The four stages of the creative process are preparation, incubation, illumination, and verification.[44] Preparation means seeking out new experiences and opportunities to learn, because creativity grows from a base of knowledge. Incubation is a process of reflective thought and is often conducted subconsciously. During incubation, the individual engages in other pursuits while the mind considers the problem and works on it. Illumination occurs when the individual senses an insight for solving the problem. Finally, verification is conducted to determine if the solution or idea is valid. Verification is accomplished by thinking through the implications of the decision, presenting the idea to another person, or trying out the decision. Momentary quieting of the brain through relaxation can increase "coherence" or the ability of different parts of the brain to work together.[45] Both individual and organizational influences affect the creative process.

**Individual Influences** Several individual variables are related to creativity. One group of factors involves the cognitive processes that creative individuals tend to use. One cognitive process is divergent thinking, meaning the individual's ability to generate several potential solutions to a problem.[46] In addition, associational abilities and the use of imagery are associated with creativity.[47] Unconscious processes such as dreams are also essential cognitive processes related to creative thinking.[48]

Personality factors have also been related to creativity in studies of individuals from several different occupations. These characteristics include intellectual and artistic values, breadth of interests, high energy, concern

**creativity**

A process influenced by individual and organizational factors that results in the production of novel and useful ideas, products, or both.

> # There is also evidence that people who are in a good mood are more creative.

with achievement, independence of judgment, intuition, self-confidence, and a creative self-image.[49] Tolerance of ambiguity, intrinsic motivation, risk taking, and a desire for recognition are also associated with creativity.[50]

There is also evidence that people who are in a good mood are more creative.[51] Positive affect is related to creativity in work teams because being in a positive mood allows team members to explore new ways of thinking.[52] Positive emotions enhance creativity by broadening your cognitive patterns and resources. These positive emotions initiate thoughts and actions that are novel and unscripted.[53] Moreover, it is a cyclical process: thinking positively makes us more creative, and being more creative makes us think positively.[54]

Conversely, it has been found that people in negative moods perform better at tasks involving considerable cognitive demands. When an individual experiences negative moods or emotions, it is a signal to the individual that all is not well, and leads to more attention and vigilance in cognitive activity.

**Organizational Influences** The organizational environment in which people work can either support creativity or impede creative efforts. Creativity killers include focusing on how work will be evaluated, being closely monitored while you are working, and competing with other people in win–lose situations. In contrast, creativity facilitators include feelings of autonomy, being part of a team with diverse skills, and having creative supervisors and coworkers.[55] High-quality, supportive relationships with supervisors are related to creativity.[56] High-quality social networks that are cohesive can have a positive impact on creative decision making. Such social networks encourage creative decision making by facilitating shared sensemaking of relevant information and consensus building.[57] Flexible organizational structures and participative decision making have also been associated with creativity.

An organization can also present impediments to creativity. These barriers include internal political problems, harsh criticism of new ideas, destructive internal competition, and avoidance of risk.[58] The physical environment can also hamper creativity. Companies such as Oticon, a Danish hearing-aid manufacturer, and Ethicon Endo-Surgery, a division of Johnson & Johnson, use open-plan offices that eliminate office walls and cubicles so that employees interact more frequently.

When people mix, ideas mix as well.[59] Organizations can therefore enhance individuals' creative decision making by providing a supportive environment, participative decision making, and a flexible structure.

**Individual/Organization Fit** Research has indicated that creative performance is highest when there is a match, or fit, between the individual and organizational influences on creativity. When individuals who desire to be creative are matched with an organization that values creative ideas, the result is more creative performance.[60]

> ## What about You? on the Chapter 10 Review Card allows you to determine whether you prefer creative or logical problem solving.

A common mistaken assumption about creativity is that either you have it or you do not. Research refutes this myth and has shown that individuals can be trained to be more creative.[61] The Disney Institute features a wide range of programs offered to organizations, and one of its best-sellers is creativity training.

Part of creativity training involves learning to open up mental locks that keep us from generating creative alternatives to a decision or problem. The following are some mental locks that diminish creativity:

> - Searching for the "right" answer
> - Trying to be logical
> - Following the rules
> - Avoiding ambiguity
> - Striving for practicality
> - Being afraid to look foolish
> - Avoiding problems outside our own expertise
> - Fearing failure
> - Believing we are not really creative
> - Not making play a part of work.[62]

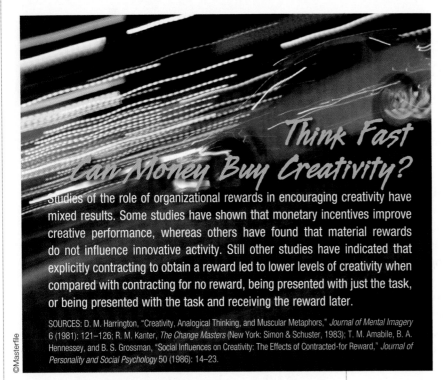

## Think Fast
## Can Money Buy Creativity?

Studies of the role of organizational rewards in encouraging creativity have mixed results. Some studies have shown that monetary incentives improve creative performance, whereas others have found that material rewards do not influence innovative activity. Still other studies have indicated that explicitly contracting to obtain a reward led to lower levels of creativity when compared with contracting for no reward, being presented with just the task, or being presented with the task and receiving the reward later.

SOURCES: D. M. Harrington, "Creativity, Analogical Thinking, and Muscular Metaphors," *Journal of Mental Imagery* 6 (1981): 121–126; R. M. Kanter, *The Change Masters* (New York: Simon & Schuster, 1983); T. M. Amabile, B. A. Hennessey, and B. S. Grossman, "Social Influences on Creativity: The Effects of Contracted-for Reward," *Journal of Personality and Social Psychology* 50 (1986): 14–23.

the organization. Contributory creativity is responding to problems presented to you because you want to be creative. Proactive creativity is discovering problems because you want to be creative.[64]

3M consistently ranks among the top ten in *Fortune*'s annual list of most admired corporations. It earned this reputation through innovation: more than one-quarter of 3M's sales are from products less than four years old. Post-It Notes, for example, were created by a worker who wanted little adhesive papers to mark hymns for church service. He thought of another worker who had perfected a light adhesive, and the two spent their "free time" developing Post-It Notes. 3M has continued its tradition of innovation with Post-It Flags, Pop-Up Tape Strips, and Nexcare Ease-Off Bandages.

Leaders can play key roles in modelling creative behaviour. Sir Richard Branson, founder and chairman of U.K.–based Virgin Group, believes that if you do not use your employees' creative potential, you are doomed to failure. At Virgin Group, the culture encourages risk taking and rewards innovation. Rules and regulations are not its thing, nor is analyzing ideas to death. Branson says an employee can have an idea in the morning and implement it in the afternoon.[65]

Note that many of these mental locks stem from values within organizations. Organizations can facilitate creative decision making in many ways. Rewarding creativity, allowing employees to fail, making work more fun, and providing creativity training are a few suggestions. Organizations can encourage creativity by exposing employees to new ideas through job rotation, for example, which moves employees through different jobs and gives them exposure to different information, projects, and teams, either within or outside of the company. Finally, managers can encourage employees to surround themselves with stimuli that they have found to enhance their creative processes. These may be music, artwork, books, or anything else that encourages creative thinking.[63]

We have seen that both individual and organizational factors can produce creativity. Creativity also means finding problems as well as fixing them. Recently, four different types of creativity have been proposed, based on the source of the trigger (internal or external) and the source of the problem (presented versus discovered). Responsive creativity means responding to a problem that is presented to you by others because it is part of your job. Expected creativity is discovering problems because you are expected to by

**synergy**
A positive force that occurs in groups when group members stimulate new solutions to problems through the process of mutual influence and encouragement within the group.

# The Group Decision-Making Process

Managers use groups to make decisions for several reasons. One is **synergy**, which occurs when group members stimulate new solutions to problems through the process of mutual influence and encouragement within the group. Another reason for using a group is to gain commitment to a decision. Groups also bring more knowledge and experience to the problem-solving situation.

Group decisions can sometimes be predicted by comparing the views of the initial group

AP Photo/Jacques Brinon

members with the final group decision. These simple relationships are known as **social decision schemes**. One social decision scheme is the majority-wins rule, in which the group supports whatever position is taken by the majority of its members. Another scheme, the truth-wins rule, predicts that the correct decision will emerge as an increasing number of members realize its appropriateness. The two-thirds-majority rule means that the decision favoured by two-thirds or more of the members is supported. Finally, the first-shift rule states that members support a decision represented by the first shift in opinion shown by a member.

Research indicates that these social decision schemes can predict a group decision as much as 80 percent of the time.[66] Current research is aimed at discovering which rules are used in particular types of tasks. For example, studies indicate that the majority-wins rule is used most often in judgment tasks (that is, when the decision is a matter of preference or opinion), whereas the truth-wins rule predicts decisions best when the task is an intellective one (that is, when the decision has a correct answer).[67]

## Advantages and Disadvantages of Group Decision Making

Group decision making has advantages and disadvantages. The advantages include (1) more knowledge and information through the pooling of group member resources; (2) increased acceptance of and commitment to the decision, because the members had a voice in it; and (3) greater understanding of the decision, because members were involved in the various stages of the decision process. The disadvantages of group decision making include (1) pressure within the group to conform and fit in; (2) domination of the group by one forceful member or a dominant clique, who may ramrod the decision; and (3) the amount of time required, because a group makes decisions more slowly than an individual.[68]

In light of these advantages and disadvantages, should an individual or a group make a decision? Substantial empirical research indicates that effectively making that determination depends on the type of task involved. For judgment tasks requiring an estimate or a prediction, groups are usually superior to individuals because of the breadth of experience that multiple individuals bring to the problem.[69] On tasks that have a correct solution, other studies have indicated that the most competent individual outperforms the group.[70] This finding has been called

> **Social decision schemes can predict a group decision as much as 80 percent of the time.**

into question, however. Much of the previous research on groups was conducted in the laboratory, where group members interacted only for short periods of time. Researchers wanted to know how a longer group experience would affect decisions. Their study showed that groups who worked together for longer periods of time outperformed the most competent member 70 percent of the time. As groups gained experience, the best members became less important to the group's success.[71] This study demonstrated that experience in the group is an important variable to consider when evaluating the individual versus group decision-making question.

Given the emphasis on teams in the workplace, many managers believe that groups produce better decisions than individuals, yet the evidence is mixed. More research needs to be conducted in organizational settings to help answer this question.

## Limits of Group Decision Making

Two potential liabilities are found in group decision making: groupthink and group polarization. These problems are discussed next.

**Groupthink** One liability of a cohesive group is its tendency to develop **groupthink**, a dysfunctional process. Irving Janis, the originator of the groupthink concept, describes groupthink as "a deterioration of mental efficiency, reality testing, and moral judgment" resulting from pressures within the group.[72]

Certain conditions favour the development of groupthink. One of the conditions is high cohesiveness. Cohesive groups tend to favour solidarity because members identify strongly with the group.[73] High-ranking teams that make decisions without outside help are especially prone to groupthink because they are likely to have shared mental models; that is, they are more likely to think alike.[74] Homogeneous groups (ones with little to no diversity among members) are more likely to suffer from groupthink.[75] Two other conditions that encourage groupthink are having to make a highly consequential decision and time constraints.[76] A highly consequential decision is one that will have a great impact on the group members and on outside parties.

**social decision schemes**
Simple rules used to determine final group decisions.

**groupthink**
A deterioration of mental efficiency, reality testing, and moral judgment resulting from pressures within the group.

When group members feel that they have a limited time in which to make a decision, they may rush through the process. These antecedents cause members to prefer concurrence in decisions and to fail to evaluate one another's suggestions critically. A group suffering from groupthink shows recognizable symptoms.

An incident cited as a prime example of groupthink is the 1986 *Challenger* disaster, in which the shuttle exploded and killed all seven crew members. A presidential commission concluded that flawed decision making was the primary cause of the accident. In 2003, the shuttle *Columbia* exploded over Texas upon reentering the earth's atmosphere, killing all seven crew members. Within days of the *Columbia* disaster, questions began to surface about the decision-making process that led flight engineers to assume that damage caused to the shuttle upon takeoff was minor and to continue the mission. The subsequent investigation of the disaster led observers to note that NASA's decision-making process appeared just as flawed in 2003 as it was in 1986, exhibiting all the classic symptoms of groupthink. The final accident report blamed the NASA culture that downplayed risk and suppressed dissent for the decision.[77]

Consequences of groupthink include an incomplete survey of alternatives, failure to evaluate the risks of the preferred course of action, biased information processing, and a failure to work out contingency plans. Evident in the *Challenger* situation, the overall result of groupthink is defective decision making. The group considered only two alternatives: launch or no launch. Group members failed to consider the risks of their decision to launch the shuttle, and they did not develop any contingency plans. Table 10.1 presents the symptoms of groupthink and

Janis's guidelines for avoiding groupthink. Many of these suggestions centre around ensuring that decisions are evaluated completely, with opportunities for discussion from all group members. This strategy encourages members to evaluate one another's ideas critically. Groups that are educated about the value of diversity tend to perform better at decision-making tasks. On the other hand, groups that are homogenous and are not educated about the value of diversity do not accrue such benefits in decision making.[78]

Janis has used the groupthink framework to conduct historical analyses of several political and military fiascoes. One review of the decision situation in the *Challenger* incident proposed that two variables, time and leadership style, are important to include.[79] When a decision must be made quickly, there is more potential for groupthink. Leadership style can either promote groupthink (if the leader makes his or her opinion known up front) or avoid groupthink (if the leader encourages open and frank discussion).

There are few empirical studies of groupthink, and most of these involved students in a laboratory setting. More applied research may be seen in the future, however, as a questionnaire has been developed to measure the constructs associated with groupthink.[80] Janis's work on groupthink has led to several interdisciplinary efforts at understanding policy decisions.[81] The work underscores the need to examine multiple explanations for failed decisions. Teams that experience cognitive (task-based) conflict are found to make better decisions than teams that experience affective (emotion-based) conflict. As such, one prescription for managers has been to encourage cognitive conflict while minimizing affective

**TABLE 10.1** Symptoms of Groupthink and How to Prevent It

### SYMPTOMS OF GROUPTHINK

- *Illusions of invulnerability.* Group members feel that they are above criticism. This symptom leads to excessive optimism and risk taking.
- *Illusions of group morality.* Group members feel they are moral in their actions and therefore above reproach. This symptom leads the group to ignore the ethical implications of their decisions.
- *Illusions of unanimity.* Group members believe there is unanimous agreement on the decisions. Silence is misconstrued as consent.
- *Rationalization.* Group members concoct explanations for their decisions to make them appear rational and correct. The results are that other alternatives are not considered, and there is an unwillingness to reconsider the group's assumptions.
- *Stereotyping the enemy.* Competitors are stereotyped as evil or stupid. This leads the group to underestimate its opposition.
- *Self-censorship.* Members do not express their doubts or concerns about the course of action. This prevents critical analysis of the decisions.
- *Peer pressure.* Any members who express doubts or concerns are pressured by other group members who question their loyalty.
- *Mindguards.* Some members take it upon themselves to protect the group from negative feedback. Group members are thus shielded from information that might lead them to question their actions.

### GUIDELINES FOR PREVENTING GROUPTHINK

- Ask each group member to assume the role of the critical evaluator who actively voices objections or doubts.
- Have the leader avoid stating his or her position on the issue prior to the group decision.
- Create several groups that work on the decision simultaneously.
- Bring in outside experts to evaluate the group process.
- Appoint a devil's advocate to question the group's course of action consistently.
- Evaluate the competition carefully, posing as many different motivations and intentions as possible.
- Once consensus is reached, encourage the group to rethink its position by reexamining the alternatives.

From JANIS. *Groupthink*, 2E. © 1982 Wadsworth, a part of Cengage Learning, Inc. Reproduced by permission. www.cengage.com/permissions.

conflict. However, these two forms of conflict can also occur together and more research is needed on how one can be encouraged while minimizing the other.[82]

### Group Polarization

Another group phenomenon was discovered by a graduate student. His study showed that groups and individuals within the group made riskier decisions and accepted greater levels of risk following a group discussion of the issue. Subsequent studies uncovered another shift—toward caution. Thus, group discussion produced shifts both toward more risky positions and toward more cautious positions.[83] Further research revealed that individual group member attitudes simply became more extreme following group discussion. Individuals who were initially against an issue became more radically opposed, and individuals who were in favour of the issue became more strongly supportive following discussion. These shifts came to be known as **group polarization**.[84]

The tendency toward polarization has important implications for group decision making. Groups whose initial views lean a certain way can be expected to adopt more extreme views following interaction.

Several ideas have been proposed to explain why group polarization occurs. One explanation is the social comparison approach. Prior to group discussion, individuals believe they hold better views than the other members. During group discussion, they see that their views are not so far from average, so they shift to more extreme positions.[85] A second explanation is the persuasive arguments view. It contends that group discussion reinforces the initial views of the members, so they take a more extreme position.[86] Both explanations are supported by research. It may be that both processes, along with others, cause the group to develop more polarized attitudes.

Group polarization leads groups to adopt extreme attitudes. In some cases, this can be disastrous. For instance, if individuals are leaning toward a dangerous decision, they are likely to support it more strongly following discussion. Both groupthink and group polarization are potential liabilities of group decision making, but several techniques can be used to help prevent or control these two liabilities.

**group polarization**
The tendency for group discussion to produce shifts toward more extreme attitudes among members.

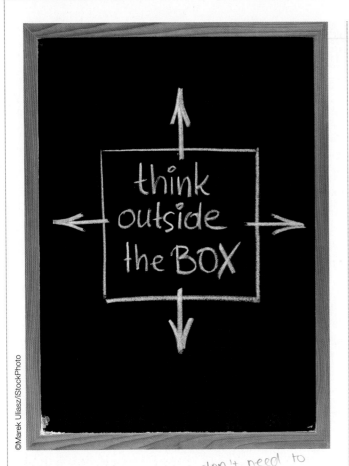

©Marek Uliasz/iStockPhoto

## Techniques for Group Decision Making

*don't need to know in depth*

Once a manager has determined that a group decision approach should be used, he or she can determine the technique that is best suited to the decision situation. <u>Seven</u> techniques will be briefly summarized: brainstorming, nominal group technique, devil's advocacy, dialectical inquiry, quality circles, quality teams, and self-managed teams.

### Brainstorming

Brainstorming is a good technique for generating alternatives. The idea behind **brainstorming** is to generate as many ideas as possible, suspending evaluation until all of the ideas have been suggested. Participants are encouraged to build upon the suggestions of others, and

imagination is emphasized. One company that benefits from brainstorming is Toyota. Despite its success with the baby-boomer generation, Toyota's executives realized that they were failing to connect with younger buyers, who viewed the firm as stodgy. In response, Toyota assembled a group of younger employees to brainstorm new products for this market. The result was the Toyota Echo, as well as Scion, an entirely new line of boxy crossover vehicles aimed at the younger set.[87] Similarly, Cirque du Soleil has a group, The Trend Group, composed of young people, to gather ideas from all over the world.[88]

Evidence suggests, however, that group brainstorming is less effective than a comparable number of individuals working alone. In groups, participants engage in discussions that can make them lose their focus.[89]

**Nominal Group Technique** A structured approach to decision making that focuses on generating alternatives and choosing one is called **nominal group technique (NGT)**. NGT involves the following discrete steps:

1. Individuals silently list their ideas.

2. Ideas are written on a chart one at a time until all ideas are listed.

3. Discussion is permitted but only to clarify the ideas. No criticism is allowed.

4. A written vote is taken.

NGT is a good technique to use in a situation where group members fear criticism from others.[90]

**Devil's Advocacy** In the **devil's advocacy** decision method, a group or individual is given the role of critic. This devil's advocate has the task of coming up with the potential problems of a proposed decision. This helps organizations avoid costly mistakes in decision making by identifying potential pitfalls in advance.[91] As we discussed in Chapter 9, a devil's advocate who challenges the CEO and top management team can help sustain the vitality and performance of the upper echelon.

**Dialectical Inquiry** **Dialectical inquiry** is essentially a debate between two opposing sets of recommendations. Although it sets up a conflict, it is a constructive approach, because it brings out the benefits and limitations of both sets of ideas.[92] When using this technique, it is important to guard against a win–lose attitude and to concentrate on reaching the most effective solution for all concerned. Research has shown that the way a decision is framed (that is, win–win versus win–lose) is very important. A decision's outcome could be viewed as a gain or a loss, depending on the way the decision is framed.[93]

---

**brainstorming**

A technique for generating as many ideas as possible on a given subject, while suspending evaluation until all the ideas have been suggested.

**nominal group technique (NGT)**

A structured approach to group decision making that focuses on generating alternatives and choosing one.

**devil's advocacy**

A technique for preventing groupthink in which a group or individual is given the role of critic during decision making.

**dialectical inquiry**

A debate between two opposing sets of recommendations.

---

## Hot Trend: Electronic Brainstorming

Electronic brainstorming overcomes two common problems that can produce group brainstorming failure: production blocking and evaluation apprehension. Production blocking occurs when you forget what *you* wanted to contribute because you were concentrating on listening to *others* in the session. In electronic brainstorming, ideas are recorded electronically, so participants can focus on the ideas they want to share free from interruption. Electronic brainstorming also overcomes evaluation apprehension, which occurs when individuals fear that others might respond negatively to their ideas. In electronic brainstorming, input is anonymous, so evaluation apprehension is reduced. Studies indicate that anonymous electronic brainstorming groups outperform face-to-face brainstorming groups in the number of ideas generated.

SOURCES: B. A. Nijstad, W. Stroebe, and H. F. M. Lodewijkx, "Production Blocking and Idea Generation: Does Blocking Interfere with Cognitive Processes?" *Journal of Experimental Social Psychology* 39 (2003): 531–549; W. H. Cooper, R. B. Gallupe, S. Pollard, and J. Cadsby, "Some Liberating Effects of Anonymous Electronic Brainstorming," *Small Group Research* 29 (1998): 147–178.

luchshen/Shutterstock

## Factors in Selecting the Appropriate Technique

Before choosing a group decision-making technique, the manager should carefully evaluate the group members and the decision situation. Only then can the best method for accomplishing the objectives of the group decision-making process be selected. If the goal is generating a large number of alternatives, for example, brainstorming would be a good choice. If group members are reluctant to contribute ideas, the nominal group technique would be appropriate. To guard against groupthink, devil's advocacy or dialectical inquiry would be effective. Decisions that concern quality or production would benefit from the advice of quality circles or the empowered decisions of quality teams. Moreover, recent research results suggests that if individuals within a team are made accountable for the process of decision making (rather than the end decision itself), then such teams are more likely to gather diverse information, share information, and eventually make better decisions.[94] Finally, a manager who wants to provide total empowerment to a group should consider self-managed teams.

## Special Decision-Making Groups

Even though in organizations many types of groups make collective decisions, quality-oriented groups and self-managed teams have higher levels of involvement and authority in group decision making.

### Quality Circles and Quality Teams

**Quality circles** are small groups that voluntarily meet to provide input for solving quality or production problems. Quality circles also extend participative decision making into teams. Managers often listen to recommendations from quality circles and implement the suggestions. Involvement in the decision-making process is the primary reward.

Quality circles are not empowered to implement their own recommendations. They operate in parallel fashion to the organization's structure, and they rely on voluntary participation.[95] In Japan, quality circles have been integrated into the organization instead of added on. This may be one reason for Japan's success with this technique. In contrast, the North American experience is not as positive. It has been estimated that 60 to 75 percent of the quality circles have failed. Reasons for the failures have included lack of top management support and lack of problem-solving skills among quality circle members.[96]

**Quality teams**, in contrast, are included in total quality management and other quality improvement efforts as part of a change in the organization's structure. Quality teams are generated from the top down and are empowered to act on their own recommendations. Whereas quality circles emphasize the generation of ideas, quality teams make data-based decisions about improving product and service quality. Various decision-making techniques are employed in quality teams. Brainstorming, flow charts, and cause-and-effect diagrams help pinpoint problems that affect quality.

Quality circles and quality teams are methods for using groups in the decision-making process. Self-managed teams take the concept of participation one step further.

### Self-Managed Teams

Another group decision-making method is the use of self-managed teams, which we discussed in Chapter 9. The decision-making activities of self-managed teams are more broadly focused than those of quality circles and quality teams. Self-managed teams make many of the decisions

**quality circle**

A small group of employees who work voluntarily on company time, typically one hour per week, to address work-related problems such as quality control, cost reduction, production planning and techniques, and even product design.

**quality team**

A team that is part of an organization's structure and is empowered to act on its decisions regarding product and service quality.

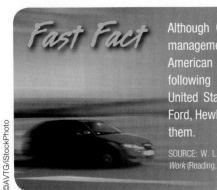

**Fast Fact**

Although QCs are typically associated with Japanese management methods, they were actually conceived by American W. Edwards Deming and exported to Japan following World War II. QCs became popular in the United States in the 1980s, when companies such as Ford, Hewlett-Packard, and Eastman Kodak implemented them.

SOURCE: W. L. Mohr and H. Mohr, *Quality Circles: Changing Images of People at Work* (Reading, Mass.: Addison-Wesley, 1983).

that were once reserved for managers, such as work scheduling, job assignments, and staffing.

Many organizations have claimed success with self-managed teams. At Nortel Networks, revenues rose 63 percent and sales increased 26 percent following the implementation of self-managed teams.[97] Research evidence shows that self-managed teams can lead to higher productivity, lower turnover among employees, and flatter organization structure.[98]

Self-managed teams, like any cohesive group, can fall victim to groupthink. The key to stimulating innovation and better problem solving in these groups is welcoming dissent among members. Dissent breaks down complacency and sets in motion a process that results in better decisions. Team members must know that dissent is permissible so that they won't fear embarrassment or ridicule.[99]

hierarchical cultures, such as India, top-level managers make decisions. In countries with low power distance, lower-level employees make many decisions. The Swedish culture exemplifies this type.

The individualist/collectivist dimension has implications for decision making. Japan, with its collectivist emphasis, favours group decisions. Canada has a more difficult time with group decisions because it is an individualistic culture. Time orientation affects the frame of reference of the decision. In China, with its long-term view, decisions are made with the future in mind. In Canada, many decisions are made considering only the short term.

The masculine/feminine dimension can be compared to the Jungian thinking/feeling preferences for decision making. Masculine cultures, as in many Latin American countries, value quick, assertive decisions. Feminine cultures, as in many Scandinavian countries, value decisions that reflect concern for others.

Research examining the effects of cultural diversity on decision making has found that when individuals in a group are racially dissimilar, they engage in more open information sharing, encourage dissenting perspectives, and arrive at better decisions than racially similar

> ## A manager who wants to provide total empowerment to a group should consider self-managed teams.

*not mentioned*

# Diversity and Culture in Decision Making

Styles of decision making vary greatly among cultures. Many of the dimensions proposed by Hofstede that were presented in Chapter 2 affect decision making. Uncertainty avoidance, for example, can affect the way people view decisions. In Canada, a culture with low uncertainty avoidance, decisions are seen as opportunities for change. In contrast, cultures such as those of Indonesia and Malaysia attempt to accept situations as they are rather than to change them.[100] Power distance also affects decision making. In more

groups.[101] Other kinds of diversity such as functional background have been studied as well. Top management teams that have members who come from a variety of functional backgrounds (for example, marketing, accounting, information systems) engage in greater debate in decision making than top management teams in which the members come from similar backgrounds. This diversity results in better financial performance for the firm.[102] Research also indicates that strategic decision making in firms can vary widely by culture. For example, one such source of variation stems from the differential emphasis placed on environmental scanning in different cultures. Furthermore, strategic decision making might appear rational but is also informed by firm level and national characteristics.[103]

# Participation in Decision Making

Effective management of people can improve a company's economic performance. Firms that capitalize on this fact share several common practices. Chief among them is participation of employees in decision making.[104] Many companies do this through highly empowered self-managed teams. Even in situations where formal teams are not feasible, decision authority can be handed down to frontline employees who have the knowledge and skills to make a difference. At Hampton Inn hotels, for example, guest services personnel are empowered to do whatever is necessary to make guests happy—without consulting their superiors.

## The Effects of Participation

**Participative decision making** occurs when individuals who are affected by decisions influence the making of those decisions. Participation buffers employees from the negative experiences of organizational politics.[105] In addition, participative management has been found to increase employee creativity, job satisfaction, and productivity.[106]

GE Capital believes in participation. Each year it holds dreaming sessions, and employees from all levels of the company attend strategy and budget meetings to discuss where the company is heading.

As our economy becomes increasingly based on knowledge work and as new technologies make it easier for decentralized decision makers to connect, participative decision making will undoubtedly increase.[107] Needing to adopt a single messaging system to meet the requirements of more than 20,000 users, one municipal organization faced a huge challenge in getting all the users to provide input into the decision. Technology helped craft a system that balanced the needs of all the groups involved, and IT planners developed a 28-page spreadsheet to pull together the needs and desires of all 60 departments into a focused decision matrix. Within two years, 90 percent of the users had agreed on and moved to a single system, reducing costs and complexity.[108]

> " Participation buffers employees from the negative experiences of organizational politics.

# Foundations for Participation and Empowerment

Organizational and individual foundations underlie empowerment that enhances task motivation and performance. The organizational foundations for empowerment include a participative, supportive organizational culture and a team-oriented work design. A supportive work environment is essential because of the uncertainty that empowerment can cause within the organization. Empowerment requires that lower-level organizational members be able to make decisions and take action on those decisions. As operational employees become empowered to make decisions, real fear, anxiety, or even terror can be created among middle managers in the organization.[109] Senior leadership must create an organizational culture that is supportive and reassuring for these middle managers as the power dynamics of the system change.

A second organizational foundation for empowerment concerns the design of work. The old factory system relied on work specialization and narrow tasks with the intent of achieving routinized efficiency.[110] This approach to the design of work had some economic advantages, but it also had some distressing disadvantages leading to monotony and fatigue. This approach to the design of work is inconsistent with participation because the individual feels absolved of much responsibility for a whole piece of work. Team-oriented work designs are a key organizational foundation because they lead to broader tasks and a greater sense of responsibility. For example, Volvo builds cars using a team-oriented work design in which each person does many different tasks and each person has direct responsibility for the finished product.[111] These work designs create a context for effective participation as long as the empowered individuals meet necessary individual prerequisites.

The three individual prerequisites for participation and empowerment are (1) the capability to become psychologically involved in participative activities, (2) the motivation to act autonomously, and (3) the capacity to see the relevance of participation for one's own well-being.[112] First, people must be psychologically equipped to become involved in participative activities if they are to be empowered and become effective team members. Not all people are so predisposed. For example, Germany has an authoritarian tradition that runs counter to participation and empowerment at the individual and group level. General Motors

**participative decision making**

Decision making in which individuals who are affected by decisions influence the making of those decisions.

encountered significant difficulties implementing quality circles in its German plants, because workers expected to be directed by supervisors, not to engage in participative problem solving. The German initiatives to establish supervisory/worker boards in corporations are intended to change this authoritarian tradition.

A second individual prerequisite is the motivation to act autonomously. People with dependent personalities are predisposed to be told what to do and to rely on external motivation rather than internal, intrinsic motivation.[113] These dependent people are not effective contributors to decision making.

Finally, if participative decision making is to work, people must be able to see how it provides a personal benefit to them. The personal payoff for the individual need not be short term. It may be a long-term benefit that results in people receiving greater rewards through enhanced organizational profitability.

Volvo Car Corporation

## What Level of Participation?

Participative decision making is complex, and managers must understand is that employees can be involved in some, or all, of the stages of the decision-making process. For example, employees could be variously involved in identifying problems, generating alternatives, selecting solutions, planning implementations, or evaluating results. Research shows that greater involvement in all five of these stages has a cumulative effect. Employees who are involved in all five processes have higher satisfaction and performance levels. And, all decision processes are not created equal. If employees can't be provided with full participation in all stages, the highest payoffs seem to come with involvement in generating alternatives, planning implementations, and evaluating results.[114] Styles of participation in decision making may need to change as the company grows or as its culture changes.

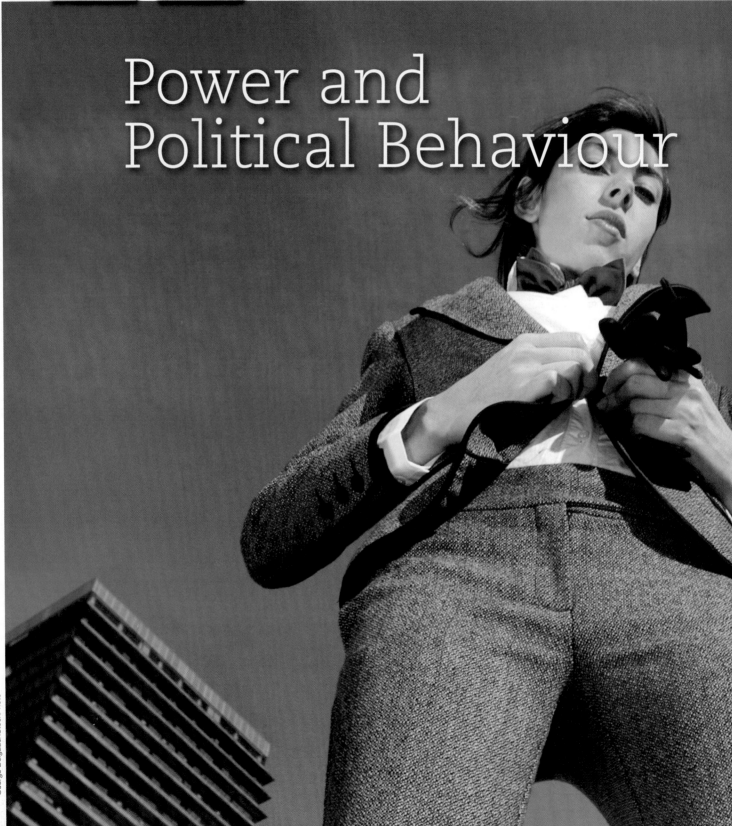

# Power and
# Political Behaviour

> ## " *Because power is an ability, individuals can learn to use it effectively.* "

# The Concept of Power

**Power** is the ability to influence someone else. As an exchange relationship, it occurs in transactions between an agent and a target. The agent is the person using the power, and the target is the recipient of the attempt to use power.[1] Power is often described as a relationship of asymmetric dependence. To the extent A depends on B, then B has power over A. Power is ". . . a dynamic quantity and its characteristics change together with the changes in the asymmetrical dependence between the object and the subject of impact."[2]

Clegg, Courpasson, and Phillips, in their seminal book, *Power and Organizations*, highlight a useful distinction about power. They distinguish between *power to* and *power over*. *Power to* suggests that power can be used for positive impact—to extend freedom—while *power over* suggests that power can be used to prohibit behaviours—to limit freedom. In our quotidian experiences in organizations, we often experience power over, as there are rules, reinforced by sanctions, that direct our activities. However, there may be individual differences in how we respond to the effects of power.

Power itself isn't 'over' or 'to' in a transcendent way; it is "over" or "to" depending on the specific situation and the contingent position of the agents involved in the relation.[3]

Because power is an ability, individuals can learn to use it effectively. **Influence** is the process of affecting the thoughts, behaviour, and feelings of another person. **Authority**

**power**
The ability to influence another person, a relationship of assymetric dependence.

**influence**
The process of affecting the thoughts, behaviour, and feelings of another person.

**authority**
The right to influence another person.

---

## LEARNING OUTCOMES

After reading this chapter, you should be able to do the following:

**1** Describe the concept of power.

**2** Identify forms and sources of power in organizations.

**3** Describe the role of ethics in using power.

**4** Identify symbols of power and powerlessness in organizations.

**5** Define *organizational politics* and understand the role of political skill and major influence tactics.

**6** Identify ways to manage political behaviour in organizations.

## Politics Can BackFIRE

Failures to understand power and politics can be costly in terms of your career. To prevent American Airlines from having to file bankruptcy, a Torontonian whose career included working at Air Canada and Canadian Pacific Railway, CEO Donald Carty successfully negotiated steep pay cuts from unions resulting in savings to the company of over a billion dollars. The announcement of the landmark agreement was tarnished, however, by the news that American Airlines executives, including Carty, had received special pension trust funding and huge retention bonuses. Carty spent the next three-and-a-half weeks apologizing and returning money before falling on his sword. Political behaviour can achieve desired results, but it can also backfire if trust is breached.

SOURCE: Reuters Limited, "Canadian Carty Had Rough Ride at American Airlines," *USA Today* (April 25, 2003), http://www.usatoday.com/travel/news/2003/2003-04-25-aa-carty-profile.htm.

the range in which attempts to influence the employee are perceived as legitimate and are acted on without a great deal of thought.[5] The term *zone of indifference* may be better described as the *zone of unquestioning compliance*. The employee accepts that the manager has the authority to request such behaviours and complies with the requests. Some requests, however, fall outside the zone of indifference, so the manager must work to enlarge the employee's zone of indifference. Enlarging the zone is accomplished with power (an ability) rather than with authority (a right).

Suppose the manager asks the employee to purchase a birthday gift for the manager's spouse or to overcharge a customer for a service call. The employee may think that the manager has no right to ask these things. These requests fall outside the zone of indifference. They're viewed as extraordinary, and the manager has to operate from outside the authority base to induce the employee to fulfill them. In some cases, no power base is enough to induce the employee to comply, especially if the behaviours requested by the manager are considered unethical by the employee.

# Forms and Sources of Power in Organizations

Individuals have many forms of power to use in their work settings. Some of them are interpersonal—used in interactions with others. One of the earliest and most influential theories of power comes from John French and Bertram Raven, who tried to determine the sources of power managers use to influence other people.

## Interpersonal Forms of Power

French and Raven identified five forms of interpersonal power that managers use. They are reward, legitimate, referent, expert, and coercive power.[6]

**Reward power** is power based on the agent's ability to control rewards that a target wants. For example, managers control the rewards of salary increases, bonuses, and promotions. Reward power can lead to better performance, but only as long as the employee sees a clear and strong link between performance and rewards. To use reward power effectively, then, the manager should be explicit about the behaviour being rewarded and should make the connection clear between the behaviour and the reward.

**Legitimate power**, which is similar to authority, is power that is based on position and mutual agreement. The

is the right to influence another person.[4] It is important to understand the subtle differences among these terms. For instance, a manager may have authority but no power. She may have the right, by virtue of her position as boss, to tell someone what to do. But she may not have the skill or ability to influence other people.

In a relationship between the agent and the target, there are many influence attempts that the target considers legitimate. Working 40 hours per week, greeting customers, solving problems, and collecting bills are actions that, when requested by the manager, are considered legitimate by a customer service representative. Requests such as these fall within the employee's **zone of indifference**—

**zone of indifference**

The range in which attempts to influence a person will be perceived as legitimate and will be acted on without a great deal of thought.

**reward power**

Power based on an agent's ability to control rewards that a target wants.

**legitimate power**

Power that is based on position and mutual agreement; agent and target agree that the agent has the right to influence the target.

> ## The most effective power bases—referent and expert— are ones that must be developed and strengthened through interpersonal relationships with employees.

agent and target agree that the agent has the right to influence the target. It doesn't matter that a manager thinks he has the right to influence his employees; for legitimate power to be effective, the employees must also believe the manager has the right to tell them what to do. In North American native societies, the chief has legitimate power; tribe members believe in his/her right to influence their decisions.

**Referent power** is an elusive power that is based on interpersonal attraction. The agent has referent power over the target because the target identifies with or wants to be like the agent. Charismatic individuals are often thought to have referent power. Interestingly, the agent need not be superior to the target in any way. People who use referent power well are most often individualistic and respected by the target.

**Expert power** is the power that exists when the agent has specialized knowledge or skills that the target needs. For expert power to work, three conditions must be in place. First, the target must trust that the expertise given is accurate. Second, the knowledge involved must be relevant and useful to the target. Third, the target's perception of the agent as an expert is crucial. Using easy-to-understand language signals to the target that the expert has an appreciation for real-world concerns and increases the target's trust in the expert.[7]

**Coercive power** is power that is based on the agent's ability to cause the target to have an unpleasant experience. To coerce someone into doing something means to force the person to do it, often with threats of punishment. Managers using coercive power may verbally abuse employees or withhold support from them.

Which type of interpersonal power is most effective? Research has focused on this question since French and Raven introduced their five forms of power. Some of the results are surprising. Reward power and coercive power have similar effects.[8] Both lead to compliance. That is, employees will do what the manager asks them to, at least temporarily, if the manager offers a reward or threatens them with punishment. Reliance on these sources of power is dangerous, however, because it may require the manager to be physically present and watchful in order to apply rewards or punishment when the behaviour occurs. Constant surveillance creates an uncomfortable situation for managers and employees and eventually results in a dependency relationship. Employees will not work unless the manager is present.

Legitimate power also leads to compliance. When told "Do this because I'm your boss," most employees will comply. However, the use of legitimate power has not been linked to organizational effectiveness or to employee satisfaction.[9] In organizations where managers rely heavily on legitimate power, organizational goals are not necessarily met.

Referent power is linked with organizational effectiveness. It is the most dangerous power, however, because it can be too extensive and intensive in altering the behaviour of others. Charismatic leaders need an accompanying sense of responsibility for others. Rick Hansen's referent power makes him a powerful spokesperson for research on spinal cord research and making communities more inclusive and accessible.

Expert power has been called the power of the future.[10] Of the five forms of power, it has the strongest relationship with performance and satisfaction. It is through expert power that vital skills, abilities, and knowledge are passed on within the organization. Employees internalize what they observe and learn from managers they perceive to be experts.

The results on the effectiveness of these five forms of power pose a challenge in organizations. The least effective power bases—legitimate, reward, and coercive—are the ones most likely to be used by managers.[11] Managers inherit these power bases as part of the position when they take a supervisory job. In contrast, the most effective power bases—referent and expert—are ones that must be developed and strengthened through interpersonal relationships with employees. Marissa Mayer, vice president of search products and user experience at Google, is well respected and liked by her colleagues. She is described as someone with a lot of technical knowledge, and she is comfortable in social environments. This represents her expert power and referent power—she has an advanced degree in computer science from Stanford University and is known for her ability to connect with people. At 33 years old, she has had a very successful career at Google

**referent power**
An elusive power that is based on interpersonal attraction.

**expert power**
The power that exists when an agent has specialized knowledge or skills that the target needs.

**coercive power**
Power that is based on an agent's ability to cause an unpleasant experience for a target.

and is one of the most powerful female executives in North America.[12] Expert power and social networks help CEOs influence their top management teams in ways that are profitable for the firm.

## Bullying in Organizations

Bullying is not a concern limited to the educational system. Bullying, a form of coercive power, has become a concern in all kinds of workplaces. Bullying behaviour can contribute to creating toxic workplaces, i.e., "a place where people come to work so they can make enough money so they can leave."[13] Bullying in the workplace has been defined as

> . . . repeated, health-harming mistreatment of a person by one or more workers that takes the form of verbal abuse; conduct or behaviours that are threatening, intimidating, or humiliating; sabotage that prevents work from getting done; or some combination of the three.[14]

According to the Workplace Bullying Institute's survey of 7,740 adults in 2007, 37 percent of workers had been bullied at work and 12 percent had witnessed bullying. Half of the reported bullying occurred in public but the other half did not. The majority of bullies were men (60 percent) and the majority who were bullied were women (57 percent). The research identified the top 10 bullying tactics in the workplace: (1) blame for errors, (2) unreasonable job demands, (3) criticism of ability, (4) inconsistent compliance with rules, (5) threatening job loss, (6) insults and put-downs, (7) discounting or denial of successes, (8) exclusion, (9) yelling and screaming, and (10) stealing credit.[15] Table 11.1 describes the main bully types and gives guidance on managing each type.

## Intergroup Sources of Power

Groups or teams within an organization can also use power from several sources. One source of intergroup power is control of *critical resources*.[16] When one group controls an important resource that another group desires, such as money, the

**strategic contingencies**
Activities that other groups depend on in order to complete their tasks.

### TABLE 11.1 Types of Bullies and Tactics to Manage Them

| BULLY TYPES | KEY TACTICS |
|---|---|
| Screamer | Ignore the anger. |
| Constant Critic | Rely on humour and get a second opinion. |
| Two-headed Snake (Backstabber, Jekyll-and-Hyde or Rule Violator) | Enlist allies and resist fighting. |
| Gatekeeper (Controller) | Discuss your feelings with gatekeeper. |

SOURCE: Adapted from Namie, G. and R. Namie, *The Bully at Work*, Second Edition (Naperville, Illinois: Sourcebooks, Inc., 2009).

first group holds power. Controlling resources needed by another group allows the power-holding group to influence the actions of the less powerful group. This process can continue in an upward spiral. Groups seen as powerful tend to be given more resources from top management.[17]

Groups also have power to the extent that they control **strategic contingencies**—activities that other groups depend on in order to complete their tasks.[18] The dean's office, for example, may control the number of faculty positions to be filled in each department of a college. The departmental hiring plans are thus contingent on approval from the dean's office. In this case, the dean's office controls the strategic contingency of faculty hiring, and thus has power.

Three factors can give a group control over a strategic contingency.[19] One is the *ability to cope with uncertainty*. If a group can help another group deal with uncertainty, it has power. One organizational group that has gained power in recent years is the legal department. Faced with increasing government regulations and fears of litigation, many other departments seek guidance from the legal department.

Another factor that can give a group control power is a *high degree of centrality* within the organization. If a group's functioning is important to the organization's success, it has high centrality. The sales force in a computer firm, for example, has power because of its immediate effect on the firm's operations and because other groups (accounting and servicing groups, for example) depend on its activities.

The third factor that can give a group power is *nonsubstitutability*—the extent to which a group performs a function that is indispensable to an organization. A team of computer specialists may be powerful because of its expertise with a system. It may have specialized experience that another team cannot provide.

The strategic contingencies model thus shows that groups hold power over other groups when they can reduce uncertainty, when their functioning is central to the organization's success, and when the group's activities are difficult to replace.[20] The key to all three of these factors, as you can see, is dependency. When one group controls something that another group needs, it creates a dependent relationship—and gives one group power over the other.

It can be useful to create influence maps so that you see the distribution of power in organizations. In one study, 3,000 managers were surveyed to see if there was a fit between their hierarchical level and their power. The study revealed that many managers were quite powerless and that their departments suffered a power vacuum.[21]

LEARNING OUTCOME 3

# Using Power Ethically

Managers can work at developing all five forms of power for future use. The key to using them well is using them ethically, as Table 11.2 shows. Coercive power, for example, requires careful administration if it is to be used in an ethical manner. Employees should be informed of the rules in advance, and any punishment should be used consistently, uniformly, and privately. The key to using all five types of interpersonal power ethically is to be sensitive to employees' concerns and to communicate well.

To French and Raven's five power sources, we can add a source that is very important in today's organizations. **Information power** is access to and control over important information. Consider, for example, the CEO's administrative assistant. He or she has information about the CEO's schedule that people need if they are going to get in to see the CEO. Central to the idea of information power is the person's position in the communication networks in the organization, both formal and informal. Also important is the idea of framing, which is the spin that managers put on information. Managers not only pass information on to subordinates but also interpret this information and influence the subordinates' perceptions of it. Information power occurs not only in the downward direction; it also may flow upward from subordinates to managers. In manufacturing plants, database operators often control information about plant metrics and shipping performance that is vital to managerial decision making. Information power can also flow laterally. Salespeople convey information from the outside environment (their customers) that is essential for marketing efforts.

Determining whether a power-related behaviour is ethical is complex. Another way to look at the ethics surrounding the use of power is to ask three questions that show the criteria for examining power-related behaviours:[22]

 *Does the behaviour produce a good outcome for people both inside and outside the organization?* This question represents the criterion of *utilitarian outcomes.* The behaviour should result in the greatest good for the greatest number of people. If the power-related behaviour serves only the individual's self-interest and fails to help the organization reach its goals, it is considered unethical.

**information power**
Access to and control over important information.

**TABLE 11.2** Guidelines for the Ethical Use of Power

| FORM OF POWER | GUIDELINES FOR USE |
|---|---|
| Reward power | Verify compliance. Make feasible, reasonable requests. Make only ethical requests. Offer rewards desired by subordinates. Offer only credible rewards. |
| Coercive power | Inform subordinates of rules and penalties. Warn before punishing. Administer punishment consistently and uniformly. Understand the situation before acting. Maintain credibility. Fit punishment to the infraction. Punish in private. |
| Legitimate power | Be cordial and polite. Be confident. Be clear and follow up to verify understanding. Make sure request is appropriate. Explain reasons for request. Follow proper channels. Exercise power consistently. Enforce compliance. Be sensitive to subordinates' concerns. |
| Referent power | Treat subordinates fairly. Defend subordinates' interests. Be sensitive to subordinates' needs and feelings. Select subordinates similar to yourself. Engage in role modelling. |
| Expert power | Maintain credibility. Act confidently and decisively. Keep informed. Recognize employee concerns. Avoid threatening subordinates' self-esteem. |

SOURCE: *Leadership in Organizations* by Gary A. Yukl. Copyright © 1981. Reprinted by permission of Pearson Education, Inc., Upper Saddle River, NJ.

>> 
> Does the behaviour produce a good outcome for people both inside and outside the organization?
> Does the behaviour respect the rights of all parties?
> Does the behaviour treat all parties equitably and fairly?

A salesperson might be tempted to discount a product deeply in order to make a sale that would win a contest. Doing so would be in his or her self-interest but would not benefit the organization.

**2** *Does the behaviour respect the rights of all parties?* This question emphasizes the criterion of *individual rights*. Free speech, privacy, and due process are individual rights that are to be respected, and power-related behaviours that violate these rights are considered unethical.

**3** Does the *behaviour treat all parties equitably and fairly?* This question represents the criterion of *distributive justice*. Power-related behaviour that treats one party arbitrarily or benefits one party at the expense of another is unethical. Granting a day of vacation to one employee in a busy week in which coworkers must struggle to cover for him or her might be considered unethical.

To be considered ethical, power-related behaviour must meet all three criteria. If the behaviour fails to meet the criteria, then alternative actions should be considered. Unfortunately, most power-related behaviours are not easy to analyze. Conflicts may exist among the criteria; for example, a behaviour may maximize the greatest good for the greatest number of people but may not treat all parties equitably. Individual rights may need to be sacrificed for the good of the organization. A CEO may need to be removed from power for the organization to be saved. Still, these criteria can be used on a case-by-case basis to sort through the complex ethical issues surrounding the use of power. The ethical use of power is one of the hottest topics in the current business arena,

**personal power**
Power used for personal gain.

due to the abuse of power by top executives at several firms such as Enron and Livent Inc.

In 2009, Garth Drabinsky and Myron Gottlieb, co-founders of Livent Inc., were convicted of fraud and forgery. The judge noted that although the two had created successful stage productions that garnered them acclaim, they had done so "on a platform of falsehoods and manipulations" by artificially overstating the company's profits and understating its costs to bilk investors of $500 million.[23]

## Positive versus Negative Power

We turn now to a theory of power that takes a strong stand on the "right" versus "wrong" kind of power to use in organizations. David McClelland has spent a great deal of his career studying the need for power and the ways managers use power. As was discussed in Chapter 5, he believes that there are two distinct faces of power, one negative and one positive.[24] The negative face of power is **personal power**—power used for personal gain. Managers who use personal power are commonly described as "power hungry." People who approach relationships with an exchange orientation often use personal power to ensure that they get at least their fair share—and often more—in the relationship. They are most interested in their own needs and interests. One way to encourage ethical behaviour in organizations is to encourage principled dissent. This refers to valid criticism that can benefit the organization rather than mere complaints about working conditions. Much like whistle-blowers, who can serve as checks on powerful people within the organization, dissenters can pinpoint wrongdoings, encourage employee voice in key issues and create a climate conducive to ethical use of power.[25]

## [ Conrad Black's Troubles ]

In 2007, Conrad Black, Lord Black of Crossharbour, was found guilty of one count of mail fraud and two counts that involved an artificial noncompete agreement that paid him and his colleagues not to compete against themselves. He was sentenced to 6.5 years and served over two years in a Florida prison until he was released on bail in July 2010. His first reported unethical behaviour occurred when he was 14 and was expelled from Upper Canada College for stealing and then selling exams to his fellow students. Black was known for his lavish lifestyle as well as being a friend of such people as Henry Kissinger and Margaret Thatcher. He renounced his Canadian citizenship in 2001 so he could become a member of the House of Lords. Before his fall, he had created the third largest newspaper company in the world, owning papers such as the *National Post*, the *Jerusalem Post* and *The Daily Telegraph*.

SOURCE: R. Siklos, "Conrad Black's Downfall Shaped by Many Battles," *The New York Times* (July 14, 2007). http://www.nytimes.com/2007/07/14/business/14react.html?_r=1&th&emc=th&oref=slogin.

Individuals who rely on personal power at its extreme might be considered Machiavellian—willing to do whatever it takes to get their own way. Niccolo Machiavelli was an Italian statesman during the 16th century who wrote *The Prince,* a guide for acquiring and using power.[26] Among his methods for using power was manipulating others, believing that it was better to be feared than loved. Machiavellians (or high Machs) are willing to manipulate others for personal gain, and are unconcerned with others' opinions or welfare.

The positive face of power is **social power**—power used to create motivation or to accomplish group goals. McClelland clearly favours the use of social power by managers. People who approach relationships with a communal orientation focus on the needs and interests of others. They rely on social power.[27] McClelland has found that managers who use power successfully have four power-oriented characteristics:

1. *Belief in the authority system.* They believe that the institution is important and that its authority system is valid. They are comfortable influencing and being influenced. The source of their power is the authority system of which they are a part.

2. *Preference for work and discipline.* They like their work and are very orderly. They have a basic value preference for the work ethic, believing that work is good for a person over and beyond its income-producing value.

3. *Altruism.* They publicly put the organization and its needs before their own needs. They are able to do so because they see their own well-being as integrally tied to the organization's well-being.

4. *Belief in justice.* They believe justice is to be sought above all else. People should receive that to which they are entitled and that which they earn.

McClelland takes a definite stand on the proper use of power by managers. When power is used for the good of the group, rather than for individual gain, it is positive.

LEARNING OUTCOME **4**

# Symbols of Power

Organization charts show who has authority, but they do not reveal much about who has power. We'll now look at two very different ideas about the symbols of power. The first one comes from Rosabeth Moss Kanter. It is a scholarly approach to determining who has power and who feels powerless. The second is a look at the tangible symbols of power by Michael Korda.

## Kanter's Symbols of Power

Kanter provides several characteristics of powerful people in organizations:[28]

1. *Ability to intercede for someone in trouble.* An individual who can pull someone out of a jam has power.

2. *Ability to get placements for favoured employees.* Getting a key promotion for an employee is a sign of power.

3. *Exceeding budget limitations.* A manager who can go above budget limits without being reprimanded has power.

4. *Procuring above-average raises for employees.* One faculty member reported that her department head distributed 10 percent raises to the most productive faculty members although the budget allowed for only 4 percent increases. "I don't know how he did it; he must have pull," she said.

5. *Getting items on the agenda at meetings.* If a manager can raise issues for action at meetings, it's a sign of power.

6. *Access to early information.* Having information before anyone else does is a signal that a manager is plugged into key sources.

**social power**
Power used to create motivation or to accomplish group goals.

©OSTILL/iStockPhoto

**What can you do when you recognize that employees are feeling powerless?**

**The key to overcoming powerlessness is to share power and delegate decision-making authority to employees.**

7. *Having top managers seek out their opinion.* When top managers have a problem, they may ask for advice from lower-level managers. The managers they turn to have power.

A theme that runs through Kanter's list is doing things for others: for people in trouble, for employees, for bosses. There is an active, other-directed element in her symbols of power.

You can use Kanter's symbols of power to identify powerful people in organizations. They can be particularly useful in finding a mentor who can effectively use power.

## Kanter's Symbols of Powerlessness

Kanter also wrote about symptoms of **powerlessness**—a lack of power—in managers at different levels of the organization. First-line supervisors, for example, often display three symptoms of powerlessness: overly close supervision, inflexible adherence to the rules, and a tendency to do the job themselves rather than training their employees to do it. Staff professionals such as accountants and lawyers display different symptoms of powerlessness. When they feel powerless, they tend to resist change and try to protect their turf. Top executives can also feel powerless. They show symptoms such as focusing on budget cutting, punishing others, and using dictatorial, top-down communication. Acting in certain ways can lead employees to believe that a manager is powerless. By making external attributions (blaming others or circumstances) for negative events, a manager looks as if he or she has no power.[29]

## Korda's Symbols of Power

Michael Korda takes a different look at symbols of power in organizations.[30] He discusses three unusual symbols: office furnishings, time power, and standing by.

Furniture is not just physically useful; it also conveys a message about power. Locked file cabinets are signs that the manager has important and confidential information in the office. A rectangular (rather than round) conference table enables the most important person to sit at the head of the table. The size of a person's desk may convey the amount of power. Most executives prefer large, expensive desks.

Time power means using clocks and watches as power symbols. Korda says that the biggest compliment a busy executive can pay a visitor is to remove his watch and place it face down on the desk, thereby communicating "my time is yours." He also notes that the less powerful the executive, the more intricate the watch; moreover, managers who are really secure in their power wear no watch at all, since they believe nothing important can happen without them. A full calendar is also proof of power. Personal planners are left open on the desk to display busy schedules.

Standing by is a game in which people are obliged to keep their cell phones, pagers, etc. with them at all times so executives can reach them. The idea is that the more you can impose your schedule on other people, the more power you have. In fact, Korda defines *power* as follows: There are more people who inconvenience themselves on your behalf than there are people on whose behalf you would inconvenience yourself. Closely tied to this is the ability to make others perform simple tasks for you, such as getting your coffee or fetching the mail.

While Kanter's symbols focus on the ability to help others, Korda's symbols focus on status—a person's relative standing in a group based on prestige and having other people defer to him or her.[31] By identifying powerful people and learning vicariously from their behaviours, you can learn the keys to power use in the organization.

# Political Behaviour in Organizations

Like power, the term *politics in organizations* may conjure up a few negative images. However, **organizational politics** is not necessarily negative; it is the use of power and influence in organizations. Because organizations are arenas in which people have competing interests, effective managers must reconcile competing interests. Organizational politics are central to managing. As people try to acquire power and expand their power base, they use various tactics and strategies. Some are sanctioned (acceptable to the organization); others are not. **Political behaviour** refers to actions not officially sanctioned by an organization that are taken to influence others in order to meet personal goals.[32] Sometimes personal goals are aligned with team or organizational goals, and they can be achieved in support of others' interests. But other times personal goals and the interests of others collide, and individuals pursue politics at the expense of others' interests.[33]

Politics is a controversial topic among managers. Some managers take a favourable view of political behaviour; others see it as detrimental to the organization. Some workers who perceive their workplace as highly political actually find the

**powerlessness**
A lack of power.

**organizational politics**
The use of power and influence in organizations.

**political behaviour**
Actions not officially sanctioned by an organization that are taken to influence others in order to meet personal goals.

use of political tactics more satisfying and report greater job satisfaction when they engage in political behaviour. Some people may therefore thrive in political environments, while others may find office politics distasteful and stressful.[34]

Most people are also amazingly good at recognizing political behaviour at all levels of the organization. Employees are not only keenly aware of political behaviour at their level but also can spot political behaviour at both their supervisor's level and the topmost levels of the organization.[35]

Many organizational conditions encourage political activity. Among them are unclear goals, autocratic decision making, ambiguous lines of authority, scarce resources, and uncertainty.[36] Even supposedly objective activities may involve politics. One such activity is the performance appraisal process. A study of 60 executives who had extensive experience in employee evaluation indicated that political considerations were nearly always part of the performance appraisal process.[37]

The effects of political behaviour in organizations can be quite negative when the political behaviour is strategically undertaken to maximize self-interest. If people within the organization are competitively pursuing selfish ends, they're unlikely to be attentive to the concerns of others. The workplace can seem less helpful, more threatening, and more unpredictable. People focus on their own concerns rather than on organizational goals. This represents the negative face of power described earlier by David McClelland as personal power. If employees view the organization's political climate as extreme, they experience more anxiety, tension, fatigue, and burnout. They are also dissatisfied with their jobs and are more likely to leave.[38] Not all political behaviour is destructive. Constructive political behaviour is selfless, rather than selfish, in nature. In this respect, it is similar to David McClelland's concept of social power. Constructive organizational politicians see the difference between ethical and unethical behaviour, understand that relationships drive the political process, and use power with a sense of responsibility.[39]

## Influence Tactics

*Influence* is the process of affecting the thoughts, behaviour, or feelings of another person. That other person could be the boss (upward influence), an employee (downward influence), or a coworker (lateral influence). There are eight basic types of influence tactics. They are listed and described in Table 11.3 on page 184.[40]

Research has shown that the four tactics used most frequently are consultation, rational persuasion, inspirational appeals, and ingratiation. Upward appeals and coalition tactics are used moderately. Exchange tactics are used least often.

Influence tactics are used for impression management, which was described in Chapter 3. In impression management, individuals use influence tactics to control others' impressions of them. One way in which people engage in impression management is through image building. Another way is to use impression management to get support for important initiatives or projects.

Ingratiation is an example of one tactic often used for impression management. Ingratiation can take many forms, including flattery, opinion conformity, and subservient behaviour.[41] Exchange is another influence tactic that may be used for impression management. Offering to do favours for someone in an effort to create a favourable impression is an exchange tactic.

Which influence tactics are most effective? It depends on the target of the influence attempt and the objective. Individuals use different tactics for different purposes, and they use different tactics for different people. Influence attempts with subordinates, for example, usually involve assigning tasks or changing behaviour. With peers, the objective is often to request help. With superiors, influence attempts are often made to request approval, resources, political support, or personal benefits. Rational persuasion and coalition tactics are used most often to get support from peers and superiors to change policy. Consultation and inspirational appeals are particularly effective for gaining support and resources for a new project.[42] Overall, the most effective tactic in terms of achieving objectives is rational persuasion. Pressure is the least effective tactic.

## TABLE 11.3 Influence Tactics Used in Organizations

| TACTICS | DESCRIPTION | EXAMPLES |
|---|---|---|
| Pressure | The person uses demands, threats, or intimidation to convince you to comply with a request or to support a proposal. | If you don't do this, you're fired. You have until 5:00 to change your mind, or I'm going without you. |
| Upward appeals | The person seeks to persuade you that the request is approved by higher management or appeals to higher management for assistance in gaining your compliance with the request. | I'm reporting you to my boss. My boss supports this idea. |
| Exchange | The person makes an explicit or implicit promise that you will receive rewards or tangible benefits if you comply with a request or support a proposal or reminds you of a prior favour to be reciprocated. | You owe me! I'll take you to lunch if you'll support me. |
| Coalition | The person seeks the aid of others to persuade you to do something or uses the support of others as an argument for you to agree also. | All the other supervisors agree with me. I'll ask you in front of the whole committee. |
| Ingratiation | The person seeks to get you in a good mood or to think favourably of him or her before asking you to do something. | Only you can do this job right. I can always count on you, so I have another request. |
| Rational persuasion | The person uses logical arguments and factual evidence to persuade you that a proposal or request is viable and likely to result in the attainment of task objectives. | This new procedure will save us $150,000 in overhead. It makes sense to hire John; he has the most experience. |
| Inspirational appeals | The person makes an emotional request or proposal that arouses enthusiasm by appealing to your values and ideals or by increasing your confidence that you can do it. | Being environmentally conscious is the right thing. Getting that account will be tough, but I know you can do it. |
| Consultation | The person seeks your participation in making a decision or planning how to implement a proposed policy, strategy, or change. | This new attendance plan is controversial. How can we make it more acceptable? What do you think we can do to make our workers less fearful of the new robots on the production line? |

SOURCE: First two columns from G. Yukl and C. M. Falbe, "Influence Tactics and Objectives in Upward, Downward, and Lateral Influence Attempts," *Journal of Applied Psychology* 75 (1990): 132–140. Copyright © 1990 by the American Psychological Association. Reprinted with permission.

Influence tactics are often used on bosses in order to get the boss to evaluate the employee more favourably or to give the employee a promotion. Two tactics—rational persuasion and ingratiation—appear to work effectively. Employees who use these tactics receive higher performance evaluations than other employees who don't use rational persuasion and ingratiation.[43] When supervisors believe an employee's motive for doing favours for the boss is simply to be a good citizen, they are likely to reward that employee. However, when the motive is seen as brownnosing (ingratiation), supervisors respond negatively.[44] And, as it becomes more obvious that the employee has something to gain by impressing the boss, the likelihood that ingratiation will succeed decreases. So, how does you use ingratiation effectively?

Results from a study conducted among supervisors and subordinates of a large agency indicate that subordinates with higher scores on political skill used ingratiation regularly and received higher performance ratings whereas individuals with lower scores on political skill who used ingratiation frequently received lower performance ratings.[45] Additionally, another research study demonstrated that supervisors rated subordinate ingratiation behaviour as less manipulative if the subordinate was highly politically skilled.[46] These results indicate that political skill might be one factor that enables people to use ingratiation effectively.

Still, a well-disguised ingratiation can be hard to resist. Attempts that are not obvious usually succeed in increasing the target's liking for the ingratiator.[47] Most people have trouble remaining neutral when someone flatters them or agrees with them. However, witnesses to the ingratiation are more likely to question the motive behind the flattery or agreement. Observers are more skeptical than the recipients of the ingratiation.

There is evidence that men and women view politics and influence attempts differently. Men tend to view political behaviour more favourably than do women. When both men and women witness political behaviour, they view it more positively if the agent is of their gender and the target is of the opposite gender.[48] Women executives often view politics with distaste and expect to be recognized and promoted only on the merit of their work. A lack of awareness of organizational politics is a barrier that holds women back in terms of moving into senior executive ranks.[49] Women may have fewer opportunities to develop political skills because of a lack of mentors and role models and because they are often excluded from informal networks.[50]

Different cultures prefer different influence tactics at work. One study found that North American managers dealing with a tardy employee tended to rely on pressure tactics such as "If you don't start reporting on time for work, I will have no choice but to start docking your pay." In contrast, Japanese managers relied on influence tactics that either appealed to the employee's sense of duty ("It is your duty as a responsible employee of this company to begin work on time.") or emphasized a consultative approach ("Is there anything I can do to help you overcome the problems that are preventing you from coming to work on time?").[51]

It is important to note that influence tactics do have some positive effects. When investors form coalitions and put pressure on firms to increase their research and development efforts, it works.[52] However, some influence tactics, including pressure, coalition building, and exchange, can have strong ethical implications. There is a fine line between being an impression manager and being seen as a manipulator.

How can a manager use influence tactics well? First, a manager can develop and maintain open lines of communication in all directions: upward, downward, and lateral. Then, the manager can treat the targets of influence attempts—whether managers, employees, or peers—with basic respect. Finally, the manager can understand that influence relationships are reciprocal—they are two-way relationships. As long as the influence attempts are directed toward organizational goals, the process of influence can be advantageous to all involved.

## Political Skill

Researchers have generated an impressive body of research on political skill.[53] **Political skill** is a distinct interpersonal attribute that is important for managerial success. Researchers suggest that that political skill should be considered in hiring and promotion decisions. They found that leader political skill has a positive effect on team performance, trust for the leader, and support for the leader.[54] Furthermore, political skill buffers the negative effects of stressors such as role conflict in work settings. This set of research findings points to the importance of developing political skill for managerial success.[55]

So what exactly is political skill? It is the ability to get things done through positive interpersonal relationships outside the formal organization. Politically skilled individuals have the ability to accurately understand others and use this knowledge to influence others in order to meet personal or organizational goals. Political skill is made up of four key dimensions; social astuteness, interpersonal influence, networking ability, and sincerity. Social astuteness refers to accurate perception and evaluation of social situations. Socially astute individuals manage social situations in ways that present them in the most favourable light.

Interpersonal influence refers to a subtle and influential personal style that is effective in getting things done. Individuals with interpersonal influence are very flexible in adapting their behaviour to differing targets of influence or differing contexts in order to achieve their goals. Networking ability is an individual's capacity to develop and retain diverse and extensive social networks. People who have networking ability are effective in building successful alliances and coalitions, thus making them skilled at negotiation and conflict resolution. Sincerity refers to an individual's ability to portray forthrightness and authenticity in all of his/her dealings. Individuals who can appear sincere inspire more confidence and trust, thus making them very successful in influencing other people.[56]

Each of the four dimensions of political skill can be learned. Some organizations now offer training to help develop their employees' political skill. And, political skill is important at all levels of the organization. The most potent cause of failure among top executives is lack of social effectiveness.[57] High self-monitors and politically savvy individuals score higher on an index of political skill, as do individuals who are emotionally intelligent.

Military settings are particularly demanding in their need for leaders who can adapt to changing situations and maintain a good reputation. In such an environment, politically skilled leaders are seen as more

**political skill**
The ability to get things done through favourable interpersonal relationships outside formally prescribed organizational mechanisms.

sincere in their motives, can more readily perceive and adapt to work events, and thus build a strong positive reputation among followers. In fact, political skill can be acquired through a social learning process and by having a strong mentor. Such a mentor then serves as a role model and helps the protégé navigate organizational politics and helps him or her learn the informal sources of power and politics in the organization.[58]

**What about You? on the Chapter 11 Review Card helps you assess your political skill.**

LEARNING OUTCOME **6**

# Managing Political Behaviour in Organizations

Politics cannot and should not be eliminated from organizations. Managers can, however, take a proactive stance and manage the political behaviour that inevitably occurs.[59]

Open communication is one key to managing political behaviour. Uncertainty tends to increase political behaviour, and communication that reduces the uncertainty is important. One way to open communication is to clarify the sanctioned and nonsanctioned political behaviours in the organization. For example, managers may want to encourage social power as opposed to personal power.[60]

Another key is to clarify expectations regarding performance. This can be accomplished through the use of clear, quantifiable goals and through the establishment of a clear connection between goal accomplishment and rewards.[61]

Participative management is yet another key. Often, people engage in political behaviour when they feel excluded from decision-making processes in the organization. By including them, you will encourage positive input and eliminate behind-the-scenes manoeuvring.

Encouraging cooperation among work groups is another strategy for managing political behaviour. Managers can instill a unity of purpose among work teams by rewarding cooperative behaviour and by implementing activities that emphasize the integration of team efforts toward common goals.[62]

Managing scarce resources well is also important. An obvious solution to the problem of scarce resources is to increase the resource pool, but few managers have this luxury. Clarifying the resource allocation process and making the connection between performance and resources explicit can help discourage dysfunctional political behaviour.

Providing a supportive organizational climate is another way to manage political behaviour effectively. A supportive climate allows employees to discuss controversial issues promptly and openly. This prevents the issue from festering and potentially causing friction among employees.[63]

Managing political behaviour at work is important. The perception of dysfunctional political behaviour can lead to dissatisfaction.[64] When employees perceive that there are dominant interest groups or cliques at work, they are less satisfied with pay and promotions. When they believe that the organization's reward practices are influenced by who you know rather than how well you perform, they are less satisfied.[65] In addition, when employees believe that their coworkers are exhibiting increased political behaviour, they are less satisfied with their coworkers. Open communication, clear expectations about performance and rewards, participative decision-making practices, work group cooperation, effective management of scarce resources, and a supportive organizational climate can help managers prevent the negative consequences of political behaviour.

## Managing Up: Managing the Boss

One of the least discussed aspects of power and politics is the relationship between an individual and his/her boss. This is a crucial relationship, because a boss is the most important link with the rest of the organization.[66] The employee–boss relationship is one of mutual dependence; an individual depends on the boss to give performance feedback, provide resources, and supply critical information. The boss depends on the individual for performance, information, and support. Because it's a mutual relationship, the individual should take an active role in managing it. Too often, the management of this relationship is left to the boss; but if the relationship doesn't meet the individual's needs, chances are that he/she hasn't taken the responsibility to manage it proactively.

Table 11.4 shows the basic steps to take in managing a relationship with the boss. The first step is to try to understand as much as possible about the boss. What are the person's goals and objectives? What kind of pressures does the person face in the job? Many individuals naively expect the boss to be perfect and are disappointed when they find that this is not the case. What are the boss's strengths, weaknesses, and blind spots? Because this is an emotionally charged relationship, it is difficult to be objective; but this is a critical step in forging an effective working relationship. What is the boss's preferred

**Table 11.4** Managing Your Relationship with Your Boss

**Make Sure You Understand Your Boss and Her Context, Including:**
Her goals and objectives.
The pressures on her.
Her strengths, weaknesses, and blind spots.
Her preferred work style.

**Assess Yourself and Your Needs, Including:**
Your own strengths and weaknesses.
Your personal style.
Your predisposition toward dependence on authority figures.

**Develop and Maintain a Relationship that:**
Fits both your needs and styles.
Is characterized by mutual expectations.
Keeps your boss informed.
Is based on dependability and honesty.
Selectively uses your boss's time and resources.

SOURCE: Reprinted by permission of *Harvard Business Review*. From "Managing Your Boss," by J. J. Gabarro and J. P. Kotter, (May-June 1993): p. 155. Copyright © 1993 by the Harvard Business School Publishing Corporation; all rights reserved.

work style? Does the person prefer everything in writing or hate detail? Does the boss prefer that workers make appointments or is dropping in acceptable? The point is to gather as much information as possible.

The second step in managing this important relationship is for the individual to assess himself and his own needs much in the same way he analyzed his boss's. What are the individual's strengths, weaknesses, and blind spots? What is his work style? How does he normally relate to authority figures? Some people have tendencies toward counterdependence; that is, they rebel against the boss as an authority and view the boss as a hindrance to their performance. Or, in contrast, they might take an overdependent stance, passively accepting the employee–boss relationship and treating the boss as an all-wise, protective parent. An individual's knowledge of how he reacts to authority figures can help him understand his interactions with his boss.

Once a worker has tried to understand his boss and done a careful self-analysis, the next step is to work to develop an effective relationship. Both parties' needs and styles must be accommodated. A fundraiser for a large volunteer organization related a story about a new boss, describing him as cold, aloof, unorganized, and inept. She made repeated attempts to meet with him and clarify expec-

tations, and his usual reply was that he didn't have the time. Frustrated, she almost looked for a new job. "I just can't reach him!" was her refrain. Then she stepped back to consider her boss's and her own styles. Being an intuitive-feeling type of person, she prefers constant feedback and reinforcement from others. Her boss, an intuitive-thinker, works comfortably without feedback from others and has a tendency not to praise or reward others. She sat down with him and cautiously discussed the differences in their needs. This discussion became the basis for working out a comfortable relationship. "I still don't like him, but I understand him better," she said.

Another aspect of managing the relationship involves working out mutual expectations. One key activity is to develop a plan for work objectives and have the boss agree to it.[67] It is important to do things right, but it is also important to do the right things. Neither party to the relationship is a mind reader, so clarifying the goals is a crucial step. Keeping the boss informed is also a priority. No one likes to be caught off guard.

The employee–boss relationship must be based on dependability and honesty. This means giving and receiving positive and negative feedback. Most of us are reluctant to give any feedback to the boss, but positive feedback is welcomed at the top. Negative feedback, while tougher to initiate, can clear the air. If given in a problem-solving format, it can even bring about a closer relationship.[68]

Finally, workers need to remember that the boss is on the same team. The golden rule is to make the boss look good, because workers expect the boss to do the same for them.

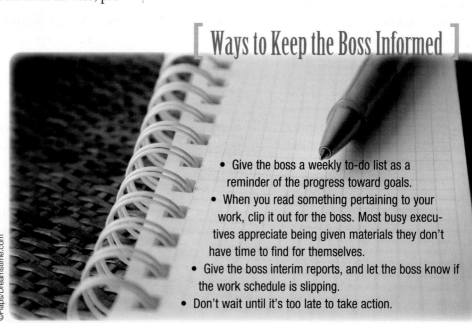

**[ Ways to Keep the Boss Informed ]**

- Give the boss a weekly to-do list as a reminder of the progress toward goals.
- When you read something pertaining to your work, clip it out for the boss. Most busy executives appreciate being given materials they don't have time to find for themselves.
- Give the boss interim reports, and let the boss know if the work schedule is slipping.
- Don't wait until it's too late to take action.

©Flaps/Dreamstime.com

## Sharing Power: Empowerment

Another positive strategy for managing political behaviour is **empowerment**—sharing power within an organization. As modern organizations grow flatter, eliminating layers of management, empowerment becomes more and more important. Jay Conger defines empowerment as "creating conditions for heightened motivation through the development of a strong sense of personal self-efficacy."[69] This means sharing power in such a way that individuals learn to believe in their ability to do the job. The driving idea of empowerment is that the individuals closest to the work and to the customers should make the decisions and that this makes the best use of employees' skills and talents. You can empower yourself by developing your sense of self-efficacy.

Four dimensions comprise the essence of empowerment: meaning, competence, self-determination, and impact.[70] *Meaning* is a fit between the work role and the employee's values and beliefs. It is the engine of empowerment through which employees become energized about their jobs. If employees' hearts are not in their work, they cannot feel empowered. *Competence* is the belief that you have the ability to do the job well. Without competence, employees will feel inadequate and lack a sense of empowerment. *Self-determination* is having control over the way employees do their work. Employees who feel they're just following orders from the boss cannot feel empowered. *Impact* is the belief that your job makes a difference within the organization. Without a sense of contributing to a goal, employees cannot feel empowered.

Employees need to experience all four of the empowerment dimensions in order to feel truly empowered. Only then will organizations reap the hoped-for rewards from empowerment efforts. The rewards sought are increased effectiveness, higher job satisfaction, and less stress.

Empowerment is easy to advocate but difficult to put into practice. Conger offers some guidelines on how leaders can empower others.

First, managers should express confidence in employees and set high performance expectations. Positive expectations can go a long way toward enabling good performance, as the Pygmalion effect shows (see Chapter 3).

Second, managers should create opportunities for employees to participate in decision making. This means participation in the forms of both voice and choice. Employees should not just be asked to contribute their opinions about any issue; they should also have a vote in the decision that is made. One method for increasing participation is using self-managed teams, as we discussed in Chapter 9.

Third, managers should remove bureaucratic constraints that stifle autonomy. Often, organizations have antiquated rules and policies that prevent employees from managing themselves. An example is a collection agency where a manager's signature was once required to approve long-term payment arrangements for delinquent customers. Collectors, who spoke directly with customers, were the best judges of whether the payment arrangements were workable, and having to consult a manager made them feel closely supervised and powerless. The rule was dropped, and collections increased.

Fourth, managers should set inspirational or meaningful goals. When individuals feel they "own" a goal, they are more willing to take personal responsibility for it.

Empowerment is a matter of degree. Jobs can be thought of in two dimensions: job content and job context. Job content consists of the tasks and procedures necessary for doing a particular job. Job context is broader. It is the reason the organization needs the job and includes the way the job fits into the organization's mission, goals, and objectives. These two dimensions are depicted in Figure 11.1 (on page 189), the employee empowerment grid.

**empowerment**

Sharing power within an organization.

## [ Gucci: Fine Fashion, Finer Management ]

Robert Polet, CEO of the Gucci Group, strongly believes in empowering his design teams, so each of Gucci's brands operates autonomously to a large extent. Each team is captained by a creative director who oversees the creative process of design, while a CEO for each team oversees the packaging and advertising part of the business. Polet has articulated a clear vision for Gucci and translated it into clearly defined roles and responsibilities for key organizational players whom he has empowered to carry out the responsibilities effectively. Most importantly, Polet has been adept at emphasizing the importance of the Gucci brand over people associated with it so that employees never lose sight of organizational goals. Polet's principles have worked. Since his arrival at Gucci, income is up 44 percent and some of the company's unprofitable brands are making a turnaround.

SOURCE: J. L. Yang, "Managing Top Talent at Gucci Group," *Fortune* (July 17, 2007). http://money.cnn.com/magazines/fortune/fortune_archive/2007/07/23/100135662/?postversion=2007071710.

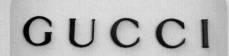

Ingo Schulz/Photolibrary

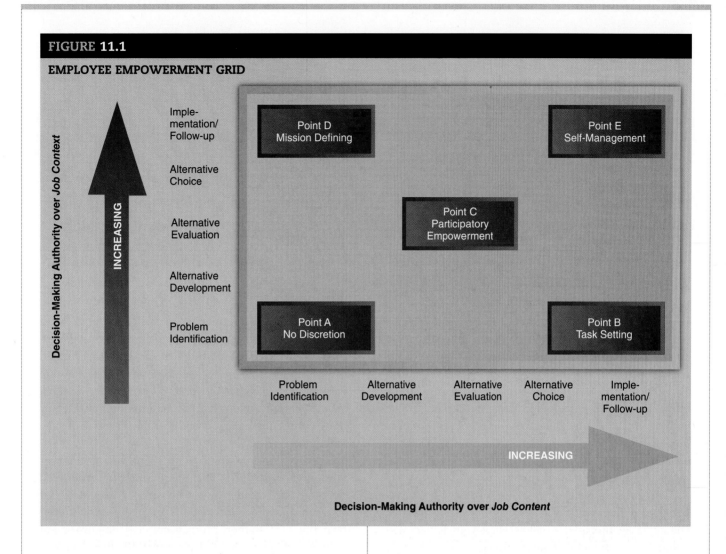

**FIGURE 11.1**

**EMPLOYEE EMPOWERMENT GRID**

*Decision-Making Authority over Job Context* — INCREASING

Imple-mentation/Follow-up
Alternative Choice
Alternative Evaluation
Alternative Development
Problem Identification

Point D — Mission Defining
Point E — Self-Management
Point C — Participatory Empowerment
Point A — No Discretion
Point B — Task Setting

Problem Identification · Alternative Development · Alternative Evaluation · Alternative Choice · Imple-mentation/Follow-up

INCREASING

**Decision-Making Authority over *Job Content***

Both axes of the grid contain the major steps in the decision-making process. As shown on the horizontal axis, decision-making authority over job content increases in terms of greater involvement in the decision-making process. Similarly, the vertical axis shows that authority over job context increases with greater involvement in that decision-making process. Combining job content and job context authority in this way produces five points that vary in terms of the degree of empowerment.[71]

No Discretion (point A) represents the traditional, assembly-line job: highly routine and repetitive, with no decision-making power. Recall from Chapter 7 that if these jobs have a demanding pace and if workers have no discretion, distress will result.

Task Setting (point B) is the essence of most empowerment programs in organizations today. In this case, the worker is empowered to make decisions about the best way to get the job done but has no decision responsibility for the job context.

Participatory Empowerment (point C) represents a situation that is typical of autonomous work groups that have some decision-making power over both job content and job context. Their involvement is in problem identi-

fication, developing alternatives, and evaluating alternatives, but the actual choice of alternatives is often beyond their power. Participatory empowerment can lead to job satisfaction and productivity.

Mission Defining (point D) is an unusual case of empowerment and is seldom seen. Here, employees have power over job context but not job content. An example would be a unionized team that is asked to decide whether their jobs could be better done by an outside vendor. Deciding to outsource would dramatically affect the mission of the company, but would not affect job content, which is specified in the union contract. Assuring these employees of continued employment regardless of their decision would be necessary for this case of empowerment.

Self-Management (point E) represents total decision-making control over both job content and job context. It is the ultimate expression of trust. One example is TXI Chaparral Steel, where employees redesign their own jobs to add value to the organization.

Empowerment should begin with job content and proceed to job context. Because the workforce is so diverse, managers should recognize that some employees

## By The Numbers

**5** types of interpersonal power

**$60,000** cost of birthday party for Conrad Black's wife, much of which allegedly came from Hollinger Inc.

**1515** year *The Prince* was published

**44%** increase in income at Gucci since Robert Polet became CEO

**8** influence tactics used in organizations

are more ready for empowerment than others. Managers must diagnose situations and determine the degree of empowerment to extend to employees. Recently, the management of change in organizations was identified as another area where empowerment can have a strong effect. Employees are more likely to support change done with them than change done to or for them. Empowered employees are more likely to participate in and facilitate change processes in organizations as they feel more committed to the organizations' success.[72]

The empowerment process also carries with it a risk of failure. When you delegate responsibility and authority, you must be prepared to allow employees to fail; and failure is not something most managers tolerate well. At Merck, some say CEO Ray Gilmartin empowered scientists too much and that their failures cost Merck

its profitability and reputation as one of *Fortune*'s Most Admired Companies. One example of this empowerment involved a diabetes drug that early research showed caused tumours in mice. Scientists argued that, despite early studies showing the drug wasn't viable, research should continue, and it did . . . until the drug was finally axed, costing the company considerably in terms of time and money.[73]

This example reminds us that "[power] in empowered organizations is not 'shared power,' where all decisions are made by consensus. It is not about throwing out procedures and letting everyone do their own thing."[74] Rather, "[organizational] empowerment is about ensuring that people can influence decisions commensurate with their positions and interests in the organization."[75]

## Visit **icanorgb.com** to find the resources you need today!

*Located at the back of the textbook are rip-out Chapter Review Cards. Make sure you also go online to check out other tools that ORGB offers to help you successfully pass your course.*

- Interactive Quizzing
- Key Term Flashcards
- PowerPoint Slides
- Audio Chapter Summaries

- Cases and Exercises
- Interactive Games
- Self-Assessments
- "On the Job" and "Bizflix" Videos

# Leadership and Followership

**Leadership** in organizations is the process of guiding and directing the behaviour of people in the work environment. The first section of the chapter distinguishes leadership from management. **Formal leadership** occurs when an organization officially bestows on a leader the authority to guide and direct others in the organization. **Informal leadership** occurs when a person is unofficially accorded power by others in the organization and uses influence to guide and direct their behaviour. Leadership is among the most researched topics in organizational behaviour and one of the least understood social processes in organizations.

LEARNING OUTCOME **1**

# Leadership versus Management

John Kotter suggests that leadership and management are two distinct, yet complementary, systems of action in organizations.[1] Specifically, he believes that effective leadership produces useful change in organizations and that good management controls complexity in the organization and its environment. Healthy organizations need both effective leadership and good management.

For Kotter, the management process involves

**leadership**
The process of guiding and directing the behaviour of people in the work environment.

**formal leadership**
Officially sanctioned leadership based on the authority of a formal position.

**informal leadership**
Unofficial leadership accorded to a person by other members of the organization.

## LEARNING OUTCOMES

After reading this chapter, you should be able to do the following:

**1** Discuss the differences between leadership and management and between leaders and managers.

**2** Explain the role of trait theory in describing leaders.

**3** Describe the role of foundational behavioural research in the development of leadership theories.

**4** Describe and compare the three contingency theories of leadership.

**5** Discuss the recent developments in leadership theory of leader–member exchange and inspirational leadership.

**6** Discuss how issues of emotional intelligence, trust, gender, and servant leadership are informing today's leadership models.

**7** Define *followership* and identify different types of followers.

**8** Synthesize historical leadership research into key guidelines for leaders.

**9** Learn about servant leadership in action.

(1) planning and budgeting, (2) organizing and staffing, and (3) controlling and problem solving. The management process reduces uncertainty and stabilizes an organization. Alfred P. Sloan's integration and stabilization of General Motors after its early growth years are an example of good management.

In contrast, the leadership process involves (1) setting a direction for the organization; (2) aligning people with that direction through communication; and (3) motivating people to action, partly through empowerment and partly through basic need gratification. The leadership process often creates uncertainty and change in an organization. Effective leaders not only control the future of the organization but also act as enablers of change in organizations. They disturb existing patterns of behaviours, promote novel ideas, and help organizational members make sense of the change process.[2]

Abraham Zaleznik proposes that leaders have distinct personalities that stand in contrast to the personalities of managers.[3] Zaleznik suggests that both leaders and managers make a valuable contribution to an organization and that each one's contribution is different. Whereas **leaders** agitate for change and new approaches, **managers** advocate stability and the status quo. There is a dynamic tension between leaders and managers that makes it difficult for each to understand the other. Leaders and managers differ along four separate dimensions of personality: attitudes toward goals, conceptions of work, relationships with other people, and sense of self. The differences between these two personality types are summarized in Table 12.1.

It has been proposed that some people are strategic leaders who embody both the stability of managers and the visionary abilities of leaders. Thus, strategic

©VisualField/iStockPhoto

leaders combine the best of both types of behaviours. The unprecedented success of both Coca-Cola and Microsoft suggests that their leaders, the late Robert Goizueta (of Coke) and Bill Gates, were strategic leaders.[4]

LEARNING OUTCOME **2**

# Early Trait Theories

The first studies of leadership attempted to identify what physical attributes, personality characteristics, and abilities distinguished leaders from other members of a group.[5] The physical attributes considered have been height,

**TABLE 12.1** Leaders and Managers

| PERSONALITY DIMENSION | MANAGER | LEADER |
|---|---|---|
| **Attitudes toward goals** | Has an impersonal, passive, functional attitude; believes goals arise out of necessity and reality | Has a personal and active attitude; believes goals arise from desire and imagination |
| **Conceptions of work** | Views work as an enabling process that combines people, ideas, and things; seeks moderate risk through coordination and balance | Looks for fresh approaches to old problems; seeks high-risk positions, especially with high payoffs |
| **Relationships with others** | Avoids solitary work activity, preferring to work with others; avoids close, intense relationships; avoids conflict | Is comfortable in solitary work activity; encourages close, intense working relationships; is not conflict averse |
| **Sense of self** | Is once born; makes a straightforward life adjustment; accepts life as it is | Is twice born; engages in a struggle for a sense of order in life; questions life |

SOURCE: Reprinted by permission of *Harvard Business Review*. From "Managers and Leaders: Are They Different?" by A. Zaleznik; (January 2004). Copyright © 2004 by the Harvard Business School Publishing Corporation; all rights reserved.

**leader**
An advocate for change and new approaches to problems.

**manager**
An advocate for stability and the status quo.

weight, physique, energy, health, appearance, and even age. Even though this line of research yielded some interesting findings, very few valid generalizations emerged from this line of inquiry. Therefore, there is insufficient evidence to conclude that leaders can be distinguished from followers on the basis of physical attributes.

Leader personality characteristics that have been examined include originality, adaptability, introversion–extroversion, dominance, self-confidence, integrity, conviction, mood optimism, and emotional control. There is some evidence that leaders may be more adaptable and self-confident than the average group member.

Attention has been devoted to leader abilities such as social skills, intelligence, scholarship, speech fluency, cooperativeness, and insight. In this area, there is some evidence that leaders are more intelligent, verbal, and cooperative and have a higher level of scholarship than the average group member.

Nonetheless, these findings are neither strong nor uniform. For each attribute or trait claimed to distinguish leaders from followers, there were always at least one or two studies with contradictory findings. For some, the trait theories are invalid, though interesting and intuitively of some relevance. The trait theories have had very limited success in being able to identify any universal, distinguishing attributes of leaders.

LEARNING OUTCOME **3**

# Behavioural Theories

Behavioural theories emerged as a response to the deficiencies of the trait theories. Trait theories told us what leaders were like, but didn't address how leaders behaved. Three theories are the foundations of many modern leadership theories: the Lewin, Lippitt, and White studies; the Ohio State studies; and the Michigan studies.

## Foundational Behavioural Research

The earliest research on leadership style, conducted by Kurt Lewin and his students, identified three basic styles: autocratic, democratic, and laissez-faire.[6] Each leader uses one of these three basic styles when approaching a group of followers in a leadership situation. The specific situation is not an important consideration, because the leader's style does not vary with the situation. The autocratic style is directive, strong, and controlling in relationships. Leaders with an autocratic style use rules and regulations to run the work environment. Followers have little discretionary influence over the nature of the work, its accomplishment, or other aspects of the work environment. The leader with a democratic style is collaborative, responsive, and interactive in relationships and

emphasizes rules and regulations less than the autocratic leader. Followers have a high degree of discretionary influence, although the leader has ultimate authority and responsibility. The leader with a laissez-faire style leads through nonleadership. A laissez-faire leader abdicates the authority and responsibility of the position, and this style often results in chaos. Laissez-faire leadership also causes role ambiguity for followers by the leader's failure to clearly define goals, responsibilities, and outcomes. It leads to higher interpersonal conflict at work.[7]

The leadership research program at The Ohio State University also measured specific leader behaviours. The initial results suggested that there were two important underlying dimensions of leader behaviours—initiating structure and consideration.[8] Initiating structure is leader behaviour aimed at defining and organizing work relationships and roles, as well as establishing clear patterns of organization, communication, and ways of getting things done. Consideration is leader behaviour aimed at nurturing friendly, warm working relationships as well as encouraging mutual trust and interpersonal respect within the work unit. These two leader behaviours are independent of each other. That is, a leader may be high on both, low on both, or high on one while low on the other.[9]

Finally, studies conducted at the University of Michigan suggest that the leader's style has very important implications for the emotional atmosphere of the work environment and, therefore, for the followers who work under that leader. Two styles of leadership were identified: production oriented and employee oriented.[10]

A production-oriented style leads to a work environment where the focus is on getting things done. The leader in this environment uses direct, close supervision or many written and unwritten rules and regulations to control behaviour.

In comparison, an employee-oriented leadership style leads to a work

**autocratic style**
A style of leadership in which the leader uses strong, directive, controlling actions to enforce the rules, regulations, activities, and relationships in the work environment.

**democratic style**
A style of leadership in which the leader takes collaborative, responsive, interactive actions with followers concerning the work and work environment.

**laissez-faire style**
A style of leadership in which the leader fails to accept the responsibilities of the position.

**initiating structure**
Leader behaviour aimed at defining and organizing work relationships and roles, as well as establishing clear patterns of organization, communication, and ways of getting things done.

**consideration**
Leader behaviour aimed at nurturing friendly, warm working relationships, as well as encouraging mutual trust and interpersonal respect within the work unit.

Use What about You? on the Chapter 12 Review Card to assess your supervisor's task- versus people-oriented styles.

environment that focuses on relationships. The leader exhibits less direct or less close supervision and establishes fewer written or unwritten rules and regulations for behaviour. Employee-oriented leaders display concern for people and their needs.

Taken together, these three groups of studies (the Lewin, Lippitt, and White studies; Ohio State studies; and Michigan studies) form the building blocks of many recent leadership theories. What the studies have in common is that two basic leadership styles were identified, with one focusing on tasks (autocratic, production-oriented, initiating structure) and one focusing on people (democratic, employee-oriented, consideration).

## The Leadership Grid: A Contemporary Extension

Robert Blake and Jane Mouton's **Leadership Grid**, originally called the Managerial Grid, was developed with a focus on attitudes.[11] The two underlying dimensions of the grid are labelled Concern for Results and Concern for People. These two attitudinal dimensions are independent of each other and in different combinations form various leadership styles. Blake and Mouton originally identified five distinct managerial styles, and further development of the grid has led to the seven distinct leadership styles shown in Figure 12.1.

The **organization man manager (5,5)** is a middle-of-the-road leader who has a medium concern for people and production. This leader attempts to balance a concern for both people and production without a commitment to either.

The **authority-compliance manager (9,1)** has great concern for production and little concern for people. This leader desires tight control in order to get tasks done efficiently and considers creativity and human relations unnecessary. Authority-compliance managers may become so focused on running an efficient organization that they actually use tactics such as bullying. Some authority-compliance managers may intimidate, verbally and mentally attack, and otherwise mistreat subordinates. This form of abuse is quite common, with one in six North American workers reporting that they have been bullied by a manager.[12] The inverse position is the **country club manager (1,9)**, who has great concern for people and little concern for production, attempts to avoid conflict, and seeks to be well liked. This leader's goal is to keep people happy through good interpersonal relations, which are more important to him or her than the task.

The **team manager (9,9)** is considered ideal and has great concern for both people and production. This leader works to motivate employees to reach their highest levels of accomplishment, is flexible, responsive to change, and understands the need for change. The **impoverished manager (1,1)** is often referred to as a laissez-faire leader. This leader has little concern for people or production, avoids taking sides, and stays out of conflicts; he or she does just enough to get by. Two new leadership styles have been added to these five original leadership styles within the grid. The **paternalistic "father knows best" manager (9+9)** promises reward for compliance and threatens punishment for noncompliance. The **opportunistic "what's in it for me" manager (Opp)** uses the style that he or she feels will return him or her the greatest self-benefits.

It's important to highlight that the grid evaluates the team manager (9,9) as the very best style of managerial behaviour. This is the basis on which the grid has been used for team building and leadership training in an organization's development. As an organizational development method, the grid aims to transform the leader in the organization to lead in the "one best way," which, according to the grid, is the team approach. The team style is one that combines optimal concern for people with optimal concern for results.

---

**Leadership Grid**
An approach to understanding a leader's or manager's concern for results (production) and concern for people.

**organization man manager (5,5)**
A middle-of-the-road leader.

**authority-compliance manager (9,1)**
A leader who emphasizes efficient production.

**country club manager (1,9)**
A leader who creates a happy, comfortable work environment.

**team manager (9,9)**
A leader who builds a highly productive team of committed people.

**impoverished manager (1,1)**
A leader who exerts just enough effort to get by.

**paternalistic "father knows best" manager (9+9)**
A leader who promises reward and threatens punishment.

**opportunistic "what's in it for me" manager (Opp)**
A leader whose style aims to maximize self-benefit.

---

| SAME BASIC IDEA, VERY DIFFERENT MANIFESTATION | |
|---|---|
| **Ohio State** | **Blake-Mouton** |
| descriptive | normative |
| nonevaluative | prescriptive |
| no attitude | attitudinal overtones |

## FIGURE 12.1

### THE LEADERSHIP GRID

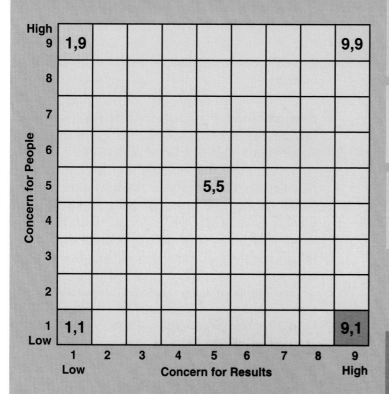

**1,9 Country Club Management:**
Thoughtful attention to the needs of the people for satisfying relationships leads to a comfortable, friendly organization atmosphere and work tempo.

**9,9 Team Management:**
Work accomplishment is from committed people; interdependence through a "common stake" in organization purpose leads to relationships of trust and respect.

**5,5 Middle-of-the-Road Management:**
Adequate organization performance is possible through balancing the necessity to get work out while maintaining morale of people at a satisfactory level.

**1,1 Impoverished Management:**
Exertion of minimum effort to get required work done is appropriate to sustain organization membership.

**9,1 Authority-Compliance Management:**
Efficiency in operations results from arranging conditions of work in such a way that human elements interfere to a minimum degree.

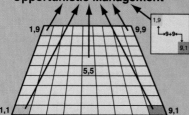

**Opportunistic Management**

In Opportunistic Management, people adapt and shift to any grid style needed to gain the maximum advantage. Performance occurs according to a system of selfish gain. Effort is given only for an advantage for personal gain.

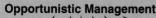

**9+9: Paternalism/Maternalism Management:**
Reward and approval are bestowed to people in return for loyalty and obedience; failure to comply leads to punishment.

SOURCE: "The Leadership Grid®" figure, Paternalism Figure and Opportunism from *Leadership Dilemmas—Grid Solutions,* by Robert R. Blake and Anne Adams McCanse (formerly The Managerial Grid by Robert R. Blake and Jane S. Mouton). Houston: Gulf Publishing Company (Grid Figure: p. 29; Paternalism Figure: p. 30, Opportunism Figure: p. 31). Copyright 1991 by Blake and Mouton, and Scientific Methods, Inc. Reproduced by permission of the owners.

---

### LEARNING OUTCOME 4

# Contingency Theories

Contingency theories involve the belief that leadership style must be appropriate for the particular situation. By their nature, contingency theories are "if–then" theories: If the situation is *x*, then the appropriate leadership

behaviour is *y*. We examine three such theories, including Fiedler's contingency theory, path–goal theory, and situational leadership theory.

## Fiedler's * not included. Contingency Theory

Fiedler's contingency theory of leadership proposes that the fit between the leader's need structure and the favourableness of the leader's situation determine the team's effectiveness in work accomplishment. This theory assumes that leaders are either task-oriented or relationship oriented, depending upon how the leaders obtain their primary need gratification.[13] Task-oriented leaders are primarily gratified by accomplishing tasks and getting work done. Relationship-oriented leaders are primarily gratified by developing good, comfortable interpersonal relationships. Therefore, the effectiveness of both types of leaders depends on the favourableness of their situation. The theory classifies the favourableness of the leader's situation according to the leader's position power, the structure of the team's task, and the quality of the leader–follower relationships.

### The Least Preferred Coworker

Fiedler classifies leaders using the Least Preferred Coworker (LPC) Scale.[14] The LPC Scale is a projective technique through which a leader is asked to think about the person with whom he or she can work the least well (the **least preferred coworker**, or **LPC**). The leader is asked to describe this least preferred coworker using 16 eight-point bipolar adjective sets. Two of these bipolar adjective sets follow (the leader marks the blank most descriptive of the least preferred coworker):

> Efficient : : : : : : : : : Inefficient
> Cheerful : : : : : : : : : Gloomy

**least preferred coworker (LPC)**

The person with whom a leader can work the least well over his or her career.

**task structure**

The degree of clarity, or ambiguity, in the work activities assigned to the group.

**position power**

The authority associated with the leader's formal position in the organization.

**leader–member relations**

The quality of interpersonal relationships among a leader and the group members.

Leaders who describe their least preferred coworker in positive terms (that is, pleasant, efficient, cheerful, and so on) are classified as high LPC, or relationship-oriented, leaders. Those who describe their least preferred coworker in negative terms (that is, unpleasant, inefficient, gloomy, and so on) are classified as low LPC, or task-oriented, leaders.

The LPC score is a controversial element in contingency theory.[15] The LPC score has been critiqued conceptually and methodologically because

it is a projective technique with low measurement reliability.

**Situational Favourableness** The leader's situation has three dimensions: task structure, position power, and leader–member relations. Based on these three dimensions, the situation is either favourable or unfavourable for the leader. **Task structure** refers to the number and clarity of rules, regulations, and procedures for getting the work done. **Position power** refers to the leader's legitimate authority to evaluate and reward performance, punish errors, and demote group members.

The quality of **leader–member relations** is measured by the Group-Atmosphere Scale, composed of nine eight-point bipolar adjective sets. Two of these bipolar adjective sets follow:

> Friendly : : : : : : : : : Unfriendly
> Accepting : : : : : : : : : Rejecting

A favourable leadership situation is one with a structured task for the work group, strong position power for the leader, and good leader–member relations. In contrast, an unfavourable leadership situation is one with an unstructured task, weak position power for the leader, and moderately poor leader–member relations. Between these two extremes, the leadership situation has varying degrees of moderate favourableness for the leader.

| | Favourable | Moderate | Unfavourable |
|---|---|---|---|
| Task structure | Structured | | Unstructured |
| Position power | Strong | | Weak |
| Leader–member relations | Good | | Poor |

**Leadership Effectiveness** The contingency theory suggests that low and high LPC leaders are each effective if placed in the right situation.[16] Specifically, low LPC (task-oriented) leaders are most effective in either very favourable or very unfavourable leadership situations. In contrast, high LPC (relationship-oriented) leaders are most effective in situations of intermediate favourableness. Figure 12.2 shows the nature of these relationships and suggests that leadership effectiveness is determined by the degree of fit between the leader and the situation. Recent research has shown that relationship-oriented

## FIGURE 12.2

### LEADERSHIP EFFECTIVENESS IN THE CONTINGENCY THEORY

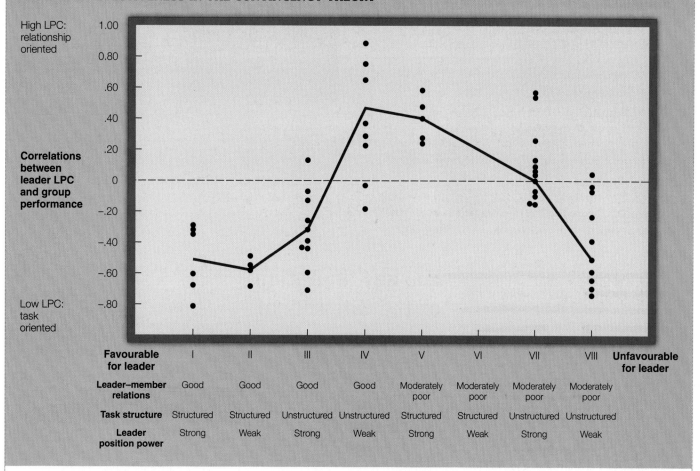

| | I | II | III | IV | V | VI | VII | VIII | |
|---|---|---|---|---|---|---|---|---|---|
| **Favourable for leader** | | | | | | | | | **Unfavourable for leader** |
| **Leader–member relations** | Good | Good | Good | Good | Moderately poor | Moderately poor | Moderately poor | Moderately poor | |
| **Task structure** | Structured | Structured | Unstructured | Unstructured | Structured | Structured | Unstructured | Unstructured | |
| **Leader position power** | Strong | Weak | Strong | Weak | Strong | Weak | Strong | Weak | |

SOURCE: F. E. Fiedler, *A Theory of Leader Effectiveness* (New York: McGraw-Hill, 1964). Reprinted with permission of the author.

leaders encourage team learning and innovativeness, which helps products get to market faster. This means that most relationship-oriented leaders perform well in leading new product development teams. In short, the right team leader can help get creative new products out the door faster, while a mismatch between the leader and the situation can have the opposite effect.[17]

What, then, is to be done if there is a misfit? That is, what happens when a low LPC leader is in a moderately favourable situation or when a high LPC leader is in a highly favourable or highly unfavourable situation? It is unlikely that the leader can be changed, according to the theory, because the leader's need structure is an enduring trait that is hard to change. Fiedler recommends that the leader's situation be changed to fit the leader's style.[18] A moderately favourable situation would be reengineered to be more favourable and therefore more suitable for the low LPC leader. A highly favourable or highly unfavourable situation would be changed to one that is moderately favourable and more suitable for the high LPC leader.

## Path–Goal Theory

Martin Evans and Robert House developed a path–goal theory of leader effectiveness based on an expectancy theory of motivation.[19] From the perspective of path–goal theory, the basic role of the leader is to clear the follower's path to the goal. The leader uses the most appropriate of four leader behaviour styles to help followers clarify the paths that lead them to work and personal goals. The key concepts in the theory are shown in Figure 12.3 on page 200.

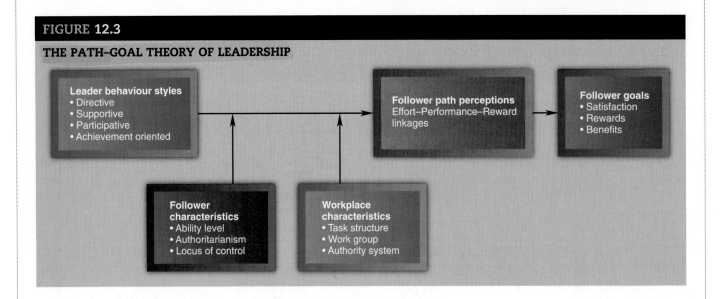

**FIGURE 12.3**

**THE PATH–GOAL THEORY OF LEADERSHIP**

**Leader behaviour styles**
- Directive
- Supportive
- Participative
- Achievement oriented

**Follower path perceptions**
Effort–Performance–Reward
linkages

**Follower goals**
- Satisfaction
- Rewards
- Benefits

**Follower characteristics**
- Ability level
- Authoritarianism
- Locus of control

**Workplace characteristics**
- Task structure
- Work group
- Authority system

A leader selects from the four leader behaviour styles, shown in Figure 12.3, the one that is most helpful to followers at a given time. The directive style is used when the leader must give specific guidance about work tasks, schedule work, and let followers know what is expected. The supportive style is used when the leader needs to express concern for followers' well-being and social status. The participative style is used when the leader must engage in joint decision-making activities with followers. The achievement-oriented style is used when the leader must set challenging goals for followers and show strong confidence in those followers.

In selecting the appropriate leader behaviour style, the leader must consider both the followers and the work environment. A few characteristics are included in Figure 12.3. Let us look at two examples. In Example 1, the followers are inexperienced and working on an ambiguous, unstructured task. The leader in this situation might best use a directive style. In Example 2, the followers are highly trained professionals, and the task is a difficult, yet achievable one. The leader in this situation might best use an achievement-oriented style. The leader always chooses the leader behaviour style that best helps followers achieve their goals.

The path–goal theory assumes that leaders adapt their behaviour and style to fit the characteristics of the followers and the environment in which they work. Actual tests of the path–goal theory and its propositions provide conflicting evidence.[20] The path–goal theory does have intuitive appeal and reinforces the idea that the appropriate leadership style depends on both the work situation and the followers. Research is focusing

> **One key limitation of the Situational Leadership® model is the absence of central hypotheses that can be tested.**

on which style works best in specific situations. For example, in small organizations, leaders who used visionary, transactional, and empowering behaviours, while avoiding autocratic behaviours, were most successful.[21]

## The Situational Leadership® Model

The Situational Leadership® model, developed by Paul Hersey and Kenneth Blanchard, suggests that the leader's behaviour should be adjusted to the maturity level of the followers.[22] The model employs two dimensions of leader behaviour as used in the Ohio State studies; one dimension is task oriented, and the other is relationship oriented. Follower maturity is categorized into four levels, as shown in Figure 12.4. Follower readiness is determined by the follower's ability and willingness to complete a specific task. Readiness can therefore be low or high depending on the particular task. In addition, readiness varies within a single person according to the task. One person may be willing and able to satisfy simple requests from customers (high readiness) but less able or willing to give highly technical advice to customers (low readiness). It is important that the leader be able to evaluate the readiness level of each follower for each task. The four styles of leader behaviour associated with the four readiness levels are depicted in the figure as well.

According to the Situational Leadership® model, a leader should use a telling style (S1) when a follower is unable and unwilling to do a certain task. This style involves providing instructions and closely monitoring performance. As such, the telling style involves considerable

**Leader Behaviours**

Relationship Behaviour (Supportive Behaviour)

(high) ... (low)

| High Relationship and Low Task | High Task and High Relationship |
| --- | --- |
| Participating | Selling |
| **S3** | **S2** |
| **S4** | **S1** |
| Delegating | Telling |
| Low Relationship and Low Task | High Task and Low Relationship |

(low) ←——— **Task Behaviour** ———→ (high)
(Directive Behaviour)

(high) ←——— **Follower Readiness** ———→ (low)

| Able and Willing or Confident | Able but Unwilling or Insecure | Unable but Willing or Confident | Unable and Unwilling or Insecure |
| --- | --- | --- | --- |
| **R4** | **R3** | **R2** | **R1** |

task behaviour and low relationship behaviour. When a follower is unable but willing and confident to do a task, the leader can use the selling style (S2) in which there is high task behaviour and high relationship behaviour. In this case, the leader explains decisions and provides opportunities for the employee to seek clarification or help. Sometimes a follower will be able to complete a task but may seem unwilling or insecure about doing so. In these cases, a participating style (S3) is warranted, which involves high relationship but low task behaviour. The leader in this case encourages the follower to participate in decision making. Finally, for tasks in which a follower is able and willing, the leader is able to use a delegating style (S4), characterized by low task behaviour and low relationship behaviour. In this case, follower readiness is high, and low levels of leader involvement (task or relationship) are needed.

One key limitation of the Situational Leadership® model is the absence of central hypotheses that can be tested, which would make it a more valid, reliable theory of leadership.[23] However, the theory has intuitive appeal and is widely used for training and development in corporations. In addition, the theory focuses attention on follower maturity as an important determinant of the leadership process.

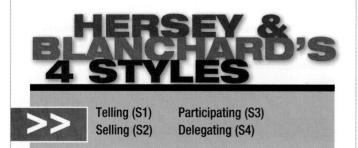

HERSEY & BLANCHARD'S 4 STYLES

>> Telling (S1)   Participating (S3)
   Selling (S2)   Delegating (S4)

LEARNING OUTCOME **5**

# Recent Leadership Theories

Many newer developments in leadership theory merit discussion here.

## Leader–Member Exchange

Leader–member exchange theory, or LMX, recognizes that leaders may form different relationships with followers. The basic idea behind LMX is that leaders form two groups of followers: in-groups and out-groups. In-group members tend to be similar to the leader and given greater responsibilities, more rewards, and more attention. They work within the leader's inner circle of communication. As a result, in-group members are more satisfied, have lower turnover, and have higher organizational commitment. In contrast, out-group members are outside the circle and receive less attention and fewer rewards. They are managed by formal rules and policies.[24]

Research on LMX is supportive. In-group members are more likely to engage in organizational citizenship behaviour, while out-group members are more likely to retaliate against the organization.[25] The type of stress varies by the group to which a subordinate belongs. In-group members' stress comes from the additional responsibilities placed on them by the leader, whereas out-group members' stress comes from being left out of the communication network.[26] One interesting finding is that more frequent communication with the boss may either help or hurt a worker's performance ratings, depending on whether the worker is in the in-group or the out-group. Among the in-group, more frequent communication generally leads to higher performance ratings, while members of the out-group who communicate more often with the superior tend to receive lower performance ratings.[27]

Employees who enjoy more frequent contact with the boss also have a better understanding of the boss's expectations. Such agreement tends to lead to better performance by the employee and fewer misunderstandings between employer and employee.[28] In-group members are also more likely to support the values of the organization and to become models of appropriate behaviour. If the leader, for example, wants to promote safety at work, in-group members model safe work practices, which leads to a climate of workplace safety.[29]

## Inspirational Leadership

Leadership is an exciting area of organizational behaviour, one in which new research is constantly emerging. Three new developments are important to understand. These are transformational leadership, charismatic leadership, and authentic leadership. These three theories can be called *inspirational leadership theories* because in each one, followers are inspired by the leader to perform well.

### Transformational Leadership
Transactional leaders are those who use rewards and punishment to strike deals with followers and shape their behaviour.

> " Leadership is an exciting area of organizational behaviour, one in which new research is constantly emerging.

In contrast, transformational leaders inspire and excite followers to high levels of performance.[30] They rely on their personal attributes instead of their official position to manage followers. There is some evidence that transformational leadership can be learned.[31] Transformational leadership consists of the following four sub-dimensions: charisma, individualized consideration, inspirational motivation, and intellectual stimulation. We describe charisma in detail below. Individualized consideration refers to how much the leader displays concern for each follower's individual needs and acts as a coach or a mentor. Inspirational motivation is the extent to which the leader is able to articulate a vision that is appealing to followers.[32]

As North American organizations increasingly operate in a global economy, there is a greater demand for leaders who can practise transformational leadership by converting their visions into reality and by inspiring followers to perform "above and beyond the call of duty."[33] Howard Schultz, founder and chairman of Starbucks Coffee, is the transformational leader and visionary heart of Starbucks. He has grown his firm from a small specialty coffee bar into one of the best-known brands in the world. With the firm hoping to continue its rapid growth pace of 25–30 percent per year, Schultz's ability to develop new leaders within the firm (which helped Starbucks get where it is today) will be sorely tested. But given the enormous market for coffee worldwide (Starbucks currently has less than 10 percent of the market), the potential for further growth exists if the company can develop the people to tap it.[34]

Leaders can be both transformational and transactional.[35] Transformational leadership adds to the effects of transactional leadership, but exceptional transactional leadership cannot substitute for transformational leadership.[36] Transformational leadership is effective because transformational leaders encourage followers to set goals congruent with the followers' own authentic interests and values. As a result, followers see their work as important and their goals as aligned with who they are.[37]

### Charismatic Leadership
Steve Jobs, the pioneer behind the Macintosh computer, the music

download market, iPods, and the iPad, has an uncanny ability to create a vision and convince others to become part of it. This was evidenced by Apple's continual overall success despite its major blunders in the desktop computer wars. Jobs's unique ability is so powerful that Apple employees coined a term in the 1980s for it—the *reality-distortion field*. This expression is used to describe the persuasive ability and peculiar charisma of managers like Steve Jobs. This reality-distortion field allows Jobs to convince even skeptics that his plans are worth supporting, no matter how unworkable they may appear. Those close to such managers become passionately committed to possibly insane projects, without regard to the practicality of their implementation or competitive forces in the marketplace.[38]

**Charismatic leadership** results when a leader uses the force of personal abilities and talents to have profound and extraordinary effects on followers.[39] Some scholars see transformational leadership and charismatic leadership as very similar, but others believe they are different. Charismatic leaders rely heavily on referent power, discussed in Chapter 11, and charismatic leadership is especially effective in times of uncertainty.[40] Charismatic leadership falls to those who are chosen (are born with the "gift" of charisma) or who cultivate that gift. Some say charismatic leaders are born, and others say they are taught.

Charismatic leadership carries with it not only great potential for high levels of achievement and performance on

the part of followers but also shadowy risks of destructive courses of action that might harm followers or other people. Several researchers have attempted to demystify charismatic leadership and distinguish its two faces.[41] The ugly face of charisma is revealed in the personalized power motivations of Adolf Hitler in Nazi Germany and James Jones of the People's Temple cult. Both men led their followers into struggle, conflict, and death. The brighter face of charisma is revealed in the Canadian unity motivations of Prime Minister Pierre Trudeau. Former U.S. President Bill Clinton and former U.K. Prime Minister Tony Blair are quite similar in their use of personal charisma to inspire followers and motivate them to pursue the leader's vision. In each case, followers perceived the leader as imbued with a unique vision and unique abilities to lead their country there.

**charismatic leadership**
A leader's use of personal abilities and talents in order to have profound and extraordinary effects on followers.

← Howard Schultz

©Kevin P. Casey/Bloomberg News/Landov

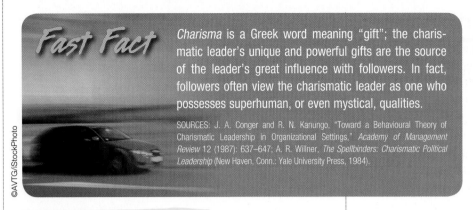
**Authentic Leadership** Recently, a new form of leadership has started to garner attention thanks to the ethical scandals rocking the business environment. In response to concerns about the potential negative side of inspirational forms of leadership, researchers have called for authentic leadership.[42] Authentic leadership includes transformational, charismatic, or transactional leadership as the situation might demand. However, authentic leadership differs from the other kinds in that such authentic leaders have a conscious and well-developed sense of values. They act in ways that are consistent with their value systems, so authentic leaders have a highly evolved sense of moral right and wrong. Their life experiences (labelled "moments that matter") lead to such authentic leadership development, and allow authentic leaders to be their true selves.[43]

Authentic leaders arouse and motivate followers to higher levels of performance by building a workforce characterized by high levels of hope, optimism, resiliency, and self-efficacy.[44] Followers also experience more positive emotions and trust leadership as a result of transparency and a collective caring climate engendered by the leader. Researchers contend that this is the kind of leadership embodied by Mahatma Gandhi, Nelson Mandela, and others like them throughout history. Only time and solid management research will tell if this approach can yield results for organizational leadership.

One recent development in the identification of authentic leaders stems from the emotions arena. Emotions act as checks on the ugly side of charisma and also provide certain cues to followers. For example, a leader who espouses benevolence (as a value) and does not display compassion (an emotion) might not be very authentic in followers' eyes.[45] Similarly, a leader who displays compassion when announcing a layoff may be seen by followers as more morally worthy and held in higher regard.[46]

Despite the warm emotions charismatic leaders can evoke, some charismatic leaders are narcissists who listen only to those who agree with them and do not seek advice from those who disagree.[47] Whereas charismatic leaders with socialized power motivation are concerned about the collective well-being of their followers, charismatic leaders with a personalized power motivation are driven by the need for personal gain and glorification.[48]

Charismatic leadership styles are associated with several positive outcomes. One study reported that firms headed by more charismatic leaders outperformed other firms, particularly in difficult economic times. Perhaps even more important, charismatic leaders were able to raise more outside financial support for their firms than noncharismatic leaders, meaning that charisma at the top may translate to greater funding at the bottom.[49]

---

**LEARNING OUTCOME 6**

# Emerging Issues in Leadership

Along with the recent developments in theory, some exciting issues have emerged of which leaders must be aware. These include emotional intelligence, trust, women leaders, and servant leadership.

## [ She's the Original ]

When Anne Mulcahy took over as Chairman and CEO of Xerox in 2000, the company was drowning in debt ($18 million in the red) and advisors were counselling her to file for bankruptcy. She had no background in finance, so she reached out to people in her company to tutor her. She started to ride with field salespeople to understand her business better. Mulcahy tempers her tenacity with humility and understanding. More than anything else, Mulcahy is known for being a consensus leader, one who seeks out several opinions and arrives at decisions on the basis of such consensus. Being perceived as an authentic leader has helped her overcome several challenges at Xerox.

SOURCE: B. George, "What Is Your True North?" *Fortune* (March 19, 2007): 125–130; CNNMoney.com, "How to Succeed in 2007?" http://money.cnn.com/popups/2006/biz2/howtosucceed/7.html.

## Emotional Intelligence

It has been suggested that effective leaders possess emotional intelligence, which is the ability to recognize and manage emotion in yourself and in others. In fact, some researchers argue that emotional intelligence is more important for effective leadership than either IQ or technical skills.[50] Emotional intelligence is made up of several competencies, including self-awareness, empathy, adaptability, and self-confidence. While most people gain emotional intelligence as they age, not everyone starts with an equal amount. Fortunately, emotional intelligence can be learned. With honest feedback from coworkers and ongoing guidance, almost any leader can improve emotional intelligence, and with it, the ability to lead in times of adversity.[51]

Emotional intelligence affects the way leaders make decisions. Under high stress, leaders with higher emotional intelligence tend to keep their cool and make better decisions, while leaders with low emotional intelligence make poor decisions and lose their effectiveness.[52] When Cito Gaston was manager of the Toronto Blue Jays, he got the most out of his team and kept his cool through two World Series wins and many losing seasons. He is still a model of emotional intelligence: compassionate, calm under stress, and a great motivator. Some are now challenging the belief that there is an important relationship between emotional intelligence and leadership. Some maintain that the claims about the importance of emotional intelligence are "hyperbolic" and unwarranted.[53] The concerns centre on the methodologies and measurements used to determine emotional intelligence. Research on emotional intelligence is only 20 years old, so much more work needs to be done to determine the nature of the relationship between leadership and emotional intelligence.

## Trust

Trust is an essential element in leadership. Trust is the willingness to be vulnerable to the actions of another.[54] This means that followers believe that their leader will act with the followers' welfare in mind. Trustworthiness is also one of the competencies in emotional intelligence. Trust among top management team members facilitates strategy implementation; that means that if team members trust each other, they have a better chance of getting "buy-in" from employees on the direction of the company.[55] And if employees trust their leaders, they will buy in more readily.

Leaders must not only come to trust their subordinates, but also express that trust. Research has shown that workers who believe their boss trusts them (called "felt trustworthiness") enjoy their work more, are

Hans Neleman/Stone/Getty Images

more productive, and are more likely to "go the extra mile" at work and perform organizational citizenship behaviours.[56]

Effective leaders also understand both *whom* to trust and *how* to trust. At one extreme, leaders often trust a close circle of advisors, listening only to them and gradually cutting themselves off from dissenting opinions. At the opposite extreme, lone-wolf leaders may trust nobody, leading to preventable mistakes. Wise leaders carefully evaluate both the competence and the position of those they trust, seeking out a variety of opinions and input.[57]

## Gender and Leadership

An important, emergent leadership question is this: Do women and men lead differently? Historical stereotypes persist, and people characterize successful managers as having more male-oriented attributes than female-oriented attributes.[58] Although legitimate gender differences may exist, the same leadership traits may be interpreted differently in a man and a woman because of stereotypes. The real issue should be leader behaviours that are not bound by gender stereotypes.

Early evidence shows that women tend to use a more people-oriented style that is inclusive and empowering. Women managers excel in positions that demand strong interpersonal skills.[59] Even though more and more women are assuming positions of leadership in organizations, interestingly, much of what we know about leadership is based on studies that were conducted on men. We need to know more about the ways women lead. In one recent study of women Aboriginal leaders in Canada, some significant differences emerged between men and

**TABLE 12.2** Key Differences between Non-Aboriginal and Aboriginal Leaders

| | NON-ABORIGINAL LEADERS | ABORIGINAL LEADERS |
|---|---|---|
| **Concept of Leader** | Individualistic | Community-oriented |
| **Concept of Leader Effectiveness** | Narrow, goal- and task-focused | Broad, long-term, and community-focused |
| **Spirituality** | Entering workplace slowly | Spirituality key driver |
| **Story-telling** | Becoming important | Central to leader communication |
| **Relationships** | Principally hierarchical | Egalitarian |
| **Focus on Person** | Employee | Whole person |

SOURCE: M. Julien, B. Wright, and D. M. Zinni, "Stories from the Circle: Leadership Lessons from Aboriginal Leaders", *The Leadership Quarterly*, 21 (2010):123.

women. While women demonstrated many of the the attributes of male Aboriginal leaders (see Table 12.2), they felt the need to outperform as leaders, as they faced sexism and racism in their work even though, traditionally, Aboriginal communities are matriarchies.[60]

Recent research reports on the phenomenon of the *Glass Cliff* (as opposed to the *Glass Ceiling* effect discussed in Chapter 2). The *Glass Cliff* represents a trend in organizations wherein more women are placed in difficult leadership situations. Women perceive these assignments as necessary due to difficulty in attaining leadership positions and lack of alternate opportunities combined with male in-group favouritism. On the other hand, men perceive that women were better suited to difficult leadership positions due to better decision making.[61]

## Servant Leadership

Robert Greenleaf was director of management research at AT&T for many years. He believed that leaders should serve employees, customers, and the community, and his essays are the basis for today's view called *servant leadership*. His personal and profes-

**followership**

The process of being guided and directed by a leader in the work environment.

## WHO'S WHO

>> Donna Dubinsky, founder and CEO of palmOne, cofounded Palm and Handspring, and is known as the mother of the handheld computer. She wants to change the world such that PDAs outsell PCs.

sional philosophy was that leaders lead by serving others. Other tenets of servant leadership are that work exists for the person as much as the person exists for work, and that servant leaders try to find out the will of the group and lead based on that. Servant leaders are also stewards who consider leadership a trust and desire to leave the organization in better shape for future generations.[62] Although Greenleaf's writings were completed 30 years ago, many have now been published and are becoming more popular.

Aboriginal leadership can be seen as a type of servant leadership that has a rich historical tradition. Aboriginal leadership has six main attributes: (1) it focuses on the community and connections, (2) social order is to be maintained by harmony, (3) spirituality has a significant role in shaping action, (4) values are guides for action, (5) actions are selected through a process of decision sharing and consensus, and (6) respect is the most important criterion for leaders. "In essence, leaders serve rather than boss."[63] Table 12.2 highlights some key differences between non-Aboriginal and Aboriginal leaders.

# Followership

In contrast to leadership, the topic of **followership** has not been extensively researched. Much of the leadership literature suggests that leader and follower roles are highly differentiated. The traditional view casts followers as passive, whereas a more contemporary view casts the follower role as an active one with potential for leadership.[64] The follower role has alternatively been cast as one of self-leadership in which the follower assumes responsibility for influencing his or her own performance.[65] This approach emphasizes the follower's individual responsibility and self-control. Self-led followers perform naturally motivating tasks and do work that must be done but that is not naturally motivating. Self-leadership enables followers to be disciplined and effective, essential first steps to become a leader. Organizational programs such as empowerment and self-managed work teams may be used to further activate the follower role.[66]

# Types of Followers

Contemporary work environments are ones in which followers recognize their interdependence with leaders and learn to challenge them while at the same time respecting the leaders' authority.[67] Effective followers are active, responsible, and autonomous in their behaviour and critical in their thinking without being insubordinate or disrespectful—in essence, they are highly engaged at work.

Effective followers and four other types of followers are identified based on two dimensions: (1) activity versus passivity and (2) independent, critical thinking versus dependent, uncritical thinking.[68] Figure 12.5 shows these follower types.

Alienated followers think independently and critically, yet are very passive in their behaviour. As a result, they become psychologically and emotionally distanced from their leaders. Alienated followers are potentially disruptive and a threat to the health of the organization. Sheep are followers who do not think independently or critically and are passive in their behaviour. They simply do as they are told by their leaders. Yes people are followers who also do not think independently or critically, yet are very active in their behaviour. They uncritically reinforce the thinking and ideas of their leaders with enthusiasm, never questioning or challenging the wisdom

## Yes people do not think independently or critically.

of the leaders' ideas and proposals. Yes people are the most dangerous to a leader because they are the most likely to give a false positive reaction and give no warning of potential pitfalls. Survivors are the least disruptive and the lowest risk followers in an organization. They perpetually sample the wind, and their motto is "better safe than sorry."

Effective followers are the most valuable to a leader and an organization because of their active contributions. Effective followers share four essential qualities. First, they practise self-management and self-responsibility. A leader can delegate to an effective follower without anxiety about the outcome. Second, they are committed both to the organization and a purpose, principle, or person outside themselves. Effective followers are not self-centred or self-aggrandizing. Third, effective followers invest in their own competence and professionalism and focus their energy for maximum impact. Effective followers look for challenges and ways in which to add to their talents or abilities. Fourth, they are courageous, honest, and credible.

Effective followers might be thought of as self-leaders who do not require close supervision.[69] The notion of self-leadership, or superleadership, blurs the distinction between leaders and followers. Caring leaders are able to develop dynamic followers.

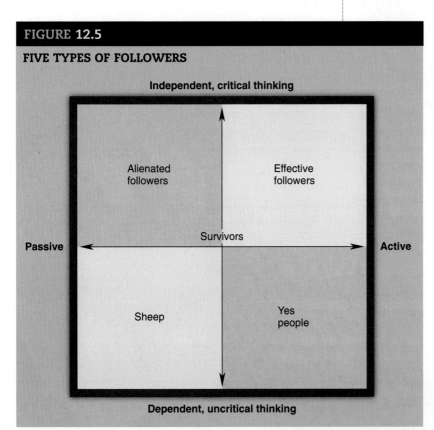

**FIGURE 12.5**

**FIVE TYPES OF FOLLOWERS**

Independent, critical thinking

Alienated followers

Effective followers

Passive — Survivors — Active

Sheep

Yes people

Dependent, uncritical thinking

SOURCE: Reprinted by permission of *Harvard Business Review*. From "In Praise of Followers" by R. E. Kelley, (November–December 1988), p. 145. Copyright © 1988 by Harvard Business School Publishing Corporation; all rights reserved.

# Guidelines for Leadership

Leadership is a key to influencing organizational behaviour and achieving organizational effectiveness. When artifacts are eliminated, studies of leadership succession show a moderately strong leader influence on organizational performance.[70] With this said, it is important to recognize that other factors also influence organizational performance. These include environmental factors (such as general economic conditions) and technological factors (such as efficiency).

Corporate leaders play a central role in setting the ethical tone and moral values for their organizations. While many corporate leaders talk about ethics, many never have to actually risk the firm's fortune on an ethical decision. In 1976, when James Burke, head of Johnson & Johnson, challenged his management team to reaffirm the company's historic commitment to ethical behaviour, he had no idea he would be asked to demonstrate that commitment in action. But six years later, when poisoned packages of Tylenol appeared on store shelves, Burke did not hesitate to act on what he had pledged. The company pulled the product from the shelves at a cost of $100 million. It also offered a reward and revamped the product's packaging. In the end, Tylenol recovered its market position and, more importantly, its credibility.

Five useful guidelines appear to emerge from the extensive leadership research of the past 60 years:

**1** Leaders and organizations should appreciate the unique attributes, predispositions, and talents of each leader. No two leaders are the same, and there is value in this diversity.

**2** Although there appears to be no single best style of leadership, there are organizational preferences in terms of style. Leaders should be chosen who challenge the organizational culture when necessary, without destroying it.

## WHO'S WHO

>> Jim Burke was recently recognized by *Fortune* as one of the 10 greatest CEOs of all time, and Johnson & Johnson continues to be rated one of the best companies for which to work.[71]

---

## [ North America's Leadership Factories: How They Do It ]

Some of North America's best known companies seem to have perfected the art of grooming and producing exceptional leaders. Companies such as General Electric, Johnson & Johnson, PepsiCo, and several others have strong leadership development programs in place that help them identify and groom employees for leadership positions. These leaders in turn are instrumental in guiding the organization to the goal of delivering on its promises.

One research study examined the internal processes of leadership development across 150 of the top leader-producing firms and identified five key principles that were common to all the organizations.

What do top leader-producing firms do? They

> Identify leaders who are proficient at setting organizational strategy and identifying talent within the company.
> Focus on customer expectations of the firm and ensure that leadership never loses sight of those expectations.
> Evaluate leader performance and effectiveness against these customer expectations.
> Develop leadership training that includes skill development specific to meeting customer expectations.
> Periodically evaluate the success of leadership development, including asking customers for feedback on company leadership.

SOURCE: D. Ulrich and N. Smallwood, "Building a Leadership Brand," *Harvard Business Review* 85(7, 8) (2007): 92–100.

Jupiter Images

**3** Participative, considerate leader behaviours that demonstrate a concern for people appear to enhance the health and well-being of followers in the work environment. This does not imply, however, that a leader must ignore the team's work tasks.

**4** Different leadership situations call for different leadership talents and behaviours. This may result in different individuals taking the leader role, depending on the specific situation in which the team finds itself.

**5** Good leaders are likely to be good followers. Although there are distinctions between their social roles, the attributes and behaviours of leaders and followers may not be as distinct as is sometimes thought.

LEARNING OUTCOME **9**

# Leadership in Action

Craig Kielburger, from Thornhill, Ontario, was 12 when he and his brother, Marc, and their friends founded Free the Children. They were motivated to combat child labour after Kielburger had read about the fate of Iqbal Masik, a former child slave who was murdered because he advocated an end to child labour. In the early days of Free the Children, it raised money through bake sales, was run by a board of students, and engaged in awareness-building activities such as letter-writing campaigns to heads of state.

Since then, Free the Children has become an international development organization that builds schools and provides education, and also engages youth in social action through a number of activities and programs such as Adopt a Village and Leaders Today. Now more than one million youth are involved in Free the Children's programs in more than 45 countries!

Its mission is "Free children from poverty. Free children from exploitation. Free children from the idea that they are powerless to change the world."[72] Its principal goal is to educate youth so that they become empowered to take action to improve the world. Free the Children has started a social enterprise, Me to We, to support its empowerment and development work. Half the profits from Me to We's products and services are given to Free the Children and the other half is used to sustain the organization. In 2009, Me to We contributed more than one million dollars to Free the Children in cash and in-kind.[73] Underlying Free the Children and Me to We is the belief that anyone of any age anywhere can make a difference to make the world a better place by taking thoughtful action. The two organizations are good examples of the principles of servant leadership in action.

# Visit **icanorgb.com** to find the resources you need today!

*Located at the back of the textbook are rip-out Chapter Review Cards. Make sure you also go online to check out other tools that ORGB offers to help you successfully pass your course.*

- Interactive Quizzing
- Key Term Flashcards
- PowerPoint Slides
- Audio Chapter Summaries

- Cases and Exercises
- Interactive Games
- Self-Assessments
- "On the Job" and "Bizflix" Videos

# 13

>>

# Conflict and
# Negotiation

# The Nature of Conflicts in Organizations

All of us have experienced conflict of various types, yet we probably fail to recognize the variety of conflicts that occur in organizations. *Conflict* is defined as any situation in which incompatible goals, attitudes, emotions, or behaviours lead to disagreement or opposition between two or more parties.[1]

Today's organizations may face greater potential for conflict than ever before in history. The marketplace, with its increasing competition and globalization, magnifies differences among people in terms of personality, values, attitudes, perceptions, languages, cultures, and national backgrounds.[2] With the increasing diversity of the workforce comes the potential for incompatibility and conflict.

## Importance of Conflict Management Skills for the Manager

Estimates show that managers spend about 21 percent of their time, or one day every week, dealing with conflict.[3] As such, conflict management skills are a major predictor of managerial success.[4] A critical indicator of a manager's ability to manage conflict is his or her emotional intelligence (EI), which is an individual's power to control his or her emotions and perceive emotions in others, adapt to change, and manage adversity. (Conflict management skills may be more a reflection of EI than of IQ.) People who lack emotional intelligence, especially empathy or the ability to see life from another person's perspective, are more likely to be causes of conflict than managers of conflict.[5]

## LEARNING OUTCOMES

After reading this chapter, you should be able to do the following:

1 Describe the nature of conflicts in organizations.

2 Explain the role structural and personal factors play in causing conflict in organizations.

3 Discuss the nature of group conflict in organizations.

4 Describe the factors that influence conflict between individuals in organizations.

5 Describe effective and ineffective techniques for managing conflict.

6 Identify five styles of conflict management.

**TABLE 13.1** Consequences of Conflict

| POSITIVE CONSEQUENCES | NEGATIVE CONSEQUENCES |
|---|---|
| • Leads to new ideas<br>• Stimulates creativity<br>• Motivates change<br>• Promotes organizational vitality<br>• Helps individuals and groups establish identities<br>• Serves as a safety valve to indicate problems | • Diverts energy from work<br>• Threatens psychological well-being<br>• Wastes resources<br>• Creates a negative climate<br>• Breaks down group cohesion<br>• Can increase hostility and aggressive behaviours |

## Functional versus Dysfunctional Conflict

Not all conflict is bad. In fact, some types of conflict encourage new solutions to problems and enhance creativity in the organization. In these cases, managers will want to encourage the conflicts. Thus, the key to conflict management is to stimulate functional conflict and prevent or resolve dysfunctional conflict. The difficulty, however, is distinguishing between dysfunctional and functional conflicts. As Table 13.1 shows, the consequences of conflict can be positive or negative.

**Functional conflict** is a healthy, constructive disagreement between two or more people. Functional conflict can produce new ideas, learning, and growth among individuals. When individuals engage in constructive conflict, they develop a better awareness of themselves and others. In addition, functional conflict can improve working relationships; when two parties work through their disagreements, they feel they have accomplished something together. By releasing tensions and solving problems in working together, morale is improved.[6] Functional conflict can lead to innovation and positive change for the organization.[7] Because it tends to encourage creativity among individuals, this positive form of conflict can translate into increased productivity.[8] A key to recognizing functional conflict is that it is often cognitive in origin; that is, it arises from someone challenging old policies or thinking of new ways to approach problems.

**Dysfunctional conflict** is an unhealthy, destructive disagreement between two or more people. Its danger is that it takes the focus away from the work to be done and places the focus on the conflict itself and the parties involved. Excessive conflict drains energy that could be used more productively. A key to recognizing a dysfunctional conflict is that its origin is often emotional or behavioural. Disagreements that involve personalized anger and resentment directed at specific individuals rather than specific ideas are dysfunctional.[9] Individuals involved in dysfunctional conflict tend to act before thinking, and they often rely on threats, deception, and verbal abuse to communicate. In dysfunctional conflict, the losses to both parties may exceed any potential gain from the conflict.

## Diagnosing Conflict

Diagnosing conflict as good or bad is not easy. The manager must look at the issue, the context of the conflict, and the parties involved. Once the manager has diagnosed the type of conflict, he or she can either work to resolve it (if it is dysfunctional) or to stimulate it (if it is functional).

>> The following questions can be used to diagnose the nature of the conflict a manager faces:
> Are the parties approaching the conflict from a hostile standpoint?
> Is the outcome likely to be a negative one for the organization?
> Do the potential losses of the parties exceed any potential gains?
> Is energy being diverted from goal accomplishment?

If the majority of the answers to these questions are yes, then the conflict is probably dysfunctional.

[ **Conflict Breaks Open New Thinking** ]

One occasion when managers should work to stimulate conflict is when they suspect their group is suffering from groupthink, discussed in Chapter 10.[10] When a group fails to consider alternative solutions and becomes stagnant in its thinking, it might benefit from healthy disagreements. Teams exhibiting symptoms of groupthink should be encouraged to consider creative problem solving and should appoint a devil's advocate to point out opposing perspectives. These actions can help stimulate constructive conflict in a group.

Kasiutek/Shutterstock

**functional conflict**

A healthy, constructive disagreement between two or more people.

**dysfunctional conflict**

An unhealthy, destructive disagreement between two or more people.

FIGURE **13.1**

## CAUSES OF CONFLICT IN ORGANIZATIONS

**Structural Factors**
• Specialization
• Interdependence
• Common resources
• Goal differences
• Authority relationships
• Status inconsistencies
• Jurisdictional ambiguities

**Conflict**

**Personal Factors**
• Skills and abilities
• Personalities
• Perceptions
• Values and ethics
• Emotions
• Communication barriers
• Cultural differences

Jim Barber/Shutterstock

It is easy to make mistakes in diagnosing conflicts. Sometimes task conflict, which is functional, can be misattributed as being personal, and dysfunctional conflict can follow. Developing trust within the work group can keep this misattribution from occurring.[11] A study of group effectiveness found that North American decision-making groups made up of friends were able to more openly engage in disagreement than groups made up of strangers, allowing the friends' groups to make more effective decisions. When group members (friends) felt comfortable and trusting enough to express conflicting opinions, optimal performance resulted. But similar groups made up of Chinese friends and strangers exhibited both high levels of conflict *and* low levels of performance, suggesting that open disagreement in these groups was not helpful. This finding should serve as a cautionary tale for managers trying to apply one country's management style and techniques in another cultural setting.[12]

# Causes of Conflict in Organizations

Conflict is pervasive in organizations. To manage it effectively, managers should understand the many sources of conflict. They can be classified into two broad categories: structural factors, which stem from the nature of the organization and the way in which work is organized, and personal factors, which arise from differences among individuals. Figure 13.1 summarizes the causes of conflict within each category.

## Structural Factors

The causes of conflict related to the organization's structure include specialization, interdependence, common resources, goal differences, authority relationships, status inconsistencies, and jurisdictional ambiguities.

**Specialization** When jobs are highly specialized, employees become experts at certain tasks. For example, a software company might have one specialist for databases, one for statistical packages, and another for expert systems. Highly specialized jobs can lead to conflict, because people have little awareness of the tasks that others perform.

A classic conflict of specialization may occur between salespeople and engineers. Engineers are technical specialists responsible for product design and quality. Salespeople are marketing experts and liaisons with customers. Salespeople are often accused of making delivery promises to customers that engineers cannot keep because the sales force lacks the technical knowledge necessary to develop realistic delivery deadlines.

**Interdependence** Work that is interdependent requires groups or individuals to depend on one another to accomplish goals.[13] Depending on other people to get work done is fine when the process works smoothly. When there is a problem, however, it becomes very easy to blame the other party, and conflict escalates.

©Rui Frias/iStockPhoto

> [ *It is as naïve to expect that you will like all of your coworkers as it is to expect that they will all like you.* ]

**Common Resources** Any time multiple parties must share resources, there is potential for conflict.[14] This potential is enhanced when the shared resources become scarce. For example, managers often share secretarial support. Not uncommonly, one secretary supports 10 or more managers, each of whom believes his or her work is most important. This puts pressure on the secretary and leads to potential conflicts in prioritizing and scheduling work.

**Goal Differences** When work groups have different goals, these goals may be incompatible. For example, in one cable television company, the salesperson's goal was to sell as many new installations as possible. This created problems for the service department, because its goal was timely installations. With increasing sales, the service department's workload became backed up, and orders were delayed. Often these types of conflicts occur because individuals do not have knowledge of another department's objectives.

**Authority Relationships** A traditional boss–employee relationship is hierarchical in nature, with a boss who is superior to the employee. For many employees, such a relationship is not a comfortable one, because another individual has the right to tell them what to do. Some people resent authority more than others, and obviously this creates conflicts. In addition, some bosses are more autocratic than others; this compounds the potential for conflict in the relationship. As organizations move toward the team approach and empowerment, there should be less potential for conflict from authority relationships.

**Status Inconsistencies** Some organizations have a strong status difference between management and nonmanagement workers. Managers may enjoy privileges—such as flexible schedules, reserved parking spaces, and longer lunch hours—that are not available to nonmanagement employees. This may result in resentment and conflict.

**Jurisdictional Ambiguities** Have you ever telephoned a company with a problem and had your call transferred through several different people and departments? This situation illustrates **jurisdictional ambiguity**—that is, unclear lines of responsibility within an organization.[15] The classic situation here involves the

**jurisdictional ambiguity**
The presence of unclear lines of responsibility within an organization.

hardware/software dilemma. You call the company that made your computer, and they inform you that the problem is caused by the software. You call the software division, and they tell you it's the hardware . . . you get the idea!

## Personal Factors

Not all conflicts arise out of structural factors in the organization. Some conflicts arise out of differences among individuals. The causes of conflict that arise from individual differences include skills and abilities, personalities, perceptions, values and ethics, emotions, communication barriers, and cultural differences.

**Skills and Abilities** Diversity in skills and abilities may be positive for the organization, but it also holds potential for conflict, especially when jobs are interdependent. Experienced, competent workers may find it difficult to work alongside new and unskilled recruits. Workers can become resentful when their new boss, fresh from college, knows a lot about managing people but is unfamiliar with the technology with which they are working.

**Personalities** Individuals do not leave their personalities at the doorstep when they enter the workplace. Personality conflicts are realities in organizations. It is as naïve to expect that you will like all of your coworkers as it is to expect that they will all like you.

One personality trait that many people find difficult to deal with is abrasiveness.[16] An abrasive person ignores the interpersonal aspects of work and the feelings of colleagues. Abrasive individuals are often achievement oriented and hardworking, but their perfectionist, critical style often leaves others feeling unimportant. This style creates stress and strain for those around the abrasive person.[17]

**Perceptions** Differences in perception can also lead to conflict. For example, managers and workers may not have a shared perception of what motivates people. In this case, the reward system can create conflicts if managers provide what they think employees want rather than what employees really want.

**Values and Ethics** Differences in values and ethics can be sources of disagreement. Older workers, for example, value company loyalty and probably would not take a sick day when they were not really ill. Younger workers, valuing mobility, like the concept of "mental health days," or calling in sick to get away from work. This may not be true for all workers, but it illustrates that differences in values can lead to conflict.

Most people have their own sets of values and ethics. The extent to which they apply these ethics in the workplace varies. Some people have strong desires for approval from others and will work to meet others' ethical standards. Some people are relatively unconcerned about approval from others and strongly apply their own ethical standards. Still others operate seemingly without regard to ethics or values.[18] When conflicts about values or ethics do arise, heated disagreement is common because of the personal nature of the differences.

**Emotions** Conflict by its nature is an emotional interaction, and the emotions of the parties involved in conflict play a pivotal role in how they perceive the negotiation and respond to one another.[19] In fact, emotions are now considered critical elements of any negotiation and must be included in any examination of the process and how it unfolds.[20]

One important research finding has been that emotion can play a problematic role in negotiations. In particular, when negotiators begin to act based on emotions rather than on cognitions, they become much more likely to reach an impasse.[21]

**Communication Barriers** Communication barriers such as physical separation and language can create distortions in messages, and these can lead to conflict. Another communication barrier is value judgment, in which a listener assigns a worth to a message before it is received. For example, suppose a team member is a chronic complainer. When this individual enters the manager's office, the manager is likely to devalue the message before it is even delivered. Conflict can then emerge, especially if the complaint is legitimate.

**Cultural Differences** Although cultural differences are assets in organizations, sometimes they can be seen as sources of conflict. Often, these conflicts stem from a lack of understanding of another culture. In one MBA class, for example, Indian students were horrified when Canadian students challenged the professor. Meanwhile, the Canadian students thought the students from India were too passive. Subsequent discussions revealed that professors in India expected to

©Jupiter Images

be treated deferentially and with great respect. While students might challenge an idea vigorously, they would rarely challenge the professor. Diversity training that emphasizes education on cultural differences can make great strides in preventing misunderstandings and teaching new behaviours.

# Forms of Group Conflict in Organizations

Conflict in an organization can take on any of several different forms, which can be sorted into two core types: conflicts that occur at the group level and conflicts that occur at the individual level. Conflicts at each level can be further classified as either *inter* or *intra*. (The prefix *inter* means "between," whereas the prefix *intra* means "within.") Conflict at the group level can occur between organizations (interorganizational), between groups (intergroup), or within a group (intragroup).

## Interorganizational Conflict

Conflict that occurs between two or more organizations is called **interorganizational conflict**. Competition can heighten interorganizational conflict. Corporate takeovers, mergers, and acquisitions can also produce interorganizational conflict. Consider the interorganizational conflict between the National Hockey League's players' union and management, which is sometimes characterized as a battle between millionaires and multimillionaires. The players regularly go on strike to extract more of the profits from management, while management cries that it is not making a dime.

## Intergroup Conflict

When conflict occurs between groups or teams, it is known as **intergroup conflict**. Conflict between groups can have positive effects within each group, such as increased group cohesiveness, increased focus on tasks, and increased loyalty to the group. There are, however, negative consequences as well. Groups in

**interorganizational conflict**
Conflict that occurs between two or more organizations.

**intergroup conflict**
Conflict that occurs between groups or teams in an organization.

conflict tend to develop an "us against them" mentality whereby each sees the other group as the enemy, becomes more hostile, and decreases its communication with the other group. Groups are even more competitive and less cooperative than individuals. The inevitable outcome is that one group gains and the other group loses.[22]

Competition between groups must be managed carefully so that it does not escalate into dysfunctional conflict. Research has shown that when groups compete for a goal that only one group can achieve, negative consequences such as territoriality, aggression, and prejudice toward the other group can result.[23] Managers should encourage and reward cooperative behaviours across groups. Some effective ways of doing this include modifying performance appraisals to include assessing intergroup behaviour and using an external supervisor's evaluation of intergroup behaviour. Group members will be more likely to help other groups when they know that the other group's supervisor will be evaluating their behaviour and that they will be rewarded for cooperation.[24] In addition, managers should encourage social interactions across groups so that trust can be developed. Trust allows individuals to exchange ideas and resources with members of other groups and results in innovation when members of different groups cooperate.[25]

**intragroup conflict**
Conflict that occurs within groups or teams.

**intrapersonal conflict**
Conflict that occurs within an individual.

**interrole conflict**
A person's experience of conflict among the multiple roles in his or her life.

# GENERATION CLASH

>>

An emerging challenge in conflict management is the intergenerational conflict brought about by the diversity in age in the North American workforce. Some sources of intergenerational conflict are

- employee benefit packages being designed to appeal more to one age group than another, or

- older employees fearing that younger new hires may take over their jobs.

Organizations should design flexible employee "cafeteria style" benefit systems that have a broader appeal to a diverse age group and encourage social interaction to reduce these perceived threats and create trust.[26]

## Intragroup Conflict

Conflict that occurs within groups or teams is called **intragroup conflict**. Some conflict within a group is functional. It can help the group avoid groupthink, as we discussed in Chapter 10. Furthermore, recall that self-managed teams are teams with a high degree of decision making and implementation authority.

Even the newest type of teams, virtual teams, are not immune to conflict. The nuances and subtleties of face-to-face communication are often lacking in these teams, and misunderstandings can result. To avoid dysfunctional conflicts, virtual teams should ensure their tasks fit their methods of interacting. Complex strategic decisions may require face-to-face meetings rather than e-mails or threaded discussions. Face-to-face and telephone interactions early on can eliminate future conflicts and allow virtual teams to move on to use electronic communication because trust has been developed.[27]

LEARNING OUTCOME **4**

# Individual Conflict in Organizations

As with groups, conflict can occur between individuals or within a single individual.

## Types of Intrapersonal Conflict

When conflict occurs within an individual, it is called **intrapersonal conflict**. There are several types of intrapersonal conflict, including interrole, intrarole, and person–role conflicts. A role is a set of expectations placed on an individual by others.[28] The person occupying the focal role is the role incumbent, and the individuals who place expectations on the person are role senders. Figure 13.2 depicts a set of role relationships.

**Interrole conflict** occurs when a person experiences conflict among the multiple roles in his or her life. One interrole conflict that many employees experience is work–life conflict, in which their role as worker clashes with their role as spouse or parent.[29] Work/home conflict has become even more common with the rise of work-at-home professionals and telecommuting because the home becomes the office, blurring the boundary between work and family life.[30] Interrole conflict can have a serious impact on an individual's health. According to Duxbury, who has studied interrole conflict extensively in Canada, "[when] we look today at people who can't balance [work and life], we find that they have substantially higher levels of perceived stress, they have higher levels of depressed mood ..."[31] Similarly, Spinks notes "We're all expending a

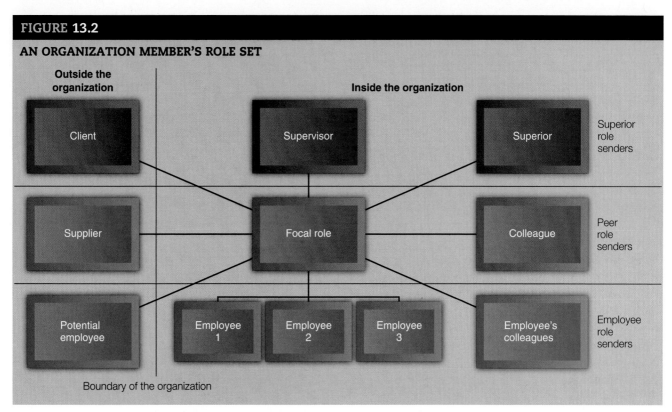

## FIGURE 13.2

### AN ORGANIZATION MEMBER'S ROLE SET

**Outside the organization**

**Inside the organization**

Client

Supervisor

Superior — Superior role senders

Supplier

Focal role

Colleague — Peer role senders

Potential employee

Employee 1

Employee 2

Employee 3

Employee's colleagues — Employee role senders

Boundary of the organization

lot of energy running over rocks and barriers, exhausting ourselves, never fully satisfied with whatever we do in our home life, our personal life, or our work life. We feel like we're never meeting the expectations that others have placed on us, that we're constantly without the necessary resources to do our jobs, which leaves us depleted, which leaves us unhappy, which again leads to all kinds of negative implications in personal relationships and in the community."[32]

Recently, organizations are levering their use of information technology to gain a competitive edge. This has

translated into ambitious and highly involved employees using office communications (e.g., voice mail, e-mail, etc.) even after hours. Such after-hours communication usage is associated with increased work–life conflict as reported by the employee and a significant other.[33]

**Intrarole conflict** is conflict within a single role. It often arises when a person receives conflicting messages from role senders about how to perform a certain role. Suppose a manager receives counsel from her department head that she needs to socialize less with the nonmanagement employees. She also is told by her project manager that she needs to be a better team member, and that she can accomplish this by socializing more with the other nonmanagement team members. This situation is one of intrarole conflict.

**Person–role conflict** occurs when an individual in a particular role is expected to perform behaviours that clash with his or her values.[34] Salespeople, for example, may be required to offer the most expensive item in the sales line first to the customer, even when it is apparent that the customer does not want or cannot afford the item. A

**intrarole conflict**

Conflict that occurs within a single role, such as when a person receives conflicting messages from role senders about how to perform a certain role.

**person–role conflict**

Conflict that occurs when an individual is expected to perform behaviours in a certain role that conflict with his or her personal values.

computer salesperson may be required to offer a large, elaborate system to a student he knows is on a tight budget. This may conflict with the salesperson's values, and he may experience person–role conflict.

Intrapersonal conflicts can have positive consequences. Often, professional responsibilities clash with deeply held values. A budget shortfall may force a manager to lay off a loyal, hardworking employee. An individual's daughter may have a piano recital on the same day his or her largest client is scheduled to be in town, visiting the office. In such conflicts, individuals often have to choose between right and right; that is, there's no correct response. These may be thought of as *defining moments* that challenge us to choose between two or more things in which we believe.[35] Character is formed in defining moments because they cause us to shape our identities. They help us crystallize our values and serve as opportunities for personal growth.

## Managing Intrapersonal Conflict

Intrapersonal conflict can be managed with careful self-analysis and diagnosis of the situation. Three actions in particular can help prevent or resolve intrapersonal conflicts.

First, job seekers should find out as much as possible about the values of the organization.[36] Many person–role conflicts centre around differences between the organization's values and the individual's values. Research has shown that when there is a good fit between the values of the individual and the organization, the individual is more satisfied and committed and is less likely to leave the organization.[37]

Second, to manage intrarole or interrole conflicts, role analysis is a good tool.[38] In role analysis, the individual asks the various role senders what they expect of him or her. The outcomes are clearer work roles and the reduction of conflict and ambiguity.[39] Role analysis is a simple tool that clarifies the expectations of both parties in a relationship and reduces the potential for conflict within a role or between roles.

Third, political skills can help buffer the negative effects of stress that stem from role conflicts. Effective politicians can negotiate role expectations when conflicts occur. All these forms of conflict can be managed. An understanding of the many forms is a first step.

**interpersonal conflict**

Conflict that occurs between two or more individuals.

## Managing Interpersonal Conflict

Conflict between two or more people, or **interpersonal conflict**, can arise from many individual differences, such as personalities, attitudes, values, perceptions, to name a few. To manage interpersonal conflict, it is helpful to understand power networks in organizations, defence mechanisms exhibited by individuals, and ways to cope with difficult people.

**Power Networks** According to Mastenbroek, individuals in organizations are organized in three basic types of power networks.[40] Based on these power relationships, certain kinds of conflict tend to emerge. Figure 13.3 illustrates three basic kinds of power relationships in organizations.

The first relationship is equal versus equal, in which there is a horizontal balance of power among the parties. An example of this type of relationship would be a conflict between individuals from two different project teams. The behavioural tendency is toward suboptimization; that is, the focus is on a win–lose approach to problems, and each party tries to maximize its power at the expense of the other party. Conflict within this type of network can lead to depression, low self-esteem, and other distress symptoms. Interventions like improving coordination between the parties and working toward common interests can help manage these conflicts.

The second power network is high versus low, or a powerful versus a less powerful relationship. Conflicts that emerge here take the basic form of the powerful individuals trying to control others, with the less powerful people trying to become more autonomous. Conflict in this network can lead to job dissatisfaction, low organizational commitment, and turnover.[41] Organizations typically respond to these conflicts by tightening the rules. However, the more successful ways of managing these conflicts are to try a different style of leadership, such as a coaching and counselling style, or to change the structure to a more decentralized one.

The third power network is high versus middle versus low. This power network illustrates the classic conflicts felt by middle managers. Two particular conflicts are evident for middle managers: role conflict, in which conflicting expectations are placed on the manager from

## FIGURE 13.3

### POWER RELATIONSHIPS IN ORGANIZATIONS

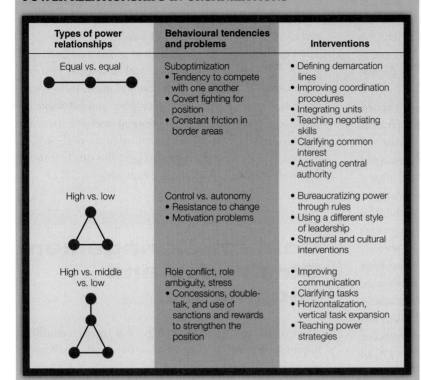

| Types of power relationships | Behavioural tendencies and problems | Interventions |
|---|---|---|
| Equal vs. equal | Suboptimization<br>• Tendency to compete with one another<br>• Covert fighting for position<br>• Constant friction in border areas | • Defining demarcation lines<br>• Improving coordination procedures<br>• Integrating units<br>• Teaching negotiating skills<br>• Clarifying common interest<br>• Activating central authority |
| High vs. low | Control vs. autonomy<br>• Resistance to change<br>• Motivation problems | • Bureaucratizing power through rules<br>• Using a different style of leadership<br>• Structural and cultural interventions |
| High vs. middle vs. low | Role conflict, role ambiguity, stress<br>• Concessions, double-talk, and use of sanctions and rewards to strengthen the position | • Improving communication<br>• Clarifying tasks<br>• Horizontalization, vertical task expansion<br>• Teaching power strategies |

SOURCE: W. F. G. Mastenbroek, *Conflict Management and Organization Development*, 1987. Copyright John Wiley & Sons Limited. Reproduced with permission.

bosses and employees, and role ambiguity, in which the expectations of the boss are unclear. Improved communication among all parties can reduce role conflict and ambiguity. In addition, middle managers can benefit from training in positive ways to influence others.

Knowing the typical kinds of conflicts that arise in various kinds of relationships can help a manager diagnose conflicts and devise appropriate ways to manage them.

### Defence Mechanisms

When individuals are involved in conflict with another human being, frustration often results.[42] Conflicts can often arise within the context of a performance appraisal session. Most people do not react well to negative feedback, as was illustrated in a classic study.[43] In this study, when employees were given criticism about their work, over 50 percent of their responses were defensive.

> " Defence mechanisms are common reactions to the frustration that accompanies conflict.

When individuals are frustrated, as they often are in interpersonal conflict, they respond by exhibiting defence mechanisms.[44] Defence mechanisms are common reactions to the frustration that accompanies conflict.

Aggressive mechanisms, such as fixation, displacement, and negativism, are aimed at attacking the source of the conflict. In **fixation**, an individual fixates on the conflict, or keeps up a dysfunctional behaviour that obviously will not solve the conflict. An example of fixation occurred in a university, where a faculty member became embroiled in a battle with the dean because the faculty member felt he had not received a large enough salary increase. He persisted in writing angry letters to the dean, whose hands were tied because of a low budget allocation. **Displacement** means directing anger toward someone who is not the source of the conflict. For example, a manager may respond harshly to an employee after a telephone confrontation with an angry customer. Another aggressive defence mechanism is **negativism**, which is active or passive resistance. Negativism is illustrated by a manager who, when appointed to a committee on which she did not want to serve, made negative comments throughout the meeting.

Compromise mechanisms, such as compensation, identification, and rationalization, are used by individuals to make the best of a conflict situation. **Compensation** occurs when an individual tries to make up for an inadequacy by putting increased energy into another activity. Compensation can be seen when a person makes up for a bad relationship at home by spending more time at the office. **Identification** occurs when one individual patterns his or her behaviour after another's. One

**fixation**
An aggressive mechanism in which an individual keeps up a dysfunctional behaviour that obviously will not solve the conflict.

**displacement**
An aggressive mechanism in which an individual directs his or her anger toward someone who is not the source of the conflict.

**negativism**
An aggressive mechanism in which a person responds with pessimism to any attempt at solving a problem.

**compensation**
A compromise mechanism in which an individual attempts to make up for a negative situation by devoting himself or herself to another pursuit with increased vigour.

**identification**
A compromise mechanism whereby an individual patterns his or her behaviour after another's.

supervisor at a construction firm, not wanting to acknowledge consciously that she was not likely to be promoted, mimicked the behaviour of her boss, even going so far as to buy a car just like the boss's. **Rationalization** involves an individual trying to justify his or her behaviour by constructing bogus reasons for it. Employees may rationalize unethical behaviour such as padding their expense accounts because "everyone else does it."

Withdrawal mechanisms are exhibited when frustrated individuals try to flee from a conflict using either physical or psychological means. Flight, conversion, and fantasy are examples of withdrawal mechanisms. Physically escaping a conflict is **flight**. An employee taking a day off after a blowup with the boss is an example. **Withdrawal** may take the form of emotionally leaving a conflict, such as exhibiting an "I don't care anymore" attitude. **Conversion** is a process whereby emotional conflicts become expressed in physical symptoms. Most of us have experienced the conversion reaction of a headache following an emotional exchange with another person. **Fantasy** is an escape by daydreaming. In the Internet age, fantasy as an escape mechanism has found new meaning. A study conducted by International Data Corporation (IDC) showed that 30 to 40 percent of all Internet surfing at work is nonwork-related and that more than 70 percent of companies have had sex sites accessed from their networks, suggesting that employees' minds aren't always focused on their jobs.[45]

When employees exhibit withdrawal mechanisms, they often fake it by pretending to agree with their bosses or coworkers in order to avoid facing an immediate conflict. Many employees fake it because the organization informally rewards agreement and punishes dissent. The long-term consequence of withdrawal and faking it is emotional distress for the employee.[46]

Knowledge of these defence mechanisms can be extremely beneficial to a manager. By understanding the ways in which people typically react to interpersonal conflict, managers can be prepared for employees' reactions and help them uncover their feelings about a conflict.

A case that is currently causing conflict within the legal profession is a lawsuit filed by Diane LaCalamita that alleges that McCarthy Tétrault LLP engaged in systemic gender-based discrimination when it fired LaCalamita.[47] The case is significant, not only for the conflict, but also because "[it is] believed to be the first time that a major Canadian law firm has been ordered to reveal confidential information related to gender ..."[48] The case is being argued with great passion on both sides and is causing bitter divisions and defensive postures. "For some—mainly men, but some women, too—it's the story of a bitter, mediocre lawyer who couldn't make the cut among the top-flight litigators at an elite firm. For others—mostly women, but some men as well—it's the kind of case that finally brings to light the subtle forms of discrimination and stereotyping that linger ..."[49]

LEARNING OUTCOME **5**

# Conflict Management Strategies and Techniques

The overall approach (or strategy) you use in a conflict is important in determining whether the conflict will have a positive or negative outcome.

These overall strategies are competitive versus cooperative strategies. Table 13.2 depicts the two strategies and four different conflict scenarios. The competitive strategy is founded on assumptions of win–lose and entails dishonest communication, mistrust, and a rigid position from both parties.[50] The cooperative strategy is founded on different assumptions: the potential for win–win outcomes, honest communication, trust, openness to risk and vulnerability, and the notion that the whole may be greater than the sum of the parts.

To illustrate the importance of the overall strategy, consider the case of two groups competing for scarce

**rationalization**

A compromise mechanism characterized by an individual trying to justify his or her behaviour by constructing bogus reasons for it.

**flight/withdrawal**

A withdrawal mechanism that entails physically escaping a conflict (flight) or psychologically escaping (withdrawal).

**conversion**

A withdrawal mechanism in which emotional conflicts are expressed in physical symptoms.

**fantasy**

A withdrawal mechanism that provides an escape from a conflict through daydreaming.

©Anna Bryukhanova/iStockPhoto

## TABLE 13.2 Win-Lose versus Win-Win Strategies

| STRATEGY | DEPARTMENT A | DEPARTMENT B | ORGANIZATION |
|---|---|---|---|
| Competitive | Lose | Lose | Lose |
| | Lose | Win | Lose |
| | Win | Lose | Lose |
| Cooperative | Win | Win | Win |

resources. Suppose budget cuts have to be made at an insurance company. The claims manager argues that the sales training staff should be cut, because agents are fully trained. The sales training manager argues that claims staff should be cut, because the company is processing fewer claims. This could turn into a dysfunctional brawl, with both sides refusing to give ground. This would constitute a win–lose, lose–win, or lose–lose scenario. Staff cuts could be made in only one department, or in both departments. In all three cases, with the competitive approach the organization winds up in a losing position.

Even in such intense conflicts as those over scarce resources, a win–win strategy can lead to an overall win for the organization. In fact, conflicts over scarce resources can be productive if the parties have cooperative goals—a strategy that seeks a winning solution for both parties. To achieve a win–win outcome, the conflict must be approached with open-minded discussion of opposing views. Through open-minded discussion, both parties integrate views and create new solutions that facilitate productivity and strengthen their relationship; the result is feelings of unity rather than separation.[51]

In the example of the conflict between the claims manager and sales training manager, open-minded discussion might reveal that there are ways to achieve budget cuts without cutting staff. Sales support might surrender part of its travel budget, and claims might cut out overtime. This represents a win–win situation for the company. The budget has been reduced, and relationships between the two departments have been preserved. Both parties have given up something, but the conflict has been resolved with a positive outcome.

You can see the importance of the broad strategy used to approach a conflict. We now move from broad strategies to more specific techniques.

©Joshua Hodge/iStockPhoto

## Ineffective Techniques

There are many specific techniques for dealing with conflict. Before turning to techniques that work, it should be recognized that some actions commonly taken in organizations to deal with conflict are not effective.[52]

**Nonaction** is doing nothing in hopes that the conflict will disappear. Generally, this is not a good technique, because most conflicts do not go away, and the individuals involved in the conflict react with frustration.

**Secrecy**, or trying to keep a conflict out of view of most people, only creates suspicion. An example is an organizational policy of pay secrecy. In some organizations, discussion of salary is grounds for dismissal. When this is the case, employees suspect that the company has something to hide.

**Administrative orbiting** is delaying action on a conflict by buying time, usually by telling the individuals involved that the problem is being worked on or that the boss is still thinking about the issue. Like nonaction, this technique leads to frustration and resentment.

**Due process nonaction** is a procedure set up to address conflicts that is so costly, time consuming, or personally risky that no one will use it. Some organizations' sexual harassment policies are examples of this technique. To file a sexual harassment complaint, detailed paperwork is required, the accuser must go through appropriate channels, and the accuser risks being branded a troublemaker. Thus, the company has a procedure for handling complaints (due process), but no one uses it (nonaction) because it is cumbersome and offputting.

---

**nonaction**
Doing nothing in hopes that a conflict will disappear.

**secrecy**
Attempting to hide a conflict or an issue that has the potential to create conflict.

**administrative orbiting**
Delaying action on a conflict by buying time.

**due process nonaction**
A procedure set up to address conflicts that is so costly, time consuming, or personally risky that no one will use it.

**Character assassination** is an attempt to label or discredit an opponent. Character assassination can backfire and make the individual who uses it appear dishonest and cruel. It often leads to name calling and accusations by both parties, and both parties end up losers in the eyes of those who witness the conflict.

## Effective Techniques

Fortunately, there are effective conflict management techniques. These include appealing to superordinate goals, expanding resources, changing personnel, changing structure, and confronting and negotiating.

### Superordinate Goals
An organizational goal that is more important to both parties in a conflict than their individual or group goals is a **superordinate goal**.[53] Superordinate goals cannot be achieved by an individual or by one group alone. The achievement of these goals requires cooperation by both parties.

One effective technique for resolving conflict is to appeal to a superordinate goal—in effect, to focus the parties on a larger issue on which they both agree. This helps them realize their similarities rather than their differences.

In the conflict between service representatives and cable television installers that was discussed earlier, appealing to a superordinate goal would be an effective technique for resolving the conflict. Both departments can agree that superior customer service is a goal worthy of pursuit and that this goal cannot be achieved unless cables are installed properly and in a timely manner, and customer complaints are handled effectively. Quality service requires that both departments cooperate to achieve the goal.

### Expanding Resources
One conflict resolution technique is so simple that it may be overlooked. If the conflict's source is common or scarce resources, providing more resources may be a solution. Of course, managers working with tight budgets may not have the luxury of obtaining additional resources. Nevertheless, it is a technique to be considered. In the example earlier in this chapter, one solution to the conflict among managers over secretarial support would be to hire more secretaries.

### Changing Personnel
In some cases, long-running severe conflict may be traced to a specific individual. For example, managers with lower levels of emotional intelligence have been demonstrated to have more negative work attitudes, to exhibit

less altruistic behaviour, and to produce more negative work outcomes. A chronically disgruntled manager who exhibits low EI may not only frustrate his employees but also impede his department's performance. In such cases, transferring or firing an individual may be the best solution, but only after due process.[54]

### Changing Structure
Another way to resolve a conflict is to change the structure of the organization. One way of accomplishing this is to create an integrator role. An integrator is a liaison between groups with very different interests. In severe conflicts, it may be best that the integrator be a neutral third party.[55] Creating the integrator role is a way of opening dialogue between groups that have difficulty communicating.

Using cross-functional teams is another way of changing the organization's structure to manage conflict. In the traditional methods of designing new products in organizations, many departments had to contribute, and delays resulted from difficulties in coordinating the activities of the various departments. Using a cross-functional team made up of members from different departments improves coordination and reduces delays by allowing many activities to be performed at the same time rather than sequentially.[56] The team approach allows members from different departments to work together and reduces the potential for conflict. However, recent research also suggests that such functional diversity can lead to slower informational processing in teams due to differences in members' perceptions of what might be required to achieve group goals. When putting together cross-functional teams, organizations should emphasize superordinate goals and train team members on resolving conflict. One such training technique could

## WHEN TO NEGOTIATE

>> Negotiating is a useful strategy under the following conditions:

> There are two or more parties. Negotiation is primarily an interpersonal or intergroup process.
> There is a conflict of interest between the parties such that what one party wants is not what the other party wants.
> The parties are willing to negotiate because each believes it can use its influence to obtain a better outcome than by simply taking the side of the other party.
> The parties prefer to work together rather than to fight openly, give in, break off contact, or take the dispute to a higher authority.

---

**character assassination**
An attempt to label or discredit an opponent.

**superordinate goal**
An organizational goal that is more important to both parties in a conflict than their individual or group goals.

> ## *There appears to be no evidence that men are better negotiators than women or vice versa. The differences lie in how negotiators are treated.*

involve educating individual members in other functional areas so that everyone in the team can have a shared language.[57] In teamwork, it is helpful to break up a big task so that it becomes a collection of smaller, less complex tasks, and to have smaller teams work on the smaller tasks. This helps to reduce conflict, and organizations can potentially improve the performance of the overall team by improving the outcomes in each subteam.[58]

**Confronting and Negotiating** Some conflicts require confrontation and negotiation between the parties. Both of these strategies require skill on the part of the negotiator and careful planning before engaging in negotiations. The process of negotiating involves an open discussion of problem solutions, and the outcome often is an exchange in which both parties work toward a mutually beneficial solution.

Negotiation is a joint process of finding a mutually acceptable solution to a complex conflict. There are two major negotiating approaches: distributive bargaining and integrative negotiation.[59] **Distributive bargaining** is an approach in which the goals of one party are in direct conflict with the goals of the other party. Resources are limited, and each party wants to maximize its share of the resources (get its part of the pie). It is a competitive or win–lose approach to negotiations. Sometimes distributive bargaining causes negotiators to focus so much on their differences that they ignore their common ground. In these cases, distributive bargaining can become counterproductive. The reality is, however, that some situations are distributive in nature, particularly when the parties are interdependent. If a negotiator wants to maximize the value of a single deal and is not worried about maintaining a good relationship with the other party, distributive bargaining may be an option.

In contrast, **integrative negotiation** is an approach in which the parties' goals are not seen as mutually exclusive and in which the focus is on making it possible for both sides to achieve their objectives. Integrative negotiation focuses on the merits of the issues and is a win–win approach. (How can we make the pie bigger?) For integrative negotiation to be successful, certain preconditions must be present. These include having a common goal, faith in your own problem-solving abilities, a belief in the validity of the other party's position, motivation to work together, mutual trust, and clear communication.[60]

According to Fisher, Ury, and Patton, in their landmark book, *Getting to Yes—Negotiating Agreement without Giving In*, a good negotiation is principled, not positional. A principled process of negotiation is characterized throughout by (1) separating the person from the problem, (2) focusing on interests rather than on positions, (3) generating several different options before coming to an agreement, and (4) ensuring that the agreement be supported by objective criteria. They note that the weaker party in the negotiation should develop a BATNA, i.e., Best Alternative to a Negotiated Agreement, so as to avoid negotiating an outcome that is worse than he/she would have gotten without negotiating![61] Increasingly, individuals and organizations are using Alternative Dispute Resolution, known as ADR, techniques to address conflicts. The three principal techniques are mediation and arbitration, as well as negotiation.[62] Table 13.3 (on page 224) highlights the main differences between various ways to address conflict.

Cultural differences in negotiation must be acknowledged. Japanese negotiators, for example, when working with North American negotiators, tend to see their power as coming from their role (buyer versus seller). North Americans, in contrast, view their power as their ability to walk away from the negotiations.[63] Neither culture understands the other very well, and the negotiations can resemble a dance in which one person is waltzing and the other doing a samba. The collectivism–individualism dimension (discussed in Chapter 2) has a great bearing on negotiations. North Americans, with their individualism, negotiate from a position of self-interest; Japanese focus on the good of the group. Cross-cultural negotiations can be more effective if you learn as much about other cultures as possible.

Gender may also play a role in negotiation. There appears to be no evidence that men are better negotiators than women or vice versa. The differences lie in how negotiators are treated. Women are blatantly discriminated against in terms of the offers made to them in negotiations.[64] Gender stereotypes also affect the negotiating process. Women may be seen as accommodating,

**distributive bargaining**
A negotiation approach in which the goals of the parties are in conflict, and each party seeks to maximize its resources.

**integrative negotiation**
A negotiation approach that focuses on the merits of the issues and seeks a win–win solution.

**TABLE 13.3** Negotiation, Mediation, Arbitration and Litigation—How They Work

| | HOW IT HAPPENS | WHO IS INVOLVED | HOW DOES THE PROCESS WORK | OUTCOME |
|---|---|---|---|---|
| **Negotiation** | By agreement/ contract | Two or more parties communicate with each other and make decisions | The parties determine the process | Contract is final and binding |
| **Mediation** | By agreement/ contract Court-ordered | A neutral third party acts as communicator and facilitator to help parties make their own decisions to resolve the dispute | A neutral third party leads the parties through stages in private, caucus, and together. 1. Opening Statements 2. Defining the issues 3. Developing understanding of issues 4. Developing solution | Written or verbal agreement which morally or legally binds the parties |
| **Arbitration** | By agreement/ contract By legislation Court-ordered | A neutral third party acts as decision-maker | By e-mail, fax and conference calls, the arbitrator leads the parties through stages: 1. Parties structure proceedings and schedule 2. Submission of claims, preliminary matters, defence, answers, evidence, argument 3. In person hearing if requested 4. Cross examination 5. Summation (unless parties agree to a less formal process). | The arbitrator's award is final and binding on the parties and enforceable by the courts |
| **Litigation** | Either party may initiate | Judge acts as decision-maker | Judge takes the parties through stages: 1. Opening statements 2. Argument/evidence 3. Examination in chief 4. Cross examination 5. Summation | A decision by the judge which is final and binding on the parties subject to the right |

SOURCE: ADR Institute of Ontario, Inc. http://www.adrontario.ca/about/faq.cfm. Retrieved March 3, 2010.

conciliatory, and emotional (negatives in negotiations) and men may be seen as assertive, powerful, and convincing (positive for negotiations) in accordance with traditional stereotypes. Sometimes, when women feel they're being stereotyped, they exhibit stereotype reactance, which is a tendency to display behaviour inconsistent with (or opposite of) the stereotype. This means they become more assertive and convincing. Alternatively, men may choke when they're expected to fulfill the stereotype, fearing that they might not be able to live up to the stereotype.

LEARNING OUTCOME **6**

# Conflict Management Styles

Managers have at their disposal a variety of conflict management styles: avoiding, accommodating, competing,

compromising, and collaborating. One way of classifying styles of conflict management is to examine the styles' assertiveness (the extent to which you want your goals met) and cooperativeness (the extent to which you want to see the other party's concerns met).[65] Figure 13.4 graphs the five conflict management styles using these two dimensions. Table 13.4 (on page 226) lists appropriate situations for using each conflict management style.

## Avoiding

Avoiding is a style low on both assertiveness and cooperativeness. Avoiding is a deliberate decision to take no action on a conflict or to stay out of a conflict situation. In recent times, Airbus, a European manufacturer of aircraft, has faced massive intraorganizational conflict stemming from major expansions that included French, German, Spanish and British subsidiaries within the same parent company. Power struggles among executives combined with massive changes in organizational structure are believed to have

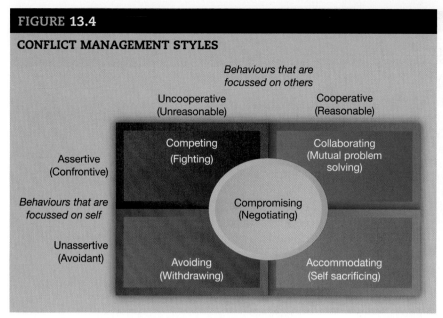

## FIGURE 13.4

### CONFLICT MANAGEMENT STYLES

Behaviours that are focussed on others

Uncooperative (Unreasonable)

Cooperative (Reasonable)

Assertive (Confrontive)

Competing (Fighting)

Collaborating (Mutual problem solving)

Behaviours that are focussed on self

Compromising (Negotiating)

Unassertive (Avoidant)

Avoiding (Withdrawing)

Accommodating (Self sacrificing)

SOURCE: Hutt, Guy K. and Robert A. Milligan. "Managing Conflict on the Farm." Managing Farm Personnel, In-service Workshop for Extension Agents and Specialists. Kansas City, 1990. Reprinted with permission.

led to this type of conflict. Airbus seems to be adopting the avoidance strategy in an effort to let these conflicts subside on their own.[66] Some relationship conflicts, such as those involving political norms and personal tastes, may distract team members from their tasks and avoiding may be an appropriate strategy.[67] When the parties are angry and need time to cool down, it may be best to use avoidance. There is a potential danger in using an avoiding style too often, however. Research shows that overuse of this style results in negative evaluations from others in the workplace.[68]

## Accommodating

A style in which you are concerned that the other party's goals be met but relatively unconcerned with getting your own way is called accommodating. It is cooperative but unassertive. Appropriate situations for accommodating include times when you find you are wrong, when you want to let the other party have his or her way so that that individual will owe you similar treatment later, or when the relationship is important. Overreliance on accommodating has its dangers. Managers who constantly defer to others may find that others lose respect for them. In addition, accommodating managers may become frustrated and resentful because their own needs are never met, and they may lose self-esteem.[69]

Shutterstock

## Competing

Competing is a style that is very assertive and uncooperative. You want to satisfy your own interests and are willing to do so at the other party's expense. In an emergency or in situations where you know you are right, it may be appropriate to put your foot down. For example, environmentalists forced Shell Oil Company (part of Royal Dutch/Shell Group) to scrap its plans to build a refinery after a bitter "To Hell with Shell" campaign.[70] Relying solely on competing strategies is dangerous, though. Managers who do so may become reluctant to admit when they are wrong and may find themselves surrounded by people who are afraid to disagree with them. In team settings, it has been noted earlier that task conflict and relationship conflict could occur together, although task conflict is seen as functional whereas relationship conflict is seen as dysfunctional for the team. In a recent study, dyads of participants were exposed to task-based conflict. One of the two members of the dyads was trained on using either the competing conflict handling style or the collaborative style. Results indicated that the competing style led to the most relationship conflict whereas the collaborative style led to the least relationship conflict after the task conflict was resolved.[71]

## Compromising

The compromising style is intermediate in both assertiveness and cooperativeness, because each party must give up something to reach a solution to the conflict. Compromises are often made in the final hours of union–management negotiations, when time is of the essence. Compromise may be an effective backup style when efforts toward collaboration are not successful.[72]

It is important to recognize that compromises are not optimal solutions. Compromise means partially surrendering your position for the sake of coming to terms. Often, when people compromise, they inflate their demands to begin with. The solutions reached may be only temporary, and often compromises do nothing to improve relationships between the parties in the conflict.

## TABLE 13.4 Uses of Five Styles of Conflict Management

| CONFLICT-HANDLING STYLE | APPROPRIATE SITUATION |
| --- | --- |
| Competing | 1. When quick, decisive action is vital (e.g., emergencies).<br>2. On important issues where unpopular actions need implementing (e.g., cost cutting, enforcing unpopular rules, discipline).<br>3. On issues vital to company welfare when you know you are right.<br>4. Against people who take advantage of noncompetitive behaviour. |
| Collaborating | 1. To find an integrative solution when both sets of concerns are too important to be compromised.<br>2. When your objective is to learn.<br>3. To merge insights from people with different perspectives.<br>4. To gain commitment by incorporating concerns into a consensus.<br>5. To work through feelings that have interfered with a relationship. |
| Compromising | 1. When goals are important but not worth the effort or potential disruption of more assertive modes.<br>2. When opponents with equal power are committed to mutually exclusive goals.<br>3. To achieve temporary settlements to complex issues.<br>4. To arrive at expedient solutions under time pressure.<br>5. As a backup when collaboration or competition is unsuccessful. |
| Avoiding | 1. When an issue is trivial or more important issues are pressing.<br>2. When you perceive no chance of satisfying your concerns.<br>3. When potential disruption outweighs the benefits of resolution.<br>4. To let people cool down and regain perspective.<br>5. When gathering information supersedes immediate decision.<br>6. When others can resolve the conflict more effectively.<br>7. When issues seem tangential or symptomatic of other issues. |
| Accommodating | 1. When you find you are wrong—to allow a better position to be heard, to learn, and to show your reasonableness.<br>2. When issues are more important to others than to yourself—to satisfy others and maintain cooperation.<br>3. To build social credits for later issues.<br>4. To minimize loss when you are outmatched and losing.<br>5. When harmony and stability are especially important.<br>6. To allow employees to develop by learning from mistakes. |

SOURCE: K. W. Thomas, "Toward Multi-Dimensional Values in Teaching: The Example of Conflict Behaviors," *Academy of Management Review* 2 (1977): 309–325. Reproduced by permission of the publisher via Copyright Clearance Center, Inc.

## Collaborating

A win–win style that is high on both assertiveness and cooperativeness is known as collaborating. Working toward collaborating involves an open and thorough discussion of the conflict and arriving at a solution that is satisfactory to both parties. Situations where collaboration may be effective include times when both parties need to be committed to a final solution or when a combination of different perspectives can be formed into a solution. Collaborating requires open, trusting behaviour and sharing information for the benefit of both parties. Long term, it leads to improved relationships and effective performance.[73]

Research on the five styles of conflict management indicates that although most managers favour a certain style, they have the capacity to change styles as the situation demands.[74] A study of project managers found that managers who used a combination of competing and avoiding styles were seen as ineffective by the engineers who worked on their project teams.[75] In another study of conflicts between R&D project managers and technical staff, competing and avoiding styles resulted in more frequent conflict and lower performance, whereas the collaborating style resulted in less frequent conflict and better performance.[76]

> The What about You? on the Chapter 13 Review Card helps you to assess your dominant conflict management style.

# GET ONLINE

The easy-to-navigate website for **ORGB** offers guidance on key topics in **Organizational Behaviour** in a variety of engaging formats. You have the opportunity to refine and check your understanding via interactive quizzes and flashcards. Videos and podcasts provide inspiration for your own further exploration. And, in order to make **ORGB** an even better learning tool, we invite you to speak up about

your experience with **ORGB** by completing a survey form and sending us your comments.

**Get online and discover the following resources:**
- Cases and Exercises
- Key Term flashcards
- Interactive Quizzing
- PowerPoint Slides
- Interactive Games

*"I think this book is awesome for students of all ages. It is a much simpler way to study."*

—Yasmine Al-Hashimi, Fanshawe College

Visit **www.icanorgb.com** to find the resources you need today!

# Jobs and the Design of Work

# Work in Organizations

**Work** is effortful, productive activity resulting in a product or a service. A **job** is defined as an employee's set of specific task activities in an organization, assigned pieces of work to be done in a specified time period. Work is an especially important human endeavour because it has a powerful effect in binding a person to reality. Through work, people become securely attached to reality and securely connected in human relationships. *Work* has different meanings for different people. For all people, work is organized into jobs, and jobs fit into the larger structure of an organization. The structure of jobs is the concern of this

> ❝ Through work, people become securely attached to reality and securely connected in human relationships.

chapter, and the structure of the organization is the concern of the next chapter. Both chapters emphasize organizations as sets of task and authority relationships through which people get work done.

## The Meaning of Work

Many big lottery winners choose to continue working. Work does not

**work**
Mental or physical activity that has productive results.

**job**
A set of specified work and task activities that engage an individual in an organization.

## LEARNING OUTCOMES

After reading this chapter, you should be able to do the following:

**1** Differentiate between *job* and *work*.

**2** Explain how job enlargement and job rotation counter Taylor's scientific management

**3** Explain the job characteristics model, and how it has been expanded by subsequent research.

**4** Describe the concepts of social information processing (SIP) and job crafting.

**5** Identify and describe contemporary issues facing

simply fulfill financial needs; it is an important element of most people's lives. It contributes to their identity, their self-esteem, social interaction and status, and the fulfillment of personal needs as well as practical ones.[1] In a study of American lottery winners, the majority (85 percent) chose to continue working, even though the average win in that group was $2.59 million. The choice to quit was certainly related to the amount won, but also strongly related to the centrality of work in the lives of the winners. Those to whom work was important chose to continue working despite no longer having the financial incentive. For example, a 64-year-old bus driver who won $20 million stated that the "lottery is just a bonus that came my way; it has not or will not affect my work habits and goals in life."[2] The key role of work in one's life is indicated by the impact on both physical and psychological health when work is lost. A longitudinal study in New Zealand followed meat-processing workers after their plants closed and compared them to similar workers in a neighbouring community who had not lost their jobs. It found a significant difference in mental distress leading to serious self-harm.[3] Other studies link involuntary job loss to the risk of stroke,[4] heart disease and arthritis,[5] depression, substance abuse, and anxiety.[6]

Several international studies assess the importance of work as compared with other aspects of people's lives and show that work is typically ranked second in importance (to family) in most countries.[7,8] One study examined 5,550 people across 10 occupational groups in 20 different countries, asking them to complete the Work Value Scales (WVS).[9] The WVS is composed of 13 items measuring various aspects of the work environment, such as responsibility and job security. The study found two common basic work dimensions across cultures. Work content is one dimension, measured by items such as "the amount of responsibility on the job." Job content is the other dimension, measured by items such as "the policies of my company." This finding suggests that people in many cultures distinguish between the nature of the work itself and elements of the context in which the work is done. This supports Herzberg's two-factor theory of motivation (see Chapter 5) and his job enrichment approach discussed later in this chapter.

## [ The Call of the Wild ]

A study of Canadian and American zookeepers illustrated the impact of work centrality so deeply personal that work is seen as a personal calling. Those zookeepers with a sense of calling found their work more significant and important. At the same time, they were more willing to sacrifice money, time, and physical comfort for their work, and were more vulnerable to exploitation by management. Devotion to the job permeated their lives, giving them great meaning but it came at a price.

SOURCE: "The Call of the Wild: Zookeepers, Callings and the Double-edged Sword of Deeply Meaningful Work," *Administrative Science Quarterly* 54 (2009): 32–57.

©Jupiter Images

## Jobs in Organizations

Task and authority relationships define an organization's structure. Jobs are the basic building blocks of this task–authority structure and are considered the micro-structural element to which employees most directly relate. Jobs are usually designed to complement and support other jobs in the organization. Isolated jobs are rare.

Jobs in organizations are interdependent and designed to make a contribution to the organization's

©James W. Porter/Corbis

overall mission and goals. For salespeople to be successful, the production people must be effective. For production people to be effective, the material department must be effective. These interdependencies require careful planning and design so that all of the "pieces of work" fit together into a whole. For example, an envelope salesperson who wants to take an order for one million envelopes from Canadian Tire Financial Services must coordinate with the production department to establish an achievable delivery date. The failure to incorporate this interdependence into his planning could create conflict and doom the company to failure in meeting Canadian Tire's expectations. The central concerns of this chapter are designing work and structuring jobs to prevent such problems and to ensure employee well-being. Inflexible jobs that are rigidly structured have an adverse effect and lead to stressed-out employees.

The larger issues in the design of organizations are the competing processes of differentiation and integration in organizations. (See Chapter 15.) Differentiation is the process of subdividing and departmentalizing the work of an organization. Jobs result from differentiation, which is necessary because no one can do it all. Even small organizations must divide work so that each person is able to accomplish a manageable piece of the whole. At the same time the organization divides up the work, it must also integrate those pieces back into a whole. Integration is the process of connecting jobs and departments into a coordinated, cohesive whole. For example, if the envelope salesperson had coordinated with the production manager before finalizing the order with Canadian Tire, the company could have met the customer's expectations, and integration would have occurred.

LEARNING OUTCOME 2

# Traditional Approaches to Job Design

The balance of integration and differentiation, decisions about who does what, can have a significant impact on behaviour in organizations. People can respond to their work positively or negatively, with consequences for the organization. We saw in Chapter 7 how excessive demands and lack of control are major sources of stress for workers. Job design underlies demands and control and, consequently, stress. Job design also offers the opportunity to create work that engages people. Many managers underestimate the importance of job design characteristics in motivating employee performance.[10]

This is ironic considering managers often have more control over the design features of their employees' jobs than over technology, organizational culture, relationships, or people themselves. We will examine how approaches to job design have changed over time, starting with the traditional approaches from the 20th century.

## Scientific Management

Scientific management, an approach to work design first advocated by Frederick Taylor, emphasized work simplification. This emphasis on simplification is rooted in the idea of division of labour advocated by early economists Smith[11] and Babbage,[12] who believed productivity would increase if work could be broken down into simple tasks. **Work simplification** is the standardization and the narrow, explicit specification of task activities for workers.[13] Jobs designed through scientific management have a limited number of tasks, and each task is scientifically specified so that the worker is not required to think or deliberate. According to Taylor, the role of management and the industrial engineer is to calibrate and define each task carefully. The role of the worker is to execute the task. Work simplification is the underlying principle of assembly-line work. The elements of scientific management, such as offering breaks for workers (which were not common in Taylor's time), differential piece-rate systems of pay, the careful selection and training of workers, and time-and-motion studies all focus on the efficient use of labour to the economic benefit of the corporation. Many of Taylor's approaches persist because they were and are successful. The time-and-motion studies have not seen continuing popularity, however, despite their contribution to scientifically reshaping work to be more effective. Consider how you would react if you were Schmidt in the following excerpt.[14] Taylor describes improving the work of pig-iron handlers at Bethlehem Steel from an average of 12 tons a day to 47.5 tons (thereby increasing the pay from $1.15 a day to $1.85 a day).

"Schmidt started to work, and all day long, and at regular intervals, was told by the man who stood over him with a watch, "Now pick up a pig and walk. Now sit down and rest. Now walk—now rest," etc. He worked when he was told to work, and rested when he was told to rest, and at half-past five in the afternoon had his 47.5 tons loaded on the car."

Work simplification has many benefits but it also has drawbacks (see box on page 232). If, imagining yourself in Schmidt's place, you felt treated like a child or a machine part, you will understand how scientific management triggered a reactionary focus on the importance of people and their feelings about work conditions. This human relations movement launched the Hawthorne

**work simplification**
Standardization and the narrow, explicit specification of task activities for workers.

Work simplification is the underlying principle of assembly-line work.

©Dusko Jovic/iStockPhoto

studies described in Chapter 1 that examined how people's work changed under varying conditions. Worker satisfaction and motivation were seen as key to the organization's success.

## Job Enlargement/ Job Rotation

Recognizing the problems created by oversimplification of work led to the use of job rotation and job enlargement.[15]

**Job enlargement** is a method of job design that increases the number of tasks in a job. **Job rotation**, a variation of job enlargement, exposes a worker to a variety of specialized job tasks

**job enlargement**
A method of job design that increases the number of activities in a job to overcome the boredom of overspecialized work.

**job rotation**
A variation of job enlargement in which workers are exposed to a variety of specialized jobs over time.

over time. The reasoning behind these approaches to the problems of overspecialization is as follows. First, the core problem with overspecialized work was believed to be lack of variety. That is, jobs designed by scientific management were too narrow and limited in the number of tasks and activities assigned to each worker. Second, a lack of variety led to understimulation and underutilization of the worker. Third, the worker would be more stimulated and better utilized by increasing the variety in the job. Variety could be increased by increasing the number of activities or by rotating the worker through different jobs. For example, job enlargement for a lathe operator in a steel plant might include selecting the steel pieces to be turned and performing all of the maintenance work on the lathe. As an example of job rotation, an employee at a small bank might take new accounts one day, serve as a cashier another day, and process loan applications on a third day.

One of the first studies of the problem of repetitive work was conducted at IBM after World War II. The company implemented a job enlargement program during the war and evaluated the effort after six years.[16] The two most important results were a significant increase in product quality and a reduction in idle time, both for people and for machines. Less obvious and measurable were the benefits of job enlargement to IBM through enhanced worker status and improved manager–worker communication. IBM concluded that job enlargement countered the problems of work specialization.

More recent work suggests that enlargement may create problems. A study with employees of an English glass manufacturer showed that job enlargement had a negative impact on self-efficacy.[17] Although work variety can be welcome, if people are given a wider range of tasks without also getting more influence over the situation, it can feel like greater pressure.

## [ Arguments for Work Simplification ]

1. Low skill requirements mean lower wages, ease in replacing absent workers, and speed in training.
2. Allows people of diverse backgrounds to work together in a systematic way.
3. Leads to production efficiency and higher profits.

## [ Limitations of Work Simplification ]

1. Undervalues worker capacity for thought and ingenuity; underutilization means loss of opportunity for the organization to gain from employee creativity and problem solving.
2. Boring, repetitive work for employees, leading to problems such as repetitive strain injuries, absenteeism, turnover, substance abuse.
3. Dehumanization.

Job rotation and cross-training programs are variations of job enlargement. Job rotation can be a proactive means for enhancing work experiences for career development and can have tangible benefits for employees in the form of salary increases and promotions.[18] In cross-training, workers are trained in different specialized tasks or activities. All three kinds of programs horizontally enlarge jobs; that is, the number and variety of an employee's tasks and activities are increased.

## Job Enrichment

Whereas job enlargement refers to expanding the scope of the job by adding tasks at the same level,[19] job enrichment refers to incorporating motivational factors into the design of the job. Job enrichment emerged from Herzberg's two-factor theory (Chapter 5) of motivation. Recall Herzberg's claim that job satisfaction is a result of motivational factors characteristic of the work itself and that job dissatisfaction results from poor hygiene factors. Job enrichment recommends increasing the recognition, responsibility and opportunity for achievement. For example, enlarging the lathe operator's job means adding maintenance activities, whereas enriching the job could mean having the operator meet with customers who buy the products.

Herzberg believes that only certain jobs should be enriched and that the first step is to select the jobs appropriate for job enrichment.[20] He recognizes that some people prefer simple jobs. Once jobs are selected for enrichment, management should brainstorm about possible changes, revise the list to include only specific changes related to motivational factors, and screen out generalities and suggestions that would simply increase activities or numbers of tasks. Those whose jobs are to be enriched should not participate in this process because of a conflict of interest.

A seven-year implementation study of job enrichment at AT&T found the approach beneficial.[21] Job enrichment required a big change in management style, and AT&T found that it could not ignore hygiene factors in the work environment just because it was enriching existing jobs. Although the AT&T experience with job enrichment was positive, a critical review of job enrichment did not find that to be the case generally.[22] One problem with job enrichment as a strategy for work design is that it is based on an oversimplified motivational theory. Another problem is the lack of consideration for individual differences among employees. Job enrichment, like scientific management's work specialization and job enlargement/job rotation, is a universal approach to the design of work and thus does not differentiate among individuals.

# Job Characteristics Theory

In the mid-60s, Hackman and Oldham created job characteristics theory, a job design approach that came to dominate the field for decades. It made a significant departure from the earlier approaches in that it emphasized the interaction between the individual and the specific attributes of the job. It is a person–job fit model rather than a universal job design model.

According to the job characteristics model (JCM), desirable work behaviours and attitudes are a result of employees experiencing three critical psychological states: they experience their work as meaningful, they feel responsible for their work actions, and they know how well they are doing (see Figure 14.1 on page 234). Five core dimensions of job design feed directly into those critical psychological states (see Figure 14.2 on page 235). A job is more meaningful if it requires a variety of skills, if it has an impact on others (task significance), and if it involves completing a whole or identifiable piece of work (task identity) that one can take pride in. Employees need a level of autonomy in order to feel personally responsible for their work. Feedback is required for employees to know how they are doing. The Job Diagnostic Survey (JDS), the most commonly used design measure, was developed to diagnose jobs by measuring the core job

**cross-training**

A variation of job enlargement in which workers are trained in different specialized tasks or activities.

**job enrichment**

Designing or redesigning jobs by incorporating motivational factors into them.

**job characteristics model (JCM)**

A framework for understanding person–job fit through the interaction of core job dimensions with critical psychological states within a person.

**Job Diagnostic Survey (JDS)**

The survey instrument designed to measure the elements in the Job Characteristics Model.

[ **Two key problems can arise in the implementation of job enrichment:** ]

1. An initial drop in performance can be expected as workers accommodate to the change.
2. First-line supervisors may experience some anxiety or hostility as a result of employees' increased responsibility.

©Qoncept/Shutterstock

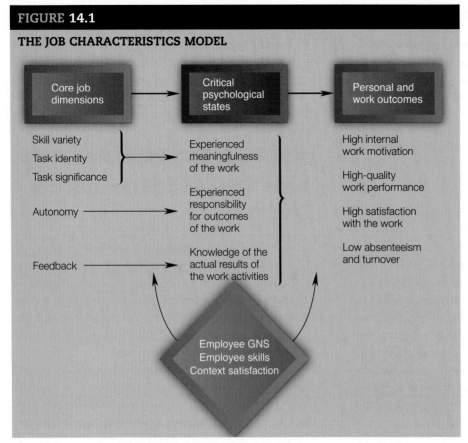

## FIGURE 14.1

### THE JOB CHARACTERISTICS MODEL

Core job dimensions

Critical psychological states

Personal and work outcomes

Skill variety
Task identity
Task significance

→ Experienced meaningfulness of the work

Autonomy —————→ Experienced responsibility for outcomes of the work

Feedback —————→ Knowledge of the actual results of the work activities

High internal work motivation

High-quality work performance

High satisfaction with the work

Low absenteeism and turnover

Employee GNS
Employee skills
Context satisfaction

Adapted from J. R. Hackman and G. R. Oldham, "The Relationship Among Core Job Dimensions, the Critical Psychological States, and On-the-Job Outcomes," *The Job Diagnostic Survey: An Instrument for the Diagnosis of Jobs and the Evaluation of Job Redesign Projects,* 1974. Reprinted by permission of Greg R. Oldham.

dimensions shown in the model. It allows the calculation of the Motivating Potential Score of a job by combining the specific core dimension scores with the following equation:

$$MPS = \frac{\left[\begin{array}{c}\text{Skill} \\ \text{variety}\end{array}\right] + \left[\begin{array}{c}\text{Task} \\ \text{identity}\end{array}\right] + \left[\begin{array}{c}\text{Task} \\ \text{significance}\end{array}\right]}{3} \times [\text{Autonomy}] \times [\text{Feedback}].$$

Hackman and his colleagues created norms for the JDS by administering it to almost 7,000 employees in 876 different jobs.[23] These norms established a baseline for comparison, allowing organizations to see whether the JDS scores of their jobs indicated a need for redesign. Using the JDS could lead immediately to suggestions for redesign by indicating which core job dimensions were weak. Hackman and Oldham suggested a number of implementing concepts to address design problems: (1) combining tasks into larger jobs, (2) forming natural work units to increase task identity and task significance, (3) establishing relationships with customers, (4) loading jobs vertically by giving more responsibility and authority, and (5) opening feedback channels for the job incumbent. For example, if an auto mechanic received little feedback on the quality of repair work performed, one redesign strategy would be to solicit customer feedback one month after each repair.

As noted earlier, the JCM is not a universal design. It does not suggest one size fits all. Note the moderator variables at the bottom of the job characteristics model in Figure 14.1: growth need strength, skills, and context satisfaction. These three factors influence whether an employee will respond positively to the five core dimensions. They must be considered before deciding to redesign a job. One of the moderators relates directly to Herzberg's theory—satisfaction with work context. It suggests that an organization cannot forget the impact of the hygiene factors. So the JDS measures satisfaction with security, pay, relations with supervisors, and relations with others. If an organization sees issues in these areas, it knows they must be addressed. An employee may quit a perfectly designed job if fed up with an unreasonable supervisor or feeling drastically underpaid. Skills and abilities also moderate the relationship between core job dimensions and outcomes. A highly motivated employee will still be limited in his/her productivity if lacking the necessary skills to achieve successful performance. The third moderator is an employee's growth need strength (GNS), the desire to grow and fully develop one's abilities. Employees with low GNS will not respond favourably to jobs with a high motivating potential. On the other hand, employees with high GNS will thrive in a job with variety and challenge.

Research shows general support for the JCM in that the core job characteristics are moderately correlated with favourable attitudes and behaviours, mediated by the three psychological states.[24,25] Interestingly, meta-analysis indicates that feedback influences all three critical psychological states, not just knowledge of results.[26] Feedback also contributes to experienced meaningfulness and a sense of greater autonomy, emphasizing its key role in proposed job redesign.

## Importance of Experienced Meaningfulness

One of the most interesting aspects of JCM research is the evidence of the importance of experienced meaningfulness

| CORE JOB CHARACTERISTIC | HIGHER | LOWER |
|---|---|---|
| **Skill Variety**<br>The degree to which a job uses different skills | Store worker manages inventory, processes sales and returns, sets up displays | Cashier only processes sales |
| **Task Significance**<br>The degree to which a job has an impact on others | Administrator processes payroll for next day | Administrator processes statistics of unknown usefulness |
| **Task Identity**<br>The degree to which a job requires the completion of a whole or identifiable part | Webmaster designs an entire website | Web designer creates parts of websites; work blends in with others' work |
| **Autonomy**<br>The degree to which a job provides freedom in decision making | Salesperson has full freedom in working with corporate clients | Salesperson is given scripts defining exact way to deal with clients |
| **Feedback from the Job Itself**<br>The degree to which doing the job provides clear information about the effectiveness of performance | Salesperson makes presentation to potential client and makes sale or does not | Office worker prepares materials for various salespeople to use in future presentations |

of work.[27] Meaningfulness has a closer link to attitudinal and behavioural outcomes than the other critical psychological states, and all five core job dimensions contribute to it. Other research supports the apparent impact of perceived meaningfulness. For example, a Swedish study of patients with chronic pain found that the perceived meaningfulness of their job was a significant influence on their motivation to return to work.[28] Manipulation of task significance in a series of experiments by Grant with lifeguards and fundraising callers demonstrated the link between significance and performance. Callers in the task significance condition earned more pledges; lifeguards in the task significance condition showed increased dedication and helping behaviour.[29]

Grant's work also indicates how organizations can enhance the task significance of a job and, subsequently, the experienced meaningfulness: by providing opportunities for employees to have a positive impact on others, and by putting workers in contact with those who benefit from their work.[30] For example, when fundraisers had one 15-minute interaction with a student explaining how the funds made an impact in her life, it resulted in more than five times the weekly donation money a full month later.[31] A medical study supports Grant's contention in a

totally different work context. When radiologists saw the photographs of patients whose imaging scans they were evaluating, they reported stronger empathy for the patients and they were more accurate in diagnosing medical problems.[32] Consider how unusual it is for radiologists to see

**Employees in contact with those who benefit from their work find the work more meaningful.**

©Slawomir Fajer/iStockPhoto

patient photographs and for fundraisers to meet fund recipients, yet how easy it is for the organization to take this step and make a significant difference in performance.

How else can we increase experienced meaningfulness? JCM research suggests that giving feedback, autonomy, skill variety, and task identity will each contribute to meaningfulness. A study of Canadian health care workers, funeral directors, and dental hygienists demonstrated that transformational leadership enhances the psychological well-being of workers through adding meaning to their work.[33] This is to be expected, since transformational leaders inspire and excite their employees (see Chapter 12).

# Expanding the Job Characteristics Model

Criticism of the JCM's narrow focus on five task attributes has prompted research into complementary areas. Morgeson, Humphrey, and colleagues have built upon the research efforts of many to create an integrative expansion of the JCM. They also created the Work Design Questionnaire (WDQ) as their version of the JDS measure.[34] The expanded model still includes the JCM original core dimensions but adds task variety, and divides autonomy into three types: work scheduling autonomy, work methods autonomy, and decision-making autonomy. The original autonomy was a vague concept that could be interpreted differently. The three specific types of autonomy capture different employee experiences more accurately. The expanded model adds three broad categories to the JCM's original task grouping: social characteristics, knowledge characteristics, and work context characteristics (see Figure 14.3).

We saw the critical impact of social factors on workers in Chapter 7's discussion of how social support prevents

stress, and acts as an important buffer in times of high demands and low control. The expanded JCM posits four specific social characteristics of importance: the degree of interdependence between an employee's job and the jobs of others, the extent of interaction outside the organization, the degree of social support, and feedback from others. Research shows that all play an important role in employees' attitudes and experiences. They are strongly linked to job satisfaction, turnover intentions, subjective performance, and organizational commitment.[35] A discussion in Chapter 6 described the key role of feedback, particularly negative feedback, in changing behaviour. Whereas managers have tended to ignore social aspects of a job, it is clear that the ways in which a job's design causes workers to interact with others is a critical element in their experience of work.

Jobs also vary in their knowledge demands—complexity, information processing, problem solving, and

## FIGURE 14.3

### MORGESON AND HUMPHREY'S EXPANSION OF THE JCM

| MORGESON AND HUMPHREY'S EXPANSION OF THE JCM | | |
|---|---|---|
| **Work Design Characteristics** | **Critical Psychological States as Mediators** | **Outcomes** |
| **Task characteristics**<br>• Task significance<br>• Task identity<br>• Task variety<br>• Autonomy:<br>  Work scheduling<br>  Work methods<br>  Decision making<br>• Feedback from job | Experiences meaningfulness<br><br>Experiences responsibility<br><br>Knowledge of results | **Behaviours**<br>• Performance<br>• Absenteeism<br>• Turnover<br><br>**Attitudes**<br>• Satisfaction with job<br>• Satisfaction with supervisor<br>• Organizational commitment<br>• Job involvement<br>• Internal work motivation |
| **Knowledge characteristics**<br>• Job complexity<br>• Information processing<br>• Specialization<br>• Problem solving<br>• Skill variety | | **Role perceptions**<br>• Role ambiguity<br>• Role conflict |
| **Social characteristics**<br>• Interdependence<br>• Feedback from others<br>• Social support<br>• Interaction outside organization | | **Well-being**<br>• Anxiety<br>• Stress<br>• Burnout/exhaustion<br>• Overload |
| **Work context characteristics**<br>• Physical demands<br>• Work conditions<br>• Ergonomics | | |

Adapted from S. E. Humphrey, J. D. Nahrgang & F. P. Morgeson, Integrating motivational, social and contextual work design features: A meta-analytic summary and theoretical extension of the work design literature, *Journal of Applied Psychology* 92 (2007): 1332–1356.

specialization. Initial research suggests that high knowledge demands promote satisfaction but may also lead to perceptions of overload. Therefore, these high knowledge demands can be both engaging and overwhelming.[36] A study of Danish managers showed that cognitively challenging activities (e.g., problem solving) are linked to the experience of "flow," an engrossing and enjoyable immersion in an activity.[37]

The physical characteristics of a job are critical in an employee's perception of his/her work[38]—for example, what are the hazards, what does the workspace look like, how fatiguing is the work? The WDQ focuses on ergonomics, physical demands, work conditions, and equipment use. Humphrey and Morgeson's[39] meta-analysis showed that these physical characteristics strongly correlate with stress, separately from all the other job characteristics, and also link to job satisfaction.

# Alternative Approaches to Job Design

This section examines alternative work design approaches that have emerged. First, it discusses the social information-processing model and a recent variation that focuses on the subjective social experience of the worker. Then we look at job crafting and i-deals, assertions that employees actually shape their own jobs to a great extent. Finally, we examine how the changing parameters of the work world are influencing job design, and how perspectives on the design of work vary internationally.

## Social Information Processing

Traditional approaches to the design of work focus on the objective characteristics of a job. The **social information-processing (SIP) model** emphasizes a job's subjective characteristics. Specifically, the SIP model says that what others tell us about our jobs is important.[40] The SIP model has four basic premises about the work environment.[41] First, other people provide cues we use to understand the work environment. Second, other people help us judge what is important in our jobs. Third, other people tell us how they see our jobs. Fourth, other people's positive and negative feedback helps us understand our feelings about our jobs. This is consistent with the dynamic model of the job design process that views it as a social one involving job holders, supervisors, and peers.[42]

People's perceptions and reactions to their jobs are shaped by information from other people in the work environment.[43] In other words, what others believe about a person's job may be important to understanding the person's perceptions of, and reactions to, the job. This does not mean that objective job characteristics are unimportant; rather, it means that others can modify the way these characteristics affect us. For example, one study of task complexity found that the objective complexity of a task must be distinguished from the subjective task complexity experienced by the employee.[44] Although objective task complexity may be a motivator, the presence of others in the work environment, social interaction, or even daydreaming may be important additional sources of motivation. The SIP model makes an important contribution to the design of work by emphasizing the importance of other people and the social context of work. For example, relational job design may motivate employees to take prosocial action and make a positive difference in other people's lives.[45] In addition, the relational aspects of the work environment may be more important than objective core job characteristics. Therefore, the subjective feedback of other people about how difficult a particular task is may be more important to a person's motivation to perform than an objective estimate of the task's difficulty.

Research for the SIP model's validity is mixed. Although some lab experiments have shown that positive social cues can improve productivity,[46,47] field experiments have not been so supportive.[48,49] Positive changes in task perceptions do not consistently result in performance improvement. The effect of social cues is considerably weaker than objective characteristics of job design, in contrast to SIP's contention.

Wrzesniewski, Dutton, and Debebe[50] have offered a model of interpersonal sensemaking as an

> **social information-processing (SIP) model**
> A model that suggests that the important job factors depend in part on what others tell a person about the job.

> *The subjective feedback of other people about how difficult a particular task is may be more important to a person's motivation to perform than an objective estimate of the task's difficulty.*

enhanced replacement of the SIP model. Rather than seeing the employee as the SIP passive recipient of social cues about job tasks, their model sees the employee as actively seeking out cues far beyond the task. Employees want to understand the meaning and value of their work and their performance, so actively construct that meaning through noticing cues from others and interpreting those cues. The words and actions of others are interpreted as either affirming (communicating regard, worth, care) or disaffirming (communicating a derogatory attribute). These interpretations shape the employees' sense of the meaning of their job, their role in the organization, and themselves. That, in turn, will influence attitudes such as job satisfaction and behaviours such as absenteeism and OCB. This model fits closely with the discussion earlier in the chapter about the importance of work's meaningfulness.

## Job Crafting and I-deals

Whereas job design approaches have typically seen job design as something an organization creates for an employee, the **job crafting** concept sees employees as the active architects of their jobs.[51] Employees take the initiative to redefine their jobs, changing the boundaries of their job in terms of how they interact with others, how they think about and approach their work, and exactly what they do. Why do they do it? Job crafting can be motivated by a desire for some control, a desire for a positive self-image (by focusing on activities in which the employee excels), and a desire for connection with others. For example, a hospital cleaner may choose to engage in interactions with patients, finding pleasure in it, and believing he is contributing to the well-being of sick and lonely patients.[52] Job crafting is more common in jobs with high autonomy and low interdependence because these jobs offer more opportunity for crafting.[53] In a study of outside salespeople, 75 percent of them reported engaging in job crafting, shaping the job to their own preferences, in ways largely unknown to management.[54] Both collaborative and individual job crafting were observed in a study of childcare workers. The collaborative job crafting led to higher performance.[55] A study of employees at different ranks yielded the unexpected result that higher ranked employees, despite having more "power," actually felt more constrained in crafting their jobs and tended to alter their own expectations and behaviours to make do. Lower-ranked employees were more likely to alter others' expectations and behaviours. The constraint felt by higher ranks may be due to the greater interdependence of their jobs and their visibility.[56]

The redefinition or shaping of an employee's job can be a process in which both employee and supervisor participate. Employees often negotiate changes in roles. Rousseau[57] describes these as idiosyncratic deals, or "**i-deals**," which are customized employment terms negotiated between employees and their supervisors. They can be formed before hiring or after and typically emerge because the employee has special life circumstances (such as a need for flexible hours) or unique skills. A study with German government employees showed that i-deals tended to focus on either scheduling or personal development, were more common in departments with individualized work arrangements already (such as telecommuting and part-time work), and were more likely to be negotiated by employees who had a personality highlighting personal initiative.[58] A further study of i-deals in German and American hospitals showed that employees were more likely to negotiate successful i-deals when they had high quality leader–member exchange relationships with their supervisors[59] (see Chapter 12).

## Job Design in the Changing World of Work

Many of today's changes have implications for job design— the movement from an economy based on manufacturing to a service base, globalization, new technology, the increasing numbers of knowledge workers, organizations remaking themselves or merging in response to competition, and the increasing use of teams. Jobs are increasingly characterized by uncertainty and complexity. There is more interdependence, and greater relations with others. Organizations are looking to employees for more initiative and creativity.

Autonomy is particularly important under the above conditions. When we are working in uncertain, ambiguous environments, a feeling of control within our work helps us cope. People react more positively to getting autonomy in uncertain conditions than they do in certain ones.[60] The combination of high interdependence and uncertainty in many jobs supports the use of self-managed work teams (Chapter 9), so the autonomy is given to a group in order to deal with uncertain conditions. Employees are more likely to be proactive in implementing ideas and solving problems when they are given autonomy and control.[61] The autonomy enhances their self-efficacy by signalling they are capable of handling responsibilities.[62,63] The autonomy also leads employees to define their role in a more flexible way.[64] A two-year longitudinal study of German employees found that initial levels of autonomy and complexity in their jobs predicted higher levels of personal initiative. Exercising personal initiative, in turn, predicted perceptions of increased autonomy and complexity over time.[65]

**job crafting**
Employees take the initiative to redefine their jobs.

**i-deals**
Customized employment terms negotiated between employees and their supervisors.

Interpersonal feedback is also critical in many of today's jobs. Uncertainty means that the task feedback in many jobs is ambiguous.[66] The majority of the population now works in service jobs where they rely on interpersonal feedback to interpret the success of their performance.[67] Feedback has a key role in all three critical psychological states of the JCM, yet is often not built into jobs, so the organization must find a way to design feedback into the workday.

Creativity is a valuable resource and increasingly needed. There is evidence that job enrichment provides the foundation for greater creativity. Oldham & Cummings found employees working in enriched jobs (high on JCM attributes) were rated as more creative, produced more patents, and offered more suggestions.[68] Job complexity can encourage initiative and creativity,[69,70] but is related to higher stress.[71] This had led some to suggest that routinized or "mindless" work may be a welcome break for those in complex, challenging jobs.[72] Intertwining routinized tasks within a complex job would provide a balance, allowing workers to relax, and may even stimulate greater proactivity and creativity by freeing up psychological resources.[73]

# International Perspectives on the Design of Work

Each nation or ethnic group has a unique way of understanding and designing work.[74] As organizations become more global and international, an appreciation of the perspectives of other nations is increasingly important. The Japanese, Germans, and Scandinavians in particular have distinctive perspectives on the design and organization of work.[75] Each country's perspective is forged within its unique cultural and economic system, and each is distinct from the approaches used in North America.

**The Japanese Approach** The Japanese began harnessing their productive energies during the 1950s by drawing on the product quality ideas of W. Edwards Deming.[76] In addition, the central government became actively involved in the economic resurgence of Japan, and it encouraged companies to conquer industries rather than to maximize profits.[77] Such an industrial policy, which built on the Japanese cultural ethic of collectivism, has implications for how work is done. Whereas Frederick Taylor and his successors in the United States emphasized the job of an individual worker, the Japanese work system emphasizes the strategic level and encourages collective and cooperative working arrangements.[78]

The Japanese emphasize performance, accountability, and other- or self-directedness in defining work, whereas North Americans emphasize the positive affect, personal identity, and social benefits of work.

The Japanese have had success with lean production methods, an approach that focuses on using committed employees with ever-expanding responsibilities to achieve zero waste, 100 percent good product, delivered on time, every time. This "do more with less" approach has drawn the attention of North American and European managers and spread rapidly. Its use outside Japan has been less successful, however. For example, one three-year evaluation of lean teams, assembly lines, and workflow formalization as lean production practices was conducted in Australia.[79] Employees in all production groups were negatively affected, and the assembly-line employees the most.

**The German Approach** The German approach to work has been shaped by Germany's unique educational system, cultural values, and economic system. The Germans are a highly educated and well-organized people. For example, their educational system has a multitrack design with technical and university alternatives. The German economic system puts a strong emphasis on free enterprise, private property rights, and management–labour cooperation. A comparison of voluntary and mandated management–labour cooperation in Germany found that productivity was superior under voluntary cooperation.[80] The Germans value hierarchy and authority relationships and, as a result, are generally disciplined.[81] Germany's workers are highly unionized, and their discipline and efficiency have enabled Germany to be highly productive while its workers labour substantially fewer hours than do North Americans.

The traditional German approach to work design was **technocentric**, an approach that placed technology and engineering at the centre of job design decisions. Recently, German industrial engineers have moved to a more **anthropocentric** approach, which places human considerations at the centre of job design decisions.

**The Scandinavian Approach** The Scandinavian cultural values and economic system stand

What about You? on the Chapter 14 Review Card provides you with an opportunity to evaluate how psychologically healthy your work environment is.

**technocentric**
Placing technology and engineering at the centre of job design decisions.

**anthropocentric**
Placing human considerations at the centre of job design decisions.

**Scheduling shifts for employees in a clockwise manner (1st, 2nd, 3rd) rather than a counterclockwise manner (1st, 3rd, 2nd) is more compatible with human biology.**

Andresr/Shutterstock

in contrast to the German system. The social democratic tradition in Scandinavia has emphasized social concern rather than industrial efficiency. The Scandinavians place great emphasis on a work design model that encourages a high degree of worker control and good social support systems for workers.[82] Lennart Levi believes that circumstantial and inferential scientific evidence provides a sufficiently strong basis for legislative and policy actions for redesigns aimed at enhancing worker well-being. An example of such an action for promoting good working environments and occupational health was Swedish Government Bill 1976/77:149, which stated, "Work should be safe both physically and mentally *but also* provide opportunities for involvement, job satisfaction, and personal development." In 1991, the Swedish Parliament set up the Swedish Working Life Fund to fund research, intervention programs, and demonstration projects in work design. For example, a study of Stockholm police on shift schedules found that going from a daily, counterclockwise rotation to a clockwise rotation was more compatible with human biology and resulted in improved sleep, less fatigue, lower systolic blood pressure, and lower blood levels of triglycerides and glucose.[83] Hence, the work redesign improved the police officers' health.

**telecommuting**

Employees work away from the company (typically at home) through the use of technology.

# Contemporary Issues in the Design of Work

A number of contemporary issues related to specific aspects of the design of work have an effect on increasing numbers of employees. Rather than addressing job design or worker well-being in a comprehensive way, these issues address one or another aspect of a job. The issues include telecommuting, alternative work patterns, technology at work, and skill development. Telecommuting and alternative work patterns such as job sharing can increase flexibility for employees. Companies use these and other approaches to the design of work as ways to manage a growing business while contributing to a better balance of work and family life for employees.

## Telecommuting

**Telecommuting** is when employees work away from the company (typically at home) through the use of technology. Telecommuting may entail working in a combination of home, satellite office, and main office locations. This flexible arrangement is designed to achieve a better fit between the needs of the individual employee and the organization's task demands.

Telecommuting has been around since the 1970s but was slower to catch on than some expected.[84] There is reluctance in some managers and employers to break the traditional visibility of work—if you cannot see them, how do you know they are actually working? Telecommuting requires a focus on performance outcomes rather than "face time." In Canada, telecommuting is not typically an all-or-nothing arrangement. Approximately 10 percent

## IN THE FUTURE, WE'LL ALL TELECOMMUTE—OR WILL WE?

>> Today, telecommuting can be ideal for a variety of careers (e.g., Web designers and coders, analysts, marketers, or financial salespeople) and in the future, the expansion of intellectual commerce and e-commerce will allow that list to grow. Leadership positions, however, may never appear on that list because the inability to work face-to-face with people at work makes telecommuting and leadership antithetical and intractable. Leadership is personal and interpersonal, requiring human interaction and face time. Followers need leaders to be there to lead, and that cannot be done through telecommuting.

SOURCE: J. Welch and S. Welch, "The Importance of Being There," *Business Week* (April 16 2007): 92.

of Canadian workers telecommute, with 71 percent of them doing so one day a week and only 3 percent doing so for a 40-hour week.[85]

Advocates of telecommuting point to the many benefits. It is easier to recruit and maintain employees, who find telecommuting appealing. Employers save overhead costs since less organizational space may be required. From the employees' point of view, telecommuting saves them time and money through less commuting time, and gives them more autonomy and flexibility in how their day is spent, thereby reducing work–family conflict.[86]

Environmental benefits add weight to the list of telecommuting advantages. The City of Calgary held its first Telework Week in 2010 to highlight the many benefits of telecommuting and encourage more employers to adopt it.[87] In an address advocating Telework Week, Alderman Diane Colley-Urquhart reported that the City of Calgary's own telework program, in less than a year, had already produced a reduction of 7,440 commuter trips and 183,000 vehicle kilometres travelled, conserving 16,000 litres of fuel and reducing carbon dioxide emissions by 42,000 kilograms.[88] This is good news to a city rated by the UN as one of the worst carbon dioxide producers in the world.[89] As part of Calgary's telework initiative, companies—including TELUS, ATB Financial, SAIT Polytechnic, Calgary Police Services, ENMAX and Calgary Economic Development—have signed the Calgary Telework Charter.[90]

> # Telecommuting and alternative work patterns such as job sharing can increase flexibility for employees.

Research supports the value of telecommuting. Telecommuting is correlated with improved satisfaction, performance, turnover intent, and role stress as well as increased autonomy and lower work–family conflict.[91] Some have feared that the social isolation of telecommuting would damage relationships and career prospects. Ironically, research suggests that telecommuting is actually associated with a higher quality of employee–supervisor relationship.[92] This could be because telecommuting is more likely to be granted to workers who are already performing well or favoured by the supervisor, or it may be that awareness of the potential for damage in the relationship triggers a focus on ensuring the relationship is maintained.[93] Coworker relationships are also maintained under most telecommuting. It is only when the telecommuting becomes more intensive (over 2.5 days a week) that coworker relationships are harmed.[94] Meta-analysis showed that telecommuting had no adverse effects on employees' perceived career prospects.[95] Not all forms of work are amenable to telecommuting. For example, firefighters and police officers must be at their duty stations to be successful in their work. Employees for whom telecommuting is not a viable option within a company may feel jealous of those able to telecommute. In addition, telecommuting may have the potential to create the sweatshops of the 21st century. Thus, telecommuting is a novel, emerging issue.

## Alternative Work Patterns

**Job sharing** is a permanent work arrangement where two or more employees voluntarily share or split one full-time position. A written agreement outlines the terms and each employee's salary and benefits are pro-rated for the hours worked. Typical job sharing means either splitting the work day with each employee working half or splitting the work week with each employee working 2.5 days. These arrangements are usually initiated by employees who want the time to deal with other life commitments (e.g., education, young children) but sometimes by employers to deal with recessionary conditions, allowing employees to keep their full-time status while saving the company money.[96]

The **compressed work week** (CWW) is an arrangement where employees work longer shifts in exchange for a reduction in the number of working days in their work cycle. For example,

©Steve Lovegrove/Shutterstock

**job sharing**
A permanent work arrangement where two or more employees voluntarily share or split one full-time position.

**compressed work week**
Employees work longer shifts in exchange for a reduction in the number of working days.

they may work four 10-hour days rather than 5 days a week. Compressed work weeks may be a standard work schedule set by the employer or an employee option. The Yukon government allows employees to request a compressed work arrangement that allows them regular days off by working longer days.[97] For instance, if an employee's schedule is normally 7.5 daily hours of work, the employee may take two days off in every two-week period and work 9.38 hours on a daily basis spread over the other eight working days. For Yukon government employees, this scheduling is a longer-term arrangement that requires the agreement of the other workers in the work area and the concurrence of the employee's deputy minister or designate. A CWW arrangement can be attractive for balancing work and family life and saving commute time and money, but regular long days can be fatiguing.

**Flextime** is the most common form of alternative work arrangement. Thirty-five percent of Canadian workers[98] have the freedom to set their daily start and stop times as long as they are present within specified core operational hours. It can lead to reduced absenteeism. Companies in highly concentrated urban areas, such as Vancouver, Toronto, and Montreal, may allow employees to set their own daily work schedules as long as they start their eight hours at any thirty-minute interval from 6:00 A.M. to 9:00 A.M. This arrangement is designed to ease traffic and commuting pressures. It also is somewhat responsive to individual biorhythms, allowing early risers to go to work early and nighthawks to work late. Even in companies without formal flextime programs, flextime may be an individual option arranged between supervisor and subordinate. For example, a first-line supervisor who wants to complete a university degree may negotiate a work schedule accommodating both job requirements and course schedules at the university. Flextime options may be more likely for high performers who assure their bosses that work quality and productivity will not suffer.[99] On the cautionary side, one study found that a woman on a flexible work schedule was perceived to have less job/career dedication and less advancement motivation, though no less ability.[100]

Research shows flexible and compressed workweek schedules have positive effects.[101] Flexible work schedules are correlated with higher employee productivity and job satisfaction, and lower employee absenteeism. However, these effects apply only to general employees, not to professionals or managers. And the positive effects with flextime may diminish over time as employees become accustomed to it. Compressed work weeks are associated with higher job satisfaction but do not seem to significantly affect productivity or absenteeism.[102]

## Technology at Work

New technologies and electronic commerce are here to stay and are changing the face of work environments—dramatically in some cases. Many government jobs expect to change, and even disappear, with the advent of e-government using Internet technology. As forces for change, new technologies are a double-edged sword that can be used to improve job performance or to create stress. On the positive side, modern technologies are helping to revolutionize the way jobs are designed and the way work gets done. The **virtual office** is a mobile platform of computer, telecommunication, and information technology and services that allows mobile workforce members to conduct business virtually anywhere, anytime, globally. While virtual offices have benefits, they may also lead to a lack of social connection or to technostress.

**Technostress** is stress caused by new and advancing technologies in the workplace, most often information technologies.[103] For example, the widespread use of electronic bulletin boards as a forum for rumours of layoffs may cause feelings of uncertainty and anxiety (technostress). However, the same electronic bulletin boards can be an important source of information and thus reduce uncertainty for workers.

New information technologies enable organizations to monitor employee work performance, even

©Radius Images/Jupiter Images

**flextime**
An alternative work pattern that enables employees to set their own daily work schedules outside core operational hours.

**virtual office**
A mobile platform of computer, telecommunication, and information technology and services.

**technostress**
The stress caused by new and advancing technologies in the workplace.

# By The Numbers

**5** core job characteristics

**47** the tons of pig iron handled daily by a worker under Taylor's approach

**75** the percentage of salespeople who reported crafting their job to their own preferences

**85** the percentage of big lottery winners who continue to work

**876** the number of occupations represented in the JDS norming process

**42,000** the kilogram reduction of carbon dioxide emissions in less than a year by the City of Calgary's telework program

©Kun Jiang/iStockPhoto

when the employee is not aware of the monitoring.[104] These new technologies also allow organizations to tie pay to performance because performance is electronically monitored.[105] Three guidelines can help make electronic workplace monitoring, especially of performance, less distressful. First, workers should participate in the introduction of the monitoring system. Second, performance standards should be seen as fair. Third, performance records should be used to improve performance, not to punish the performer. In the extreme, new technologies that allow for virtual work in remote locations take employees beyond such monitoring.[106]

## Skill Development

Problems in work system design are often seen as the source of frustration for those dealing with technostress.[107] However, system and technical problems are not the only sources of technostress in new information technologies. Some experts see a growing gap between the skills demanded by new technologies and the skills possessed by employees in jobs using these technologies.[108] Although technical skills are important and are emphasized in many training programs, the largest sector of the economy is actually service-oriented, and service jobs require interpersonal skills. Managers also need a wide range of nontechnical skills to be effective in their work.[109] Therefore, any discussion of jobs and the design of work must recognize the importance of incumbent skills and abilities to meet the demands of the work. Organizations must consider the talents and skills of their employees when they engage in job design efforts. The two issues of employee skill development and job design are interrelated. The knowledge and information requirements for jobs of the future are especially high.

# Visit **icanorgb.com** to find the resources you need today!

*Located at the back of the textbook are rip-out Chapter Review Cards. Make sure you also go online to check out other tools that ORGB offers to help you successfully pass your course.*

- Interactive Quizzing
- Key Term Flashcards
- PowerPoint Slides
- Audio Chapter Summaries

- Cases and Exercises
- Interactive Games
- Self-Assessments
- "On the Job" and "Bizflix" Videos

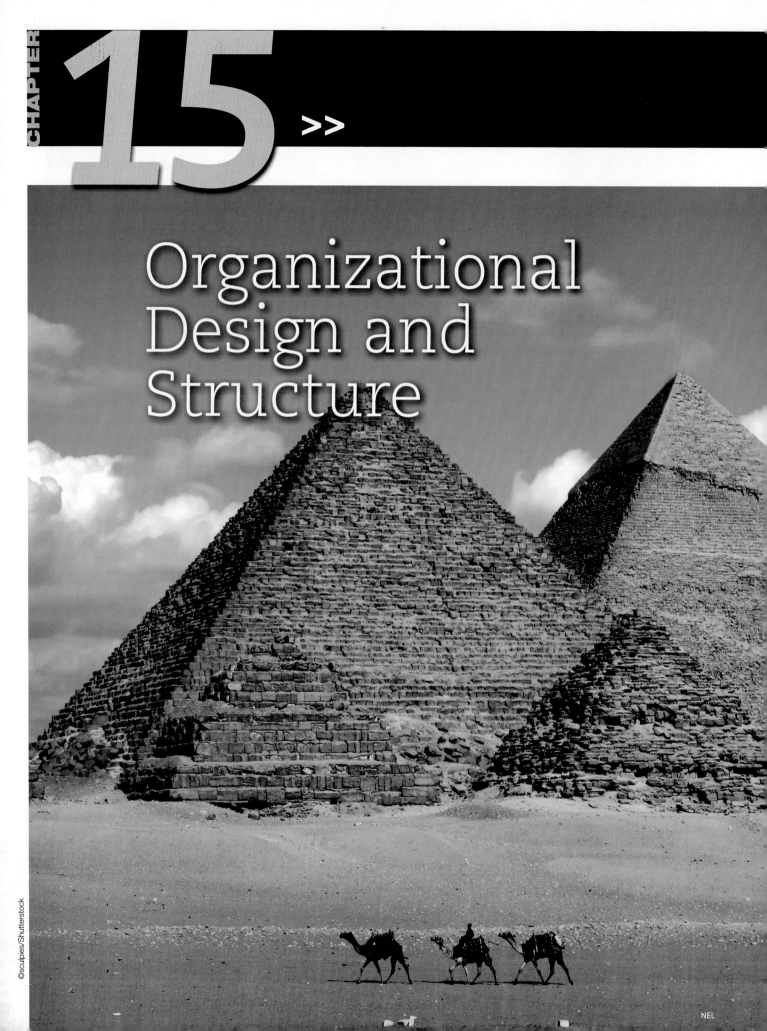

# Organizational Design and Structure

> **❝** *The organizational structure is designed to prevent chaos through an orderly set of reporting relationships and communication channels.* **❞**

**Organizational design** is the process of constructing and adjusting an organization's structure to achieve its goals. The design process begins with the organization's goals. These goals are broken into tasks as the basis for jobs, as discussed in Chapter 14. Jobs are grouped into departments, and departments are linked to form the **organizational structure**.

The most visible representation of an organization's structure is the organizational chart. Figure 15.1 (on page 246) shows the organizational chart for the Toronto Zoo. Most organizations have a series of organizational charts showing reporting relationships throughout the system (not all jobs are visible on the Zoo chart). The underlying components are (1) formal lines of authority and responsibility (the organizational structure designates reporting relationships by the way jobs and departments are grouped) and (2) formal systems of communication, coordination, and integration (the structure designates the expected patterns of formal interaction among employees). The organizational structure is designed to prevent chaos through an orderly set of reporting relationships and communication channels.[1]

LEARNING OUTCOME 1

# Impact of Structure on Employees

The way an organization is structured has an impact on the daily lives of the people within it. It influences what people do and what skills are needed in their position. It determines who they interact

**organizational design**
The process of constructing and adjusting an organization's structure to achieve its goals.

**organizational structure**
The linking of departments and jobs within an organization.

## LEARNING OUTCOMES

After reading this chapter, you should be able to do the following:

**1** Explain what aspects of organizational structure are represented on an organizational chart.

**2** Discuss the basic design dimensions managers must consider in structuring an organization.

**3** Describe the basic organizational structures: simple, functional, divisional, matrix

**4** Describe four contextual variables that influence organizational structure.

**5** Explain the forces reshaping organizations.

**6** Identify and describe emerging organizational structures.

**7** Identify the consequences of an inappropriate structure.

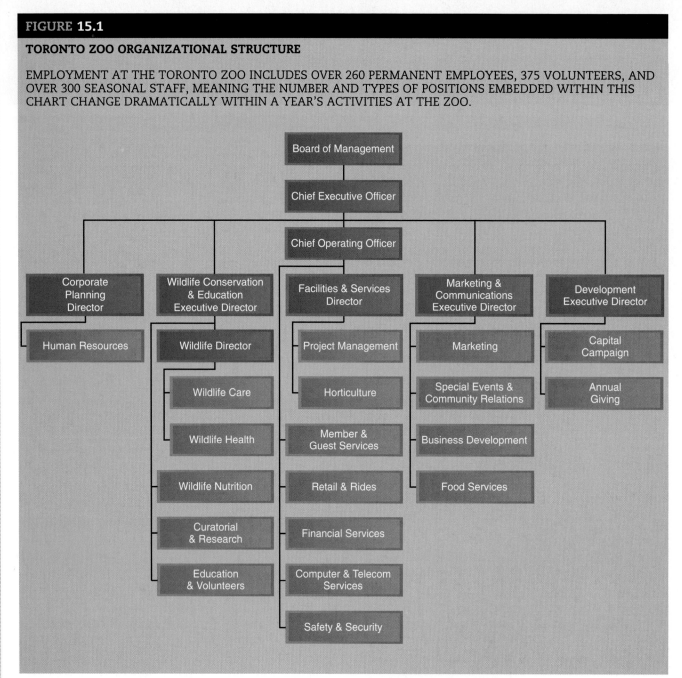

SOURCE: Reprinted by permission of The Toronto Zoo.

with, what information they have access to, and who they are accountable to. It influences leadership behaviour and organizational culture. Employees may "craft" their job (see Chapter 14) to create a better fit for themselves, but the organizational structure will put boundaries on just how far an employee can modify the job and its interactions. There is no ideal structure—the fact that different organizations achieve success within the same industry with different structures indicates this. But a poor structure can cause economic and social difficulties for the organization, holding it back from achieving its goals and frustrating its employees. And no structure will appeal to everyone. As in every other topic discussed in this book, individual differences play a role.

Thinking of the experiences of students in different educational structures helps us to reflect on the interaction between structure and individual differences. High school students and university students are all educated within structures that include classes, courses, timetables, and rules. But the experience is vastly different. Consider someone you know who was highly successful in high school but found the transition to university difficult and whose grades showed it. Consider another person who did not perform well in high school but blossomed within the university context. High school is a highly structured

Jupiter Images

environment with small classes, extensive contact with school staff, lots of rules, and little autonomy for students. University offers much more freedom to students and relative anonymity within the large-class setting. Some students feel stifled by the high school context and thrive in the opportunities provided by university. Other students feel safe and connected in the earlier structure and find the flexible, open structure of university cold and overwhelming. The two structures are necessarily different as they are dealing with different age groups and have different goals. Neither one is "better." But individuals have different levels of comfort with the different types of structure, which can affect their performance. A parallel occurs in work settings. In some organizations, employees know exactly what they are expected to do, when and how; their activities are predictable, and their relations with others are defined. This may provide security and low stress on the one hand, or boredom on the other. Other employees work in a context of ill-defined duties and are expected to work to changing expectations with a varying group of people, resources, and deadlines. This may be exciting and stimulating, or it may be stressful. This chapter examines how and why organizational structures vary, and the interplay with employee behaviour and attitudes.

LEARNING OUTCOME **2**

# Basic Design Dimensions

The appropriate structure to meet an organization's goals will mean an appropriate combination of differentiation and integration. As discussed in Chapter 14, **differentiation** refers to the process of deciding how to divide the work in an organization. The organization exists because no one person can achieve all the demands, so the work must be spread among organizational members. At the same time, the various parts of the organization must work together to achieve organizational success. Thus integration must be created; the different parts of the organization must be coordinated to form a structure that supports goal accomplishment. Every manager and organization looks for the best combination of differentiation and **integration** for accomplishing the goals of the organization. There are many ways to split up work and coordinate the various activities. In order to understand the underlying characteristics of the various organizational structures, it is important that we begin by considering the basic structural dimensions.

[ *Every manager and organization looks for the best combination of differentiation and integration for accomplishing the goals of the organization.* ]

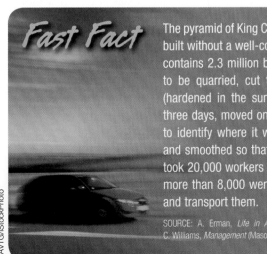

*Fast Fact*

The pyramid of King Cheops of Egypt could not have been built without a well-conceived organization. The pyramid contains 2.3 million blocks of stone, each of which had to be quarried, cut to precise size and shape, cured (hardened in the sun), transported by boat for two to three days, moved onto the construction site, numbered to identify where it would be placed, and then shaped and smoothed so that it would fit perfectly into place. It took 20,000 workers 23 years to complete this pyramid; more than 8,000 were needed just to quarry the stones and transport them.

SOURCE: A. Erman, *Life in Ancient Egypt* (London: Macmillan & Co., 1984); C. Williams, *Management* (Mason, OH: Cengage Learning, 2008).

©AVTG/iStockPhoto

**differentiation**

The process of deciding how to divide work in the organization.

**integration**

The process of coordinating the different parts of the organization.

**1** Formalization: The degree to which an employee's role is defined by formal documentation (procedures, job descriptions, manuals, and regulations).

**2** Centralization: The extent to which decision-making authority has been delegated to lower levels of an organization. An organization is centralized if the decisions are made at the top of the organization and decentralized if decision making is pushed down to lower levels in the organization.

**3** Specialization: The degree to which organizational tasks are subdivided into separate jobs. The division of labour and the degree to which formal job descriptions spell out job requirements indicate the level of specialization in the organization.

**4** Standardization: The extent to which work activities are described and performed routinely in the same way. Highly standardized organizations have little variation in the defining of jobs.

**5** Complexity: The number of activities within the organization and the amount of differentiation needed within the organization.

**6** Hierarchy of authority: The degree of vertical differentiation through reporting relationships and the span of control within the structure of the organization.[2]

These concepts relate closely to differentiation and integration. The more specialization occurs, the greater the differentiation. Differentiation can occur horizontally so different units at the same level have jobs with different training and scope (e.g., an engineer and accountant in different departments with similar levels of responsibility but specialized jobs). Differentiation can also occur vertically (through creating differences in hierarchy and authority) and spatially (through locating parts of the organization in different places). The greater the differentiation is, the greater the complexity will be and the greater the need for integration. Formalization, centralization, standardization, and authority are all potential ways of achieving integration. The organization can ensure employee behaviours are aligned with organizational goals by creating explicit rules and procedures (formalization) or by standardizing activities so there is seldom any variation.

Top management could insist on making all important decisions (centralization), leaving few decisions to employees. The organization could ask supervisors to monitor and guide employee behaviours (using their authority). These are not the only ways in which to achieve integration. Others include using the management information system, liaison roles (such as a project manager), task forces, or teams. One of the interesting research results on authority is that the **span of control** (number of people reporting to a supervisor) is related to integration in opposite ways in different circumstances. A large span of control can mean improved performance in some situations because employees feel less monitored and appreciate the freedom to do their job.[3,4] Their activities are coordinated through other means, such as routine and procedures or teamwork. However, for groups that are interdependent and for whom coordination is critical, a smaller span of control supports the group coordination.[5] The manager is more available to staff and is more likely to work alongside the staff, to offer coaching and feedback, and to have frequent and timely communication with staff, thereby creating shared goals.[6] A study with cross-functional flight departure teams (e.g., baggage handlers, pilots, cabin cleaners, ticketing agents) at a variety of airlines demonstrated that those with smaller spans of control achieved better performance in terms of gate time per departure, staff time per departure, customer complaints, and late arrivals.[7] When span of control increases, managers have less opportunity for interacting with individual subordinates,[8] tend to become more autocratic in their decision making,[9] and are more likely to handle problems with subordinates in a formalized, impersonal way, using warnings and punishments instead of coaching and feedback.[10,11]

Henry Mintzberg believes that the following questions can guide managers in designing formal structures that fit an organization's unique set of circumstances:

1. How many tasks should a given position in the organization contain, and how specialized should each task be?

**formalization**

The degree to which the organization has official rules, regulations, and procedures.

**centralization**

The degree to which decisions are made at the top of the organization.

**specialization**

The degree to which jobs are narrowly defined and depend on unique expertise.

**standardization**

The degree to which work activities are accomplished in a routine fashion.

**complexity**

The degree to which many different types of activities occur in the organization.

**hierarchy of authority**

The degree of vertical differentiation across levels of management.

**span of control**

The number of employees reporting to a supervisor.

©Inspirestock/Jupiter Images

2. How standardized should the work content of each position be?

3. What skills, abilities, knowledge, and training should be required for each position?

4. What should be the basis for the grouping of positions within the organization into units, departments, divisions, and so on?

5. How large should each unit be, and what should the span of control be (that is, how many individuals should report to each manager)?

6. How much standardization should be required in the output of each position?

7. What mechanisms should be established to help individuals in different positions and units to adjust to the needs of other individuals?

8. How centralized or decentralized should decision-making power be in the chain of authority? Should most of the decisions be made at the top of the organization (centralized) or be made down in the chain of authority (decentralized)? [12]

The manager who can answer these questions has a good understanding of how the organization should implement the basic structural dimensions. These basic design dimensions act in combination with one another and are not entirely independent characteristics of an organization.

# Basic Structures

Most companies begin their existence as a simple structure. All power rests in the entrepreneur (centralization) whose few staff do whatever is needed. There are no job descriptions or written procedures. The owner decides what will be done and how as the need arises. An example of a **simple structure** would be a small computer consulting company. The owner works with three technicians to help small businesses "fix" computer applications and to make decisions regarding computer hardware and software that meet their needs (Figure 15.2). The owner supervises the work and works alongside the technicians as needed. Some specialized functions, such as the bookkeeping and advertising, are contracted out rather than done in-house.

As a business grows, it adds people, including middle managers to relieve the pressure on the owner. The staff becomes more specialized, dividing up the duties rather than jointly doing whatever is needed. Staff are grouped (or departmentalized) for the purpose of supervision and resource sharing. This grouping can take several forms: functional, divisional, or matrix.

A **functional structure** groups people according to their function in the organization. The computer consulting company expands and takes back the functions it had outsourced when it was small. It groups people into consulting, finance, and marketing (Figure 15.3).

**Divisional structures** create self-contained units that focus on products, services, clients, or geographical regions. One way in which the computer consulting company could divisionalize is by opening up several offices that provide services within particular geographical areas (Figure 15.4 on page 250). Other divisional structures would see the company structured according to specific specialty services, e.g., computer applications, web design, IT training (Figure 15.5 on page 250) or according to clients (Figure 15.6 on page 250).

**simple structure**
A centralized form of organization that emphasizes direct supervision and low formalization.

**functional structure**
A form of organization that groups people according to the function they perform.

**divisionalized structure**
A form of organization that groups employees according to product, service, client, or geography.

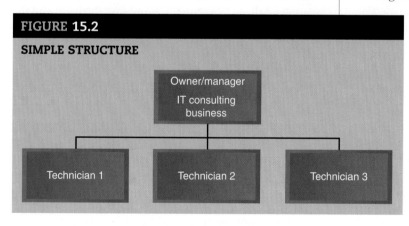

**FIGURE 15.2**

**SIMPLE STRUCTURE**

Owner/manager
IT consulting business

Technician 1 — Technician 2 — Technician 3

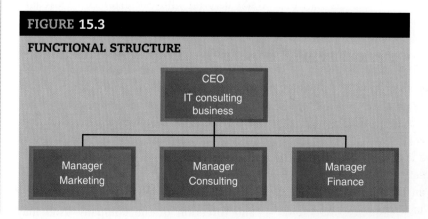

**FIGURE 15.3**

**FUNCTIONAL STRUCTURE**

CEO
IT consulting business

Manager Marketing — Manager Consulting — Manager Finance

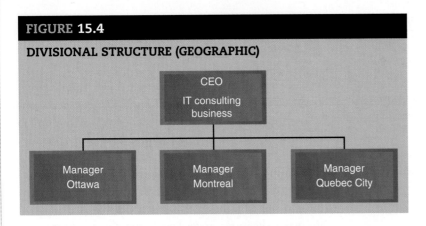

**FIGURE 15.4**

**DIVISIONAL STRUCTURE (GEOGRAPHIC)**

CEO
IT consulting business

Manager
Ottawa

Manager
Montreal

Manager
Quebec City

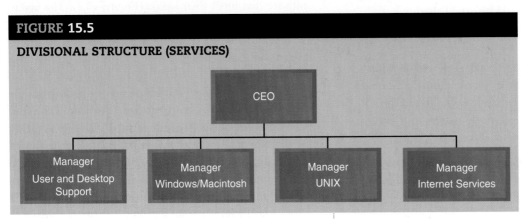

**FIGURE 15.5**

**DIVISIONAL STRUCTURE (SERVICES)**

CEO

Manager
User and Desktop Support

Manager
Windows/Macintosh

Manager
UNIX

Manager
Internet Services

**Matrix structures** are dual-authority structures that combine functional and divisional approaches. For example, an employee in Internet services could be assigned as a web designer to a project team working on a major project for Client A (Figure 15.7). That web designer would work with a multidisciplinary team pulled together to meet these particular project needs and would report on a daily basis to the project manager (who reports to the person in charge of Client A). The

**matrix structure**

A dual-authority form of structure that combines functional and divisional structures, typically through project teams.

web designer is also under the supervision of the Internet services manager, who can provide technical facilitation that the project manager could not. When this project is completed, the web designer will be assigned to another project. A matrix design can also be more permanent. For example, the human resources manager of a large manufacturing plant can report both to the plant manager and to the corporate human resources director (who oversees human resources at the company's six plants to ensure consistency and quality).

Once an organizational structure grows beyond a simple structure, it often combines several structural designs rather than following one, thereby creating a hybrid structure. For instance, the sales force is likely to be grouped on a geographical basis, whereas headquarters may have a functional structure for the staff functions contained there (e.g., human resources, finance), and the plants may be divided according to product.

## Experiences with Structure

To give you a sense of what each structure is like, its pros and cons, and the experience for an employee within it, let's look at an employee who gets the opportunity to work in each of the structures. Shay is hired as a marketing assistant in a start-up promotional company. Besides the owner, there are three staff members. Shay is hired to manage client promotion campaigns but also finds herself helping with client pitches and client management, office accounting, and the hiring of contract workers. Because it is a simple structure there are few rules, no job description, and her work varies daily; all major decisions are made by the owner but the frequent office interaction means Shay has input into many decisions. There is no bureaucracy to deal with. She sees that the company is very adaptable, able to move quickly when a need is identified. Her future career depends on the success and direction of the company—she may

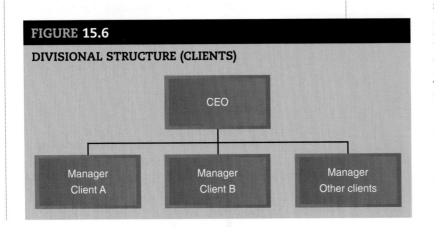

**FIGURE 15.6**

**DIVISIONAL STRUCTURE (CLIENTS)**

CEO

Manager
Client A

Manager
Client B

Manager
Other clients

## FIGURE 15.7

### MATRIX STRUCTURE

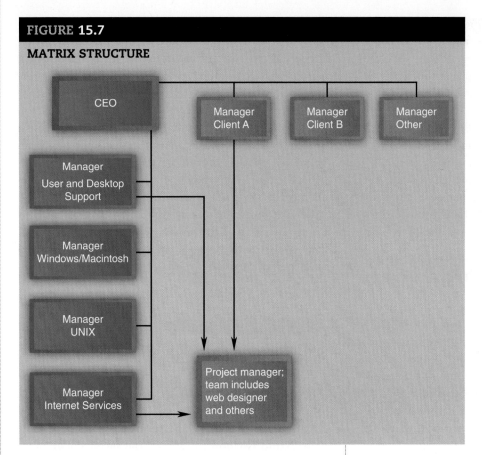

but she also misses the variety of interaction from her old job and being stretched to undertake roles that are outside her expertise. Also, she does not get the same sense of being close to the action because corporate decisions are far removed from her. She realizes, because of her experience at the small company, that the disadvantage of the functional structure is the narrow focus of each department—each one seems to focus more on its own success than the success of the company as a whole and there seems to be competitiveness among them. She sees a lack of coordination and communication between the departments, which she has heard called a "silo" mentality.

Reorganization and layoffs led to Shay once again looking for a job, this time in a company divisionalized according to product. She now works for a large consumer products company within a self-contained subunit that is focused on a particular product line. So now she specializes in marketing that particular product. She finds that the various functions in the large subunit are well coordinated and focused on jointly making the product successful. There is a sensitivity to the needs of its market, with a willingness to adapt as needed. But she has limited contact with the other functional people in her subunit (such as production and finance) and usually interacts only with marketers. She sees the silo mentality again here, but in a different form. This time the conflict lies between company product divisions. It seems to generate a lot of politicking. She also sees some duplication between product divisions; for example, why do they each have a human resources function when it would probably be more efficient to have a central human resource department supporting all parts of the company? In terms of Shay's future career, she can move up within the marketing group assigned to this product division but would like to ultimately get a broader experience.

When, once again, Shay changes employment, she moves to a matrix organization. She is now providing marketing expertise within a series of project teams with others of different functional backgrounds. For example, in a recent new product project team she worked with operations people (e.g., production

end up doing far more complex work, she may enter management as it grows, or she may lose her job if the company has difficulties. Shay likes the variety in her activities and the close atmosphere of the small group. She knows her contribution to the company's success. She gets to stretch her skills and is learning constantly. On the other hand, Shay is frustrated at the hours. The owner expects long hours from all staff and it is difficult to say no. There is no one to complain to when she is annoyed with her boss. Shay sees the risks with this structure: the owner is good at many things but not everything, yet he has the final say, and, if he is absent, the organization is handicapped because no one else has full information or power.

Looking for experience with a much larger, established organization, Shay takes a job as a marketing assistant in a functional structure. Now working in a marketing department separated from the other parts of the organization, she is managed by a supervisor who is a marketer. Shay works only with marketers, works within clear procedures and defined activities, has specified tasks and responsibilities, and ends up specializing in labelling. She is able to learn from the experts in her area, watching them handle more challenging assignments than she is ready to deal with. Her career direction is a clear progression through marketing positions. It is comforting to be with people similar to her

planning, engineering design, and product design). Shay now has two supervisors: one is the marketing manager and the other is the project manager. She likes the teamwork involved, the range of projects she works on over the course of a year, and the variety of people with whom she interacts, as well as the security of having an expert in her area as backup. But sometimes her project manager and marketing manager have different priorities for her, and she wishes there was closer communication between them when it comes to doing her performance review. Her functional manager (the marketer) does the actual review even though the project manager is much more familiar with what she has been doing over the last months.

## Mechanistic and Organic Structures

The six basic structural dimensions can be combined into two broad and contrasting descriptive categories, mechanistic and organic organizations.[13] **Mechanistic structures** have a cluster of formalization, centralization, standardization, hierarchy, and specialization. As in a machine, every part has a specific, well-defined role and no room for variation. Communication is mostly top down. The traditional automobile-manufacturing facility with an assembly line setup fits this description. Organic organizations act more like living things than machines. As living things survive through adaptation to their environment (Darwin's survival of the fittest), organic organizations continuously adjust their operations as needed and can do so because they have a flat structure with decentralization, low formalization, low

standardization, and low specialization. They emphasize open communication and de-emphasize hierarchy. Decisions are linked more to expertise than formal authority. A consulting firm that uses its staff interchangeably on project teams tends to have a more **organic structure**. Activities are not bound by job descriptions, rules, or standardized procedures. Each project is a new challenge and handled jointly by team members, with support rather than interference coming from the top. In fact, no organizations are purely organic or mechanistic, with a more varied combination of the six basic dimensions likely. But these contrasting concepts are useful short forms for the typical clustering of characteristics that have implications for efficiency and innovation (to be discussed later).

LEARNING OUTCOME **4**
## Contextual Variables

The basic design dimensions and the resulting structural configurations play out in the context of the organization's internal and external environments. Four **contextual variables** influence the success of an organization's design: size, technology, environment, and strategy and goals. These variables provide a manager with key considerations for the right organizational design, although they do not determine the structure. The amount of change in the contextual variables throughout the life of the organization influences the amount of change needed in the basic dimensions of

**mechanistic structure**

An organizational design that emphasizes structured activities, specialized tasks, and centralized decision making.

**organic structure**

An organizational design that emphasizes teamwork, open communication, and decentralized decision making.

**contextual variables**

A set of characteristics that influence the organization's design processes.

## [ A Small Organization Stretches Across Canada ]

The Delta Synergy Group delivers team-building and corporate training programs to clientele across Canada and North America, and around the globe. Compelling experiential activities (such as building a bridge or rappelling down a cliff) form the basis for reflection on interaction and leadership, risk, trust, support, teamwork, and communication. From its creation in 1994, Delta's structure has evolved to a geographic divisionalization with offices in Calgary, Vancouver, and Toronto. This was partially to meet the needs of local clients and partially to take advantage of the local training resources (e.g., mountains and lakes).

Photo courtesy of Delta Synergy Group

the organization's structure. For example, competitive pressures in many industries have led to outsourcing, labelled one of the greatest shifts in organization structure in a century.[14]

## Size

In organizational structure, size is defined as the total number of employees. This is logical, because people and their interactions are the building blocks of structure. Other measures, such as net assets, production rates, and total sales, are usually highly correlated with the total number of employees but may not reflect the actual number of interpersonal relationships that are necessary to effectively structure an organization.

When exploring structural alternatives, what should the manager know about designing structures for large and small organizations?

Formalization, specialization, and standardization all tend to be greater in larger organizations because they are necessary to control activities within the organization. For example, larger organizations are more likely to use documentation, rules, written policies and procedures, and detailed job descriptions than to rely on personal observation by the manager. McDonald's has several volumes that describe how to make all its products, how to greet customers, how to maintain the facilities, and so on. This level of standardization, formalization, and specialization helps McDonald's maintain the same quality of product no matter where a restaurant is located. In contrast, at a small, locally owned café, your hamburger and French fries may taste a little different every time you visit. This is evidence of a lack of standardization.

Formalization and specialization also help a large organization decentralize decision making. Because of the complexity and number of decisions in a large organization, formalization and specialization are used to set parameters for decision making at lower levels. By decentralizing decision making, the larger organization adds horizontal and vertical complexity, but not necessarily spatial complexity. However, it is more common for a large organization to have more geographic dispersion.

Hierarchy of authority is another dimension of design related to complexity. As size increases, complexity increases; thus, more levels are added to the

©LIU, CHIN-CHENG/Shutterstock

hierarchy of authority. This keeps the span of control from getting too large. However, there is a balancing force, because formalization and specialization are added. The more formalized, standardized, and specialized the roles within the organization, the wider the span of control can be.

## Technology

An organization's technology is an important contextual variable in determining the organization's structure.[16] Technology is defined as the tools, techniques, and actions used by an organization to transform inputs into outputs.[17] The inputs of the organization include human resources, machines, materials, information, and money. The outputs are the products and services that the organization offers to the external environment. Determining the relationship between technology and structure is complicated, because different departments may employ very different technologies. As organizations become larger, there is greater variation in technologies across units in the organization. Joan Woodward, Charles Perrow, and James Thompson have developed ways to understand traditional organizational technologies.

Woodward introduced one of the best-known classification

schemes for technology, identifying three types: unit, mass, or process production. Unit technology is small-batch manufacturing technology and, sometimes, made-to-order production. Examples include Island View Design, a custom furniture and cabinet-making shop near Halifax, and Vancouver's KIMBO Design, a full-service design firm specializing in branding and website design. Mass technology is large-batch manufacturing technology. Examples include automotive assembly lines and latex glove production. Process production is continuous-production processes. Examples include oil refining and beer making. Woodward classified unit technology as the least complex, mass technology as more complex, and process technology as the most complex. The more complex the organization's technology, the more complex the administrative component or structure of the organization needs to be.

Perrow proposed an alternative to Woodward's scheme based on two variables: task variability and problem analyzability. Task variability considers the number of exceptions encountered in doing the tasks within a job. Problem analyzability examines the types of search procedures followed to find ways to respond to task exceptions. For example, for some exceptions encountered while doing a task, the appropriate response is easy to find. If you are driving down a street and see a sign that says, "Detour—Bridge Out," it is very easy to respond to the task variability, so analyzability is low (i.e., limited analysis is needed). By contrast, when Alexander Graham Bell was designing the first telephone, the problem analyzability was very high for his task.

Perrow went on further to identify the four key aspects of structure that could be modified to the technology. These structural elements are (1) the amount of discretion that an individual can exercise to complete a task, (2) the power of groups to control the unit's goals and strategies, (3) the level of interdependence among groups, and (4) the extent

to which organizational units coordinate work using either feedback or planning. Figure 15.8 summarizes Perrow's findings about types of technology and basic design dimensions.[18]

Thompson offered yet another view of technology and its relationship to organizational design. This view is based on the concept of **technological interdependence** (i.e., the degree of interrelatedness of the organization's various technological elements) and the pattern of an organization's work flows. Thompson's research suggests that greater technological interdependence leads to greater organizational complexity and that the problems of this greater complexity may be offset by decentralized decision making.[19]

The research of these three early scholars on the influence of technology on organizational design can be combined into one integrating concept—routineness in the process of changing inputs into outputs in an organization. This routineness has a very strong relationship with organizational structure. The more routine and repetitive the tasks of the organization, the higher the degree of formalization that is possible; the more centralized, specialized, and standardized the organization can be; and the more hierarchical levels with wider spans of control that are possible.

Essentially, the more routine the technology, the more effective a mechanistic structure will be in supporting

**technological interdependence**

The degree of interrelatedness of the organization's various technological elements.

---

### FIGURE 15.8

**SUMMARY OF PERROW'S FINDINGS ABOUT THE RELATIONSHIP BETWEEN TECHNOLOGY AND BASIC DESIGN DIMENSIONS**

Task Variability

| Problem Analyzability | Few Exceptions | Many Exceptions |
|---|---|---|
| **Ill-defined and Unanalyzable** | Craft<br>1. Mod. formalization<br>2. Mod. centralization<br>3. Mod. specialization<br>4. Low-mod. standardization<br>5. High complexity<br>6. Low hierarchy | Nonroutine<br>1. Low formalization<br>2. Low centralization<br>3. Low specialization<br>4. Low standardization<br>5. High complexity<br>6. Low hierarchy |
| **Well-defined and Analyzable** | Routine<br>1. High formalization<br>2. High centralization<br>3. Mod. specialization<br>4. High standardization<br>5. Low complexity<br>6. High hierarchy | Engineering<br>1. Mod. formalization<br>2. Mod. centralization<br>3. High specialization<br>4. Mod. standardization<br>5. Mod. complexity<br>6. Mod. hierarchy |

SOURCE: Built from C. Perrow, "A Framework for the Comparative Analysis of Organizations," *American Sociological Review* (April 1967): 194–208.

organizational success. The less routine the technology, the more likely an organic structure is appropriate.

## Environment

The third contextual variable for organizational design is **environment**. The environment of an organization is most easily defined as anything outside the boundaries of that organization. Different aspects of the environment have varying degrees of influence on the organization's structure. The general environment includes all conditions that may have an impact on the organization. These conditions could include economic factors, political considerations, ecological changes, sociocultural demands, and governmental regulation.

### Environmental Uncertainty

The level of **environmental uncertainty** is the contextual variable of environment that most influences organizational design. Some organizations have relatively static environments with little uncertainty, whereas others are so dynamic that no one is sure what tomorrow may bring. Binney & Smith, for example, has made relatively the same product for more than 50 years, with very few changes in the product design or packaging. The environment for its Crayola products is relatively static. In fact, customers rebelled when the company tried to get rid of some old colours and add new ones. In contrast, in the last two decades, competitors in the airline industry have encountered deregulation, mergers, bankruptcies, safety changes, changes in cost and price structures, changes in customer and employee demographics, and changes in global competition. In such uncertain conditions, fast-response organizations must use expertise coordination practices to ensure that distributed expertise is managed and applied in a timely manner.[20]

The amount of uncertainty in the environment influences the structural dimensions. A functional structure is superior in a predictable environment because it enhances efficiencies, but a divisional structure's (e.g., geography/product) customized focus allows it to respond more quickly in an unpredictable environment.[21]

If the organization's environment is uncertain, dynamic, and complex, and resources are scarce, the manager needs an organic structure that is better able to adapt to its environment. Such a structure allows the manager to monitor the environment from a number of internal perspectives, thus helping the organization maintain flexibility in responding to environmental changes.[22]

This finding has been replicated recently in Chinese companies.[23] Although an organic structure's flexibility makes it suitable to meet the need for timely responsiveness, research suggests that there remains a need for some structure and it may be better to err on the side of too much structure rather than too little.[24] Some suggest the use of a "simple rules" structure that can be robust in a number of environments.[25]

The organization's perceptions of its environment and the actual environment may not be the same. The environment that the manager perceives is the environment that the organization responds to and organizes for.[26] Therefore, two organizations may be in relatively the same environment from an objective standpoint, but if the managers perceive differences, the organizations may enact very different structures to deal with this same environment. For example, one company may decentralize and use monetary incentives for managers

**environment**
Anything outside the boundaries of an organization.

**environmental uncertainty**
The amount and rate of change in the organization's environment.

## [ How to Determine Environmental Uncertainty ]

Dess and Beard defined three dimensions of environment that should be measured in assessing the degree of uncertainty: capacity, volatility, and complexity.[27] The capacity of the environment reflects the abundance or scarcity of resources. If resources abound, the environment supports expansion, mistakes, or both. In contrast, in times of scarcity, the environment demands survival of the fittest. Volatility is the degree of instability. The airline industry is in a volatile environment. This makes it difficult for managers to know what needs to be done. The complexity of the environment refers to the differences and variability among environmental elements.

that lead it to be competitively aggressive while another company may centralize and use incentives for managers that lead it to be less intense in its rivalry.[28]

## Strategy and Goals

The fourth contextual variable that influences how the design dimensions of structure should be enacted is the strategies and goals of the organization. Strategies and goals provide legitimacy to the organization, as well as employee direction, decision guidelines, and criteria for performance.[29] In addition, strategies and goals help the organization fit into its environment.

Different strategies will lead to different emphases on efficiency versus innovation. If a company follows a cost leadership strategy, aiming at selling more because its products are the least expensive, it needs efficiency to lower its costs. It will typically lean toward a mechanistic structure in order to gain this efficiency. On the other hand, if it emphasizes differentiation from the competition through a unique or innovative product, an organic structure with decentralization and low formalization will encourage the creativity and quick responsiveness needed.[30, 31]

For example, when Apple Computer introduced personal computers to the market, its strategies were very innovative. The structure of the organization was relatively flat and very informal. Apple had Friday afternoon beer and popcorn discussion sessions, and eccentric behaviour was easily accepted. As the personal computer market became more competitive, however,

the structure of Apple changed to help it control costs. The innovative strategies and structures devised by Steve Jobs, one of Apple's founders, were no longer appropriate. The board of directors recruited John Scully, a marketing expert from PepsiCo, to help Apple better compete in the market it had created. In 1996 and 1997, Apple reinvented itself again and brought back Jobs to try to restore its innovative edge. Since his return, Apple has become a major player in the digital music market with its introduction of several models of iPod, the iPhone, and the iPad.

Limitations exist, however, on the extent to which strategies and goals influence structure. Because the structure of the organization includes the formal information-processing channels in the organization, it stands to reason that the need to change strategies may not be communicated throughout the organization. In such a case, the organization's structure influences its strategic choice. Changing the organization's structure may not unlock value but rather drive up costs and difficulties. Therefore, strategic success may hinge on choosing an organization design that works reasonably well, and then fine tuning the structure through a strategic system.[32]

The inefficiency of the structure to perceive environmental changes may even lead to organizational failure. Examples of how different design dimensions can affect the strategic decision process are listed in Table 15.1.

The four contextual variables—size, technology, environment, and strategy and goals—combine to influence the design process. However, the existing structure of

| **TABLE 15.1** Examples of How Structure Affects the Strategic Decision Process |
|---|
| **Formalization** |
| As the level of formalization increases, so does the probability of the following: <br> 1. The strategic decision process will become reactive to crisis rather than proactive through opportunities. <br> 2. Strategic moves will be incremental and precise. <br> 3. Differentiation in the organization will not be balanced with integrative mechanisms. <br> 4. Only environmental crises that are in areas monitored by the formal organizational systems will be acted upon. |
| **Centralization** |
| As the level of centralization increases, so does the probability of the following: <br> 1. The strategic decision process will be initiated by only a few dominant individuals. <br> 2. The decision process will be goal-oriented and rational. <br> 3. The strategic process will be constrained by the limitations of top managers. |
| **Complexity** |
| As the level of complexity increases, so does the probability of the following: <br> 1. The strategic decision process will become more politicized. <br> 2. The organization will find it more difficult to recognize environmental opportunities and threats. <br> 3. The constraints on good decision processes will be multiplied by the limitations of each individual within the organization. |

SOURCE: Republished with permission of Academy of Management, Briarcliff Manor. "The Strategic Decision Process and Organizational Structure" (Table), J. Fredrickson, *Academy of Management Review* (1986): 284. Reproduced by permission of the publisher via Copyright Clearance Center, Inc.

the organization influences how the organization interprets and reacts to information about each of the variables. Each of the contextual variables has management researchers who claim that it is the most important variable in determining the best structural design. Because of the difficulty in studying the interactions of the four contextual dimensions and the complexity of organizational structures, the argument about which variable is most important continues.

What is apparent is that there must be some level of fit between the structure and the contextual dimensions of the organization. The better the fit, the more likely the organization will achieve its short-run goals. In addition, the better the fit, the more likely the organization will process information and design appropriate organizational roles for long-term prosperity, as indicated in Figure 15.9.

## Interaction Between Structure and People

One can also apply the idea of fit between structures and people. In studies of Americans, they were more attracted to organizations with decentralized structures,[33] and their job satisfaction was inversely related to the level of bureaucracy in the work. Individual differences showed that the low job satisfaction—bureaucracy link was particularly pronounced in those individuals who place a high value on individuality, freedom, and independence.[34] In contrast, research investigating the high failure rate of development projects in developing countries attributed many of the difficulties in Nepalese projects to the mismatch between the high bureaucratic orientation of the Nepalese and the Western project-management structure.[35] Finnish research showed that individuals with a high personal need for structure experience more job strain in highly complex work circumstances.[36] An individual's level of self-esteem seems related to the influence of organization structural dimensions, with low-self-esteem people more sensitive to those cues.[37]

Structure influences leadership. Charismatic leaders are more likely to emerge in organic structures than in mechanistic ones.[38] Flat structures reward those managers who favour sharing information and objectives with employees by promoting them faster than those managers who do not believe in making information and objectives explicit to those below them. The opposite was observed in tall structures.[39] Leadership also influences structure. CEOs with a high need for achievement are more likely to use centralization, formalization, and integration. Because they want to meet standards of excellence and want to have control over events affecting performance, they try to accomplish their work in an interactive way

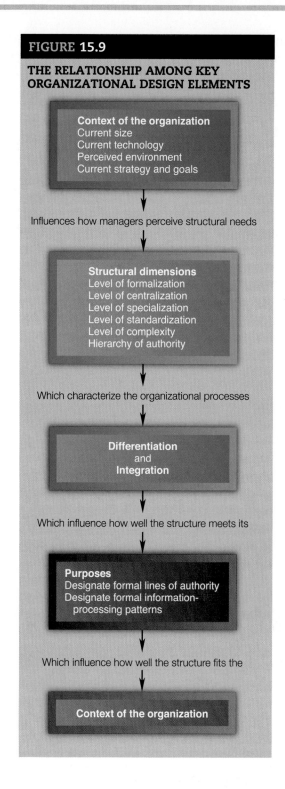

**FIGURE 15.9**

**THE RELATIONSHIP AMONG KEY ORGANIZATIONAL DESIGN ELEMENTS**

**Context of the organization**
Current size
Current technology
Perceived environment
Current strategy and goals

Influences how managers perceive structural needs

**Structural dimensions**
Level of formalization
Level of centralization
Level of specialization
Level of standardization
Level of complexity
Hierarchy of authority

Which characterize the organizational processes

**Differentiation and Integration**

Which influence how well the structure meets its

**Purposes**
Designate formal lines of authority
Designate formal information-processing patterns

Which influence how well the structure fits the

**Context of the organization**

(because they like feedback) and an analytical/rational way (suggesting a focus on good procedures and linking mechanisms).[40]

Structure also influences justice expectations and perceptions. Decentralized organizations are seen as more procedurally fair than centralized.[41] Individuals are more sensitive to procedural justice in mechanistic structures because formal procedures are part of the daily work landscape. Individuals are more sensitive to interactional justice in organic structures because organic structure is based on interpersonal interactions.[42]

# Forces Reshaping Organizations

Several forces reshaping organizations are causing managers to go beyond the traditional frameworks and to examine ways to make organizations more responsive to customer needs. Some of these forces include shorter organizational life cycles, globalization, and rapid changes in information technology. These forces together increase the demands on process capabilities within the organization and emerging organizational structures. To successfully retain their health and vitality, organizations must function as open systems that are responsive to their task environment.[43]

## Life Cycles in Organizations

Organizations are dynamic entities. As such, they ebb and flow through different stages. Usually, researchers think of these stages as **organizational life cycles**. The total organization has a life cycle that begins at birth, moves through growth and maturity to decline, and possibly experiences revival.[44]

Organizational subunits may have very similar life cycles. Because of changes in technology and product design, many organizational subunits, especially those that are product based, are experiencing shorter life cycles. Hence, the subunits that compose the organization are changing more rapidly than in the past. These shorter life cycles enable the organization to respond quickly to external demands and changes.

When a new organization or subunit is born, the structure is organic and informal. If the organization or subunit is successful, it grows and matures. This usually leads to formalization, specialization, standardization, complexity, and a more mechanistic structure. If the environment changes, however, the organization must be able to respond. A mechanistic structure is not able to respond to a dynamic environment as well as an organic one. If the organization or subunit does respond, it becomes more organic and revives; if not, it declines and possibly dies.

Shorter life cycles put more pressure on the organization to be both flexible and efficient at the same time. Further, as flexible organizations use design to their competitive advantage, discrete organizational life cycles may give way to a kaleidoscope of continuously emerging, efficiency-seeking organizational designs.[45] The manager's challenge in this context becomes one of creating congruency among various organizational design dimensions to fit continuously changing markets and locations.

## Globalization

Another force that is reshaping organizations is the process of globalization. In other words, organizations operate worldwide rather than in just one country or region. Global corporations can become pitted against sovereign nations when rules and laws conflict across national borders. Globalization makes spatial differentiation even more of a reality for organizations. Besides the obvious geographic differences, there may be deep cultural and value system differences. This adds another type of complexity to the structural design process and necessitates the creation of integrating mechanisms so that people are able to understand and interpret one another, as well as coordinate with one another.

The choice of structure for managing an international business is generally based on choices concerning the following three factors:

1. *The level of vertical differentiation.* A hierarchy of authority must be created that clarifies the responsibilities of both domestic and foreign managers.

2. *The level of horizontal differentiation.* Foreign and domestic operations should be grouped in such a way that the company effectively serves the needs of all customers.

3. *The degree of formalization, specialization, standardization, and centralization.* The global structure must allow decisions to be made in the most appropriate area of the organization. However, controls must be in place that reflect the strategies and goals of the parent firm.[46]

## Changes in Information-Processing Technologies

Many of the changes in information-processing technologies have allowed organizations to move into new product and market areas more quickly. However, just as shorter life cycles and globalization have caused new concerns for designing organizational structures, so has the increased availability of advanced information-processing technologies.

Organizational structures are already feeling the impact of advanced information-processing technologies. More integration and coordination are evident, because managers worldwide can be connected through computerized networks. The basic design dimensions

**organizational life cycle**

The differing stages of an organization's life from birth to death.

have also been affected as follows:

1. The hierarchy of authority has been flattened.

2. The basis of centralization has been changed. Now managers can use technology to acquire more information and make more decisions, or they can use technology to push information and decision making lower in the hierarchy and thus decrease centralization. In fact, decentralized structures do make greater use of information technology than do centralized structures.[47]

3. Less specialization and standardization are needed, because people using advanced information-processing technologies have more sophisticated jobs that require a broader understanding of how the organization gets work done.[48]

Advances in information processing are leading to knowledge-based organizations that incorporate virtual enterprising, dynamic teaming, and knowledge networking.[49]

## Demands on Organizational Processes

Because of the forces reshaping organizations, managers find themselves trying to meet what seem to be conflicting goals: an efficiency orientation that results in on-time delivery *and* a quality orientation that results in customized, high-quality goods or services.[50] Traditionally, managers have seen efficiency and customization as conflicting demands.

To meet these conflicting demands, organizations need to become "dynamically stable."[51] To do so, an organization must have managers who see their roles as architects who clearly understand the "how" of the organizing process. Managers must combine long-term thinking with flexible and quick responses that help improve process and know-how (see Table 15.2). The organizational structure must help define, at least to some degree, roles for managers who hope to successfully address the conflicting demands of dynamic stability.

**TABLE 15.2** Structural Roles of Managers Today versus Managers of the Future

| Roles of Managers Today | |
|---|---|
| | 1. Strictly adhering to boss–employee relationships. |
| | 2. Getting things done by giving orders. |
| | 3. Carrying messages up and down the hierarchy. |
| | 4. Performing a prescribed set of tasks according to a job description. |
| | 5. Having a narrow functional focus |
| | 6. Going through channels, one by one by one. |
| | 7. Controlling subordinates. |
| **Roles of Future Managers** | |
| | 1. Having heirarchical relationships subordinated to functional and peer relationships. |
| | 2. Getting things done by negotiating. |
| | 3. Solving problems and making decisions. |
| | 4. Creating the job by developing entrepreneurial projects. |
| | 5. Having broad cross-functional collaboration. |
| | 6. Emphasizing speed and flexibility. |
| | 7. Coaching their workers. |

SOURCE: Reprinted by permission of the publisher, from *Management Review*, January 1991 © 1991. Thomas R. Horton. American Management Association, New York. All rights reserved.

# Emerging Organizational Structures

The demands on managers and on process capabilities place demands on structures. The emphasis in organizations is shifting to organizing around processes. This process orientation emerges from the combination of three streams of applied organizational design: high-performance, self-managed teams; managing processes rather than functions; and the evolution of information technology. Information technology and advanced communication systems have led to inter-networking. In a study of 469 firms, deeply inter-networked firms were found to be more focused and specialized, less hierarchical, and more engaged in external partnering.[52] Two emerging organizational structures associated with these changes are network organizations and virtual organizations.

Network organizations are weblike structures that contract some or all of their operating functions to other organizations and then coordinate their activities through managers and other employees at their headquarters. Information technology is the basis for building the weblike structure of the network organization and business unit managers that are essential to the success of these systems. This type of organization has arisen in the age of electronic commerce and brought into practice transaction cost economics, interorganizational collaborations, and strategic alliances. Network organizations can be global in scope.[53]

Virtual organizations are temporary network organizations consisting of independent enterprises. Many dot-coms were virtual organizations designed to come together swiftly to exploit an apparent market opportunity. They may function much like a theatrical troupe that comes together for a "performance."[54] Trust can be a challenge for virtual organizations because it is a complex phenomenon involving ethics, morals, emotions, values, and natural attitudes. However, trust and trustworthiness are important connective issues in virtual environments. Three key ingredients for the development of trust in virtual organizations are technology that can communicate emotion; a sharing of values, vision, and organizational identity; and a high standard of ethics.[55]

## FIGURE 15.10

### PRECISION BIOLOGIC ORGANIZATIONAL FRAMEWORK

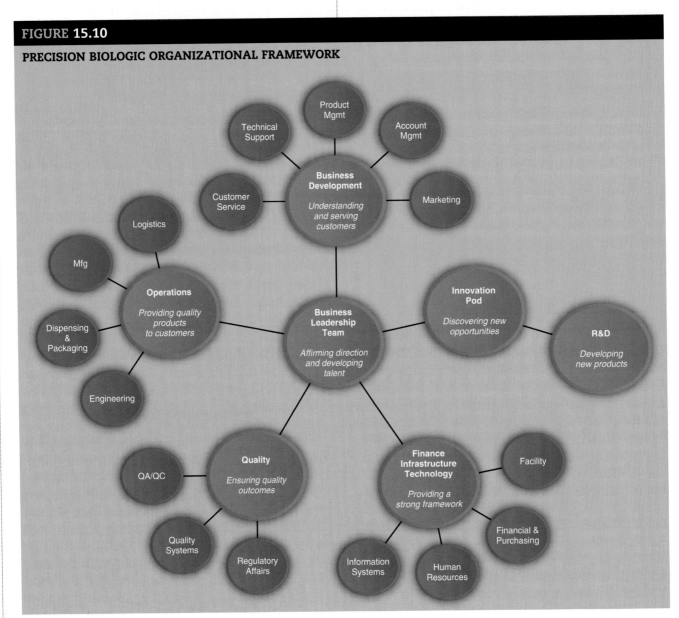

SOURCE: Reprinted by permission of Precision Biologic

Other new structures do not fit either the network or virtual models. In sharp contrast to the Toronto Zoo organizational structure which you examined at the start of the chapter is the organizational framework of Precision Biologic seen in Figure 15.10. Precision Biologic of Dartmouth, Nova Scotia was named one of the best employers in Canada for 2010. The developer and manufacturer of medical lab products has an unusual hub-and-spokes organizational structure that de-emphasizes hierarchy and promotes collaboration in a working relationship approach that resembles a molecular structure. More organizations will be experimenting with unusual structures like this in order to meet demands for responsiveness, flexibility, and innovation.

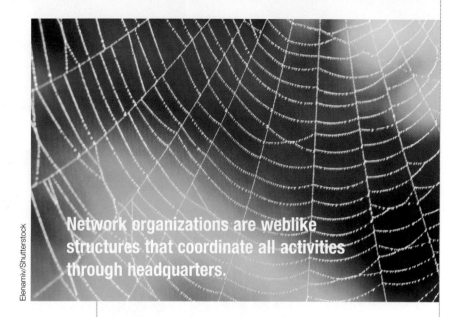

Elenamiv/Shutterstock

Network organizations are weblike structures that coordinate all activities through headquarters.

# Consequences of a Poor Structure

This chapter has identified the purposes of structure, the processes of organizational design, and the dimensions and contexts that must be considered in structure. In addition, it has looked at forces and trends in organizational design. A cautionary note is important for the student of organizational behaviour. An organizational structure may be weak or deficient. In general, if the structure is out of alignment with its contextual variables, one or more of the following four symptoms appears.

> Decision making is delayed because the hierarchy is overloaded and too much information is being funnelled through one or two channels.

> Decision making lacks quality because information linkages are not providing the correct information to the right person in the right format.

> The organization does not respond innovatively to a changing environment, especially when coordinated effort is lacking across departments.

> A great deal of conflict is evident when departments are working against one another rather than working for the strategies and goals of the organization as a whole; the structure is often at fault.

 Visit **icanorgb.com** to find the resources you need today!

*Located at the back of the textbook are rip-out Chapter Review Cards. Make sure you also go online to check out other tools that ORGB offers to help you successfully pass your course.*

- Interactive Quizzing
- Key Term Flashcards
- PowerPoint Slides
- Audio Chapter Summaries

- Cases and Exercises
- Interactive Games
- Self-Assessments
- "On the Job" and "Bizflix" Videos

# Organizational Culture

> **"** *Just as there are cultures in larger human society, there are cultures within organizations.* **"**

The concept of organizational culture has its roots in cultural anthropology. Just as there are cultures in larger human society, there are cultures within organizations. Like societal cultures, they are shared, communicated through symbols, and passed down from generation to generation of employees.

The concept of cultures in organizations was alluded to as early as the Hawthorne studies, which described work group culture. The topic came into its own during the early 1970s, when managers and researchers alike began to search for keys to survival for organizations in a competitive and turbulent environment. Then, in the early 1980s, several books on corporate culture were published, including Deal and Kennedy's *Corporate Cultures*,[1] Ouchi's *Theory Z*,[2] and Peters and Waterman's *In Search of Excellence*.[3] These books found wide audiences, and research began in earnest on the elusive topic of organizational cultures. Executives indicated that these cultures were real and could be managed.[4]

# Levels of Organizational Culture

Many definitions of *organizational culture* have been proposed. Most of them agree that there are several levels of culture and that these levels differ in terms of their visibility and their ability to be changed. The definition adopted in this chapter is that **organizational (corporate) culture**

**organizational (corporate) culture**
A pattern of basic assumptions that are considered valid and that are taught to new members as the way to perceive, think, and feel in the organization.

## LEARNING OUTCOMES

After reading this chapter, you should be able to do the following:

**1** Identify the three levels of culture and evaluate the roles they play in an organization.

**2** Describe the four functions of culture within an organization.

**3** Explain the relationship between organizational culture and corporate performance.

**4** Describe five ways leaders reinforce organizational culture.

**5** Describe the three stages of organizational socialization and the ways culture is communicated in each step.

**6** Discuss how managers assess their organization's culture.

**7** Explain actions managers can take to change organizational culture.

**8** Identify the challenges organizations face developing positive, cohesive cultures.

FIGURE **16.1**

## LEVELS OF ORGANIZATIONAL CULTURE

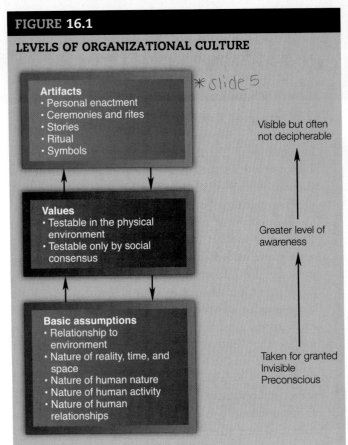

*slide 5

**Artifacts**
- Personal enactment
- Ceremonies and rites
- Stories
- Ritual
- Symbols

Visible but often not decipherable

**Values**
- Testable in the physical environment
- Testable only by social consensus

Greater level of awareness

**Basic assumptions**
- Relationship to environment
- Nature of reality, time, and space
- Nature of human nature
- Nature of human activity
- Nature of human relationships

Taken for granted Invisible Preconscious

SOURCE: From Edgar H. Schein, *Organizational Culture and Leadership: A Dynamic View.* Copyright © 1985 Jossey-Bass, Inc. Reprinted with permission of John Wiley & Sons, Inc.

is a pattern of basic assumptions that are considered valid and that are taught to new members as the way to perceive, think, and feel in the organization.[5]

Edgar Schein, in his comprehensive book on organizational culture and leadership, suggests that organizational culture has three levels. His view of culture is presented in Figure 16.1. The levels range from visible artifacts and creations to testable values to invisible and even preconscious basic assumptions. To achieve a complete understanding of an organization's culture, all three levels must be studied.

## Artifacts – what you see.

Cultural symbols in the physical and social work environments are called **artifacts**. They are the most visible and accessible level of culture.

**artifacts**

Symbols of culture in the physical and social work environments.

The key to understanding culture through artifacts lies in figuring out their meanings. Artifacts are also the most frequently studied manifestation of organizational culture, perhaps because of their accessibility. See what cultural artifacts or symbols you can identify in the following story.

The corporate culture of the Great Little Box Company (GLBC) is apparent in the facility on Mitchell Island, Richmond, B.C. that houses its head office, manufacturing, and warehouse activities. Open-concept offices are arranged in a horseshoe design so employees have a view of the Fraser River; there's a gym open 24 hours a day; the manufacturing and warehouse facilities are clean, with abundant natural light; and there's an outdoor gazebo, volleyball and basketball courts, horseshoe pitch and dock for kayaking commuters, a nap room for quiet time, free coffee, tea, and snacks. GLBC sets a common goal each year for the company and if they beat the goal, every employee goes on an all-expenses-paid vacation to a sunny destination. Open-book management means employees know where the company stands financially. A profit-sharing program includes all employees. The company-subsidized social committee organizes many events (e.g., golf tournament, paintball competition, summer barbeques, summer cruises on president's boat), and the social calendar reflects the cultural diversity of the firm with its annual celebrations of the Chinese New Year and the Sikh festival of Vaisakhi. Employees receive individual performance reviews every three months, 360 feedback is invited, and exceptional performance and cost-saving ideas are rewarded. Benefits include full tuition subsidies for courses completed at outside institutions, academic scholarships for employees' children, flexible working hours, reduced summer hours, compressed work weeks and phased-in retirement. GLBC donates and matches employee donations to numerous charitable and community initiatives, with employees helping to select the charitable groups assisted each year. The company planted over 4,000 trees and shrubs on its new site and is reducing its carbon footprint through an internal scrap recovery program and shipping pallet repair program.[6] The artifacts at GLBC reinforce the notion that GLBC

Photo courtesy of The Great Little Box Company

cares about excellence but at the same time cares about employees and the environment, seeking a balance that creates a fine quality of life for all.

Among the artifacts of culture are personal enactment, ceremonies and rites, stories, rituals, and symbols.[7]

**Personal Enactment** Culture can be understood, in part, through an examination of the behavior of organization members. Personal enactment is behaviour that reflects the organization's values. In particular, personal enactment by the top managers provides insight into these values. At Digital Extremes, a game development studio in London, Ontario, the company's CEO recently donated one month of his salary to assist an employee who needed home renovations to ensure accessibility for a loved one with disabilities.[8] At NepApp Canada Ltd., the co-chairman of the company makes an average of 30 personal thank-you calls a week to individual employees.[9] Each year Kish Kapoor, the president of Winnipeg-based boutique investment company Wellington West, goes on the road to visit each of the 31 cities in which the company has an office. There he holds a three- or four-hour town hall meeting at which employees are guaranteed an answer to any question.[10, 11]

Modelled behaviour is a powerful learning tool for employees, as Bandura's social learning theory demonstrated.[12] As we saw in Chapter 6, individuals learn vicariously by observing others' behaviour and patterning their own behaviour similarly. Culture can be an important leadership tool. Managerial behaviour can clarify what is important and coordinate the work of employees, in effect negating the need for close supervision.[13]

**Ceremonies and Rites** Relatively elaborate sets of activities that are repeatedly enacted on important occasions are known as organizational ceremonies and rites.[14] These occasions provide opportunities to reward and recognize employees whose behaviour is congruent with the values of the company. Ceremonies and rites send a message that individuals who both espouse and exhibit corporate values are heroes to be admired.

Ceremonies and rites also bond organizational members together. Edmonton-based Intuit Canada creates financial and tax preparation software, including the popular QuickTax. This means that during tax season the whole company must pull together to meet the intense demand to field calls from customers. To make this annual challenge more palatable, during the last week of tax season employees are treated to free ice cream sundaes in the lobby, juggling lessons, and other games.[15] Diavik Diamond Mines in the Northwest Territories has celebrations to recognize employees who achieve safety record milestones.[16] At Burnaby-based Ames Tile & Stone Ltd, when the company has a record sales month, the president and GM bring in an espresso machine, personally make everyone their favourite coffee, and present each person with a gift card and letter of thanks.[17] Research in Motion has celebrated significant milestones with "RIM ROCKS" concerts, featuring past performances from U2, the Tragically Hip, Aerosmith, and the Barenaked Ladies.[18] Six kinds of rites in organizations (see below) have been identified.[19]

**Stories** Some researchers have argued that the most effective way to reinforce organizational values is through stories.[20] As they are retold, stories give meaning

## [ Rites in Organizations ]

| Rite | Role | Example |
|------|------|---------|
| *Rites of passage* | show that an individual's status has changed | retirement dinners |
| *Rites of enhancement* | reinforce the achievement of individuals | awarding certificates to sales contest winners |
| *Rites of renewal* | emphasize change in the organization and commitment to learning and growth | opening a new corporate training centre |
| *Rites of integration* | unite diverse groups or teams within the organization and renew commitment to the larger organization | company functions such as annual picnics |
| *Rites of conflict reduction* | dealing with conflicts or disagreements that arise naturally in organizations | grievance hearings and the negotiation of union contracts |
| *Rites of degradation* | used to visibly punish persons who fail to adhere to values and norms of behaviour | publicly replacing a CEO for unethical conduct or for failure to achieve organizational goals |

Research in Motion celebrates significant milestones with "RIM ROCKS" concerts.

Dave M. Benett/Getty Images

and identity to organizations and are especially helpful in orienting new employees. Part of the strength of organizational stories is that the listeners are left to draw their own conclusions—a powerful communication tool.[21]

Research by Joanne Martin and her colleagues has indicated that certain themes appear in stories across different types of organizations:[22]

1. *Stories about the boss.* These stories may reflect whether the boss is "human" or how the boss reacts to mistakes.

2. *Stories about getting fired.* Events leading to employee firings are recounted.

3. *Stories about how the company deals with employees who have to relocate.* These stories relate to the company's actions toward employees who have to move—whether the company is helpful and takes family and other personal concerns into account.

4. *Stories about whether lower-level employees can rise to the top.* Often, these stories describe a person who started out at the bottom and eventually became the CEO.

5. *Stories about how the company deals with crisis situations.* These stories show how the company overcomes obstacles.

6. *Stories about how status considerations work when rules are broken.* When Tom Watson, Sr., was CEO of IBM, he was once confronted by a security guard because he was not wearing an ID badge.

These are the themes that can emerge when stories are passed down. The information from these stories serves to guide the behaviour of organization members.

To be effective cultural tools, stories must be credible. You can't tell a story about your flat corporate hierarchy and then have reserved parking spaces for managers. Stories that aren't backed by reality can lead to cynicism and mistrust.

Effective stories are not only motivational but also can reinforce culture and create renewed energy. Lucasfilm is the home of director and producer George Lucas and the birthplace of such blockbusters as *Star Wars* and *Forrest Gump*. Stories of the company's legendary accomplishments are used to reinforce the creative culture and to rally the troops. When Gail Currey, former head of the company's digital division, found her 300 designers were grumbling, she reminded them of how they did *Gump* when everyone else said it was impossible and what a hit the film was. The geniuses would then head back to their computers to add to the company's success.[23]

**Rituals** Everyday, repetitive, organizational practices are rituals. They are usually unwritten, but they send a clear message about "the way we do things around here." While some companies insist that people address each other by their titles (Mr., Mrs., Ms., Miss) and surnames to reinforce a professional image, others prefer that employees operate on a first-name basis—from the top manager on down. At Winnipeg's Protegra, employees consider themselves partners in the IT company (many do own shares in the private company) and the company's success depends on everyone contributing ideas for improved efficiency and performance. So titles are discarded. Even CEO Wadood Ibrahim is "just Wadood" to the staff.[24]

As everyday practices, rituals reinforce the organizational culture. Insiders who commonly practise the rituals may be unaware of their subtle influence, but outsiders recognize it easily.

**Symbols** Symbols communicate organizational culture through unspoken messages. The organizational chart quickly communicates its emphasis on hierarchy and status. The company dress code represents its relative concern with formality. Physical expressions of culture can be strong symbols. For example, Miele Canada's

## [ Storytelling Savvy ]

To maintain its renowned level of customer service and create lifelong customers, the Ritz-Carlton chain of hotels trains its employees every *day* on the value of such service. In fifteen-minute training sessions called "lineups," employees are encouraged to share one "wow" story for the day in which someone in their work group went above and beyond the call of duty. Stories from each hotel's daily lineup are then shared with other Ritz-Carlton locations across the world as a way to reinforce organizational service and teamwork values. Ritz-Carlton is investing thousands of hours in training employees and using storytelling as a tool to reinforce the company's culture and values.

SOURCE: C. Gallo, "How Ritz-Carlton Maintains Its Mystique," *BusinessWeek* (February 13, 2007), http://www.businessweek.com/print/smallbiz/content/feb2007/sb20070213_171606.htm

**For decades, the mantra of the Ritz Carlton has been "Ladies and gentlemen serving ladies and gentlemen."**

glass walls in all the work areas and the president's office encourage open communication and collaboration.[25] A similar message comes from the wall-less pods at Sapient Canada, an IT consulting firm, where coworkers are arranged according to the projects they are undertaking.[26] At Sophos, which provides custom computer programming services in Vancouver, the employee lounge is open 24/7 and features music, a pool table, table hockey, foosball, video games, and a self-service lunch area with free coffee and teas, cookies, and fresh fruit. This suggests a work-hard, play-hard, creative culture that does not abide by normal clocks.[27] ISL Engineering and Land Services provides a company Smart car for staff who walk, bike, transit, or carpool to work if they need to drive on company business around Edmonton. It is a visible symbol of the company's environmental concerns.[28] Alberta-Pacific Forest Industries reception area houses a large aquarium filled with treated wastewater and stocked with native fish from the nearby river as a unique demonstration of the advanced waste water treatment facilities at its pulp mill.[29] Everyone who walks past and sees it is reminded of the company's environmental sensibility.

Symbols can also be literal in the illustrative symbols an organization chooses to represent itself. For example, Red Frog Solutions uses an appealing character to match its name on its website, a symbol that represents the innovation, creativity, and uniqueness of a Vancouver firm that provides services in branding, graphic design, marketing, and advertising.[30] Graphic symbols are representative of organizational identity and membership to employees. Nike's trademark "swoosh" is proudly tattooed above the ankles of some Nike employees. Symbols are used to build solidarity in the organizational culture.[31] Personal enactment, rites and ceremonies, stories, rituals, and symbols serve to reinforce the values that are the next level of culture.

## Values

Values are the second, deeper, level of culture. They reflect a person's inherent beliefs of what should or should not be. Values are often consciously articulated, both in conversation and in a company's mission statement or annual report. However, there may be a difference between a company's **espoused values** (what the members say they value) and its **enacted values** (values reflected in the way the members actually behave).[32] Values also may be reflected in the behaviour of individuals, which is an artifact of culture. One study investigating the gender gap in a Canadian sports organization found that coaches and athletes had come to believe that the inequity between espoused and enacted values was normal or natural. Or they completely denied it existed, even though such inequities were widely prevalent. This was because even though the organization espoused gender equity as a value, its practices did not enact gender equity.[33]

How a firm promotes and publicizes its values may also affect how workers feel about their jobs and themselves. A study of 180 managers evaluated their employers' effectiveness in communicating concern for employees' welfare. Managers in organizations that consistently communicated concern for workers' well-being and that focused on treating employees fairly reported feeling better about themselves and their role in the organization.[34] The lesson? *Treat* employees like valuable team members, and they are more likely to *feel* like valuable team members.

Some organizational cultures are characterized by values that support healthy lifestyle behaviours. When the workplace culture values worker health and psychological needs, there is enhanced potential for high performance and improved well-being.[35] Husky Injection Molding Systems of Bolton, Ontario not only encourages use of its on-site fitness centre but also provides an incentive to keep fit by providing an extra vacation day for people who meet criteria for a certain level of fitness.[36]

**espoused values**

What members of an organization say they value.

**enacted values**

Values reflected in the way individuals actually behave.

## Assumptions

**Assumptions** are the deeply held beliefs that guide behaviour and tell members of an organization how to perceive situations and people. As the deepest and most fundamental level of an organization's culture, according to Edgar Schein, they are the essence of culture. Assumptions are so strongly held that a member behaving in a fashion that would violate them is unthinkable. Another characteristic of assumptions is that they are often unconscious. Organization members may not be aware of their assumptions and may be reluctant or unable to discuss them or change them.

While unconscious assumptions often guide a firm's actions and decisions, some companies are quite explicit in their assumptions about employees. Urban Systems includes several of these assumptions on its website. Based in Kamloops, Urban Systems has seven offices across Alberta and British Columbia providing services in civil engineering, community planning, and landscape architecture. Its unique culture has been deliberately nurtured to attract some of the best in the industry and has led it to being ranked one of the "Best Workplaces in Canada" for several years. The firm assumes that people want fulfilling work, opportunity, and meaningful rewards; that personal growth and development are good both for the company and the individual; that success will come from a work atmosphere where people want to work hard and love to have fun; and that work–life balance is a critical underpinning for all.[37]

**assumptions**

Deeply held beliefs that guide behaviour and tell members of an organization how to perceive and think about things.

# Functions of Organizational Culture

In an organization, culture serves four basic functions. First, culture provides a sense of identity to members and increases their commitment to the organization.[38] When employees internalize the values of the company, they find their work intrinsically rewarding and identify with their fellow workers. Motivation is enhanced, and employees are more committed.[39]

Second, culture provides a way for employees to interpret the meaning of organizational events.[40] Leaders can use organizational symbols such as corporate logos to help employees understand the changing nature of their organizational identity. Sometimes symbols can remain the same to ensure that some things stay constant despite changing conditions; other times, symbols may have to change to reflect the new culture in the organization.

Third, culture reinforces the values in the organization. Finally, culture serves as a control mechanism for shaping behaviour. Norms that guide behaviour are part of culture. If the norm the company wants to promote is teamwork, then its culture must reinforce that norm. The company's culture must be characterized by open communication, cooperation between teams, and integration of teams.[41] Culture can also be used as a powerful tool to discourage dysfunctional and deviant behaviours in organizations. Norms can send clear messages that certain behaviours are unacceptable.[42]

# The Relationship of Culture to Corporate Performance

The effects of organizational culture are hotly debated by organizational behaviourists and researchers. It seems that, although managers attest strongly to the positive effects of culture in organizations, it is difficult to quantify these effects. John Kotter and James Heskett have reviewed three theories about the relationship between organizational culture and performance and the evidence that either supports or refutes these theories.[43] The three are the strong culture perspective, the fit perspective, and the adaptation perspective.

## Hot Trend: Rebranding

The most prominent symbol of a company is its logo. Some logos never change (McDonalds golden arches have been the logo since its inception in 1955), but some logos get modified to reflect changes in the company's direction. United Parcel Service has used four logos in its 97-year history. The company most recently altered its logo with the bow-tied package to focus on its growth into areas other than parcel delivery, like supply chain management.

SOURCES: http://www.mcdonalds.com/corp/about/mcd_history_pg1.html; http://www.pressroom.ups.com/mediakits/factsheet/0,2305,1060,000.html

*Express Box*
*Boîte UPS Express*

*26*

## The Strong Culture Perspective

The strong culture perspective states that organizations with "strong" cultures perform better than other organizations.[44] A **strong culture** is an organizational culture with a consensus on the values that drive the company and with an intensity that is recognizable even to outsiders. Thus, a strong culture is deeply held and widely shared. It also is highly resistant to change.

Strong cultures are thought to facilitate performance for three reasons. First, these cultures are characterized by goal alignment; that is, all employees share common goals. Second, strong cultures create a high level of motivation because of the values shared by the members. Third, strong cultures provide control without the oppressive effects of a bureaucracy.

There is evidence to support this model. Kotter and Heskett found that, examining organizations in a variety of industries over a 10-year period, those perceived to have strong cultures had greater average levels of return on investment, net income growth, and change in share price.[45] A reanalysis of their data showed that the link between culture and performance was particularly strong in highly competitive markets and could be attributed to the increased efficiency of routine execution.[46] Another study found that the performance of insurance companies increased to the extent there was consensus surrounding cultural values, an indication of strength.[47]

There are also two perplexing questions about the strong culture perspectives. First, what can be said about evidence showing that strong economic performance can create strong cultures, rather than the reverse? Second, what if the strong culture leads the firm down the wrong path? Sears, for example, is an organization with a strong culture, but in the 1980s, it focused inward, ignoring competition and consumer preferences and damaging its performance. Changing Sears' strong but stodgy culture has been a tough task, with financial performance only recently showing an upward trend.[48]

## The Fit Perspective

The "fit" perspective argues that a culture is good only if it fits the industry or the firm's strategy. For example, a culture that values a traditional hierarchical structure and stability would not work well in the computer manufacturing industry, which demands fast response and a lean, flat organization. Three particular industry characteristics may affect culture: the competitive environment, customer requirements, and societal expectations.[49]

A study of 12 large U.S. firms indicated that cultures consistent with industry conditions help managers make better decisions. It also indicated that cultures need not change as long as the industry doesn't change. If the industry does change, however, many cultures change too slowly to avoid negative effects on firms' performance.[50]

The fit perspective is useful in explaining short-term performance but not long-term performance. It also indicates that it is difficult to change culture quickly, especially if the culture is widely shared and deeply held. But it doesn't explain how firms can adapt to environmental change.

## The Adaptation Perspective

The adaptation perspective states that only cultures that help organizations adapt to environmental change are associated with

3M is a company with an adaptive culture—it encourages new product ideas from all levels within the company. (BTW, 3M invented the Post-It.)

**strong culture**

An organizational culture with a consensus on the values that drive the company and with an intensity that is recognizable even to outsiders.

| TABLE 16.1 | Adaptive versus Nonadaptive Organizational Cultures | |
|---|---|---|
| | **ADAPTIVE ORGANIZATIONAL CULTURES** | **NONADAPTIVE ORGANIZATIONAL CULTURES** |
| **Core values** | Most managers care deeply about customers, stockholders, and employees. They also strongly value people and processes that can create useful change (e.g., leadership up and down the management hierarchy). | Most managers care mainly about themselves, their immediate work group, or some product (or technology) associated with that work group. They value the orderly and risk-reducing management process much more highly than leadership initiatives. |
| **Common behaviour** | Managers pay close attention to all their constituencies, especially customers, and initiate change when needed to serve their legitimate interests, even if that entails taking some risks. | Managers tend to behave somewhat insularly, politically, and bureaucratically. As a result, they do not change their strategies quickly to adjust to or take advantage of changes in their business environments. |

SOURCE: Reprinted with the permission of The Free Press, a Division of Simon & Schuster, Adult Publishing Group, from *Corporate Culture and Performance* by John P. Kotter and James L. Heskett. Copyright © 1992 by Kotter Associates, Inc. and James L. Heskett. All rights reserved.

excellent performance. An **adaptive culture** is a culture that encourages confidence and risk taking among employees,[51] has leadership that produces change,[52] and focuses on the changing needs of customers.[53]

To test the adaptation perspective, Kotter and Heskett interviewed industry analysts about the cultures of 22 firms. The contrast between adaptive cultures and nonadaptive cultures was striking. The results of the study are summarized in Table 16.1.

Adaptive cultures facilitate change to meet the needs of three groups of constituents: stockholders, customers, and employees. Nonadaptive cultures are characterized by cautious management that tries to protect its own interests. Adaptive firms showed significantly better long-term economic performance in Kotter and Heskett's study. Given that high-performing cultures are adaptive ones, it is important to know how managers can develop adaptive cultures.

Analysis of data from 339 Canadian corporate bankruptcies supports the adaptation perspective. Whereas young firms tended to fail due to a lack of managerial knowledge or financial management abilities, failure among older firms seems to be due to an inability to adapt to environmental change.[54]

## Impact of Culture on Employees

Perception of personal fit with an organization's culture influences whether a person is attracted to the organization as a potential employer. Data from a wide range of students looking for positions showed small but consistent links between culture and personality.[55] For example, highly extraverted students were attracted to aggressive and team-oriented culture and less so to supportive cultures. Those high on neuroticism were less attracted to innovative and decisive cultures. Those high on openness to experience were attracted to innovative cultures. A study with British adults supported the contention that people are attracted to organizations with features similar to their own personality.[56] Perception of employee fit with the culture also seems to influence the hiring organization's decision to offer employment.[57] There seems to be validity to this since, once hired, the fit perception continues to influence employees. A longitudinal study demonstrated that fit of individual values with organizational culture predicts job satisfaction and organizational commitment one year later and predicts the likelihood of turnover two years later.[58] A meta-analysis of studies showed that person–culture fit has a strong correlation with job satisfaction and organizational commitment, and a moderate relationship to coworker satisfaction, trust in managers, indicators of strain, and intention to quit.[59] The perception of not "fitting in" with a company's values seems to generate a level of stress and dissatisfaction.

Culture influences the interaction and relative influence of the people within it. For example, a study looking at co-worker ratings of influence found that extraverted employees exert a lot of influence in a team-oriented consulting firm. Extraversion also predicted influence somewhat in a detail-oriented engineering department but not nearly as strongly. On the other hand, conscientiousness was related to influence in the engineering department but not at all in the consulting firm.[60] Culture affects the way in which people address each other, how much status influences communication, whether information is shared and with whom, how much people "joke around," and whether employees are likely to see each other socially and consider each other friends or as simply colleagues. This leads us to the consideration of subcultures.

**adaptive culture**

An organizational culture that encourages confidence and risk taking among employees, has leadership that produces change, and focuses on the changing needs of customers.

A **subculture** is the culture created within a small subset of employees within the organization. It is tied to how the organization's structure groups people, so different functions tend to develop their own subcultures (consider how the seasonal celebrations may differ between sales and finance) and different teams tend to do so as well. This links to Chapter 9's discussion of group norms. Consider the parallel with different educational classes you have been part of. One may have had a serious, competitive culture that encouraged student effort whereas another emphasized doing as little as possible, leading students to hide academic interests or accomplishments for fear of ridicule. These subcultures can have a powerful influence. For example, a study of nurses and hospital ward staff in three large American health organizations found that subcultures were more important than overall organizational culture in motivating transfer of learning.[61] Supportive and innovative subcultures were positively related to the transfer of learning, whereas bureaucratic subcultures negatively affected the motivation to transfer learning. In a study that examined the job satisfaction of employees in a consulting firm who worked in competency groups, fit with subculture values was just as important to employee job satisfaction as was fit with the firm's overall culture.[62] Management itself may be considered a subculture with its own set of values in contrast to nonmanagers. Two studies with Dutch employees suggest that women may be deterred from entering management more than men because of a perception that management's "masculine" culture of competitiveness, task orientation, and focusing on status and hierarchy is less of a fit with their own values.[63] Subcultures can fit well within an organization's culture or can take on values that oppose the larger group, making it a counterculture. Subcultures are often functional in adapting the subset to the demands of their particular jobs (e.g., a risk-averse subculture for the accountants) and also in challenging the values of the overall organization. One of the reasons that strong cultures have difficulty adapting as needed is because they may be less likely to have nonconformist subcultures that recognize the need for change and challenge the status quo or, even if they are offered insights from counterculture types, those insights may be ignored because they oppose the firm's culture.[64]

---

### LEARNING OUTCOME 4

# The Leader's Role in Shaping and Reinforcing Culture

According to Edgar Schein, leaders play crucial roles in shaping and reinforcing culture.[65] The five most important elements in managing culture are (1) what leaders pay attention to; (2) how leaders react to crises; (3) how leaders behave; (4) how leaders allocate rewards; and (5) how leaders hire and fire individuals.

## What Leaders Pay Attention To

Leaders in an organization communicate their priorities, values, and beliefs through the themes that consistently emerge from their focus. These themes are reflected in what they notice, comment on, measure, and control. If leaders are consistent in their focus, employees receive clear signals about what is important in the organization. If, however, leaders are inconsistent, employees spend a lot of time trying to decipher and find meaning in the inconsistent signals.

## How Leaders React to Crises

The way leaders deal with crises communicates a powerful message about culture. Emotions are heightened during a crisis, and learning is intense.

Difficult economic times present crises for many companies and illustrate their different values. Some organizations avoid at all costs laying off workers. Others may claim that employees are important but quickly institute major layoffs at the first signal of an economic downturn. Employees may perceive that the company shows its true colours in a crisis and thus may pay careful attention to the reactions of their leaders.

## How Leaders Behave

Through role modelling, teaching, and coaching, leaders reinforce the values that support the organizational culture. Employees often emulate leaders' behaviour and look to the leaders for cues to appropriate behaviour. Many companies encourage employees to be more entrepreneurial, using more initiative and innovation. A study showed that if managers want employees to be more entrepreneurial, they must demonstrate such behaviors themselves.[66] This is the case with any cultural value. Employees observe the behaviour of leaders to find out what the organization values.

## How Leaders Allocate Rewards

To ensure that values are accepted, leaders should reward behaviour that is consistent with the values. Some companies, for example, may claim that they use a pay-for-performance system that distributes rewards on

**subculture**
A subculture is the culture created within a subset of employees within the organization.

the basis of performance. When the time comes for raises, however, the increases are awarded according to length of service with the company. Imagine the feelings of a high-performing newcomer who receives only a tiny raise after hearing company leaders espouse the value of rewarding individual performance.

Some companies may value teamwork. They form cross-functional teams and empower these teams to make important decisions. However, when performance is appraised, the criteria for rating employees focus on individual performance. This sends a confusing signal to employees about the company's culture: Is individual performance valued, or is teamwork the key?

## How Leaders Hire and Fire Individuals

A powerful way that leaders reinforce culture is through the selection of newcomers to the organization. With the advent of electronic recruitment practices, applicant perceptions of organizational culture are shaped by what the organization advertises on its recruitment website. Typical perception-shaping mechanisms are organizational values, policies, awards, and goals.[67] Leaders often unconsciously look for individuals who are similar to current organizational members in terms of values and assumptions. Some companies hire individuals on the recommendation of a current employee; this tends to perpetuate the culture because the new employees typically hold similar values. Janice Webster, the vice president of talent management and retention, brought a new approach to WestJet's recruiting efforts that better matched its culture. WestJet emphasizes personality in their flight-staff and other employees who deal with clients, yet their impersonal panel interviews did not allow those personalities to show through. So Webster changed the one-on-three panel interviews to three-hour

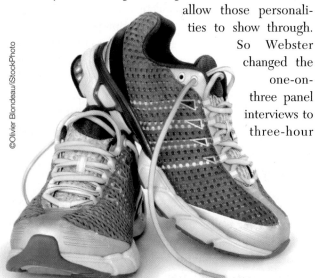

**If you want to interview at WestJet, wear comfortable shoes: you'll be participating in some games.**

sessions with groups of 20 to 30 applicants. Potential hires engage in games, team tasks, individual tasks, and presentations and WestJet looks for the personalities revealed in the interactions. This approach is used for flight attendants, call centre and counter employees, and luggage handlers.[68]

The way a company fires an employee and the rationale behind the firing also communicate the culture. Some companies deal with poor performers by trying to find a place within the organization where they can perform better and make a contribution. Other companies seem to operate under the philosophy that those who cannot perform are out quickly.

Don Gordon is vice president of operations of Cooper Construction in Oakville, Ontario, and knows that the challenges of the construction industry mean layoffs are inevitable at times. Disliking the necessity of terminating good employees due to lack of work, he takes the approach of making it as easy as possible for them to find other work and as attractive as possible for them to consider returning to the company once business improves. For example, he will go into the termination discussion having looked for possible openings for the employee elsewhere and even having passed on contacts and job postings. There is no surprise and the employee feels supported. Don has been rewarded over the years by a loyal group that includes several who have been terminated and chosen to return.

The reasons for terminations may not be directly communicated by the employer to other employees, but curiosity leads to speculation. An employee who displays unethical behaviour and is caught may simply be reprimanded even though such behaviour is clearly against the organization's values. Other employees may view this as a failure to reinforce the values within the organization.

In summary, leaders play a critical role in shaping and reinforcing organizational culture. Managers need to create a positive culture through what they pay attention to, how they react to crises, how they behave, the way they allocate rewards, and how they hire and fire employees. Transformational leaders create a more adaptive culture, which in turn increases business unit performance.[69]

LEARNING OUTCOME 5

# Organizational Socialization

We have seen that leaders play key roles in shaping an organization's culture. Another process that perpetuates culture is the way it is passed on from generation to generation of employees. Newcomers learn the culture through **organizational socialization**— the process by which newcomers are transformed from outsiders to participating, effective members of the organization.[70] As we saw earlier, cultural socialization begins with the careful selection of newcomers who are likely to reinforce the organizational culture.[71] Once selected, newcomers pass through the socialization process.

# The Stages of the Socialization Process

The organizational socialization process is generally described as having three stages: anticipatory socialization, encounter, and change and acquisition. Figure 16.2 presents a model of the process and the key concerns at each stage of it.[72] It also describes the outcomes of the process, which will be discussed in the next section of the chapter.

**Anticipatory Socialization** *Anticipatory socialization*, the first stage, encompasses all of the learning that takes place prior to the newcomer's first day on the job. It includes the newcomer's expectations. The two key concerns at this stage are realism and congruence.

*Realism* is the degree to which a newcomer holds realistic expectations about the job and organization. One thing newcomers should receive information about during entry into the organization is the culture. Information about values at this stage can help newcomers begin to construct a scheme for interpreting their organizational experiences. A deeper understanding of the organization's culture will be possible through time and experience in the organization.

There are two types of *congruence* between an individual and an organization: congruence between the individual's abilities and the demands of the job, and the fit between the individual's values and the organization's values. Organizations disseminate information about their values through their Web pages, annual reports, and recruitment brochures.[73] Value congruence is particularly important for organizational culture. It is also important in terms of newcomer adjustment. Newcomers whose values match the company's values are more satisfied with their new jobs, adjust more quickly, and say they intend to remain with the firm longer.[74]

**Encounter** The second stage of socialization, *encounter*, is when newcomers learn the tasks associated with the job, clarify their roles, and establish new relationships at work. This stage commences on the first day at work and is thought to encompass the first six

## FIGURE 16.2

### THE ORGANIZATIONAL SOCIALIZATION PROCESS: STAGES AND OUTCOMES

SOURCE: Reprinted from *Organizational Dynamics*, Autumn 1989, "An Ethical Weather Report: Assessing the Organization's Ethical Climate" by John B. Cullen et al. Copyright © 1989, with permission from Elsevier Science.

to nine months on the new job. Newcomers face task demands, role demands, and interpersonal demands during this period.

Task demands involve the actual work performed. Learning to perform tasks is related to the organization's culture. In some organizations, where creativity is valued, newcomers are given considerable latitude to experiment with new ways to do their job. In others, newcomers are expected to learn the established procedures for their tasks. Early experiences with trying to master task demands can affect employees' entire careers. Auditors, for example, are often forced to choose between being thorough and being fast in completing their work. By pressuring auditors in this way, firms often set themselves up for problems later, when these pressures may lead auditors to make less-than-ethical decisions.

*Role demands* involve the expectations placed on

**organizational socialization**
The process by which newcomers are transformed from outsiders to participating, effective members of the organization.

**anticipatory socialization**
The first socialization stage, which encompasses all of the learning that takes place prior to the newcomer's first day on the job.

**encounter**
The second socialization stage in which the newcomer learns the tasks associated with the job, clarifies roles, and establishes new relationships at work.

**At the end of the socialization process, newcomers are considered insiders.**

Philip Date/Shutterstock

newcomers. Newcomers may not know exactly what is expected of them (role ambiguity) or may receive conflicting expectations from other individuals (role conflict). The way newcomers approach these demands depends in part on the culture of the organization. Are newcomers expected to operate with considerable uncertainty, or is the manager expected to clarify the newcomers' roles? Some cultures even put newcomers through considerable stress in the socialization process, including humility-inducing experiences, so newcomers will be more open to accepting the firm's values and norms. Long hours, tiring travel schedules, and an overload of work are part of some socialization practices.

*Interpersonal demands* arise from relationships at work. Politics, leadership style, and group pressure are interpersonal demands. All of them reflect the values and assumptions that operate within the organization. Most organizations have basic assumptions about the nature of human relationships. The Korean chaebol LG Group strongly values harmony in relationships and in society, and its decision-making policy emphasizes unanimity.

In the encounter stage, the expectations formed in anticipatory socialization may clash with the realities of the job. It is a time of facing the task, role, and interpersonal demands of the new job.

**Change and Acquisition** In the third and final stage of socialization, **change and acquisition**, newcomers begin to master the demands of the job. They become proficient at managing their tasks, clarifying and negotiating their roles, and engaging in relationships at work. The time when the socialization process is completed varies widely, depending on the

**change and acquisition**
The third socialization stage, in which the newcomer begins to master the demands of the job.

individual, the job, and the organization. The end of the process is signalled by newcomers being considered by themselves and others as organizational insiders.

## Outcomes of Socialization

Newcomers who are successfully socialized should exhibit good performance, high job satisfaction, and the intention to stay with the organization. In addition, they should exhibit low levels of distress symptoms.[75] High levels of organizational commitment are also marks of successful socialization.[76] This commitment is facilitated throughout the socialization process by the communication of values that newcomers can buy into. Successful socialization is also signalled by mutual influence; that is, the newcomers have made adjustments in the job and organization to accommodate their knowledge and personalities. Newcomers are expected to leave their mark on the organization and not be completely conforming.

When socialization is effective, newcomers understand and adopt the organization's values and norms. This ensures that the company's culture, including its central values, survives. It also provides employees a context for interpreting and responding to things that happen at work, and it ensures a shared framework of understanding among employees.[77]

Newcomers adopt the company's norms and values more quickly when they receive positive support from organizational insiders. Sometimes this is accomplished through informal social gatherings.[78]

LEARNING OUTCOME **6**

# Assessing Organizational Culture

Although some organizational scientists argue for assessing organizational culture with quantitative methods, others say that organizational culture must be assessed with qualitative methods.[79] Quantitative methods, such as questionnaires, are valuable because of their precision, comparability, and objectivity. Qualitative methods, such as interviews and observations, are valuable because of their detail, descriptiveness, and uniqueness.

Two widely used quantitative assessment instruments are the Organizational Culture Inventory (OCI) and the Kilmann-Saxton Culture-Gap Survey. Both assess the behavioural norms of organizational cultures, as opposed to the artifacts, values, or assumptions of the organization.

## Organizational Culture Inventory

The OCI focuses on behaviours that help employees fit into the organization and meet the expectations of coworkers. Using Maslow's motivational need hierarchy as its basis, it measures 12 cultural styles. The two underlying dimensions of the OCI are task/people and security/satisfaction. There are four satisfaction cultural styles and eight security cultural styles.

A self-report instrument, the OCI contains 120 questions. It provides an individual assessment of culture and may be aggregated to the work group and to the organizational level.[80] It has been used in firms throughout North America, Western Europe, New Zealand, and Thailand, as well as in U.S. military units, and nonprofit organizations.

## Kilmann-Saxton Culture-Gap Survey

The Kilmann-Saxton Culture-Gap Survey focuses on what actually happens and on the expectations of others in the organization.[81] Its two underlying dimensions are technical/human and time (the short term versus the long term). With these two dimensions, the actual operating norms and the ideal norms in four areas are assessed. The areas are task support (short-term technical norms), task innovation (long-term technical norms), social relationships (short-term human orientation norms), and personal freedom (long-term human orientation norms). Significant gaps in any of the four areas are used as a point of departure for cultural change to improve performance, job satisfaction, and morale.

A self-report instrument, the Gap Survey provides an individual assessment of culture and may be aggregated to the work group.

## Triangulation

A study of a rehabilitation centre in a 400-bed hospital incorporated triangulation (the use of multiple methods to measure organizational culture) to improve inclusiveness and accuracy in measuring the organizational culture.[82] Triangulation has been used by anthropologists, sociologists, and other behavioural scientists to study organizational culture. Its name comes from the navigational technique of using multiple reference points to locate an object. In the rehabilitation centre study, the three methods used to triangulate on the culture were (1) obtrusive observations by eight trained observers, which provided an outsider perspective; (2) self-administered questionnaires, which provided quantitative insider information; and (3) personal interviews with the centre's staff, which provided qualitative contextual information.

The study showed that each of the three methods made unique contributions toward the discovery of the rehabilitation centre's culture. The complete picture could not have been drawn with just a single technique. Triangulation can lead to a better understanding of the phenomenon of culture and is the best approach to assessing organizational culture.

# Changing Organizational Culture

With rapid environmental changes such as globalization, workforce diversity, and technological innovation, the fundamental assumptions and basic values that drive the organization may need to be altered.

Changing an organization's culture is feasible but difficult.[83] One reason for the difficulty is that assumptions—the deepest level of culture—are often unconscious. As such, they are often nonconfrontable and nondebatable. Another reason for the difficulty is that culture is deeply ingrained and behavioural norms and rewards are well learned.[84] In a sense, employees must unlearn the old norms before they can learn new ones. Managers who want to change the culture should look first to the ways culture is maintained. Research among American hospitals found that change was welcomed in private hospitals with a collaborative culture whereas change was met with opposition in public hospitals with an autocratic culture.[85]

A model for cultural change that summarizes the interventions managers can use is presented in Figure 16.3. In this model, the numbers represent the actions managers can take. There are two basic approaches to changing the existing culture: (1) helping current members buy into a new set of values (actions 1, 2, and 3); or (2) adding newcomers and socializing them into the organization and removing current members as appropriate (actions 4 and 5).[86]

The first action is to change behaviour in the organization. Even if behaviour does change, however, this change is not sufficient for cultural change to occur. Behaviour is an artifact (level 1) of culture. Individuals may change their behaviour but

**triangulation**
The use of multiple methods to measure organizational culture.

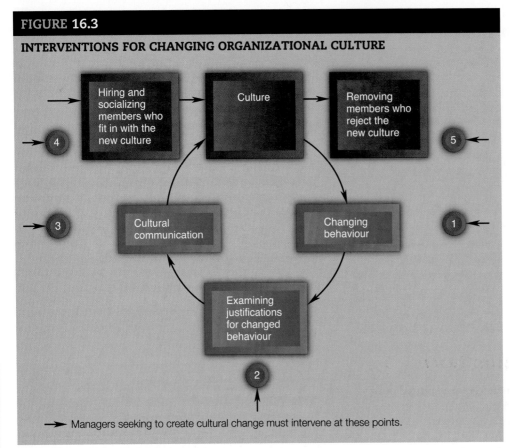

## FIGURE 16.3

### INTERVENTIONS FOR CHANGING ORGANIZATIONAL CULTURE

Hiring and socializing members who fit in with the new culture

Culture

Removing members who reject the new culture

4

5

Cultural communication

Changing behaviour

3

1

Examining justifications for changed behaviour

2

→ Managers seeking to create cultural change must intervene at these points.

SOURCE: From Vijay Sathe, "How to Decipher and Change Corporate Culture," Chap. 13 in *Gaining Control of the Corporate Culture* (R. H. Kilmann et al., eds.), Fig. 1, p. 245. Copyright © 1985 Jossey-Bass Inc. Reprinted with permission of John Wiley & Sons, Inc.

not the values that drive it. They may rationalize, "I'm only doing this because my manager wants me to."

Therefore, managers must use action 2, which is to examine the justifications for the changed behaviour. Are employees buying into the new set of values, or are they just complying?

The third action, cultural communication, is extremely important. All of the artifacts (personal enactment, stories, rites and ceremonies, rituals, and symbols) must send a consistent message about the new values and beliefs. It is crucial that the communication be credible; that is, managers must live the new values and not just talk about them. Leaders should pay attention to the informal social networks more so than structural positions in leading organizational change. These informal network communication channels combined with employees' values, and beliefs that managers are highly committed to the change effort, can go a long way in making the change a success.[87]

The two remaining actions (4 and 5) involve shaping the workforce to fit the intended culture. First, the organization can revise its selection strategies to more accurately reflect the new culture. Second, the organization can identify individuals who resist the cultural change or who are no longer comfortable with the values in the

organization. Reshaping the workforce should not involve a ruthless pursuit of nonconforming employees; it should be a gradual and subtle change that takes considerable time. Changing personnel in the organization is a lengthy process; it cannot be done effectively in a short period of time without considerable problems.

Evaluating the success of cultural change may be best done by looking at behaviour. Cultural change can be assumed to be successful if the behaviour is intrinsically motivated—on "automatic pilot." If the new behaviour were to persist even if rewards were not present, and if the employees have internalized the new value system, then the behaviour is probably intrinsically motivated. If employees automatically respond to a crisis in ways consistent with the corporate culture, then the cultural change effort can be deemed successful.

Given the current business environment, managers may want to focus on three particular cultural modifications: (1) support for a global view of business, (2) reinforcement of ethical behaviour, and (3) empowerment of employees to excel in product and service quality.

### LEARNING OUTCOME 8

# Challenges to Developing a Positive, Cohesive Culture

Developing an organizational culture is challenging in its own right, but certain factors pose additional challenges to managers in their pursuit of positive, cohesive cultures: mergers and acquisition, globalization, ethics, and empowerment and quality.

## [ Farmers Once Suspicious of Big Business Create Their Own ]

Mayo Schmidt, the CEO of Viterra, has piloted a cultural transformation of the organization formerly known as the Saskatchewan Wheat Pool. The members of the farmers' co-operative that was on the brink of financial disaster agreed to relinquish their voting control, allowing Schmidt to shape it into a global agribusiness corporation. He divested businesses and went on to accomplish a hostile takeover of much-larger rival, Agricore United.

Dave Reede/First Light/Getty Images

SOURCE: L. Cameron, J. Castaldo and A. Wahl, "All-star Execs," *Canadian Business,* November 23, 2009, 82(20), http://www. canadianbusiness.com/managing/strategy/article.jsp?content=20091123_10024_10024.

## Merger or Acquisition

One particular situation that may require cultural change is a merger or acquisition. The blending of two distinct organizational cultures may prove difficult.

Despite good-faith efforts, combining cultures is difficult. AIM Trimark's tumble from second-largest mutual fund company in Canada is attributed to a culture clash. Trimark was sold in 2000 to global fund manager Amvescap PLC and became AIM Trimark. As Sean Silcoff says in the *National Post,* "The investing style didn't change but everything else did."[88] Amvescap focused on sales and marketing; the head of its Canadian unit started his career in consumer packaging and was not a money manager.[89] Trimark's people were careful career investors. Whereas Trimark had encouraged salespeople and fund managers to share insights in the tight-knit firm, the new structure stated that the salespeople were not to bother the portfolio managers. By 2008, most of the Trimark star fund managers and senior executives had defected. As a consequence, a lot of skill critical to AIM Trimark's business went with them.[90]

Organizational culture also affects international joint venture performance. A study of 127 joint ventures between Indian corporations and their partners in 21 other countries showed that both organizational culture and national culture had significant impact on the success of the ventures. Organizational culture differences tended to have a negative impact because they reflected ongoing differences in values and norms that resulted in conflicting expectations, misunderstandings, and interaction problems. One critical area of difference was in communication climate and whether the culture treated communication as part of an open or closed system.

Information sharing is critical to venture success. Interestingly, although national culture differences could be a source of friction, they can also be a source of admiration and a positive challenge leading to higher levels of communication and more sustained collaboration.[91]

Alterations in culture may also be required when an organization employs people from different countries. Research indicates that some organizational cultures actually enhance differences in national cultures.[92] One study compared foreign employees working in a multinational organization with employees working in different organizations within their own countries. The assumption was that the employees from various countries working for the same multinational organization would be more similar than employees working in diverse organizations in their native countries. The results were surprising, in that there were significantly greater differences among the employees of the multinational than among managers working for different companies within their native countries. In the multinational, Swedes became more Swedish, Americans became more American, and so forth. It appears that employees enhance their national culture traditions even when working within a single organizational culture.[93] This is more likely to occur when diversity is moderate. When diversity is very high, employees are more likely to develop a shared identity in the organization's culture instead of relying on their own national culture.[94]

## Developing a Global Organizational Culture

The values that drive the organizational culture should support a global view of the company and its efforts. Management should embody the shared values and reward employees who support the global view. Finally, the values should be consistent over time. Consistent values give an organization a unifying theme that competitors may be unable to emulate.[95] Because global corporations suffer from the conflicting pressures of centralization and decentralization, an overarching corporate culture that integrates the decentralized subsidiaries in locations around the world can be an asset in the increasingly competitive global marketplace.

> What is the ethical climate of an organization you belong to? Do What about You? on the Chapter 16 Review Card to find out.

## Developing an Ethical Organizational Culture (3)

The organizational culture can have profound effects on the ethical behaviour of organization members.[96] When a company's culture promotes ethical norms, individuals behave accordingly. Managers can encourage ethical behaviour by being good role models for employees. They can institute the philosophy that ethical behaviour makes good business sense and puts the company in congruence with the larger values of society.[97] Managers can also communicate that rationalizations for unethical behaviour are not tolerated.

Trust is another key to effectively managing ethical behaviour, especially in cultures that encourage whistle-blowing (as we saw in Chapter 2). Employees must trust that whistle-blowers will be protected, that procedures used to investigate ethical problems will be fair, and that management will take action to solve problems that are uncovered.

At John Deere & Company, a simple idea guides the firm's ethics and decision making: "No smoke, no mirrors, no tricks: just right down the middle of the field," as Robert Lane, chairman and CEO, puts it. John Deere's decision to donate a multimillion-dollar parcel of land to a university, rather than selling it to a developer, demonstrates its values and is one of the reasons the firm made the top five in *Corporate Responsibility* magazine's list of the "100 Best Corporate Citizens for 2008."[98]

Many companies have implemented a code of ethics to help their employees discern right from wrong, but the impact of these codes is not always as positive as might be expected. The implementation of formal ethics guidelines might be expected to improve ethical behaviour, yet some studies have shown the exact opposite—institution of formal ethics codes can actually lead to less ethical behaviour among employees. There appear to be two main reasons for this: in some cases employees see the code of ethics as simply a management showpiece, leading to cynicism and resentment. In other cases, a heavy reliance on a strict set of rules may reduce the perceived need for employees to think about and be involved in ethical decision making, leading to inferior choices in the long run.[99]

## Developing a Culture of Empowerment and Quality (4)

Throughout this book, we have seen that successful organizations promote a culture that empowers employees and excels in product and service quality. Empowerment serves to unleash employees' creativity and productivity.

## [ The Dog Ate My Homework and Other Excuses for Unethical Conduct ]

### Excuses

The reasons (excuses) most often cited for unethical corporate conduct are:

> It's not really unethical.
> It's in the organization's best interest.
> No one will find out.
> The organization will support it because it offers a good outcome for the organization.

### How to Squash These Excuses

An ethical corporate culture can eliminate the viability of these excuses in a number of ways:

> The company clearly communicates the boundaries of ethical conduct.
> The firm selects employees who support the ethical culture.
> Management rewards organization members who exhibit ethical behaviour.
> Management conspicuously punishes members who engage in unethical behaviour.

SOURCE: S. W. Gellerman, "Why Good Managers Make Bad Ethical Choices," *Harvard Business Review* 64 (1986): 85–90.

Micimakin/Shutterstock

# By The Numbers

**3** levels of organizational culture

**120** questions on the OCI

**6** types of rites in organizations

**17** the number of Lee Valley tools in Bell's plastic surgery clinic

**~15** minutes for a Ritz-Carlton employee "lineup"

**4** logos used by UPS since the company's founding

---

It requires eliminating traditional hierarchical notions of power. Cultures that emphasize empowerment and quality are preferred by Canadian employees. Companies that value empowerment and continuous improvement have cultures that promote high product and service quality.[100] For example, the high quality of a Lee Valley tool is not merely an artifact of better shop practices. It results from a culture that nurtures empowerment and quality. The company has been creating and distributing unique, high-quality woodworking and gardening tools since its 1978 start in Ottawa. Integrity and excellence are principles upon which its reputation is based. Full guarantees mean any product may be returned within three months at no cost to the customer. No one is on commission and there are no minimum sales targets built into anyone's job descriptions because that would conflict with good advice to customers. Product descriptions truly describe the product, e.g., "... handle with hardwood scales complete with spots of wood filler. A tough, ugly tool that is perfect for the person whose usual solution is to use a larger hammer."[101] Lee Valley shows that every employee is valued by distributing 25 percent of pre-tax profits equally among all employees, whether a senior manager or warehouse staff. Employees are involved in decision making in their own areas of expertise and at the project level. No one punches a clock, including the people working in assembly. Decisions focus on doing the right thing and following the golden rule—treating others (whether customers or employees) as they would want to be treated.[102] Always responsive to customer questions and feedback, founder Leonard Lee was intrigued to discover that plastic surgeon Michael Bell was using 17 Lee Valley tools for surgery, finding them superior to commercially available surgical tools. Invited by Bell to visit the clinic, Lee brought along a group of tool designers. This led ultimately to the creation of a new organization, Canica Design, that develops innovative medical devices.[103]

---

# Visit **icanorgb.com** to find the resources you need today!

*Located at the back of the textbook are rip-out Chapter Review Cards. Make sure you also go online to check out other tools that ORGB offers to help you successfully pass your course.*

- Interactive Quizzing
- Key Term Flashcards
- PowerPoint Slides
- Audio Chapter Summaries

- Cases and Exercises
- Interactive Games
- Self-Assessments
- "On the Job" and "Bizflix" Videos

# Managing Change

> **❝ In the past, organizations could succeed by claiming excellence in one area. This is not the case today. ❞**

LEARNING OUTCOME 1

# Forces for Change in Organizations

Change has become the norm in most organizations. Many Canadian companies have experienced plant closings, business failures, mergers and acquisitions, or downsizing. *Adaptiveness, flexibility,* and *responsiveness* are characteristics of the organizations that will succeed in meeting the competitive challenges that businesses face.[1] In the past, organizations could succeed by claiming excellence in one area—quality, reliability, or cost, for example—but this is not the case today. The current environment demands excellence in all areas and vigilant leaders. A recent survey of CEOs who were facing crises found that 50 percent of them said they believed the problems arrived "suddenly" and that they had not prepared adequately for them. More than 10 percent said they were, in fact, the last to know about the problems.[2]

Change has become the norm, and yet successful change can be elusive. Some estimate that 50 to 75 percent of mergers fail their financial objectives and the success rate of large-scale change interventions is about 50 percent.[3]

As we saw in Chapter 1, change is what's on managers' minds. The pursuit of organizational effectiveness through downsizing, restructuring, reengineering, productivity management, cycle-time reduction, and other efforts is paramount. Organizations are in a state of tremendous turmoil and transition, and all members are affected. Continued downsizings may have left firms leaner but not necessarily richer. Though downsizing can increase shareholder value by better aligning costs with revenues, firms may suffer from public criticism for their actions. Laying off employees may be accompanied by increases in CEO pay and stock options, linking the misery of employees with the financial success of owners and management.[4]

## LEARNING OUTCOMES

After reading this chapter, you should be able to do the following:

1 Identify the major external and internal forces for change in organizations.

2 Describe how different types of change vary in scope.

3 Discuss methods organizations can use to manage

4 Explain Lewin's organizational change model.

5 Explain how companies determine the need to conduct an organizational development intervention.

6 Discuss the major group-focused techniques for organization development intervention.

7 Discuss the major individual-focused techniques for organization development intervention.

Organizations must also deal with ethical, environmental, and other social issues. Competition is fierce, and companies can no longer afford to rest on their laurels. General Electric holds off-site WorkOut sessions with groups of managers and employees whose goal is to make GE a faster, less complex organization that can respond effectively to change. In the WorkOut sessions, employees recommend specific changes, explain why they are needed, and propose ways the changes can be implemented. Top management must make an immediate response: an approval, a disapproval (with an explanation), or a request for more information. The GE WorkOut sessions eliminate the barriers that keep employees from contributing to change.

There are two basic forms of change in organizations. **Planned change** results from a deliberate decision to alter the organization. Companies that wish to move from a traditional hierarchical structure to one that facilitates self-managed teams must use a proactive, carefully orchestrated approach. **Unplanned change** is imposed on the organization and is often unforeseen. Changes in government regulations and changes in the economy, for example, are often unplanned. Responsiveness to unplanned change requires tremendous flexibility and adaptability on the part of organizations. Managers must be prepared to handle both planned and unplanned forms of change in organizations.

Forces for change can come from many sources. Some of these are external, arising from outside the company, whereas others are internal, arising from sources within the organization.

## External Forces

The four major managerial challenges we have described throughout the book are major external forces for change. Globalization, workforce diversity, technological change, and managing ethical behaviour are challenges that precipitate change in organizations.

**Globalization** Globalization brings the opportunities of new markets, the threat of new competition, and the necessity of adaptive response. Canadian businesses have been affected in varying ways. The Canadian clothing industry has seen huge job losses (a 36 percent drop from 2000 to 2005).[6] But, even there, the survivors are the ones that learned to play the global game. Gildan Activewear Inc., headquartered in Montreal, strategically anticipated the changing global competition and searched out the various trade agreements to place its plants where they could ship duty-free into North America, the EU countries, and Australia. The combination of advanced technology and relatively low wages in Honduras, Dominican Republic, Haiti, Mexico, and Nicaragua has meant Gilden has been able to survive the threat from low-cost Chinese labour.[7] Canadian industries based in knowledge or commodities have also done well in the new economic circumstances. For example, Montreal-based CGI Group is one of the world's largest independent IT and business process services firms, employing 26,000 people around the world.[8] Also based in Montreal, SNC-Lavalin is one of the world's largest engineering companies. Globalization means its expertise now finds wider markets.

Tube-Mac, out of Stoney Creek, Ontario, wanted to take its nonwelded hydraulic piping systems global, but to do so had to earn new certifications, such as those from Lloyd's Registry, American Bureau of Shipping, and Chinese Classification Society. Tube-Mac built a test lab in Ontario and invited the associations to audit its product testing.[9] The company hasn't looked back. Choosing to embrace global opportunities rather than let globalization destroy you requires a different mindset. Brad Miller, CEO of IMW Industries Ltd., demonstrated this. Although the poor economy and soaring Canadian dollar suggested he should lay off staff at his natural gas equipment company in Chilliwack, B.C., he chose to "rethink the business and dramatically lower the costs and get aggressive and go after the global market in a much bigger way."[10] IMW invested in redesigns and more efficient machinery instead of downsizing, bought a larger factory in Chilliwack, built another in China, and aggressively marketed to developing markets. "Pack your Pepto Bismol, get on a plane and meet the people. The world is full of good people eager to do business with Canadian companies."[11]

**Fast Fact**

Fortune magazine named Research in Motion the fastest growing company in the world.[5]

**planned change**

Change resulting from a deliberate decision to alter the organization.

**unplanned change**

Change that is imposed on the organization and is often unforeseen.

Coca-Cola faced a crisis when it introduced its Dasani bottled water in Great Britain. Coke had chosen a particularly compelling theme for its advertising, touting Dasani as even more pure than other bottled waters. After Coke had invested more than seven million pounds in this project, government regulators found that the water contained illegally high levels of bromate, a potentially cancer-causing chemical. To make matters worse, Coke was forced to admit that the contamination was introduced by its own production process. Coke's response was swift: it quickly pulled half a million bottles of Dasani from London shelves and postponed plans for product launches in France and Germany. Some British writers rank Coke's introduction of Dasani among the worst marketing disasters in Britain's history.[12]

**Workforce Diversity** Related to globalization is the challenge of workforce diversity. As we have seen throughout this book, workforce diversity is a powerful force for change in organizations. Changes in Canadian demographics mean the labour force is aging and becoming more culturally diverse. Census figures from 2006 show that the Canadian workforce has slipped into middle age, with the median age now over 41.[13] Population projections indicate that, by about 2017, Canada may have more people at the age where they can leave the labour force than at the age where they can enter it.[14] Labour shortages are anticipated, as is a shortage of entrepreneurs.[15] Statistics Canada predicts substantial increases in the number of foreign-born and visible-minority citizens in metropolitan areas. For example, from 2006 to 2031, it predicts the percentage of visible minorities in Ottawa will rise from 19 percent to 36 percent, in Calgary from 22 percent to 38 percent, and in Toronto from 43 percent to 63 percent.[16] Current statistics on Toronto show a surprisingly rich multicultural diversity. Residents come from over 200 distinct ethnic origins. Toronto is home to 20 percent of all immigrants living in Canada and 23 percent of all visible minorities living in Canada.[17] Toronto hotels provide an example of the benefits and complexities of this diversity for employers. Immigrant groups provide a large source of potential labour that meets the needs of a diverse group of customers. Also, new market segments are attracted to culturally diverse hotels. However, cultural groups tend to cluster in certain departments, which can lead to communication problems and conflict and can create less incentive for the employees to learn English. These concentrations are counterproductive to diversity goals. Differences in cultural styles have implications for management, since subordinates with varying degrees of power distance (Chapter 2) interact differently with their supervisors.

Differences in behavioural style also influence how the employees get along.[18] The hotels have learned that providing English as a Second Language courses, paying for at least partial attendance, and rewarding successful completion leads to a more skilled and flexible immigrant workforce. Fostering a culture that is inclusive and supportive also helps.

Many Canadian companies are taking steps to welcome and integrate new Canadians. For example, Canadian Imperial Bank of Commerce was selected as one of the Best Employers for New Canadians because of its initiatives. These include providing career-track internships for foreign professionals, hiring newcomers with international credentials in finance through a five-week job readiness training program, participating in a unique "speed mentoring" program where new Canadians meet one-on-one with employee mentors, and seeking out immigrant job seekers through job fairs, online channels, information sessions, and partnerships with community organizations.[19]

**Technological Change** Rapid technological innovation is another force for change in organizations, and those that fail to keep pace can quickly fall behind. Pressures to remain competitive push organizations to find cost savings and improve productivity where possible. Table 17.1 describes some significant changes brought in by Canadian Pacific Railways and their impact on workers and corporate productivity.[20] At one point CPR and its employees were protected from the full impact of technological change by a heavily regulated, noncompetitive environment. Because of the North American Free Trade Agreement and general worldwide tariff reduction, the competitive landscape for CPR (and other North American rail companies) has been dramatically altered, accelerating the pace of change.[21] Many Canadian companies find themselves in similar positions.

Technological innovations bring about profound change because the innovation process promotes associated changes in work relationships and organizational structures.[22] The team approach adopted by many organizations leads to flatter structures, decentralized decision making, and more open communication between leaders and team members.

| TABLE 17.1 | Examples of Significant Technological Changes at CPR, 1950–2000 | |
| --- | --- | --- |
| **TECHNOLOGY INTRODUCED** | **IMPLEMENTATION PERIOD** | **IMPACT** |
| Diesel locomotives replaced steam locomotives | Late 1950s | Eliminated job of fireman<br>Increased speed, productivity, and safety |
| Highly automated track maintenance equipment | Late 1950s | Increased productivity per worker |
| Computer assisted traffic control | 1970s | Reduced need for traffic controllers |
| End of train IT (radio signals at front apply brakes at rear) | Mid to late 1980s | Eliminated cabooses, reducing crew size |
| Hot box detector (measures wheel temperature) | Mid to late 1980s | Impact on crew size, track and rolling stock maintenance |
| Remote control locomotive system | Early 1990s | Jobs of yardmen & locomotive engineers changed |
| New office computer systems | Early 1990s | E-billing, EDI & HRIS reduced need for certain functions |
| Automatic Equipment Identification (rolling stock tracked through sensors) | Early 1990s | Reduces need to visually track and manually record serial numbers in yard or past checkpoints; tracking errors reduced |

Adapted from A. T. Timur & A. Ponak, Labor Relations and Technological Change at Canadian Pacific Railway, *Journal of Labor Research* 23 (2002): 535–557.

**Managing Ethical Behaviour** Recent ethical scandals have brought ethical behaviour in organizations to the forefront of public consciousness. Ethical issues, however, are not always public and monumental. Employees face ethical dilemmas in their daily work lives. The need to manage daily ethical behaviour has brought about several changes in organizations. Most centre around the idea that an organization must create a culture that encourages ethical behaviour.

All public companies issue annual financial reports. Gap Inc. has gone a step further by issuing an annual ethical report. The clothing industry is almost synonymous with the use of sweatshops, but what sets Gap apart is its candid admission that none of its 3,000 suppliers fully complies with the firm's ethical code of conduct. But rather than retreat from these problems, Gap has chosen to work with its suppliers to improve conditions overseas. The firm has more than 90 full-time employees charged with monitoring supplier operations around the world.[23]

The annual report includes extensive descriptions of workers' activities, including which factories were monitored, violations that were found, and which factories are no longer used by Gap because of the violations. It also addresses media reports critical of Gap and its operations.

Gap tries to improve worker conditions by providing training and encouraging suppliers to develop their own conduct codes. For example, in China it has encouraged lunchtime sessions in which workers are advised of their rights. While most facilities respond positively to these efforts, some don't, and Gap pulled its business from 136 factories it concluded were not going to improve. It also terminated contracts with two factories that had verifiable use of child labour. Gap's approach to overseas labour offers a model for other garment firms.[24]

© All Canada Photos/Alamy

Lynn Amaral/Shutterstock

experiences its third quarterly loss within a fiscal year is undoubtedly motivated to do something about it. Some companies react by instituting layoffs and massive cost-cutting programs, whereas others look at the bigger picture, view the loss as symptomatic of an underlying problem, and seek the cause of the problem.

A crisis may also stimulate change in an organization. Strikes or walkouts may lead management to change the wage structure. The resignation of a key decision maker may cause the company to rethink the composition of its management team and its role in the organization.

Changes in employee expectations can also trigger change in organizations. A company that hires a group of young newcomers may find that their expectations are very different from those expressed by older workers. The workforce is more educated than ever before. Although this has its advantages, workers with more education demand more of employers. Today's workers are also concerned with career and family balance issues, such as dependent care. The many sources of workforce diversity hold potential for a host of differing expectations among employees.

Changes in the work climate at an organization can also stimulate change. A workforce that seems lethargic, unmotivated, and dissatisfied is showing symptoms of larger problems that must be addressed. Such symptoms are common in organizations that have experienced layoffs. Workers who have escaped a layoff may grieve for those who have lost their jobs and may find it hard to continue to be productive. They may fear that they will be laid off as well, and many feel insecure in their jobs.

The Canadian Centre for Ethics and Corporate Policy notes many specific steps that an organization can take to guide ethical behaviour in addition to the code of conduct. These include ethics training, creating decision aids for likely ethical dilemmas, appointing an ethics officer or ombudsperson, and creating a protected whistle-blowing program.[25] For example, Magna International, the automotive parts supplier headquartered in Aurora, Ontario, has created a "Good Business Line." Stakeholders are encouraged to use this confidential communications tool to report any concerns about questionable business practices.[26]

Society expects organizations to maintain ethical behaviour both internally and in relationships with other organizations, as well as with customers, the environment, and society. These expectations may be informal, or they may come in the form of increased regulation. In addition to the pressure from societal expectations, legal developments, changing stakeholder expectations, and shifting consumer demands can also lead to change.[27] And some companies change simply because others are changing.[28] Other powerful forces for change originate from within the organization.

## Internal Forces

Pressures for change that originate inside the organization are generally recognizable. A declining effectiveness is a pressure to change. A company that

### [ Greener Arches? ]

In response to market pressures, McDonald's Europe has implemented several socially responsible business practices. The company buys all of its coffee from the world's poorest farmers and from farms sanctioned by the Rainforest Alliance. McDonald's Europe mostly buys locally raised beef and meat that is not genetically altered. The chain has also introduced more organic products to its menu. Surprisingly, a large chicken nuggets and French fries in the U.S. contains almost ten times the trans fat as the same meal in Denmark, so McDonald's Europe committed to matching Denmark's trans fat content throughout the organization by 2008. Such proactive strategies to addressing change have made McDonald's Europe very profitable.

SOURCE: K. Capell, "McDonald's Offers Ethics with Those Fries," *BusinessWeek*, January 9, 2007; http://www.businessweek.com/globalbiz/content/jan2007/gb20070109_958716.htm.

# The Scope of Change

Change can be of a relatively small scope, such as a modification in a work procedure (an **incremental change**). Such changes are a fine-tuning of the organization. Schweitzer-Mauduit Canada (SMC) a flax straw processing company, is receiving financial support from the federal and Manitoba governments to upgrade and expand its plants in Winkler and Carman, Manitoba. With this new equipment, it will be able to produce a line of renewable, sustainable biomaterials to serve the growing bio-economy, expanding its current business.[29] While radical change is more exciting and interesting to discuss, most research on change has focused on evolutionary (incremental) rather than revolutionary change.[30] Change can also be of a larger scale, such as the restructuring of an organization (a **strategic change**).[31] In strategic change, the organization moves from an old state to a known new state during a controlled period of time. Strategic change usually involves a series of transition steps. In the United States, AT&T, the granddaddy of long distance companies, made a strategic decision in 2004 to get out of the residential long distance market entirely. Rather than simply cutting off its existing customers, the firm has stopped advertising to consumers and raised residential rates sharply.[32]

The most massive scope of change is **transformational change**, in which the organization moves to a radically different, and sometimes unknown, future state.[33] In transformational change, the organization's mission, culture, goals, structure, and leadership may all change dramatically.[34] Several industries are undergoing transformational change due to the Internet, including financial services, publishing, and the music industry. The digital environment, easy access to inexpensive recording equipment, ease of distribution through the Internet, widespread practices of illegal copying, and the new ways in which audiences access music mean that the power of the major record companies has been challenged. They cannot stop the technological developments and must design a business model that responds appropriately to the new environment.[35] Record labels are transforming themselves from vendors of physical goods to licensors of digital

**incremental change**

Change of a relatively small scope, such as making small improvements.

**strategic change**

Change of a larger scale, such as organizational restructuring.

**transformational change**

Change in which the organization moves to a radically different, and sometimes unknown, future state.

**change agent**

The individual or group that undertakes the task of introducing and managing a change in an organization.

Jupiter Images

media.[36] The organization must shift from a command and control approach focused on low costs to a loop of connections and collaboration with consumers and partners.[37]

One of the toughest decisions faced by leaders is the proper "pace" of change. Some scholars argue that rapid change is more likely to succeed, since it creates momentum,[38] while others argue that these short, sharp changes are actually rare and not experienced by most firms.[39] Still others observe that change in a large organization may occur incrementally in parts of the firm and quickly in others.[40] In summary, researchers agree that the pace of change is important, but they can't quite agree on which pace of change is most beneficial.

Very little long-term research has looked at change over a significant time period. One 12-year study looked at change in the structure of Canadian National Sports Organizations (NSOs). It found that within NSOs, radical transition did not always require a fast pace of change. It also found that successful transitions often involve changing the high-impact elements of an organization (in this case, their decision-making structures) early in the process.[41]

## The Change Agent's Role

The individual or group that introduces and manages change in an organization is known as a **change agent**. Change agents can be internal, such as managers or employees who are appointed to oversee the change process.

Internal change agents have certain advantages in managing the change process. They know the organization's past history, its political system, and its culture. Because they must live with the results of their change efforts, internal change agents are likely to be very careful about managing change. There are disadvantages, however, to using internal change agents. They may be associated with certain factions within the organization, be accused of favouritism, or be too close to the situation to have an objective view of what needs to be done.

Change leaders within organizations tend to be creative people with positive self-concepts and high risk tolerance.[42] In fact, a study of Israeli firms found that risk aversion and self-centredness in leaders are both associated with resistance to change and, consequently, organizational decline.[43] A transformational leadership style is particularly effective at gaining employee commitment to a change when the impact on employees is high.[44] A high number of change leaders are women. Change managers are more flexible than ordinary general managers and much more people-oriented. Using a balance of technical and interpersonal skills, they are tough decision makers who focus on performance results. They also know how to energize people and get them aligned in the same direction. In addition, they have the ability to operate in more than one leadership style and can shift from a team mode to command and control, depending on the situation. They are also comfortable with uncertainty.[45]

If change is large scale or strategic in nature, it may take a team of leaders to make change happen. A team assembling leaders with a variety of skills, expertise, and influence that can work together harmoniously may be needed to accomplish change of large scope.[46]

*External change agents* bring an outsider's objective view to the organization. They may be preferred by employees because of their impartiality. When an organization wants a new approach and a fresh perspective, it is important that it choose a change leader who has no psychological connection to the previous decision maker(s). In Chapter 10 you learned that one way in which to minimize escalation of commitment is to separate project decisions so different people make the decisions at different stages. However, intriguing research has recently demonstrated that if the subsequent decision maker has any psychological connection to that initial person, he or she is likely to get trapped in repeating and justifying that person's errors. This suggests that an internal change leader may be unconsciously tied to the previous leader's actions. Perhaps only an outsider can truly make a clean break with the past.[47] External change agents face certain problems, however; not only is their knowledge of the organization's history limited, but they may also be viewed with suspicion by organization members. External change agents have more power in directing changes if employees perceive the change agents as being trustworthy, possessing important expertise, having a track record that establishes credibility, and being similar to them.[48]

Different change agent competencies are required at different stages of the change process. Leadership, communication, training, and participation have varying levels of impact as the change proceeds, meaning change agents must

> ## "Nobody likes change except a wet baby."
> —Mark Smith

be flexible in how they work through the different phases of the process.[49] Effective change leaders build strong relationships within their leadership team, between the team and organizational members, and between the team and key environmental players. Maintaining all three relationships simultaneously is quite difficult, so successful leaders are continually "coupling" and "uncoupling" with the different groups as the change process proceeds. Adaptability is a key skill for both internal and external change leaders.[50]

## LEARNING OUTCOME 3

# Resistance to Change

Resistance to change is an expected human response. As Mark Smith, a change specialist at KPMG Canada says, "Nobody likes change except a wet baby."[51] The resistance can be quite rational, motivated by self-interest or by the best interests of the organization. A change that seems the exciting start of something new for the change leader can mean an end to the employee—an end to the way he or she is used to doing things. The change proposal can be interpreted as indicating that the employee was somehow failing.[52] Employee resistance is a natural response, so preventing it is unlikely. Instead, knowing resistance will occur, organizations need to deal with it and work toward gaining employee commitment and support for the change. Employees emotionally opposed to a change may not only undermine the change implementation, but also are likely to withdraw and lose trust in both management and the organization.[53]

## Major Reasons People Resist Change

There are several commonly found reasons people resist change. They include:

**Fear of the Unknown** Change often brings with it substantial uncertainty. Employees facing a technological change may resist the change because it introduces ambiguity into what was once a comfortable situation for them. We know from Chapter 7 how stressful uncertainty is. Research shows that employees who feel uncertain because the change seems poorly planned or there seems to be a high frequency of changes have lower job satisfaction and are more likely to consider quitting.[54]

**Fear of Loss** Some employees may fear losing their jobs with impending change, especially when an advanced technology like robotics is introduced. Employees may also fear losing their status because of a change.[55] Computer systems experts, for example, may feel threatened when they feel their expertise is eroded by the installation of a more user-friendly networked information system. Another common fear is that changes may diminish the positive qualities the individual enjoys in the job.

**Fear of Failure** Some employees fear changes because they fear their own failure. Employees may fear that changes will result in increased workloads or increased task difficulty, and subsequently may question their own competencies. They may also fear that performance expectations will be elevated following the change, and that they may not measure up.[56]

Anticipating that a change (even a positive one) will increase demands is quite justified. A study of over 2,000 working Norwegians showed that organizational change increased stress, principally through increasing job demands, no matter how well the change was implemented or how desirable the change was.[57] Employees resist even changes with favourable outcomes if they require significant personal adaptation.[58]

**Disruption of Interpersonal Relationships** Employees may resist change that threatens to limit meaningful interpersonal relationships on the job. Librarians facing automation feared that once the computerized system was implemented, they would not be able to interact as they did when they had to go to another floor of the library to get help finding a resource.

**Personality and Justice Issues** When the change agent's personality creates negativity, employees may resist the change. A change agent who appears insensitive to employee concerns may meet considerable resistance, because employees perceive that their needs are not being taken into account. Resistance to change can also derive from a perception that the outcomes are unfair or the way it is being implemented is unfair.[59,60,61] In fact, resistance can arise long before the change from the simple anticipation that it will not be handled fairly, based on employees' past experiences with management.[62]

**Politics** Organizational change may also shift the existing balance of power in the organization. Individuals or groups empowered under the current arrangement may be threatened with losing these political advantages in the advent of change.

**Cultural Assumptions and Values** Sometimes cultural assumptions and values can be impediments to change, particularly if the assumptions underlying the change are alien to employees. Other times, employees might interpret strategic change initiatives from the standpoint of the organization's value system and ideologies of the management team. What an organization chooses to change and how it implements the change both express something about the company's values. How well an employee's values match those of the organization during change influences the employee's perceptions of how well he or she fits into that organization.[63] Resistance based on cultural values can be very difficult to overcome because some cultural assumptions are unconscious. As we discussed in Chapter 2, some cultures tend to avoid uncertainty. In Mexican and Greek cultures, for example, change that creates a great deal of uncertainty may be met with great resistance.

We have described several sources of resistance to change. The reasons for resistance are as diverse as the workforce itself and vary with different individuals and organizations. The challenge for managers is introducing change in a positive manner and managing employee resistance.

## Managing Resistance to Change

The traditional view of resistance to change treated it as something to be overcome, and many organizational attempts to reduce the resistance have served only to intensify it. The contemporary view holds that resistance is simply a form of feedback and that this feedback can be used very productively to manage the change process.[64] One key to managing resistance is to plan for it and to be ready with a variety of strategies for using the

**[ Characteristics of an Effective Change Message ]**

| | |
|---|---|
| Appropriateness: | The desired change is right for the organization |
| Discrepancy: | We need to change |
| Self-efficacy: | We have the capability to successfully change |
| Personal valence: | It is in our best interest to change |
| Principle support: | Those affected are behind the change |

SOURCE: A. A. Armenakis and A. G. Bedeian, "Organizational Change: A Review of Theory and Research in the 1990s," *Journal of Management* 25 (1999): 293–315.

resistance as feedback and helping employees negotiate the transition. Three key strategies for managing resistance to change are communication, participation, and empathy and support.[65]

Communication about impending change is essential if employees are to adjust effectively.[66] The details and, equally importantly, the rationale of the change should be provided. Accurate and timely information can help prevent unfounded fears and potentially damaging rumours from developing. Conversely, announcement delay and witholding information can serve to fuel the rumour mill. Open communication in a culture of trust is a key ingredient for successful change.[67] Managers should pay attention to the informal communication networks in an organization because they can serve as power channels for disseminating change-related information.[68] All employees (especially those high in organizational identification) want information about a change that will affect them, not only on what will happen and why but also how the change will be implemented.[69] This will influence their perception of fairness and reduce feelings of uncertainty. A study looking at employees voluntarily adopting a new self-service technology found that, before the change, information on ease of use affected their support for the change. Both before and after the change, information on the usefulness of the change was important to support.[70] In a merger situation, the information provided in realistic merger previews can help employees prepare for the change, giving a greater sense of certainty and control and reducing the stress.[71] A change message gives the manager the opportunity to influence employee perception of the change, to see it as an opportunity rather than a threat,[72] to see the benefits in the change, and to have confidence in dealing with the change.[73]

There is substantial research support underscoring the importance of participation in the change process. Employees must be engaged and involved in order for change to work—as supported by the notion "That which we create, we support." Participation helps employees become involved in the change and establishes a feeling of ownership in the process. It also guarantees they will become more informed on the what, how, and why of the change, thereby reducing uncertainty.

Another strategy for managing resistance is to provide empathy and support to employees who have trouble dealing with the change. Active listening is an excellent tool for identifying the reasons behind resistance and for uncovering fears. An expression of concerns about the change can provide important feedback that managers can use to improve the change process. Emotional support and encouragement can help an employee deal with the anxiety that is a natural response to change. Supportive leadership actually changes employee perceptions of the change so they experience less uncertainty, less frequency of change, and a greater sense that the change is well planned.[74] Management patience is an important aspect of support. Relapses are typical. People often slide back into old habits several times before they maintain the new behaviour.[75] The stress of a change affects management as well as employees, and supervisors may not always feel up to supporting their employees. In fact, research indicates that middle managers tend to withdraw during large-scale change processes in an attempt to get the situation under control for themselves.[76] Managers responsible for downsizing often engage in avoidance tactics to avoid needy or upset employees.[77] Yet manager availability is a key component in an effective change management process.[78]

The employee–supervisor relationship in general is critical to how the employee reacts to a specific change. In a high-quality relationship, the employee is more accepting of supervisor change influence tactics, believing they must be justified. In a poor-quality relationship, the employee is more suspicious and resistant.[79] Past experience with a supervisor shapes employee expectations of how fairly a change will be handled and colours his or her actual experience of fairness when the change occurs.[80] When employees trust their supervisors, it serves as a social support mechanism and they are more committed to the organization even if they feel they can't control the change process.[81]

The above approaches to managing change have actually been made into law in Norway. The *Working Environment Act* implemented in Norway in 2006 ensures the rights of employees during a reorganization process. In a reorganization that involves significant changes to employees' working situation, the employer must ensure provision of necessary information to employees, participation of the employees in the process, and competence development to meet the requirements of a fully satisfactory working environment.[82] Sponsored research to guide the labour inspection authorities in dealing with these change situations found that a healthy change process cannot prevent adaptation demands but it can reduce stress and increase perceptions of support and control (in line with Karasek's job demand-control-support model of stress in Chapter 7).[83]

## LEARNING OUTCOME 4

# Lewin's Model for Managing Change

**unfreezing**

The first step in Lewin's change model, in which individuals are encouraged to discard old behaviours by shaking up the equilibrium state that maintains the status quo.

Kurt Lewin developed a model of the change process that has stood the test of time and continues to influence the way organizations manage planned change. Lewin's model is based on the idea of force field analysis.[84] Figure 17.1

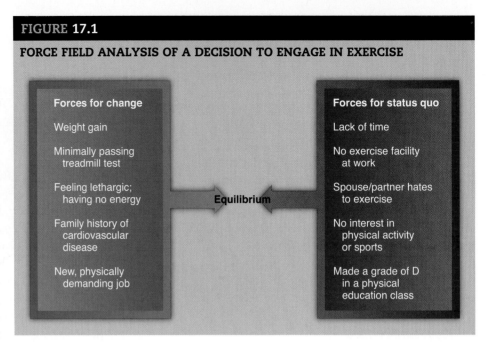

**FIGURE 17.1**

**FORCE FIELD ANALYSIS OF A DECISION TO ENGAGE IN EXERCISE**

Forces for change
Weight gain
Minimally passing treadmill test
Feeling lethargic; having no energy
Family history of cardiovascular disease
New, physically demanding job

Equilibrium

Forces for status quo
Lack of time
No exercise facility at work
Spouse/partner hates to exercise
No interest in physical activity or sports
Made a grade of D in a physical education class

shows a force field analysis of a decision to engage in exercise behaviour.

This model contends that a person's behaviour is the product of two opposing forces: One force pushes toward preserving the status quo, and the other force pushes for change. When the two opposing forces are approximately equal, current behaviour is maintained. For behavioural change to occur, the forces maintaining the status quo must be overcome. This can be accomplished by increasing the forces for change, by weakening the forces for the status quo, or by a combination of these actions.

Lewin's change model is a three-step process, as shown in Figure 17.2. The process begins with **unfreezing**, which is a crucial first hurdle in the change process. Unfreezing involves encouraging individuals to discard old behaviours by shaking up the equilibrium state that maintains the status quo. Change management literature has long advocated that certain individuals have personalities that make them more resistant to change. However, recent research indicates that only a small portion of a study's respondents (23 percent) displayed consistency in their reactions to three different kinds of change: structural, technological, and office relocation. The majority of respondents (77 percent) reacted differently to these differing kinds of change, suggesting that reactions to change might be more situationally driven than was previously thought.[85] Organizations often accomplish unfreezing by eliminating the rewards for current behaviour and showing that current behaviour is not valued. In essence, individuals surrender by allowing the boundaries of their status quo to be opened in preparation for change.[86]

## FIGURE 17.2

### LEWIN'S CHANGE MODEL

| Unfreezing | Moving | Refreezing |
|---|---|---|
| Reducing forces for status quo | Developing new attitudes, values, and behaviours | Reinforcing new attitudes, values, and behaviours |

The second step in the change process is **moving**. In the moving stage, the change is implemented and new attitudes, values, and behaviours are substituted for old ones. Adapting to the change at this second stage is much easier if unfreezing was effective. Employees know what is changing and why, and what their role is to be.

**Refreezing** is the final step in the change process. In this step, new attitudes, values, and behaviours are established as the new status quo. The new ways of operating are cemented in and reinforced. Managers should ensure that the organizational culture and formal reward systems encourage the new behaviours. Changes in the reward structure may be needed to ensure that the organization is not rewarding the old behaviours and merely hoping for the new behaviours. A study by Exxon Research and Engineering showed that framing and displaying a mission statement in managers' offices may eventually change the behaviour of 2 percent of the managers. In contrast, changing managers' evaluation and reward systems will change the behaviour of 55 percent of the managers almost overnight.[87]

The approach used by Monsanto to increase opportunities for women within the company is an illustration of how to use Lewin's model effectively. First, Monsanto emphasized unfreezing by helping employees debunk negative stereotypes about women in business. This also helped overcome resistance to change. Second, Monsanto moved employees' attitudes and behaviours by diversity training in which differences were emphasized as positive, and supervisors learned ways of training and developing female employees. Third, Monsanto changed its reward system so that managers were evaluated and paid according to how they coached and promoted women, which helped refreeze the new attitudes and behaviours.

Following through all three stages of Lewin's model is not easy or typical. A review of change management practices at the Correctional Services of Canada examined four specific change initiatives. It found that the early stages of change initiatives were well handled (for example, making the case for change, and articulating and communicating the vision). However, there was mixed success in sustaining the change. There was inconsistency in continuing the communications, generating early wins to build momentum, and keeping the focus needed to institutionalize the change.[88]

One frequently overlooked issue is whether or not the change is consistent with the company's deeply held core values. Value consistency is critical to making a change "stick." Organizations whose members perceive the changes to be consistent with the firm's values adopt the changes much more easily and fully. Conversely, organizations whose members' values conflict with the changes may display "superficial conformity," in which members pay lip service to the changes but ultimately revert to their old behaviours.[89]

Organizations that wish to change can select from a variety of methods to make a change become reality. Organization development is an approach that consists of various programs for making organizations more effective.

**moving**

The second step in Lewin's change model, in which new attitudes, values, and behaviours are substituted for old ones.

**refreezing**

The final step in Lewin's change model, in which new attitudes, values, and behaviours are established as the new status quo.

# Determining the Need for Organization Development Interventions

Organization development (OD) is a systematic approach to organizational improvement that applies behavioural science theory and research in order to increase individual and organizational well-being and effectiveness.[90] This definition implies certain characteristics. First, OD is a systematic approach to planned change. It is a structured cycle of diagnosing organizational problems and opportunities and then applying expertise to them. Second, OD is grounded in solid research and theory. It involves the application of behavioural science knowledge to the challenges that organizations face. Third, OD recognizes the reciprocal relationship between individuals and organizations. It acknowledges that for organizations to change, individuals must change. Finally, OD is goal oriented. It is a process that seeks to improve both individual and organizational well-being and effectiveness.

Prior to deciding on a method of intervention, managers must carefully diagnose the problem they are attempting to address. Diagnosis and needs analysis is a critical first step in any OD intervention. Following this, an intervention method is chosen and applied. Finally, a thorough follow-up of the OD process is conducted.

## Diagnosis and Needs Analysis

Before any intervention is planned, a thorough organizational diagnosis should be conducted. Diagnosis is an essential first step for any organization development intervention.[91] The term *diagnosis* comes from *dia* (through) and *gnosis* (knowledge of). Thus, the diagnosis should pinpoint specific problems and areas in need of improvement. Six areas to examine carefully are the organization's purpose, structure, reward system, support systems, relationships, and leadership.[92]

**organization development (OD)**

A systematic approach to organizational improvement that applies behavioural science theory and research in order to increase individual and organizational well-being and effectiveness.

Harry Levinson's diagnostic approach asserts that the process should begin by identifying where the pain (the problem) in the organization is, what it is like, how long it has been happening, and what has already been done about it.[93] Then a four-part, comprehensive diagnosis can begin. The first part of the diagnosis involves achieving an understanding of the organization's history. In the second part, the organization as a whole is analyzed to obtain data about its structure and processes. In the third part, interpretive data about attitudes, relationships, and current organizational functioning are gathered. In the fourth part of the diagnosis, the data are analyzed and conclusions are reached. In each stage of the diagnosis, the data can be gathered using a variety of methods, including observation, interviews, questionnaires, and archival records.

A needs analysis is another crucial step in managing change. This is an analysis of the skills and competencies that employees must have to achieve the goals of the change.

 The diagnostic process may yield the conclusion that change is necessary. As part of the diagnosis, it is important to address the following issues:

> What are the forces for change?
> What are the forces preserving the status quo?
> What are the most likely sources of resistance to change?
> What are the goals to be accomplished by the change?

This information constitutes a force field analysis, as discussed earlier in the chapter.

A needs analysis is essential because interventions such as training programs must target these skills and competencies.

Hundreds of alternative OD intervention methods exist. One way of classifying these methods is by the target of change. The target of change may be the organization, groups within the organization, or individuals.

LEARNING OUTCOME **6**

# Group-Focused Techniques for OD Intervention

Some OD intervention methods emphasize changing the organization itself or changing the work groups within the organization. Intervention methods in this category include survey feedback, management by objectives, product and service quality programs, team building, and process consultation.

## Survey Feedback

**Survey feedback** is a widely used intervention method whereby employee attitudes are solicited using a questionnaire. Once the data are collected, they are analyzed and fed back to the employees to diagnose problems and plan other interventions. Survey feedback is often used as an exploratory tool and then is combined with some other intervention. The effectiveness of survey feedback in actually improving outcomes (absenteeism or productivity, for example) increases substantially when this method is combined with other interventions.[94] The effectiveness of this technique is contingent upon trust between management and subordinates, and this can be reinforced through the anonymity and confidentiality of survey responses.

For survey feedback to be an effective method, certain guidelines should be used. Employees must be assured that their responses to the questionnaire will be confidential and anonymous. Feedback should be reported in a group format. Employees must be able to trust that negative repercussions will not result from their responses. Employees should be informed of the purpose of the survey. Failing to do this can set up unrealistic expectations about the changes that might come from the surveys.

In addition, management must be prepared to follow up on the survey results. If some things cannot be changed, the rationale (for example, prohibitive cost) must be explained to the employees. Without appropriate follow-through, employees will not take the survey process seriously the next time.

## Management by Objectives

As an organization-wide technique, **management by objectives (MBO)** involves joint goal setting between employees and managers. The MBO process (discussed in Chapter 6) includes the setting of initial objectives, periodic progress reviews, and problem solving to remove any obstacles to goal achievement.[95] All these steps are joint efforts between managers and employees.

MBO is a valuable intervention because it meets three needs. First, it clarifies what is expected of employees. This reduces role conflict and ambiguity. Second, MBO provides knowledge of results, an essential ingredient in effective job performance. Finally, MBO provides an opportunity for coaching and counselling by the manager. The problem-solving approach encourages open communication and discussion of obstacles to goal achievement.[96]

One company that has used MBO successfully is General Electric. The success of MBO in effecting organizational results hinges on the linking of individual goals to the goals of the organization.[97] MBO programs should be used with caution, however. An excessive emphasis on goal achievement can result in cutthroat competition among employees, falsification of results, and striving for results at any cost.

## Product and Service Quality Programs

**Quality programs**—programs that embed product and service quality excellence in the organizational culture—are assuming key roles in the organization development efforts of many companies. For example, the success or failure of a service company may depend on the quality of customer service it provides.[98]

Toyota Motor Corporation constantly finds ways to integrate cutting-edge technological innovations with the growing pains of global expansion. The famed "Toyota Way" of doing business is focused on two key principles: continuous improvement focused on innovation and respect for people.[99]

**survey feedback**
A widely used method of intervention whereby employee attitudes are solicited using a questionnaire.

**management by objectives (MBO)**
An organization-wide intervention technique that involves joint goal setting between employees and managers.

**quality program**
A program that embeds product and service quality excellence in the organizational culture.

This cord is called an andon cord. It runs the length of every Toyota assembly line, and any worker who encounters a quality problem is allowed to pull it and stop the line.

©AP Photo/Willie Riggle

Some suggest that Toyota's recent problems with defective parts and major recalls arose because Toyota had been focusing on growth instead of its traditional devotion to quality.[100] Hyundai, on the other hand, has turned around its fortunes and reputation because of its focus on quality. Once the butt of jokes in the 1980s with its poorly made compact cars, Hyundai committed itself to quality. In 2000, it adopted the Six Sigma management discipline, using intense statistical analysis to identify flaws in the manufacturing process. The Korean company has now surpassed Ford to become the fourth-largest car manufacturer in the world.[101]

## Team Building

**Team building** programs can improve the effectiveness of work groups. Team building usually begins with a diagnostic process through which team members identify problems, and continues with the team planning actions to take in order to resolve those problems. The OD practitioner in team building serves as a facilitator, and the work itself is completed by team members.[102]

Team building is a very popular OD method. A survey of Fortune 500 companies indicated that human resource managers consid-

ered team building the most successful OD technique.[103] Managers are particularly interested in building teams that can learn. To build learning teams, members must be encouraged to seek feedback, discuss errors, reflect on successes and failures, and experiment with new ways of performing. Mistakes should be analyzed for ways to improve, and a climate of mutual support should be developed. Leaders of learning teams are good coaches who promote a climate of psychological safety so that team members feel comfortable discussing problems.[104]

One popular technique for team building is the use of outdoor challenges. Participants go through a series of outdoor activities, such as climbing a 4-metre wall. Similar physical challenges require the participants to work as a team and focus on trust, communication, decision making, and leadership. GE and Weyerhaeuser use outdoor challenges at the beginning of their team-building courses, and later in the training, team members apply what they have learned to actual business situations.[105] One innovative firm called Teambuilding Inc. uses rowing as team building exercise. It enlisted the services of an Olympic gold medalist to design a seminar focused on team building using rowing as the central organizing theme. This activity encourages participants to practise leadership, communication, goal setting, conflict management and motivation. GE Healthcare, ING Direct, and Wyeth Corporate Communications have all used this technique for their team-building programs.[106] Preliminary studies indicate that team building can improve group processes.[107]

## Process Consultation

Pioneered by Edgar Schein, **process consultation** is an OD method that helps managers and employees improve the processes that are used in organizations.[108] The processes most often targeted are communication, conflict resolution, decision making, group interaction, and leadership.

One of the distinguishing features of the process consultation approach is that an outside consultant is used. The role of the consultant is to help employees help themselves. In this way, the ownership of a successful outcome rests with the employees.[109] The consultant guides the organization members in examining the processes in the organization and in refining them. The steps in process

**team building**
An intervention designed to improve the effectiveness of a work group.

**process consultation**
An OD method that helps managers and employees improve the processes that are used in organizations.

consultation are entering the organization, defining the relationship, choosing an approach, gathering data and diagnosing problems, intervening, and gradually leaving the organization.

Process consultation is an interactive technique between employees and an outside consultant, so it is seldom used as a sole OD method. Most often, it is used in combination with other OD interventions.

--------------------------------

All the preceding OD methods focus on changing the organization or the work group. The following OD methods are aimed toward individual change.

LEARNING OUTCOME 7

# Individual-focused Techniques for OD Intervention

Organization development efforts that are targeted toward individuals include skills training, leadership training and development, executive coaching, job redesign, health promotion programs, and career planning.

## Skills Training

The key question addressed by **skills training** is "What knowledge, skills, and abilities are necessary to do this job effectively?" Skills training is accomplished either in formal classroom settings or on the job. The challenge is integrating skills training into organization development in today's rapidly changing environments that most organizations face. The job knowledge in most positions requires continual updates to keep pace with rapid change.

wavebreakmedia ltd/Shutterstock

## Leadership Training and Development

Companies invest millions of dollars in **leadership training and development**, a term that encompasses a variety of techniques that are designed to enhance individuals' leadership skills. One popular technique is sending future leaders to off-site training classes. Research shows that this type of education experience can have some impact, but participants' enthusiastic return to work may be short lived due to the challenges and realities of work life. Classroom learning alone thus has a limited effect on leadership skills.

The best leadership training and development programs combine classroom learning with on-the-job experiences. One way of accomplishing development is through the use of action learning, a technique that was pioneered in Europe.[110] In action learning, leaders take on unfamiliar problems or familiar problems in unfamiliar settings. The leaders work on the problems and meet weekly in small groups made up of individuals from different parts of the organizations. The outcome of action learning is that leaders learn about themselves through the challenges of their comrades. Other techniques that provide active learning for participants are simulation, business games, role-playing, and case studies.[111]

Eli Lilly has an action learning program that pulls together 18 future company leaders and gives them a strategic business issue to resolve. For six weeks, the trainees meet with experts, best-practices organizations, and customers, and then present their recommendations to top brass. One action learning team was charged with coming up with an e-business strategy; their plan was so good that executives immediately implemented it. At Eli Lilly and other firms, action learning programs provide developmental experiences for leaders and result in useful initiatives for the company.[112]

Leadership training and development is an ongoing process that takes considerable time and effort. There are no quick fixes. At IBM, managers are held accountable for leadership development. In fact, IBM's managers will not be considered for promotion into senior executive positions unless they have a record of developing leaders. Top management must be committed to the process of leadership training and development if they want to create a pipeline of high-potential employees to fill leadership positions.[113]

**skills training**
Increasing the job knowledge, skills, and abilities that are necessary to do a job effectively.

**leadership training and development**
A variety of techniques that are designed to enhance individuals' leadership skills.

## Executive Coaching

Executive coaching is a technique in which managers or executives are paired with a coach in a partnership to help the executive perform more effectively at work. Although coaching is usually done in a one-on-one manner, it is sometimes attempted in groups. The popularity of executive coaching has increased dramatically in recent years. The International Coach Federation, a group that trains and accredits executive coaches, in just two years of existence doubled its membership, which is now at 7,000 members in 35 countries.[114]

Coaching is typically a special investment in top-level managers. Coaches provide another set of eyes and ears and help executives see beyond their own blinders. They elicit solutions and ideas from the client rather than making suggestions; thus, they develop and enhance the talents and capabilities within the client. Many coaching arrangements focus on developing the emotional intelligence of the client executive and may use a 360-degree assessment in which the executive, his or her boss, peers, subordinates, and even family members rate the executive's emotional competencies.[115] This information is then fed back to the executive, and along with the coach, a development plan is put in place.

Good coaches form strong connections with clients, exhibit professionalism, and deliver forthright, candid feedback. The top reasons executives seek out coaches are to make personal behaviour changes, enhance their effectiveness, and foster stronger relationships. Does executive coaching pay off? Evidence suggests that successful coaching can result in sustained changes in executives' behaviour, increased self-awareness and understanding, and more effective leadership competencies.[116] In one study, for example, executives who worked with executive coaches were more likely to set specific goals, ask for feedback from their supervisors, and rated as better performers by their supervisors and subordinates when compared to executives who simply received feedback from surveys.[117] Effective coaching relationships depend on a professional, experienced coach, an executive who is motivated to learn and change, and a good fit between the two.

## Job Redesign

As an OD intervention method, job redesign emphasizes the fit between individual skills and the demands of the job. Chapter 14 outlined several approaches to job design.

> **Coaching is typically a special investment in top-level managers.**

Many of these methods are used as OD techniques for realigning task demands and individual capabilities or for redesigning jobs to fit new techniques or organizational structures better.

Ford Motor Company has redesigned virtually all of its manufacturing jobs, shifting workers from individual to team-based roles in which they have greater control of their work and can take the initiative to improve products and production techniques. Ford began trying this technique more than a decade ago and found that it improved not only employee job satisfaction but also productivity and product quality.

Another form of job redesign is telecommuting. Companies including Telus, Bell Canada, and IBM Canada have significant numbers of employees who work this way. Research reported by the Canadian Telework Association indicates that 1.5 million Canadians telecommute at least one day a week and 77 percent of them claim it increases job satisfaction.[118]

## Health Promotion Programs

As organizations have become increasingly concerned with the costs of distress in the workplace, health promotion programs have become a part of larger organization development efforts. Companies that have successfully integrated health promotion programs into their organizations include both large and small firms. KPMG, an established accounting and professional services firm with over 5,000 full-time employees in Canada, helps employees with a generous fitness participation subsidy (up to 1.25 percent of salary) that can be used for health-club memberships, weight loss support, and home equipment purchases. It also supports a number of employee sports teams, from cricket to hockey.[119] With only 96 employees, Digital Extremes, a London, Ontario–based company offering custom computer programming services, also recognizes the benefits of a healthy workforce; it offers fitness club subsidies as well as a bonus (up to $450) to encourage employees to get fit and stay fit.[120] Hershey's Nova Scotia plant (makers of Pot of Gold chocolates) introduced a comprehensive wellness program. It started with over 500 employees completing a voluntary health risk assessment that provided data for developing wellness programs, and benchmarks to note improvements. This led to the creation of weight management, smoking cessation, and fitness programs.[121]

Although companies have long recognized the importance of maintenance on their machinery, many are only recently learning that their human assets need maintenance as well, in the form of employee wellness and health promotion activities. All are focused on helping employees manage their stress and health in a preventive manner.

## Career Planning

Matching an individual's career aspirations with the opportunities in the organization is career planning. This proactive approach to career management is often part of an organization's development efforts. Career planning is a joint responsibility of organizations and individuals.

Career-planning activities benefit both the organization and its individuals. Through counselling sessions, employees identify their skills and skill deficiencies. The organization then can plan its training and development efforts based on this information. In addition, the process can be used to identify and nurture talented employees for potential promotion.

- - - - - - - - - - - - - - - - - - - - - - - - - - - - - -

Managers can choose from a host of organization development techniques to facilitate organizational change. Large-scale changes in organizations require the use of

©Juice Images—Fotolia.com

multiple techniques. For example, implementing a new technology such as robotics may require simultaneous changes in the structure of the organization, the configuration of work groups, and individual attitudes.

We should recognize at this point that the organization development methods just described are means to an end. Programs do not drive change; business needs do. The OD methods are merely vehicles for moving the organization and its employees in a more effective direction.

## ARE ORGANIZATION DEVELOPMENT EFFORTS EFFECTIVE?

>> Since organization development is designed to help organizations manage change, it is important to evaluate the effectiveness of these efforts. The success of any OD intervention depends on a host of factors, including the technique used, the competence of the change agent, the organization's readiness for change, and top management commitment. No single method of OD is effective in every instance. Instead, multiple-method OD approaches are recommended because they allow organizations to capitalize on the benefits of several approaches.[122]

Efforts to evaluate OD effects have focused on outcomes such as productivity. One review of more than 200 interventions indicated that worker productivity improved in 87 percent of the cases.[123] We can conclude that when properly applied and managed, organization development programs have positive effects on performance.[124]

# Visit **icanorgb.com** to find the resources you need today!

*Located at the back of the textbook are rip-out Chapter Review Cards. Make sure you also go online to check out other tools that ORGB offers to help you successfully pass your course.*

- Interactive Quizzing
- Key Term Flashcards
- PowerPoint Slides
- Audio Chapter Summaries

- Cases and Exercises
- Interactive Games
- Self-Assessments
- "On the Job" and "Bizflix" Videos

# 18

>>

# Career Management

# "A career is more a journey than a destination"

A **career** is a pattern of work-related experiences that span the course of a person's life.[1] A career is more a journey than a destination. The two elements in a career are the objective element and the subjective element.[2] The objective element of the career is the observable, concrete environment. For example, you can manage a career by getting training to improve your skills. In contrast, the subjective element involves your perception of the situation. Rather than getting training (an objective element), you might change your aspirations (a subjective element). Therefore, both objective events and the individual's perception of those events are important in defining a career.

**Career management** is a lifelong process of learning about self, jobs, and organizations; setting personal career goals; developing strategies for achieving the goals; and revising the goals based on work and life experiences.[3] Whose responsibility is career management? It is tempting to place the responsibility on individuals, and it is appropriate. However, it is also the organization's responsibility to form partnerships with individuals in managing their careers. Careers are made up of exchanges between individuals and organizations. Inherent in these exchanges is the idea of reciprocity, or give and take.

Whether we approach it as managers or as employees, career management is an integral activity

**career**

The pattern of work-related experiences that span the course of a person's life.

**career management**

A lifelong process of learning about self, jobs, and organizations; setting personal career goals; developing strategies for achieving the goals, and revising the goals based on work and life experiences.

## LEARNING OUTCOMES

After reading this chapter, you should be able to do the following:

1 Explain occupational and organizational choice decisions.

2 Identify foundations for a successful career.

3 Explain the career-stage model.

4 Explain the major tasks facing individuals in the establishment stage of the career model.

5 Identify the issues confronting individuals in the advancement stage of the career model.

6 Describe how individuals can navigate the challenges of the maintenance stage of the career model.

7 Explain how individuals withdraw from the workforce.

8 Explain how career anchors help form a career identity.

9 Become familiar with some current tools and practices that will help you develop your own career.

in our lives. There are three reasons it is important to understand careers:

> If we know what to look forward to over the course of our careers, we can take a proactive approach to planning and managing them.

> As managers, we need to understand the experiences of our employees and colleagues as they pass through the various stages of careers over their life spans.

> Career management is good business. It makes good financial sense to have highly trained employees keep up with their fields so that organizations can protect valuable investments in human resources.

# Occupational and Organizational Choice Decisions

The time of the fast track to the top of the hierarchical organization is past. Also gone is the idea of lifetime employment in a single organization. Today's environment demands leaner organizations. The paternalistic attitude that organizations take care of employees no longer exists. Individuals now take on more responsibility for managing their own careers. The concept of the career is undergoing a paradigm shift, as shown in Table 18.1.

**TABLE 18.1**  The New versus Old Career Paradigms

| NEW CAREER PARADIGM | OLD CAREER PARADIGM |
| --- | --- |
| **Discrete exchange means:**<br>• Explicit exchange of specified rewards in return for task performance<br>• Basing job rewards on the current market value of the work being performed<br>• Engaging in disclosure and renegotiation on both sides as the employment relationship unfolds<br>• Exercising flexibility as each party's interests and market circumstances change | **The mutual loyalty contract meant:**<br>• Implicit trading of employee compliance in return for job security<br>• Allowing job rewards to be routinely deferred into the future<br>• Leaving the mutual loyalty assumptions as a political barrier to renegotiation<br>• Assuming employment and career opportunities are standardized and prescribed by the organization |
| **Occupational excellence means:**<br>• Performance of current jobs in return for developing new occupational expertise<br>• Employees identifying with and focusing on what is happening in their adopted occupation<br>• Emphasizing occupational skill development over the local demands of any particular firm<br>• Getting training in anticipation of future job opportunities; having training lead jobs | **The one-employer focus meant:**<br>• Relying on the organization to specify jobs and their associated occupational skill base<br>• Employees identifying with and focusing on what is happening in their particular organization<br>• Foregoing technical or functional development in favour of firm-specific learning<br>• Doing the job first to be entitled to new training: making training follow jobs |
| **Organizational empowerment means:**<br>• Strategic positioning is dispersed to separate business units<br>• Everyone is responsible for adding value and improving competitiveness<br>• Business units are free to cultivate their own markets<br>• New enterprise, spinoffs, and alliance building are broadly encouraged | **The top-down firm meant:**<br>• Strategic direction is subordinated to "corporate headquarters"<br>• Competitiveness and added value are the responsibility of corporate experts<br>• Business unit marketing depends on the corporate agenda<br>• Independent enterprise is discouraged, and likely to be viewed as disloyalty |
| **Project allegiance means:**<br>• Shared employer and employee commitment to the overarching goal of the project<br>• A successful outcome of the project is more important than holding the project team together<br>• Financial and reputational rewards stem directly from project outcomes<br>• Upon project completion, organization and reporting arrangements are broken up | **Corporate allegiance meant:**<br>• Project goals are subordinated to corporate policy and organizational constraints<br>• Being loyal to the work group can be more important than the project itself<br>• Financial and reputational rewards stem from being a "good soldier" regardless of results<br>• Social relationships within organizational boundaries are actively encouraged |

The old career is giving way to a new career characterized by discrete exchange, occupational excellence, organizational empowerment, and project allegiance.[4] Moreover, one recent study found that both individuals and organizations are actively involved in the management of the new career of employees. As such, the new career involves a type of participatory management technique on the part of the individual; the organization responds to each individual's needs and thus is more flexible in its career development programs.[5]

Discrete exchange occurs when an organization gains productivity while a person gains work experience. It is a short-term arrangement that recognizes that job skills change in value and that renegotiation of the relationship must occur as conditions change. This contrasts sharply with the mutual loyalty contract of the old career paradigm in which employee loyalty was exchanged for job security.

Occupational excellence means continually honing skills that can be marketed across organizations. The individual identifies more with the occupation (I am an engineer) than the organization (I am an RIMer). In contrast, the old one-employer focus meant that training was company specific rather than preparing the person for future job opportunities. A recent research study that focused on ethnographic data (interviews and stories) was conducted among software engineers in three European firms and two North American firms. Software engineers did not have much regard for their immediate supervisors, the organization, or formal dress codes. The only thing they did believe in was occupational excellence so that they could be better at what they do. In this regard, the authors of the study note that software engineers represent a unique group in terms of career development and that they fit well within the model of the "new career."[6]

Organizational empowerment means that power flows down to business units and in turn to employees. Employees are expected to add value and help the organization remain competitive by being innovative and creative. The old top-down approach meant that control and strategizing were done only by the top managers, and individual initiative might be viewed as disloyalty or disrespect.

Project allegiance means that both individuals and organizations are committed to the successful completion of a project. The organization's gain is the project outcome; the individual's gain is experience and shared success. On project completion, the project team breaks up as individuals move on to new projects. Under the old paradigm, organizational allegiance was paramount. The needs of projects were overshadowed by policies and procedures. Work groups were long term, and keeping the group together was often as important a goal as project completion.

## Preparing for the World of Work

When viewed from one perspective, you might say that we spend our youth preparing for the world of work. Educational experiences and personal life experiences help an individual develop the skills and maturity needed to enter a career. Preparation for work is a developmental process that gradually unfolds over time.[8] As the time approaches for beginning a career, individuals face two difficult decisions: the choice of occupation and the choice of organization.

## Occupational Choice

In choosing an occupation, individuals assess their needs, values, abilities, and preferences and attempt to match them with an occupation that provides a fit. Personality plays a role in the selection of occupation. John Holland's theory of occupational choice contends that there are six types of personalities and that each personality is characterized by a set of interests and values.[9]

Holland also states that occupations can be classified using this typology. For example, realistic occupations include mechanic, restaurant server, and mechanical engineer. Artistic occupations include architect, voice coach, and interior designer. Investigative occupations include physicist, surgeon, and economist. Real estate

*Hot Trend*

In today's business environment, job hopping and company hopping are becoming more the norm. In fact, U.S. college graduates typically change jobs 4 times in their first 10 years of work, a number that is projected to increase. At that rate, you could easily hold 20 different jobs in a typical career. The stigma associated with frequent job changes has largely disappeared, and some recruiters now view a résumé littered with different companies and locations as a sign of a smart self-promoter. The key is to know "why" you are making each job move, including both what it will cost and gain for you. By presenting your job-hopping career path as a growth process, rather than a series of impulsive changes, you may set yourself apart in the minds of recruiters.[7]

# HOLLAND'S SIX TYPES

>>

**1** *Realistic:* stable, persistent, and materialistic

**2** *Artistic:* imaginative, emotional, and impulsive

**3** *Investigative:* curious, analytical, and independent

**4** *Enterprising:* ambitious, energetic, and adventurous

**5** *Social:* generous, cooperative, and sociable

**6** *Conventional:* efficient, practical, and obedient

agent, human resource manager, and lawyer are enterprising occupations. The social occupations include counsellor, social worker, and religious leader. Conventional occupations include word processor, accountant, and data entry operator.

Holland's typology has been used to predict career choices with a variety of international participants, including Mexicans, Australians, Indians, New Zealanders, Taiwanese, Pakistanis, South Africans, and Germans.[10]

An assumption that drives Holland's theory is that people choose occupations that match their own personalities. People who fit Holland's social types are those who prefer jobs that are highly interpersonal in nature. They may see careers in physical and math sciences, for example, as not affording the opportunity for interpersonal relationships.[11] To fulfill the desire for interpersonal work, they may instead gravitate toward jobs in customer service or counselling in order to better match their personalities. Although personality is a major influence on occupational choice, it is not the only influence. There are a host of other influences, including social class, parents' occupations, economic conditions, and geography.[12] Once a choice of occupation has been made, another major decision individuals face is the choice of organizations.

## Organizational Choice and Entry

Several theories of how individuals choose organizations exist, ranging from theories that postulate very logical and rational choice processes to those that offer seemingly irrational processes. Expectancy theory, which we discussed in Chapter 5, can be applied to organizational choice.[13] According to the expectancy theory view, individuals choose organizations that maximize positive outcomes and avoid negative outcomes. Job candidates calculate the probability that an organization will provide a certain outcome and then compare the probabilities across organizations.

Other theories propose that people select organizations in a much less rational fashion. Job candidates may satisfice, that is, select the first organization that meets one or two important criteria and then justify their choice by distorting their perceptions.[14]

The method of selecting an organization varies greatly among individuals and may reflect a combination of the expectancy theory and theories that postulate less rational approaches. Entry into an organization is further complicated by the conflicts that occur between individuals and organizations during the process. Figure 18.1 illustrates these potential conflicts. The arrows in the figure illustrate four types of conflicts that can occur as individuals choose organizations and organizations choose individuals. The first two conflicts (1 and 2) occur between individuals and organizations. The first is a conflict between the organization's effort to attract candidates and the individual's choice of an organization. The individual needs complete and accurate information to make a good choice, but the organization may well not provide it. The organization is trying to attract a large number of qualified candidates, so it presents itself in an overly attractive way.

The second conflict is between the individual's attempt to attract several organizations and the organization's need to select the best candidate. Individuals want good offers, so they do not disclose their faults. They

### FIGURE 18.1

**CONFLICTS DURING ORGANIZATIONAL ENTRY**

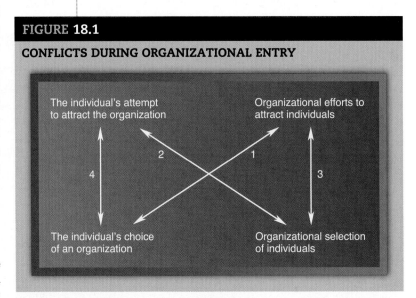

SOURCE: Figure in L. W. Porter, E. E. Lawler III, and J. R. Hackman, *Behavior in Organizations*, New York: McGraw-Hill, Inc., 1975, p. 134. Reproduced with permission of The McGraw-Hill Companies.

describe their preferred job in terms of the organization's opening instead of describing a job they would really prefer.

Conflicts 3 and 4 are conflicts internal to the two parties. The third is a conflict between the organization's desire to recruit a large pool of qualified applicants and the organization's need to select and retain the best candidate.

In recruiting, organizations tend to give only positive information, and this results in mismatches between the individual and the organization. The fourth conflict is internal to the individual; it is between the individual's desire for several job offers and the need to make a good choice. When individuals present themselves as overly attractive, they risk being offered positions that are poor fits in terms of their skills and career goals.[15]

The organizational choice and entry process is very complex due to the nature of these conflicts. Partial responsibility for preventing these conflicts rests with the individual. Individuals should conduct thorough research of the organization through published reports and industry analyses. Individuals also should conduct a careful self-analysis and be as honest as possible with organizations to ensure a good match. The job interview process can be stressful, but also informative.

Partial responsibility for good matches also rests with the organization. One way of avoiding the conflicts and mismatches is to use a realistic job preview.

**Realistic Job Previews** The conflicts just discussed may result in unrealistic expectations on the part of the candidate. People entering the world of work may expect, for example, that they will receive explicit directions from their boss, only to find that they are left with ambiguity about how to do the job. They may expect that promotions will be based on performance and find that promotions are based mainly on political considerations. Some new hires expect to be given managerial responsibilities right away; however, this is not often the case.

Giving potential employees a realistic picture of the job they are applying for is known as a **realistic job preview (RJP)**. When candidates are given both positive and negative information, they can make more effective job choices.

Traditional recruiting practices produce unrealistically high expectations, which produce low job satisfaction when these unrealistic expectations meet the reality of the job situation. RJPs tend to create expectations that are much closer to reality, and they increase the numbers of candidates who withdraw from further consideration.[16]

## If new recruits know what to expect in the new job, they can prepare for the experience.

This occurs because candidates with unrealistic expectations tend to look for employment elsewhere. Shell Canada's website provides a realistic job preview through a series of scenarios and questions. "By covering a range of topics, such as diversity, ethics and standards, and career aspirations, the Realistic Job Preview allows you to make a more educated and valued decision on your future, with Shell and beyond." For example, question 1 of 10 on expectations asks:

*Joining Shell as a new hire, you'll be treated from day one like any other Shell employee. Unlike some companies, we don't give our new joiners any particular special treatment. Instead, we believe that everyone should be treated with equal respect and that a person's skills and actions should determine their role in the company. How do you feel about this?*

1. *I think I'll find it easier to fit in if I'm treated just like everyone else.*
2. *As a new hire, I think that my educational qualifications and the fact that I made it through the tough selection process should allow me to be fast-tracked to senior roles.*
3. *I think that it's only fair that I be afforded some special opportunities as a new hire to the company.*[17]

RJPs can also be thought of as inoculation against disappointment. If new recruits know what to expect in the new job, they can prepare for the experience. Newcomers who were not given RJPs may find that their jobs don't measure up to their expectations. They may then believe that their employer was deceitful in the hiring process, become unhappy and mishandle job demands, and ultimately leave the organization.[18] Reverse résumé viewing is an intriguing additional process that organizations might consider to enhance their RJPs.[19] It involves the job candidate reviewing the résumés of current employees such as his/her supervisor, peers, and/or subordinates. That way, the job candidate can make a more informed decision about his/her fit with the organization. There are, of course, significant privacy issues to address and résumés could not be used without the employee's consent.

Job candidates who receive RJPs view the organization as honest and also have a greater ability to cope with the demands of the job.[20] RJPs perform another important function: they reduce uncertainty.[21]

> **realistic job preview (RJP)**
> Both positive and negative information given to potential employees about the job they are applying for, thereby giving them a more realistic picture of the job.

Knowing what to expect, both good and bad, gives a newcomer a sense of control that is important to job satisfaction and performance. With today's emphasis on ethics, organizations need to do all they can to be seen as operating consistently and honestly. Realistic job previews are one way in which companies can provide ethically required information to newcomers. Ultimately, RJPs result in more effective matches, lower turnover, and higher organizational commitment and job satisfaction.[22] There is much to gain, and little to risk, in providing realistic job information.[23] In summary, the needs and goals of individuals and organizations can clash during entry into the organization. To avoid potential mismatches, individuals should conduct a careful self-analysis and provide accurate information about themselves to potential employers. Organizations should present realistic job previews to show candidates both the positive and negative aspects of the job, along with the potential career paths available to the employee.

LEARNING OUTCOME **2**

# Foundations for a Successful Career

In addition to planning and preparation, building a career takes attention and self-examination. One way you can build a successful career is by becoming your own career coach; another is by developing your emotional intelligence, which is an important attribute if you want to succeed in your organization.

> **>>** The key to survival is to add more value every day and to be flexible. Use What about You? on the Chapter 18 Review Card to assess the current state of your flexibility skills.

## Becoming Your Own Career Coach

The best way to stay employed is to see yourself as being in business for yourself, even if you work for someone else. Know what skills you can package for other employers and what you can do to ensure that your skills are current. Organizations need employees who have acquired multiple skills and are adept at more than one job. Employers want employees who have demonstrated competence in dealing with change.[24] To be successful, think of organizational change not as a disruption to your work but instead as the central focus of your

work, as we discussed in Chapter 17. You will also need to develop self-reliance, as we discussed in Chapter 7, to deal effectively with the stress of change. Self-reliant individuals take an interdependent approach to relationships and are comfortable both giving and receiving support from others.

The people who will be most successful in the new career paradigm are individuals who are flexible, team oriented (rather than hierarchical), energized by change, and tolerant of ambiguity. Those who will become frustrated in the new career paradigm are individuals who are rigid in their thinking and learning styles and who have high needs for control. A commitment to continuous, lifelong learning will prevent you from becoming a professional dinosaur.[25] An intentional and purposeful commitment to taking charge of your professional life will be necessary in managing the new career paradigm.

Behaving in an ethical manner, standing by your values, and building a professional image of integrity is also very important. Major organizations conduct extensive reference checks on their applicants—not only with the references supplied by the applicants, but also with friends of such references. Behaving ethically is not only a benefit to your job application, but also can help you withstand pressures that might endanger your career. One study suggests that executives succumb to the temptation of fraud because they feel pressure to keep up with inflated expectations and changes in cultural norms, short-term versus long-term orientations, board of directors' composition, and senior leadership in the organization.[26]

## Emotional Intelligence and Career Success

Almost 40 percent of new managers fail within the first 18 months on the job.[27] What are the reasons for the failure? Newly hired managers flame out because they fail to build good relationships with peers and subordinates (82 percent of failures), are confused or uncertain about what their bosses expect (58 percent of failures), lack political skills (50 percent of failures), and are unable to achieve the two or three most important objectives of the new job (47 percent of failures).[28] You'll note that these failures are all due to a lack of human (rather than technical) skills.

In Chapter 13, we discussed the concept of emotional intelligence (EI) as an important determinant of conflict management skills. Daniel Goleman argues that emotional intelligence is a constellation of the qualities that mark a star performer at work. These attributes include self-awareness, self-control, trustworthiness, confidence, and empathy, among others. Goleman's belief

## [ Emotional Intelligence as a Selection Tool ]

L'Oréal has found emotional intelligence to be a profitable selection tool. Salespeople selected on the basis of emotional competence outsold those selected using the old method by an average of $91,370 per year. As an added bonus for the firm, these salespeople also had 63 percent less turnover during the first year than those selected in the traditional way.

SOURCE: "What's your EQ?," Time Magazine, Oct. 2, 1995, cover. Copyright TIME INC. Reprinted by permission. TIME is a registered trademark of Time Inc. All rights reserved.

are providing training in emotional intelligence competencies. American Express began sending managers through an emotional competence training program. It found that trained managers outperformed those who lacked this training. In the year after completing the course, managers trained in emotional competence grew their businesses by an average of 18.1 percent compared to 16.2 percent for those businesses whose managers were untrained.[34]

is that emotional competencies are twice as important to people's success today as raw intelligence or technical know-how. He also argues that the further up the ranks you go, the more important emotional intelligence becomes.[29] Employers, either consciously or unconsciously, look for emotional intelligence during the hiring process. In addition to traditionally recognized competencies such as communication and social skills, interns with higher levels of emotional intelligence are rated as more hireable by their host firms than those with lower levels of EI.[30] Neither gender seems to have cornered the market on EI. Both men and women who can demonstrate high levels of EI are seen as particularly gifted and may be promoted more rapidly.[31] For example, organizations such as Wrigley, CIBC, Canada Life, McDonnell Douglas, and Merrill Lynch use EI in hiring and training.[32]

Emotional intelligence is important to career success in many cultures. A recent study in Australia found that high levels of emotional intelligence are associated with job success. EI improves your ability to work with other team members and to provide high-quality customer service, and workers with high EI are more likely to take steps to develop their skills. This confirms North American studies that portray high emotional intelligence as an important attribute for the upwardly mobile worker.[33]

The good news is that emotional intelligence can be developed and does tend to improve throughout life. Some companies

# The Career Stage Model

A common way of understanding careers is viewing them as a series of stages through which individuals pass during their working lives.[35] Figure 18.2 presents the career stage model, which will form the basis for our discussion in the remainder of this chapter.[36] The career stage model shows that individuals pass through four stages in their careers: establishment, advancement, maintenance, and withdrawal. It is important to note that the age ranges shown are approximations; that is, the timing of the career transitions varies greatly among individuals.

**FIGURE 18.2**

**THE CAREER STAGE MODEL**

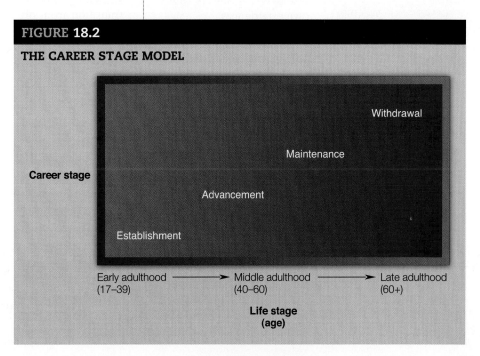

**Establishment** is the first stage of a person's career. The activities that occur in this stage centre around learning the job and fitting into the organization and occupation. **Advancement** is a high achievement–oriented stage in which people focus on increasing their competence. The **maintenance** stage finds the individual trying to maintain productivity while evaluating progress toward career goals. The **withdrawal** stage involves contemplation of retirement or possible career change.

Along the horizontal axis in Figure 18.2 are the corresponding life stages for each career stage. These life stages are based on the pioneering research on adult development conducted by Levinson and his colleagues. Levinson conducted extensive biographical interviews to trace the life stages of men and women. He interpreted his research in two books, *The Seasons of a Man's Life* and *The Seasons of a Woman's Life*.[37] Levinson's life stages are characterized by an alternating pattern of stability and transition.[38] Throughout the discussion of career stages that follows, we weave in the transitions of Levinson's life stages. Work and personal life are inseparable, and to understand a person's career experiences, we must also examine the unfolding of the person's own experiences.

You can see that adult development provides unique challenges for the individual and that there may be considerable overlap between the stages. Now let us examine each career stage in detail.

LEARNING OUTCOME **4**

# The Establishment Stage

During the establishment stage, the individual begins a career as a newcomer to the organization. This is a period of great dependence on others, as the individual is learning about the job and the organization. The establishment stage usually occurs during the beginning of the early adulthood years (ages 18 to 25). During this time, Levinson notes, an important personal life transition into adulthood occurs: the individual begins to separate from his/her parents and becomes less emotionally and financially dependent. Following this period is a fairly stable time of exploring the adult role and settling down. The transition from school to work is a part of the establishment stage. Many graduates find the transition to be a memorable experience. The following description was provided by a newly graduated individual who went to work at a large public utility:

> *We all tried to one-up each other about jobs we had just accepted . . . bragging that we had the highest salary, the best management training program, the most desirable coworkers, the most upward mobility . . . and believed we were destined to become future corporate leaders. . . . Every Friday after work we met for happy hour to visit and relate the events of the week. It is interesting to look at how the mood of those happy hours changed over the first few months . . . at first, we jockeyed for position in terms of telling stories about how great these new jobs were, or how weird our bosses were. . . . Gradually, things quieted down at happy hour. The mood went from "Wow, isn't this great?" to "What in the world have we gotten ourselves into?" There began to be general agreement that business wasn't all it was cracked up to be.[39]*

Establishment is thus a time of big transitions in both personal and work life. At work, three major tasks face the newcomer: negotiating effective psychological contracts, managing the stress of socialization, and making a transition from organizational outsider to organizational insider.

## Psychological Contracts

A **psychological contract** is an implicit agreement between the individual and the organization that specifies what each is expected to give and to receive in the relationship.[40] Individuals expect to receive salary, status, advancement opportunities, and challenging work to meet their needs. Organizations expect to receive time, energy, talents, and loyalty in order to meet their goals. Working out the psychological contract with the organization begins with entry, but the contract is modified as the individual proceeds through the career.

Psychological contracts can also form and exist between individuals.[41] During the establishment stage, newcomers form attachment relationships with many people in the organization. Working out

**establishment**

The first stage of a person's career in which the person learns the job and begins to fit into the organization and occupation.

**advancement**

The second, high achievement–oriented career stage in which people focus on increasing their competence.

**maintenance**

The third stage in an individual's career in which the individual tries to maintain productivity while evaluating progress toward career goals.

**withdrawal**

The final stage in an individual's career in which the individual contemplates retirement or possible career changes.

**psychological contract**

An implicit agreement between an individual and an organization that specifies what each is expected to give and receive in the relationship.

effective psychological contracts within each relationship is important. Newcomers need social support in many forms and from many sources. Table 18.2 shows the type of psychological contracts, in the form of social support, that newcomers may work out with key insiders in the organization.

One common newcomer concern, for example, is whose behaviour to watch for cues to appropriate behaviour. Senior colleagues can provide modelling support by displaying behaviour that the newcomer can emulate. This is only one of many types of support that newcomers need. Newcomers should contract with others to receive each of the needed types of support so that they can adjust to the new job. Organizations should help newcomers form relationships early and should encourage the psychological contracting process between newcomers and insiders. The influence of a broken psychological contract is often felt even after an employee leaves a job. Laid-off employees who feel that a psychological contract breach has occurred are not only unhappy with their former firms but may also be both more cynical and less trusting of their new employers.[42]

## [ For Boring Jobs, Apply Elsewhere ]

When Reed Hastings founded Netflix, he swore that it would never turn into a boring, bureaucratic place to work. To keep that from happening, Hastings uses a rather unorthodox management style to attract and retain key talent.

### To Attract:
Newcomers can design their compensation system, and there is no upper limit on how much Netflix will pay for the brightest minds in the industry. In fact, Netflix regularly collects in-house salary data and then resets those salaries substantially higher than current market rates. That practice has created a team of some of the best minds in the software business.

### To Retain:
Netflix has done away with formal performance reviews, offers unlimited raises to people who produce, and provides a severance package for people who don't (not a warning or a write up—they actually let people go if they do not perform). Employees are free to take as much vacation time as they like.

### Does It Work?
Netflix employees typically produce the work equivalent to that of four people in similar firms! Many employees liken the atmosphere at Netflix to that of the movie *Oceans 11* with Reed Hastings as the influential leader who drives everyone to do their best using unconventional means. Industry analysts believe that it is these competitive edges in terms of the brainpower and unique company culture that will help Netflix compete against Blockbuster and other competitors.

©AP Photo/Paul Sakuma

SOURCE: M. Conlin, "Netflix: Recruiting and Retaining the Best Talent," *BusinessWeek Online*, September 13, 2007; http://www.businessweek.com/managing/content/sep2007/ca20070913_564868.htm?chan=careers_managing+index+page_managing+your+team.

---

**TABLE 18.2** Newcomer-Insider Psychological Contracts for Social Support

| TYPE OF SUPPORT | FUNCTION OF SUPPORTIVE ATTACHMENTS | NEWCOMER CONCERN | EXAMPLES OF INSIDER RESPONSE/ACTION |
|---|---|---|---|
| Protection from stressors | Direct assistance in terms of resources, time, labour, or environmental modification | What are the major risks/threats in this environment? | *Supervisor* cues newcomer to risks/threats. |
| Informational | Provision of information necessary for managing demands | What do I need to know to get things done? | *Mentor* provides advice on informal political climate in organization. |
| Evaluative | Feedback on both personal and professional role performances | How am I doing? | *Supervisor* provides day-to-day performance feedback during first week on new job. |
| Modelling | Evidence of behavioural standards provided through modelled behaviour | Whom do I follow? | Newcomer is apprenticed to *senior colleague*. |
| Emotional | Empathy, esteem, caring, or love | Do I matter? Who cares if I'm here or not? | *Other newcomers* empathize with and encourage individual when reality shock sets in. |

SOURCE: Table from D. L. Nelson, J. C. Quick, and J. R. Joplin, "Psychological Contracting and Newcomer Socialization: An Attachment Theory Foundation," from *Journal of Social Behavior and Personality* 6 (1991): 65. Reprinted with permission.

# The Advancement Stage

The advancement stage is a period when many individuals strive for achievement. They seek greater responsibility and authority and strive for upward mobility. Usually around age 30, an important life transition occurs.[43] Individuals reassess their goals and feel the need to make changes in their career dreams. The transition at age 30 is followed by a period of stability during which the individual tries to find a role in adult society and wants to succeed in a career. During this stage, several issues are important: exploring career paths, finding a mentor, working out dual-career partnerships, and managing conflicts between work and personal life.

## Career Paths and Career Ladders

**Career paths** are sequences of job experiences along which employees move during their careers.[44] At the advancement stage, individuals examine their career dreams and the paths they must follow to achieve those dreams. For example, suppose a person's dream is to become a top executive in the pharmaceutical industry. She majors in chemistry in undergraduate school and takes a job with a nationally recognized firm.

After she has adjusted to her job as a quality control chemist, she reevaluates her plan and decides that further education is necessary. She plans to pursue an MBA degree part-time, hoping to gain expertise in management. From there, she hopes to be promoted to a supervisory position within her current firm. If this does not occur within five years, she will consider moving to a different pharmaceutical company. An alternate route would be to try to transfer to a sales position, from which she might advance into management.

A **career ladder** is a structured series of job positions through which an individual progresses in an organization. For example, a person may go through a series of alternating line and staff supervisory assignments to advance toward upper management. Supervisors in customer service might be assigned next to the training staff and then rotate back as line supervisors in network services to gain experience in different departments.

Some companies use the traditional concept of career ladders to help employees advance in their careers. Other organizations take a more contemporary approach to career advancement. Sony encourages creativity from its engineers by using nontraditional career paths. At Sony, individuals have the freedom to move on to interesting and challenging job assignments without notifying their supervisors. If they join a new project team, their current boss is expected to let them move on. This self-promotion philosophy at Sony is seen as a key to high levels of innovation and creative new product designs.

There has been heightened interest in international assignments by multinational corporations in response to globalization and global staffing issues. One challenge in this regard has been that most expatriate assignments are not successful and organizations have been facing the challenge of properly training and preparing individuals for such assignments. Alternative international work assignments (e.g., commuter work assignments, virtual assignments, short-term assignments, etc.) can be used to help individuals gain international work experience in preparation for higher levels in the organization.[45]

Another approach used by some companies to develop skills is the idea of a "career lattice"—an approach to building competencies by moving laterally through different departments in the organization or by moving through different projects. Top management support for the career lattice is essential, because in traditional terms an employee who has made several lateral moves might not be viewed with favour. However, the career lattice approach is an effective way to develop an array of skills to ensure your employability.[46]

The career paths of many women have moved from working in large organizations to starting their own businesses. Currently, there are about one million women-owned businesses in Canada. Women are at the forefront of two primary drivers of current small business growth: the rise in one-person operations and "seniorpreneurs" (small business owners over the age of 55).[47] The main reasons for this exodus to entrepreneurship are to seek additional challenge and self-fulfillment and to have more self-determination and freedom.[48]

Exploring career paths is one important activity in advancement. Another crucial activity during advancement is finding a mentor.

## Finding a Mentor

A **mentor** is an individual who provides guidance, coaching, counselling, and friendship to a protégé. Mentors are important to career success because they perform both career and psychosocial functions.[49]

**career path**
A sequence of job experiences that an employee moves along during his or her career.

**career ladder**
A structured series of job positions through which an individual progresses in an organization.

**mentor**
An individual who provides guidance, coaching, counselling, and friendship to a protégé.

The career functions provided by a mentor include sponsorship, facilitating exposure and visibility, coaching, and protection. Sponsorship means actively helping the individual get job experiences and promotions. Facilitating exposure and visibility means providing opportunities for the protégé to develop relationships with key figures in the organization in order to advance. Coaching involves providing advice in both career and job performance. Protection is provided by shielding the protégé from potentially damaging experiences. A more positive strategy is to focus on career functions through career coaching. One study found that the amount of career coaching received by protégés was related to more promotions, and higher salaries four years later.[50] Career functions are particularly important to the protégé's future success.

©Alex Slobodkin/iStockPhoto

> **While it may be tempting to go after the "top dog" as your mentor, personality compatibility is also an important factor in the success or failure of a mentoring relationship.**

The mentor also performs psychosocial functions. Role modelling occurs when the mentor displays behaviour for the protégé to emulate. This facilitates social learning. Acceptance and confirmation is important to both the mentor and protégé. When the protégé feels accepted by the mentor, it fosters a sense of pride. Likewise, positive regard and appreciation from the junior colleague provide a sense of satisfaction for the mentor. Counselling by a mentor helps the protégé explore personal issues that arise and require assistance. Friendship is another psychosocial function that benefits both mentor and protégé alike.

In effective mentoring relationships, there is regular contact between mentor and protégé that has clearly specified purposes. Mentoring should be consistent with the organization's goals and culture. Both mentors and protégés alike should be trained in ways to manage the relationship. Mentors should be held accountable and rewarded for their role. Mentors should be perceived

(accurately) by protégés as having considerable influence within the organization.[51] While it may be tempting to go after the "top dog" as your mentor, personality compatibility is also an important factor in the success or failure of a mentoring relationship. Mentors who are similar to their protégés in terms of personality traits such as extraversion, and whose expectations are largely met by the relationship, are more likely to show interest in continuing the arrangement.[52] RBC, for example, has a mentoring program called RBC Diversity Dialogues. It is a reciprocal mentoring program currently involving 180 employees. The program connects two people with different professional experiences and backgrounds to learn about leadership and diversity from each other.[53]

Mentoring programs are also effective ways of addressing the challenge of workforce diversity. The mentoring process, however, presents unique problems, including the availability of mentors, issues of language and acculturation, and cultural sensitivity. Negative stereotypes can limit racialized members' access to mentoring relationships and the benefits associated with mentoring.[54] To address this problem, companies can facilitate access to mentors in organizations. Informal mentoring programs identify pools of mentors and protégés, provide training in the development of effective mentoring and diversity issues, and then provide informal opportunities for the development of mentoring relationships.

Network groups are another avenue for mentoring. Network groups help members identify with those few others who are like them within an organization, build relationships with them, and build social support. Network groups enhance the chance that minorities will find mentors.[55] IBM Canada, for example, has an Aboriginal Peoples Network Group, Black IBM Network Group, Blue Q (Gay, Lesbian, Bisexual, and Transgender employees), East Asian Diversity Network Group, Latin American Network Group, South Asian Network Group, Men's Association, and a People Enablement Network Group focused on Persons with Disabilities.[56]

Networks also increase the likelihood that individuals have more than one mentor. Individuals with multiple mentors, such as those gained from mentoring networks, have even greater career success than those with only one mentor.[57]

Some companies have formal mentoring programs. PricewaterhouseCoopers (PwC) uses the mentoring model to help its interns. Each intern is assigned both a peer mentor to help with day-to-day questions and an experienced mentor to help with larger issues such as career path development. As an international firm,

PwC also employs similar methods overseas. In PwC's Czech Republic operations, a team of two mentors—one of whom is called a "counsellor"—fills the same guidance role as the two mentors generally fill for its other employees.[58]

Mentoring has had a strong impact in shaping the identities of the major accounting firms. In one study, every partner who was interviewed reported having at least one mentor who played a critical role in his/her attainment of the partnership and beyond. Protégés' identities are shaped through mentoring, and their work goals, language, and even lifestyles reflect the imperatives of the firm.[59] Protégés are schooled on partners' "hot buttons" (what not to talk about), what to wear, to "tuck in the tie," and not to cut the grass without wearing a shirt.

Although some companies have formal mentoring programs, junior employees more often are left to negotiate their own mentoring relationships. The barriers to finding a mentor include lack of access to mentors, fear of initiating a mentoring relationship, and fear that supervisors or coworkers might not approve of the mentoring relationship. Individuals may also be afraid to initiate a mentoring relationship because it might be misconstrued as a sexual advance by the potential mentor or others. This is a fear of potential mentors as well. Some are unwilling to develop a relationship because of their own or because of the protégé's gender. Women report more of these barriers than men, and individuals who lack previous experience report more barriers to finding a mentor.[60]

Organizations can encourage junior workers to approach mentors by providing opportunities for them to interact with senior colleagues. The immediate supervisor is not often the best mentor for an individual, so exposure to other senior workers is important. Seminars, multilevel teams, and social events can serve as vehicles for bringing together potential mentors and protégés.

Mentoring relationships go through a series of phases: initiation, cultivation, separation, and redefinition. There is no fixed time length for each phase, because each relationship is unique. In the initiation phase, the mentoring relationship begins to take on significance for both the mentor and the protégé. In the cultivation phase, the relationship becomes more meaningful, and the protégé shows rapid progress because of the career and psychosocial support provided by the mentor. Protégés influence mentors as well.

In the separation phase, the protégé feels the need to assert independence and work more autonomously. Separation can be voluntary, or it can result from an involuntary change (the protégé or mentor may be promoted or transferred). The separation phase can be difficult if it is resisted, either by the mentor (who is reluctant to let go of the relationship) or by the protégé (who resents the mentor's withdrawal of support).

The redefinition phase occurs if separation has been successful. In this phase, the relationship takes on a new identity as both parties consider themselves colleagues or friends. The mentor feels pride in the protégé, and the protégé develops a deeper appreciation for the support from the mentor.

Why are mentors so important? Aside from the support they provide, the research shows that mentors are important to the protégé's future success. For example, studies have demonstrated that individuals with mentors have higher promotion rates and higher incomes than individuals who do not have mentors.[61] Professionals who have mentors earn between $5,600 and $22,000 more per year than those who do not.[62] Individuals with mentors also are better decision makers.[63] It is not just the presence of the mentor that yields these benefits. The quality of the relationship is most important.[64]

## Dual-Career Partnerships

During the advancement stage, many individuals face another transition: they settle into a relationship with a life partner. This lifestyle transition requires adjustment in many respects: learning to live with another person, being concerned with someone else, dealing with an extended family, and many other demands. The partnership can be particularly stressful if both members are career oriented.

The two-career lifestyle has increased in recent years due in part to the need for two incomes to maintain a preferred standard of living. **Dual-career partnerships** are relationships in which both people have important career roles. This type of partnership can be mutually beneficial, but it can also be stressful. Often these stresses centre around lingering stereotypes that providing income is a man's responsibility and taking care of the home is the woman's domain. Among married couples, working women's satisfaction with the marriage is affected by how much the husband contributes with childcare. Men who adhere to traditional gender beliefs may be threatened if the wife's income exceeds their own. Beliefs about who should do what in the partnership complicate the dual-career issue.[65]

One stressor in a dual-career partnership is time pressure. When both partners work outside the home, there may be a time crunch fitting in work, family, and leisure time. Another potential problem is jealousy. When one partner's career blooms before the other's, the partner

**dual-career partnership**

A relationship in which both people have important career roles.

may feel threatened.[66] Another issue to work out is whose career takes precedence. For example, what happens if one partner is transferred to another city? Must the other partner make a move that might threaten his/her own career in order to be with the individual who was transferred? Who, if anyone, will stay home and take care of a new baby?

Working out a dual-career partnership takes careful planning and consistent communication between the partners. Each partner must serve as a source of social support for the other. Couples can also turn to other family members, friends, and professionals for support if the need arises.

## Work–Home Conflicts

An issue related to dual-career partnerships that is faced throughout the career cycle, but often first encountered in the advancement phase, is the conflicts that occur between work and personal life. Experiencing a great deal of work–home conflict negatively affects an individual's overall quality of life. Work–home conflicts can lead to emotional exhaustion. Dealing with customer complaints all day, failed sales calls, and missed deadlines can magnify negative events at home, and vice versa.[67] Responsibilities at home can clash with responsibilities at work, and these conflicts must be planned for. For example, suppose a child gets sick at school. Who will pick up the child and stay home with him/her? Couples must work together to resolve these conflicts. Even at Eli Lilly and Co., only 36 percent of workers said it is possible to get ahead in their careers and still devote sufficient time to family. This is surprising, because Lilly has a reputation as one of the world's most family-friendly workplaces.[68]

>> People in the advancement stage are also dealing with developmental and life-stage changes. The midlife transition, which takes place approximately between ages 40 and 45, is often a time of crisis. Levinson points out three major changes that contribute to the midlife transition:

> People realize that their lives are half over and that they are mortal.
> Age forty is considered by people in their twenties and thirties to be "over the hill" and not part of the youthful culture.
> People reassess their dreams and evaluate how close they have come to achieving their dreams.

Midlife transition can add a layer of stress to the challenges employees face during the advancement stage.

Work–home conflicts are particular problems for working women.[69] Women have been quicker to share the provider role than men have been to share responsibilities at home.[70] When working women experience work–home conflict, their performance declines, and they suffer more strain.

Work–home conflict is a broad topic. It can be narrowed further into work–family conflict, in which work interferes with family, versus family–work conflict, in which family or home life interferes with work.[71] Cultural differences arise in these types of conflicts. One study showed that while North Americans experience more family–work conflict, Chinese experience more work–family conflict.[72] For example, women in management positions in China were very positive about future advancements and carried a strong belief in their ability to succeed. This, in turn, caused them to reevaluate their personal and professional identities. Such an identity transformation is marked by happiness associated with career advancement, even though many women foresaw emotional costs with such career advancement. This study indicated that female Chinese managers experience work–family conflict in part because the Chinese culture emphasizes close social ties and *guanxi*.[73]

©Corbis/Jupiter Images

**Ways to Manage Work–Home Conflict** To help individuals deal with work–home conflict, companies can offer **flexible work schedules**.[74] Programs such as flextime, which we discussed in Chapter 14, give employees freedom to take care of personal concerns while still getting their work done. Organization-sponsored childcare is another way to help. Organizations with on-site daycare centres include Johnson & Johnson, University of Toronto, and Campbell Soup. Syscon Justice Systems, a software firm located in Richmond, B.C., has an onsite daycare centre. According to Syscon's CEO, Floyd Sully, "[childcare] is not a women's issue, it's a business issue. . . . It's a parental issue. . . . The fact that women have to go out and work puts it into stark relief."[75] While large organizations may offer corporate day care, small ones can also assist their workers by providing referral services for locating the type of childcare the workers need. For smaller organizations, this can be a cost-effective alternative.[76] At the very least, organizations need to be sensitive to work–home conflicts and handle them on a case-by-case basis with flexibility and concern.

A program of increasing interest that organizations can provide is **eldercare**. Often workers find themselves part of the sandwich generation as they are expected to care for both their children and their elderly parents. Approximately one million Canadians care for both their children and their parents.[77] This extremely stressful role is reported more often by women than men.[78] The impact of caring for an aging loved one is often underestimated. But 17 percent of those who provide care eventually quit their jobs due to time constraints, and another 15 percent cut back their work hours for the same reason.[79] Caring for an elderly relative at home can create severe work–home conflicts for employees and also takes a toll on the employee's own well-being and performance at work. This is especially the case if the organization is not one that provides a supportive climate for discussion of eldercare issues.[80] Harvard University has taken steps to help its faculty and staff deal with eldercare issues by contracting with Parents In A Pinch, a firm that specializes in nanny services and now also offers eldercare.[81] Catholic Children's Aid Society of Greater Toronto offers compassionate top-up leave payments (to 70 percent for 8 weeks) for employees taking time off to care for a loved one.[82]

John Beatrice is one of a handful of men making work fit their family, rather than trying to fit family around career. John remembers his father working most of the night so he could be at John's athletic events during the day, and John wants the same for his family. So while job sharing, flexible scheduling, and telecommuting have traditionally been viewed as meeting the needs of working mothers, John and other men are increasingly taking advantage of such opportunities. In John's case, flexible work hours at Ernst & Young allow him to spend part of his mornings and afternoons coaching a high school hockey team. In John's assessment, flexible work hours actually led him to work more hours than he would otherwise, and he's happier about doing it. Not surprisingly, John's employer also benefits from the arrangement; after 19 years, John is more loyal than ever and still loves what he does.[83]

Alternative work arrangements such as flextime, compressed workweeks, work-at-home arrangements, part-time hours, job sharing, and leave options can help employees manage work–home conflicts. Managers must not let their biases get in the way of these benefits. Top managers may be less willing to grant alternative work arrangements to men than to women, to supervisors than to subordinates, and to employees caring for elderly parents rather than children. It is important that family-friendly policies be applied fairly.[84]

# The Maintenance Stage

*Maintenance* may be a misnomer for this career stage, because some people continue to grow in their careers, although the growth is usually not at the rate it was earlier. A career crisis at midlife may accompany the midlife transition. A senior product manager at Borden found himself in such a crisis and described it this way: "When I was in college, I had thought in terms of being president of a company. . . . But at Borden I felt used and cornered. Most of the guys in the next two rungs above me had either an MBA or fifteen to twenty years of experience in the food business. My long-term plans stalled."[85]

Some individuals who reach a career crisis are burned out, and a month's vacation will help, according to Carolyn Smith Paschal, who owns an executive search firm. She recommends that organizations give employees in this stage sabbaticals instead of bonuses to help rejuvenate them.

Some individuals reach the maintenance stage with a sense of achievement and contentment, feeling no need to strive for further upward mobility. Whether the maintenance stage is a time of crisis or contentment, however, there are two issues to grapple with: sustaining performance and becoming a mentor.

**flexible work schedule**
A work schedule that allows employees discretion in order to accommodate personal concerns.

**eldercare**
Assistance in caring for elderly parents and/or other elderly relatives.

## Sustaining Performance

Remaining productive is a key concern for individuals in the maintenance stage. This becomes challenging when you reach a **career plateau**, a point where the probability of moving further up the hierarchy is low. Some people handle career plateauing fairly well, but others may become frustrated, bored, and dissatisfied with their jobs.

To keep employees productive, organizations can provide challenges and opportunities for learning. Lateral moves are one option. Another option is to involve the employee in project teams that provide new tasks and skill development. The key is to keep the work stimulating and involving. Individuals at this stage also need continued affirmation of their value to the organization. They need to know that their contributions are significant and appreciated.[86]

## Becoming a Mentor

During maintenance, individuals can make a contribution by sharing their wealth of knowledge and experience with others. Opportunities to be mentors to new employees can keep senior workers motivated and involved in the organization. It is important for organizations to reward mentors for the time and energy they expend. Some employees adapt naturally to the mentor role, but others may need training on how to coach and counsel junior workers.

Maintenance is a time of transition, like all career stages. It can be managed by individuals who know what to expect and plan to remain productive, as well as by organizations that focus on maximizing employee involvement in work. According to Levinson, during the latter part of the maintenance stage, another life transition occurs. The age-50 transition is another time of reevaluating the dream and working further on the issues raised in the midlife transition. Following the age-50 transition is a fairly stable period. During this time, individuals begin to plan seriously for withdrawing from their careers.

> " It is important for organizations to reward mentors for the time and energy they expend.

## FOUR KEYS TO A SUCCESSFUL MENTORING PROGRAM

>>> Kathy Kram notes that there are four keys to the success of a formal mentoring program:

> Participation should be voluntary. No one should be forced to enter a mentoring relationship, and careful matching of mentors and protégés is important.
> Support from top executives is needed to convey the intent of the program and its role in career development.
> Training should be provided to mentors so they understand the functions of the relationship.
> A graceful exit should be provided for mismatches or for people in mentoring relationships that have fulfilled their purpose.[87]

LEARNING OUTCOME 7

## The Withdrawal Stage

The withdrawal stage usually occurs later in life and signals that a long period of continuous employment will soon come to a close. Older workers may face discrimination and stereotyping. They may be viewed by others as less productive, more resistant to change, and less motivated. However, older workers are one of the most undervalued groups in the workforce. They can provide continuity in the midst of change and can serve as mentors and role models to younger generations of employees.

Discrimination against older workers is prohibited. Organizations must create a culture that values older workers' contributions. With their level of experience, strong work ethic, and loyalty, these workers have much to contribute. In fact, older workers have lower rates of tardiness and absenteeism, are more safety conscious, and are more satisfied with their jobs than are younger workers.[88]

## Planning for Change

The decision to retire is an individual one, but the need for planning is universal. A retired sales executive from Boise Cascade said that the best advice is to "plan no

**career plateau**

A point in an individual's career in which the probability of moving further up the hierarchy is low.

unplanned retirement."[89] This means carefully planning not only the transition but also the activities an individual will be involved in once the transition is made. All options should be open for consideration. One recent trend is the need for temporary top-level executives. Some companies are hiring senior managers from the outside on a temporary basis. The qualities of a good temporary executive include substantial high-level management experience, financial security that allows the executive to choose only assignments that really interest him/her, and a willingness to relocate.[90] Some individuals at the withdrawal stage find this an attractive option.

Planning for retirement should include not only financial planning but also a plan for psychologically withdrawing from work. The pursuit of hobbies and travel, volunteer work, or more time with extended family can all be part of the plan. The key is to plan early and carefully, as well as to anticipate the transition with a positive attitude and a full slate of desirable activities.

## Retirement

There are several retirement trends right now, ranging from early retirement to phased retirement to never retiring. Some adults are choosing a combination of these options, leaving their first career for some time off before reentering the workforce either part-time or full-time doing something they enjoy. For more and more North Americans, the idea of a retirement spent sitting beside a swimming pool sounds—for lack of a better word—boring. Factors that influence the decision of when to retire include company policy, financial considerations, family support or pressure, health, and opportunities for other productive activities.[91]

During the withdrawal stage, the individual faces a major life transition that Levinson refers to as the late adulthood transition (ages 60 to 65). A person's own mortality becomes a major concern and the loss of family members

and friends becomes more frequent. The person works to achieve a sense of integrity in life—that is, the person works to find the encompassing meaning and value in life.

Retirement need not be a complete cessation of work. Many alternative work arrangements can be considered, and many companies offer flexibility in these options. **Phased retirement** is a popular option for retirement-age workers who want to gradually reduce their hours and/or responsibilities. There are many forms of phased retirement, including reduced workdays or workweeks, job sharing, and consulting and mentoring arrangements. Many organizations cannot afford the loss of large numbers of experienced employees at once. This means there is an increase in **bridge employment**, which is employment that takes place after a person retires from a full-time position but before the person's permanent withdrawal from the workforce. Bridge employment is related to retirement satisfaction and overall life satisfaction.[92]

Some companies are helping employees transition to retirement in innovative ways. Retired individuals can continue their affiliation with the organization by serving as mentors to employees who are embarking on retirement planning or other career transitions. This helps diminish the fear of loss some people have about retirement, because the retiree has an option to serve as a mentor or consultant to the organization.

**phased retirement**
An arrangement that allows employees to reduce their hours and/or responsibilities in order to ease into retirement.

**bridge employment**
Employment that takes place after a person retires from a full-time position but before the person's permanent withdrawal from the workforce.

©Jupiter Images

Some retirement-agers may go through a second midlife crisis. Vickie Ianucelli, for example, bought a condo on a Mexican beach, celebrated a birthday in Paris, bought herself a 9.5-karat ring, and got plastic surgery. And, it's her second midlife crisis. She's a psychologist who is also a 60-plus grandmother of two.[93]

Lawrence Livermore National Labs (LLNL) employs some of the best research minds in the world. And when these great minds retire from full-time work, they have numerous opportunities to continue contributing. LLNL's retiree program website lists a wide variety of requests, ranging from guiding tours and making phone calls to providing guidance on current research and helping researchers make contact with other researchers.[94] Programs like this one help LLNL avoid the typical knowledge drain that takes place when seasoned veteran employees retire.

## LEARNING OUTCOME 8

# Career Anchors

Much of an individual's self-concept rests upon a career. Over the course of the career, career anchors are developed. **Career anchors** are self-perceived talents, motives, and values that guide an individual's career decisions.[95] Edgar Schein developed the concept of career anchors based on a 12-year study of MBA graduates from the Massachusetts Institute of Technology (MIT). Schein found great diversity in the graduates' career histories but great similarities in the way they explained the career decisions they had made.[96] From

## FIVE GOOD WEBSITES FOR MANAGING YOUR CAREER

> http://www.workopolis.com—jobs and career resources
> http://www.vault.com—career intelligence
> http://www.canadastop100.com/index.html— Canada's top 100 employers
> http://www.shatterbox.com—"Stories of innovative young people who love what they do."
> http://talentegg.ca—recent graduates

extensive interviews with the graduates, Schein developed five career anchors.

Career anchors emerge over time and may be modified by work or life experiences.[97] The importance of knowing your career anchor is that it can help you find a match between you and an organization. For example, individuals with creativity as an anchor may find themselves stifled in bureaucratic organizations. Textbook sales may not be the place for an individual with a security anchor because of the frequent travel and seasonal nature of the business.

## LEARNING OUTCOME 9

In the last section of the book, the focus will move from the theoretical to the applied. There are some key individual, team and organizational skills required to manage your career well.

First you need to develop a good understanding of who you are, what you value, what you do well, and what you need to improve. In addition to the material in Part 2 of the book, there are many tools to help you. The most popular is Richard N. Bolles' *What Color is My*

## FIVE CAREER ANCHORS

**1** *Technical/functional competence.* Individuals who hold this career anchor want to specialize in a given functional area (for example, finance or marketing) and become competent. The idea of general management does not interest them.

**2** *Managerial competence.* Adapting this career anchor means individuals want general management responsibility. They want to see their efforts have an impact on organizational effectiveness.

**3** *Autonomy and independence.* Freedom is the key to this career anchor, and often these individuals are uncomfortable working in large organizations. Autonomous careers such as writer, professor, or consultant attract these individuals.

**4** *Creativity.* Individuals holding this career anchor feel a strong need to create something. They are often entrepreneurs.

**5** *Security/stability.* Long-term career stability, whether in a single organization or in a single geographic area, fits people with this career anchor. Some government jobs provide this type of security.

©Jupiter Images

# By The Numbers

**17%** of workers responsible for elder-care in their families quit their jobs

**1 million** women-owned businesses in Canada

**$91,370** more in average sales for L'Oréal employees with high emotional competence than for those without

**5** career anchors in Schein's theory

**6** personalities in Holland's typology

©Kun Jiang/iStockPhoto

*Parachute? 2010: A Practical Manual for Job-Hunters and Career-Changers.* It was originally self-published in 1970, is updated annually and now sells 20,000 copies monthly! Another valuable resource is Daniel Pink's *The Adventures of Johnny Bunko—The Last Career Guide You'll Ever Need*, a manga-style business book that has been translated into more than 10 languages and received many awards.

As much of your work will be done in teams, it is vital that you understand team dynamics and team decision making, discussed in Chapters 9 and 10. In addition, there are many books on teams. One that has become popular for its storytelling style, coupled with its rich insights, is Patrick M. Lencioni's *The Five Dysfunctions of a Team: A Leadership Fable.* He identifies five significant and typical problems in teams and then suggests way to address them.

In Chapter 16, you learned about organizational culture and its impact on shaping behaviour in organizations. It is vitally important that you understand the nuances of organizational life so that you don't make career-limiting errors or engage in career-killer behaviours. To address career-limiting or -killing behaviour, you have to be brutally honest with yourself to assess, for example, if you are self-absorbed, needy, boring, mechanical, judgmental, insensitive, or overly self-promoting.[98]

As you prepare for the world of work, take time for self-assessment, work on your team skills, and research in detail the organizations you are interested in and then determine the extent to which you fit. Remember, your career is a journey and there will be many good times if you work hard at managing your career. Throughout your career, be sure to have regular discussions with your mentor and/or your boss about your career path and your progress on the path.[99]

# Visit **icanorgb.com** to find the resources you need today!

*Located at the back of the textbook are rip-out Chapter Review Cards. Make sure you also go online to check out other tools that ORGB offers to help you successfully pass your course.*

- Interactive Quizzing
- Key Term Flashcards
- PowerPoint Slides
- Audio Chapter Summaries
- Cases and Exercises
- Interactive Games
- Self-Assessments
- "On the Job" and "Bizflix" Videos

# Notes

## Chapter 1

1. H. Schwartz, "The Clockwork or the Snakepit: An Essay on the Meaning of Teaching Organizational Behavior," *Organizational Behavior Teaching Review* 11, No. 2 (1987): 19–26.

2. M. Matcho, "Idea Fest," *Fast Company 66* (January 2003): 95–105, http://www.fastcompany.com/online/66/ideafest.html.

3. H. G. Barkem, J. A. C. Baum, and E. A. Mannix, "Management Challenges in a New Time," *Academy of Management Journal* 45 (2002): 916–930.

4. K. Lewin, "Field Theory in Social Science," selected theoretical papers (edited by Dorin Cartwright) (New York: Harper, 1951).

5. N. Schmitt, ed., Industrial/Organizational Section in *Encyclopedia of Psychology* (Washington, D.C.: American Psychological Association, and New York: Oxford University Press, 2000).

6. R. M. Yerkes, "The Relation of Psychology to Military Activities," *Mental Hygiene* 1 (1917): 371–376.

7. Merton, R. (1957). The Role-Set: Problems in Sociological Theory, *British Journal of Sociology*, 8, 106–120.

8. N. Gross, W. Mason, and A. McEachen, *Explorations in Role Analysis: Studies of the School Superintendency Role* (New York: Wiley, 1958).

9. J. S. Adams, A. Tashchian, and T. H. Stone, "Codes of Ethics as Signals for Ethical Behavior," *Journal of Business Ethics* 29 (2001): 199–211.

10. F. W. Taylor, *The Principles of Scientific Management* (New York: Norton, 1911).

11. E. A. Locke and G. P. Latham, *A Theory of Goal Setting and Task Performance* (Englewood Cliffs, N.J.: Prentice-Hall, 1990).

12. A. L. Wilkins and W. G. Ouchi, "Efficient Cultures: Exploring the Relationship between Culture and Organizational Performance," *Administrative Science Quarterly* 28 (1983): 468–481.

13. M. F. R. Kets de Vries and D. Miller, "Personality, Culture, and Organization," *Academy of Management Review* 11 (1986): 266–279.

14. H. Schwartz, *Narcissistic Process and Corporate Decay: The Theory of the Organizational Ideal* (New York: NYU Press, 1990).

15. J. G. March and H. A. Simon, *Organizations* (New York: Wiley, 1958).

16. H. B. Elkind, *Preventive Management: Mental Hygiene in Industry* (New York: B. C. Forbes, 1931).

17. J. C. Quick, "Occupational Health Psychology: Historical Roots and Future Directions," *Health Psychology* 18 (1999).

18. V. Graham, Hershey Canada Inc. "Fit For Life" Worksite Wellness Program, presented at Canadian Labour and Business Centre (CLBC) Workplace Health Works, November 18–19, 2003.

19. D. R. Ilgen, "Health Issues at Work," *American Psychologist* 45 (1990): 273–283.

20. B. M. Staw, L. E. Sandelands, and J. E. Dutton, "Threat-Rigidity Effects in Organizational Behavior: A Multilevel Analysis," *Administrative Science Quarterly* 26 (1981): 501–524.

21. D. Kirkpatrick, "The Net Makes It All Easier–Including Exporting U.S. Jobs," *Fortune* (May 26, 2003): 146.

22. E. V. Brown, Vice President of Global Business Development, Alberto Culver, Inc., "Commencement Address—College of Business Administration, the University of Texas at Arlington" (December 2003).

23. T. Reay, K. Golden-Biddle, and K. Germann, "Legitimizing a New Role: Small Wins and Microprocesses of Change," *Academy of Management Journal* 49 (2006): 977–998.

24. R. L. A. Sterba, "The Organization and Management of the Temple Corporations in Ancient Mesopotamia," *Academy of Management Review* 1 (1976): 16–26; S. P. Dorsey, *Early English Churches in America* (New York: Oxford University Press, 1952).

25. Sir I. Moncreiffe of That Ilk, *The Highland Clans: The Dynastic Origins, Chiefs, and Background of the Clans and of Some Other Families Connected to Highland History*, rev. ed. (New York: C. N. Potter, 1982).

26. D. Shambaugh, "The Soldier and the State in China: The Political Work System in the People's Liberation Army," *Chinese Quarterly* 127 (1991): 527–568.

27. L. L'Abate, ed., *Handbook of Developmental Family Psychology and Psychopathology* (New York: Wiley, 1993).

28. J. A. Hostetler, *Communitarian Societies* (New York: Holt, Rinehart & Winston, 1974).

29. J. M. Lewis, "The Family System and Physical Illness," in *No Single Thread: Psychological Health in Family Systems* (New York: Brunner/Mazel, 1976).

30. D. Katz and R. L. Kahn, *The Social Psychology of Organizations*, 2nd ed. (New York: John Wiley, 1978; H. J. Leavitt, "Applied Organizational Change in Industry: Structural, Technological, and Humanistic Approaches," in J. G. March, ed., *Handbook of Organizations* (Chicago: Rand McNally, 1965), 1144–1170.

31. J. D. Thompson, *Organizations in Action* (New York: McGraw-Hill, 1967).

32. F. J. Roethlisberger and W. J. Dickson, *Management and the Worker* (Cambridge, Mass.: Harvard University Press, 1939).

33. W. L. French and C. H. Bell, *Organization Development*, 4th ed. (Englewood Cliffs, N.J.: Prentice-Hall, 1990).

34. S. G. Barsade and D. E. Gibson, "Why Does Affect Matter in Organizations?," *Academy of Management Perspectives*, 21 (2007): 36–59.

35. J. P. Kotter, "Managing External Dependence," *Academy of Management Review* 4 (1979): 87–92.

36. H. K. Steensma and D. G. Corley, "Organizational Context as a Moderator of Theories on Firm Boundaries for Technology Sourcing," *Academy of Management Journal* 44 (2001): 271–291.

37. "Canada GDP Growth Rate," http://www.tradingeconomics.com/Economics/GDP-Growth.aspx?Symbol=CAD.

38. T. B. Lawrence and V. Corwin, "Being There: The Acceptance and Marginalization of Part-Time Professional Employees," *Journal of Organizational Behavior* 24 (2003): 923–943.

39. M. K. Gowing, J. D. Kraft, and J. C. Quick, *The New Organizational Reality: Downsizing, Restructuring and Revitalization* (Washington, D.C.: American Psychological Association, 1998); T. Tang and R. M. Fuller, "Corporate Downsizing: What Managers Can Do to Lessen the Negative Effects of Layoffs," *SAM Advanced Management Journal* 60 (1995): 12–15, 31.

40. L. R. Offermann and M. K. Gowing, "Organizations of the Future," *American Psychologist* 45 (1990): 95–108.

41. J. Chatman, J. Polzer, S. Barsade, and M. Neale, "Being Different Yet Feeling Similar: The Influence of Demographic Composition and Organizational Culture on Work Processes and Outcomes," *Administrative Science Quarterly* 43 (1998): 749–780.

42. L. E. Thurow, *Head to Head: The Coming Economic Battle among Japan, Europe, and America* (New York: William Morrow, 1992).

43. J. E. Patterson, *Acquiring the Future: America's Survival and Success in the Global Economy* (Homewood, Ill.: Dow Jones-Irwin, 1990); H. B. Stewart, *Recollecting the Future: A View of Business, Technology, and Innovation in the Next 30 Years* (Homewood, Ill.: Dow Jones-Irwin, 1989).

44. D. Ciampa, *Total Quality* (Reading, Mass.: Addison-Wesley, 1992).

45. Aguntuk, "Toyota President Akio Toyoda Tearful After Congressional Hearing, Vows to Regain Customer Trust," February 25, http://thetechjournal.com/off-topic/toyota-president-akio-toyoda-tearful-after-congressional-hearing-vows-to-regain-customer-trust.xhtml.

46. T. J. Douglas and W. Q. Judge, Jr., "Total Quality Management Implementation and Competitive Advantage: The Role of Structural Control and Exploration," *Academy of Management Journal* 44 (2001): 158–169.

47. American Management Association, *Blueprints for Service Quality: The Federal Express Approach* (New York: American Management Association, 1991); P. R. Thomas, L. J. Gallace, and K. R. Martin, *Quality Alone Is Not Enough* (New York: American Management Association, 1992).

48. "2009 Canada Awards for Excellence Recipients", http://www.nqi.ca/galadinner2009/2009CAEVideos.aspx.

49. J. de Mast, "A Methodological Comparison of Three Strategies for Quality Improvement," *International Journal of Quality & Reliability Management* 21 (2004): 198–213.

50. M. Barney, "Motorola's Second Generation," *Six Sigma Forum Magazine* 1(3) (May 2002): 13.

51. J. A. Edosomwan, "Six Commandments to Empower Employees for Quality Improvement," *Industrial Engineering* 24 (1992): 14–15.

52. "About Us", NQI, http://www.nqi.ca/aboutus/info/mission.aspx.

53. See also the five articles in the Special Research Forum on Teaching Effectiveness in the Organizational Sciences, *The Academy of Management Journal* 40 (1997): 1265–1398.

54. L. Proserpio and D. A. Gioia, "Teaching the Virtual Generation," *Academy of Management Learning & Education* 6 (2007): 69–80.

55. R. M. Steers, L. W. Porter, and G. A. Bigley, *Motivation and Leadership at Work* (New York: McGraw-Hill, 1996).

56. H. Levinson, *Executive Stress* (New York: New American Library, 1975).

57. "Understanding Essential Skills" (2009) http://www.hrsdc.gc.ca/eng/workplaceskills/essential_skills/general/understanding_es.shtml.

58. C. Argyris and D. A. Schon, *Organizational Learning: A Theory of Action Perspective* (Reading, Mass.: Addison-Wesley, 1978).

59. A. Y. Kolb and D. A. Kolb, "Learning Styles and Learning Spaces: Enhancing Experiential Learning in Higher Education, *Academy of Management Learning & Education* 4 (2005): 193–212.

60. B. Breen, "The Business of Design," *Fast Company,* (April 1, 2005) http://www.fastcompany.com/magazine/93/design.html.

61. Ibid.

62. "The Academic: Roger Martin," *BusinessWeek* (August 1, 2005), http://www.businessweek.com/magazine/content/05_31/b3945417.htm.

63. C. Atkinson, "Software Firm Provides Time for 'Personal Pet Projects,'" *Report on Business* (June 2, 2010) http://www.theglobeandmail.com/report-on-business/your-business/grow/new-product-development/fusenet-creates-friday-labs-to-spur-enterprising-staffers/article1589169/?cmpid=rss1.

# Chapter 2

1. M. A. Hitt, R. E. Hoskisson, and J. S. Harrison, "Strategic Competitiveness in the 1990s: Challenges and Opportunities for U.S. Executives," *Academy of Management Executive* 5 (1991): 7–22.

2. H. G. Barkem, J. A. C. Baum, and E. A. Mannix, "Management Challenges in a New Time," *Academy of Management Journal* 45 (2002): 916–930.

3. "The Post-recession Outlook: Canada's Key Economic Strengths and Challenges," remarks prepared for the Honourable John Manley, CEO of CCCE, http://www.ceocouncil.ca/en/view/?area_id=1&document_id=1396.

4. K. Sera, "Corporate Globalization: A New Trend," *Academy of Management Executive* 6 (1992): 89–96.

5. K. Ohmae, *Borderless World: Power and Strategies in the Interlinked Economy* (New York: Harper & Row, 1990).

6. C. A. Bartlett and S. Ghoshal, *Managing across Borders: The Transnational Solution* (Boston: Harvard Business School Press, 1989).

7. H. W. Arthurs, (nd) "The Hollowing out of Corporate Canada?", http://www.yorku.ca/robarts/archives/pub_domain/pdf/apd_arthurs.pdf.

8. F. Warner, "Learning How to Speak to Gen Y," *Fast Company* 72 (July 2003): 36–37.

9. K. R. Xin and J. L. Pearce, "Guanxi: Connections as Substitutes for Formal Institutional Support," *Academy of Management Journal* 39 (1996): 1641–1658.

10. P. S. Chan, "Franchise Management in East Asia," *Academy of Management Executive* 4 (1990): 75–85.

11. H. Weihrich, "Europe 1992: What the Future May Hold," *Academy of Management Executive* 4 (1990): 7–18.

12. E. H. Schein, "Coming to a New Awareness of Organizational Culture," *MIT Sloan Management Review* 25 (1984): 3–16.

13. S. S. Sarwano and R. M. Armstrong, "Microcultural Differences and Perceived Ethical Problems: An International Business Perspective," *Journal of Business Ethics* 30 (2001): 41–56.

14. R. Sharpe, "Hi-Tech Taboos," *The Wall Street Journal* (October 31, 1995): A1.

15. G. Hofstede, *Culture's Consequences: International Differences in Work-Related Values* (Beverly Hills, Calif.: Sage Publications, 1980).

16. G. Hofstede, "Motivation, Leadership, and Organization: Do American Theories Apply Abroad?" *Organizational Dynamics* (Summer 1980): 42–63.

17. G. M. Spreitzer, M. W. McCall, Jr., and J. D. Mahoney, "Early Identification of International Executive Potential," *Journal of Applied Psychology* 82 (1997): 6–29.

18. M. A. Hitt, L. Bierman, K. Uhlenbruck, and K. Shimizu, "The Importance of Resources in the Internationalization of Professional Service Firms: The Good, the Bad, and the Ugly," *Academy of Management Journal* 49 (2006): 1137–1157.

19. A. J. Michel, "Goodbyes Can Cost Plenty in Europe," *Fortune* (April 6, 1992): 16.

20. "Hofstede's Cultural Dimensions, Understanding Workplace Values Around the World," http://www.mindtools.com/pages/article/newLDR_66.htm.

21. G. Hofstede, "Gender Stereotypes and Partner Preferences of Asian Women in Masculine and Feminine Countries," *Journal of Cross Cultural Psychology* 27 (1996): 533–546.

22. G. Hofstede, "Cultural Constraints in Management Theories," *Academy of Management Executive* 7 (1993): 81–94.

23. E. Brandt, "Global HR," *Personnel Journal* 70 (1991): 38–44.

24. L. Hartley, "The Roots of Conflict: A Conversation with Michelle LeBaron," *Fieldnotes* (April 1–4, 2005), 9.

25. P. Chattopadhyay, "Can Dissimilarity Lead to Positive Outcomes: The Influence of Open versus Closed Minds," *Journal of Organizational Behavior* 24 (2003): 295–312.

26. J. C. Quick, J. H. Gavin, C. L. Cooper, and J. D. Quick, "Working Together: Balancing Head and Heart," in R. H. Rozensky, N. G. Johnson, C. D. Goodheart, and W. R. Hammond, eds., *Psychology Builds a Healthy World: Opportunities for Research and Practice* (Washington, D.C.: American Psychological Association, 2004): 219–232.

27. R. Caballero and R. Yerema (2010) "Agrium," http://www.eluta.ca/diversity-at-agrium.

28. StatsCan (2008) "Some Facts about the Demographic and Ethnocultural Composition of the Population," http://www.statcan.gc.ca/pub/91-003-x/2007001/4129904-eng.htm#2.

29. S. Block (2010) "How Do Race and Gender Factor into Income Inequality?" http://www.policyalternatives.ca/sites/default/files/uploads/publications/reports/docs/The%20Role%20of%20Race%20Ontario%20Growing%20Gap.pdf.

30. S. Caudron, "Task Force Report Reveals Coke's Progress on Diversity," *Workforce* 82 (2003): 40, http://www.workforceonline.com/section/03/feature/23/42/44/234246.html.

31. T. Perkins, "How RBC Became a Champion of Diversity," *Report on Business* (March 24, 2010) http://www.theglobeandmail.com/report-on-business/managing/how-rbc-became-a-champion-of-diversity/article1508812.

32. The Canadian Press, "Women Outnumber Men in Canadian Workforce" (September 5, 2009) http://www.ctv.ca/servlet/ArticleNews/story/CTVNews/20090905/women_workforce_090905/20090905?hub=Canada.

33. "Catalyst Releases 2005 Censuses of Women Board Directors and Corporate Officers," Perspective, Catalyst.org, http://www.catalyst.org/bookstore/perspective/06August.pdf.

34. Ibid.

35. U.S. Department of Labor, "Highlights of Women's Earnings in 2005," Report 995 (September 2006) 33; Catalyst, *Catalyst Census of Women Corporate Officers and Top Earners* (2001).

36. A. M. Morrison, R. P. White, E. Van Velsor, and the Center for Creative Leadership, *Breaking the Glass Ceiling: Can Women Reach the Top of America's Largest Corporations?* (Reading, Mass.: Addison-Wesley, 1987).

37. Catalyst "Quick Takes—Women and Law" (2009)://www.catalyst.org/publication/234/women-in-law-in-canada.

38. "Women CEOs who Broke the Glass Ceiling in India," (December 1, 2009) http://business.rediff.com/slide-show/2009/dec/01/slide-show-1-more-women-ceos-in-india-than-abroad.htm#contentTop.

39. Ibid.

40. L. L. Martins and C. K. Parsons, "Effects of Gender Diversity Management on Perceptions of Organizational Attractiveness: The Role of Individual Differences in Attitudes and Beliefs," *Journal of Applied Psychology* 92 (2007): 865–875.

41. A. Eyring and B. A. Stead, "Shattering the Glass Ceiling: Some Successful Corporate Practices," *Journal of Business Ethics* 17 (1998): 245–251.

42. Catalyst, *Advancing Women in Business: The Catalyst Guide* (San Francisco: Jossey-Bass, 1998).

43. D. L. Nelson and M. A. Hitt, "Employed Women and Stress: Implications for Enhancing Women's Mental Health in the Workplace," in J. C. Quick, L. R. Murphy, and J. J. Hurrell, Jr., eds., *Stress and Well-Being at Work* (Washington, D.C.: American Psychological Association, 1992): 164–177.

44. Statscan "Demographic Change," (2010) http://www.statcan.gc.ca/pub/82-229-x/2009001/demo/int1-eng.htm.

45. W. B. Johnston, "Global Workforce 2000: The New World Labor Market," *Harvard Business Review* 69 (1991): 115–127.

46. S. E. Jackson and E. B. Alvarez, "Working through Diversity as a Strategic Imperative," in S. E. Jackson, ed., *Diversity in the Workplace: Human Resources Initiatives* (New York: Guilford Press, 1992), 13–36.

47. "Managing Generational Diversity," *HR Magazine* 36 (1991): 91–92.

48. K. Tyler, "The Tethered Generation," *HR Magazine* (May 2007): 41–46.

49. S. R. Rhodes, "Age-Related Differences in Work Attitudes and Behavior: A Review and Conceptual Analysis," *Psychological Bulletin* 93 (1983): 338–367.

50. B. L. Hassell and P. L. Perrewe, "An Examination of Beliefs about Older Workers: Do Stereotypes Still Exist?" *Journal of Organizational Behavior* 16 (1995): 457–468.

51. HRSDC "Canadians in Context—People with Disabilities," (2006) http://www4.hrsdc.gc.ca/.3ndic.1t.4r@-eng.jsp?iid=40.

52. *J. O'Connor, "Brian McKeever's Olympic Dream Over," National Post, (February 27, 2010) http://www.cbc.ca/olympics/blogs/joeoconnor/2010/02/brian-mckeevers-olympic-dream-over.html.*

53. J. J. Laabs, "The Golden Arches Provide Golden Opportunities," *Personnel Journal* (July 1991): 52–57.

54. J. E. Rigdon, "PepsiCo's KFC Scouts for Blacks and Women for Its Top Echelons," *The Wall Street Journal* (November 13, 1991): A1.

55. P. A. Galagan, "Tapping the Power of a Diverse Workforce," *Training and Development Journal* 26 (1991): 38–44.

56. C. L. Holladay, J. L. Knight, D. L. Paige, and M. A. Quinones, "The Influence of Framing on Attitudes Toward Diversity Training," *Human Resource Development Quarterly* 14 (2003): 245–263.

57. Ibid.

58. R. Thomas, "From Affirmative Action to Affirming Diversity," *Harvard Business Review* 68 (1990): 107–117.

59. T. H. Cox, Jr., *Cultural Diversity in Organizations: Theory, Research and Practice* (San Francisco: Berrett-Koehler, 1994).

60. Merck Annual Report 2000, http://www.anrpt2000.com/18.htm.

61. M. R. Fusilier, C. D. Aby, Jr., J. K. Worley, and S. Elliott, "Perceived Seriousness of Business Ethics Issues," *Business and Professional Ethics Journal* 15 (1996): 67–78.

62. J. S. Mill, *Utilitarianism, Liberty, and Representative Government* (London: Dent, 1910).

63. K. H. Blanchard and N. V. Peale, *The Power of Ethical Management* (New York: Morrow, 1988).

64. A. Smith, *An Inquiry into the Nature and Causes of the Wealth of Nations,* vol. 10 of The Harvard Classics, ed. C. J. Bullock (New York: P. F. Collier & Son, 1909).

65. C. Fried, *Right and Wrong* (Cambridge, Mass.: Harvard University Press, 1978).

66. I. Kant, *Groundwork of the Metaphysics of Morals,* trans. H. J. Paton (New York: Harper & Row, 1964).

67. R. C. Solomon, "Corporate Roles, Personal Virtues: Aristotelean Approach to Business Ethics," *Business Ethics Quarterly* 2 (1992): 317–339; R. C. Solomon, *A Better Way to Think about Business: How Personal Integrity Leads to Corporate Success* (New York: Oxford University Press, 1999).

68. D. Kemp, "Employers and AIDS: Dealing with the Psychological and Emotional Issues of AIDS in the Workplace," *American Review of Public Administration* 25 (1995): 263–278.

69. J. J. Koch, "Wells Fargo's and IBM's HIV Policies Help Protect Employees' Rights," *Personnel Journal* (April 1990): 40–48.

70. "Global Business Coalition Member Profiles," http://www.gbcimpact.org/itcs_type/9/506/member_profiles.

71. U.S. EEOC, "Discrimination Because of Sex under Title VII of the 1964 Civil Rights Act as Amended: Adoption of Interim Guidelines—sexual harassment," *Federal Register* 45 (1980): 25024–25025; S. J. Adler, "Lawyers Advise Concerns to Provide Precise Written Policy to Employees," *The Wall Street Journal* (October 9, 1991): B1.

72. L. F. Fitzgerald, F. Drasgow, C. L. Hulin, M. J. Gelfand, and V. J. Magley, "Antecedents and Consequences of Sexual Harassment in Organizations: A Test of an Integrated Model," *Journal of Applied Psychology* 82 (1997): 578–589.

73. E. Felsenthal, "Rulings Open Way for Sex-Harass Cases," *The Wall Street Journal* (June 29, 1998): A10.

74. Canadian Human Rights Commission, Anti-Harassment Policies for the Workplace: An Employer's Guide March 2006, http://www.chrc-ccdp.ca/publications/anti_harassment_toc-en.asp#23.

75. K. T. Schneider, S. Swan, and L. F. Fitzgerald, "Job-Related and Psychological Effects of Sexual Harassment in the Workplace: Empirical Evidence from Two Organizations," *Journal of Applied Psychology* 82 (1997): 401–415.

76. A. M. O'Leary-Kelly, R. L. Paetzold, and R. W. Griffin, "Sexual Harassment as Aggressive Behavior: An Actor-Based Perspective," *Academy of Management Review* 25 (2000): 372–388.

77. Marsh, B. (1996) ICN, Chairman Settle 2nd Sexual Harassment Case, *Los Angeles Times*, July 2, http://articles.latimes.com/1996-07-02/business/fi-20479_1_sexual-harassment.

78. L. M. Goldenhar, N. G. Swanson, J. J. Hurrell, Jr., A. Ruder, and J. Deddens, "Stressors and Adverse Outcomes for Female Construction Workers," *Journal of Occupational Health Psychology* 3 (1998): 19–32; C. S. Piotrkowski, "Gender Harassment, Job Satisfaction and Distress Among Employed White and Minority Women," *Journal of Occupational Health Psychology* 3 (1998): 33–42.

79. R. A. Posthuma, C. P. Maertz, Jr., and J. B. Dworkin, "Procedural Justice's Relationship with Turnover: Explaining Past Inconsistent Findings," *Journal of Organizational Behavior* 28 (2007): 381–398.

80. D. Fields, M. Pang, and C. Chio, "Distributive and Procedural Justice as Predictors of Employee Outcomes in Hong Kong," *Journal of Organizational Behavior* 21 (2000): 547–562.

81. H. L. Laframboise, "Vile Wretches and Public Heroes: The Ethics of Whistleblowing in Government," *Canadian Public Administration* (Spring 1991): 73–78.

82. D. B. Turban and D. W. Greening, "Corporate Social Performance and Organizational Attractiveness to Prospective Employees," *Academy of Management Journal* 40 (1996): 658–672.

83. "Ivey Pledge" (nd) http://www.ivey.uwo.ca/alumni/downloads/pledge.pdf.

84. Task Force on Management of Innovation, *Technology and Employment: Innovation and Growth in the U.S. Economy* (Washington, D.C.: U.S. Government Research Council, 1987).

85. C. H. Ferguson, "Computers and the Coming of the U.S. Keiretsu," *Harvard Business Review* 68 (1990): 55–70.

86. J. Collins, *Good to Great: Why Some Companies Make the Leap . . . and Others Don't* (New York: HarperCollins, 2001).

87. J. A. Senn, *Information Systems in Management,* 4th ed. (Belmont, Calif.: Wadsworth, 1990).

88. D. K. Sorenson, O. Bouhaddou, and H. R. Warner, *Knowledge Engineering in Health Informatics* (New York: Springer, 1999).

89. M. T. Damore, "A Presentation and Examination of the Integration of Unlawful Discrimination Practices in the Private Business Sector with Artificial Intelligence" (Thesis, Oklahoma State University, 1992).

90. IEEE Robotics and Automation Society, "FR. Statistics Report Optimistic About Robotics Industry Growth in 2011–12."

91. E. Fingleton, "Jobs for Life: Why Japan Won't Give Them Up," *Fortune* (March 20, 1995): 119–125.

92. M. Iansitu, "How the Incumbent Can Win: Managing Technological Transitions in the Semiconductor Industry," *Management Science* 46 (2000): 169–185.

93. M. B. W. Fritz, S. Narasimhan, and H. Rhee, "Communication and Coordination in the Virtual Office," *Journal of Management Information Systems* 14 (1998): 7–28.

94. "Telus Finds Telecommuting Good for Planet and the Bottom Line," *The Vancouver Sun*, (June 25, 2007) http://www.working.com/vancouver/story.html?id=bc7b53a1-4cf4-4624-9c23-b28c6ee8e559&k=31069.

95. M. Apgar, IV, "The Alternative Workplace: Changing Where and How People Work," *Harvard Business Review* (May–June 1998): 121–136.

96. D. L. Nelson, "Individual Adjustment to Information-Driven Technologies: A Critical Review," *MIS Quarterly* 14 (1990): 79–98.

97. S. Armour, "Hi, I'm Joan and I'm a Workaholic," *USA Today* (May 23, 2007).

98. M. Allen, "Legislation Could Restrict Bosses from Snooping on Their Workers," *The Wall Street Journal* (September 24, 1991): B1–B8.

99. K. D. Hill and S. Kerr, "The Impact of Computer-Integrated Manufacturing Systems on the First Line Supervisor," *Journal of Organizational Behavior Management* 6 (1984): 81–87.

100. J. Anderson, "How Technology Brings Blind People into the Workplace," *Harvard Business Review* 67 (1989): 36–39.

101. D. L. Nelson and M. G. Kletke, "Individual Adjustment during Technological Innovation: A Research Framework," *Behavior and Information Technology* 9 (1990): 257–271.

102. D. Mankin, T. Bikson, B. Gutek, and C. Stasz, "Managing Technological Change: The Process Is the Key," *Datamation* 34 (1988): 69–80.

# Chapter 3

1. K. Lewin, "Formalization and Progress in Psychology," in D. Cartwright, ed., *Field Theory in Social Science* (New York: Harper, 1951).

2. N. S. Endler and D. Magnusson, "Toward an Interactional Psychology of Personality," *Psychological Bulletin* 83 (1976): 956–974.

3. J. R. Terborg, "Interactional Psychology and Research on Human Behavior in Organizations," *Academy of Management Review* 6 (1981): 561–576.

4. F. L. Schmidt and J. Hunter, "General Mental Ability in the World of Work: Occupational Attainment and Job Performance," *Journal of Personality and Social Psychology* 86(1) (2004): 162–173.

5. C. Bertua, N. Anderson, and J. F Salgado, "The Predictive Validity of Cognitive Ability Tests: A UK Meta-Analysis," *Journal of Occupational and Organizational Psychology* 78 (2004): 387–409.

6. T. J. Bouchard, Jr., "Twins Reared Together and Apart: What They Tell Us about Human Diversity," in S. W. Fox, ed., *Individuality and Determinism* (New York: Plenum Press, 1984); R. D. Arvey, T. J. Bouchard, Jr., N. L. Segal, and L. M. Abraham, "Job Satisfaction: Environmental and Genetic Components," *Journal of Applied Psychology* 74 (1989): 235–248.

7. T. A. Judge, C. Hurst, and L. S. Simon, "Does It Pay to Be Smart, Attractive or Confident (or All Three)? Relationships Among General Mental Ability, Physical Attractiveness, Core Self-Evaluations, and Income," *Journal of Applied Psychology* 94(3) (2009): 742–755.

8. J. M. Digman, "Personality Structure: Emergence of a Five-Factor Model," *Annual Review of Psychology* 41 (1990): 417–440.

9. T. A. Judge, J. J. Martocchio, and C. J. Thoresen, "Five-Factor Model of Personality and Employee Absence," *Journal of Applied Psychology* 82 (1997): 745–755.

10. H. J. Bernardin, D. K. Cooke, and P. Villanova, "Conscientiousness and Agreeableness as Predictors of Rating Leniency," *Journal of Applied Psychology* 85 (2000): 232–234.

11. S. E. Seibert and M. L. Kraimer, "The Five-Factor Model of Personality and Career Success," *Journal of Vocational Behavior* 58 (2001): 1–21.

12. T. A. Judge and R. Ilies, "Relationships of Personality to Performance Motivation: A Meta-Analytic Review," *Journal of Applied Psychology* 87 (2002): 797–807.

13. G. M. Hurtz and J. J. Donovan, "Personality and Job Performance: The Big Five Revisited," *Journal of Applied Psychology* 85 (2000): 869–879.

14. S. T. Bell, "Deep-Level Composition Variables as Predictors of Team Performance: A Meta-Analysis," *Journal of Applied Psychology* 92(3) (2007): 595–615.

15. D. P. Schmitt, J. Allik, R. R. McCrae and V. Benet-Martinez. "The Geographic Distribution of Big Five Personality Traits: Patterns and Profiles of Human Self-Description across 56 Nations." *Journal of Cross-Cultural Psychology* 38(2) (2007): 173–212.

16. M. R. Barrick and M. K. Mount, "The Big Five Personality Dimensions and Job Performance: A Meta-Analysis," *Personnel Psychology* 44 (1991): 1–26.

17. D. D. Clark and R. Hoyle, "A Theoretical Solution to the Problem of Personality-Situational Interaction," *Personality and Individual Differences* 9 (1988): 133–138.

18. D. Byrne and L. J. Schulte, "Personality Dimensions as Predictors of Sexual Behavior," in J. Bancroft, ed., *Annual Review of Sexual Research,* vol. 1 (Philadelphia: Society for the Scientific Study of Sex, 1990).

19. T. A., Judge, E. A. Locke, and C. C. Durham, "The Dispositional Causes of Job Satisfaction: A Core Self-Evaluation Approach," *Research in Organizational Behavior* 19 (1997):151–88.

20. B. A. Scott and T. A. Judge, "The Popularity Contest at Work: Who Wins, Why, and What Do They Receive?" *Journal of Applied Psychology* 94(1) (2009): 20–33.

21. T. A. Judge and C. Hurst, "How the Rich (and Happy) Get Richer (and Happier): Relationship of Core Self-Evaluations to Trajectories in Attaining Work Success," *Journal of Applied Psychology* 93(4) (2008): 849–863.

22. C. J. Resick, D. S. Whitman, S. M. Weingarden, and N. J. Hiller, "The Bright-Side and the Dark-Side of CEO Personality: Examining Core Self-Evaluations, Narcissism, Transformational Leadership and Strategic Influence," *Journal of Applied Psychology* 94(6) (2009): 1365–1381.

23. J. B. Rotter, "Generalized Expectancies for Internal vs. External Control of Reinforcement," *Psychological Monographs* 80, whole No. 609 (1966).

24. T. W. H. Ng, K. L. Sorensen, and L. T. Eby, "Locus of Control at Work: A Meta-Analysis," *Journal of Organizational Behavior* 27 (2006): 1057–1087.

25. G. Chen, S. M. Gully, J. Whiteman, and R. N. Kilcullen, "Examination of Relationships Among Trait-Like Individual Differences, State-Like Individual Differences, and Learning Performance," *Journal of Applied Psychology* 85 (2000): 835–847; G. Chen, S. M. Gully, and D. Eden, "Validation of a New General Self-Efficacy Scale," *Organizational Research Methods* 4 (2001): 62–83.

26. A. Bandura, *Self-Efficacy: The Exercise of Control* (San Francisco: Freeman, 1997).

27. D. R. Avery, "Personality as a Predictor of the Value of Voice," *The Journal of Psychology* 137 (2003): 435–447.

28. T. A. Judge and J. E. Bono, "Relationship of Core Self-Evaluations Traits—Self-Esteem, Generalized Self-Efficacy, Locus of Control, and Emotional Stability—with Job Satisfaction and Job Performance: A Meta-Analysis," *Journal of Applied Psychology* 86 (2001): 80–92.

29. B. W. Pelham and W. B. Swann, Jr., "From Self-Conceptions to Self-Worth: On the Sources and Structure of Global Self-Esteem," *Journal of Personality and Social Psychology* 57 (1989): 672–680.

30. A. H. Baumgardner, C. M. Kaufman, and P. E. Levy, "Regulating Affect Interpersonally: When Low Esteem Leads to Greater Enhancement," *Journal of Personality and Social Psychology* 56 (1989): 907–921.

31. J. Schimel, T. Pyszczynski, J. Arndt, and J. Greenberg, "Being Accepted for Who We Are: Evidence that Social Validation of the Intrinsic Self Reduces General Defensiveness," *Journal of Personality and Social Psychology* 80 (2001): 35–52.

32. P. Tharenou and P. Harker, "Moderating Influences of Self-Esteem on Relationships between Job Complexity, Performance, and Satisfaction," *Journal of Applied Psychology* 69 (1984): 623–632.

33. R. A. Ellis and M. S. Taylor, "Role of Self-Esteem within the Job Search Process," *Journal of Applied Psychology* 68 (1983): 632–640.

34. J. Brockner and T. Hess, "Self-Esteem and Task Performance in Quality Circles," *Academy of Management Journal* 29 (1986): 617–623.

35. B. R. Schlenker, M. F. Weingold, and J. R. Hallam, "Self-Serving Attributions in Social Context: Effects of Self-Esteem and Social Pressure," *Journal of Personality and Social Psychology* 57 (1990): 855–863.

36. M. K. Duffy, J. D. Shaw, and E. M. Stark, "Performance and Satisfaction in Conflicted Interdependent Groups: When and How Does Self-Esteem Make a Difference?" *Academy of Management Journal* 43 (2000): 772–782.

37. C. J. Resick, D. S. Whitman, S. M. Weingarden, and N. J. Hiller, "The Bright-Side and the Dark-Side of CEO Personality: Examining Core Self-Evaluations, Narcissism, Transformational Leadership and Strategic Influence," *Journal of Applied Psychology* 94(6) (2009): 1365–1381.

38. M. Erez and T. A. Judge, "Relationship of Core Self-Evaluations to Goal Setting, Motivation and Performance," *Journal of Applied Psychology* 86 (2001): 1270–79.

39. M. Snyder and S. Gangestad, "On the Nature of Self-Monitoring: Matters of Assessment, Matters of Validity." *Journal of Personality and Social Psychology* (1986): 125–139.

40. G. Toegel, N. Anand, and M. Kilduff, "Emotion Helpers: The Role of High Positive Affectivity and High Self-monitoring Managers," *Personnel Psychology* 60(2) (2007): 337–365.

41. J. E. Bono and M. A. Vey, "Personality and Emotional Performance: Extraversion, Neuroticism and Self-Monitoring," *Journal of Occupational Health Psychology* 12(2) (2007): 177–192.

42. A. Mehra, M. Kilduff, and D. J. Brass, "The Social Networks of High and Low Self-Monitors: Implications for Workplace Performance," *Administrative Science Quarterly* 46 (2001): 121–146.

43. W. H. Turnley and M. C. Bolino, "Achieving Desired Images While Avoiding Undesired Images: Exploring the Role of Self-Monitoring in Impression Management," *Journal of Applied Psychology* 86 (2001): 351–360.

44. M. Kilduff and D. V. Day, "Do Chameleons Get Ahead? The Effects of Self-Monitoring on Managerial Careers," *Academy of Management Journal* 37 (1994): 1047–1060.

45. A. H. Church, "Managerial Self-Awareness in High-Performing Individuals in Organizations," *Journal of Applied Psychology* 82 (1997): 281–292.

46. C. Douglas and W. L. Gardner, "Transition to Self-Directed Work Teams: Implications of Transition Time and Self-Monitoring for Managers' Use of Influence Tactics," *Journal of Organizational Behavior* 25 (2004): 45–67.

47. A. M. Isen and R. A. Baron, "Positive Affect and Organizational Behavior," in B. M. Staw and L. L. Cummings, eds., *Research in Organizational Behavior*, vol. 12 (Greenwich, Conn.: JAI Press, 1990).

48. D. Watson and L. A. Clark, "Negative Affectivity: The Disposition to Experience Aversive Emotional States," *Psychological Bulletin* 96 (1984): 465–490.

49. R. Ilies and T. Judge, "On the Heritability of Job Satisfaction: The Mediating Role of Personality," *Journal of Applied Psychology* 88 (2003): 750–759.

50. J. M. George, "State or Trait," *Journal of Applied Psychology* 76 (1991): 299–307.

51. J. M. George, "Mood and Absence," *Journal of Applied Psychology* 74 (1989): 287–324.

52. S. Lyubormirsky, L. King, and L. E. Diener, "The Benefits of Frequent Positive Affect: Does Happiness Lead to Success?" *Psychological Bulletin* 131(6) (2005): 803–855.

53. S. Barsade, A. Ward, J. Turner, and J. Sonnenfeld, "To Your Heart's Content: A Model of Affective Diversity in Top Management Teams," *Administrative Science Quarterly* 45 (2000): 802–836.

54. W. Mischel, "The Interaction of Person and Situation," in D. Magnusson and N. S. Endler, eds., *Personality at the Crossroads: Current Issues in Interactional Psychology* (Hillsdale, N.J.: Erlbaum, 1977).

55. G. L. Stewart and A. K. Nandkeolyar, "Adaptation and Intraindividual Variation in Sales Outcomes: Exploring the Interactive Effects of Personality and Environmental Opportunity," *Personnel Psychology* 59 (2006): 307–332.

56. F. P. Morgeson, M. C. Campion, R. L. Dipboye, J. R. Hollenbeck, K. Murphy, and N. Schmitt, "Reconsidering the Use of Personality Tests in Personnel Selection Contexts," *Personnel Psychology* 60, (2007): 683–729.

57. N. M. Dudley, K. A. Orvis, J. E. Lebiecki, and J. M. Cortina, "A Meta-Analytic Investigation of Conscientiousness in the Prediction of Job Performance: Examining the Intercorrelations and the Incremental Validity of Narrow Traits," *Journal of Applied Psychology* 91(1) (2006): 40–57.

58. R. P. Tett, D. N. Jackson, M. Rothstein, and J. R. Reddon, "Meta-Analysis of Bidirectional Relations in Personality-Job Performance Research," *Human Performance* 12(1) (1999): 1–29.

59. J. W. Westerman and B. L. Simmons, "The Effects of the Work Environment on the Personality-Performance Relationship: An Exploratory Study," *Journal of Managerial Issues* 19(2) (2007): 288–305.

60. C. G. Jung, *Psychological Types* (New York: Harcourt & Brace, 1923).

61. www.cpp.com/products/mbti/index.aspx.

62. R. Benfari and J. Knox, *Understanding Your Management Style* (Lexington, Mass.: Lexington Books, 1991).

63. T. N. Osborn, D. B. Osborn, and B. Twillman, "MBTI, FIRO-B, and NAFTA: Psychological Profiles of Not-So-Distant Neighbors," *Journal of Psychological Type* 36 (1996): 3–15.

64. P. Rosati, "Academic Progress of Canadian Engineering Students in terms of MBTI Personality Type," *International Journal of Engineering Education* 14(5) (1998): 322–327.

65. S. Hirsch and J. Kummerow, *Life Types* (New York: Warner Books, 1989).

66. J. B. Murray, "Review of Research on the Myers-Briggs Type Indicator," *Perceptual and Motor Skills* 70 (1990): 1187–1202; J. G. Carlson, "Recent Assessment of the Myers-Briggs Type Indicator," *Journal of Personality Assessment* 49 (1985): 356–365.

67. P. Rosati, "Academic Progress of Canadian Engineering Students in terms of MBTI Personality Type," *International Journal of Engineering Education* 14(5) (1998): 322–327.

68. C. Walck, "Training for Participative Management: Implications for Psychological Type," *Journal of Psychological Type* 21 (1991): 3–12.

69. J. Michael, "Using the Myers-Briggs Indicator as a Tool for Leadership Development: Apply with Caution," *Journal of Leadership & Organizational Studies* 10 (2003): 68–78.

70. E. C. Webster, *The Employment Interview: A Social Judgment Process* (Schomberg, Canada: SIP, 1982).

71. A. J. Ward, M. J. Lankau, A. C. Amason, J. A. Sonnenfeld, and B. R. Agle, "Improving the Performance of Top Management Teams," *MIT Sloan Management Review* 48(3) (2007): 85–90.

72. J. E. Edwards and D. M. Cable, "The Value of Value Congruence," *Journal of Applied Psychology* 94(3) (2009): 654–677.

73. P. E. Spector, T. D. Allen, S. A. Y. Poelmans, L. M. Lapierre, C. L. Cooper, M. O'Driscoll, J. I. Sanchez, N. Abarca, M. Alexandrova, B. Beham, P. Brough, P. Ferreiro, G. Fraile, C. Lu, L. Lu, I. Moreno-Velazquez, M. Pagon, H. Pitariu, V. Salamatov, S. Shima, A. S. Simoni, O. L. Siu and M. Widerszal-Bazyl, "Cross-National Differences in Relationships of Work Demands, Job Satisfaction, and Turnover Intentions with Work-Family Conflict," *Personnel Psychology* 60 (2007): 805–835.

74. D. Cohen, R. E. Nisbett, B. F. Bowdle, and N. Schwarz, "Insult, Aggression, and the Southern Culture of Honor: An Experimental Ethnography," *Journal of Personality and Social Psychology* 70 (1996): 945–960.

75. H. I. Jzerman, W. W. van Dijk, and M. Gallucci, "A bumpy train ride: A field experiment on insult, honor, and emotional reactions," *Emotion* 7(4) (2007): 869–875.

76. J. Park and M. R. Banaji, "Mood and Heuristics: The Influence of Happy and Sad States on Sensitivity and Bias in Stereotyping," *Journal of Personality and Social Psychology* 78 (2000): 1005–1023.

77. M. W. Levine and J. M. Shefner, *Fundamentals of Sensation and Perception* (Reading, Mass.: Addison-Wesley, 1981).

78. R. L. Dipboye, H. L. Fromkin, and K. Willback, "Relative Importance of Applicant Sex, Attractiveness, and Scholastic Standing in Evaluations of Job Applicant Resumes," *Journal of Applied Psychology* 60 (1975): 39–43; I. H. Frieze, J. E. Olson, and J. Russell, "Attractiveness and Income for Men and Women in Management," *Journal of Applied Social Psychology* 21 (1991): 1039–1057.

79. J. H. Langlois, L. Kalakanis, A. J. Rubenstein, A. Larson, M. Hallam, and M. Smoot, "Maxims or Myths of Beauty? A Meta-Analytic and Theoretical Review," *Psychological Bulletin* 126(3) (2000): 390–423.

80. P. Ekman and W. Friesen, *Unmasking the Face* (Englewood Cliffs, N.J.: Prentice-Hall, 1975).

81. J. E. Rehfeld, "What Working for a Japanese Company Taught Me," *Harvard Business Review* (November–December 1990): 167–176.

82. M. W. Morris and R. P. Larrick, "When One Cause Casts Doubt on Another: A Normative Analysis of Discounting in Causal Attribution," *Psychological Review* 102 (1995): 331–355.

83. G. B. Sechrist and C. Stangor, "Perceived Consensus Influences Intergroup Behavior and Stereotype Accessibility," *Journal of Personality and Psychology* 80 (2001): 645–654; A. Lyons and Y. Kashima, "How Are Stereotypes Maintained through Communication? The Influence of Stereotype Sharedness," *Journal of Personality and Social Psychology* 85 (2003): 989–1005.

84. L. Copeland, "Learning to Manage a Multicultural Workforce," *Training* (May 1988): 48–56.

85. S. Ferrari, "Human Behavior in International Groups," *Management International Review* 7 (1972): 31–35.

86. A. Feingold, "Gender Differences in Effects of Physical Attractiveness on Romantic Attraction: A Comparison across Five Research Paradigms," *Journal of Personality and Social Psychology* 59 (1990): 981–993.

87. M. Snyder, "When Belief Creates Reality," *Advances in Experimental Social Psychology* 18 (1984): 247–305.

88. J. H. Langlois, L. Kalakanis, A. J. Rubenstein, A. Larson, M. Hallam, and M. Smoot, "Maxims or Myths of Beauty? A Meta-Analytic and Theoretical Review," *Psychological Bulletin* 126(3) (2000): 390–423.

89. E. Burnstein and Y. Schul, "The Informational Basis of Social Judgments: Operations in Forming an Impression of Another Person," *Journal of Experimental Social Psychology* 18 (1982): 217–234.

90. G. L. Stewart, S. L. Dustin, M. R. Barrick, and T. C. Darnold, "Exploring the Handshake in Employment Interviews," *Journal of Applied Psychology* 93(5) (2008): 1139–1146.

91. R. L. Gross and S. E. Brodt, "How Assumptions of Consensus Undermine Decision Making," *MIT Sloan Management Review* 42 (Winter 2001): 86–94.

92. R. Rosenthal and L. Jacobson, *Pygmalion in the Classroom: Teacher Expectations and Pupils' Intellectual Development* (New York: Holt, Rinehart & Winston, 1968).

93. D. Eden, "Pygmalion without Interpersonal Contrast Effects: Whole Groups Gain from Raising Manager Expectations," *Journal of Applied Psychology* 75 (1990): 394–398.

94. R. A. Giacolone and P. Rosenfeld, eds., *Impression Management in Organizations* (Hillsdale, N.J.: Erlbaum, 1990); J. Tedeschi and V. Melburg, "Impression Management and Influence in the Organization," in S. Bacharach and E. Lawler, eds., *Research in the Sociology of Organizations* (Greenwich, Conn.: JAI Press, 1984), 31–58.

95. A. Colella and A. Varma, "The Impact of Subordinate Disability on Leader–Member Exchange Relationships," *Academy of Management Journal* 44 (2001): 304–315.

96. D. C. Gilmore and G. R. Ferris, "The Effects of Applicant Impression Management Tactics on Interviewer Judgments," *Journal of Management* (December 1989): 557–564; C. K. Stevens and A. L. Kristof, "Making the Right Impression: A Field Study of Applicant Impressions Management during Job Interviews," *Journal of Applied Psychology* 80 (1995): 587–606.

97. S. J. Wayne and R. C. Liden, "Effects of Impression Management on Performance Ratings: A Longitudinal Study," *Academy of Management Journal* 38 (1995): 232–260.

98. M. R. Barrick, J. A. Shaffer, and S. W. DeGrassi, "What You See May Not Be What You Get: Relationships Among Self-Presentation Tactics and Ratings of Interview and Job Performance," *Journal of Applied Psychology* 94(6) (2009):1394–1411.

99. F. Heider, *The Psychology of Interpersonal Relations* (New York: Wiley, 1958).

100. B. Weiner, "An Attributional Theory of Achievement Motivation and Emotion," *Psychological Review* (October 1985): 548–573.

101. P. D. Sweeney, K. Anderson, and S. Bailey, "Attributional Style in Depression: A Meta-Analytic Review," *Journal of Personality and Social Psychology* 51 (1986): 974–991.

102. P. Rosenthal, D. Guest, and R. Peccei, "Gender Differences in Managers' Causal Explanations for Their Work Performance," *Journal of Occupational and Organizational Psychology* 69 (1996): 145–151.

103. L. Ross, "The Intuitive Psychologist and His Shortcomings: Distortions in the Attribution Process," in L. Berkowitz, ed., *Advances in Experimental Social Psychology* (New York: Academic Press, 1977); M. O'Sullivan, "The Fundamental Attribution Error in Detecting Deception: The Boy-Who-Cried-Wolf Effect," *Personality & Social Psychology Bulletin* 29 (2003): 1316–1327.

104. D. T. Miller and M. Ross, "Self-Serving Biases in the Attribution of Causality: Fact or Fiction?" *Psychological Bulletin* 82 (1975): 313–325.

105. J. R. Schermerhorn, Jr., "Team Development for High-Performance Management," *Training and Development Journal* 40 (1986): 38–41.

106. J. G. Miller, "Culture and the Development of Everyday Causal Explanation," *Journal of Personality and Social Psychology* 46 (1984): 961–978.

107. G. Si, S. Rethorst, and K. Willimczik, "Causal Attribution Perception in Sports Achievement: A Cross-Cultural Study on Attributional Concepts in Germany and China," *Journal of Cross-Cultural Psychology* 26 (1995): 537–553.

108. M. J. Martinko and W. L. Gardner, "The Leader/Member Attributional Process," *Academy of Management Review* 12 (1987): 235–249.

109. K. N. Wexley, R. A. Alexander, J. P. Greenawalt, and M. A. Couch, "Attitudinal Congruence and Similarity as Related to Interpersonal Evaluations in Manager-Subordinate Dyads," *Academy of Management Journal* 23 (1980): 320–330.

110. H. H. Kelley, *Attribution in Social Interaction* (New York: General Learning Press, 1971); H. H. Kelley, "The Processes of Causal Attribution," *American Psychologist* 28 (1973): 107–128.

111. S. D. Salamon and S. L. Robinson, "Trust That Binds: The Impact of Collective Felt Trust on Organizational Performance," *Journal of Applied Psychology* 93(3) (2008): 593–601.

112. D. R. Avery and P. F. McKay, "Target Practice: An Organizational Impression Management Approach to Attracting Minority and Female Job Applicants," *Personnel Psychology* 59 (2006): 157–187.

113. L. H. Nishii, D. P. Lepak and B. Schneider, "Employee Attributions of the "Why" of HR Practices: Their Effects on Employee Attitudes and Behaviors, and Customer Satisfaction," *Personnel Psychology* 61 (2008): 503–545.

114. A. M. Grant, S. Parker, and C. Collins, "Getting Credit for Proactive Behavior: Supervisor Reactions Depend on What You Value and How You Feel," *Personnel Psychology* 62 (2009): 31–55.

# Chapter 4

1. A. H. Eagly and S. Chaiken, *The Psychology of Attitudes* (Orlando, Fla.: Harcourt Brace Jovanovich, 1993).

2. M. J. Rosenberg, C. I. Hovland, W. J. McGuire, R. P. Abelson, and J. H. Brehm, *Attitude Organization and Change* (New Haven, Conn.: Yale University Press, 1960).

3. L. Festinger, *A Theory of Cognitive Dissonance* (Evanston, Ill.: Row, Peterson, 1957).

4. R. H. Fazio and M. P. Zanna, "On the Predictive Validity of Attitudes: The Roles of Direct Experience and Confidence," *Journal of Personality* 46 (1978): 228–243.

5. A. Tversky and D. Kahneman, "Judgment under Uncertainty: Heuristics and Biases," in D. Kahneman, P. Slovic, and A. Tversky, eds., *Judgment under Uncertainty* (New York: Cambridge University Press, 1982), 3–20.

6. I. Ajzen and M. Fishbein, "Attitude–Behavior Relations: A Theoretical Analysis and Review of Empirical Research," *Psychological Bulletin* 84 (1977): 888–918.

7. M. A. Adam and D. Rachman-Moore, "The Methods Used to Implement an Ethical Code of Conduct and Employee Attitudes," *Journal of Business Ethics* 54 (2004): 225–244.

8. Ajzen and Fishbein, "Attitude-Behavior Relations": 888–918.

9. B. T. Johnson and A. H. Eagly, "Effects of Involvement on Persuasion: A Meta-Analysis," *Psychological Bulletin* 106 (1989): 290–314.

10. K. G. DeBono and M. Snyder, "Acting on One's Attitudes: The Role of History of Choosing Situations," *Personality and Social Psychology Bulletin* 21 (1995): 629–636.

11. I. Ajzen and M. Fishbein, *Understanding Attitudes and Predicting Social Behavior* (Englewood Cliffs, N.J.: Prentice-Hall, 1980).

12. I. Ajzen, "From Intentions to Action: A Theory of Planned Behavior," in J. Kuhl and J. Beckmann, eds., *Action-Control: From Cognition to Behavior* (Heidelberg: Springer, 1985).

13. I. Ajzen, "The Theory of Planned Behavior," *Organizational Behavior and Human Decision Processes* 50 (1991): 1–33.

14. L. M. Saari and T. A. Judge, "Employee Attitudes and Job Satisfaction," *Human Resource Management* 43 (2004): 395–407.

15. J. W. Harter, F. L. Schmidt, and T. L. Hayes, "Business-unit-level Relationship Between Employee Satisfaction, Employee Engagement, and Business Outcomes: A Meta-analysis," *Journal of Applied Psychology* 87 (2002): 268–279.

16. A. Sagie and M. Krausz, "What Aspects of the Job Have Most Effect on Nurses?" *Human Resource Management Journal* 13 (2003): 46–62.

17. C. P. Parker, B. B. Baltes, S. A. Young, J. W. Huff, R. A. Altman, H. A. LaCost, and J. E. Roberts, "Relationships between Psychological Climate Perceptions and Work Outcomes: A Meta-Analytic Review," *Journal of Organizational Behavior* 24 (2003): 389–416.

18. J. Lemmick and J. Mattsson, "Employee Behavior, Feelings of Warmth and Customer Perception in Service Encounters," *International Journal of Retail & Distribution Management* 30 (2002): 18–44.

19. E. A. Locke, "The Nature and Causes of Job Satisfaction," in M. Dunnette, ed., *Handbook of Industrial and Organizational Psychology* (Chicago: Rand McNally, 1976).

20. P. C. Smith, L. M. Kendall, and C. L. Hulin, *The Measurement of Satisfaction in Work and Retirement* (Skokie, Ill.: Rand McNally, 1969).

21. A. Sousa-Poza and A. A. Sousa-Poza, "Well-being at Work: A Cross-national Analysis of the Levels and Determinants of Job Satisfaction," *Journal of Socio-Economics* 29 (2000): 517–538.

22. D. Chiaburu and D. A. Harrison, "Do Peers Make the Place? Conceptual Synthesis and Meta-analysis of Coworker Effects on Perceptions, Attitudes, OCB's and Performance," *Journal of Applied Psychology* 93 (2008): 1082–1103.

23. P. Warr, "Work Values: Some Demographic and Cultural Correlates," *Journal of Occupational and Organizational Psychology* 81 (2008): 751–775.

24. Ibid.

25. T. A. Judge and J. E. Bono, "Relationship of Core Self-Evaluation Traits—Self-esteem, Generalized Self-efficacy, Locus of Control, and Emotional Stability—with Job Satisfaction and Job Performance: A Meta-analysis," *Journal of Applied Psychology* 86 (2001): 80–92.

26. R. Ilies and T. A. Judge, "On the Heritability of Job Satisfaction: The Mediating Role of Personality," *Journal of Applied Psychology* 88 (2003): 750–759.

27. I. Levin and J. P. Stokes, "Dispositional Approach to Job Satisfaction: Role of Negative Affectivity," *Journal of Applied Psychology* 74 (1989): 752–758.

28. B. M. Staw, N. E. Bell, and J. A. Clausen, "The Dispositional Approach to Job Attitudes: A Lifetime Longitudinal Test," *Administrative Science Quarterly* 31 (1986): 56–77.

29. T. A. Judge, C. J. Thoresen, J. E. Bono, and G. K. Patton, "The Job Satisfaction-Job Performance Relationship: A Qualitative and Quantitative Review," *Psychological Bulletin* 127 (2001): 376–407.

30. C. Ostroff, "The Relationship between Satisfaction, Attitudes and Performance: An Organizational Level Analysis," *Journal of Applied Psychology* 77 (1992): 963–974.

31. R. Griffin and T. Bateman, "Job Satisfaction and Organizational Commitment," in C. Cooper and I. Robertson, eds., *International Review of Industrial and Organizational Psychology* (New York: Wiley, 1986).

32. A. R. Wheeler, V. C. Gallagher, R. L. Brouer, & C. J. Sablynski, "When Person-Organization (Mis)Fit and (Dis)Satisfaction Lead to Turnover: The Moderating Role of Perceived Job Mobility," *Journal of Managerial Psychology* 22 (2) 203–219.

33. L. A. Bettencourt, K. P. Gwinner, and M. L. Meuter, "A Comparison of Attitude, Personality, and Knowledge Predictors of Service-Oriented Organizational Citizenship Behaviors," *Journal of Applied Psychology* 86 (2001): 29–41.

34. D. W. Organ, *Organizational Citizenship Behavior: The Good Soldier Syndrome* (Lexington, Mass.: Lexington Books, 1988).

35. P. M. Podsakoff, S. B. Mackenzie, and C. Hui, "Organizational Citizenship Behaviors and Managerial Evaluations of Employee Performance: A Review and Suggestions for Future Research," G. Ferris, ed., in *Research in Personnel and Human Resources Management* (Greenwich, Conn.: JAI Press, 1993), 1–40.

36. O. Christ, R. Van Dick, and U. Wagner, "When Teachers Go the Extra Mile: Foci of Organizational Identification as Determinants of Different Forms of Organizational Citizenship Behavior among Schoolteachers," *British Journal of Educational Psychology* 73 (2003): 329–341.

37. G. L. Blakely, M. C. Andrews, and J. Fuller, "Are Chameleons Good Citizens: A Longitudinal Study of the Relationship between Self-Monitoring and Organizational Citizenship Behavior," *Journal of Business & Psychology* 18 (2003): 131–144.

38. W. H. Bommer, E. W. Miles, and S. L. Grover, "Does One Good Turn Deserve Another? Coworker Influences on Employee Citizenship," *Journal of Organizational Behavior* 24 (2003): 181–196.

39. N. P. Podsakoff, S. W. Whiting, P. M. Podsakoff, and B. D. Blume, "Individual- and Organizational-level Consequences of Organizational Citizenship Behaviors: A Meta-analysis," *Journal of Applied Psychology* 94 (2009): 122–141.

40. T. D. Allen, J. D. Facteau, and C. L. Facteau, "Structured Interviewing for OCB: Construct Validity, Faking and the Effects of Question Type," *Human Performance* 17 (2004): 247–260.

41. D. W. Organ, P. M. Podsakoff, and S. B Mackenzie, *Organizational Citizenship Behavior: Its Nature, Antecedents and Consequences.* (Thousand Oaks, CA: Sage 2006).

42. S. L. Robinson, and R. J. Bennett, "A Typology of Deviant Workplace Behaviors: A Multidimensional Scaling Study," *Academy of Management Journal*, 38(2) (1995), 555.

43. M. E. Heilman, and V. B. Alcott, "What I Think You Think of Me: Women's Reactions to Being Viewed as Beneficiaries of Preferential Selection," *Journal of Applied Psychology* 86 (2001): 574–582; M. E. Heilman, C. J. Block, & P. Stathatos, "The Affirmative Action Stigma of Incompetence: Effects of Performance Information Ambiguity," *Academy of Management Journal,* 40, (1997): 603–625.

44. R. T. Mowday, L. W. Porter, and R. M. Steers, *Employee–Organization Linkages: The Psychology of Commitment* (New York: Academic Press, 1982).

45. H. S. Becker, "Notes on the Concept of Commitment," *American Journal of Sociology* 66 (1960): 32–40.

46. J. P. Meyer, N. J. Allen, and C. A. Smith, "Commitment to Organizations and Occupations: Extension and Test of a Three-Component Model," *Journal of Applied Psychology* 78 (1993): 538–551.

47. J. P. Meyer, D. S. Stanley, L. Herscovitch, and L. Topolnytsky, "Affective, Continuance and Normative Commitment to the Organization: A Meta-analysis of Antecedents, Correlates and Consequences," *Journal of Vocational Behavior,* 61 (2002): 20–52.

48. F. Stinglhamber and C. Vandenberghe, "Organizations and Supervisors as Sources of Support and Targets of Commitment," *Journal of Organizational Behavior* 24 (2003): 251–270.

49. R. Eisenberger et al., "Reciprocation of Perceived Organizational Support," *Journal of Applied Psychology* 86 (2001): 42–51; J. E. Finegan, "The Impact of Person and Organizational Values on Organizational Commitment," *Journal of Occupational and Organizational Psychology* 73 (2000): 149–169.

50. E. Snape and T. Redman, "Too Old or Too Young? The Impact of Perceived Age Discrimination," *Human Resource Management Journal* 13 (2003): 78–89.

51. J. A. Conger, "The Necessary Art of Persuasion," *Harvard Business Review* 76 (1998): 84–96.

52. J. Cooper and R. T. Croyle, "Attitudes and Attitude Change," *Annual Review of Psychology* 35 (1984): 395–426.

53. K. M. Kniffen and D. S. Wilson, "The Effect of Nonphysical Traits on the Perception of Physical Attractiveness: Three Naturalistic Studies," *Evolution and Human Behavior* 25 (2004): 88–101.

54. E. M. Whitener, S. E. Brodt, M. A. Korsgaard, and J. M. Werner, "Managers as Initiators of Trust: An Exchange Relationship Framework for Understanding Managerial Trustworthy Behavior," *Academy of Management Review* 23 (1998): 513–530.

55. D. M. Mackie and L. T. Worth, "Processing Deficits and the Mediation of Positive Affect in Persuasion," *Journal of Personality and Social Psychology* 57 (1989): 27–40.

56. J. W. Brehm, *Responses to Loss of Freedom: A Theory of Psychological Reactance* (New York: General Learning Press, 1972).

57. D. DeSteno, R. E. Petty, and D. D. Rucker, "Discrete Emotions and Persuasion: The Role of Emotion-Induced Expectancies," *Journal of Personality & Social Psychology* 86 (2004): 43–56.

58. R. Petty, D. T. Wegener, and L. R. Fabrigar, "Attitudes and Attitude Change," *Annual Review of Psychology* 48 (1997): 609–647.

59. P. Brinol and R. E. Petty, "Overt Head Movements and Persuasion: A Self-Validation Analysis," *Journal of Personality & Social Psychology* 84 (2003): 1123–1139.

60. W. Wood, "Attitude Change: Persuasion and Social Influence," *Annual Review of Psychology* 51 (2000): 539–570.

61. N. H. Frijda, "Moods, Emotion Episodes, and Emotions," in M. Lewis and J. M. Haviland (Eds.), *Handbook of Emotions* (New York: Guilford Press, 1993) 381–403.

62. A. Ortony, G. L. Clore, and A. Collins, "The Cognitive Structure of Emotions (Cambridge, England: Cambridge University Press, 1988).

63. R. S. Lazarus, *Emotion and Adaptation* (New York: Oxford University Press, 1991).

64. H. M. Weiss, K. Suckow, and R. Cropanzano, "Effects of Justice Conditions on Discrete Emotions," *Journal of Applied Psychology*, 84 (1999), 786–794.

65. M. M. Pillutla and J. K. Murnighan, "Unfairness, Anger, and Spite: Emotional Rejections of Ultimatum Offers," *Organizational Behavior Human Decision Process* 68 (1996): 208–224.

66. T. B. Lawrence, and S. L. Robinson, "Ain't Misbehavin: Workplace Deviance as Organizational Resistance," *Journal of Management*, 33 (2007): 378–394.

67. B. L. Fredrickson, and C. Brannigan, "Positive Emotions," in. G. Bonnano & T. Mayne (eds.) *Emotions: Current Issues and Future Directions* (New York: Guilford Press, 2001) 123–152.

68. A. M. Isen, and R. A. Baron, "Positive Affect as a Factor in Organizational Behavior," *Research in Organizational Behavior*, 13 (1991): 1–53.

69. S. G. Barsade and D. E. Gibson "Why Does Affect Matter in Organizations?" *The Academy of Management Perspectives*, 21 (2007 ): 36–59.

70. A. Grandey, "When "The Show Must Go On": Surface and Deep Acting as Predictors of Emotional Exhaustion and Service Delivery," *Academy of Management Journal* 46 (2003): 86–96.

71. A. R. Hochschild, *The Managed Heart: Commercialization of Human Feeling.* (Berkeley, CA: University of California Press, 1983).

72. D. L. Joseph and D. A. Newman, "Emotional Intelligence: An Integrative Meta-analysis and Cascading Model," *Journal of Applied Psychology* 95 (2010): 54–78.

73. D. Matsumoto, S. H. Yoo, and J. Fontaine, "Mapping Expressive Differences Around the World: The Relationship Between Emotional Display Rules and Individualism versus Collectivism," *Journal of Cross-Cultural Psychology*, 39 (2008): 55–74.

74. S. Safdar, W. Friedlmeier, D. Matsumoto, S. H. Yoo, C. T. Kwantes, H. Kakai, and E. Shigemasu, "Variations of Emotional Display Rules Within and Across Cultures: A Comparison Between Canada, USA and Japan," *Canadian Journal of Behavioral Science,* 41 (2009): 1–10.

75. J. E. Dutton, P. J. Frost, M. C. Worline, J. M. Lilius, and J. M. Kanov, "Leading in Times of Trauma," *Harvard Business Review,* Vol. 80 (2002), Issue 1.

76. T. A. Stewart, "The Highway of the Mind," *Harvard Business Review,* 82 (2004): 116.

77. F. Navran, "Your Role in Shaping Ethics," *Executive Excellence* 9 (1992): 11–12.

78. C. H. J. Schwepker, "Ethical Climate's Relationship to Job Satisfaction, Organizational Commitment and Turnover in the Sales Force," *Journal of Business Research* 54 (2001): 39–52.

79. D. B. Turban and D. M. Cable, "Firm Reputation and Applicant Pool Characteristics," *Journal of Organizational Behavior* 24 (2003): 733–751.

80. E. A. Lind, J. Greenberg, K. S. Scott, and T. D. Welchans, "The Winding Road from Employee to Complainant: Situational and Psychological Determinants of Wrongful-Termination Claims," *Administrative Science Quarterly* 45 (2000): 557–590.

81. J. O. Cherrington and D. J. Cherrington, "A Menu of Moral Issues: One Week in the Life of *The Wall Street Journal,*" *Journal of Business Ethics* 11 (1992): 255–265.

82. P. Pelosi, *Corporate Karma: How Business Can Move Forward by Giving Back.* (Toronto: Orenda Publishing, 2007).

83. M. Easwaramoorthy, C. Barr, M. Runte, and D. Basil, *Business Support for Employee Volunteers in Canada: Results of a National Survey.* (Imagine Canada, 2006).

84. B. L. Flannery and D. R. May, "Environmental Ethical Decision Making in the U.S. Metal-Finishing Industry," *Academy of Management Journal* 43 (2000): 642–662.

85. K. R. Andrews, "Ethics in Practice," *Harvard Business Review* (September–October 1989): 99–104.

86. M. Rokeach, *The Nature of Human Values* (New York: Free Press, 1973).

87. S. P Eisner (2005), "Managing Generation Y," S.A.M. *Advanced Management Journal,* 70(4), 4–15.

88. R. H. Doktor, "Asian and American CEOs: A Comparative Study," *Organizational Dynamics* 18 (1990): 46–56.

89. R. L. Tung, "Handshakes across the Sea: Cross-Cultural Negotiating for Business Success," *Organizational Dynamics* (Winter 1991): 30–40.

90. C. Gomez, B. L. Kirkman, and D. L. Shapiro, "The Impact of Collectivism and In-Group/Out-Group Membership on the Evaluation Generosity of Team Members," *Academy of Management Journal* 43 (2000): 1097–1106; J. Zhou and J. J. Martocchio, "Chinese and American Managers' Compensation Award Decisions: A Comparative Policy-Capturing Study," *Personnel Psychology* 54 (2001): 115–145.

91. A. J. Ali and M. Amirshahi, "The Iranian Manager: Work Values and Orientations," *Journal of Business Ethics* 40 (2002): 133–143.

92. R. Neale and R. Mindel, "Rigging Up Multicultural Teamworking," *Personnel Management* (January 1992): 27–30.

93. G. W. England, "Organizational Goals and Expected Behavior of American Managers," *Academy of Management Journal* 10 (1967): 107–117.

94. B. M. Meglino, E. C. Ravlin, and C. L. Adkins, "A Work Values Approach to Corporate Culture: A Field Test of the Value Congruence Process and its Relationship to Individual Outcomes," *Journal of Applied Psychology* 74(1989): 424–432.

95. D. R. Avery, M. Hernandez, and M. R. Hebl, "Who's Watching the Race? Racial Salience in Recruitment Advertising," *Journal of Applied Social Psychology,* 34 (2004): 146–161.

96. P. F. McKay and D. R. Avery, "Warning! Diversity Recruitment Could Backfire," *Journal of Management Inquiry,* 14 (2005): 330–336.

97. J. B. Rotter, "Generalized Expectancies for Internal versus External Control of Reinforcement," *Psychological Monographs* 80 (1966): 1–28.

98. L. K. Trevino and S. A. Youngblood, "Bad Apples in Bad Barrels: A Causal Analysis of Ethical Decision-Making Behavior," *Journal of Applied Psychology* 75 (1990): 378–385.

99. H. M. Lefcourt, *Locus of Control: Current Trends in Theory and Research,* 2nd ed. (Hillsdale, N.J.: Erlbaum, 1982).

100. N. Machiavelli, *The Prince,* trans. George Bull (Middlesex, England: Penguin Books, 1961).

101. R. Christie and F. L. Geis, *Studies in Machiavellianism* (New York: Academic Press, 1970).

102. R. A. Giacalone and S. B. Knouse, "Justifying Wrongful Employee Behavior: The Role of Personality in Organizational Sabotage," *Journal of Business Ethics* 9 (1990): 55–61.

103. S. B. Knouse and R. A. Giacalone, "Ethical Decision Making in Business: Behavioral Issues and Concerns," *Journal of Business Ethics* 11 (1992): 369–377.

104. L. Kohlberg, "Stage and Sequence: The Cognitive Developmental Approach to Socialization," in D. A. Goslin, ed., *Handbook of Socialization Theory and Research* (Chicago: Rand McNally, 1969), 347–480.

105. C. I. Malinowski and C. P. Smith, "Moral Reasoning and Moral Conduct: An Investigation Prompted by Kohlberg's Theory," *Journal of Personality and Social Psychology* 49 (1985): 1016–1027.

106. M. Brabeck, "Ethical Characteristics of Whistleblowers," *Journal of Research in Personality* 18 (1984): 41–53.

107. W. Y. Penn and B. D. Collier, "Current Research in Moral Development as a Decision Support System," *Journal of Business Ethics* 4 (1985): 131–136; Trevino and Youngblood, "Bad Apples in Bad Barrels."

108. D. F. Spake, C. M. Megehee, and G. R. Franke, "Students' Views of Ethical Behavior and the Impact of Association," *Marketing Education Review,* 17 (2007): 33–47.

# Chapter 5

1. U. Klehe and N. Anderson, "Working Hard and Working Smart: Motivation and Ability During Typical and Maximum Performance," *Journal of Applied Psychology* 92 (2007): 978–99.

2. D. M. McGregor, *The Human Side of Enterprise* (New York: McGraw-Hill, 1960).

3. J. P. Campbell and R. D. Pritchard, "Motivation Theory in Industrial and Organizational Psychology," in M. D. Dunnette, ed., *Handbook of Industrial and Organizational Psychology* (Chicago: Rand McNally, 1976), 63–130.

4. M. Weber, *The Protestant Ethic and the Spirit of Capitalism* (London: Talcott Parson, tr., 1930).

5. S. Freud, *Civilization and Its Discontents,* trans. and ed. J. Strachey (New York: Norton, 1961).

6. P. D. Dunlop and K. Lee, "Workplace Deviance, Organizational Citizenship Behavior, and Business Unit Performance: The Bad Apples Do Spoil the Whole Barrel," *Journal of Organizational Behavior* 25 (2004): 67–80.

7. A. H. Maslow, "A Theory of Human Motivation," *Psychological Review* 50 (1943): 370–396.

8. C. P. Alderfer, *Human Needs in Organizational Settings* (New York: Free Press, 1972).

9. B. Schneider and C. P. Alderfer, "Three Studies of Need Satisfactions in Organizations," *Administrative Science Quarterly* 18 (1973): 489–505.

10. D. C. McClelland, *Motivational Trends in Society* (Morristown, N.J.: General Learning Press, 1971).

11. J. P. Chaplin and T. S. Krawiec, *Systems and Theories of Psychology* (New York: Holt, Rinehart & Winston, 1960).

12. D. C. McClelland, "Achievement Motivation Can Be Learned," *Harvard Business Review* 43 (1965): 6–24.

13. E. A. Ward, "Multidimensionality of Achievement Motivation among Employed Adults," *Journal of Social Psychology* 134 (1997): 542–544.

14. A. Sagie, D. Elizur, and H. Yamauchi, "The Structure and Strength of Achievement Motivation: A Cross-Cultural Comparison," *Journal of Organizational Behavior* 17 (1996): 431–444.

15. D. C. McClelland and D. Burnham, "Power Is the Great Motivator," *Harvard Business Review* 54 (1976): 100–111; J. Hall and J. Hawker, *Power Management Inventory* (The Woodlands, Tex.: Teleometrics International, 1988).

16. S. Schachter, *The Psychology of Affiliation* (Stanford, Calif.: Stanford University Press, 1959).

17. G. G. Alpander and K. D. Carter, "Strategic Multi-National Intra-Company Differences in Employee Motivation," *Journal of Managerial Psychology* 6 (1991): 25–32.

18. M. E. Enzle and S. C. Anderson, "Surveillance Intentions and Intrinsic Motivation," *Journal of Personality and Social Psychology* 64 (1993): 257–266.

19. F. Herzberg, B. Mausner, and B. Snyderman, *The Motivation to Work* (New York: Wiley, 1959).

20. F. Herzberg, *Work and the Nature of Man* (Cleveland: World, 1966).

21. J. Marquez, "Winning Women Back," *Workforce Management* 86(7) (2007): 20–21.

22. F. J. Leach and J. D. Westbrook, "Motivation and Job Satisfaction in One Government Research and Development Environment," *Engineering Management Journal* 12 (2000): 3–8.

23. J. S. Adams, "Inequity in Social Exchange," in L. Berkowitz, ed., *Advances in Experimental Social Psychology,* Vol. 2 (New York: Academic Press, 1965), 267–299; J. S. Adams, "Toward an Understanding of Inequity," *Journal of Abnormal and Social Psychology* 67 (1963): 422–436.

24. Pay Equity Legislation in Canada, Human Resources and Skills Development Canada, (March 28, 2010), http://www.hrsdc.gc.ca/eng/labour/labour_law/esl/pay_equity.shtml

25. D. van Dierendonck, W. B. Schaufeli, and H. J. Sixma, "Burnout among General Practitioners: A Perspective from Equity Theory," *Journal of Social and Clinical Psychology* 13 (1994): 86–100.

26. J. Greenberg, "Approaching Equity and Avoiding Inequity in Groups and Organizations." In J. Greenberg and R. L. Cohen, eds., *Equity and Justice in Social Behavior.* 337–351. New York: Academic Press, 1982.

27. P. D. Sweeney, D. B. McFarlin, and E. J. Inderrieden, "Using Relative Deprivation Theory to Explain Satisfaction with Income and Pay Level: A Multistudy Examination," *Academy of Management Journal* 33 (1990): 423–436.

28. R. C. Huseman, J. D. Hatfield, and E. A. Miles, "A New Perspective on Equity Theory: The Equity Sensitivity Construct," *Academy of Management Review* 12 (1987): 222–234.

29. D. McLoughlin and S. C. Carr, "Equity and Sensitivity and Double Demotivation," *Journal of Social Psychology* 137 (1997): 668–670.

30. K. E. Weick, M. G. Bougon, and G. Maruyama, "The Equity Context," *Organizational Behavior and Human Performance* 15 (1976): 32–65.

31. R. Coles, *Privileged Ones* (Boston: Little, Brown, 1977).

32. O. H. Akan, R. S. Allen, and C. S. White, "Equity Sensitivity and Organizational Citizenship Behavior in a Team Environment," *Small Group Research* 40 (2009): 94–112.

33. W. C King, E. W. Miles, and D. D. Day, "A Test and Refinement of the Equity Sensitivity Construct," *Journal of Organizational Behavior* 14 (1993): 301–317.

34. L. Y. Fok, S. J. Hartman, M. F. Villere, and R. C. Freibert, "A Study of the Impact of Cross Cultural Differences on Perceptions of Equity and Organizational Citizenship Behavior," *International Journal of Management* 13 (1996): 3–14.

35. J. Greenberg, "Who Stole the Money, and When? Individual and Situational Determinants of Employee Theft," *Organizational Behavior and Human Decision Processes* 89 (2002): 985–1003.

36. M. L. Ambrose, M. A. Seabright, and M. Schminke, "Sabotage in the Workplace: The Role of Organizational Justice," *Organizational Behavior and Human Decision Processes* 89 (2002): 947–965.

37. D. P. Skarlicki and R. Folger, "Retaliation in the Workplace: The Roles of Distributive, Procedural and Interactional Justice," *Journal of Applied Psychology* 82 (1997): 434–443.

38. R. J. Sanchez, D. M. Truxillo, and T. N. Bauer, "Development and Examination of an Expectancy-Based Measure of Test-Taking Motivation," *Journal of Applied Psychology* 85 (2000): 739–750.

39. V. H. Vroom, *Work and Motivation* (New York: Wiley, 1964/1970).

40. U. R. Larson, "Supervisor's Performance Feedback to Subordinates: The Effect of Performance Valence and Outcome Dependence," *Organizational Behavior and Human Decision Processes* 37 (1986): 391–409.

41. W. VanEerde and H. Thierry, "Vroom's Expectancy Models and Work-Related Criteria: A Meta-Analysis," *Journal of Applied Psychology* 81 (1996): 575–586.

42. E. D. Pulakos and N. Schmitt, "A Longitudinal Study of a Valence Model Approach for the Prediction of Job Satisfaction of New Employees," *Journal of Applied Psychology* 68 (1983): 307–312; F. J. Landy and W. S. Becker, "Motivation Theory Reconsidered," in L. L. Cummings and B. M. Staw, eds., *Research in Organizational Behavior* 9 (Greenwich, Conn.: JAI Press, 1987), 1–38.

43. L. Kohlberg, "The Cognitive-Developmental Approach to Socialization," in D. A. Goslin, ed., *Handbook of Socialization Theory and Research* (Chicago: Rand McNally, 1969).

44. D. C. Zetik and A. Schumacher, "Goal-setting and Negotiation Performance: A Meta-analysis," *Group Process and Intergroup Relationships* 5 (2002): 35–52.

45. G. P. Latham and S. B. Kinne, "Improving Job Performance through Training in Goal Setting," *Journal of Applied Psychology* 59 (1974): 187–191.

46. G. P. Latham and J. Baldes, "The 'Practical Significance' of Locke's Theory of Goal-setting," *Journal of Applied Psychology* 60 (1975): 122–124.

47. E. A. Locke and G. P. Latham, "Building a Practically Useful Theory of Goal Setting and Task Motivation: A 35-year Odyssey," *American Psychologist* 57 (2002): 705–717.

48. R. Kanfer and P. L. Ackerman, "Motivation and Cognitive Abilities: An Integrative Aptitude Treatment Interaction Approach to Skill Acquisition," *Journal of Applied Psychology* 74 (1989): 657–690.

49. D. Winters and G. P. Latham, "The Effect of Learning versus Outcome Goals on a Simple versus a Complex Task," *Group and Organization Management* 21 (1996): 236–250.

50. J. Hollenbeck, C. Williams, and H. Klein, "An Empirical Examination of the Antecedents of Commitment to Difficult Goals," *Journal of Applied Psychology* 74 (1989): 18–23.

51. E. A. Locke and G. P. Latham, "Building a Practically Useful Theory of Goal Setting and Task Motivation: A 35-year Odyssey," *American Psychologist* 57 (2002): 705–717.

52. Ibid.

53. N. J. Adler, *International Dimensions of Organizational Behavior,* 4th ed. (Mason, Ohio: South-Western, 2001).

54. G. Hofstede, "Motivation, Leadership, and Organization: Do American Theories Apply Abroad?" *Organizational Dynamics* 9 (1980): 42–63.

55. G. H. Hines, "Cross-Cultural Differences in Two-Factor Theory," *Journal of Applied Psychology* 58 (1981): 313–317.

56. M. C. Bolino and W. H. Turnley, "Old Faces, New Places: Equity Theory in Cross-Cultural Contexts," *Journal of Organizational Behavior* (In Press).

57. M. Erez, "A Culture-based Approach to Work Motivation." In C. P. Early and M. Erez, eds., *New Perspectives on International Industrial/Organizational Psychology,* 192–242, Jossey-Bass Publishers, 1997.

58. H. Thierry, "Payment by Results: A Review of Research 1945–1985," *Applied Psychology: An International Review* 36 (1987): 91–108.

59. K. Y. Thornblum, D. Jonsson, and U. G. Foa, "Nationality Resource Class, and Preferences among Three Allocation Rules: Sweden vs. USA," *International Journal of Intercultural Relations* 9 (1985): 51–77.

60. J. J. Berman and P. Singh, "Cross-cultural Similarities and Differences in Perceptions of Fairness," *Journal of Cross-Cultural Psychology* 16 (1985): 55–67.

61. U. M. Gluskinos, "Cultural and Political Considerations in the Introduction of Western Technologies: The Mekorot Project," *Journal of Management Development* 6 (1988): 34–46.

62. M. Erez and C. P. Earley, "Comparative Analysis of Goal-setting Strategies across Cultures," *Journal of Applied Psychology* 71 (1987): 658–665.

# Chapter 6

1. B. F. Skinner, "Operant Behavior," *American Psychologist* 18 (1963): 503–515.

2. B. F. Skinner, "Reinforcement Today," *American Psychologist* 13 (1958): 94–99.

3. Research summarized in A. Poling and D. Braatz, Chapter 2: Principles of Learning: Respondent and Operant Conditioning and Human Behavior, In *Handbook of Organizational Performance: Behavior Analysis and Management,* C. Merle Johnson, William K. Redmon, and Thomas C. Mawhinney, eds. Binghampton, N.Y.: The Haworth Press, 2001, 23–50.

4. G. P. Latham and V. L. Huber, "Schedules of Reinforcement: Lessons from the Past and Issues for the Future," *Journal of Organizational Behavior Management* 12 (1991): 125–149.

5. M. Maccoby, J. Hoffer Gittell, and M. Ledeen, "Leadership and the Fear Factor," *Sloan Management Review* 148 (Winter 2004): 14–18.

6. A. Bandura, *Social Learning Theory* (Englewood Cliffs, N.J.: Prentice-Hall, 1977); A. Bandura, "Self-Efficacy: Toward a Unifying Theory of Behavioral Change," *Psychological Review* 84 (1977): 191–215.

7. J. J. Martocchio and E. J. Hertenstein, "Learning Orientation and Goal Orientation Context: Relationships with Cognitive and Affective Learning Outcomes," *Human Resource Development Quarterly* 14 (2003): 413–434.

8. A. Bandura, "Regulation of Cognitive Processes through Perceived Self-Efficacy," *Developmental Psychology* (September 1989): 729–735.

9. J. M. Phillips and S. M. Gully, "Role of Goal Orientation, Ability, Need for Achievement, and Locus of Control in the Self-Efficacy and Goal-Setting Process," *Journal of Applied Psychology* 82 (1997): 792–802.

10. J. C. Weitlauf, R. E. Smith, and D. Cervone, "Generalization Effects of Coping-Skills Training: Influence of Self-Defense Training on Women's Efficacy Beliefs, Assertiveness, and Aggression," *Journal of Applied Psychology* 85 (2000): 625–633.

11. V. Gecas, "The Social Psychology of Self-Efficacy," *Annual Review of Sociology* 15 (1989): 291–316.

12. T. Sitzmann, B. Bell, K. Kraiger, and A. Kanar, "A Multilevel Analysis of the Effect of Prompting Self-regulation in Technology-delivered Instruction," *Personnel Psychology* 62 (2009), 697–734.

13. T. Sitzmann and K. Ely, "Sometimes You Need a Reminder: The Effects of Prompting Self-regulation on Regulatory Processes, Learning and Attrition," *Journal of Applied Psychology* 95 (2010), 132–144.

14. N. Keith and M. Frese, "Effectiveness of Error Management Training: A Meta-analysis," *Journal of Applied Psychology* 93 (2008), 59–69.

15. N. Keith and M. Frese, "Self-regulation in Error Management Training: Emotion Control and Metacognition as Mediators of Performance Effects," *Journal of Applied Psychology* 90 (2005), 677–691.

16. S. Ellis, Y. Ganzach, E. Castle, and G. Sekely, "The Effect of Filmed versus Personal After-event Reviews on Task Performance: The Mediating and Moderating Role of Self-efficacy," *Journal of Applied Psychology,* 95 (2010), 122–131.

17. S. Ellis and I Davidi, "After-event Reviews: Drawing Lessons from Successful and Failed Experience," *Journal of Applied Psychology* 90 (2005), 857–871.

18. S. Ellis, R. Mendel, and M. Nir, "Learning from Successful and Failed Experience: The Moderating Role of Kind of After-event Review," *Journal of Applied Psychology* 91 (2006): 669–680.

19. S. Ellis, Y. Ganzach, E. Castle and G. Sekely, "The Effect of Filmed versus Personal After-event Reviews on Task Performance: The Mediating and Moderating Role of Self-Efficacy," *Journal of Applied Psychology,* 95 (2010), 122–131.

20. L. Baird, P. Holland, and S. Deacon, "Imbedding More Learning into the Performance Fast Enough to Make a Difference," *Organizational Dynamics,* Spring 1999: 19–32.

21. R. L. Cardy, *Performance Management: Concepts, Skills, and Exercises* (Armonk, New York and London, England: M. E. Sharpe, 2004).

22. G. S. Odiorne, *Management by Objectives: A System of Managerial Leadership* (New York: Pitman, 1965).

23. J. C. Quick, "Dyadic Goal Setting and Role Stress," *Academy of Management Journal* 22 (1979): 241–252.

24. P. F. Drucker, *The Practice of Management* (New York: Harper & Bros., 1954).

25. R. D. Prichard, P. L. Roth, S. D. Jones, P. J. Galgay, and M. D. Watson, "Designing a Goal-Setting System to Enhance Performance: A Practical Guide," *Organizational Dynamics* 17 (1988): 69–78.

26. C. L. Hughes, *Goal Setting: Key to Individual and Organizational Effectiveness* (New York: American Management Association, 1965).

27. M. E. Tubbs and S. E. Ekeberg, "The Role of Intentions in Work Motivation: Implications for Goal-Setting Theory and Research," *Academy of Management Review* 16 (1991): 180–199.

28. S. Vatave, "Managing Risk," *Supervision* 65 (2004): 6–9.

29. J. R. Hollenbeck and A. P. Brief, "The Effects of Individual Differences and Goal Origin on Goal Setting and Performance," *Organizational Behavior and Human Decision Processes* 40 (1987): 392–414.

30. G. D. Nord, T. F. McCubbins, and J. Horn Nord, "E-monitoring in the Workplace: Privacy, Legislation and Surveillance Software," *Communications of the ACM,* 49 (2006): 74–77.

31. C. Spitzmuller and J. M. Stanton, "Examining Employee Compliance with Organizational Surveillance and Monitoring," *Journal of Occupational and Organizational Psychology* 79 (2006), 245–272.

32. H. H. Meyer, E. Kay, and J. R. P. French, "Split Roles in Performance Appraisal," *Harvard Business Review* 43 (1965): 123–129.

33. S. L. Rynes, B. Gerhart, and L. Parks, "Personnel Psychology: Performance Evaluation and Pay for Performance," *Annual Review of Psychology* 56 (2005), 571–600.

34. A. N. Kluger and A. DeNisi, "The Effects of Feedback Interventions on Performance: A Historical Review, a Meta-analysis and a Preliminary Feedback Intervention Theory," *Psychological Bulletin* 119 (1996): 254–284.

35. W. A. Fisher, J. C. Quick, L. L. Schkade, and G. W. Ayers, "Developing Administrative Personnel through the Assessment Center Technique," *Personnel Administrator* 25 (1980): 44–46, 62.

36. G. A. Van Kleef, A. C. Homan, B. Beersma, D. Van Knippenberg, and F. Damen, "Searing Sentiment or Cold Calculation? The Effects of Leader Emotional Displays on Team Performance Depend on Follower Epistemic Motivation," *Academy of Management Journal* 52 (2009), 562–580.

37. K. Byron, S. Khazanchi, and D. Nazarian, "The Relationship between Stressors and Creativity: A Meta-analysis Examining Competitive Theoretical Models," *Journal of Applied Psychology* 95 (2010), 201–212.

38. M. B. DeGregorio and C. D. Fisher, "Providing Performance Feedback: Reactions to Alternative Methods," *Journal of Management* 14 (1988): 605–616.

39. G. C. Thornton, "The Relationship between Supervisory and Self-Appraisals of Executive Performance," *Personnel Psychology* 21 (1968): 441–455.

40. A. S. DeNisi and A. N. Kluger, "Feedback Effectiveness: Can 360-Degree Appraisals Be Improved?" *Academy of Management Executive* 14 (2000): 129–140.

41. S. L. Rynes, B. Gerhart, and L. Parks, "Personnel Psychology: Performance Evaluation and Pay for Performance," *Annual Review of Psychology* 56 (2005), 571–600.

42. F. Luthans and S. J. Peterson, "360-Degree Feedback with Systematic Coaching: Empirical Analysis Suggests a Winning Combination," *Human Resource Management* 42 (2003): 243–256.

43. G. Toegel and J. A. Conger, "360-Degree Assessment: Time for Reinvention," *Academy of Management Learning and Education* 2 (2003): 297–311.

44. L. Hirschhorn, "Leaders and Followers in a Postindustrial Age: A Psychodynamic View," *Journal of Applied Behavioral Science* 26 (1990): 529–542.

45. F. M Jablin, "Superior-Subordinate Communication: The State of the Art," *Psychological Bulletin* 86 (1979): 1201–1222.

46. J. Pfeffer, "Six Dangerous Myths about Pay," *Harvard Business Review* 76 (1998): 108–119.

47. E. A. Locke, D. B. Feren, V. M. McCaleb, K. N. Shaw, and A. T. Denny, "The Relative Effectiveness of Four Ways of Motivating Employee Performance." In *Changes in Working Life*, K. D. Duncan, M. M. Gruenberg, and D. Wallis, eds., New York: Wiley, 1960, 363–388.

48. D. G. Jenkins Jr., A. Mitra, N. Gupta, and J. D. Shaw, "Are Financial Incentives Related to Performance? A Meta-analytic Review of Empirical Research," *Journal of Applied Psychology* 83 (1998): 777–787.

49. J. D. Shaw and N. Gupta, "Pay System Characteristics and Quit Patterns of Good, Average and Poor Performers," *Personnel Psychology* 60 (2007): 903–928.

50. E. P. Lazear, "Salaries and Piece Rates," *Journal of Business* 59 (1986): 405–431.

51. R. D. Bretz, R. A. Ash, and G. F. Dreher, "Do People Make the Place? An Examination of the Attraction-selection-attrition Hypothesis," *Personnel Psychology* 42 (1989): 561–581.

52. D. M. Cable and T. A. Judge, "Pay Preferences and Job Search Decisions: A Person-Organization Fit Perspective," *Personnel Psychology* 47 (1994): 317–348.

53. C. B. Cadsby, F. Song, and F. Tapon, "Sorting and Incentive Effects of Pay for Performance: An Experimental Investigation," *Academy of Management Journal* 50 (2007): 387–405.

54. R. T. Kaufman, "The Effects of Improshare on Productivity," *Industrial Labour Relations Review* 45 (1992): 311–322.

55. M. J. Pearsall, M. S. Christian, and A. P. J. Ellis, "Motivating Interdependent Teams: Individual Rewards, Shared Rewards, or Something In-between," *Journal of Applied Psychology* 95 (2010), 183–191.

56. S. Kerr, "On the Folly of Rewarding A, While Hoping for B," *Academy of Management Journal* 18 (1975): 769–783.

57. J. M. Bardwick, *Danger in the Comfort Zone* (New York: American Management Association, 1991).

58. B. Raabe and T. A. Beehr, "Formal Mentoring versus Supervisor and Coworker Relationships: Differences in Perceptions and Impact," *Journal of Organizational Behavior* 24 (2003): 271–293.

59. A. M. Young and P. L. Perrewe, "What Did You Expect? An Examination of Career-Related Support and Social Support among Mentors and Protégés," *Journal of Management* 26 (2000): 611–633.

60. K. Doherty, "The Good News about Depression," *Business and Health* 3 (1989): 1–4.

61. K. E. Kram, "Phases of the Mentor Relationship," *Academy of Management Journal* 26 (1983): 608–625.

62. T. D. Allen, L. T. Eby, M. L. Poteet, E. Lentz, and L. Lima, "Career Benefits Associated with Mentoring for Protégés: A Meta-Analysis," *Journal of Applied Psychology* 89 (2004): 127–136.

63. T. N. Bauer and S. G. Green, "Development of Leader–Member Exchange: A Longitudinal Test," *Academy of Management Journal* 39 (1996): 1538–1567.

64. K. E. Kram and L. A. Isabella, "Mentoring Alternatives: The Role of Peer Relationships in Career Development," *Academy of Management Journal* 28 (1985): 110–132.

65. J. Greco, "Hey, Coach!" *Journal of Business Strategy* 22 (2001): 28–32.

# Chapter 7

1. J. C. Quick, J. D. Quick, D. L. Nelson, and J. J. Hurrell, Jr., *Preventive Stress Management in Organizations* (Washington, D.C.: American Psychological Association, 1997).

2. J. Park, "Work Stress and Job Performance," *Perspectives on Labour and Income*, Statistics Canada, December 2007, catalogue no. 75–001-XIE, http://www.statcan.gc.ca/pub/75-001-x/75-001-x2007112-eng.htm.

3. C. Higgins, L. Duxbury, and S. Lyons, "Reducing Work-life Conflict: What Works? What Doesn't?" Health Canada, 2008, available at http://www.hc-sc.gc.ca/ewh-semt/pubs/occup-travail/balancing-equilibre/sum-res-eng.php.

4. Cited in C. Williams, "Sources of Workplace Stress," *Perspectives on Labour and Income*, Statistics Canada, June 2003, http://www.statcan.gc.ca/pub/75-001-x/00603/6533-eng.html.

5. A. Ostry, S. Maggi, J. Tansey, J. Dunn, R. Hershler, L. Chen, and C. Hertzman, "The Impact of Psychosocial and Physical Work Experience on Mental Health: A Nested Case Control Study," *Canadian Journal of Community Mental Health* 25 (2006): 59–70.

6. L. Duxbury, C. Higgins, and S. Lyons, "The Etiology and Reduction of Role Overload in Canada's Health Care Sector, 2010," http://www.sprott.carleton.ca/news/2010/docs/complete-report.pdf.

7. S. A Murphy, L. Duxbury, and C. Higgins, "The Individual and Organizational Consequences of Stress, Anxiety and Depression in the Workplace: A Case Study," *Canadian Journal of Community Mental Health* 25 (2006): 143–157.

8. European Foundation for the Improvement of Living and Working Conditions, Work-related stress, 2007, http://www.eurofound.europa.eu/ewco/reports/TN0502TR01/TN0502TR01.pdf

9. F. Green and S McIntosh, "The intensification of work in Europe," *Labour Economics* 8 (2001): 291–308.

10. M. Dollard, N. Skinner, M. R. Tuckey, and T. Bailey, "National Surveillance of Psychosocial Risk Factors in the Workplace: An International Overview," *Work and Stress* 21 (2007): 1–29.

11. J. Sun, S. Wang, J. Zhang, and W. Li, "Assessing the Cumulative Effects of Stress: The Association Between Job Stress and Allostatic Load in a Large Sample of Chinese Employees," *Work and Stress* 21 (2007): 333–347.

12. K. Peltzer, O. Shisana, K. Zuma, B. Van Wyk, and N. Zungu-Dirwayi, "Job Sress, Job Satisfaction and Stress-related Illnesses among South African Educators," *Stress and Health* 25 (2009): 247–257.

13. European Social Partners, "Implementation of the European Autonomous Framework Agreement on Work-Related Stress," June 2008, http://www.etuc.org/IMG/pdf_Final_Implementation_report.pdf.

14. Health and Safety Executive, "Managing the Causes of Work-related Stress," United Kingdom, 2007, http://www.hse.gov.uk/pubns/priced/hsg218.pdf.

15. S. Leka, A. Griffiths, and T. Cox (Institute of Work, Health and Organisations; World Health Organization), *Work Organisation and Stress: Systematic Problem Approaches for Employers, Managers and Trade Union Representatives*, World Health Organisation, 2003.

16. S. Sri Kantha, "Productivity Drive," *Nature* (April 30, 1992): 738.

17. S. Sri Kantha, "Clues to Prolific Productivity Among Prominent Scientists," *Medical Hypotheses* 39 (1992): 159–163.

18. H. Selye, *The Stress of Life* (New York, McGraw-Hill, 1956).

19. W. B. Cannon, "Stresses and Strains of Homeostasis," *American Journal of the Medical Sciences* 189 (1935): 1–14.

20. W. B. Cannon, *The Wisdom of the Body* (New York: Norton, 1932).

21. R. S. Lazarus, *Psychological Stress and the Coping Process* (New York: McGraw-Hill, 1966).

22. T. R. Schneider, "The Role of Neuroticism on Psychological and Physiological Stress Responses," *Journal of Experimental Social Psychology* 40 (2004): 795–804.

23. D. Katz and R. L. Kahn, *The Social Psychology of Organizations*, 2nd ed. (New York: Wiley, 1978), 185–221.

24. H. Levinson, "A Psychoanalytic View of Occupational Stress," *Occupational Mental Health* 3 (1978): 2–13.

25. S. Cohen, D. Janicki-Deverts, and G. E. Miller, "Psychological Stress and Disease," *Journal of the American Medical Association* 298 (2007): 1685–1687.

26. T. L. Friedman, *The Lexus and the Olive Tree* (New York: Vintage Anchor, 2000).

27. S. Zuboff, *In the Age of the Smart Machine: The Future of Work and Power* (New York: Basic Books, 1988).

28. D. T. Hall and J. Richter, "Career Gridlock: Baby Boomers Hit the Wall," *Academy of Management Executive* 4 (1990): 7–22.

29. N. P. Podsakoff, J. A. LePine, and M. A. LePine, "Differential Challenge Stressor-Hindrance Stressor Relationships with Job Attitudes, Turnover Intentions, Turnover, and Withdrawal Behavior: A Meta-Analysis," *Journal of Applied Psychology* 92 (2007): 438–454.

30. R. L. Kahn, D. M. Wolfe, R. P. Quinn, J. D. Snoek, and R. A. Rosenthal, *Organizational Stress: Studies in Role Conflict and Ambiguity* (New York: Wiley, 1964).

31. L. B. Hammer, T. N. Bauer, and A. A. Grandey, "Work-Family Conflict and Work-Related Withdrawal Behaviors," *Journal of Business and Psychology* 17 (2003): 419–436.

32. R. B. Reid, "Mental Stress in the Workplace," Lancaster, Brooks and Welch, 2004. http://www.lbwlawyers.com/publications/mentalstressintheworkplace.php.

33. Quoted in J. Burton, *The Business Case for a Healthy Workplace*, Industrial Accident Prevention Association, 2008. http://www.iapa.ca/pdf/fd_business_case_healthy_workplace.pdf .

34. P. J. Frost, *Toxic Emotions at Work: How Compassionate Managers Handle Pain and Conflict* (Boston: Harvard Business School Press, 2003).

35. S. Grebner, N. K. Semmer, L. L. Faso, S. Gut, W. Kalin, and A. Elfering, "Working Conditions, Well-Being, and Job-Related Attitudes Among Call Centre Agents," *European Journal of Work and Organizational Psychology* 12 (2003): 341–365.

36. M. P. Bell, J. C. Quick, and C. Cycota, "Assessment and Prevention of Sexual Harassment: An Applied Guide to Creating Healthy Organizations," *International Journal of Selection and Assessment* 10 (2002): 160–167.

37. L. T. Hosmer, "Trust: The Connecting Link between Organizational Theory and Philosophical Ethics," *Academy of Management Review* 20 (1995): 379–403; V. J. Doby and R. D. Caplan, "Organizational Stress as Threat to Reputation: Effects on Anxiety at Work and at Home," *Academy of Management Journal* 38 (1995): 1105–1123.

38. R. T. Keller, "Cross-Functional Project Groups in Research and New Product Development: Diversity, Communications, Job Stress, and Outcomes," *Academy of Management Journal* 33 (2001): 547–555.

39. J. Burton, *The Business Case for a Healthy Workplace*, Industrial Accident Prevention Association, 2008.

40. M. F. Peterson and P. B. Smith, "Does National Culture or Ambient Temperature Explain Cross-National Differences in Role Stress? No Sweat!" *Academy of Management Journal* 40 (1997): 930–946.

41. K. K. Gillingham, "High-G Stress and Orientational Stress: Physiologic Effects of Aerial Maneuvering," *Aviation, Space, and Environmental Medicine* 59 (1988): A10–A20.

42. R. S. DeFrank, "Executive Travel Stress: Perils of the Road Warrior," *Academy of Management Executive* 14 (2000): 58–72; M. Westman, "Strategies for Coping with Business Trips: A Qualitative Exploratory Study," *International Journal of Stress Management* 11 (2004): 167–176.

43. R. S. Bhagat, S. J. McQuaid, S. Lindholm, and J. Segovis, "Total Life Stress: A Multimethod Validation of the Construct and Its Effect on Organizationally Valued Outcomes and Withdrawal Behaviors," *Journal of Applied Psychology* 70 (1985): 202–214.

44. J. C. Quick, J. R. Joplin, D. A. Gray, and E. C. Cooley, "The Occupational Life Cycle and the Family," in L. L'Abate, ed., *Handbook of Developmental Family Psychology and Psychopathology* (New York: John Wiley, 1993).

45. S. A. Lobel, "Allocation of Investment in Work and Family Roles: Alternative Theories and Implications for Research," *Academy of Management Review* 16 (1991): 507–521.

46. G. Porter, "Organizational Impact of Workaholism: Suggestions for Researching the Negative Outcomes of Excessive Work," *Journal of Occupational Health Psychology* 1 (1996): 70–84.

47. R. A. Karasek, "Job Demands, Job Decision Latitude, and Mental Strain: Implications for Job Redesign." *Administrative Science Quarterly* 24 (1979): 285–310.

48. T. Theorell, A. Tsutsumi, J. Hallquist, C. Reuterwall, C. Hagstedt, P. Fredlund, N. Emlund, and J. V. Johnson, "Decision Latitude, Job Strain, and Myocardial Infarction: A Study of Working Men in Stockholm," *American Journal of Public Health* 88 (1998): 382–388.

49. C. Aboa-Eboule, C. Brisson, E. Maunsell, B. Masse, R. Bourbonnais, M. Vezina, A. Milot, P. Theroux, and G. Dagenais, "Job Strain and Risk of Recurrent Coronary Heart Disease Events," *Journal of the American Medical Association* 298 (2007): 1652–1660.

50. H. Kuper, and M. Marmot, "Job Strain, Job Demands, Decision Latitude, and Risk of Coronary Heart Disease Within the Whitehall II Study," *Journal of Epidemiology and Community Health* 57 (2003): 147–153.

51. A. Ostry, S. Maggi, J. Tansey, J. Dunn, R. Hershler, L. Chen and C. Hertzman, "The Impact of Psychosocial and Physical Work Experience on Mental Health: A Nested Case Control Study," *Canadian Journal of Community Mental Health* 25 (2006): 59–70.

52. J. L. Wang, A. Lesage, N. Schmitz, and A. Drapeau, "The Relationship between Work Stress and Mental Disorders in Men and Women: Findings from a Population-based Study," *Journal of Epidemiology and Community Health* 62 (2008): 42–47.

53. J. J. Hakanen, W. B. Schaufeli, and K. Ahola, "The Job Demands-resources Model: A Three-year Cross-lagged Study of Burnout, Depression, Commitment, and Work Engagement," *Work and Stress* 22 (2008): 224–241.

54. D. G. J. Beckers, D. van der Linden, P. G. W. Smulders, M. A. J. Kompier, T. W. Taris, and S. A. E. Geurts, "Voluntary or Involuntary? Control over Overtime and Rewards for Overtime in Relation to Fatigue and Work Satisfaction," *Work and Stress* 22 (2008): 33–50.

55. H. K. Knudsen, L. J. Ducharme, and P. M. Roman, "Turnover Intention and Emotional Exhaustion "At the Top": Adapting the Job Demands-resources Model to Leaders of Addiction Treatment Organizations," *Journal of Occupational Health Psychology* 14 (2009): 84–95.

56. S. B. Bacharach, P. A. Bamberger, and E. Doveh, "Firefighters, Critical Incidents, and Drinking to Cope: The Adequacy of Unit-level Performance Resources as a Source of Vulnerability and Protection," *Journal of Applied Psychology* 93 (2008): 155–169.

57. D. de Bacquer, E. Pelfrene, E. Clays, R. Mak, M. Moreau, P. de Smet, M. Kornitzer, and G. de Backer, "Perceived Job Stress and Incidence of Coronary Events: 3-year Follow-up of the Belgian Stress Project Cohort," *American Journal of Epidemiology* 161 (2005): 434–441.

58. N. W. Van Yperen and M. Hagedoorn, "Do High Job Demands Increase Intrinsic Motivation or Fatigue or Both? The Role of Job Control and Job Social Support," *Academy of Management Journal* 46 (2003): 339–348.

59. V. Rousseau, S. Salek, C. Aube, and E. M. Morin, "Distributive Justice, Procedural Justice, and Psychological Distress: The Moderating Effect of Coworker Support and Work Autonomy," *Journal of Occupational Health Psychology* 14 (2009): 305–317.

60. J. Siegrist, "Adverse Health Effects of High Effort/Low Reward Conditions," *Journal of Occupational Health Psychology* 1 (1996): 27–41.

61. K. Schmidt, B. Neubach, and H. Heuer, "Self-control Demands, Cognitive Control Deficits, and Burnout, *Work and Stress* 21 (2007): 142–154.

62. S. Diestel and K. Schmidt, "Mediator and Moderator Effects of Demands on Self-control in the Relationship between Work Load and Indicators of Strain," *Work and Stress* 23 (2009): 60–79.

63. I. Godin, F. Kittel, Y. Coppieters, and J. Siegrist, "A Prospective Study of Cumulative Job Stress in Relation to Mental Health," *BMC Public Health* 5 (2005): 67.

64. H. Kuper, A. Singh-Manoux, J. Siegrist, and M. Marmot, "When Reciprocity Fails: Effort-reward Imbalance in Relation to Coronary Heart Disease and Health Functioning in the Whitehall II Study," *Occupational and Environmental Medicine* 59 (2002): 777–784.

65. R. Rugulies and N. Krause, "Effort-reward Imbalance and Incidence of Low Back and Neck Injuries in San Francisco Transit Operators," *Occupational and Environmental Medicine* 65 (2008): 525–533.

66. A. S. Ostry, S. Kelly, P. A. Demers, C. Mustard, and C. Hertzman, "A Comparison between the Effort-reward Imbalance and Demand Control Models," *BMC Public Health* 3 (2003): 10.

67. C. Maslach and M. P Leiter, "Early Predictors of Job Burnout and Engagement," *Journal of Applied Psychology* 93 (2008): 498–512.

68. Health Canada, "Best Advice for Stress Risk Management," Cat. No.: H39-546/2000E, 2000. http://www.hc-sc.gc.ca/ewh-semt/pubs/occup-travail/stress-part-1/index-eng.php.

69. J. Loehr and T. Schwartz, "The Making of a Corporate Athlete," *Harvard Business Review* 79 (2001): 120–129.

70. J. D. Quick, R. S. Horn, and J. C. Quick, "Health Consequences of Stress," *Journal of Organizational Behavior Management* 8 (1986): 19–36.

71. R. M. Yerkes and J. D. Dodson, "The Relation of Strength of Stimulus to Rapidity of Habit-Formation," *Journal of Comparative Neurology and Psychology* 18 (1908): 459–482.

72. J. D. Cresswell, W. T. Welch, S. E. Taylor, D. K. Sherman, T. L. Gruenewald, and T. Mann, "Affirmation of Personal Values Buffers Neuroendocrine and Psychological Stress Responses," *Psychological Science* 16 (2005): 846–851.

73. M. B. Ford and N. L. K. Collins, "Self-esteem Moderates Neuroendocrine and Psychological Responses to Interpersonal Rejection," *Journal of Personality and Social Psychology* 98 (2010): 405–419.

74. Y. E. Shen, "Relationships between Self-efficacy, Social Support and Stress Coping Strategies in Chinese Primary and Secondary School Teachers," *Stress and Health* 25 (2009): 129–138.

75. J. L. Xie, J. Schaubroeck, and S. S. K. Lam, "Theories of Job Stress, and the Role of Traditional Values: A Longitudinal Study in China," *Journal of Applied Psychology* 93 (2008): 831–848.

76. K. L. Zellars, J. A. Meurs, P. L. Perrewe, C. J. Kacmar, and A. M. Rossi, "Reacting to and Recovering from a Stressful Situation: The Negative Affectivity-physiological Arousal Relationship," *Journal of Occupational Health Psychology* 14 (2009): 11–22.

77. N. A. Bowling and K. J. Eschleman, "Employee Personality as a Moderator of the Relationships between Work Stressors and Counterproductive Work Behavior," *Journal of Occupational Health Psychology* 15 (2010): 91–103.

78. Ibid.

79. M. D. Friedman and R. H. Rosenman, *Type A Behavior and Your Heart* (New York: Knopf, 1974).

80. L. Wright, "The Type A Behavior Pattern and Coronary Artery Disease," *American Psychologist* 43 (1988): 2–14.

81. J. M. Ivancevich and M. T. Matteson, "A Type A–B Person–Work Environment Interaction Model for Examining Occupational Stress and Consequences," *Human Relations* 37 (1984): 491–513.

82. S. O. C. Kobasa, "Conceptualization and Measurement of Personality in Job Stress Research," in J. J. Hurrell, Jr., L. R. Murphy, S. L. Sauter, and C. L. Cooper, eds., *Occupational Stress: Issues and Developments in Research* (New York: Taylor & Francis, 1988), 100–109.

83. J. Borysenko, "Personality Hardiness," *Lectures in Behavioral Medicine* (Boston: Harvard Medical School, 1985).

84. J. S. House, K. R. Landis, and D. Umberson, "Social Relationships and Health," *Science* 241 (1988): 540–545.

85. J. Bowlby, *A Secure Base* (New York: Basic Books, 1988).

86. C. Hazan and P. Shaver, "Love and Work: An Attachment-Theoretical Perspective," *Journal of Personality and Social Psychology* 59 (1990): 270–280.

87. J. C. Quick, D. L. Nelson, and J. D. Quick, *Stress and Challenge at the Top: The Paradox of the Successful Executive* (Chichester, England: Wiley, 1990).

88. J. C. Quick, J. R. Joplin, D. L. Nelson, and J. D. Quick, "Self-Reliance for Stress and Combat" (*Proceedings of the 8th Combat Stress Conference*, U.S. Army Health Services Command, Fort Sam Houston, Texas, September 23–27, 1991): 1–5.

89. L. Duxbury, C. Higgins, and D. Coghill, "Voices of Canadians: Seeking Work-life Balance," Human Resources Canada Cat. No. RH54-12, 2003.

90. S. D. Tvedt, P. O. Saksvik, and K. Nytro, "Does Change Process Healthiness Reduce the Negative Effects of Organizational Change on the Psychosocial Environment?" *Work and Stress* 23 (2009): 80–98.

91. M. Fugate, A. J. Kinicki, and G. E. Prussia, "Employee Coping with Organizational Change: An Examination of Alternative Theoretical Perspectives and Models," *Personnel Psychology* 61 (2008): 1–36.

92. L. Duxbury, C. Higgins, and S. Lyons, "The Etiology and Reduction of Role Overload in Canada's Health Care Sector, 2010," http://www.sprott.carleton.ca/news/2010/docs/complete-report.pdf. .

93. J. Halpern, M. Gurevich, B. Schwartz, and P. Brazeau, "Interventions for Critical Incident Stress in Emergency Medical Services: A Qualitative Study," *Stress and Health* 25(2009): 139–149.

94. Health and Safety Executive, "Managing the Causes of Work-related Stress," United Kingdom, 2007, http://www.hse.gov.uk/pubns/priced/hsg218.pdf.

95. M. Fugate, A. J. Kinicki, and G. E. Prussia, "Employee Coping with Organizational Change: An Examination of Alternative Theoretical Perspectives and Models," *Personnel Psychology* 61 (2008): 1–36.

96. J. C. Wallace, B. D. Edwards, T. Arnold, M. L. Frazier, and D. M. Finch, "Work Stressors, Role-based Performance and the Moderating Influence of Organizational Support," *Journal of Applied Psychology* 94 (2009): 254–262.

97. M. A. Glynn, "Effects of Work Task Cues and Play Task Cues on Information Processing, Judgment and Motivation," *Journal of Applied Psychology* 79 (1994): 34–45.

98. R. Bourbonnais, C. Brisson, A. Vinet, M. Vezina, B. Abdous, and M. Gaudet, "Effectiveness of a Participative Intervention on Psychosocial Work Factors to Prevent Mental Health Problems in a Hospital Setting," *Occupational and Environmental Medicine* 63 (2006): 335–342.

99. C. Maslach and M. P Leiter, "Early Predictors of Job Burnout and Engagement," *Journal of Applied Psychology* 93 (2008): 498–512.

100. R. Bourbonnais, C. Brisson, A. Vinet, M. Vezina, B. Abdous, and M. Gaudet, "Effectiveness of a Participative Intervention on Psychosocial Work Factors to Prevent Mental Health Problems in a Hospital Setting," *Occupational and Environmental Medicine* 63 (2006): 335–342.

101. S. Leka, A. Griffiths, and T. Cox (Institute of Work, Health and Organisations; World Health Organization), *Work Organisation and Stress: Systematic Problem Approaches for Employers, Managers and Trade Union Representatives*, World Health Organisation, 2003.

102. WorksafeBC, "Coping with Critical Incident Stress at Work," Workers Compensation Board, BC, 2002 http://www.worksafebc.com/publications/health_and_safety/by_topic/assets/pdf/critical_incident_stress.pdf.

103. J. C. Quick and C. L. Cooper, *FAST FACTS: Stress and Strain*, 2nd ed. (Oxford, England: Health Press, 2003).

104. M. E. P. Seligman, *Learned Optimism* (New York: Knopf, 1990).

105. W. T. Brooks and T. W. Mullins, *High-Impact Time Management* (Englewood Cliffs, N.J.: Prentice-Hall, 1989).

106. M. Westman and D. Eden, "Effects of a Respite from Work on Burnout: Vacation Relief and Fade-Out," *Journal of Applied Psychology* 82 (1997): 516–527.

107. C. P. Neck and K. H. Cooper, "The Fit Executive: Exercise and Diet Guidelines for Enhancing Performance," *Academy of Management Executive* 14 (2000): 72–84.

108. M. Davis, E. R. Eshelman, and M. McKay, *The Relaxation and Stress Reduction Workbook*, 3rd ed. (Oakland, Calif.: New Harbinger, 1988).

109. H. Benson, "Your Innate Asset for Combating Stress," *Harvard Business Review* 52 (1974): 49–60.

110. J. W. Pennebaker, *Opening Up: The Healing Power of Expressing Emotions* (New York: Guilford, 1997).

111. M. E. Francis and J. W. Pennebaker, "Putting Stress into Words: The Impact of Writing on Physiological, Absentee, and Self-Reported Emotional Well-Being Measures," *American Journal of Health Promotion* 6 (1992): 280–287.

112. Z. Solomon, B. Oppenheimer, and S. Noy, "Subsequent Military Adjustment of Combat Stress Reaction Casualties: A Nine-Year Follow-Up Study," in N. A. Milgram, ed., *Stress and Coping in Time of War: Generalizations from the Israeli Experience* (New York: Brunner/Mazel, 1986), 84–90.

# Chapter 8

1. D. L. Whetzel, "The Department of Labor Identifies Workplace Skills," *The Industrial/Organizational Psychologist* (July 1991): 89–90.

2. M. Macik-Frey, J. C. Quick, and J. D. Quick, "Interpersonal Communication: The Key to Unlocking Social Support for Preventive Stress Management," in C. L. Cooper, ed., *Handbook of Stress, Medicine, and Health, rev. ed.* (Boca Raton, FL: CRC Press, 2004).

3. *Richness* is a term originally coined by W. D. Bodensteiner, "Information Channel Utilization under Varying Research and Development Project Conditions" (Ph.D. diss., University of Texas at Austin, 1970).

4. B. Barry and I. S. Fulmer, "The Medium and the Message: The Adaptive Use of Communication Media in Dyadic Influence," *Academy of Management Review* 29 (2004): 272–292.

5. R. Reik, *Listen with the Third Ear* (New York: Pyramid, 1972).

6. E. Rautalinko and H. O. Lisper, "Effects of Training Reflective Listening in a Corporate Setting," *Journal of Business and Psychology* 18 (2004): 281–299.

7. A. G. Athos and J. J. Gabarro, *Interpersonal Behavior: Communication and Understanding in Relationships* (Englewood Cliffs, N.J.: Prentice-Hall, 1978).

8. A. D. Mangelsdorff, "Lessons Learned from the Military: Implications for Management" (Distinguished Visiting Lecture, University of Texas at Arlington, 29 January 1993).

9. "How Maple Leaf Foods Is Handling the Listeria Outbreak" (August 28, 2008) http://www.cbc.ca/money/story/2008/08/27/f-crisisresponse.html.

10. "Maple Leaf Promises 'to Never Forget' Listeriosis Outbreak" (August 24, 2009) http://www.timescolonist.com/story_print.html?id=1924918&sponsor.

11. A. Auriemmo, "Care and Feeding of the Organizational Grapevine," *Industrial Management,* (March 1, 1999) http://www.allbusiness.com/human-resources/workforce-management/280885-1.html.

12. D. A. Morand, "Language and Power: An Empirical Analysis of Linguistic Strategies Used in Superior–Subordinate Communication," *Journal of Organizational Behavior* 21 (2000): 235–249.

13. S. Bates, "How Leaders Communicate Big Ideas to Drive Business Results," *Employment Relations Today* 33 (Fall 2006): 13–19.

14. F. Luthans, "Successful versus Effective Real Managers," *Academy of Management Executive* 2 (1988): 127–132.

15. L. E. Penley, E. R. Alexander, I. E. Jernigan, and C. I. Henwood, "Communication Abilities of Managers: The Relationship of Performance," *Journal of Management* 17 (1991): 57–76.

16. J. A. LePine and L. Van Dyne, "Voice and Cooperative Behavior as Contrasting Forms of Contextual Performance: Evidence of Differential Relationships with Big Five Personality Characteristics and Cognitive Ability," *Journal of Applied Psychology* 86 (2001): 326–336.

17. F. M. Jablin, "Superior-Subordinate Communication: The State of the Art," *Psychological Bulletin* 86 (1979): 1201–1222; W. C. Reddin, *Communication within the Organization: An Interpretive Review of Theory and Research* (New York: Industrial Communication Council, 1972).

18. B. Barry and J. M. Crant, "Dyadic Communication Relationships in Organizations: An Attribution Expectancy Approach," *Organization Science* 11 (2000): 648–665.

19. J. Silvester, F. Patterson, A. Koczwara, and E. Ferguson, "'Trust Me . . .': Psychological and Behavioral Predictors of Perceived Physician Empathy," *Journal of Applied Psychology* 92 (2007): 519–527.

20. A. Furhham and P. Stringfield, "Congruence in Job-Performance Ratings: A Study of 360 Degree Feedback Examining Self, Manager, Peers, and Consultant Ratings," *Human Relations* 51 (1998): 517–530.

21. J. W. Gilsdorf, "Organizational Rules on Communicating: How Employees Are—and Are Not—Learning the Ropes," *Journal of Business Communication* 35 (1998): 173–201.

22. D. Tannen, *That's Not What I Mean! How Conversational Style Makes or Breaks Your Relations with Others* (New York: Morrow, 1986); D. Tannen, *You Just Don't Understand* (New York: Ballantine, 1990).

23. D. G. Allen and R. W. Griffeth, "A Vertical and Lateral Information Processing: The Effects of Gender, Employee Classification Level, and Media Richness on Communication and Work Outcomes," *Human Relations* 50 (1997): 1239–1260.

24. K. L. Ashcraft, "Empowering 'Professional' Relationships," *Management Communication Quarterly* 13 (2000): 347–393.

25. G. Hofstede, *Culture's Consequences: International Differences in Work-Related Values* (Beverly Hills, Calif.: Sage Publications, 1980).

26. G. Hofstede, "Motivation, Leadership, and Organization: Do American Theories Apply Abroad?" *Organizational Dynamics* 9 (1980): 42–63.

27. H. Levinson, *Executive* (Cambridge, Mass.: Harvard University Press, 1981).

28. P. Benimadhu, "Adding Value through Diversity: An Interview with Bernard F. Isautier," *Canadian Business Review* 22 (1995): 6–11.

29. M. J. Gannon and Associates, *Understanding Global Cultures: Metaphorical Journeys through 17 Countries* (Thousand Oaks, Calif.: Sage Publications, 1994).

30. M. LeBaron "Cross-Cultural Communication," *Beyond Intractability*. eds. Guy Burgess and Heidi Burgess. Conflict Research Consortium, University of Colorado, Boulder (July 2003) http://www.beyondintractability.org/essay/cross-cultural_communication/.

31. Ibid.

32. Right to Play, "Mission, Vision and Values," http://www.righttoplay.com/canada/about-us/Pages/mission.aspx.

33. "UN Inter-Agency Task force on Sport for Development and Peace," *Sport as a Tool for Development and Peace: Towards Achieving the United Nations Millennium Development Goals* (nd) http://www.un.org/sport2005/resources/task_force.pdf.

34. T. Wells, *Keeping Your Cool under Fire: Communicating Nondefensively* (New York: McGraw-Hill, 1980).

35. R. D. Laing, *The Politics of the Family and Other Essays* (New York: Pantheon, 1971).

36. H. S. Schwartz, *Narcissistic Process and Corporate Decay: The Theory of the Organizational Ideal* (New York: New York University Press, 1990).

37. W. R. Forrester and M. F. Maute, "The Impact of Relationship Satisfaction on Attribution, Emotions, and Behaviors Following Service Failure," *Journal of Applied Business Research* (2000): 1–45.

38. M. L. Knapp, *Nonverbal Communication in Human Interaction* (New York: Holt, Rinehart & Winston, 1978); J. McCroskey and L. Wheeless, *Introduction to Human Communication* (New York: Allyn & Bacon, 1976).

39. A. M. Katz and V. T. Katz, eds., *Foundations of Nonverbal Communication* (Carbondale, Ill.: Southern Illinois University Press, 1983).

40. M. D. Lieberman, "Intuition: A Social Cognitive Neuroscience Approach," *Psychological Bulletin* (2000): 109–138.

41. E. T. Hall, *The Hidden Dimension* (Garden City, N.Y.: Doubleday Anchor, 1966).

42. E. T. Hall, "Proxemics," in A. M. Katz and V. T. Katz, eds., *Foundations of Nonverbal Communication* (Carbondale, Ill.: Southern Illinois University Press, 1983).

43. R. T. Barker and C. G. Pearce, "The Importance of Proxemics at Work," *Supervisory Management* 35 (1990): 10–11.

44. R. L. Birdwhistell, *Kinesics and Context* (Philadelphia: University of Pennsylvania Press, 1970).

45. M. G. Frank and P. Ekman, "Appearing Truthful Generalizes across Different Deception Situations," *Journal of Personality and Social Psychology* 86 (2004): 486–495.

46. P. Ekman and W. V. Friesen, "Research on Facial Expressions of Emotion," in A. M. Katz and V. T. Katz, eds., *Foundations of Nonverbal Communication* (Carbondale, Ill.: Southern Illinois University Press, 1983).

47. H. H. Tan, M. D. Foo, C. L. Chong, and R. Ng, "Situational and Dispositional Predictors of Displays of Positive Emotions," *Journal of Organizational Behavior* 24 (2003): 961–978.

48. C. Barnum and N. Wolniansky, "Taking Cues from Body Language," *Management Review* 78 (1989): 59.

49. Katz and Katz, *Foundations of Nonverbal Communication,* 181.

50. J. J. Lynch, *A Cry Unheard: New Insights into the Medical Consequences of Loneliness* (Baltimore, MD: Bancroft Press, 2000).

51. J. C. Quick, J. H. Gavin, C. L. Cooper, and J. D. Quick, "Working Together: Balancing Head and Heart," in N. G. Johnson, R. H. Rozensky, C. D. Goodheart, and R. Hammond, eds., *Psychology Builds a Healthy World:* (Washington, D.C.: American Psychological Association, 2004), 219–232.

52. J. C. Quick, C. L. Cooper, J. D. Quick, and J. H. Gavin, *The Financial Times Guide to Executive Health* (London, UK: Financial Times–Prentice Hall, 2003).

53. K. M. Wasylyshyn, "Coaching the Superkeepers," in L. A. Berger and D. R. Berger, eds., *The Talent Management Handbook: Creating Organizational Excellence by Identifying, Developing, and Positioning Your Best People* (New York: McGraw-Hill, 2003), 320–336.

54. J. C. Quick and M. Macik-Frey, "Behind the Mask: Coaching through Deep Interpersonal Communication," *Consulting Psychology Journal: Practice and Research* 56 (2004): 67–74.

55. B. Drake and K. Yuthas, "It's Only Words—Impacts of Information Technology on Moral Dialogue," *Journal of Business Ethics* 23 (2000): 41–60.

56. C. Brod, *Technostress: The Human Cost of the Computer Revolution* (Reading, Mass.: Addison-Wesley, 1984).

57. S. Kiesler, "Technology and the Development of Creative Environments," in Y. Ijiri and R. L. Kuhn, eds., *New Directions in Creative and Innovative Management* (Cambridge, Mass.: Ballinger Press, 1988).

58. S. Kiesler, J. Siegel, and T. W. McGuire, "Social Psychological Aspects of Computer-Mediated Communication," *American Psychologist* 39 (1984): 1123–1134.

# Chapter 9

1. J. R. Katzenbach and D. K. Smith, "The Discipline of Teams," *Harvard Business Review* 71 (1993): 111–120.

2. S. S. Webber and R. J. Klimoski, "Crews: A Distinct Type of Work Team," *Journal of Business and Psychology* 18 (2004): 261–279.

3. P. F. Drucker, "There's More than One Kind of Team," *The Wall Street Journal* (February 11, 1992): A16.

4. A. Boynton and B. Fischer, *Virtuoso Teams—Lessons from Teams that Changed their Worlds* (Harlow, Pearson Education, 2005), 3.

5. T. Appleby, "Highly Specialized OPP Unit Credited for Speedy Arrest," *The Globe and Mail* (February 11, 2010), http://www.theglobeandmail.com/news/national/highly-specialized-opp-unit-credited-for-speedy-arrest/article1464081.

6. A. M. Towsend, S. M. DeMarie, and A. R. Hendrickson, "Virtual Teams: Technology and the Workplace of the Future," *Academy of Management Executive* 12 (1998): 17–29.

7. B. L. Kirkman, C. B. Gibson, and D. L. Shapiro, "'Exporting' Teams: Enhancing the Implementation and Effectiveness of Work Teams in Global Affiliates," *Organizational Dynamics* 30 (2001): 12–29.

8. A. Taylor and H. R. Greve, "Superman or the Fantastic Four? Knowledge Combination and Experience in Innovative Teams," *Academy of Management Journal,* 49 (2006): 723–740.

9. P. Shaver and D. Buhrmester, "Loneliness, Sex-Role Orientation, and Group Life: A Social Needs Perspective," in P. Paulus, ed., *Basic Group Processes* (New York: Springer-Verlag, 1985), 259–288.

10. K. L. Bettenhausen and J. K. Murnighan, "The Development and Stability of Norms in Groups Facing Interpersonal and Structural Challenge," *Administrative Science Quarterly* 36 (1991): 20–35.

11. I. Adarves-Yorno, T. Postmes, and S. A. Haslam, "Creative Innovation or Crazy Irrelevance? The Contribution of Group Norms and Social Identity to Creative Behavior," *Journal of Experimental Social Psychology* 43 (2007): 410–416.

12. D. Tjosvold and Z. Yu, "Goal Interdependence and Applying Abilities for Team In-Role and Extra-Role Performance in China," *Group Dynamics: Theory, Research, and Practice* 8 (2004): 98–111.

13. V. U. Druskat and S. B. Wolff, "Building the Emotional Intelligence of Groups," *Harvard Business Review* 79 (2001): 80–90.

14. I. Summers, T. Coffelt, and R. E. Horton, "Work-Group Cohesion," *Psychological Reports* 63 (1988): 627–636.

15. D. C. Man and S. S. K. Lam, "The Effects of Job Complexity and Autonomy on Cohesiveness in Collectivistic and Individualistic Work Groups: A Cross-Cultural Analysis," *Journal of Organizational Behavior* 24 (2003): 979–1001.

16. K. H. Price, "Working Hard to Get People to Loaf," *Basic and Applied Social Psychology* 14 (1993): 329–344.

17. R. Albanese and D. D. Van Fleet, "Rational Behavior in Groups: The Free-Riding Tendency," *Academy of Management Review* 10 (1985): 244–255.

18. E. Diener, "Deindividuation, Self-Awareness, and Disinhibition," *Journal of Personality and Social Psychology* 37 (1979): 1160–1171.

19. C. H. Farnsworth, "Torture by Army Peacekeepers in Somalia Shocks Canada," *The New York Times* (November 27, 1994), http://www.nytimes.com/1994/11/27/world/torture-by-army-peacekeepers-in-somalia-shocks-canada.html?pagewanted=1.

20. S. Prentice-Dunn and R. W. Rogers, "Deindividuation and the Self-Regulation of Behavior," in P. Paulus, ed., *Psychology of Group Influence* (Hillsdale, N.J.: Erlbaum, 1989), 87–109.

21. B. M. Bass and E. C. Ryterband, *Organizational Psychology*, 2nd ed. (Boston: Allyn & Bacon, 1979).

22. W. G. Bennis and H. A. Shepard, "A Theory of Group Development," *Human Relations* 9 (1956): 415–438.

23. *Early Reading Strategy*, http://www.edu.gov.on.ca/eng/document/reports/reading.

24. D. L. Fields and T. C. Bloom, "Employee Satisfaction in Work Groups with Different Gender Composition," *Journal of Organizational Behavior* 18 (1997): 181–196.

25. A. Shrouder, "Sexual Orientation Can Be Office Minefield," *Business Edge,* 7, 14, http://www.businessedge.ca/printArticle.ctm/newsID/15806.ctm.

26. D. C. Lau and J. K. Murnighan, "Demographic Diversity and Faultlines: The Compositional Dynamics of Organizational Groups," *Academy of Management Review* 23 (1998): 325–340.

27. B. Tuckman, "Developmental Sequence in Small Groups," *Psychological Bulletin* 63 (1965): 384–399; B. Tuckman and M. Jensen, "Stages of Small-Group Development," *Group and Organizational Studies* 2 (1977): 419–427.

28. D. Nichols, "Quality Program Sparked Company Turnaround," *Personnel* (October 1991): 24. For a commentary on Wallace's hard times and subsequent emergence from Chapter 11 bankruptcy, see R. C. Hill, "When the Going Gets Tough: A Baldrige Award Winner on the Line," *Academy of Management Executive* 7 (1993): 75–79.

29. S. Weisband and L. Atwater, "Evaluating Self and Others in Electronic and Face-to-Face Groups," *Journal of Applied Psychology* 84 (1999): 632–639.

30. C. J. G. Gersick, "Time and Transition in Work Teams: Toward a New Model of Group Development," *The Academy of Management Journal* 31 (1988): 9–41.

31. M. Hardaker and B. K. Ward, "How to Make a Team Work," *Harvard Business Review* 65 (1987): 112–120.

32. C. R. Gowen, "Managing Work Group Performance by Individual Goals and Group Goals for an Interdependent Group Task," *Journal of Organizational Behavior Management* 7 (1986): 5–27.

33. K. L. Bettenhausen and J. K. Murnighan, "The Emergence of Norms in Competitive Decision-Making Groups," *Administrative Science Quarterly* 30 (1985): 350–372; K. L. Bettenhausen, "Five Years of Groups Research: What We Have Learned and What Needs to Be Addressed," *Journal of Management* 17 (1991): 345–381.

34. J. E. McGrath, *Groups: Interaction and Performance* (Englewood Cliffs, N.J.: Prentice-Hall, 1984).

35. K. L. Gammage, A. V. Carron, and P. A. Estabrooks, "Team Cohesion and Individual Productivity," *Small Group Research* 32 (2001): 3–18.

36. CBC, "Liberals, NDP, Bloc Sign Deal on Proposed Coalition," CBC (December 1, 2008), http://www.cbc.ca/canada/story/2008/12/01/coalition.tlaks.html.

37. S. M. Klein, "A Longitudinal Study of the Impact of Work Pressure on Group Cohesive Behaviors," *International Journal of Management* 12 (1996): 68–75.

38. N. Steckler and N. Fondas, "Building Team Leader Effectiveness: A Diagnostic Tool," *Organizational Dynamics* 23 (1995): 20–35.

39. A. Carter and S. Holmes, "Curiously Strong Teamwork," *Business Week* 4023 (February 26, 2007): 90–92.

40. W. R. Lassey, "Dimensions of Leadership," in W. R. Lassey and R. Fernandez, eds., *Leadership and Social Change* (La Jolla, Calif.: University Associates, 1976), 10–15.

41. J. D. Quick, G. Moorhead, J. C. Quick, E. A. Gerloff, K. L. Mattox, and C. Mullins, "Decision Making among Emergency Room Residents: Preliminary

Observations and a Decision Model," *Journal of Medical Education* 58 (1983): 117–125.

42. W. J. Duncan and J. P. Feisal, "No Laughing Matter: Patterns of Humor in the Workplace," *Organizational Dynamics* 17 (1989): 18–30.

43. L. Hirschhorn, *Managing in the New Team Environment* (Upper Saddle River, N.J.: Prentice-Hall, 1991), 521A.

44. G. Chen and R. J. Klimoski, "The Impact of Expectations on Newcomer Performance in Teams as Mediated by Work Characteristics, Social Exchanges, and Empowerment," *Academy of Management Journal* 46 (2003): 591–607.

45. B. Beersma, J. R. Hollenbeck, S. E. Humphrey, H. Moon, D. E. Conlon, and D. R. Ilgen, "Cooperation, Competition, and Team Performance: Toward a Contingency Approach," *Academy of Management Journal* 46 (2003): 572–590.

46. G. Parker, *Team Players and Teamwork* (San Francisco: Jossey-Bass, 1990).

47. N. R. F. Maier, "Assets and Liabilities in Group Problem Solving: The Need for an Integrative Function," *Psychological Review* 74 (1967): 239–249.

48. T. A. Stewart, "The Search for the Organization of Tomorrow," *Fortune* (May 18, 1992): 92–98.

49. P. Chattopadhyay, M. Tluchowska, and E. George, "Identifying the Ingroup: A Closer Look at the Influence of Demographic Dissimilarity on Employee Social Identity," *Academy of Management Review* 29 (2004): 180–202.

50. E. V. Hobman, P. Bordia, and C. Gallois, "Consequences of Feeling Dissimilar from Others in a Work Team," *Journal of Business and Psychology* 17 (2003): 301–325.

51. A. E. Randel and K. S. Jaussi, "Functional Background Identity, Diversity, and Individual Performance in Cross-Functional Teams," *Academy of Management Journal* 46 (2003): 763–774.

52. J. S. Bunderson, "Team Member Functional Background and Involvement in Management Teams: Direct Effects and the Moderating Role of Power Centralization," *Academy of Management Journal* 46 (2003): 458–474.

53. G. S. Van Der Vegt, E. Van De Vliert, and A. Oosterhof, "Informational Dissimilarity and Organizational Citizenship Behavior: The Role of Intrateam Interdependence and Team Identification," *Academy of Management Journal* 46 (2003): 715–727.

54. F. Balkundi, M. Kilduff, Z. I. Barsness, and J. H. Michael, "Demographic Antecedents and Performance Consequences of Structural Holes in Work Teams," *Journal of Organizational Behavior* 28 (2007): 241–260.

55. A. Pirola-Merlo and L. Mann, "The Relationship between Individual Creativity and Team Creativity: Aggregating across People and Time," *Journal of Organizational Behavior* 25 (2004): 235–257.

56. L. Thompson, "Improving the Creativity of Organizational Work Groups," *Academy of Management Executive* 17 (2003): 96–111.

57. C. Ford and D. M. Sullivan, "A Time for Everything: How the Timing of Novel Contributions Influences Project Team Outcomes," *Journal of Organizational Behavior* 25 (2004): 279–292.

58. K. W. Thomas and B. A. Velthouse, "Cognitive Elements of Empowerment: An 'Interpretive' Model of Intrinsic Task Motivation," *Academy of Management Review* 15 (1990): 666–681.

59. R. R. Blake, J. S. Mouton, and R. L. Allen, *Spectacular Teamwork: How to Develop the Leadership Skills for Team Success* (New York: Wiley, 1987).

60. American Management Association, *Blueprints for Service Quality: The Federal Express Approach,* AMA Management Briefing (New York: AMA, 1991).

61. W. C. Byham, *ZAPP! The Human Lightning of Empowerment* (Pittsburgh, Pa.: Developmental Dimensions, 1989).

62. F. Shipper and C. C. Manz, "Employee Self-Management without Formally Designated Teams: An Alternative Road to Empowerment," *Organizational Dynamics* (Winter 1992): 48–62.

63. P. Block, *The Empowered Manager: Positive Political Skills at Work* (San Francisco: Jossey-Bass, 1987).

64. V. J. Derlega and J. Grzelak, eds., *Cooperation and Helping Behavior: Theories and Research* (New York: Academic Press, 1982).

65. G. S. Van der Vegt, J. S. Bunderson, and A. Oosterhof, "Expertness Diversity and Interpersonal Helping in Teams: Why Those Who Need the Most Help End Up Getting the Least," *Academy of Management Journal* 49 (2006): 877–893.

66. A. G. Athos and J. J. Gabarro, *Interpersonal Behavior: Communication and Understanding in Relationships* (Englewood Cliffs, N.J.: Prentice-Hall, 1978).

67. C. Douglas and W. L. Gardner, "Transition to Self-Directed Work Teams: Implications of Transition Time and Self-Monitoring for Managers' Use of Influence Tactics," *Journal of Organizational Behavior* 25 (2004): 47–65.

68. C. Douglas, J. S. Martin, and R. H. Krapels, "Communication in the Transition to Self-Directed Work Teams," *Journal of Business Communication* 43 (2006): 295–321.

69. J. L. Cordery, W. S. Mueller, and L. M. Smith, "Attitudinal and Behavioral Effects of Autonomous Group Working: A Longitudinal Field Study," *Academy of Management Journal* 34 (1991): 464–476.

70. G. Moorhead, C. P. Neck, and M. S. West, "The Tendency toward Defective Decision Making within Self-Managing Teams: The Relevance of Groupthink for the 21st Century," *Organizational Behavior & Human Decision Processes* 73 (1998): 327–351.

71. B. M. Staw and L. D. Epstein, "What Bandwagons Bring: Effects of Popular Management Techniques on Corporate Performance, Reputation, and CEO Pay," *Administrative Science Quarterly* 45 (2000): 523–556.

72. R. M. Robinson, S. L. Oswald, K. S. Swinehart, and J. Thomas, "Southwest Industries: Creating High-Performance Teams for High-Technology Production," *Planning Review* 19, published by the Planning Forum (November–December 1991): 10–47.

73. D. C. Hambrick and P. Mason, "Upper Echelons: The Organization as a Reflection of Its Top Managers," *Academy of Management Review* 9 (1984): 193–206.

74. D. C. Hambrick, "The Top Management Team: Key to Strategic Success," *California Management Review* 30 (1987): 88–108.

75. A. D. Henderson and J. W. Fredrickson, "Top Management Team Coordination Needs and the CEO Pay Gap: A Competitive Test of Economic and Behavioral Views," *Academy of Management Journal* 44 (2001): 96–117.

76. D. C. Hambrick and G. D. S. Fukutomi, "The Seasons of a CEO's Tenure," *Academy of Management Review* 16 (1991): 719–742.

77. J. C. Quick, D. L. Nelson, and J. D. Quick, "Successful Executives: How Independent?" *Academy of Management Executive* 1 (1987): 139–145.

78. L. G. Love, "The Evolving Pinnacle of the Corporation: An Explanatory Study of the Antecedents, Processes, and Consequences of Co-CEOs," 2003 (The University of Texas at Arlington).

79. N. J. Adler, *International Dimensions of Organizational Behavior* (Mason, Ohio: South-Western, 2001).

80. I. D. Steiner, *Group Process and Productivity* (New York: Academic Press, 1972).

81. Kricher, L. D. "Best Practices of Team-Based Organizations," Whitepaper, DDI, (2007), http://www.camcinstitute.org/university/pages/toolkit/0407/ddi_bestpracticesteambasedorganizations_wp.pdf.

82. Ibid., p. 2.

# Chapter 10

1. H. A. Simon, *The New Science of Management Decision* (New York: Harper & Row, 1960).

2. "What is Blue Ocean Strategy?" *The Wall Street Journal Online* (2009), http://guides.wsj.com/management/strategy/what-is-blue-ocean-strategy.

3. G. Pitts, "Daniel Lamarre: Cirque du Soleil," *The Globe and Mail* (August 27, 2007), http://www.theglobeandmail.com/report-on-business/article778263.ece.

4. G. Huber, *Managerial Decision Making* (Glenview, Ill.: Scott, Foresman, 1980).

5. H. A. Simon, *Administrative Behavior* (New York: Macmillan, 1957).

6. E. F. Harrison, *The Managerial Decision-Making Process* (Boston: Houghton Mifflin, 1981).

7. V. H. Vroom, and P. W. Yetton, *Leadership and Decision Making* (Pittsburgh, University of Pittsburgh, 1973).

8. V. H. Vroom, "Leadership and the Decision-Making Process," *Organizational Dynamics* 28 (2000): 82–94.

9. R. L. Ackoff, "The Art and Science of Mess Management," *Interfaces* (February 1981): 20–26.

10. R. M. Cyert and J. G. March, eds., *A Behavioral Theory of the Firm* (Englewood Cliffs, N.J.: Prentice-Hall, 1963).

11. M. D. Cohen, J. March, and J. P. Olsen, "A Garbage Can Model of Organizational Choice," *Administrative Science Quarterly*, 17, 1, 1–25.

12. "'Garbage Can' Models: Multiple Stream Theory" (nd), http://faculty.chass.ncsu.edu/parson?PA/65?garbagecan.htm.

13. M. Lipson, *A Garbage Can Model of UN Peacekeeping*, (2004), http://www.allacademic.com/meta/p_mla_apa_research_citation/0/7/3/1/5/p73159_index.html.

14. B. M. Staw, "Knee-Deep in the Big Muddy: A Study of Escalating Commitment to a Chosen Course of Action," *Organizational Behavior and Human Performance* 16 (1976): 27–44; B. M. Staw, "The Escalation of Commitment to a Course of Action," *Academy of Management Review* 6 (1981): 577–587.

15. B. M. Staw and J. Ross, "Understanding Behavior in Escalation Situations," *Science* 246 (1989): 216–220.

16. T. Freemantle and M. Tolson, "Space Station Had Political Ties in Tow," *Houston Chronicle* (August 4, 2003), http://www.chron.com/cs/CDA/ssistory.mpl/space/2004947.

17. L. Festinger, *A Theory of Cognitive Dissonance* (Evanston, Ill.: Row, Peterson, 1957).

18. B. M. Staw, "The Escalation of Commitment: An Update and Appraisal," in Z. Shapira, ed., *Organizational Decision Making* (Cambridge, England: Cambridge University Press, 1997).

19. D. M. Boehne and P. W. Paese, "Deciding Whether to Complete or Terminate an Unfinished Project: A Strong Test of the Project Completion Hypothesis," *Organizational Behavior and Human Decision Processes* 81 (2000): 178–194; H. Moon, "Looking Forward and Looking Back: Integrating Completion and Sunk Cost Effects within an Escalation-of-Commitment Progress Decision," *Journal of Applied Psychology* 86 (2000): 104–113.

20. D. M. Rowell, "Concorde: An Untimely and Unnecessary Demise" (April 11, 2003), http://www.thetravelinsider.info/2003/0411.htm.

21. G. McNamara, H. Moon, and P. Bromiley, "Banking on Commitment: Intended and Unintended Consequences of an Organization's Attempt to Attenuate Escalation of Commitment," *Academy of Management Journal* 45 (2002): 443–452.

22. G. Whyte, "Diffusion of Responsibility: Effects on the Escalation Tendency," *Journal of Applied Psychology* 76 (1991): 408–415.

23. D. van Knippenberg, B. van Knippenberg, and E. van Dijk, "Who Takes the Lead in Risky Decision Making? Effects of Group Members' Risk Preferences and Prototypicality," *Organizational Behavior and Human Decision Processes* 83 (2000): 213–234.

24. K. R. MacCrimmon and D. Wehrung, *Taking Risks* (New York: Free Press, 1986).

25. T. S. Perry, "How Small Firms Innovate: Designing a Culture for Creativity," *Research Technology Management* 28 (1995): 14–17.

26. A. Saleh, "Brain Hemisphericity and Academic Majors: A Correlation Study," *College Student Journal* 35 (2001): 193–200.

27. N. Khatri, "The Role of Intuition in Strategic Decision Making," *Human Relations* 53 (2000): 57–86.

28. H. Mintzberg, "Planning on the Left Side and Managing on the Right," *Harvard Business Review* 54 (1976): 51–63.

29. D. J. Isenberg, "How Senior Managers Think," *Harvard Business Review* 62 (1984): 81–90.

30. R. N. Beck, "Visions, Values, and Strategies: Changing Attitudes and Culture," *Academy of Managment Executive* 1 (1987): 33–41.

31. K. G. Ross, G. A. Klein, P. Thunholm, J. F. Schmitt, and H. C. Baxter, "The Recognition-Primed Decision Model," *Military Review, Fort Leavenworth* 84 (2004): 6–10.

32. C. I. Barnard, *The Functions of the Executive* (Cambridge, Mass.: Harvard University Press, 1938).

33. R. Rowan, *The Intuitive Manager* (New York: Little, Brown, 1986).

34. W. H. Agor, *Intuition in Organizations* (Newbury Park, Calif.: Sage, 1989).

35. Isenberg, "How Senior Managers Think," 81–90.

36. H. A. Simon, "Making Management Decisions: The Role of Intuition and Emotion," *Academy of Management Executive* 1 (1987): 57–64.

37. J. L. Redford, R. H. McPhierson, R. G. Frankiewicz, and J. Gaa, "Intuition and Moral Development," *Journal of Psychology* 129 (1994): 91–101.

38. W. H. Agor, "How Top Executives Use Their Intuition to Make Important Decisions," *Business Horizons* 29 (1986): 49–53.

39. R. Wild, "Naked Hunch; Gut Instinct Is Vital to Your Business," *Success* (June 1998), http://www.findarticles.com/cf_dls/m3514/n6_v45/20746158/p1/article.html.

40. O. Behling and N. L. Eckel, "Making Sense Out of Intuition," *Academy of Management Executive* 5 (1991): 46–54.

41. L. R. Beach, *Image Theory: Decision Making in Personal and Organizational Contexts* (Chichester, England: Wiley, 1990).

42. E. Bonabeau, "Don't Trust Your Gut," *Harvard Business Review* 81 (2003): 116–126.

43. L. Livingstone, "Person-Environment Fit on the Dimension of Creativity: Relationships with Strain, Job Satisfaction, and Performance" (Ph.D. diss., Oklahoma State University, 1992).

44. G. Wallas, *The Art of Thought* (New York: Harcourt Brace, 1926).

45. H. Benson and W. Proctor, *The Break-Out Principle* (Scribner: New York, 2003); G. L. Fricchione, B. T. Slingsby, and H. Benson, "The Placebo Effect and the Relaxation Response: Neural Processes and Their Coupling to Constitutive Nitric Oxide," *Brain Research Reviews* 35 (2001): 1–19.

46. M. D. Mumford and S. B. Gustafson, "Creativity Syndrome: Integration, Application, and Innovation," *Psychological Bulletin* 103 (1988): 27–43.

47. T. Poze, "Analogical Connections—The Essence of Creativity," *Journal of Creative Behavior* 17 (1983): 240–241.

48. I. Sladeczek and G. Domino, "Creativity, Sleep, and Primary Process Thinking in Dreams," *Journal of Creative Behavior* 19 (1985): 38–46.

49. F. Barron and D. M. Harrington, "Creativity, Intelligence, and Personality," *Annual Review of Psychology* 32 (1981): 439–476.

50. R. J. Sternberg, "A Three-Faced Model of Creativity," in R. J. Sternberg, ed., *The Nature of Creativity* (Cambridge, England: Cambridge University Press, 1988), 125–147.

51. A. M. Isen, "Positive Affect and Decision Making," in W. M. Goldstein and R. M. Hogarth, eds., *Research on Judgment and Decision Making* (Cambridge, England: Cambridge University Press, 1997).

52. G. L. Clore, N. Schwartz, and M. Conway, "Cognitive Causes and Consequences of Emotion," In R. S. Wyer, and T. K. Srull (eds.), *Handbook of Social Cognition* (Hillsdale, N.J.: Erlbaum, 1994), 323–417.

53. B. L. Frederickson, "What Good Are Positive Emotions?" *Review of General Psychology* 2 (1998): 300–319; B. L. Frederickson, "The Role of Positive Emotions in Positive Psychology," *American Psychologist* 56 (2001): 218–226.

54. T. M. Amabile, S. G. Barsade, J. S. Mueller, and B. M. Staw, "Affect and Creativity at Work," *Administrative Science Quarterly* 50(3) (2005): 367–403

55. J. Zhou, "When the Presence of Creative Coworkers Is Related to Creativity: Role of Supervisor Close Monitoring, Developmental Feedback, and Creative Personality," *Journal of Applied Psychology* 88 (2003): 413–422.

56. C. Axtell, D. Holman, K. Unsworth, T. Wall, and P. Waterson, "Shopfloor Innovation: Facilitating the Suggestion and Implementation of Ideas," *Journal of Occupational Psychology* 73 (2000): 265–285.

57. B. Kijkuit and J. van den Ende, "The Organizational Life of an Idea: Integrating Social Network, Creativity and Decision-Making Perspectives," *Journal of Management Studies* 44(6) (2007): 863–882.

58. T. M. Amabile, R. Conti, H. Coon, J. Lazenby, and M. Herron, "Assessing the Work Environment for Creativity," *Academy of Management Journal* 39 (1996): 1154–1184.

59. T. Tetenbaum and H. Tetenbaum, "Office 2000: Tear Down the Wall," *Training* (February 2000): 58–64.

60. Livingstone, "Person-Environment Fit."

61. R. L. Firestein, "Effects of Creative Problem-Solving Training on Communication Behaviors in Small Groups," *Small Group Research* (November 1989): 507–521.

62. R. Von Oech, *A Whack on the Side of the Head* (New York: Warner, 1983).

63. A. G. Robinson and S. Stern, *How Innovation and Improvement Actually Happen* (San Francisco: Berrett Koehler, 1997).

64. K. Unsworth, "Unpacking Creativity," *Academy of Management Review* 26 (2001): 289–297.

65. M. F. R. Kets de Vries, R. Branson, and P. Barnevik, "Charisma in Action: The Transformational Abilities of Virgin's Richard Branson and ABBS's Percy Barnevik," *Organizational Dynamics* 26 (1998): 7–21.

66. G. Stasser, L. A. Taylor, and C. Hanna, "Information Sampling in Structured and Unstructured Discussion of Three- and Six-Person Groups," *Journal of Personality and Social Psychology* 57 (1989): 67–78.

67. E. Kirchler and J. H. Davis, "The Influence of Member Status Differences and Task Type on Group Consensus and Member Position Change," *Journal of Personality and Social Psychology* 51 (1986): 83–91.

68. R. F. Maier, "Assets and Liabilities in Group Problem Solving," *Psychological Review* 74 (1967): 239–249.

69. M. E. Shaw, *Group Dynamics: The Psychology of Small Group Behavior,* 3rd ed. (New York: McGraw-Hill, 1981).

70. P. W. Yetton and P. C. Bottger, "Individual versus Group Problem Solving: An Empirical Test of a Best Member Strategy," *Organizational Behavior and Human Performance* 29 (1982): 307–321.

71. W. Watson, L. Michaelson, and W. Sharp, "Member Competence, Group Interaction, and Group Decision Making: A Longitudinal Study," *Journal of Applied Psychology* 76 (1991): 803–809.

72. I. Janis, *Victims of Groupthink* (Boston: Houghton Mifflin, 1972); M. Kostera, M. Proppe, and M. Szatkowski, "Staging the New Romantic Hero in the Old Cynical Theatre: On Managers, Roles, and Change in Poland," *Journal of Organizational Behavior* 16 (1995): 631–646.

73. M. A. Hogg and S. C. Hains, "Friendship and Group Identification: A New Look at the Role of Cohesiveness in Groupthink," *European Journal of Social Psychology* 28 (1998): 323–341.

74. P. E. Jones and H. M. P. Roelofsma, "The Potential for Social Contextual and Group Biases in Team Decision Making: Biases, Conditions, and Psychological Mechanisms," *Ergonomics* 43 (2000): 1129–1152; J. M. Levine, E. T. Higgins, and H. Choi, "Development of Strategic Norms in Groups," *Organizational Behavior and Human Decision Processes* 82 (2000): 88–101.

75. A. L. Brownstein, "Biased Predecision Processing," *Psychological Bulletin* 129 (2003): 545–568.

76. C. P. Neck and G. Moorhead, "Groupthink Remodeled: The Importance of Leadership, Time Pressure, and Methodical Decision-Making Procedures," *Human Relations* 48 (1995): 537–557.

77. J. Schwartz and M. L. Ward, "Final Shuttle Report Cites 'Broken Safety Culture' at NASA," *New York Times* (August 26, 2003), http://www.nytimes.com/2003/08/26/national/26CND-SHUT.html?ex=1077253200&en=882575f2c17ed8ff&ei=5070; C. Ferraris and R. Carveth, "NASA and the Columbia Disaster: Decision Making by Groupthink?" in Proceedings of the 2003 Convention of the Association for Business Communication Annual Convention, http://www.businesscommunication.org/conventions/Proceedings/2003/PDF/03ABC03.pdf.

78. A. C. Homan, D. van Knippenberg, G. A. Van Kleef, and K. W. C. De Dreu, "Bridging Faultlines by Valuing Diversity: Diversity Beliefs, Information Elaboration, and Performance in Diverse Work Groups," *Journal of Applied Psychology* 92(5) (2007):1189–1199.

79. G. Moorhead, R. Ference, and C. P. Neck, "Group Decision Fiascoes Continue: Space Shuttle Challenger and a Revised Groupthink Framework," *Human Relations* 44 (1991): 539–550.

80. J. R. Montanari and G. Moorhead, "Development of the Groupthink Assessment Inventory," *Educational and Psychological Measurement* 49 (1989): 209–219.

81. P. t'Hart, "Irving L. Janis' Victims of Groupthink," *Political Psychology* 12 (1991): 247–278.

82. A. C. Mooney, P. J. Holahan, and A. C. Amason, "Don't Take It Personally: Exploring Cognitive Conflict as a Mediator of Affective Conflict," *Journal of Management Studies* 44(5) (2007): 733–758.

83. J. A. F. Stoner, "Risky and Cautious Shifts in Group Decisions: The Influence of Widely Held Values," *Journal of Experimental Social Psychology* 4 (1968): 442–459.

84. S. Moscovici and M. Zavalloni, "The Group as a Polarizer of Attitudes," *Journal of Personality and Social Psychology* 12 (1969): 125–135.

85. G. R. Goethals and M. P. Zanna, "The Role of Social Comparison in Choice of Shifts," *Journal of Personality and Social Psychology* 37 (1979): 1469–1476.

86. A. Vinokur and E. Burnstein, "Effects of Partially Shared Persuasive Arguments on Group-Induced Shifts: A Problem-Solving Approach," *Journal of Personality and Social Psychology* 29 (1974): 305–315;

J. Pfeffer, "Seven Practices of Successful Organizations," *California Management Review* 40 (1998): 96–124.

87. L. Armstrong, "Toyota's Scion: A Siren to Young Buyers?" *Business Week* (March 4, 2002), http://www.businessweek.com/bwdaily/dnflash/mar2002/nf2002034_8826.htm; Edmunds.com, Inc., "Toyota Courts NetGen Youth with Echo Subcompact" (January 1, 1999), http://www.edmunds.com/news/autoshows/articles/44460/page020.html; B. Young, "Mixing It Up: Crossover Vehicles Borrow Best of Cars, SUVs, Trucks," *Los Angeles Times,* http://www.latimes.com/extras/autoleasing/mixing.html.

88. G. Pitts, "Daniel Lamarre: Cirque du Soleil," *The Globe and Mail* (August 27, 2007): http://www.theglobeandmail.com/report-on-business/article778263.ece.

89. K. Dugosh, P. Paulus, E. Roland, and H. Yang, "Cognitive Stimulation in Brainstorming," *Journal of Personality and Social Psychology* 79 (2000): 722–735.

90. A. Van de Ven and A. Delbecq, "The Effectiveness of Nominal, Delphi and Interacting Group Decision-Making Processes," *Academy of Management Journal* 17 (1974): 605–621.

91. R. A. Cosier and C. R. Schwenk, "Agreement and Thinking Alike: Ingredients for Poor Decisions," *Academy of Management Executive* 4 (1990): 69–74.

92. D. M. Schweiger, W. R. Sandburg, and J. W. Ragan, "Group Approaches for Improving Strategic Decision Making: A Comparative Analysis of Dialectical Inquiry, Devil's Advocacy, and Consensus," *Academy of Management Journal* 29 (1986): 149–159.

93. G. Whyte, "Decision Failures: Why They Occur and How to Prevent Them," *Academy of Management Executive* 5 (1991): 23–31.

94. L. Scholten, D. van Knippenberg, B. A. Nijstad, and K. W. C. De Dreu, "Motivated Information Processing and Group Decision-Making: Effects of Process Accountability on Information Processing and Decision Quality," *Journal of Experimental Social Psychology* 43(4) (2007): 539–552.

95. E. E. Lawler III and S. A. Mohrman, "Quality Circles: After the Honeymoon," *Organizational Dynamics* (Spring 1987): 42–54.

96. T. L. Tang and E. A. Butler, "Attributions of Quality Circles' Problem-Solving Failure: Differences among Management, Supporting Staff, and Quality Circle Members," *Public Personnel Management* 26 (1997): 203–225.

97. J. Schilder, "Work Teams Boost Productivity," *Personnel Journal* 71 (1992): 67–72; S. L. Christensen, "Finding Competitive Advantage in Self-Managed Work Teams," *Business Forum,* (December 22, 2005), retrieved from http://www.allbusiness.com/human-resources/employee-development-team-building/620469-/html.

98. L. I. Glassop, "The Organizational Benefits of Teams," *Human Relations* 55 (2002): 225–249.

99. C. J. Nemeth, "Managing Innovation: When Less Is More," *California Management Review* 40 (1997): 59–68.

100. N. Adler, *International Dimensions of Organizational Behavior,* 3rd ed. (Mason, Ohio: South-Western, 1997).

101. K. W. Phillips and D. L. Lloyd, "When Surface- and Deep-Level Diversity Collide: The Effects on Dissenting Group Members," *Organizational Behavior and Human Decision Processes* 99(2) (2006): 143–160.

102. T. Simons, L. H. Pelled, and K. A Smith, "Making Use of Difference: Diversity, Debate, and Decision Comprehensiveness in Top Management Teams," *Academy of Management Journal* 42(6) (1999): 662–673.

103. S. Elbanna and J. Child, "The Influence of Decision, Environmental and Firm Characteristics on the Rationality of Strategic Decision-Making," *Journal of Management Studies* 44(4) (2007): 561–591.

104. J. Pfeffer, "Seven Practices of Successful Organizations," *California Management Review* 40 (1998): 96–124.

105. L. A. Witt, M. C. Andrews, and K. M. Kacmar, "The Role of Participation in Decision Making in the Organizational Politics—Job Satisfaction Relationship," *Human Relations* 53 (2000): 341–358.

106 C. R. Leana, E. A. Locke, and D. M. Schweiger, "Fact and Fiction in Analyzing Research on Participative Decision Making: A Critique of Cotton, Vollrath, Froggatt, Lengnick-Hall, and Jennings," *Academy of Management Review* 15 (1990): 137–146; J. L. Cotton, D. A. Vollrath, M. L. Lengnick-Hall, and K. L. Froggatt, "Fact: The Form of Participation Does Matter—A Rebuttal to Leana, Locke, and Schweiger," *Academy of Management Review* 15 (1990): 147–153.

107. T. W. Malone, "Is Empowerment Just a Fad? Control, Decision Making, and Information Technology," *Sloan Management Review* 38 (1997): 23–35.

108. IBM Customer Success Stories, "City and County of San Francisco Lower Total Cost of Ownership and Build on Demand Foundation" (February 3, 2004), http://www-306.ibm.com/software/success/cssdb.nsf/cs/LWRT-5VTLM2?OpenDocument&Site=lotusmandc.

109. T. L. Brown, "Fearful of 'Empowerment': Should Managers Be Terrified?" *IndustryWeek* (June 18, 1990): 12.

110. L. Hirschhorn, "Stresses and Patterns of Adjustment in the Postindustrial Factory." In G. M. Green and F. Baker, eds., *Work, Health, and Productivity* (New York: Oxford University Press, 1991), 115–126.

111. P. G. Gyllenhammar, *People at Work* (Reading, Mass.: Addison-Wesley, 1977).

112. R. Tannenbaum and F. Massarik, "Participation by Subordinates in the Managerial Decision-Making Process," *Canadian Journal of Economics and Political Science* 16 (1950): 408–418.

113. H. Levinson, *Executive* (Cambridge, Mass.: Harvard University Press, 1981).

114. J. S. Black and H. B. Gregersen, "Participative Decision Making: An Integration of Multiple Dimensions," *Human Relations* 50 (1997): 859–878.

# Chapter 11

1. G. C. Homans, "Social Behavior as Exchange," *American Journal of Sociology* 63 (1958): 597–606.

2. E. N. Kocev, "Modern Concept of Power as a Social and Economic Category," (2002) http://www.ejournalnet.com/Contents/Issue_2/4/4_2002.htm.

3. S. R. Clegg, D. Courpasson, and N. Phillips, *Power and Organizations* (London: Sage, 2006), 191.

4. R. D. Middlemist and M. A. Hitt, *Organizational Behavior: Managerial Strategies for Performance* (St. Paul, Minn.: West Publishing, 1988).

5. C. Barnard, *The Functions of the Executive* (Cambridge, Mass.: Harvard University Press, 1938).

6. J. R. P. French and B. Raven, "The Bases of Social Power," in D. Cartwright, ed., *Group Dynamics: Research and Theory* (Evanston, Ill.: Row Peterson, 1962); T. R. Hinkin and C. A. Schriesheim, "Development and Application of New Scales to Measure the French and Raven (1959) Bases of Social Power," *Journal of Applied Psychology* 74 (1989): 561–567.

7. K. D. Elsbach and G. Elofson, "How the Packaging of Decision Explanations Affects Perceptions of Trustworthiness," *Academy of Management Journal* 43(1) (2000): 80–89.

8. P. M. Podsakoff and C. A. Schriesheim, "Field Studies of French and Raven's Bases of Power: Critique, Reanalysis, and Suggestions for Future Research," *Psychological Bulletin* 97 (1985): 387–411.

9. M. A. Rahim, "Relationships of Leader Power to Compliance and Satisfaction with Supervision: Evidence from a National Sample of Managers," *Journal of Management* 15 (1989): 545–556.

10. C. Argyris, "Management Information Systems: The Challenge to Rationality and Emotionality," *Management Science* 17 (1971): 275–292; J. Naisbitt and P. Aburdene, *Megatrends 2000* (New York: Morrow, 1990).

11. P. P. Carson, K. D. Carson, E. L. Knight, and C. W. Roe, "Power in Organizations: A Look through the TQM Lens," *Quality Progress* (November 1995): 73–78.

12. Feature "Marissa Mayer: The Talent Scout," *Business Week Online* (June19, 2006), http://www.businessweek.com/magazine/content/06_25/b3989422.htm.

13. A. Webber, "Danger: Toxic Company," *Fast Company* (October 31, 1998) http://www.fastcompany.com/magazine/19/toxic.html?page=0%2C0.

14. G. Namie and R. Namie, *The Bully at Work*, 2nd ed. (Naperville, Illinois: Sourcebooks, 2009), 3.

15. Ibid., p. 27.

16. J. Pfeffer and G. Salancik, *The External Control of Organizations* (New York: Harper & Row, 1978).

17. T. M. Welbourne and C. O. Trevor, "The Roles of Departmental and Position Power in Job Evaluation," *Academy of Management Journal* 43(4) (2000): 761–771.

18. R. H. Miles, *Macro Organizational Behavior* (Glenview, Ill.: Scott, Foresman, 1980).

19. D. Hickson, C. Hinings, C. Lee, R. E. Schneck, and J. M. Pennings, "A Strategic Contingencies Theory of Intraorganizational Power," *Administrative Science Quarterly* 14 (1971): 219–220.

20. C. R. Hinings, D. J. Hickson, J. M. Pennings, and R. E. Schneck, "Structural Conditions of Intraorganizational Power," *Administrative Science Quarterly* 19 (1974): 22–44.

21. M. Segalia, "Vision Statement: Find the Real Power in Your Organization," *Harvard Business Review* (2010), http://hbr.org/2010/05/vision-statement-find-the-real-power-in-your-organization/ar/pr.

22. M. Velasquez, D. J. Moberg, and G. F. Cavanaugh, "Organizational Statesmanship and Dirty Politics: Ethical Guidelines for the Organizational Politician," *Organizational Dynamics* 11 (1982): 65–79.

23. CBC News, "Livent co-founders Drabinsky, Gottlieb Convicted of Fraud and Forgery," (March 25, 2009), http://www.cbc.ca/money/story/2009/03/25/livent-decision-fraud.html.

24. D. E. McClelland, *Power: The Inner Experience* (New York: Irvington, 1975).

25. N. Shahinpoor and B. F. Matt, "The Power of One: Dissent and Organizational Life," *Journal of Business Ethics* 74(1) (2007): 37–49.

26. N. Machiavelli, *The Prince*, trans. by G. Bull (Middlesex, England: Penguin Books, 1961).

27. S. Chen, A. Y. Lee-Chai, and J. A. Bargh, "Relationship Orientation as a Moderator of the Effects of Social Power," *Journal of Personality and Social Psychology* 80(2) (2001): 173–187.

28. R. Kanter, "Power Failure in Management Circuits," *Harvard Business Review* (July–August 1979): 31–54.

29. F. Lee and L. Z. Tiedens, "Who's Being Served? 'Self-Serving' Attributions in Social Hierarchies," *Organizational Behavior and Human Decision Processes* 84(2) (March 2001): 254–287.

30. M. Korda, *Power: How to Get It, How to Use It* (New York: Random House, 1975).

31. S. R. Thye, "A Status Value Theory of Power in Exchange Relations," *American Sociological Review* (2000): 407–432.

32. B. T. Mayes and R. T. Allen, "Toward a Definition of Organizational Politics," *Academy of Management Review* 2 (1977): 672–678.

33. M. Valle and P. L. Perrewe, "Do Politics Perceptions Relate to Political Behaviors? Tests of an Implicit Assumption and Expanded Model," *Human Relations* 53 (2000): 359–386.

34. W. A. Hochwarter, "The Interactive Effects of Pro-Political Behavior and Politics Perceptions on Job Satisfaction and Affective Commitment," *Journal of Applied Social Psychology* 33 (2003): 1360–1378.

35. W. A. Hochwarter, K. M. Kacmar, D. C. Treadway, and T. S. Watson, "It's All Relative: The Distinction and Prediction of Political Perceptions across Levels," *Journal of Applied Social Psychology* 33 (2003): 1955–2016.

36. D. A. Ralston, "Employee Ingratiation: The Role of Management," *Academy of Management Review* 10 (1985): 477–487; D. R. Beeman and T. W. Sharkey, "The Use and Abuse of Corporate Politics," *Business Horizons* (March–April 1987): 25–35.

37. C. O. Longnecker, H. P. Sims, and D. A. Gioia, "Behind the Mask: The Politics of Employee Appraisal," *Academy of Management Executive* 1 (1987): 183–193.

38. M. Valle and P. L. Perrewe, "Do Politics Perceptions Relate to Political Behaviors? Tests of an Implicit Assumption and Expanded Model," *Human Relations* 53(3) (2000): 359–386.

39. D. Butcher and M. Clarke, "Organizational Politics: The Cornerstone for Organizational Democracy," *Organizational Dynamics* 31 (2002): 35–46.

40. D. Kipnis, S. M. Schmidt, and I. Wilkinson, "Intraorganizational Influence Tactics: Explorations in Getting One's Way," *Journal of Applied Psychology* 65 (1980): 440–452; D. Kipnis, S. Schmidt, C. Swaffin-Smith, and I. Wilkinson, "Patterns of Managerial Influence: Shotgun Managers, Tacticians, and Bystanders," *Organizational Dynamics* (Winter 1984): 60–67; G. Yukl and C. M. Falbe, "Influence Tactics and Objectives in Upward, Downward, and Lateral Influence Attempts," *Journal of Applied Psychology* 75 (1990): 132–140.

41. G. R. Ferris and T. A. Judge, "Personnel/Human Resources Management: A Political Influence Perspective," *Journal of Management* 17 (1991): 447–488.

42. G. Yukl, P. J. Guinan, and D. Sottolano, "Influence Tactics Used for Different Objectives with Subordinates, Peers, and Superiors," *Groups & Organization Management* 20 (1995): 272–296.

43. C. A. Higgins, T. A. Judge, and G. R. Ferris, "Influence Tactics and Work Outcomes: A Meta-Analysis," *Journal of Organizational Behavior* 24 (2003): 89–106.

44. K. K. Eastman, "In the Eyes of the Beholder: An Attributional Approach to Ingratiation and Organizational Citizenship Behavior," *Academy of Management Journal* 37 (1994): 1379–1391.

45. K. J. Harris, K. M. Kacmar, S. Zivnuska, and J. D Shaw, "The Impact of Political Skill on Impression Management Effectiveness," *Journal of Applied Psychology* 92(1) (2007): 278–285.

46. D. C. Treadway, G. R. Ferris, A. B. Duke, G. L. Adams, and J. B. Thatcher, "The Moderating Role of Subordinate Political Skill on Supervisors' Impressions of Subordinate Ingratiation and Ratings of Subordinate Interpersonal Facilitation," *Journal of Applied Psychology* 92(3) (2007): 848–855.

47. R. A. Gordon, "Impact of Ingratiation on Judgments and Evaluations: A Meta-Analytic Investigation," *Journal of Personality and Social Psychology* 71(1996): 54–70.

48. A. Drory and D. Beaty, "Gender Differences in the Perception of Organizational Influence Tactics," *Journal of Organizational Behavior* 12 (1991): 249–258.

49. S. Wellington, M. B. Kropf, and P. R. Gerkovich, "What's Holding Women Back?" *Harvard Business Review* (June 2003): 2–4.

50. P. Perrewe and D. Nelson, "Gender and Career Success: The Facilitative Role of Political Skill," *Organizational Dynamics* 33 (2004): 366–378.

51. R. Y. Hirokawa and A. Miyahara, "A Comparison of Influence Strategies Utilized by Managers in American and Japanese Organizations," *Communication Quarterly* 34 (1986): 250–265.

52. P. David, M. A. Hitt, and J. Gimeno, "The Influence of Activism by Institutional Investors on R&D," *Academy of Management Journal* 44(1) (2001): 144–157.

53. G. R. Ferris, P. L. Perrewe, W. P. Anthony, and D. C. Gilmore, "Political Skill at Work," *Organizational Dynamics* 28 (2000): 25–37.

54. D. C. Treadway, W. A. Hochwarter, G. R. Ferris, C. J. Kacmar, C. Douglas, A. P. Ammeter, and M. R. Buckley, "Leader Political Skill and Employee Reactions," *Leadership Quarterly* 15 (2004): 493–513; K. K. Ahearn, G. R. Ferris, W. A. Hochwarter, C. Douglas, and A. P. Ammeter, "Leader Political Skill and Team Performance," *Journal of Management* 30(3) (2004): 309–327.

55. P. L. Perrewé, K. L. Zellars, G. R. Ferris, A. M. Rossi, C. J. Kacmar, and D. A. Ralston, "Neutralizing Job Stressors: Political Skill as an Antidote to the Dysfunctional Consequences of Role Conflict Stressors," *Academy of Management Journal* 47 (2004): 141–152.

56. G. R. Ferris, D. C. Treadway, R. W. Kolodinsky, W. A. Hochwarter, C. J. Kacmar, C. Douglas, and D. D. Frink, "Development and Validation of the Political Skill Inventory," *Journal of Management* 31 (2005): 126–152.

57. G. Ferris, S. Davidson, and P. Perrewé, "Developing Political Skill at Work," *Training* 42 (2005) : 40–45.

58. F. R. Blass and G. R. Ferris, "Leader Reputation: The Role of Mentoring, Political Skill, Contextual Learning, and Adaptation," *Human Resource Management* 46(1) (2007): 5–19.

59. K. Kumar and M. S. Thibodeaux, "Organizational Politics and Planned Organizational Change," *Group and Organization Studies* 15 (1990): 354–365.

60. McClelland, *Power*.

61. Beeman and Sharkey, "Use and Abuse of Corporate Politics," 37.

62. C. P. Parker, R. L. Dipboye, and S. L. Jackson, "Perceptions of Organizational Politics: An Investigation of Antecedents and Consequences," *Journal of Management* 21 (1995): 891–912.

63. S. J. Ashford, N. P. Rothbard, S. K. Piderit, and J. E. Dutton, "Out on a Limb: The Role of Context and Impression Management in Selling Gender-Equity Issues," *Administrative Science Quarterly* 43 (1998): 23–57.

64. J. Zhou and G. R. Ferris, "The Dimensions and Consequences of Organizational Politics Perceptions: A Confirmatory Analysis," *Journal of Applied Social Psychology* 25 (1995): 1747–1764.

65. M. L. Seidal, J. T. Polzer, and K. J. Stewart, "Friends in High Places: The Effects of Social Networks on Discrimination in Salary Negotiations," *Administrative Science Quarterly* 45 (2000): 1–24.

66. J. J. Gabarro and J. P. Kotter, "Managing Your Boss," *Harvard Business Review* (January–February 1980): 92–100.

67. P. Newman, "How to Manage Your Boss," Peat, Marwick, Mitchell & Company's Management Focus (May–June 1980): 36–37.

68. F. Bertolome, "When You Think the Boss Is Wrong," *Personnel Journal* 69 (1990): 66–73.

69. J. Conger and R. Kanungo, *Charismatic Leadership: The Elusive Factor in Organizational Effectiveness* (New York: Jossey-Bass, 1988).

70. G. M. Spreitzer, M. A. Kizilos, and S. W. Nason, "A Dimensional Analysis of the Relationship between Psychological Empowerment and Effectiveness, Satisfaction, and Strain," *Journal of Management* 23 (1997): 679–704.

71. R. C. Ford and M. D. Fottler, "Empowerment: A Matter of Degree," *Academy of Management Executive* 9 (1995): 21–31.

72. M. Holbrook, "Employee Commitment Is Crucial," *Human Resources* (May 2007).

73. J. Simons, "Merck's Man in the Hot Seat," *Fortune* (February 23, 2004): 111–114.

74. G. R. Bushe, Power and the Empowered Organization: "The Design of Power in Highly Adaptive Organizations," *The Organization Development Practitioner,* 30:4 (1998): 37.

75. Ibid. 32.

# Chapter 12

1. J. P. Kotter, "What Leaders Really Do," *Harvard Business Review* 68 (1990): 103–111.

2. D. A. Plowman, S. Solansky, T. E Beck, L. Baker, M. Kulkarni, and D. V. Travis, "The Role of Leadership in Emergent, Self-Organization," *Leadership Quarterly* 18(4) (2007): 341–356.

3. A. Zaleznik, "HBR Classic—Managers and Leaders: Are They Different?" *Harvard Business Review* 70 (1992): 126–135.

4. W. G. Rowe, "Creating Wealth in Organizations: The Role of Strategic Leadership," *Academy of Management Executive* 15 (2001): 81–94.

5. R. M. Stogdill, "Personal Factors Associated with Leadership: A Survey of the Literature," *Journal of Psychology* 25 (1948): 35–71.

6. K. Lewin, R. Lippitt, and R. K. White, "Patterns of Aggressive Behavior in Experimentally Created 'Social Climates,'" *Journal of Social Psychology* 10 (1939): 271–299.

7. S. D. Sidle, "The Danger of Do Nothing Leaders," *The Academy of Management Perspectives* 21(2) (2007): 75–77.

8. A. W. Halpin and J. Winer, "A Factorial Study of the Leader Behavior Description Questionnaire," in R. M. Stogdill and A. E. Coons, eds., *Leader Behavior: Its Description and Measurement,* research monograph no. 88 (Columbus, Ohio: Bureau of Business Research, The Ohio State University, 1957), 39–51.

9. E. A. Fleishman, "Leadership Climate, Human Relations Training, and Supervisory Behavior," *Personnel Psychology* 6 (1953): 205–222.

10. R. Kahn and D. Katz, "Leadership Practices in Relation to Productivity and Morale," in D. Cartwright and A. Zander, eds., *Group Dynamics, Research and Theory* (Elmsford, NY: Row, Paterson, 1960).

11. R. R. Blake and J. S. Mouton, *The Managerial Grid III: The Key to Leadership Excellence* (Houston: Gulf, 1985).

12. W. Vandekerckhove and R. Commers, "Downward Workplace Mobbing: A Sign of the Times?" *Journal of Business Ethics* 45 (2003): 41–50.

13. F. E. Fiedler, *A Theory of Leader Effectiveness* (New York: McGraw-Hill, 1964).

14. F. E. Fiedler, *Personality, Motivational Systems, and Behavior of High and Low LPC Persons,* tech. rep. no. 70-12 (Seattle: University of Washington, 1970).

15. J. T. McMahon, "The Contingency Theory: Logic and Method Revisited," *Personnel Psychology* 25 (1972): 697–710; L. H. Peters, D. D. Hartke, and J. T. Pohlman, "Fiedler's Contingency Theory of Leadership: An Application of the Meta-Analysis Procedures of Schmidt and Hunter," *Psychological Bulletin* 97 (1985): 224–285.

16. F. E. Fiedler, "The Contingency Model and the Dynamics of the Leadership Process," in L. Berkowitz, ed., *Advances in Experimental and Social Psychology,* vol. 11 (New York: Academic Press, 1978).

17. S. Arin and C. McDermott, "The Effect of Team Leader Characteristics on Learning, Knowledge Application, and Performance of Cross-Functional New Product Development Teams," *Decision Sciences* 34 (2003): 707–739.

18. F. E. Fiedler, "Engineering the Job to Fit the Manager," *Harvard Business Review* 43 (1965): 115–122.

19. R. J. House, "A Path–Goal Theory of Leader Effectiveness," *Administrative Science Quarterly* 16 (1971): 321–338; R. J. House and T. R. Mitchell, "Path–Goal Theory of Leadership," *Journal of Contemporary Business* 3 (1974): 81–97. M. Evans, "The Effects of Supervisory Behavior on the Path-Goal Relationship," *Organizational Behavior and Human Performance* 5, 3 (1970): 277–298.

20. C. A. Schriescheim and V. M. Von Glinow, "The Path–Goal Theory of Leadership: A Theoretical and Empirical Analysis," *Academy of Management Journal* 20 (1977): 398–405; E. Valenzi and G. Dessler, "Relationships of Leader Behavior, Subordinate Role Ambiguity, and Subordinate Job Satisfaction," *Academy of Management Journal* 21 (1978): 671–678; N. R. F. Maier, *Leadership Methods and Skills* (New York: McGraw-Hill, 1963).

21. J. P. Grinnell, "An Empirical Investigation of CEO Leadership in Two Types of Small Firms," *S.A.M. Advanced Management Journal* 68 (2003): 36–41.

22. P. Hersey and K. H. Blanchard, "Life Cycle Theory of Leadership," *Training and Development* 23 (1969): 26–34; P. Hersey, K. H. Blanchard, and D. E. Johnson, *Management of Organizational Behavior: Leading Human Resources,* 8th ed. (Upper Saddle River, N.J.: Prentice-Hall, 2001).

23. B. M. Bass, *Bass and Stogdill's Handbook of Leadership: Theory, Research, and Managerial Applications,* 3rd ed. (New York: Free Press, 1990).

24. G. B. Graen and M. Uhl-Bien, "Relationship-Based Approach to Leadership: Development of Leader–Member Exchange (LMX) Theory of Leadership over 25 Years," *Leadership Quarterly* 6 (1995): 219–247; C. R. Gerstner and D. V. Day, "Meta-Analytic Review of Leader–Member Exchange Theory: Correlates and Construct Issues," *Journal of Applied Psychology* 82 (1997): 827–844; R. C. Liden, S. J. Wayne, and R. T. Sparrowe, "An Examination of the Mediating Role of Psychological Empowerment on the Relations between the Job, Interpersonal Relationships, and Work Outcomes," *Journal of Applied Psychology* 85 (2001): 407–416.

25. J. Townsend, J. S. Phillips, and T. J. Elkins, "Employee Retaliation: The Neglected Consequence of Poor Leader–Member Exchange Relations," *Journal of Occupational Health Psychology* 5 (2000): 457–463.

26. D. Nelson, R. Basu, and R. Purdie, "An Examination of Exchange Quality and Work Stressors in Leader–Follower Dyads," *International Journal of Stress Management* 5 (1998): 103–112.

27. K. M. Kacmar, L. A. Witt, S. Zivnuska, and S. M. Gully, "The Interactive Effect of Leader–Member Exchange and Communication Frequency on Performance Ratings," *Journal of Applied Psychology* 88 (2003): 764–772.

28. A. G. Tekleab and M. S. Taylor, "Aren't There Two Parties in an Employment Relationship? Antecedents and Consequences of Organization–Employee Agreement on Contract Obligations and Violations," *Journal of Organizational Behavior* 24 (2003): 585–608.

29. D. A. Hoffman, S. J. Gerras, and F. P. Morgeson, "Climate as a Moderator of the Relationship between Leader–Member Exchange and Content Specific Citizenship: Safety Climate as an Exemplar," *Journal of Applied Psychology* 88 (2003): 170–178.

30. J. M. Burns, *Leadership* (New York: Harper & Row, 1978); T. O. Jacobs, *Leadership and Exchange in Formal Organizations* (Alexandria, Va.: Human Resources Research Organization, 1971).

31. B. M. Bass, "From Transactional to Transformational Leadership: Learning to Share the Vision," *Organizational Dynamics* 19 (1990): 19–31; B. M. Bass, *Leadership and Performance beyond Expectations* (New York: Free Press, 1985).

32. P. M. Podsakoff, S. B. MacKenzie, and W. H. Bommer, "Transformational Leader Behaviors and Substitutes for Leadership as Determinants of Employee Satisfaction, Commitment, Trust, and Organizational Citizenship Behaviors," *Journal of Management* 22 (1996): 259–298.

33. W. Bennis, "Managing the Dream: Leadership in the 21st Century," *Training* 27 (1990): 43–48; P. M. Podsakoff, S. B. MacKenzie, R. H. Moorman, and R. Fetter, "Transformational Leader Behaviors and Their Effects on Followers' Trust in Leader, Satisfaction, and Organizational Citizenship Behaviors," *Leadership Quarterly* 1 (1990): 107–142.

34. MyPrimeTime, Inc., "Great Entrepreneurs—Biography: Howard Schultz, Starbucks," http://www.myprimetime.com/work/ge/schultzbio/index.shtml.

35. C. P. Egri and S. Herman, "Leadership in the North American Environmental Sector: Values, Leadership Styles, and Contexts of Environmental Leaders and Their Organizations," *Academy of Management Journal* 43 (2000): 571–604.

36. T. A. Judge and J. E. Bono, "Five-Factor Model of Personality and Transformational Leadership," *Journal of Applied Psychology* 85 (2001): 751–765.

37. J. E. Bono and T. A. Judge, "Self-Concordance at Work: Toward Understanding the Motivational Effects of Transformational Leaders," *Academy of Management Journal* 46 (2003): 554–571.

38. The Jargon Dictionary, "The R Terms: Reality-Distortion Field," http://info. astrian.net/jargon/terms/r/reality-distortion_field.html.

39. R. J. House and M. L. Baetz, "Leadership: Some Empirical Generalizations and New Research Directions," in B. M. Staw, ed., *Research in Organizational Behavior,* vol. 1 (Greenwood, Conn.: JAI Press, 1979), 399–401.

40. D. Waldman, G. G. Ramirez, R. J. House, and P. Puranam, "Does Leadership Matter? CEO Leadership Attributes and Profitability under Conditions of Perceived Environmental Uncertainty," *Academy of Management Journal* 44 (2001): 134–143.

41. J. M. Howell, "Two Faces of Charisma: Socialized and Personalized Leadership in Organizations," in J. A. Conger, ed., *Charismatic Leadership: Behind the Mystique of Exceptional Leadership* (San Francisco: Jossey-Bass, 1988).

42. F. Luthans and B. J. Avolio, "Authentic Leadership: A Positive Development Approach," in K. S. Cameron, J. E. Dutton, and R. E. Quinn, eds., *Positive Organizational Scholarship: Foundations of a New Discipline* (San Francisco: Berrett-Koehler, 2004), 241–261.

43. W. L. Gardner, B. J. Avolio, F. Luthans, D. R. May, and F. O. Walumbwa, "Can You See the Real Me? A Self-Based Model of Authentic Leader and Follower Development," *The Leadership Quarterly* 16 (2005): 343–372.

44. B. J. Avolio, W. L. Gardner, F. O. Walumbwa, F. Luthans, and D. R. May, "Unlocking the Mask: A Look at the Process by Which Authentic Leaders Impact Follower Attitudes and Behaviors," *The Leadership Quarterly* 15 (2004): 801–823.

45. S. Michie and J. Gooty, "Values, Emotions and Authentic Leadership Behaviors: Will the Real Leader Please Stand Up?" *The Leadership Quarterly* 16 (2005): 441–457.

46. S. Michie and D. L. Nelson, "The Effects of Leader Compassion Display on Follower Attributions: Building a Socialized Leadership Image," Paper presented at the *Academy of Management Conference* in Honolulu, Hawaii (2005).

47. M. Maccoby, "Narcissistic Leaders: The Incredible Pros, the Inevitable Cons," *Harvard Business Review* 78 (2000): 68–77.

48. D. Sankowsky, "The Charismatic Leader as Narcissist: Understanding the Abuse of Power," *Organizational Dynamics* 23 (1995): 57–71.

49. F. J. Flynn and B. M. Staw, "Lend Me Your Wallets: The Effect of Charismatic Leadership on External Support for an Organization," *Strategic Management Journal* 25 (2004): 309–330.

50. D. Goleman, "What Makes a Leader?" *Harvard Business Review* 82 (2004): 82–91.

51. D. Goleman, "Never Stop Learning," *Harvard Business Review* 82 (2004): 28–30.

52. C. L. Gohm, "Mood Regulation and Emotional Intelligence: Individual Differences," *Journal of Personality and Social Psychology* 84 (2003): 594–607.

53. J. Antonakis, N. M. Ashkanasy, and M. T. Dasborough, "Does Leadership Need Emotional Intelligence?" *The Leadership Quarterly,* 20 (2009): 247–261.

54. R. C. Mayer, J. H. Davis, and F. D. Schoorman, "An Integrative Model of Organizational Trust," *Academy of Management Review* 20 (1995): 709–734.

55. R. S. Dooley and G. E. Fryxell, "Attaining Decision Quality and Commitment from Dissent: The Moderating Effects of Loyalty and Competence in Strategic Decision-Making Teams," *Academy of Management Journal* 42 (1999): 389–402.

56. S. W. Lester and H. H. Brower, "In the Eyes of the Beholder: The Relationship between Subordinates' Felt Trustworthiness and Their Work Attitudes and Behaviors," *Journal of Leadership & Organizational Studies* 10 (2003): 17–33.

57. Saj-nicole A. Joni, "The Geography of Trust," *Harvard Business Review* 82 (2003): 82–88.

58. M. E. Heilman, C. J. Block, R. F. Martell, and M. C. Simon, "Has Anything Changed? Current Characteristics of Men, Women, and Managers," *Journal of Applied Psychology* 74 (1989): 935–942.

59. A. H. Eagly, S. J. Darau, and M. Makhijani, "Gender and the Effectiveness of Leaders: A Meta-Analysis," *Psychological Bulletin* 117 (1995): 125–145.

60. M. Julien, D. Zinni, and B. Wright, "Keeper of the Drums: Female Aboriginal Leadership and the Salience of Gender: *Advancing Women in Leadership Journal* 27 (2009) http://advancingwomen.com/awl/awl_wordpress/keeper-of-the-drums-female-aboriginal-leadership-and-the-salience-of-gender.

61. M. K. Ryan, S. A. Haslam, and T. Postmes, "Reactions to the Glass Cliff: Gender Differences in the Explanations for the Precariousness of Women's Leadership Positions," *Journal of Organizational Change Management* 20(2) (2007): 182–197.

62. R. K. Greenleaf, L. C. Spears, and D. T. Frick, eds., *On Becoming a Servant-Leader* (San Francisco: Jossey-Bass, 1996).

63. M. Julien, B. Wright, and D. M. Zinni, "Stories from the Circle: Leadership Lessons from Aboriginal Leaders," *The Leadership Quarterly,* 21 (2009): 115.

64. E. P. Hollander and L. R. Offerman, "Power and Leadership in Organizations: Relationships in Transition," *American Psychologist* 45 (1990): 179–189.

65. H. P. Sims, Jr., and C. C. Manz, *Company of Heros: Unleashing the Power of Self-Leadership* (New York: John Wiley & Sons, 1996).

66. C. C. Manz and H. P. Sims, "Leading Workers to Lead Themselves: The External Leadership of Self-Managing Work Teams," *Administrative Science Quarterly* 32 (1987): 106–128.

67. L. Hirschhorn, "Leaders and Followers in a Postindustrial Age: A Psychodynamic View," *Journal of Applied Behavioral Science* 26 (1990): 529–542.

68. R. E. Kelley, "In Praise of Followers," *Harvard Business Review* 66 (1988): 142–148.

69. C. C. Manz and H. P. Sims, "SuperLeadership: Beyond the Myth of Heroic Leadership," *Organizational Dynamics* 20 (1991): 18–35.

70. G. A. Yukl, *Leadership in Organizations,* 2nd ed. (Upper Saddle River, N.J.: Prentice-Hall, 1989).

71. Harvard Business School, "James E. Burke," *Working Knowledge* (October 27, 2003), http://hbswk.hbs.edu/pubitem.jhtml?id=3755&t=leadership.

72. "Free the Children's Mission Statement 2010," http://www.freethechildren.com/aboutus/misson.php.

73. *Me to We Annual Report 2009,* http://www.metowe.com/aboutus, p. 5.

# Chapter 13

1. Definition adapted from D. Hellriegel, J. W. Slocum, Jr., and R. W. Woodman, *Organizational Behavior* (St. Paul: West, 1992) and from R. D. Middlemist and M. A. Hitt, *Organizational Behavior* (St. Paul: West, 1988).

2. D. Tjosvold, *The Conflict-Positive Organization* (Reading, Mass.: Addison-Wesley, 1991).

3. K. Thomas and W. Schmidt, "A Survey of Managerial Interests with Respect to Conflict," *Academy of Management Journal* 19 (1976): 315–318; G. L. Lippitt, "Managing Conflict in Today's Organizations," *Training and Development Journal* 36 (1982): 66–74.

4. M. Rajim, "A Measure of Styles of Handling Interpersonal Conflict," *Academy of Management Journal* 26 (1983): 368–376.

5. D. Goleman, *Emotional Intelligence* (New York: Bantam Books, 1995); J. Stuller, "Unconventional Smarts," *Across the Board* 35 (1998): 22–23.

6. Tjosvold, *The Conflict-Positive Organization,* 4.

7. R. A. Cosier and D. R. Dalton, "Positive Effects of Conflict: A Field Experiment," *International Journal of Conflict Management* 1 (1990): 81–92.

8. D. Tjosvold, "Making Conflict Productive," *Personnel Administrator* 29 (1984): 121–130.

9. A. C. Amason, W. A. Hochwarter, K. R. Thompson, and A. W. Harrison, "Conflict: An Important Dimension in Successful Management Teams," *Organizational Dynamics* 24 (1995): 25–35.

10. I. Janis, *Groupthink,* 2nd ed. (Boston: Houghton Mifflin, 1982).

11. T. L. Simons and R. S. Peterson, "Task Conflict and Relationship Conflict in Top Management Teams: The Pivotal Role of Intergroup Trust," *Journal of Applied Psychology* 85 (2000): 102–111.

12. R. Nibler and K. L. Harris, "The Effects of Culture and Cohesiveness on Intragroup Conflict and Effectiveness," *The Journal of Social Psychology* 143 (2003): 613–631.

13. J. D. Thompson, *Organizations in Action* (New York: McGraw-Hill, 1967).

14. G. Walker and L. Poppo, "Profit Centers, Single-Source Suppliers, and Transaction Costs," *Administrative Science Quarterly* 36 (1991): 66–87.

15. R. Miles, *Macro Organizational Behavior* (Glenview, Ill.: Scott, Foresman, 1980).

16. H. Levinson, "The Abrasive Personality," *Harvard Business Review* 56 (1978): 86–94.

17. J. C. Quick and J. D. Quick, *Organizational Stress and Preventive Management* (New York: McGraw-Hill, 1984).

18. F. N. Brady, "Aesthetic Components of Management Ethics," *Academy of Management Review* 11 (1986): 337–344.

19. J. R. Ogilvie and M. L. Carsky, "Building Emotional Intelligence in Negotiations," *The International Journal of Conflict Management* 13 (2002): 381–400.

20. A. M. Bodtker and R. L. Oliver, "Emotion in Conflict Formation and Its Transformation: Application to Organizational Conflict Management," *International Journal of Conflict Management* 12 (2001): 259–275.

21. D. E. Conlon and S. H. Hunt, "Dealing with Feeling: The Influence of Outcome Representations on Negotiation," *International Journal of Conflict Management* 13 (2002): 35–58.

22. J. Schopler, C. A. Insko, J. Wieselquist, et al., "When Groups Are More Competitive than Individuals: The Domain of the Discontinuity Effect," *Journal of Personality and Social Psychology* 80 (2001): 632–644.

23. M. Sherif and C. W. Sherif, *Social Psychology* (New York: Harper & Row, 1969).

24. C. Song, S. M. Sommer, and A. E. Hartman, "The Impact of Adding an External Rater on Interdepartmental Cooperative Behaviors of Workers," *International Journal of Conflict Management* 9 (1998): 117–138.

25. W. Tsai and S. Ghoshal, "Social Capital and Value Creation: The Role of Intrafirm Networks," *Academy of Management Journal* 41 (1998): 464–476.

26. M. A. Zarate, B. Garcia, A. A. Garza, and R. T. Hitlan, "Cultural Threat and Perceived Realistic Group Conflict as Dual Predictors of Prejudice," *Journal of Experimental Social Psychology* 40 (2004): 99–105; J. C. Dencker, A. Joshi, and J. J. Martocchio, "Employee Benefits as Context for Intergenerational Conflict," *Human Resource Management Review* 17(2) (2007): 208–220.

27. M. L. Maznevski and K. M. Chudoba, "Bridging Space over Time: Global Virtual-Team Dynamics and Effectiveness," *Organization Science* 11 (2000): 473–492.

28. D. Katz and R. Kahn, *The Social Psychology of Organizations,* 2nd ed. (New York: Wiley, 1978).

29. D. L. Nelson and J. C. Quick, "Professional Women: Are Distress and Disease Inevitable?" *Academy of Management Review* 10 (1985): 206–218; D. L. Nelson and M. A. Hitt, "Employed Women and Stress: Implications for Enhancing Women's Mental Health in the Workplace," in J. C. Quick, J. Hurrell, and L. A. Murphy, eds., *Stress and Well-Being at Work: Assessments and Interventions for Occupational Mental Health* (Washington, D.C.: American Psychological Association, 1992).

30. M. G. Pratt and J. A. Rosa, "Transforming Work-Family Conflict into Commitment in Network Marketing Organizations," *Academy of Management Journal* 46 (2003): 395–418.

31. "Leader Profiles and 'Quotable Quotes': Linda Duxbury," Carleton University School of Business, http://www.rhdcc.gc.ca/eng/lp/spila/wlb/ell/15linda_duxbury.shtml.

32. "Leader Profiles and 'Quotable Quotes': Nora Spinks, Work Life Harmony Enterprises" http://www.rhdcc.gc.ca/eng/lp/spila/wlb/ell/23nora_spinks.shtml.

33. W. R. Boswell and J. B. Olson-Buchanan, "The Use of Communication Technologies after Hours: The Role of Work Attitudes and Work-Life Conflict," *Journal of Management* 33(4) (2007): 592–610.

34. R. L. Kahn et al., *Organizational Stress: Studies in Role Conflict and Ambiguity* (New York: Wiley, 1964).

35. J. L. Badaracco, Jr., "The Discipline of Building Character," *Harvard Business Review* (March–April 1998): 115–124.

36. B. Schneider, "The People Make the Place," *Personnel Psychology* 40 (1987): 437–453.

37. C. A. O'Reilly, J. Chatman, and D. F. Caldwell, "People and Organizational Culture: A Profile Comparison Approach to Assessing Person-Organization Fit," *Academy of Management Journal* 34 (1991): 487–516.

38. I. Dayal and J. M. Thomas, "Operation KPE: Developing a New Organization," *Journal of Applied Behavioral Science* 4 (1968): 473–506.

39. R. H. Miles, "Role Requirements as Sources of Organizational Stress," *Journal of Applied Psychology* 61 (1976): 172–179.

40. W. F. G. Mastenbroek, *Conflict Management and Organization Development* (Chichester, England: Wiley, 1987).

41. M. R. Frone, "Interpersonal Conflict at Work and Psychological Outcomes: Testing a Model among Young Workers," *Journal of Occupational Health Psychology* 5 (2000): 246–255.

42. K. Thomas, "Conflict and Conflict Management," in M. D. Dunnette, ed., *Handbook of Industrial and Organizational Psychology* (New York: Wiley, 1976).

43. H. H. Meyer, E. Kay, and J. R. P. French, "Split Roles in Performance Appraisal," *Harvard Business Review* 43 (1965): 123–129.

44. T. W. Costello and S. S. Zalkind, *Psychology in Administration: A Research Orientation* (Englewood Cliffs, N.J.: Prentice-Hall, 1963).

45. Snapshot Spy, "Employee Computer & Internet Abuse Statistics," http://www.snapshotspy.com/employee-computer-abuse-statistics.htm; Data sources include U.S. Department of Commerce—Economics and Statistics Administration and the National Telecommunications and Information Administration—Greenfield and Rivet, "Employee Computer Abuse Statistics."

46. P. F. Hewlin, "And the Award for Best Actor Goes to ... : Facades of Conformity in Organizational Settings," *Academy of Management Review* 28 (2003): 633–642.

47. K. Kidd, "Woman's Fight Opens Legal Titans' Secret Files," *Toronto Star* (September 3, 2009) http://www.thestar.com/news/gta/article/690286.

48. Ibid.

49. K. Pullen. "The Problem with Women," *Toronto Life* (May 2010), 44.

50. C. A. Insko, J. Scholper, L. Gaertner, et al., "Interindividual–Intergroup Discontinuity Reduction through the Anticipation of Future Interaction," *Journal of Personality and Social Psychology* 80 (2001): 95–111.

51. D. Tjosvold and M. Poon, "Dealing with Scarce Resources: Open-Minded Interaction for Resolving Budget Conflicts," *Group and Organization Management* 23 (1998): 237–255.

52. Miles, *Macro Organizational Behavior; R. Steers, Introduction to Organizational Behavior,* 4th ed. (Glenview, Ill.: Harper-Collins, 1991).

53. A. Tyerman and C. Spencer, "A Critical Text of the Sherrif's Robber's Cave Experiments: Intergroup Competition and Cooperation between Groups of Well-Acquainted Individuals," *Small Group Behavior* 14 (1983): 515–531; R. M. Kramer, "Intergroup Relations and Organizational Dilemmas: The Role of Categorization Processes," in B. Staw and L. Cummings, eds., *Research in Organizational Behavior* 13 (Greenwich, Conn.: JAI Press, 1991), 191–228.

54. A. Carmeli, "The Relationship between Emotional Intelligence and Work Attitudes, Behavior and Outcomes: An Examination among Senior Managers," *Journal of Managerial Psychology* 18 (2003): 788–813.

55. R. Blake and J. Mouton, "Overcoming Group Warfare," *Harvard Business Review* 64 (1984): 98–108.

56. D. G. Ancona and D. Caldwell, "Improving the Performance of New Product Teams," *Research Technology Management* 33 (1990): 25–29.

57. M. A. Cronin and L. R. Weingart, "Representational Gaps, Information Processing and Conflict in Functionally Diverse Teams," *Academy of Management Review* 32(3) (2007), 761–773.

58. C. K. W. DeDreu and L. R. Weingart, "Task versus Relationship Conflict, Team Performance, and Team Member Satisfaction: A Meta-Analysis," *Journal of Applied Psychology* 88 (2003): 741–749.

59. R. J. Lewicki, J. A. Litterer, J. W. Minton, and D. M. Saunders, *Negotiation,* 2nd ed. (Burr Ridge, Ill.: Irwin, 1994).

60. C. K. W. De Dreu, S. L. Koole, and W. Steinel, "Unfixing the Fixed Pie: A Motivated Information-Processing Approach to Integrative Negotiation," *Journal of Personality and Social Psychology* 79 (2000): 975–987.

61. R. Fisher, W. Ury, and B. Patton, *Getting to Yes: Negotiating Agreement without Giving In* (2nd ed.) New York: Penguin Books, 1991.

62. ADR Institute of Ontario, FAQ, http://www.adrontario.ca/about/faq.cfm.

63. M. H. Bazerman, J. R. Curhan, D. A. Moore, and K. L. Valley, "Negotiation," *Annual Review of Psychology* 51 (2000): 279–314.

64. I. Ayers and P. Siegelman, "Race and Gender Discrimination in Bargaining for a New Car," *American Economic Review* 85 (1995): 304–321.

65. K. W. Thomas, "Conflict and Conflict Management," in M. D. Dunnette, ed., *Handbook of Industrial and Organizational Psychology* (Chicago: Rand McNally, 1976), 900.

66. Gladwin and Walter, "How Multinationals Can Manage," 228.

67. L. A. Dechurch, K. L. Hamilton, and C. Haas, "Effects of Conflict Management Strategies on Perceptions of Intragroup Conflict," *Group Dynamics: Theory, Research, and Practice* 11(1) (2007): 66–78.

68. S. Alper, D. Tjosvold, and K. S. Law, "Conflict Management, Efficacy, and Performance in Organizational Teams," *Personnel Psychology* 53 (2000): 625–642.

69. W. King and E. Miles, "What We Know and Don't Know about Measuring Conflict," *Management Communication Quarterly* 4 (1990): 222–243.

70. J. Barker, D. Tjosvold, and I. R. Andrews, "Conflict Approaches of Effective and Ineffective Project Managers: A Field Study in a Matrix Organization," *Journal of Management Studies* 25 (1988): 167–178.

71. M. Chan, "Intergroup Conflict and Conflict Management in the R&D Divisions of Four Aerospace Companies," *IEEE Transactions on Engineering Management* 36 (1989): 95–104.

72. S. L. Phillips and R. L. Elledge, *The Team Building Source Book* (San Diego: University Associates, 1989).

73. S. Steinberg, "Airbus Workers in France, Germany Strike against Massive Job Cuts," http://www.wsws.org/articles/2007/mar2007/airb-m01.shtml, March 1, 2007.

74. C. K. W. De Dreu and A. E. M. Van Vianen, "Managing Relationship Conflict and the Effectiveness of Organizational Teams," *Journal of Organizational Behavior* 22 (2001): 309–328.

75. R. A. Baron, S. P. Fortin, R. L. Frei, L. A. Hauver, and M. L. Shack, "Reducing Organizational Conflict: The Role of Socially Induced Positive Affect," *International Journal of Conflict Management* 1 (1990): 133–152.

76. K. W. Thomas, "Toward Multidimensional Values in Teaching: The Example of Conflict Behaviors," *Academy of Management Review* 2 (1977): 484–490.

# Chapter 14

1. I. Harpaz and X. Fu, "The Structure of the Meaning of Work: A Relative Stability Amidst Change," *Human Relations* 55 (2002): 639–668.

2. R. D. Arvey, I. Harpaz and H. Liao, "Work Centrality and Post-award Work Behavior of Lottery Winners," *The Journal of Psychology* 138 (2004): 404–420.

3. V. Keefe, P. Reid, C. Ormsby, B. Robson, G. Purdie, J. Baxter, and Ngäti Kahungunu Iwi Incorporated, "Serious Health Events Following Involuntary Job Loss in New Zealand Meat Processing Workers," *International Journal of Epidemiology* 31 (2002): 1155–1161.

4. W. T. Gallo, H. M. Teng, T. A. Falba, S. V. Kasl, H. M. Krumholz, and E. H. Bradley, "The Impact of Late Career Job Loss on Myocardial Infarction and Stroke: A 10 Year Follow up Using the Health and Retirement Survey," *Occupational and Environmental Medicine* 63 (2006): 683–687.

5. K. W. Strully, "Job Loss and Health in the U.S. Labor Market," *Demography* 46 (2009): 221–246.

6. Various research described in D. L. Blustein, "The Role of Work in Psychological Health and Well-being," *American Psychologist* 63 (2008): 228–240.

7. S. A. Ruiz-Quintanilla and B. Wilpert, "Are Work Meanings Changing?" *European Work and Organizational Psychology* 1, (1991): 91–109; MOW—International Research Team, *The Meaning of Working.* London: Academic Press, 1987.

8. S. H. Harding and F. J. Hikspoors, "New Work Values: In Theory and in Practice," *International Social Science Journal* 47 (1995), 441–455.

9. L. R. Gomez-Mejia, "The Cross-Cultural Structure of Task-Related and Contextual Constructs," *Journal of Psychology* 120 (1986): 5–19.

10. A. M. Grant, Y. Fried, and T. Juillerat, "Job Design in Classic and Contemporary Perspectives," A*PA Handbook of Industrial and Organizational Psychology,* American Psychological Association, 2010.

11. A. Smith, *An Inquiry into the Nature and Causes of the Wealth of Nations,* London:, W. Strahan and T. Cadell, 1776.

12. C. Babbage, *On the Economy of Machinery and Manufacturing,* London: Knight, 1835.

13. F. W. Taylor, *The Principles of Scientific Management* (New York: Norton, 1911).

14. From F. W. Taylor, *The Principles of Scientific Management* (New York: Harper, 1911) quoted in C. Williams, A. Kondra, and C. Vibert, *Management* (1st ed.), Nelson, 2004.

15. T. Bell, *Out of This Furnace* (Pittsburgh: University of Pittsburgh Press, 1941).

16. C. R. Walker, "The Problem of the Repetitive Job," *Harvard Business Review* 28 (1950): 54–58.

17. C. M. Axtell and S. K. Parker, "Promoting Role Breadth Self-efficacy through Involvement, Work Redesign and Training," *Human Relations* 56 (2003): 113–131.

18. M. A. Campion, L. Cheraskin, and M. J. Stevens, "Career-Related Antecedents and Outcomes of Job Rotation," *Academy of Management Journal* 37 (1994): 1518–1542.

19. A. M. Grant, Y. Fried, and T. Juillerat, "Job Design in Classic and Contemporary Perspectives," *APA Handbook of Industrial and Organizational Psychology,* American Psychological Association, 2010.

20. F. Herzberg, "One More Time: How Do You Motivate Employees?" *Harvard Business Review* 46 (1968): 53–62.

21. R. N. Ford, "Job Enrichment Lessons from AT&T," *Harvard Business Review* 51 (1973): 96–106.

22. R. J. House and L. A. Wigdor, "Herzberg's Dual-Factor Theory of Job Satisfaction and Motivation: A Review of the Evidence and a Criticism," *Personnel Psychology* 20 (1967): 369–389.

23. G. R. Oldham, J. R. Hackman, and L. P. Stepina, "Norms for the Job Diagnostic Survey," Technical Report No. 16, School of Organization and Management, Yale University, 1978, http://www.dtic.mil/cgi-bin/GetTRDoc?AD=ADA057268andLocation=U2anddoc=GetTRDoc.pdf.

24. S. E. Humphrey, J. D. Nahrgang, and F. P. Morgeson, "Integrating Motivational, Social and Contextual Work Design Features: A Meta-Analytic Summary and Theoretical Extension of the Work Design Literature," *Journal of Applied Psychology* 92 (2007): 1332–1356.

25. Y. Fried and G. R. Ferris, "The Validity of the Job Characteristics Model: A Review and Meta-Analysis," *Personnel Psychology* 40 (1987): 287–322.

26. Ibid.

27. S. E. Humphrey, J. D. Nahrgang, and F. P. Morgeson, "Integrating Motivational, Social and Contextual Work Design Features: A Meta-Analytic Summary and Theoretical Extension of the Work Design Literature," J*ournal of Applied Psychology* 92 (2007): 1332–1356.

28. G. Gard and A. C. Sandberg, "Motivating Factors for Return to Work," *Physiotherapy Research International* 3 (2006): 100–108.

29. A. M. Grant, "The Significance of Task Significance: Job Performance Effects, Relational Mechanisms, and Boundary Conditions," *Journal of Applied Psychology* 93 (2008): 108–124.

30. A. M. Grant, "Designing Jobs to Do Good: Dimensions and Psychological Consequences of Prosocial Job Characteristics," *The Journal of Positive Psychology* 3 (2008): 19–39.

31. A. M. Grant, "Employees without a Cause: The Motivational Effects of Prosocial Impact in Public Service," *International Public Management Journal* 11 (2008): 48–66.

32. Y. N. Turner, I. Hadas-Halperin, and D. Raveh, "Patient Photos Spur Radiologist Empathy and Eye for Detail," paper presented at annual meeting of the Radiological Society of North America, November 2008, reported in A. M. Grant and S. K. Parker, "Redesigning Work Theories: The Rise of Relational and Proactive Perspectives," *The Academy of Management Annals* 3 (2009): 317–375.

33. K. A. Arnold, N. Turner, J. Barling, E. K. Kelloway, and M. C. McKee, "Transformational Leadership and Psychological Well-Being: The Mediating Role of Meaningful Work," *Journal of Occupational Health Psychology* 12 (2007): 193–203.

34. F. P. Morgeson and S. E. Humphrey, "The Work Design Questionnaire (WDQ): Developing and Validating a Comprehensive Measure for Assessing Job Design and the Nature of Work," *Journal of Applied Psychology* 91 (2006): 1321–1339.

35. S. E. Humphrey, J. D. Nahrgang, and F. P. Morgeson, "Integrating Motivational, Social and Contextual Work Design Features: A Meta-Analytic Summary and Theoretical Extension of the Work Design Literature," *Journal of Applied Psychology* 92 (2007): 1332–1356.

36. Ibid.

37. K. Nielsen and B. Cleal, "Predicting Flow at Work: Investigating the Activities and Job Characteristics that Predict Flow States at Work," *Journal of Occupational Health Psychology* 15 (2010): 180–190.

38. E. F. Stone and H. G. Gueutal, "An Empirical Derivation of the Dimensions Along Which Characteristics of Jobs Are Perceived," *Academy of Management Journal* 28 (1985): 376–396.

39. S. E. Humphrey, J. D. Nahrgang, and F. P. Morgeson, "Integrating Motivational, Social and Contextual Work Design Features: A Meta-analytic Summary and Theoretical Extension of the Work Design Literature," *Journal of Applied Psychology* 92 (2007): 1332–1356.

40. G. R. Salancik and J. Pfeffer, "A Social Information Processing Approach to Job Attitudes and Task Design," *Administrative Science Quarterly* 23 (1978): 224–253.

41. J. Pfeffer, "Management as Symbolic Action: The Creation and Maintenance of Organizational Paradigms," in L. L. Cummings and B. M. Staw, eds., *Research in Organizational Behavior,* vol. 3 (Greenwich, Conn.: JAI Press, 1981), 1–52.

42. C. Clegg and C. Spencer, "A Circular and Dynamic Model of the Process of Job Design," *Journal of Occupational & Organizational Psychology* 80 (2007): 321–339.

43. J. Thomas and R. Griffin, "The Social Information Processing Model of Task Design: A Review of the Literature," *Academy of Management Review* 8 (1983): 672–682.

44. D. J. Campbell, "Task Complexity: A Review and Analysis," *Academy of Management Review* 13 (1988): 40–52.

45. A. M. Grant, "Relational Job Design and the Motivation to Make a Prosocial Difference," *Academy of Management Review* 32 (2007): 393–417.

46. S. E. White and T. R. Mitchell, "Job Enrichment versus Social Cues: A Comparison and Competitive Test," *Journal of Applied Psychology* 64 (1979): 1–9.

47. S. E. White, T. R. Mitchell, and C. H. Bell, "Goal Setting, Evaluation Apprehension, and Social Cues as Determinants of Job Performance and Job Satisfaction in a Simulated Organization," *Journal of Applied Psychology* 62 (1977): 665–673.

48. R. W. Griffin, "Objective and Social Sources of Information in Task Redesign: A Field Experiment," *Administrative Science Quarterly* 28 (1983): 184–200.

49. S. M. Jex and P. E. Spector, "The Generalizability of Social Information Processing to Organizational Settings: A Summary of Two Field Experiments," *Perceptual and Motor Skills* 69 (1989): 883–893.

50. A. Wrzesniewski, J. E. Dutton, and G. Debebe, "Interpersonal Sensemaking and the Meaning of Work, *Research in Organizational Behavior* 25 (2003): 93–135.

51. A. Wrzesniewski and J. E. Dutton, "Crafting a Job: Revisioning Employees as Active Crafters of their Work," *Academy of Management Review* 26 (2001): 179–201.

52. Ibid.

53. Ibid.

54. P. Lyons, "The Crafting of Jobs and Individual Differences," *Journal of Business and Psychology* 23 (2008): 25–36.

55. C. Leana, E. Appelbaum, and I. Shevchuk, "Work Process and Quality of Care in Early Childhood Education: The Role of Job Crafting," *Academy of Management Journal* 52 (2009): 1169–1192.

56. J. M. Berg, A. Wrzesniewski, and J. E. Dutton, "Perceiving and Responding to Challenges in Job crafting at Different Ranks: When Proactivity Requires Adaptivity," *Journal of Organizational Behavior* 31 (2010): 158–186.

57. D. M. Rouseau, V. T. Ho, and J. Greenberg, "I-deals: Idiosyncratic Terms in Employment Relationships," *Academy of Management Review* 31 (2006): 977–994.

58. S. Hornung, D. M. Rousseau, and J. Glaser, "Creating Flexible Work Arrangements through Idiosyncratic Deals," *Journal of Applied Psychology* 93 (2008): 655–664.

59. S. Hornung, D. M. Rousseau, J. Glaser, P. Angerer, and M. Weigl, "Beyond Top-down and Bottom-up Work Redesign: Customizing Job Content through Idiosyncratic Deals," *Journal of Organizational Work Behavior* 30 (2009): 187–215.

60. B. M. Wright and J. L. Cordery, "Production Uncertainty as a Contextual Moderator of Employee Reactions to Job Design," *Journal of Applied Psychology* 84 (1999): 456–463.

61. D. Fay and M. Frese, "The Concept of Personal Initiative: An Overview of Validity Studies," *Human Performance* 14 (2001): 97–124.

62. S. K. Parker," Enhancing Role-breadth Efficacy: The Roles of Job Enrichment and Other Organizational Interventions," *Journal of Applied Psychology* 83 (1998): 835–852.

63. F. P. Morgeson, K. Delaney-Klinger, and M. A. Hemingway, "The Importance of Job Autonomy, Cognitive Ability, and Job-related Skill for Predicting Role Breadth and Job Performance," *Journal of Applied Psychology* 90 (2005): 399–406.

64. S. K. Parker, T. D. Wall, and P. R. Jackson, "That's Not My Job": Developing Flexible Employee Work Orientations," *Academy of Management Journal* 40 (1997): 899–929.

65. M. Frese, H. Garst, and D. Fay, "Making Things Happen: Reciprocal Relationships Between Work Characteristics and Personal Initiative in a Four-Wave Longitudinal Structural Equation Model," *Journal of Applied Psychology* 92 (2007): 1084–1102.

66. S. J. Ashford, R. Blatt, and D. VandeWalle, "Reflections on the Looking Glass: A Review of Research on Feedback-Seeking Behavior in Organizations," *Journal of Management* 29 (2003): 769–799.

67. D. M. Mayer, M. G. Ehrhart, and B. Schneider, "Service Attribute Boundary Conditions of the Service Climate-Customer Satisfaction Link," *Academy of Management Journal* 52 (2008): 1034–1050.

68. G. R. Oldham, and A. Cummings, "Employee Creativity: Personal and Contextual Factors at Work," *Academy of Management Journal* 39 (1996): 607–634.

69. M. Frese, H. Garst, and D. Fay, "Making Things Happen: Reciprocal Relationships Between Work Characteristics and Personal Initiative in a Four-Wave Longitudinal Structural Equation Model," *Journal of Applied Psychology* 92 (2007): 1084–1102.

70. C. E. Shalley, J. Zhou, and G. R. Oldham, "The Effects of Personal and Contextual Characteristics on Creativity: Where Should We Go from Here?" *Journal of Management* 30 (2004): 933–958.

71. J. L. Xie and G. Johns, "Job Scope and Stress: Can Job Scope Be Too High?" *Academy of Management Journal* 38 (1995): 1288–1309.

72. K. D. Elsbach and A. B. Hargadon, "Enhancing Creativity through "Mindless" Work: A Framework of Workday Design," *Organization Science* 17 (2006): 470–483.

73. S. Ohly, S. Sonnentag, and F. Pluntke, "Routinization, Work Characteristics and Their Relationships with Creative and Proactive Behaviors," *Journal of Organizational Behavior* 27 (2006): 259–279.

74. B. Kohut, *Country Competitiveness: Organizing of Work* (New York: Oxford University Press, 1993).

75. J. C. Quick and L. E. Tetrick, eds., *Handbook of Occupational Health Psychology* (Washington, D.C.: American Psychological Association, 2002).

76. W. E. Deming, *Out of the Crisis* (Cambridge, Mass.: MIT Press, 1986).

77. L. Thurow, *Head to Head: The Coming Economic Battle among Japan, Europe, and America* (New York: Morrow, 1992).

78. M. A. Fruin, *The Japanese Enterprise System—Competitive Strategies and Cooperative Structures* (New York: Oxford University Press, 1992).

79. S. K. Parker, "Longitudinal Effects of Lean Production on Employee Outcomes and the Mediating Role of Work Characteristics," *Journal of Applied Psychology* 88 (2003): 620–634.

80. E. Furubotn, "Codetermination and the Modern Theory of the Firm: A Property-Rights Analysis," *Journal of Business* 61 (1988): 165–181.

81. H. Levinson, *Executive: The Guide to Responsive Management* (Cambridge, Mass.: Harvard University Press, 1981).

82. B. Gardell, "Scandinavian Research on Stress in Working Life" (Paper presented at the IRRA Symposium on Stress in Working Life, Denver, September 1980).

83. L. Levi, "Psychosocial, Occupational, Environmental, and Health Concepts; Research Results and Applications," in G. P. Keita and S. L. Sauter, eds., *Work and Well-Being: An Agenda for the 1990s* (Washington, D.C.: American Psychological Association, 1992), 199–211.

84. Y. Baruch, "The Status of Research on Teleworking and an Agenda for Future Research," *International Journal of Management Review* 3 (2000): 113–129.

85. E. B. Akyeampong, "Perspectives on Labour and Income June 2007," Statistics Canada Cat. No. 75-001-XIE.

86. R. S. Gajendran and D. A. Harrison, "The Good, the Bad, and the Unknown about Telecommuting: Meta-analysis of Psychological Mediators and Individual Consequences," *Journal of Applied Psychology* 92 (2007): 1524–1541.

87. M Toneguzzi, "Initiative Aims to Make Calgary a World Leader in Telework," *The Calgary Herald,* April 20, 2010, http://www.calgaryherald.com/life/Spring+shootie+blends+fashion+with+function/2729973/Initiative+aims+make+Calgary+world+leader+telework/2924782/story.html.

88. http://www.publicaccess.calgary.ca/

89. "Calgary Among World's Highest CO2 Emitters," *CBC News,* April 6, 2010, http://www.cbc.ca/technology/story/2010/04/06/calgary-un-report-carbon-dioxide-greenhouse-emissions.html.

90. Calgary Economic Development (April 19, 2010) http://www.calgaryeconomicdevelopment.com/global_news_template.cfm?page=0520200974952.

91. R. S. Gajendran and D. A. Harrison, "The Good, the Bad, and the Unknown about Telecommuting: Meta-analysis of Psychological Mediators and Individual consequences," *Journal of Applied Psychology* 92 (2007): 1524–1541.

92. Ibid.

93. Ibid.

94. Ibid.

95. Ibid.

96. B. Hill, "Recession Gets Real with Job-sharing," *Ottawa Citizen* (January 11, 2010), http://www.working.com/national/sectors/Recession+gets+real+with+sharing/1356914/story.html.

97. Yukon Public Service Commission, http://www.psc.gov.yk.ca/services/compressed_work.html.

98. Statistics Canada 2006, http://www.statcan.gc.ca/pub/71-222-x/2006001/4069843-eng.htm.

99. S. M. Pollan and M. Levine, "Asking for Flextime," *Working Women* (February 1994): 48.

100. S. A. Rogier and M. Y. Padgett, "The Impact of Utilizing a Flexible Work Schedule on the Perceived Career Advancement Potential of Women," *Human Resource Development Quarterly* 15 (2004): 89–106.

101. B. Baltes, T. E. Briggs, J. W. Huff, J. A. Wright, and G. A. Neuman, "Flexible and Compressed Workweek Schedules: A Meta-Analysis of Their Effects on Work-Related Criteria," *Journal of Applied Psychology* 84 (1999): 496–513.

102. Ibid.

103. S. Zuboff, *In the Age of the Smart Machine: The Future of Work and Power* (New York: Basic Books, 1988).

104. B. A. Gutek and S. J. Winter, "Computer Use, Control over Computers, and Job Satisfaction," in S. Oskamp and S. Spacapan, eds., *People's Reactions to Technology in Factories, Offices, and Aerospace: The Claremont Symposium on Applied Social Psychology* (Newbury Park, Calif.: Sage, 1990), 121–144.

105. L. M. Schleifer and B. C. Amick, III, "System Response Time and Method of Pay: Stress Effects in Computer-Based Tasks," *International Journal of Human-Computer Interaction* 1 (1989): 23–39.

106. K. Voight, "Virtual Work: Some Telecommuters Take Remote Work to the Extreme," *The Wall Street Journal Europe* (February 1, 2001): 1.

107. G. Salvendy, *Handbook of Industrial Engineering: Technology and Operations Management* (New York: John Wiley & Sons, 2001).

108. D. M. Herold, "Using Technology to Improve Our Management of Labor Market Trends," in M. Greller, ed., "Managing Careers with a Changing Workforce," *Journal of Organizational Change Management* 3 (1990): 44–57.

109. D. A. Whetten and K. S. Cameron, *Developing Management Skills,* 6th ed. (Upper Saddle River, N.J.: Prentice Hall, 2004).

# Chapter 15

1. J. Child, *Organization* (New York: Harper & Row, 1984).

2. D. Pugh, D. Hickson, C. Hinnings, and C. Turner, "Dimensions of Organization Structure," *Administrative Science Quarterly* 13 (1968): 65–91; B. Reimann, "Dimensions of Structure in Effective Organizations: Some Empirical Evidence," *Academy of Management Journal* 17 (1974): 693–708; S. Robbins, *Organization Theory: The Structure and Design of Organizations,* 3rd ed. (Englewood Cliffs, N.J.: Prentice-Hall, 1990).

3. T. D. Wall, N. J. Kemp, P. R. Jockron, and C. W. Clegg, "Outcomes of Autonomous Work Groups: A Long-Term Field Experiment," *Academy of Management Journal* 42 (1986): 127–137.

4. R. I. Beekun, "Assessing the Effectiveness of Sociotechnical Interventions: Antidote or Fad?" *Human Relations* 47 (1989): 877–897.

5. L. Porter and E. Lawler, "The Effects of 'Tall' versus 'Flat' Organization Structures on Managerial Job Satisfaction," *Personnel Psychology* 17 (1964): 135–148.

6. J. H. Gittell, "Supervisory Span, Relational Coordination, and Flight Departure Performance: A Reassessment of Postbureaucracy Theory," *Organization Science* 12 (2001): 468–483.

7. Ibid.

8. J. D. Ford, "Department Context and Formal Structure as Constraints on Leader Behavior," *Academy of Management Journal* 24 (1981): 274–288.

9. F. Heller and G. Yukl, "Participation, Managerial Decision-making and Situational Variables," *Organizational Behavior and Human Performance* 2 (1969): 227–241.

10. D. Kipnis and J. Cosentino, "Use of Leadership Powers in Industry," *Journal of Applied Psychology* 53 (1969): 460–466.

11. D. Kipnis and W. P. Lane, "Self Confidence and Leadership," *Journal of Applied Psychology* 46 (1962): 291–295.

12. H. Mintzberg, *The Structuring of Organizations* (Englewood Cliffs, N.J.: Prentice-Hall, 1979).

13. T. Burns and G. Stalker, *The Management of Innovation* (London: Tavistock, 1961); Mintzberg, Structuring of Organizations.

14. C. B. Clott, "Perspectives on Global Outsourcing and the Changing Nature of Work," *Business and Society Review* 109 (2004): 153–170.

15. B. A. Pasternack and A. J. Viscio, *The Centerless Corporation: A New Model for Transforming Your Organization for Growth and Prosperity* (New York: Simon & Schuster, 1999).

16. J. Woodward, *Industrial Organization: Theory and Practices* (London: Oxford University Press, 1965).

17. C. Perrow, "A Framework for the Comparative Analysis of Organizations," *American Sociological Review* 32 (1967): 194–208; D. Rosseau, "Assessment of Technology in Organizations: Closed versus Open Systems Approaches," *Academy of Management Review* 4 (1979): 531–542.

18. Perrow, "A Framework for the Comparative Analysis of Organizations," 194–208.

19. J. D. Thompson, *Organizations in Action* (New York: McGraw-Hill, 1967).

20. S. Faraj and Y. Xiao, "Coordination in Fast-Response Organizations," *Management Science* 52 (2006): 1155–1169.

21. J. R. Hollenbeck, H. Moon, A. P. J. Ellis, B. J. West, D. R. Ilgen, L. Sheppard, C. O. L. H. Porter, and J. A. Wagner III, "Structural Contingency Theory and Individual Differences: Examination of External and Internal Person-Team Fit," *Journal of Applied Psychology* 87 (2002): 599–606.

22. J. Courtright, G. Fairhurst, and L. Rogers, "Interaction Patterns in Organic and Mechanistic Systems," *Academy of Management Journal* 32 (1989): 773–802.

23. T. C. Head, "Structural Changes in Turbulent Environments: A Study of Small and Mid-Size Chinese Organizations," *Journal of Leadership and Organizational Studies* 12 (2005): 82–93.

24. J. P. Davis, K. M. Eisenhardt, and C. B. Bingham, "Optimal Structure, Market Dynamism, and the Strategy of Simple Rules," *Administrative Science Quarterly* 54 (1009): 413–452.

25. K. M. Eisenhardt and D. Sull, "Strategy as Simple Rules," *Harvard Business Review* 79 (2001): 107–116.

26. H. Downey, D. Hellriegel, and J. Slocum, Jr., "Environmental Uncertainty: The Construct and Its Application," *Administrative Science Quarterly* 20 (1975): 613–629.

27. G. Dess and D. Beard, "Dimensions of Organizational Task Environments," *Administrative Science Quarterly* 29 (1984): 52–73.

28. G. Vroom, "Organizational Design and the Intensity of Rivalry," *Management Science* 52 (2006): 1689–1702.

29. R. Daft, *Organization Theory and Design,* 7th ed. (Mason, Ohio: South-Western, 2000).

30. M. Porter, *Competitive Strategy,* New York: The Free Press, 1980.

31. D. Miller, "Configurations of Strategy and Structure," *Strategic Management Journal* 7 (1986): 233–249.

32. R. S. Kaplan & D. P. Norton, "How to Implement a New Strategy without Disrupting Your Organization," *Harvard Business Review,* (March 2006): 100–109.

33. D. B. Turban and T. L. Keon, "Organizational Attractiveness: An Interactionist Perspective," *Journal of Applied Psychology* 78 (1993): 184–193.

34. N. Dimarco and S. Norton, "Life Style, Organization Structure, Congruity and Job Satisfaction," *Personnel Psychology* 27 (1974): 581–591.

35. C. Allinson and J. Hayes, "Transferring the Western Model of Project Organisation to a Bureaucratic Culture: The Case of Nepal," *International Journal of Project Management* 14 (1996): 53–57.

36. M. Elovainio and M. Kivimäki, "Personal Need for Structure and Occupational Strain: An Investigation of Structural Models and Interaction with Job Complexity," *Personality and Individual Differences* 26 (1998): 209–222.

37. D. B. Turban and T. L. Keon, "Organizational Attractiveness: An Interactionist Perspective," *Journal of Applied Psychology* 78 (1993): 184–193.

38. B. Shamir and J. M. Howell, "Organizational and Contextual Influences on the Emergence and Effectiveness of Charismatic Leadership," *Leadership Quarterly* 10 (1999): 257–284.

39. E. E. Ghiselli and J. P. Siegel, "Leadership and Managerial Success in Tall and Flat Organization Structures," *Personnel Psychology* 25 (1972): 617–614.

40. D. Miller, C. Droge, and J. M. Toulouse, "Strategic Process and Content as Mediators Between Organizational Context and Structure," *Academy of Management Journal* 31 (1988): 544–569.

41. M. Schminke, M. L. Ambrose, and R. Cropanzano, "The Effect of Organizational Structure on Perceptions of Procedural Fairness," *Journal of Applied Psychology* 85 (2000): 294–304.

42. M. L. Ambrose and M. Schminke, "Organizational Structure as a Moderator of the Relationship Between Procedural Justice, Interactional Justice, Perceived Organizational Support, and Supervisory Trust," *Journal of Applied Psychology* 88 (2003): 295–305.

43. W. R. Scott, *Organizations: Rational, Natural, and Open Systems,* 4th ed. (Upper Saddle River, N.J.: Prentice-Hall, 1997).

44. D. Miller and P. Friesen, "A Longitudinal Study of the Corporate Life Cycle," *Management Science* 30 (1984): 1161–1183.

45. M. H. Overholt, "Flexible Organizations: Using Organizational Design as a Competitive Advantage," *Human Resource Planning* 20 (1997): 22–32; P. W. Roberts and R. Greenwood, "Integrating Transaction Cost and Institutional Theories: Toward a Constrained-Efficiency Framework for Understanding Organizational Design Adoption," *Academy of Management Review* 22 (1997): 346–373.

46. C. W. L. Hill and G. R. Jones, *Strategic Management Theory,* 5th ed. (Boston: Houghton Mifflin, 2000).

47. E. Brynjolfsson, and L. Hitt, *Information Technology and Organizational Design: Evidence from Micro Data,* MIT Sloan School Working Paper, 1998, http://www2.dse.unibo.it/santarel/BrynjolfssonHitt1998.pdf.

48. Daft, *Organization Theory and Design.*

49. C. M. Savage, *5th Generation Management, Revised Edition: Co-creating through Virtual Enterprising, Dynamic Teaming, and Knowledge Networking* (Boston: Butterworth-Heinemann, 1996).

50. S. M. Davis, *Future Perfect* (Perseus Publishing, 1997).

51. A. Boynton and B. Victor, "Beyond Flexibility: Building and Managing a Dynamically Stable Organization," *California Management Review* 8 (Fall 1991): 53–66.

52. P. J. Brews and C. L. Tucci, "Exploring the Structural Effects of Internetworking," *Strategic Management Journal* 25 (2004): 429–451.

53. J. Fulk, "Global Network Organizations: Emergence and Future Prospects," *Human Relations* 54 (2001): 91–100.

54. The use of the theatrical troupe as an analogy for virtual organizations was first used by David Mack, circa 1995.

55. E. C. Kasper-Fuehrer and N. M. Ashkanasy, "Communicating Trustworthiness and Building Trust in Interorganizational Virtual Organizations," *Journal of Management* 27 (2001): 235–254.

# Chapter 16

1. T. E. Deal and A. A. Kennedy, *Corporate Cultures* (Reading, Mass.: Addison-Wesley, 1982).

2. W. Ouchi, *Theory Z* (Reading, Mass.: Addison-Wesley, 1981).

3. T. J. Peters and R. H. Waterman, *In Search of Excellence* (New York: Harper & Row, 1982).

4. M. Gardner, "Creating a Corporate Culture for the Eighties," *Business Horizons* (January–February 1985): 59–63.

5. Definition adapted from E. H. Schein, *Organizational Culture and Leadership* (San Francisco: Jossey-Bass, 1985), 9.

6. R. Yerema and R. Caballero, "Great Little Box Company," at http://www.canadastop100.com/national, used with permission from the organizer of the Canada's Top 100 Employers competition, Mediacorp Canada Inc., 2010.

7. C. D. Sutton and D. L. Nelson, "Elements of the Cultural Network: The Communicators of Corporate Values," *Leadership and Organization Development* 11 (1990): 3–10.

8. R. Yerema and R. Caballero, "Digital Extremes," at http://www.canadastop100.com/national, used with permission from the organizer of the Canada's Top 100 Employers competition, Mediacorp Canada Inc., 2010.

9. Great Place to Work Institute Canada, "The Best Places to Work in Canada," *The Globe and Mail,* April 13, 2010: GPTW 6. http://v1.theglobeandmail.com/partners/free/sr/greatplacestowork/great-places-to-work-2010.pdf.

10. A. Holloway, "Recruiting: Let Them Have Pie," *Profit* (June 2008). http://www.wellingtonwest.com/documents/PROFIT_Article_07-08.pdf.

11. P. Brent, "Who's on Top? Wellington West Holdings Inc.," *Workopolis,* May 14, 2008 http://www.workopolis.com/work.aspx?action=TransferandView=Content/Common/ArticlesDetailViewandlang=ENandarticleId=brent20080514File1Article1.

12. A. Bandura, *Social Learning Theory* (Englewood Cliffs, N.J.: Prentice-Hall, 1977).

13. J. A. Chatman, "Leading by Leveraging Culture," *California Management Review* 45 (2003): 20–34.

14. J. M. Beyer and H. M. Trice, "How an Organization's Rites Reveal Its Culture," *Organizational Dynamics* 16 (1987): 5–24.

15. S. Hasulo, "Workplace Balance: The Intuit-ive Approach," *Canadian Business Online,* January 8, 2007, http://www.canadianbusiness.com/article.jsp?content=20070108_132428_5568.

16. R. Yerema and R. Caballero, "Diavik," at http://www.canadastop100.com/national, used with permission from the organizer of the Canada's Top 100 Employers competition, Mediacorp Canada Inc., 2010.

17. Great Place to Work Institute Canada ,The Best Places to Work in Canada, *The Globe and Mail,* April 13, 2010: GPTW 6. http://v1.theglobeandmail.com/partners/free/sr/greatplacestowork/great-places-to-work-2010.pdf.

18. R. Yerema and R. Caballero, "Research in Motion," at http://www.canadastop100.com/national, used with permission from the organizer of the Canada's Top 100 Employers competition, Mediacorp Canada Inc., 2010.

19. H. M. Trice and J. M. Beyer, "Studying Organizational Cultures through Rites and Ceremonials," *Academy of Management Review* 9 (1984): 653–669.

20. H. Levinson and S. Rosenthal, *CEO: Corporate Leadership in Action* (New York: Basic Books, 1984).

21. V. Sathe, "Implications of Corporate Culture: A Manager's Guide to Action," *Organizational Dynamics* 12 (1987): 5–23.

22. J. Martin, M. S. Feldman, M. J. Hatch, and S. B. Sitkin, "The Uniqueness Paradox in Organizational Stories," *Administrative Science Quarterly* 28 (1983): 438–453.

23. B. Durrance, "Stories at Work," *Training and Development* (February 1997): 25–29.

24. W. Immen, "The 50 Best Employers to Work for in Canada," *The Globe and Mail,* January 14, 2009, http://www.theglobeandmail.com/report-on-business/article965105.ece.

25. Ibid.

26. A. Wahl, Z. Olijnyk, P. Evans, A. Holloway, and E. Pooley, "Best Workplaces 2006: Lessons from Some of the Best," *Canadian Business Online* (April 26, 2006), http://www.canadianbusiness.com/managing/employees/article.jsp?content=20060410_76257_76257.

27. R. Yerema and R. Caballero, "Sophos," at http://www.canadastop100.com/national, used with permission from the organizer of the Canada's Top 100 Employers competition, Mediacorp Canada Inc., 2010.

28. http://www.onesimpleact.alberta.ca/success-stories/isl-engineering.asp.

29. R. Yerema and R. Caballero, "Alberta-Pacific Forest Industries Inc.", at http://www.canadastop100.com/national, used with permission from the organizer of the Canada's Top 100 Employers competition, Mediacorp Canada Inc., 2010.

30. http://www.redfrogsolutions.com.

31. R. Goffee and G. Jones, "What Holds the Modern Company Together?" *Harvard Business Review* (November–December 1996): 133–143.

32. C. Argyris and D. A. Schon, *Organizational Learning* (Reading, Mass.: Addison-Wesley, 1978).

33. L. Hoeber, "Exploring the Gaps between Meanings and Practices of Gender Equity in a Sport Organization," *Gender Work and Organization* 14(3) (2007): 259–280.

34. D. J. McAllister and G. A. Bigley, "Work Context and the Definition of Self: How Organizational Care Influences Organization-Based Self-Esteem," *Academy of Management Journal* 45 (2002): 894–905.

35. M. Peterson, "Work, Corporate Culture, and Stress: Implications for Worksite Health Promotion," *American Journal of Health Behavior* 21 (1997): 243–252.

36. Human Resources and Skills Development Canada, *Organizational Profiles: Husky Injection Molding Systems,* http://www.hrsdc.gc.ca/eng/lp/spila/wlb/ell/08husky_injection_molding_systems.shtml.

37. http://www.urban-systems.com.

38. L. Smircich, "Concepts of Culture and Organizational Analysis," *Administrative Science Quarterly* (1983): 339–358.

39. Y. Weiner and Y. Vardi, "Relationships between Organizational Culture and Individual Motivation: A Conceptual Integration," *Psychological Reports* 67 (1990): 295–306.

40. M. R. Louis, "Surprise and Sense Making: What Newcomers Experience in Entering Unfamiliar Organizational Settings," *Administrative Science Quarterly* 25 (1980): 209–264.

41. T. L. Doolen, M. E. Hacker, and E. M. van Aken, "The Impact of Organizational Context on Work Team Effectiveness: A Study of Production Teams," *IEEE Transactions on Engineering Management* 50 (2003): 285–296.

42. D. D. Van Fleet and R. W. Griffin, "Dysfunctional Organization Culture: The Role of Leadership in Motivating Dysfunctional Work Behaviors," *Journal of Managerial Psychology* 21(8) (2006): 698–708.

43. J. P. Kotter and J. L. Heskett, *Corporate Culture and Performance* (New York: Free Press, 1992).

44. Deal and Kennedy, *Corporate Cultures.*

45. J. P. Kotter and J. L. Heskett, *Corporate Culture and Performance,* New York: Free Press, 1992.

46. R. S. Burt, S. S. Gabbay, G. Holt, and P. Moran, "Contingent Organization as a Network Theory: The Culture Performance Contingency Function," *Acta Sociologica* 37 (1994): 345–370.

47. G. G. Gordon and N. DiTomaso, "Predicting Corporate Performance from Organizational Culture," *Journal of Management Studies* 29 (1992): 783–799.

48. A. J. Rucci, S. P. Kim, and R. T. Quinn, "The Employee–Customer Profit Chain at Sears." *Harvard Business Review* 76 (1998): 82–97.

49. G. G. Gordon, "Industry Determinants of Organizational Culture," *Academy of Management Review* 16 (1991): 396–415.

50. G. Donaldson and J. Lorsch, *Decision Making at the Top* (New York: Basic Books, 1983).

51. R. H. Kilman, M. J. Saxton, and R. Serpa, eds., *Gaining Control of the Corporate Culture* (San Francisco: Jossey-Bass, 1986).

52. J. P. Kotter, *A Force for Change: How Leadership Differs from Management* (New York: Free Press, 1990); R. M. Kanter, *The Change Masters* (New York: Simon & Schuster, 1983).

53. T. Peters and N. Austin, *A Passion for Excellence: The Leadership Difference* (New York: Random House, 1985).

54. S. Thornhill and R. Amit, "Learning about Failure: Bankruptcy, Firm Age, and the Resource-based View," *Organization Science* 14 (2003): 497–509.

55. T. A. Judge and D. M. Cable, "Applicant Personality, Organizational Culture, and Organization Attraction," *Personnel Psychology* 50 (1997): 359–394.

56. P. Warr and A. Pearce, "Preferences for Careers and Organizational Cultures as a Function of Logically Related Personality Traits," *Applied Psychology: An International Review 53* (2004): 423–435.

57. A. L. Kristof-Brown, R. D. Zimmerman, and E. C. Johnson, "Consequences of Individuals' Fit at Work: A Meta-Analysis of Person-job, Person-organization, Person-group, and Person-supervisor Fit," *Personnel Psychology* 58 (2005): 281–342.

58. C. A. O'Reilly, J. Chatman, and D. F. Caldwell, "People and Organizational Culture: A Profile Comparison Approach to Assessing Person-organization Fit," *Academy of Management Journal* 34 (1991): 487–516.

59. A. L. Kristof-Brown, R. D. Zimmerman, and E. C. Johnson, "Consequences of Individuals' Fit at Work: A Meta-analysis of Person-job, Person-organization, Person-group, and Person-supervisor fit," *Personnel Psychology* 58 (2005): 281–342.

60. C. Anderson, S. E. Spataro, and F. J. Flynn, "Personality and Organizational Culture as Determinants of Influence," *Journal of Applied Psychology* 93 (2008): 702–710.

61. T. Egan, "The Relevance of Organizational Subculture for Motivation to Transfer Learning," *Human Resource Development Quarterly* 19 (2008): 299–322.

62. B. Adkins and D. Caldwell, "Firm or Subgroup Culture: Where Does Fitting in Matter Most?" *Journal of Organizational Behavior* 25 (2004): 969–978.

63. A. E. M. van Vianen and A. H. Fischer, "Illuminating the Glass Ceiling: The Role of Organizational Culture Preferences," *Journal of Occupational and Organizational Psychology* 75 (2002): 315–337.

64. J. B. Sorensen, "The Strength of Corporate Culture and the Reliability of Firm Performance," *Administrative Science Quarterly* 47 (2002): 70–91.

65. Schein, *Organizational Culture and Leadership.*

66. J. A. Pearce II, T. R. Kramer, and D. K. Robbins, "Effects of Managers' Entrepreneurial Behavior on Subordinates," *Journal of Business Venturing* 12 (1997): 147–160.

67. P. W. Braddy, A. W. Meade, and C. M. Kroustalis, "Organizational Recruitment Website Effects on Viewers' Perceptions of Organizational Culture," *Journal of Business and Psychology* 20(4) (2006): 525–543.

68. P. Brent, "WestJet Culture Gets Employees On-board," *Workopolis,* http://www.workopolis.com/work.aspx?action=Transfer&View=Content/Common/ArticlesDetailView&lang=EN&articleId=brent20071128File1Article1.

69. A. Xenikou and M. Simosi, "Organizational Culture and Transformational Leadership as Predictors of Business Unit Performance," *Journal of Managerial Psychology* 21(6) (2006): 566–579.

70. D. C. Feldman, "The Multiple Socialization of Organization Members," *Academy of Management Review* 6 (1981): 309–318.

71. R. Pascale, "The Paradox of Corporate Culture: Reconciling Ourselves to Socialization," *California Management Review* 27 (1985): 26–41.

72. D. L. Nelson, "Organizational Socialization: A Stress Perspective," *Journal of Occupational Behavior* 8 (1987): 311–324.

73. D. M. Cable, L. Aiman-Smith, P. W. Mulvey, and J. R. Edwards, "The Sources and Accuracy of Job Applicants' Beliefs about Organizational Culture," *Academy of Management Journal* 43 (2000): 1076–1085.

74. J. Chatman, "Matching People and Organizations: Selection and Socialization in Public Accounting Firms," *Administrative Science Quarterly* 36 (1991): 459–484.

75. D. L. Nelson, J. C. Quick, and M. E. Eakin, "A Longitudinal Study of Newcomer Role Adjustment in U.S. Organizations," *Work and Stress* 2 (1988): 239–253.

76. N. J. Allen and J. P. Meyer, "Organizational Socialization Tactics: A Longitudinal Analysis of Links to Newcomers' Commitment and Role Orientation," *Academy of Management Journal* 33 (1990): 847–858.

77. T. N. Bauer, E. W. Morrison, and R. R. Callister, "Organizational Socialization: A Review and Directions for Future Research," *Research in Personnel and Human Resources Management* 16 (1998): 149–214.

78. D. M. Cable and C. K. Parsons, "Socialization Tactics and Person–Organization Fit," *Personnel Psychology* 54 (2001): 1–23.

79. D. M. Rousseau, "Assessing Organizational Culture: The Case for Multiple Methods," in B. Schneider, ed., *Organizational Climate and Culture* (San Francisco: Jossey-Bass, 1990).

80. R. A. Cooke and D. M. Rousseau, "Behavioral Norms and Expectations: A Quantitative Approach to the Assessment of Organizational Culture," *Group and Organizational Studies* 12 (1988): 245–273.

81. R. H. Kilmann and M. J. Saxton, *Kilmann-Saxton Culture-Gap Survey* (Pittsburgh: Organizational Design Consultants, 1983).

82. W. J. Duncan, "Organizational Culture: 'Getting a Fix' on an Elusive Concept," *Academy of Management Executive* 3 (1989): 229–236.

83. P. Bate, "Using the Culture Concept in an Organization Development Setting," *Journal of Applied Behavior Science* 26 (1990): 83–106.

84. K. R. Thompson and F. Luthans, "Organizational Culture: A Behavioral Perspective," in B. Schneider, ed., *Organizational Climate and Culture* (San Francisco: Jossey-Bass, 1990).

85. S. Seren and U. Baykal, "Relationships between Change and Organizational Culture in Hospitals," *Journal of Nursing Scholarship* 39(2) (2007): 191–197.

86. V. Sathe, "How to Decipher and Change Corporate Culture," in R. H. Kilman et al., *Managing Corporate Cultures* (San Francisco: Jossey-Bass, 1985).

87. M. E. Johnson-Cramer, S. Parise, and R. L. Cross, "Managing Change through Networks and Values," *California Management Review* 49(3) (2007): 85–109.

88. S. Silcoff, "The Troubles at Trimark: Company's Chronic Culture Clash," *National Post* (August 2, 2008).

89. D. Decloet, "More Than One Way to Craft a Takeover," *Mutual Fund News* (August 30, 2007) http://fund.ci.com/servlet/story/GFGAM.20070830.RDECLOET30/GFStory?query.

90. S. Silcoff, "The Troubles at Trimark: Company's Chronic Culture Clash," *National Post,* August 2, 2008.

91. V. Pothukuchi, F. Damanpour, J. Choi, C. C. Chen, and S. H. Park, "National and Organizational Culture Differences and International Joint Venture Performance," *Journal of International Business Studies* 33 (2002): 243–265.

92. N. J. Adler, *International Dimensions of Organizational Behavior,* 2nd ed. (Boston: PWS Kent, 1991).

93. A. Laurent, "The Cultural Diversity of Western Conceptions of Management," *International Studies of Management and Organization* 13 (1983): 75–96.

94. P. C. Earley and E. Mosakowski, "Creating Hybrid Team Cultures: An Empirical Test of Transnational Team Functioning," *Academy of Management Journal* 43 (2000): 26–49.

95. D. Lei, J. W. Slocum, Jr., and R. W. Slater, "Global Strategy and Reward Systems: The Key Roles of Management Development and Corporate Culture," *Organizational Dynamics* 19 (1990): 27–41.

96. L. K. Trevino and K. A. Nelson, *Managing Business Ethics: Straight Talk about How to Do It Right* (New York: John Wiley & Sons, 1995).

97. A. Bhide and H. H. Stevenson, "Why Be Honest if Honesty Doesn't Pay?" *Harvard Business Review* (September–October 1990): 121–129.

98. http://www.thecro.com/node/615.

99. A. Pater and A. van Gils, "Stimulating Ethical Decision Making in a Business Context: Ethics of Ethical and Professional Codes," *European Management Journal* 21 (December 2003): 762–772.

100. J. R. Detert, R. G. Schroeder, and J. J. Mauriel, "A Framework for Linking Culture and Improvement Initiatives in Organizations," *Academy of Management Review* 25 (2000): 850–863.

101. http://www.leevalley.com/en/home/about.aspx.

102. E. Lowe, "Working by the Golden Rule: Lee Valley Tools," *Social Innovations,* (October 2005), http://www.vifamily.ca/library/social/lee_valley.pdf.

103. S. B. Evenson, "The Red Green Show Meets ER," *National Post,* February 7, 2004.

# Chapter 17

1. M. A. Verespej, "When Change Becomes the Norm," *Industry Week* (March 16, 1992): 35–38.

2. P. Mornell, "Nothing Endures But Change," *Inc.* 22 (July 2000): 131–132, http://www.inc.com/magazine/20000701/19555.html.

3. D. Fay and H. Luhrmann, "Current Themes in Organizational Change," *European Journal of Work and Organizational Psychology,* 13 (2004): 113–119.

4. H. J. Van Buren, III, "The Bindingness of Social and Psychological Contracts: Toward a Theory of Social Responsibility in Downsizing," *Journal of Business Ethics* 25 (2000): 205–219.

5. C. Sorensen, "Fortune Smiles on RIM's Growth," *Toronto Star* (August 18, 2009). http://www.thestar.com/article/682353.

6. D. Crane, "Don't Discount the Positive Side of Globalization," *Toronto Star,* (December 31, 2006). http://www.thestar.com/article/166599.

7. J. Sanford, "Beat China On Cost: Gildan Taps Other Labour Pool—and Trade Pacts," *Canadian Business Online* (November 7, 2005), http://www.canadianbusiness.com/managing/strategy/article.jsp?content=20060109_155539_4340.

8. The Canadian Press, "CGI Wins US Contract " *The Globe and Mail* (May 18, 2010), http://www.theglobeandmail.com/globe-investor/cgi-wins-us-contract/article1572757/?utm_source=twitterfeed&utm_medium=twitter.

9. "Pipes Done Right," *Canadian Business Journal* (March 2009), www.canadianbusinessjournal.ca/business_in_action/march_09/tube_mac_industries.html.

10. D. Nice, "Brad Miller on Expanding in Lean Times," *The Globe and Mail* (April 9, 2009), http://v1.theglobeandmail.com/servlet/story/RTGAM.20090402.onRecord07/BNStory/breakthrough.

11. Ibid.

12. M. McCarthy, "PR Disaster as Coke Withdraws 'Purest' Bottled Water in Britain," *The New Zealand Herald* (March 20, 2004), http://www.nzherald.co.nz/business/businessstorydisplay.cfm?storyID=3555911&thesection=business&thesubsection=world&thesecondsubsection=europe.

13. F. Kopun, "Workforce Officially over the 40-plus Hill," *Toronto Star* (March 5, 2008), http://www.thestar.com/news/gta/article/309506.

14. Statistics Canada, "2006 Census: Age and Sex," *The Daily* (July 17, 2007), http://www.statcan.gc.ca/daily-quotidien/070717/dq070717a-eng.htm.

15. B. Doskoch, "Canada Can Adapt to Aging Workforce, Experts Say," http://www.ctv.ca/servlet/ArticleNews/story/CTVNews/20070717/labour_age_070717/20070717.

16. Statistics Canada, "Study: Projections of the Diversity of the Canadian Population," *The Daily* (March 9, 2010), http://www.statcan.gc.ca/daily-quotidien/100309/dq100309a-eng.htm.

17. http://www.toronto.ca/toronto_facts/diversity.htm.

18. J. Gandz, "A Business Case for Diversity," Human Resources and Skills Development Canada, Fall 2001, http://www.hrsdc.gc.ca/eng/lp/lo/lswe/we/special_projects/RacismFreeInitiative/BusinessCase-e.shtml#toronto hotels.

19. R. Caballero and R. Yerema, "Canadian Imperial Bank of Commerce/CIBC," April 7, 2010, http://www.eluta.ca/new-canadians-at-canadian-imperial-bank-of-commerce used with permission from the organizer of the Canada's Top 100 Employers for New Canadians competition, Mediacorp Canada Inc., 2010.

20. A. T. Timur and A. Ponak, "Labor Relations and Technological Change at Canadian Pacific Railway," *Journal of Labor Research* 23 (2002): 535–557.

21. Ibid.

22. R. M. Kanter, "Improving the Development, Acceptance, and Use of New Technology: Organizational and Interorganizational Challenges," in *People and Technology in the Workplace* (Washington, D.C.: National Academy Press, 1991), 15–56.

23. Gap Inc. press release, "Gap Inc. Joins the Ethical Trading Initiative," *CSRwire* (April 28, 2004), http://www.csrwire.com/article.cgi/2683.html.

24. "Gap Inc. 2003 Social Responsibility Report," *Gap Inc.* (September 17, 2004), http://ccbn.mobular.net/ccbn/7/645/696/index.html.

25. L. J. Brooks and D. Selley, *Ethics and Governance: Developing and Maintaining an Ethical Corporate Culture,* 3rd ed., Canadian Centre for Ethics and Corporate Policy, Toronto, 2008.

26. www.magna.com/magna/en/employee/foremployees/fyiline/default.aspx.

27. S. A. Mohrman and A. M. Mohrman, Jr., "The Environment as an Agent of Change," in A. M. Mohrman, Jr., et al., eds., *Large-Scale Organizational Change* (San Francisco: Jossey-Bass, 1989), 35–47.

28. T. D'Aunno, M. Succi, and J. A. Alexander, "The Role of Institutional and Market Forces in Divergent Organizational Change," *Administrative Science Quarterly* 45 (2000): 679–703.

29. Agriculture and Agri-Food Canada, "Major Flax Straw Processing Plant Expansion Supported by Federal and Provincial Governments," Canada News Centre (May 21, 2010), http://news.gc.ca/web/article-eng.do?m=/indexandnid=534439.

30. Q. N. Huy, "Emotional Balancing of Organizational Continuity and Radical Change: The Contribution of Middle Managers," *Administrative Science Quarterly* 47 (March 1, 2002): 31–69.

31. D. Nadler, "Organizational Frame-Bending: Types of Change in the Complex Organization," in R. Kilmann and T. Covin, eds., *Corporate Transformation* (San Francisco: Jossey-Bass, 1988), 66–83.

32. K. Belson, "AT&T Plans to Raise Its Rates for Residential Calling Plans," *The New York Times* (August 4, 2004), http://www.nytimes.com/2004/08/04/business/04phone.html.

33. L. Ackerman, "Development, Transition, or Transformation: The Question of Change in Organizations," *OD Practitioner* (December 1986): 1–8.

34. T. D. Jick, *Managing Change* (Homewood, Ill.: Irwin, 1993), 3.

35. G. Graham, "Music Industry Supply Chain: A Major Label Perspective, Executive Briefing 2006–06 for Supply Chain Management Research Group, Manchester Business School," http://www.mbs.ac.uk/research/supplychain/documents/MusicIndustry.pdf.

36. A. Bruno, "Digital Entertainment: The Future of Music: Industry Transformation Is Just Getting Started," (December 3, 2005)_http://www.allbusiness.com/retail-trade/miscellaneous-retail-retail-stores-not/4554798-1.html.

37. http://www.sap.com/about/vision/pdf/FTI1878_evolve_bus_netwrk_wp_v1.pdf.

38. D. Miller and M. J. Chen, "Sources and Consequences of Competitive Inertia. A Study of the U.S. Airline Industry," *Administrative Science Quarterly* 39 (1994): 1–23.

39. S. L. Brown and K. M. Eisenhardt, "The Art of Continuous Change: Linking Complexity Theory and Time-Paced Evolution in Relentlessly Shifting Organizations," *Administrative Science Quarterly* 42 (1997): 1–34.

40. J. Child and C. Smith, "The Context and Process of Organizational Transformation: Cadbury Ltd. In Its Sector," *Journal of Management Studies* 12 (1987): 12–27.

41. J. Amis, T. Slack, and C. R. Hinings, "The Pace, Sequence, and Linearity of Radical Change," *Academy of Management Journal* 47 (2004): 15–39.

42. T. A. Judge, C. J. Thoresen, V. Pucik and T. M. Welbourne, "Managerial Coping with Organizational Change: A Dispositional Perspective," *Journal of Applied Psychology* 84 (1999): 107–122.

43. A. Carmeli and Z. Sheaffer, "How Leadership Characteristics Affect Organizational Decline and Downsizing," *Journal of Business Ethics* 86 (2009): 363–378.

44. D. M. Herold, D. B. Fedor, S. Caldwell, and Y. Liu, "The Effects of Transformational and Change Leadership on Employees' Commitment to a Change: A Multi-level Study," *Journal of Applied Psychology* 93 (2008): 346–357.

45. J. R. Katzenbach, *Real Change Leaders* (New York: Times Business, 1995).

46. J. L. Denis, L. Lamothe, and A. Langley, "The Dynamics of Collective Leadership and Strategic Change in Pluralistic Organizations," *Academy of Management Journal* 44 (2001): 809–837.

47. B. C. Gunia, N. Sivanathan, and A. D. Galinsky, "Vicarious Entrapment: Your Sunk Costs, My Escalation of Commitment," *Journal of Experimental Social Psychology* 45 (2009): 1238–1244.

48. M. Beer, *Organization Change and Development: A Systems View* (Santa Monica, Calif.: Goodyear, 1980), 78.

49. K. Whalen-Berry and C. R. Hinings, "The Relative Effect of Change Drivers in Large-Scale Organizational Change: An Empirical Study," in W. Passmore and

R. Goodman, eds., *Research in Organizational Change and Development* 14 (New York: JAI Press, 2003): 99–146.

50. Denis et al., "The Dynamics of Collective Leadership and Strategic Change in Pluralistic Organizations."

51. G. Pitts, "The Fine Art of Managing Change," *The Globe and Mail* (January 4, 2010) available at http://www.kpmg.com/Ca/en/IssuesAndInsights/ArticlesPublications/Documents/The_fine_art_of_managing_change.pdf.

52. K. E. Weick and R. E. Quinn, "Organizational Change and Development," *Annual Review of Psychology* 59 (1999): 361–386.

53. T. Kiefer, "Feeling Bad: Antecedents and Consequences of Negative Emotions in Ongoing Change," *Journal of Organizational Behavior* 26 (2005): 875–897.

54. A. E. Rafferty and M. A. Griffin, "Perceptions of Organizational Change: A Stress and Coping Perspective," *Journal of Applied Psychology* 91 (2006): 1154–1162.

55. J. A. Klein, "Why Supervisors Resist Employee Involvement," *Harvard Business Review* 62 (1984): 87–95.

56. B. L. Kirkman, R. G. Jones, and D. L. Shapiro, "Why Do Employees Resist Teams? Examining the 'Resistance Barrier' to Work Team Effectiveness," *International Journal of Conflict Management* 11 (2000): 74–92.

57. S. D. Tvedt, P. O. Saksvik, and K. Nytro, "Does Change Process Healthiness Reduce the Negative Effects of Organizational Change on the Psychosocial Work Environment?" *Work & Stress* 23 (2009): 80–98.

58. D. B. Fedor, S. Caldwell, and D. M. Herold, "The Effects of Organizational Changes on Organizational Commitment: A Multilevel Investigation," *Personnel Psychology* 59 (2006): 1–29.

59. J. Brockner, "Making Sense of Procedural Fairness: How High Procedural Fairness Can Reduce or Heighten the Influence of Outcome Favorability," *Academy of Management Review* 27 (2002): 58–76.

60. J. Brockner, M. Konovsky, R. Cooper-Schneider, R. Folger, C. Martin, and R. J. Bies, "Interactive Effects of Procedural Justice and Outcome Negativity on Victims and Survivors of Job Loss," *Academy of Management Journal* 37 (1994): 397–409.

61. D. B. Fedor, S. Caldwell, and D. M. Herold, "The Effects of Organizational Changes on Organizational Commitment: A Multilevel Investigation," *Personnel Psychology* 59 (2006): 1–29.

62. J. B. Rodell and J. A. Colquitt, "Looking Ahead in Times of Uncertainty: The Role of Anticipatory Justice in an Organizational Change Context," *Journal of Applied Psychology* 94 (2009): 989–1002.

63. S. D. Caldwell, D. M. Herold, and D. B. Fedor, "Toward an Understanding of the Relationships among Organizational Change, Individual Differences, and Changes in Person-environment Fit: A Cross-level Study," *Journal of Applied Psychology* 89 (2004): 868–882.

64. D. Klein, "Some Notes on the Dynamics of Resistance to Change: The Defender Role," in W. G. Bennis, K. D. Benne, R. Chin, and K. E. Corey, eds., *The Planning of Change,* 3rd ed. (New York: Holt, Rinehart & Winston, 1969), 117–124.

65. T. G. Cummings and E. F. Huse, *Organizational Development and Change* (St. Paul, Minn.: West, 1989).

66. N. L. Jimmieson, D. J. Terry, and V. J. Callan, "A Longitudinal Study of Employee Adaptation to Organizational Change: The Role of Change-Related Information and Change-Related Self Efficacy," *Journal of Occupational Health Psychology* 9 (2004): 11–27.

67. N. DiFonzo and P. Bordia, "A Tale of Two Corporations: Managing Uncertainty during Organizational Change," *Human Resource Management* 37 (1998): 295–303.

68. J. de Vries, C. Webb, and J. Eveline, "Mentoring for Gender Equality and Organisational Change," *Employee Relations* 28(6) (2006): 573–587.

69. B. van Knippenberg, L. Martin, and T. Tyler, "Process-orientation versus Outcome-orientation during Organizational Change: The Role of Organizational Identification," *Journal of Organizational Behavior* 27 (2006): 685–704.

70. J. H. Marler, S. L. Fisher, and W. Ke, "Employee Self-service Technology Acceptance: A Comparison of Pre-implementation and Post-implementation Relationships," *Personnel Psychology* 62 (2009): 327–358.

71. D. Schweiger and A. DeNisi, "Communication with Employees Following a Merger: A Longitudinal Field Experiment," *Academy of Management Journal* 34 (1991): 110–135.

72. M. Fugate, A. J. Kinicki, and G. E. Prussia, "Employee Coping with Organizational Change: An Examination of Alternative Theoretical Perspectives and Models," *Personnel Psychology* 61 (2008): 1–36.

73. D. M. Herold, D. B. Fedor, and S. D. Caldwell, "Beyond Change Management: A Multilevel Investigation of Contextual and Personal Influences on Employees' Commitment to Change," *Journal of Applied Psychology* 92 (2007): 942–951.

74. A. E. Rafferty and M. A. Griffin, "Perceptions of Organizational Change: A Stress and Coping Perspective," *Journal of Applied Psychology* 91 (2006): 1154–1162.

75. K. E. Weick, and R. E. Quinn, "Organizational Change and Development," *Annual Review of Psychology* 59 (1999): 361–386.

76. M. F. R. Kets de Vries and K. Balazs, "The Downside of Downsizing," *Human Relations* 50 (1997): 11–50.

77. J. A. Clair and R. L. Dufresne, "Playing the Grim Reaper: How Employees Experience Carrying Out a Downsizing," *Human Relations* 57 (2004): 1597–1625.

78. P. O. Saksvik, S. D. Tvedt, K. Nytro, G. R. Andersen, T. K. Andersen, M. P. Buvik, and H. Torvatn, "Developing Criteria for Healthy Organizational Change," *Work and Stress* 21 (2007): 243–263.

79. S. A. Furst and D. M. Cable, "Employee Resistance to Organizational Change: Managerial Influence Tactics and Leader-member Exchange," *Journal of Applied Psychology* 93 (2008): 453–462.

80. J. B. Rodell and J. A. Colquitt, "Looking Ahead in Times of Uncertainty: The Role of Anticipatory Justice in an Organizational Change Context," *Journal of Applied Psychology* 94 (2009): 989–1002.

81. P. Neves and A. Caetano, "Social Exchange Processes in Organizational Change: The Roles of Trust and Control." *Journal of Change Management* 6(4) (2006): 351–364.

82. European Working Conditions Observatory, "Key Factors in Successful Organisational Change, http://www.eurofound.europa.eu/ewco/2008/12/NO0812039I.htm.

83. S. D. Tvedt, P. O. Saksvik, and K. Nytro, "Does Change Process Healthiness Reduce the Negative Effects of Organizational Change on the Psychosocial Work Environment?" *Work & Stress* 23 (2009): 80–98.

84. K. Lewin, "Frontiers in Group Dynamics," *Human Relations* 1 (1947): 5–41.

85. C. Bareil, A. Savoie, and S. Meunier, "Patterns of Discomfort with Organizational Change," *Journal of Change Management* 7(1) (2007):13–24.

86. W. McWhinney, "Meta-Praxis: A Framework for Making Complex Changes," in A. M. Mohrman, Jr., et al., eds., *Large-Scale Organizational Change* (San Francisco: Jossey-Bass, 1989), 154–199.

87. B. Bertsch and R. Williams, "How Multinational CEOs Make Change Programs Stick," *Long Range Planning* 27 (1994): 12–24.

88. Correctional Service Canada, Review of Change Management Practices, Internal Audit Branch 378-1-239 (April 3, 2008). http://www.csc-scc.gc.ca/text/pa/adt-rvw-chng-mgmnt-378-1-239/rvw-chng-mgmnt-378-1-239-eng.shtml.

89. J. Amis, T. Slack, and C. R. Hinings, "Values and Organizational Change," *Journal of Applied Behavioral Science* 38 (2002): 356–385.

90. W. L. French and C. H. Bell, *Organization Development: Behavioral Science Interventions for Organization Improvement,* 4th ed. (Englewood Cliffs, N.J.: Prentice-Hall, 1990); W. W. Burke, *Organization Development: A Normative View* (Reading, Mass.: Addison-Wesley, 1987).

91. A. O. Manzini, *Organizational Diagnosis* (New York: AMACOM, 1988).

92. M. R. Weisbord, "Organizational Diagnosis: Six Places to Look for Trouble with or without a Theory," *Group and Organization Studies* (December 1976): 430–444.

93. H. Levinson, *Organizational Diagnosis* (Cambridge, Mass.: Harvard University Press, 1972).

94. J. Nicholas, "The Comparative Impact of Organization Development Interventions," *Academy of Management Review* 7 (1982): 531–542.

95. G. Odiorne, *Management by Objectives* (Marshfield, Mass.: Pitman, 1965).

96. E. Huse, "Putting in a Management Development Program that Works," *California Management Review* 9 (1966): 73–80.

97. J. P. Muczyk and B. C. Reimann, "MBO as a Complement to Effective Leadership," *Academy of Management Executive* (May 1989): 131–138.

98. L. L. Berry and A. Parasuraman, "Prescriptions for a Service Quality Revolution in America," *Organizational Dynamics* 20 (1992): 5–15.

99. T. A. Stewart, and A. P. Raman, "Lessons from Toyota's Long Drive," *Harvard Business Review* 85(7/8) (2007): 74–83.

100. G. Pitts, "Toyota: Too Big, Too Fast," *The Globe and Mail* (February 5, 2010). http://www.theglobeandmail.com/report-on-business/toyota-too-big-too-fast/article1458221.

101. J. Daley and M. Moxley, "How Hyundai Became the Auto Industry's Pacesetter," *The Globe and Mail* (April 29, 2010). http://www.theglobeandmail.com/report-on-business/rob-magazine/how-hyundai-became-the-auto-industrys-pacesetter/article1548295/.

102. W. G. Dyer, *Team Building: Issues and Alternatives,* 2nd ed. (Reading, Mass.: Addison-Wesley, 1987).

103. E. Stephan, G. Mills, R. W. Pace, and L. Ralphs, "HRD in the *Fortune* 500: A Survey," *Training and Development Journal* (January 1988): 26–32.

104. A. Edmondson, "Psychological Safety and Learning Behavior in Work Teams," *Administrative Science Quarterly* 44 (1999): 350–383.

105. M. Whitmire and P. R. Nienstedt, "Lead Leaders into the '90s," *Personnel Journal* (May 1991): 80–85.

106. http://www.teambuildinginc.com/services4_teamconcepts.htm; http://www.teambuildinginc.com/services5.htm.

107. E. Salas, T. L. Dickinson, S. I. Tannenbaum, and S. A. Converse, *A Meta-Analysis of Team Performance and Training, Naval Training System Center Technical Reports* (Orlando, Fla.: U.S. Government, 1991).

108. E. Schein, *Its Role in Organization Development, vol. 1 of Process Consultation* (Reading, Mass.: Addison-Wesley, 1988).

109. H. Hornstein, "Organizational Development and Change Management: Don't Throw the Baby Out with the Bath Water," *Journal of Applied Behavioral Science* 37 (2001): 223–226.

110. R. W. Revans, *Action Learning* (London: Blonde & Briggs, 1980).

111. I. L. Goldstein, *Training in Organizations,* 3rd ed. (Pacific Grove, Calif.: Brooks/Cole, 1993).

112. J. A. Conger and R. M. Fulmer, "Developing Your Leadership Pipeline," *Harvard Business Review* 81 (2003): 76–84.

113. D. A. Ready and J. A. Conger, "Why Leadership Development Efforts Fail," *MIT Sloan Management Review* 44 (2003): 83–89.

114. http://coachfederation.org.

115. M. Jay, "Understanding How to Leverage Executive Coaching," *Organization Development Journal* 21 (2003): 6–13; D. Goleman, R. Boyaysis, and A. McKee, *Primal Leadership: Learning to Lead with Emotional Intelligence* (Harvard Business School Press, 2004).

116. K. M. Wasylyshyn, "Executive Coaching: An Outcome Study," *Consulting Psychology Journal* 55 (2003): 94–106.

117. J. W. Smither, M. London, R. Flautt, Y. Vargas, and I. Kucine, "Can Working with an Executive Coach Improve Multisource Feedback Ratings over Time? A Quasi-Experimental Field Study," *Personnel Psychology* 56 (2003): 23–44.

118. "You Might Actually Like This Homework," *Edmonton Journal,* July 7, 2007, http://www.working.com/edmonton/story.html?id=28132444-c8c3-492c-9670-77786f048147&andk=56195.

119. R. Yerema and R. Caballero, "KPMG," at http://www.canadastop100.com/national, used with permission from the organizer of the Canada's Top 100 Employers competition, Mediacorp Canada Inc., 2010.

120. R. Yerema and R. Caballero, "Digital Extremes," at http://www.canadastop100.com/national, used with permission from the organizer of the Canada's Top 100 Employers competition, Mediacorp Canada Inc., 2010.

121. V. Graham, Hershey Canada Inc. "Fit for Life" Worksite Wellness Program, presentation to Canadian Labour and Business Centre Workplace Health Works, November 18–19, 2003.

122. A. M. Pettigrew, R. W. Woodman, and K. S. Cameron, "Studying Organizational Change and Development: Challenges for Future Research," *Academy of Management Journal* 44 (2001): 697–713.

123. R. A. Katzell and R. A. Guzzo, "Psychological Approaches to Worker Productivity," *American Psychologist* 38 (1983): 468–472.

124. Goldstein, *Training in Organizations.*

# Chapter 18

1. J. H. Greenhaus, *Career Management* (Hinsdale, Ill.: CBS College Press, 1987).

2. D. T. Hall, *Careers in Organizations* (Pacific Palisades, Calif.: Goodyear, 1976).

3. Greenhaus, *Career Management;* T. G. Gutteridge and F. L. Otte, "Organizational Career Development: What's Going on Out There?" *Training and Development Journal* 37 (1983): 22–26.

4. M. B. Arthur, P. H. Claman, and R. J. DeFillippi, "Intelligent Enterprise, Intelligent Careers," *Academy of Management Executive* (November 1995): 7–22.

5. M. Lips-Wiersma and D. T. Hall, "Organizational Career Development Is Not Dead: A Case Study on Managing the New Career during Organizational Change," *Journal of Organizational Behavior* 28(6) (2007): 771–792.

6. D. Jemielniak, "Managers as Lazy, Stupid Careerists?" *Journal of Organizational Change Management* 20(4) (2007): 491–508.

7. T. Lee, "Should You Stay Energized by Changing Jobs Frequently?" *CareerJournal* (January 11, 1998), http://www.careerjournal.com/jobhunting/strategies/19980111-reisberg.html.

8. D. E. Super, *The Psychology of Careers* (New York: Harper & Row, 1957); D. E. Super and M. J. Bohn, Jr., *Occupational Psychology* (Belmont, Calif.: Wadsworth, 1970).

9. J. L. Holland, *The Psychology of Vocational Choice* (Waltham, Mass.: Blaisdell, 1966); J. L. Holland, *Making Vocational Choices: A Theory of Careers* (Englewood Cliffs, N.J.: Prentice-Hall, 1973).

10. F. T. L. Leong and J. T. Austin, "An Evaluation of the Cross-Cultural Validity of Holland's Theory: Career Choices by Workers in India," *Journal of Vocational Behavior* 52 (1998): 441–455.

11. C. Morgan, J. D. Isaac, and C. Sansone, "The Role of Interest in Understanding the Career Choices of Female and Male College Students," *Sex Roles* 44 (2001): 295–320.

12. S. H. Osipow, *Theories of Career Development* (Englewood Cliffs, N.J.: Prentice-Hall, 1973).

13. J. P. Wanous, T. L. Keon, and J. C. Latack, "Expectancy Theory and Occupational/Organizational Choices: A Review and Test," *Organizational Behavior and Human Performance* 32 (1983): 66–86.

14. P. O. Soelberg, "Unprogrammed Decision Making," *Industrial Management Review* 8 (1967): 19–29.

15. J. P. Wanous, *Organizational Entry: Recruitment, Selection, and Socialization of Newcomers* (Reading, Mass.: Addison-Wesley, 1980).

16. S. L. Premack and J. P. Wanous, "A Meta-Analysis of Realistic Job Preview Experiments," *Journal of Applied Psychology* 70 (1985): 706–719.

17. "Realistic Job Preview," Shell Canada, from http://www.shell.ca/home/content/can-en/aboutshell/careers/students_and_graduates/useful_tools/realistic_job.

18. P. W. Hom, R. W. Griffeth, L. E. Palich, and J. S. Bracker, "An Exploratory Investigation into Theoretical Mechanisms Underlying Realistic Job Previews," *Personnel Psychology* 41 (1998): 421–451.

19. J. G. Pesek, C. Farinacci, and C. Anderson, "Reverse Resume Viewing: An Overlooked Aspect of Realistic Job Preview," *Review of Business*, 17, 2, (Winter, 1995), pp. 37–41.

20. J. A. Breaugh, "Realistic Job Previews: A Critical Appraisal and Future Research Directions," *Academy of Management Review* 8 (1983): 612–619.

21. G. R. Jones, "Socialization Tactics, Self-Efficacy, and Newcomers' Adjustment to Organizations," *Academy of Management Journal* 29 (1986): 262–279.

22. M. R. Buckley, D. B. Fedor, J. G. Veres, D. S. Wiese, and S. M. Carraher, "Investigating Newcomer Expectations and Job-Related Outcomes," *Journal of Applied Psychology* 83 (1998): 452–461.

23. M. R. Buckley, D. B. Fedor, S. M. Carraher, D. D. Frink, and D. Marvin, "The Ethical Imperative to Provide Recruits Realistic Job Previews," *Journal of Managerial Issues* 9 (1997): 468–484.

24. P. Buhler, "Managing in the '90s," *Supervision* (July 1995): 24–26.

25. D. T. Hall and J. E. Moss, "The New Protean Career Contract: Helping Organizations and Employees Adapt," *Organizational Dynamics* (Winter 1998): 22–37.

26. S. A. Zahra, R. L. Priem, and A. A. Rasheed, "Understanding the Causes and Effects of Top Management Fraud," *Organizational Dynamics* 36(2) (2007): 122–139.

27. A. Fisher, "Don't Blow Your New Job," *Fortune* (June 22, 1998): 159–162.

28. Ibid.

29. D. Goleman, *Working with Emotional Intelligence* (New York: Bantam, 1998); A. Fisher, "Success Secret: A High Emotional IQ," *Fortune* (October 26, 1998): 293–298.

30. M. L. Maynard, "Emotional Intelligence and Perceived Employability for Internship Curriculum," *Psychological Reports* 93 (December 2003): 791–792.

31. K. V. Petrides, A. Furnham, and G. N. Martin, "Estimates of Emotional and Psychometric Intelligence," *Journal of Social Psychology* 144 (April 2004): 149–162.

32. D. M. Lucy, "Leadership Landscape: Expanding Your Leadership Styles to Achieve Organizational Effectiveness," (2008) CMI Consulting Services, from http://www.ncsi.gov.tw/NcsiWebFileDocuments/f6ce0676278ad0315a33b84f67f3d41e.pdf.

33. C. Chermiss, "The Business Case for Emotional Intelligence," *The Consortium for Research on Emotional Intelligence in Organizations* (2003), http://www.eiconsortium.org/research/business_case_for_ei.htm; L. M. Spencer, Jr. and S. Spencer, *Competence at Work: Models for Superior Performance* (New York: John Wiley & Sons, 1993); L. M. Spencer, Jr., D. C. McClelland, and S. Kelner, *Competency Assessment Methods: History and State of the Art* (Boston, MA: Hay/McBer, 1997).

34. Chermiss, "The Business Case for Emotional Intelligence."

35. J. O. Crites, "A Comprehensive Model of Career Adjustment in Early Adulthood," *Journal of Vocational Behavior* 9 (1976): 105–118; S. Cytrynbaum and J. O. Crites, "The Utility of Adult Development in Understanding Career Adjustment Process," in M. B. Arthur, D. T. Hall, and B. S. Lawrence, eds., *Handbook of Career Theory* (Cambridge: Cambridge University Press, 1989), 66–88.

36. D. E. Super, "A Life-Span, Life-Space Approach to Career Development," *Journal of Vocational Behavior* 16 (1980): 282–298; L. Baird and K. Kram, "Career Dynamics: Managing the Superior/Subordinate Relationship," *Organizational Dynamics* 11 (1983): 46–64.

37. D. J. Levinson, *The Seasons of a Man's Life* (New York: Knopf, 1978); D. J. Levinson, *The Seasons of a Woman's Life*, 1997.

38. D. J. Levinson, "A Conception of Adult Development," *American Psychologist* 41 (1986): 3–13.

39. D. L. Nelson, "Adjusting to a New Organization: Easing the Transition from Outsider to Insider," in J. C. Quick, R. E. Hess, J. Hermalin, and J. D. Quick, eds., *Career Stress in Changing Times* (New York: Haworth Press, 1990), 61–86.

40. J. P. Kotter, "The Psychological Contract: Managing the Joining Up Process," *California Management Review* 15 (1973): 91–99.

41. D. M. Rousseau, "New Hire Perceptions of Their Own and Their Employers' Obligations: A Study of Psychological Contracts," *Journal of Organizational Behavior* 11 (1990): 389–400; D. L. Nelson, J. C. Quick, and J. R. Joplin, "Psychological Contracting and Newcomer Socialization: An Attachment Theory Foundation," *Journal of Social Behavior and Personality* 6 (1991): 55–72.

42. S. D. Pugh, D. P. Skarlicki, and B. S. Passell, "After the Fall: Layoff Victims' Trust and Cynicism in Reemployment," *Journal of Occupational and Organizational Psychology* 76 (June 2003): 201–212.

43. Levinson, "A Conception of Adult Development," 3–13.

44. J. W. Walker, "Let's Get Realistic about Career Paths," *Human Resource Management* 15 (1976): 2–7.

45. D. G. Collings, H. Scullion, and M. J. Morley, "Changing Patterns of Global Staffing in the Multinational Enterprise: Challenges to the Conventional Expatriate Assignment and Emerging Alternatives," *Journal of World Business* 42 (2) (2007): 198–213.

46. B. Filipczak, "You're on Your Own," *Training* (January 1995): 29–36.

47. CIBC Small Business (2005) "Women Entrepreneurs: Leading the Charge," http://www.cibc.com/ca/pdf/women-entrepreneurs-en.pdf.

48. E. H. Buttner and D. P. Moore, "Women's Organizational Exodus to Entrepreneurship: Self-Reported Motivations and Correlates," *Journal of Small Business Management* 35 (1997): 34–46; Center for Women's Business

Research Press Release, "Privately Held, 50% or More Women-Owned Businesses in the United States," 2004, http://www.nfwbo.org/pressreleases/nationalstatetrends/total.htm.

49. K. E. Kram, *Mentoring at Work: Developmental Relationships in Organizational Life* (Glenview, Ill.: Scott, Foresman, 1985).

50. C. Orpen, "The Effects of Monitoring on Employees' Career Success," *Journal of Social Psychology* 135 (1995): 667–668.

51. J. Arnold and K. Johnson, "Mentoring in Early Career," *Human Resource Management Journal* 7 (1997): 61–70.

52. B. P. Madia and C. J. Lutz, "Perceived Similarity, Expectation–Reality Discrepancies, and Mentors' Expressed Intention to Remain in the Big Brothers/Big Sisters Programs," *Journal of Applied Social Psychology* 34 (March 2004): 598–622.

53. RBC Diversity Dialogues, from http://www.rbc.com/responsibility/workplace/diversity.html.

54. B. R. Ragins, "Diversified Mentoring Relationships in Organizations: A Power Perspective," *Academy of Management Review* 22 (1997): 482–521.

55. R. Friedman, M. Kan, and D. B. Cornfield, "Social Support and Career Optimism: Examining the Effectiveness of Network Groups Among Black Managers," *Human Relations* 51 (1998): 1155–1177.

56. "Diversity & Inclusion @ IBM Frequently Asked Questions," January 2007, from http://www-03.ibm.com/employment/ca/en/newhire/diversity_faq.pdf.

57. S. E. Seibert, M. L. Kraimer, and R. C. Liden, "A Social Capital Theory of Career Success," *Academy of Management Journal* 44 (2001): 219–237.

58. PricewaterhouseCoopers Czech Republic, "Graduate Recruitment—FAQs," http://www.pwcglobal.com/cz/eng/car-inexp/main/faq.html.

59. M. A. Covaleski, M. W. Dirsmuth, J. B. Heian, and S. Samuel, "The Calculated and the Avowed: Techniques of Discipline and Struggles over Identity in Big Six Public Accounting Firms," *Administrative Science Quarterly* 43 (1998): 293–327.

60. B. R. Ragins and J. L. Cotton, "Easier Said than Done: Gender Differences in Perceived Barriers to Gaining a Mentor," *Academy of Management Journal* 34 (1991): 939–951; S. D. Phillips and A. R. Imhoff, "Women and Career Development: A Decade of Research," *Annual Review of Psychology* 48 (1997): 31–43.

61. W. Whiteley, T. W. Dougherty, and G. F. Dreher, "Relationship of Career Mentoring and Socioeconomic Origin to Managers' and Professionals' Early Career Progress," *Academy of Management Journal* 34 (1991): 331–351; G. F. Dreher and R. A. Ash, "A Comparative Study of Mentoring among Men and Women in Managerial, Professional, and Technical Positions," *Journal of Applied Psychology* 75 (1990): 539–546; T. A. Scandura, "Mentorship and Career Mobility: An Empirical Investigation," *Journal of Organizational Behavior* 13 (1992): 169–174.

62. G. F. Dreher and T. H. Cox, Jr., "Race, Gender and Opportunity: A Study of Compensation Attainment and Establishment of Mentoring Relationships," *Journal of Applied Psychology* 81 (1996): 297–309.

63. D. D. Horgan and R. J. Simeon, "Mentoring and Participation: An Application of the Vroom-Yetton Model," *Journal of Business and Psychology* 5 (1990): 63–84.

64. B. R. Ragins, J. L. Cotton, and J. S. Miller, "Marginal Mentoring: The Effects of Type of Mentor, Quality of Relationship, and Program Design on Work and Career Attitudes," *Academy of Management Journal* 43 (2000): 1177–1194.

65. R. T. Brennan, R. C. Barnett, and K. C. Gareis, "When She Earns More than He Does: A Longitudinal Study of Dual-Earner Couples," *Journal of Marriage and Family* 63 (2001): 168–182.

66. F. S. Hall and D. T. Hall, *The Two-Career Couple* (Reading, Mass.: Addison-Wesley, 1979).

67. J. S. Boles, M. W. Johnston, and J. F. Hair, Jr., "Role Stress, Work–Family Conflict and Emotional Exhaustion: Inter-Relationships and Effects on Some Work-Related Consequences," *Journal of Personal Selling and Sales Management* 17 (1998): 17–28.

68. B. Morris, "Is Your Family Wrecking Your Career? (And Vice Versa)," *Fortune* (March 17, 1997): 70–80.

69. D. L. Nelson, J. C. Quick, M. A. Hitt, and D. Moesel, "Politics, Lack of Career Progress, and Work/Home Conflict: Stress and Strain for Working Women," *Sex Roles* 23 (1990): 169–185.

70. L. E. Duxbury and C. A. Higgins, "Gender Differences in Work–Family Conflict," *Journal of Applied Psychology* 76 (1991): 60–74.

71. R. G. Netemeyer, J. S. Boles, and R. McMurrian, "Development and Validation of Work–Family Conflict and Family–Work Conflict Scales," *Journal of Applied Psychology* 81 (1996): 400–410.

72. N. Yang, C. C. Chen, J. Choi, and Y. Zou, "Sources of Work–Family Conflict: A Sino–U.S. Comparison of the Effects of Work and Family Demands," *Academy of Management Journal* 43 (2000): 113–123.

73. A. Iris Aaltion and H. Jiehua Huang, "Women Managers' Careers in Information Technology in China: High Flyers with Emotional Costs?" *Journal of Organizational Change Management* (20) (2) (2007): 227–244.

74. D. L. Nelson and M. A. Hitt, "Employed Women and Stress: Implications for Enhancing Women's Mental Health in the Workplace," in J. C. Quick, L. R. Murphy, and J. J. Hurrell, eds., *Stress and Well-Being at Work: Assessments and Interventions for Occupational Mental Health* (Washington, D.C.: American Psychological Association, 1992), 164–177.

75. P. Woolley, "Is Workplace Daycare a Workable Solution?" (2007) from http://www.straight.com/print/124530.

76. Mitchell Gold Co., "Day Care," http://www.mitchellgold.com/daycare.asp.

77. C. Williams, "The Sandwich Generation," Statistics Canada Catalogue No. 11-008, *Canadian Social Trends* (Summer 2005).

78. E. M. Brody, M. H. Kleban, P. T. Johnsen, C. Hoffman, and C. B. Schoonover, "Work Status and Parental Care: A Comparison of Four Groups of Women," *Gerontological Society of America* 27 (1987): 201–208; J. W. Anastas, J. L. Gibson, and P. J. Larson, "Working Families and Eldercare: A National Perspective in an Aging America," *Social Work* 35 (1990): 405–411.

79. Cincinnati Area Senior Services, "Corporate Elder Care Program," http://www.senserv.org/elder.htm.

80. E. E. Kossek, J. A. Colquitt, and R. A. Noe, "Caregiving, Well-Being, and Performance: The Effects of Place and Provider as a Function of Dependent Type and Work–Family Climates," *Academy of Management Journal* 44 (2001): 29–44.

81. Harvard University Office of Human Resources, "Work/Life Support Services—Elder Care Resources," http://atwork.harvard.edu/worklife/eldercare/.

82. The Catholic Children's Society of Greater Toronto, "Canada's Top Family-Friendly Employers," from http://www.eluta.ca/top-employer-ccas.

83. M. Richards, "'Daddy Track' Is Road Taken More Often," *The Morning Call* (July 28, 2004), http://www.mcall.com/business/local/all-daddyjul28,0,1869593.story?coll=all-businesslocal-hed.

84. L. J. Barham, "Variables Affecting Managers' Willingness to Grant Alternative Work Arrangements," *Journal of Social Psychology* 138 (1998): 291–302.

85. M. B. Arthur and K. E. Kram, "Reciprocity at Work: The Separate Yet Inseparable Possibilities for Individual and Organizational Development," in M. B. Arthur, D. T. Hall, and B. S. Lawrence, eds., *Handbook of Career Theory* (Cambridge U.K.: Cambridge University Press, 1989).

86. K. E. Kram, "Phases of the Mentoring Relationship," *Academy of Management Review* 26 (1983): 608–625.

87. B. Rosen and T. Jerdee, *Older Employees: New Roles for Valued Resources* (Homewood, Ill.: Irwin, 1985).

88. J. W. Gilsdorf, "The New Generation: Older Workers," *Training and Development Journal* (March 1992): 77–79.

89. J. F. Quick, "Time to Move On?" in J. C. Quick, R. E. Hess, J. Hermalin, and J. D. Quick, eds., *Career Stress in Changing Times* (New York: Haworth Press, 1990), 239–250.

90. D. Machan, "Rent-an-Exec," *Forbes* (January 22, 1990): 132–133.

91. E. McGoldrick and C. L. Cooper, "Why Retire Early?" in J. C. Quick, R. E. Hess, J. Hermalin, and J. D. Quick, eds., *Career Stress in Changing Times* (New York: Haworth Press, 1990), 219–238.

92. S. Kim and D. C. Feldman, "Working in Retirement: The Antecedents of Bridge Employment and Its Consequences for Quality of Life in Retirement," *Academy of Management Journal* 43 (2000): 1195–1210.

93. E. Daspin, "The Second Midlife Crisis," *The Baltimore Sun* (originally published in *The Wall Street Journal*) (May 10, 2004), http://www.baltimoresun.com/business/bal-crisis051004,0,614944.story?coll=bal-business-headlines.

94. Lawrence Livermore Retiree Program, "Tasks Requested by Lab Programs," http://www.llnl.gov/aadp/retiree/tasks.html.

95. E. Schein, *Career Anchors* (San Diego: University Associates, 1985).

96. G. W. Dalton, "Developmental Views of Careers in Organizations," in M. B. Arthur, D. T. Hall, and B. S. Lawrence, eds., *Handbook of Career Theory* (Cambridge U.K.: Cambridge University Press, 1989), 89–109.

97. D. C. Feldman, "Careers in Organizations: Recent Trends and Future Directions," *Journal of Management* 15 (1989): 135–156.

98. B. Moses, "Career Killers: Behavior to Change," *The Globe and Mail*, (July 15, 2005) http://www.bbmcareerdev.com/booksarticles_articles_detail.php?article=8.

99. C. Crawshaw, "It's Time to Sit Your Boss Down for a Career Chat," *The Globe and Mail* (May 21, 2010), B15.

# Index

## A

ABC Model of Attitudes, 57–58
Ability diversity, 26
Aboriginal leadership, 206
Accommodating, conflict management style, 225
Achievement-oriented individuals, 52
Achievement-oriented style, leader behaviour, 200
Achilles' heel phenomenon, 112–113
Acquisition challenges, 277
Adams's Theory of Inequity, 83–84
Adaptation perspective, 269–270
Adaptive culture, 269–270
Adjourning stage
    five-stage group model, 144
Administrative orbiting, 221
Aerobic exercise, effects, 119
Affect, 57–58
    negative moods, 163
    positive, 163
Affective commitment, 63
After-events review (AER), 96
Age diversity, 25–26
Aggressive mechanisms, 219–220
Agor, Weston, 162
Agreeable individuals, 39
Alderfer, Clayton, 78
Algorithms, 15
Alternative work arrangements, 33, 312
Alternative work patterns, 241–243
Altruistic managers, 181
Anthropocentric, job design, 239
Anthropology, 5
Anticipatory socialization, 273
Arbitration, 224
Aristotle, 29
Artifacts, 264–267
Assumptions, 268
Attitudes, 57–58
    and behaviour, 59–60
    and decision making, 161
    changing, 58, 63–64
    cultural differences, 21–22
    formation, 59
    social perception, 49
    work, 60
Attractiveness, 49, 50
Attribution
    external, 52
    internal, 52, 54
Attribution theory, 52. *See also* Kelley's attribution
      theory
Attributional biases, 52–53
    cultural differences, 53
Authentic leadership theory, 204
Authority relationships, conflict, 214
Authority, defined, 175
Authority-compliance manager, 196

## B

Autocratic style of leadership, 195
Autonomous work groups, 151
Autonomy, 235
    employees and, 238
    personal initiative and, 238
    types, 236–237
Avoiding, conflict management style, 224–225

Baby boomers, 26
Baby boomlet, 26
Baby bust generation, 26
Bandura, Albert, 94
Bandura's social learning theory, 94
Barnard, Chester, 162
Barriers to communication, 128
Beck, Robert, 161
Behaviour, 37
    at work, 11–12
    effect of communication technologies, 135–137
    ethical power-related-, 179–180
    norms of, 141–142
Behavioural intentions, 58
Behavioural norms, 145
Behavioural theories, 195–196
Benevolent individual, 84
Benson, Herbert, 120
Biases
    attributional, 52–53
    stereotypes, 50
Big Five personality traits, 39
Blake, Robert, 196
Blanchard, Kenneth, 200
Blue ocean approach, decision making, 156
Bounded rationality model, 157
Braille, Louis, 34
Brain hemispheres, functions of, 161
Brainstorming, 168
    electronic, 169
Bridge employment, 314
Briggs, Katherine, 44
Bullies
    tactics to manage, 178
    types, 178
Bullying
    in organizations, 178–179
Bureaucracy. *See* Organizational structure

## C

Cannon, Walter, 106
Career anchors, 315
Career ladders, 308
Career management, 299
    foundations for, 304–305
    occupational choice, 301–302
    organizational choice, 302–304

Career paths, 308
Career planning, 297
Career plateau, 313
Career stage model, 305–306
    advancement stage, 306, 308–312
    establishment stage, 306–307
    maintenance stage, 306, 312–313
    withdrawal stage, 306, 313–315
Careers, 299
    enhancing, 100–101
    management. *See* Career management
    new *vs.* old paradigms, 300, 301
    successful careers, foundations for, 304–305
    websites managing, 315
Cell phones, 136
Central route, persuasion, 65
Centrality, group power and, 178
Centralization, 248
    and strategic decision process, 256
CEOs, tenure stages, 152
Challenges, 3
    for managers, 9, 18
    social and political changes, 18
    women's success and, 25
Change, 3
    attitude, 63–64
    behaviour in times of, 5–6
    employees, helping adjust, 34
    empowerment and employees, 190
    forces of, 281–285
    information-processing technology, 258–259
    job design in a changing world, 238–239
    managing. *See* Change management
    opportunities and risk in, 9–10
    organizational and stress, 116
    organizational cultures and, 275–276
    planning for/retirement, 313–314
    resistance to, 287–290
    scope of, 286–287
    social and political, 18
    technological, 283
Change agents, 286–287
Change and acquisition, socialization stage, 274
Change leaders, 287
Change management, 12
    Lewin's model for, 290–291
    managers/employees and new technology, 34–35
    needs analysis, 292–293
    resistance to change, 287–290
Change managers, 287
Change message, effective, 288
Changing personnel
    as conflict management, 222
Changing structure
    as conflict management, 222–223
Character assassination, 222
Character theories of ethics, 29
Character theory, 29
Charisma, 203

# E

# D

Growth need strength (GNS), 234
*Guanxi,* 18

## R

# Key Terms

**opportunities**
Favourable times or chances for progress and advancement.

**change**
The transformation or modification of an organization and/or its stakeholders.

**challenge**
The call to competition, contest, or battle.

**organizational behaviour**
The study of individual behaviour and group dynamics in organizations.

**psychology**
The science of human behaviour.

**sociology**
The science of society.

**engineering**
The applied science of energy and matter.

**anthropology**
The science of the learned behaviour of human beings.

**management**
The study of overseeing activities and supervising people in organizations.

**medicine**
The applied science of healing or treatment of diseases to enhance an individual's health and well-being.

**structure**
The systems of communication, authority, and workflow.

**technology**
The tools, knowledge, and/or techniques used to transform inputs into outputs.

**people**
The human resources of the organization.

**task**
An organization's mission, purpose, or goal for existing.

# Organizational Behaviour and Opportunity

**1** Define *organizational behaviour*.

Organizational behaviour (OB) is individual behaviour and group dynamics in organizations. The foundation of organizational behaviour is human behaviour, so the study of OB involves understanding workers' behaviour in terms of their history and personal value systems and examining the external factors to which a person is subject. Organizational behaviour has grown out of contributions from psychology, sociology, engineering, anthropology, management, and medicine.

**2** Identify four action steps for responding positively in times of change.

Change is an opportunity when a person has a positive attitude, asks questions, listens, and is committed to succeed. People in change situations often become rigid and reactive, rather than open and responsive. This behaviour works well in the face of gradual, incremental change. However, rigid and well-learned behaviour may be counterproductive responses to significant change.

**3** Identify the important system components of an organization.

Organizations are open systems composed of people, structure, and technology committed to a task. The organization as a system also has an external task environment composed of different constituents, such as suppliers, customers, and federal regulators. The organization system takes inputs, converts them into throughputs, and delivers outputs to its task environment.

**4** Describe the formal and informal elements of an organization.

Organizations have formal and informal elements within them. The *formal organization* is the official, legitimate, and most visible part that enables people to think of organizations in logical and rational ways. The *informal organization* is unofficial and less visible. The informal elements of the organization are often points of diagnostic and intervention activities in organization development.

**5** Understand the diversity of organizations in the economy.

Canada's GDP is worth $1400 billion or 2.26 percent of the world economy. It is composed of manufacturing organizations, service organizations, privately owned companies, and nonprofit organizations; all contribute to our national well-being. Understanding a variety of organizations will help you develop a greater appreciation for your own organization and for others in the world of private business enterprises and nonprofit organizations.

**6** Evaluate the opportunities that change creates for organizational behaviour.

The changes and challenges facing managers are driven by international competition and customer demands. Managers in this environment must be aware of the risks associated with downsizing and marginalization of part-time workers. Organizations also face regular challenges in the areas of globalization, workforce diversity, ethics and character, and technological innovation.

**7** Demonstrate the value of objective knowledge and skill development in the study of organizational behaviour.

Although organizational behaviour is an applied discipline, a student is not "trained" in organizational behaviour. Rather, he or she is "educated" in organizational behaviour and is a coproducer in learning. To enrich your study of organizational behaviour, take the learning styles assessment on the back of this card.

**8** Explain the process of organizational design thinking.

Design thinking is an important new idea and practice. It requires managers to think more like designers when they handle problems. Managers need to use heuristics rather than algorithms when they look at organizational challenges.

**formal organization**
The official, legitimate, and most visible part of the system.

**informal organization**
The unofficial and less visible part of the system.

**Hawthorne studies**
Studies conducted during the 1920s and 1930s that discovered the existence of the informal organization.

**objective knowledge**
Knowledge that results from research and scientific activities.

**skill development**
The mastery of abilities essential to successful functioning in organizations.

## Learning organizational behaviour involves the following:

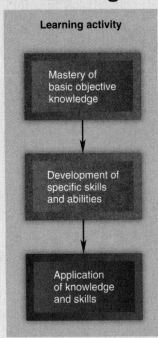

**Learning activity**

Mastery of basic objective knowledge

↓

Development of specific skills and abilities

↓

Application of knowledge and skills

## What about You? Learning Style Inventory

This 24-item survey is not timed. Answer each question as honestly as you can using one of the following words:

| OFTEN | SOMETIMES | SELDOM |
|---|---|---|

1.  Can remember more about a subject through the lecture method with information, explanations, and discussion. _____
2.  Prefer information to be written on the chalkboard, with the use of visual aids and assigned readings. _____
3.  Like to write things down or to take notes for visual review. _____
4.  Prefer to use posters, models, or actual practice and some activities in class. _____
5.  Require explanations of diagrams, graphs, or visual directions. _____
6.  Enjoy working with my hands or making things. _____
7.  Am skillful with and enjoy developing and making graphs and charts. _____
8.  Can tell if sounds match when presented with pairs of sounds. _____
9.  Remember best by writing things down several times. _____
10. Can understand and follow directions on maps. _____
11. Do better at academic subjects by listening to lectures and tapes. _____
12. Play with coins or keys in pockets. _____
13. Learn to spell better by repeating the word out loud than by writing the word on paper. _____
14. Can better understand a news development by reading about it in the paper than by listening to the radio. _____
15. Chew gum, smoke, or snack during studies. _____
16. Feel the best way to remember is to picture it in your head. _____
17. Learn spelling by "finger spelling" words. _____
18. Would rather listen to a good lecture or speech than read about the same material in a textbook. _____
19. Am good at working and solving jigsaw puzzles and mazes. _____
20. Grip objects in hands during learning period. _____
21. Prefer listening to the news on the radio rather than reading about it in the newspaper. _____
22. Obtain information on an interesting subject by reading relevant materials. _____
23. Feel very comfortable touching others, hugging, shaking hands, etc. _____
24. Follow oral directions better than written ones. _____

### Scoring Procedures

On the line next to each of your answers, write the corresponding point value. Score 5 points for each OFTEN, 3 points for each SOMETIMES, and 1 point for each SELDOM, then total your scores for the following groups of questions:

*Visual Preference* questions 2 + 3 + 7 + 10 + 14 + 16 + 19 + 22 = _____

*Auditory Preference* questions 1 + 5 + 8 + 11 + 13 + 18 + 21 + 24 = _____

*Tactile Preference* questions 4 + 6 + 9 + 12 + 15 + 17 + 20 + 23 = _____

SOURCE: Adapted from J. N. Gardner and A. J. Jewler, *Your College Experience: Strategies for Success,* 3rd concise ed. (Belmont, Calif.: Wadsworth/ITP, 1998), pp. 62–63; E. Jensen, *Student Success Secrets,* 4th ed. (Hauppauge, N.Y.: Barron's, 1996), pp. 33–36.

# Chapter 2

## >> In Review

## Challenges for Individuals

**1** Describe the factors that affect organizations competing in the global economy.

Globalization suggests that the world is free from national boundaries and is borderless. In transnational organizations, the global viewpoint supersedes national issues; organizations operate across long distances and employ a multicultural mix of workers. Social and political issues affect global operations and strategy development.

**2** Explain how cultural differences form the basis of work-related attitudes.

Individualistic cultures emphasize and encourage individual achievement whereas collectivist cultures view group loyalty and unity as paramount. Other factors affecting work-related attitudes are *power distance, uncertainty avoidance, masculinity versus femininity, and time orientation*. Developing cross-cultural sensitivity training, cultural task forces, and global human resource management is critical to success.

**3** Describe the diverse groups that make up today's business environment.

*Diversity* encompasses all forms of differences among individuals, including culture, gender, age, ability, religion, personality, social status, and sexual orientation. Benefits from diversity include human talent, marketing, creativity and innovation, problem solving, and flexibility. Potential problems include resistance to change, lack of cohesiveness, communication, conflicts, and decision making.

**4** Discuss the role of ethics, character, and personal integrity in the organization.

Ethical theories help us understand, evaluate, and classify moral arguments; make decisions; and then defend conclusions about what is right and wrong. Ethical theories can be classified as consequential, rule-based, or character.

**5** Explain five issues that pose ethical dilemmas for managers and employees.

Organizations experience a variety of ethical and moral dilemmas such as employee rights, sexual harassment, organizational justice, whistle-blowing, and social responsibility. Managers can use ethical theories to guide them through moral choices and ethical decisions.

**6** Describe the effects of technological advances on today's workforce.

Technological advances have prompted alternative work arrangements, improved working conditions, increased skilled jobs, and brought disadvantaged individuals into the workforce. It has also generated stress, workaholism, and fear of being replaced by technology or being displaced into jobs of lower skill levels.

## Key Terms

**transnational organization**
An organization in which the global viewpoint supersedes national issues.

**guanxi**
The Chinese practice of building networks for social exchange.

**expatriate manager**
A manager who works in a country other than his or her home country.

**individualism**
A cultural orientation in which people belong to loose social frameworks, and their primary concern is for themselves and their families.

**collectivism**
A cultural orientation in which individuals belong to tightly knit social frameworks, and they depend strongly on large extended families or clans.

**power distance**
The degree to which a culture accepts unequal distribution of power.

**uncertainty avoidance**
The degree to which a culture tolerates ambiguity and uncertainty.

**masculinity**
The cultural orientation in which assertiveness and materialism are valued.

**femininity**
The cultural orientation in which relationships and concern for others are valued.

**time orientation**
Whether a culture's values are oriented toward the future (long-term orientation) or toward the past and present (short-term orientation).

**diversity**
All forms of individual differences, including culture, gender, age, ability, religion, personality, social status, and sexual orientation.

>>

**glass ceiling**
A transparent barrier that keeps women from rising above a certain level in organizations.

**consequential theory**
An ethical theory that emphasizes the consequences or results of behavior.

**rule-based theory**
An ethical theory that emphasizes the character of the act itself rather than its effects.

**character theory**
An ethical theory that emphasizes the character, personal virtues, and integrity of the individual.

**distributive justice**
The fairness of the outcomes that individuals receive in an organization.

**procedural justice**
The fairness of the process by which outcomes are allocated in an organization.

**whistle-blower**
An employee who informs authorities of the wrongdoings of his or her company or coworkers.

**social responsibility**
The obligation of an organization to behave in ethical ways.

**technology**
The intellectual and mechanical processes used by an organization to transform inputs into products or services that meet organizational goals.

**expert system**
A computer-based application that uses a representation of human expertise in a specialized field of knowledge to solve problems.

**robotics**
The use of robots in organizations.

**telecommuting**
Electronically transmitting work from a home computer to the office.

**reinvention**
The creative application of new technology.

## What about You? Planning for a Global Career

Think of a country you would like to work in, do business in, or visit. Find out about its culture, using Hofstede's dimensions as guidelines. You can use a variety of sources to accomplish this, particularly your school library, government offices, faculty members, or others who have global experience. You will want to answer the following questions:

1. Is the culture individualistic or collectivist?
2. Is the power distance high or low?
3. Is uncertainty avoidance high or low?
4. Is the country masculine or feminine in its orientation?
5. Is the time orientation short-term or long-term?
6. How did you arrive at your answers to the first five questions?
7. How will these characteristics affect business practices in the country you chose to investigate?

## What about You? How Much Do You Know about Sexual Harassment?

Indicate whether you believe each statement below is true (T) or false (F).

_____ 1. Sexual harassment is unprofessional behaviour.
_____ 2. Sexual harassment is against the law in Canada.
_____ 3. Sexual advances are a form of sexual harassment.
_____ 4. A request for sexual activity is a form of sexual harassment.
_____ 5. Verbal or physical conduct of a sexual nature may be sexual harassment.
_____ 6. Sexual harassment occurs when submission to sex acts is a condition of employment.
_____ 7. Sexual harassment occurs when submission to or rejection of sexual acts is a basis for performance evaluation.
_____ 8. Sexual harassment occurs when such behaviour interferes with an employee's performance or creates an intimidating, hostile, and offenseive environment.
_____ 9. Sexual harassment includes physical contact of a sexual nature, such as touching.
_____ 10. Sexual harassment requires that a person have the intent to harass, harm, or intimidate.

All of the items are true except item 10, which is false. While somewhat ambiguous, sexual harassment is defined in the eyes of the beholder. Give yourself 1 point for each correct answer. This score reflects how much you know about sexual harassment. Scores can range from 0 (poorly informed about sexual harassment) to 10 (well informed about sexual harassment). If your score was less than 5, you need to learn more about sexual harassment.

SOURCE: See W. O'Donohue, ed., Sexual Harassment (Boston: Allyn and Bacon, 1997) for theory, research and treatment.

## Key Terms

**individual differences**
The way in which factors such as skills, abilities, personalities, perceptions, attitudes, values, and ethics differ from one individual to another.

**interactional psychology**
The psychological approach that emphasizes that in order to understand human behaviour, we must know something about the person and about the situation.

**personality**
A relatively stable set of characteristics that influence an individual's behaviour.

**integrative approach**
The broad theory that describes personality as a composite of an individual's psychological processes.

**core self-evaluation**
The positiveness of one's self-concept; comprised of locus of control, self-esteem, self-efficacy and emotional stability.

**locus of control**
An individual's generalized belief about internal control (self-control) versus external control (control by the situation or by others).

**general self-efficacy**
An individual's general belief that he or she is capable of meeting job demands in a wide variety of situations.

**self-esteem**
An individual's general feeling of self-worth.

**self-monitoring**
The extent to which people base their behaviour on cues from other people and situations.

**positive affect**
An individual's tendency to accentuate the positive aspects of himself or herself, other people, and the world in general.

**negative affect**
An individual's tendency to accentuate the negative aspects of himself or herself, other people, and the world in general.

## Personality, Perception, and Attribution

**1** Describe individual differences and their importance in understanding behaviour.

Individual differences are skills, abilities, personalities, perceptions, attitudes, emotions, and ethics. To understand human behaviour, we must know something about the person and something about the organization, work group, personal life situation, job characteristics, and environmental influences. These all interact in determining behaviour.

**2** Explain how personality influences behaviour in organizations.

Personality is an individual difference that lends consistency to a person's behaviour. Traits such as extraversion, conscientiousness, and core self-evaluation influence performance and attitudes.

**3** Discuss the practical application of personality theories in organizations.

An understanding of personality enhances the understanding of individuals and how they interact with situations and other people. With this knowledge, managers can choose appropriate ways to handle the employee.

**4** Define *social perception* and explain the factors that affect it.

*Social perception* is the process of interpreting information about another person. Management perceptions are affected by familiarity with the target, attitude, mood, and cognitive structure. The target's physical appearance, communication skills, and perceived intentions as well as characteristics of the situation influence perception. In an organization, virtually all management activities rely on perception.

**5** Identify seven common barriers to social perception.

In organizations, expectations of an individual affect both the manager's behaviour toward the individual and the individual's response. Seven barriers to social perception are selective perception, stereotyping, first-impression error, recency effect, contrast effect, projection, and self-fulfilling prophecies. Understanding social perception in organizations may help individuals who compete for jobs, favourable performance evaluations, and salary increases.

**6** Explain the attribution process and how attributions affect managerial behaviour.

Attribution theory explains how we pinpoint the causes of our own behaviour (and our performance) and that of others. Attribution theory has many applications in the workplace. We can attribute events to an internal source of responsibility or an external source. We typically err in our attributions by overestimating the impact of internal causes of others' behaviour.

**strong situation**
A situation that overwhelms the effects of individual personalities by providing strong cues for appropriate behaviour.

**Myers-Briggs Type Indicator (MBTI)® instrument**
An instrument developed to measure Carl Jung's theory of individual differences.

**extraversion**
A preference indicating that an individual is energized by interaction with other people.

**introversion**
A preference indicating that an individual is energized by time alone.

**sensing**
Gathering information through the five senses.

**intuition**
Gathering information through a "sixth sense" and focusing on what could be rather than what actually exists.

**thinking**
Making decisions in a logical, objective fashion.

**feeling**
Making decisions in a personal, value-oriented way.

**judging**
Preferring closure and completion in making decisions.

**perceiving**
Preferring to explore many alternatives and flexibility.

**social perception**
The process of interpreting information about another person.

**discounting principle**
The assumption that an individual's behaviour is accounted for by the situation.

**selective perception**
The process of selecting information that supports our individual viewpoints while discounting information that threatens our viewpoints.

**stereotype**
A generalization about a group of people.

**first-impression error**
The tendency to form lasting opinions about an individual based on initial perceptions.

**recency effect**
The tendency to weigh recent events more than earlier events.

**contrast effect**
The tendency to diminish or enhance the measure of one target through comparison with another recently observed target.

## What about You? Are You a High or Low Self-Monitor?

For the following items, circle T (true) if the statement is characteristic of your behaviour. Circle F (false) if the statement does not reflect your behaviour.

1. I find it hard to imitate the behaviour of other people. T  F
2. At parties and social gatherings, I do not attempt to do or say things that others will like. T  F
3. I can argue only for ideas that I already believe. T  F
4. I can make impromptu speeches even on topics about which I have almost no information. T  F
5. I guess I put on a show to impress or entertain others. T  F
6. I would probably make a good actor. T  F
7. In a group of people, I am rarely the centre of attention. T  F
8. In different situations and with different people, I often act like very different persons. T  F
9. I am not particularly good at making other people like me. T  F
10. I am not always the person I appear to be. T  F
11. I would not change my opinions (or the way I do things) in order to please others or win their favour. T  F
12. I have considered being an entertainer. T  F
13. I have never been good at games like charades or at improvisational acting. T  F
14. I have trouble changing my behaviour to suit different people and different situations. T  F
15. At a party, I let others keep the jokes and stories going. T  F
16. I feel a bit awkward in company and do not show up quite as well as I should. T  F
17. I can look anyone in the eye and tell a lie with a straight face (if it is for a good cause). T  F
18. I may deceive people by being friendly when I really dislike them. T  F

### Scoring

To score this questionnaire, give yourself 1 point for each of the following items that you answered T (true): 4, 5, 6, 8, 10, 12, 17, and 18. Now give yourself 1 point for each of the following items that you answered F (false): 1, 2, 3, 7, 9, 11, 13, 14, 15, and 16. Add both subtotals to find your overall score. If you scored 11 or above, you are probably a *high self-monitor*. If you scored 10 or under, you are probably a *low self-monitor*.

Source: From *Public Appearances, Private Realities: The Psychology of Self-Monitoring* by M. Snyder. Copyright © 1987 by W. H. Freeman and Company. Used with permission.

**projection**
Overestimating the number of people who share our own beliefs, values, and behaviours.

**self-fulfilling prophecy**
The situation in which our expectations about people affect our interaction with them in such a way that our expectations are fulfilled.

**impression management**
The process by which individuals try to control the impressions others have of them.

**attribution theory**
A theory that explains how individuals pinpoint the causes of their own behaviour and that of others.

**fundamental attribution error**
The tendency to make attributions to internal causes when focusing on someone else's behaviour.

**self-serving bias**
The tendency to attribute one's own successes to internal causes and one's failures to external causes.

**consensus**
An informational cue indicating the extent to which peers in the same situation behave in a similar fashion.

**distinctiveness**
An informational cue indicating the degree to which an individual behaves the same way in other situations.

**consistency**
An informational cue indicating the frequency of behaviour over time.

# Key Terms

**attitude**
A psychological tendency expressed by evaluating an entity with some degree of favour or disfavour.

**affect**
The emotional component of an attitude.

**cognitive dissonance**
A state of tension that is produced when an individual experiences conflict between attitudes and behaviour.

**social learning**
The process of deriving attitudes from family, peer groups, and culture.

**job satisfaction**
A pleasurable or positive emotional state resulting from the appraisal of one's job or job experiences.

**organizational citizenship behaviour**
Behaviour that is above and beyond the call of duty.

**organizational commitment**
The strength of an individual's identification with an organization.

**affective commitment**
The type of organizational commitment that is based on an individual's desire to remain in an organization.

**continuance commitment**
The type of organizational commitment that is based on the fact that an individual cannot afford to leave.

**normative commitment**
The type of organizational commitment that is based on an individual's perceived obligation to remain with an organization.

**emotions**
Mental states that typically include feelings, physiological changes, and the inclination to act.

**emotional labour**
The need to manage emotions in order to perform one's job effectively.

## Attitudes, Emotions, and Ethics

**1** Explain the ABC model of an attitude.

The ABC model says attitudes have three components: the affective (feeling) part, the cognitive (thinking) part, and the behavioural (intention to act) part. Knowing a person's attitudes about something means recognition that there is a positive or negative response to it connected to certain beliefs that make one likely to act in predictable ways. Because we are interested in employee behaviours (such as effort and attendance), we are interested in knowing what their attitudes are and in influencing those attitudes through changing emotional responses and beliefs.

**2** Describe how attitudes are formed.

Attitudes are learned. Influences on attitudes are direct experience and social learning. Culture also plays a definitive role in attitude development. Attitude–behaviour correspondence depends on five things: attitude specificity, attitude relevance, timing of measurement, personality factors, and social constraints. Attitudes affect work behaviour. Demanding jobs over which employees have little control negatively affect employees' work attitudes. A positive psychological climate can generate positive attitudes and good performance.

**3** Identify sources and consequences of job satisfaction.

*Job satisfaction* is a pleasurable or positive emotional state resulting from the appraisal of one's job or job experiences. It has been treated as a general attitude and as satisfaction with specific dimensions of the job, like pay, the work itself, promotion opportunities, supervision, and coworkers. Rewards are key to influencing both job satisfaction and work performance if valued by employees and tied directly to performance. Job satisfaction correlates with organizational performance, organizational citizenship behaviour, turnover, and attendance.

**4** Distinguish between organizational citizenship and workplace deviance behaviours.

Individuals who identify strongly with the organization are more likely to perform *organizational citizenship behaviour*—behaviour above and beyond the call of duty. *Workplace deviance behaviour* is a result of negative attitudes and consists of counterproductive behaviour that violates organizational norms and harms others or the organization.

**5** Identify the characteristics of the source, target, and message that affect persuasion.

Through persuasion, one individual (the source) tries to change the attitude of another person (the target). Three major characteristics of the source affect persuasion: expertise, trustworthiness, and attractiveness. Targets with low self-esteem or in a good mood are easier to persuade. Individuals with extreme attitudes or high self-esteem are more resistant. The elaboration likelihood model proposes that persuasion occurs through the central route and the peripheral route differentiated by the amount of elaboration, scrutiny, or motivation in the message.

**6** Discuss the definition and importance of emotions at work.

Emotions are mental states including feelings, physiological changes, and the inclination to act and are normal parts of human functioning and decision making. Positive emotions that travel through a work group produce cooperation and task performance. The opposite also occurs when negative emotions destroy morale and performance. Many jobs require emotional labour, expressing particular emotions even if they are not being truly felt. Doing so is easier if one is emotionally intelligent, a set of skills that refer to recognizing and managing both one's own emotions and those of others. Accurate recognition of others' emotions can be difficult if one is not aware of the emotional display rules they are following.

>>

## Glossary

**emotional dissonance**
Conflict between what one feels and what one is expected to express.

**emotional intelligence**
A set of abilities related to the understanding and management of emotions in oneself and others.

**emotional display rules**
Expectations regarding what emotions are appropriate to express in specific situations.

**emotional contagion**
A dynamic process through which the emotions of one person are transferred to another, either consciously or unconsciously, through nonverbal channels.

**ethical behaviour**
Acting in ways consistent with one's personal values and the commonly held values of the organization and society.

**values**
Enduring beliefs that a specific mode of conduct or end state of existence is personally or socially preferable to an opposite or converse mode of conduct or end state of existence.

**Machiavellianism**
A personality characteristic indicating one's willingness to do whatever it takes to get one's own way.

**cognitive moral development**
The process of moving through stages of maturity in terms of making ethical decisions.

**7** Describe the consequences of individual and organizational ethical behaviour.

*Ethical behaviour* is acting in ways consistent with one's personal values and the commonly held values of the organization and society. Firms with better reputations attract more applicants, creating a larger hiring pool, and evidence suggests that respected firms can choose higher-quality applicants. Unethical behaviour by employees can affect individuals, work teams, and even the organization.

**8** Identify the factors that affect ethical behaviour.

Factors that influence an individual's ethical behaviour are values, locus of control, *Machiavellianism* (one's willingness to do whatever it takes to get one's own way), and an individual's level of *cognitive moral development*. Organizations can offer guidance by encouraging ethical behaviour through codes of conduct, ethics committees, ethics communication systems, training, norms, modelling, rewards and punishments, and corporate social responsibility programs.

## What about You? Assess Your Job Satisfaction

Think of the job you have now or a job you've had in the past. Indicate how satisfied you are with each aspect of your job below, using the following scale:

1 = Extremely dissatisfied   2 = Dissatisfied   3 = Slightly dissatisfied   4 = Neutral
5 = Slightly satisfied   6 = Satisfied   7 = Extremely satisfied

1. The amount of job security I have.
2. The amount of pay and fringe benefits I receive.
3. The amount of personal growth and development I get in doing my job.
4. The people I talk to and work with on my job.
5. The degree of respect and fair treatment I receive from my boss.
6. The feeling of worthwhile accomplishment I get from doing my job.
7. The chance to get to know other people while on the job.
8. The amount of support and guidance I receive from my supervisor.
9. The degree to which I am fairly paid for what I contribute to this organization.
10. The amount of independent thought and action I can exercise in my job.
11. How secure things look for me in the future in this organization.
12. The chance to help other people while at work.
13. The amount of challenge in my job.
14. The overall quality of the supervision I receive on my work.

Now, compute your scores for the facets of job satisfaction.

*Pay satisfaction:*
Q2 + Q9 = ___ Divided by 2: ___

*Security satisfaction:*
Q1 + Q11 = ___ Divided by 2: ___

*Social satisfaction:*
Q4 + Q7 + Q12 = ___ Divided by 3: ___

*Supervisory satisfaction:*
Q5 + Q8 + Q14 = ___ Divided by 3: ___

*Growth satisfaction:*
Q3 + Q6 + Q10 + Q13 = ___ Divided by 4: ___

Scores on the facets range from 1 to 7. (Scores lower than 4 suggest there is room for change.)

This questionnaire is an abbreviated version of the Job Diagnostic Survey, a widely used tool for assessing individuals' attitudes about their jobs. Compare your scores on each facet to the following norms for a large sample of managers.

Pay satisfaction: 4.6   Security satisfaction: 5.2   Social satisfaction: 5.6
Supervisory satisfaction: 5.2   Growth satisfaction: 5.3

How do your scores compare? Are there actions you can take to improve your job satisfaction?

SOURCE: *Work Redesign* by Hackman/Oldham, © 1980. Reprinted by permission of Pearson Education, Inc., Upper Saddle River, N.J.

## Key Terms

**motivation**
The energizing forces that influence the direction, intensity, and persistence of effort.

**Theory X**
A set of assumptions that workers are lazy and dislike responsibility.

**Theory Y**
A set of assumptions that workers like work and will seek responsibility.

**needs theories**
Identify internal factors, typically deficiencies, that influence motivation.

**process theories**
Identify how internal factors interact with the environment to influence motivation.

**psychoanalysis**
Sigmund Freud's method for delving into the unconscious mind to better understand a person's motives and needs.

**need for achievement**
A need that concerns individuals' desire for excellence, competition, challenging goals, persistence, and overcoming difficulties.

**need for power**
A need that concerns an individual's need to make an impact on others, influence others, change people or events, and make a difference in life.

**need for affiliation**
A need that concerns an individual's need to establish and maintain warm, close, intimate relationships with other people.

**motivation factor**
A work condition related to satisfaction of the need for psychological growth.

**hygiene factor**
A work condition related to dissatisfaction caused by discomfort or pain.

## Motivation at Work

**1** Define *motivation*.

*Motivation* describes the energizing forces that influence the direction, intensity, and persistence of effort. Motivation theories may be broadly classified into needs theories and process theories. Motivation is a complex interaction between the individual and the environment and not something that management can "make" happen.

**2** Discuss the needs for achievement, power, and affiliation.

David McClelland identified three learned or acquired needs. The *need for achievement* encompasses excellence, competition, challenging goals, persistence, and overcoming difficulties. The *need for power* includes the desire to influence others, the urge to change people or events, and the wish to make a difference in life. The *need for affiliation* means an urge to establish and maintain warm, close, intimate relationships with others.

**3** Describe the two-factor theory of motivation.

Frederick Herzberg's two-factor theory examined experiences that satisfied or dissatisfied people at work. Motivation factors relate to job satisfaction; hygiene factors relate to job dissatisfaction. Motivation factors were responsibility, achievement, recognition, advancement, and the work itself. Hygiene factors were company policy and administration, technical supervision, salary, interpersonal relations with one's supervisor, working conditions, salary, and status. Excellent hygiene factors result in employees' being not dissatisfied.

**4** Describe the role of inequity in motivation.

Equity theory is a process theory of motivation that focuses on perceived fairness in the individual–environment interaction. Individuals and organizations want an equitable arrangement for both members of the relationship. Inequity occurs when a person receives more, or less, than the person believes he or she deserves based on effort and/or contribution. Because inequity is uncomfortable, it motivates behaviour to restore equity.

**5** Describe the expectancy theory of motivation.

Vroom's expectancy theory of motivation focuses on personal perceptions of the performance process. Performers are more motivated 1) if they see a strong link between their efforts and results (expectancy), 2) see that different performance results leads to different outcomes (instrumentality), and 3) value the outcomes or rewards attached to results (valence).

**6** Explain how goal setting can motivate performance.

People with specific challenging goals outperform those with general "do your best goals" or no goals at all. Higher goals lead to higher motivation and better performance, as long as the goals are accepted and the performer has the necessary skills. Goal setting directs attention to relevant activities, energizes the performer and enhances persistence.

**7** Describe the cultural differences in motivation.

Most motivation theories in use today have been developed by and about Americans. When researchers have examined the universality of these theories, they have found that the studies did not replicate the results found in the United States due to cultural differences.

## Glossary (margin)

**inequity**
The situation in which a person perceives he or she is receiving less than he or she is giving, or is giving less than he or she is receiving.

**equity sensitive**
An individual who prefers an equity ratio equal to that of his or her comparison other.

**benevolent**
An individual who is comfortable with an equity ratio less than that of his or her comparison other.

**entitled**
An individual who is comfortable with an equity ratio greater than that of his or her comparison other.

**procedural justice**
Fairness in how things are done.

**interactional justice**
Fairness in how people are treated.

**valence**
The value or importance one places on a particular reward.

**expectancy**
The belief that effort leads to performance.

**instrumentality**
The belief that performance is related to rewards.

**goal setting**
The process of establishing desired results that guide and direct behaviour.

**moral maturity**
The measure of a person's cognitive moral development.

---

## What about You? How Strong Is Your Protestant Work Ethic?

Rate the following statements from 1 (for *disagree completely*) to 6 (for *agree completely*).

_____ **1.** When the workday is finished, people should forget their jobs and enjoy themselves.

_____ **2.** Hard work makes us better people.

_____ **3.** The principal purpose of people's jobs is to provide them with the means for enjoying their free time.

_____ **4.** Wasting time is as bad as wasting money.

_____ **5.** Whenever possible, a person should relax and accept life as it is rather than always striving for unreachable goals.

_____ **6.** A good indication of a person's worth is how well he or she does his or her job.

_____ **7.** If all other things are equal, it is better to have a job with a lot of responsibility than one with little responsibility.

_____ **8.** People who "do things the easy way" are the smart ones.

_____ Total your score for the pro-Protestant ethic items (2, 4, 6, and 7).

_____ Total your score for the non-Protestant ethic items (1, 3, 5, and 8).

A pro-Protestant ethic score of 20 or over indicates that you have a strong work ethic; 15–19 indicates a moderately strong work ethic; 9–14 indicates a moderately weak work ethic; 8 or less indicates a weak work ethic.

A non-Protestant ethic score of 20 or over indicates you have a strong non-work ethic; 15–19 indicates a moderately strong non-work ethic; 9–14 indicates a moderately weak non-work ethic; 8 or less indicates a weak non-work ethic.

SOURCE: M. R. Blood, "Work Values and Job Satisfaction," *Journal of Applied Psychology* 53 (1969): 456–459. Copyright © 1969 by the American Psychological Association. Reprinted with permission.

---

## What about You? What's Important to Employees?

There are many possible job rewards that employees may receive. Listed below are 10 possible job reward factors. Rank these factors three times. First, rank them as you think the average employee would rank them. Second, rank them as you think the average employee's supervisor would rank them for the employee. Finally, rank them according to what you consider important. Your instructor has normative data for 1,000 employees and their supervisors that will help you interpret your results and place the results in the context of Maslow's need hierarchy and Herzberg's two-factor theory of motivation.

| Employee | Supervisor | You | |
|---|---|---|---|
| 2 | 2 | 5 | **1.** job security |
| 7 | | 9 | **2.** full appreciation of work done |
| 5 | | 6 | **3.** promotion and growth in the organization |
| 1 | 1 | 3 | **4.** good wages |
| 6 | | 1 | **5.** interesting work |
| 3 | | 2 | **6.** good working conditions |
| 8 | | 4 | **7.** tactful discipline |
| 4 | | 8 | **8.** sympathetic help with personal problems |
| 9 | | 10 | **9.** personal loyalty to employees |
| 10 | | 7 | **10.** a feeling of being in on things |

SOURCE: "Crossed Wires on Employee Motivation," *Training and Development* 49 (1995): 59–60. American Society for Training and Development. Reprinted with permission. All rights reserved.

## Key Terms

**learning**
A change in behaviour acquired through experience.

**operant conditioning**
Modifying behaviour through the use of positive or negative consequences following specific behaviours.

**positive reinforcement**
Attempting to strengthen desirable behaviour by bestowing positive consequences.

**negative reinforcement**
Attempting to strengthen desirable behaviour by withholding negative consequences.

**punishment**
Attempting to eliminate or weaken undesirable behaviour by bestowing negative consequences or withholding positive consequences.

**extinction**
Attempting to eliminate or weaken undesirable behaviour by attaching no consequences to it.

**task-specific self-efficacy**
An individual's beliefs and expectancies about his or her ability to perform a specific task effectively.

**self-regulation prompting**
Questions that encourage the learner to reflect on what and how he/she is learning.

**error management training**
Immersion in a safe training environment where learners are encouraged to deliberately make mistakes and see what happens.

**after-events review**
Procedure where, following an experience, the learner systematically analyzes how his/her actions and decisions contributed to the success and failure of the performance.

# Learning and Performance Management

**1**  Describe reinforcement theory's approach to learning.

Reinforcement theory applies operant conditioning principles to learning. Knowing people change their behaviour in order to gain positive consequences and avoid negative consequences, an organization can deliberately manipulate consequences in order to motivate learning. Basic strategies include positive reinforcement, negative reinforcement, punishment, and extinction.

**2**  Describe Bandura's social learning theory.

Bandura claims people learn through watching others' behaviour and its consequences and then modelling that behaviour. His theory focuses on the importance of task-specific self-efficacy, an individual's beliefs and expectancies about his/her ability to perform a specific task effectively.

**3**  Describe evidence showing that thinking about learning seems to influence the learning process.

Evidence comes from three areas of research: self-regulation prompts in online training, error management training, and after-events reviews. Interspersing prompts in online training that trigger the learner to reflect on the learning leads to better learning and lower dropout. Learners encouraged to make mistakes in a safe training environment transfer the learning better to novel situations and learn to take failure in stride. After-event reviews that ask the learner to reflect on how his/her specific actions and decisions contributed to the event's success and failure show enhanced learning.

**4**  Explain the aspects of performance management.

Performance management is the process of defining, measuring, appraising, providing feedback, and responding to performance. By taking actions that clarify organizational expectations, indicate results and impact, and support and reward effective performance, the organization can guide the performer's actions to better align with the organization's wishes.

**5**  Explain the importance of performance feedback and how it can be delivered effectively.

Feedback can have a powerful influence on behaviour. Good performance appraisal systems develop people, enhance careers, and boost individual and team achievements in an organization. Effective performance appraisal systems have five key characteristics: validity, reliability, responsiveness, flexibility, and equitability. The supervisor must establish mutual trust, be vulnerable and open to challenge, and be a skilled, empathetic listener who encourages employees to discuss their aspirations.

**6**  Identify ways managers can reward performance.

Individual reward systems (such as commission and merit pay) foster higher effort and are particularly appealing to workers with a high need for achievement and high self-efficacy, but they can also undermine cooperation. Team reward systems (such as gainsharing and profit sharing) encourage cooperation and the sharing of information and expertise but are less motivating for individual contributions. Hybrid plans combine both individual and group reward systems.

**performance management**
A process of defining, measuring, appraising, providing feedback on, and responding to performance.

**management by objectives (MBO)**
A goal-setting program based on interaction and negotiation between employees and managers.

**360-degree feedback**
A process of self-evaluation and evaluations by a manager, peers, direct reports, and possibly customers.

**mentoring**
A work relationship that encourages development and career enhancement for people moving through the career cycle.

**7** Describe how to correct poor performance.

Supervisors need first to identify the cause of the poor performance and then develop a plan for addressing the cause. In determining the cause, the supervisor must be careful to avoid the fundamental attribution error, which may lead to blaming the worker inappropriately. Performance problems are often not self-motivated and may be due to the circumstances. For example, the supervisor may need to address training practices, equipment issues, role ambiguity, or role conflicts.

**What about You?** How Do You Correct Poor Performance?

At one time or another, each of us has had a poor performance of some kind. It may have been a poor test result in school, a poor presentation at work, or a poor performance in an athletic event. Think of a poor performance event that you have experienced and work through the following three steps.

**Step 1.** Briefly describe the specific event in some detail. Include why you label it a poor performance (bad score? someone else's evaluation?).

**Step 2.** Analyze the poor performance.

    **a.** List all the possible contributing causes to the poor performance. Be specific, such as the room was too hot, you did not get enough sleep, you were not told how to perform the task, etc. You might ask other people for possible ideas, too.

        1. _____

        2. _____

        3. _____

        4. _____

        5. _____

        6. _____

        7. _____

    **b.** Is there a primary cause for the poor performance? What is it?

**Step 3.** Plan to correct the poor performance.

Develop a step-by-step plan of action that specifies what you can change or do differently to improve your performance the next time you have an opportunity. Include seeking help if it is needed. Once your plan is developed, look for an opportunity to execute it.

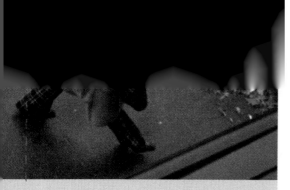

# Key Terms

**stress**
The unconscious preparation to fight or flee that a person experiences when faced with any demand.

**stressor**
The person or event that triggers the stress response.

**distress**
The adverse psychological, physical, behavioural, and organizational consequences that may arise as a result of stressful events.

**strain**
Distress.

**homeostasis**
A steady state of bodily functioning and equilibrium.

**ego-ideal**
The embodiment of a person's perfect self.

**self-image**
How a person sees himself or herself, both positively and negatively.

**workaholism**
An imbalanced preoccupation with work at the expense of home and personal life satisfaction.

**job demand-control-support model (JDCS)**
This stress model asserts that high demands, low control, and low support all contribute to strain.

**effort-reward imbalance model (ERI)**
This stress model attributes strain to a combination of high effort and low reward.

**Type A behaviour pattern**
A complex of personality and behavioural characteristics, including competitiveness, time urgency, social status insecurity, aggression, hostility, and a quest for achievements.

## Stress and Well-Being at Work

**1** Define *stress*, *stressor*, and *distress*

*Stress,* or the stress response, is the unconscious preparation to fight or flee experienced when faced with any demand. A *stressor,* or demand, is the person or event triggering the stress response. *Distress* or *strain* refers to adverse psychological, physical, behavioural, and organizational consequences that *may* occur as a result of stressful events.

**2** Compare four different approaches to stress.

There are four principal approaches to stress. Walter B. Cannon developed the homeostatic/medical approach because he believed stress resulted when an external, environmental demand upset the body's balance, or *homeostasis.* Richard Lazarus's cognitive appraisal approach emphasized perception and interpretation in classifying persons or events as stressful. Robert Kahn's person-environment fit approach claimed confusing and conflicting expectations of social roles create stress. Harry Levinson's psychoanalytic approach believed the *ego-ideal* and the *self-image* interact to cause stress.

**3** Explain the psychophysiology of the stress response.

The stress response begins with the release of chemical messengers, primarily adrenaline, into the bloodstream. These messengers activate the sympathetic nervous system and endocrine (hormone) system to trigger mind–body changes to prepare the person for fight or flight. As the body responds, the person shifts from a neutral posture to an offensive posture.

**4** Identify work and nonwork causes of stress.

Major categories of work demands that cause stress are role conflict, role ambiguity, task demands, role demands, interpersonal demands, and physical demands. Nonwork demands may broadly be identified as home demands from an individual's personal life environment and personal demands that are self-imposed.

**5** Explain the JDCS and ERI models that link stress to negative consequences.

The job-demands-control-support (JDCS) model sees stress caused by high demands, low control, and low support. Preventing or alleviating negative stress symptoms (such as anxiety, absenteeism) can be achieved by reducing demands, enhancing control, and offering support. The effort-reward imbalance (ERI) model attributes strain to a combination of high effort and low reward. Consequently, efforts by the organization to reduce the efforts required and improve the rewards offered can right the balance and reduce stress.

**6** Describe the consequences of stress.

Positive stress can create eustress, improving performance. Negative stress creates distress, which can lead to medical, performance, and behavioural problems.

**7** Discuss individual factors that influence a person's response to stress and strain.

Individual differences, such as negative affectivity and Type A behaviour pattern, enhance vulnerability to strain under stressful conditions. Other individual differences, such as personality hardiness, self-esteem, self-efficacy, and self-reliance, reduce vulnerability to strain under stressful conditions.

**personality hardiness**
A personality resistant to distress and characterized by commitment, control, and challenge.

**transformational coping**
A way of managing stressful events by changing them into less subjectively stressful events.

**self-reliance**
A healthy, secure, *interdependent* pattern of behaviour related to how people form and maintain supportive attachments with others.

**counterdependence**
An unhealthy, insecure pattern of behaviour that leads to separation in relationships with other people.

**overdependence**
An unhealthy, insecure pattern of behaviour that leads to preoccupied attempts to achieve security through relationships.

**preventive stress management**
An organizational philosophy that holds that people and organizations should take joint responsibility for promoting health and preventing distress and strain.

**primary prevention**
The stage in preventive stress management designed to reduce, modify, or eliminate the demand or stressor causing stress.

**secondary prevention**
The stage in preventive stress management designed to alter or modify the response to a demand or stressor.

**tertiary prevention**
The stage in preventive stress management designed to heal symptoms of distress and strain.

**8** Identify the stages of preventive stress management.

The three stages of prevention are primary, secondary, and tertiary prevention. *Primary prevention* is intended to reduce, modify, or eliminate the demand or stressor causing stress. *Secondary prevention* is intended to alter or modify the response to a demand or stressor. *Tertiary prevention* is intended to heal symptoms of distress and strain.

## What about You? The Frazzle Factor: How Stressed Are You?

Read each of the following statements and rate yourself on a scale of 0 to 3, giving the answer that best describes how you generally feel (3 points for *always,* 2 points for *often,* 1 point for *sometimes,* and 0 points for *never*). Answer as honestly as you can, and do not spend too much time on any one statement.

**Am I Overstressed?**

_____ **1.** I have to make important snap judgments and decisions.
_____ **2.** I am not consulted about what happens on my job or in my classes.
_____ **3.** I feel I am underpaid.
_____ **4.** I feel that no matter how hard I work, the system will mess it up.
_____ **5.** I do not get along with some of my coworkers or fellow students.
_____ **6.** I do not trust my superiors at work or my professors at school.
_____ **7.** The paperwork burden on my job or at school is getting to me.
_____ **8.** I feel people outside the job or the university do not respect what I do.

**Am I Angry?**

_____ **1.** I feel that people around me make too many irritating mistakes.
_____ **2.** I feel annoyed because I do good work or perform well in school, but no one appreciates it.
_____ **3.** When people make me angry, I tell them off.
_____ **4.** When I am angry, I say things I know will hurt people.
_____ **5.** I lose my temper easily.
_____ **6.** I feel like striking out at someone who angers me.
_____ **7.** When a coworker or fellow student makes a mistake, I tell him or her about it.
_____ **8.** I cannot stand being criticized in public.

### SCORING

To find your level of anger and potential for aggressive behaviour, add your scores from both quiz parts.

40–48: The red flag is waving, and you had better pay attention. You are in the danger zone. You need guidance from a counsellor or mental health professional, and you should be getting it now.

30–39: The yellow flag is up. Your stress and anger levels are too high, and you are feeling increasingly hostile. You are still in control, but it would not take much to trigger a violent flare of temper.

10–29: Relax, you are in the broad normal range. Like most people, you get angry occasionally, but usually with some justification. Sometimes you take overt action, but you are not likely to be unreasonably or excessively aggressive.

0–9: Congratulations! You are in great shape. Your stress and anger are well under control, giving you a laid-back personality not prone to violence.

SOURCE: Questionnaire developed by C. D. Spielberger. Appeared in W. Barnhill, "Early Warning," *The Washington Post* (August 11, 1992): B5.

# Chapter 8

## Key Terms

**communication**
The evoking of a shared or common meaning in another person.

**interpersonal communication**
Communication between two or more people in an organization.

**communicator**
The person originating a message.

**receiver**
The person receiving a message.

**perceptual screen**
A window through which we interact with people that influences the quality, accuracy, and clarity of the communication.

**message**
The thoughts and feelings that the communicator is attempting to elicit in the receiver.

**feedback**
Information fed back that completes two-way communication.

**language**
The words, their pronunciation, and the methods of combining them used and understood by a group of people.

**data**
Uninterpreted and unanalyzed facts.

**information**
Data that have been interpreted, analyzed, and have meaning to some user.

**richness**
The ability of a medium or channel to elicit or evoke meaning in the receiver.

**reflective listening**
A skill intended to help the receiver and communicator clearly and fully understand the message sent.

**two-way communication**
A form of communication in which the communicator and receiver interact.

# >> In Review

## Communication

**1** Describe the interpersonal communication process and the role of listening in the process.

Interpersonal communication is reflective, objective, and perceptual. The conceptual and emotional component of messages is affected by verbal and nonverbal communication and is key to understanding and verifying the message. Reflective listening enables the listener to understand the communicator's meaning, reduce perceptual distortions, and overcome interpersonal barriers that lead to communication failures.

**2** Describe the five communication skills of effective supervisors.

Five communication skills that distinguish "good" from "bad" supervisors include being expressive speakers, empathetic listeners, persuasive leaders, sensitive people, and informative managers.

**3** Explain five communication barriers and gateways through them.

Barriers to communication in the workplace are physical separation, status differences, gender differences, cultural diversity, and language. Awareness and recognition are the first steps in overcoming barriers. Other gateways are recognizing gender-specific conversation style differences, clarification of meaning, understanding cultural differences, and avoiding technical terms and jargon.

**4** Distinguish between defensive and nondefensive communication.

*Defensive communication* includes aggressive and angry communication as well as passive, withdrawing communication. *Nondefensive communication* is an assertive, direct, powerful form of communication.

**5** Explain the impact of nonverbal communication.

Most meaning in a message is conveyed nonverbally. *Nonverbal communication* includes all elements of communication, such as gestures and the use of space, that do not involve words or do not involve language. The four basic kinds of nonverbal communication that managers need to understand and decipher are proxemics, kinesics, facial and eye behaviour, and paralanguage.

**6** Explain positive, healthy communication.

James Lynch suggests that the heart may be equally or more important than cognition in the communications process. According to Lynch, positive, healthy communication is exemplified by trust and truthfulness, core values and beliefs, strong ethical character, personal integrity, openness, and simplicity in communication.

**7** Identify communication technologies and how they affect the communication process.

Technologies such as cell phones, e-mail, voice mail, faxes, computers, and databases provide instant exchange of volumes of information and render geographic boundaries and time zones irrelevant. Lack of personal interaction and nonverbal cues alter the social context of exchange and remove organizational barriers. The potential for information overload, constant accessibility to work, and multitasking also affect behaviour.

**one-way communication**

Communication in which a person sends a message to another person and no feedback, questions, or interaction follows.

**organizational grapevine**

Informal, uncensored communication network.

**barriers to communication**

Aspects of the communication content and context that can impair effective communication in a workplace.

**gateways to communication**

Pathways through barriers to communication and antidotes to communication problems.

**defensive communication**

Communication that can be aggressive, attacking, and angry, or passive and withdrawing.

**nondefensive communication**

Communication that is assertive, direct, and powerful.

**nonverbal communication**

All elements of communication that do not involve words.

**communicative disease**

The absence of heartfelt communication in human relationships leading to loneliness and social isolation.

**information communication technology (ICT)**

The various new technologies, such as e-mail, voice mail, teleconferencing, and wireless access, which are used for interpersonal communication.

## What about You? Are You an Active Listener?

Reflective listening is a skill that you can practise and learn. Here are ten tips to help you become a better listener.

1. Stop talking. You cannot listen if your mouth is moving.
2. Put the speaker at ease. Break the ice to help the speaker relax. Smile!
3. Show the speaker you want to listen. Put away your work. Do not look at your watch. Maintain good eye contact.
4. Remove distractions. Close your door. Do not answer the telephone.
5. Empathize with the speaker. Put yourself in the speaker's shoes.
6. Be patient. Not everyone delivers messages at the same pace.
7. Hold your temper. Do not fly off the handle.
8. Go easy on criticism. Criticizing the speaker can stifle communication.
9. Ask questions. Paraphrase and clarify the speaker's message.
10. Stop talking. By this stage, you are probably very tempted to start talking, but do not. Be sure the speaker has finished.

Think of the last time you had a difficult communication with someone at work or school. Evaluate yourself in that situation against each of the ten items. Which one(s) do you need to improve on the most?

# Key Terms

**group**
Two or more people with common interests, objectives, and continuing interaction.

**work team**
A group of people with complementary skills who are committed to a common mission, performance goals, and approach for which they hold themselves mutually accountable.

**teamwork**
Joint action by a team of people in which individual interests are subordinated to team unity.

**psychological intimacy**
Emotional and psychological closeness to other team or group members.

**integrated involvement**
Closeness achieved through tasks and activities.

**norms of behaviour**
The standards that a work group uses to evaluate the behaviour of its members.

**group cohesion**
The "interpersonal glue" that makes members of a group stick together.

**social loafing**
The failure of a group member to contribute personal time, effort, thoughts, or other resources to the group.

**loss of individuality**
A social process in which individual group members lose self-awareness and its accompanying sense of accountability, inhibition, and responsibility for individual behaviour.

**status structure**
The set of authority and task relations among a group's members.

**task function**
An activity directly related to the effective completion of a team's work.

## Work Teams and Groups

**1** Define *group* and *work team*.

A *group* is two or more people having common interests, objectives, and continuing interaction. A *work team* is a group of people with complementary skills who are committed to a common mission, performance goals, and approach for which they hold themselves mutually accountable.

**2** Explain the benefits organizations and individuals derive from working in teams.

Teams are very useful in performing work that is complicated, complex, interrelated, and/or more voluminous than one person can handle. Teams combine knowledge, talent, skills, and abilities dispersed across organizational members and integrate effort for task accomplishment. On an individual level, members benefit from psychological intimacy and achieving integrated involvement.

**3** Identify the factors that influence group behaviour.

*Group norms* of cooperative behaviour facilitate team performance and effectiveness. *Group cohesion* can enhance job satisfaction and improve productivity. Social loafing, member failure to contribute time, effort, thoughts, or other resources to a group, may negate the group's efforts and achievements. With loss of individuality, members may lose the sense of accountability, inhibition, and responsibility for individual behaviour.

**4** Describe how groups form and develop.

Groups, formal and informal, go through stages of development to become mature and productive units. Mature groups work through the necessary interpersonal, task, and authority issues to achieve at high levels. Demographic diversity and group fault lines are potential predictors of the sensemaking process, subgroup formation patterns, and nature of group conflict at various stages of group development.

**5** Explain how task and maintenance functions influence group performance.

Effective groups carry out various task functions to perform work successfully and do maintenance functions to ensure member satisfaction and a sense of team spirit. Teams that successfully fulfill these functions afford members the potential for the social benefits of psychological intimacy and integrated involvement.

**6** Discuss the factors that influence group effectiveness.

Work team effectiveness in the new team environment requires management's attention to both work team structure and work team process. In addition to how the team is structured and what the team does, diversity and creativity are two areas with significant impact on team performance.

**7** Describe how empowerment relates to self-managed teams.

Empowerment, an organizational attribute, encourages participation, an essential ingredient for teamwork. Empowered *self-managed teams,* designed to take on responsibilities and address issues traditionally reserved for management, succeed through development of competence skills, process skills, communication skills, and cooperative and helping behaviours.

**maintenance function**
An activity essential to effective, satisfying interpersonal relationships within a team or group.

**self-managed team**
A team that makes decisions that were once reserved for managers.

**upper echelon**
A top-level executive team in an organization.

**8** Explain the importance of upper echelons and top management teams.

Self-managed teams at the top of the organization are referred to as *upper echelons.* Organizations are often a reflection of these upper echelons. Upper echelon theory argues that background characteristics of the top management team can predict organizational characteristics and set standards for values, competence, ethics, and unique characteristics throughout the organization.

## What about You? How Cohesive Is Your Group?

Think about a group of which you are a member. Answer each of the following questions in relation to this group by circling the number next to the alternative that best reflects your feelings.

**1.** Do you feel that you are really a part of your group?
   5—Really a part of the group.
   4—Included in most ways.
   3—Included in some ways, but not in others.
   2—Do not feel I really belong.
   1—Do not work with any one group of people.

**2.** If you had a chance to do the same activities in another group, for the same pay if it is a work group, how would you feel about moving?
   1—Would want very much to move.
   2—Would rather move than stay where I am.
   3—Would make no difference to me.
   4—Would rather stay where I am than move.
   5—Would want very much to stay where I am.

**3.** How does your group compare with other groups with which you are familiar on each of the following points?
   • The way people get along together.
     5—Better than most.
     3—About the same as most.
     1—Not as good as most.
   • The way people stick together.
     5—Better than most.
     3—About the same as most.
     1—Not as good as most.
   • The way people help one another on the job.
     5—Better than most.
     3—About the same as most.
     1—Not as good as most.

Add up your circled responses. If you have a number of 20 or above, you view your group as highly cohesive. If you have a number between 10 and 19, you view your group's cohesion as average. If you have a number of 7 or less, you view your group as very low in cohesion.

SOURCE: From S. E. Seashore, *Group Cohesiveness in the Industrial Work Group,* University of Michigan, 1954. Reprinted by permission.

# Chapter 10

## Key Terms

**programmed decision**
A simple, routine matter for which a manager has an established decision rule.

**nonprogrammed decision**
A new, complex decision that requires a creative solution.

**effective decision**
A timely decision that meets a desired objective and is acceptable to those individuals affected by it.

**rationality**
A logical, step-by-step approach to decision making, with a thorough analysis of alternatives and their consequences.

**bounded rationality**
A theory that suggests that there are limits to how rational a decision maker can actually be.

**satisfice**
To select the first alternative that is "good enough," because the costs in time and effort are too great to optimize.

**heuristics**
Shortcuts in decision making that save mental activity.

**garbage can model**
Decision making is a process of organizational anarchy.

**escalation of commitment**
The tendency to continue to support a failing course of action.

**cognitive style**
An individual's preference for gathering information and evaluating alternatives.

**risk aversion**
The tendency to choose options that entail fewer risks and less uncertainty.

**intuition**
A fast, positive force in decision making that is utilized at a level below consciousness and involves learned patterns of information.

## >> In Review

### Decision Making by Individuals and Groups

**1** Identify the steps in the decision-making process.

The decision-making process involves *programmed decisions* and *nonprogrammed decisions*. The first step is recognizing the problem or realizing a decision must be made. Second, the objective of the decision is identified. The third step is gathering information relevant to the problem. The fourth step is listing and evaluating alternative courses of action. Finally, the manager selects the alternative that best meets the decision objective.

**2** Describe various models of decision making.

The *rational model* of decision making contends that the decision maker is completely rational in his or her approach. *Bounded rationality* theory suggests that constraints force decision makers to be less rational, and assumes that managers satisfice and develop heuristics. The Vroom-Yetton-Jago model is normative and gives managers guidance on the appropriate degree of employee participation in decision-making. The Z problem-solving model capitalizes on the strengths of four separate preferences (sensing, intuiting, thinking, and feeling), allowing managers to use preferences and nonpreferences to make decisions. The garbage can model emphasizes the chaotic nature of decision making where problems and solutions are often loosely coupled.

**3** Discuss the individual influences that affect decision making.

Decisions reflect the people who make them. The individual influences that affect decision making are comfort for risk, cognitive style, personality, intuition, and creativity.

**4** Explain how groups make decisions.

Group decisions are utilized for several reasons: *synergy,* to gain commitment to a decision, and to maximize knowledge and experience in problem-solving situations. Seven techniques utilized in group decisions are brainstorming, nominal group technique, devil's advocacy, dialectical inquiry, quality circles, quality teams, and self-managed teams.

**5** Describe the role culture plays in decision making.

Styles of decision making vary greatly among cultures and affect the way people view decisions. The dimensions proposed by Hofstede in Chapter 2 that affect decision making are uncertainty avoidance, power distance, individualist/collectivist, time orientation, and masculine/feminine.

**6** Explain how organizations can improve the quality of decisions through participation.

*Participative decision making* can include employees identifying problems, generating alternatives, selecting solutions, planning implementations, and/or evaluating results. Participative management can increase employee creativity, job satisfaction, productivity, and improve an organization's economic performance.

## Glossary (left column)

**creativity**
A process influenced by individual and organizational factors that results in the production of novel and useful ideas, products, or both.

**synergy**
A positive force that occurs in groups when group members stimulate new solutions to problems through the process of mutual influence and encouragement within the group.

**social decision schemes**
Simple rules used to determine final group decisions.

**groupthink**
A deterioration of mental efficiency, reality testing, and moral judgment resulting from pressures within the group.

**group polarization**
The tendency for group discussion to produce shifts toward more extreme attitudes among members.

**brainstorming**
A technique for generating as many ideas as possible on a given subject, while suspending evaluation until all the ideas have been suggested.

**nominal group technique (NGT)**
A structured approach to group decision making that focuses on generating alternatives and choosing one.

**devil's advocacy**
A technique for preventing groupthink in which a group or individual is given the role of critic during decision making.

**dialectical inquiry**
A debate between two opposing sets of recommendations.

**quality circle**
A small group of employees who work voluntarily on company time, typically one hour per week, to address work-related problems such as quality control, cost reduction, production planning and techniques, and even product design.

**quality team**
A team that is part of an organization's structure and is empowered to act on its decisions regarding product and service quality.

**participative decision making**
Decision making in which individuals who are affected by decisions influence the making of those decisions.

## What about You? Creative or Logical Problem Solving: What Is Your Preference?

Try the following creative problem-solving challenge.

Each of the following problems is an equation that can be solved by substituting the appropriate words for the letters. Have fun with them!

Examples:   3F = 1Y (3 feet = 1 yard.)        4LC = GL (4 leaf clover = Good luck.)

1. "1B in the H = 2 in the B."
2. 8D − 24H = 1W.
3. 3P = 6.
4. HH & MH at 12 = N or M.
5. 4J + 4Q + 4K = All the FC.
6. S & M & T & W & T & F & S are D of W.
7. T = LS State.
8. 23Y − 3Y = 2D.
9. E − 8 = Z.
10. Y + 2D = T.
11. C + 6D = NYE.
12. Y − S − S − A = W.
13. A & E were in the G of E.
14. My FL and South P are both MC.
15. "NN = GN."
16. 1 + 6Z = 1M.
17. "R = R = R."
18. N + V + P + A + A + C + P + I = P of S.

Now try the following logical problem-solving exercise, entitled "Who Owns the Fish?", which is attributed to Albert Einstein.

There are five houses in a row and in five different colours. In each house lives a person from a different country. Each person drinks a certain drink, plays a certain game, and keeps a certain pet. No two people drink the same drink, play the same game, or keep the same pet.

> The English person lives in a red house.
> The Swede keeps dogs.
> The Dane drinks tea.
> The green house is on the left of the white house.
> The green house owner drinks coffee.
> The person who plays tennis rears birds.
> The owner of the yellow house plays chess.
> The man living in the house right in the center drinks milk.
> The Norwegian lives in the first house.
> The man who plays poker lives next to the man who keeps cats.
> The man who keeps horses lives next to the one who plays chess.
> The man who plays billiards drinks beer.
> The German plays golf.
> The Norwegian lives next to the blue house.
> The man who plays poker has a neighbour who drinks water.

**Question:** Who owns the fish?
**Answer:** Your instructor can provide the solutions to this exercise.

SOURCE: From A Whack on the Side of the Head by Roger Von Oech. Copyright © 1983, 1990, 1998 by Roger Von Oech. By permission of Warner Books.

SOURCE: By E. O. Welles, © 2004 Gruner 1 Jahr USA Publishing. "The Billionaire Next Door," first published in Inc. Magazine 23(6) (May 2001): pp. 80–85. Reprinted with permission.

## Key Terms

**power**
The ability to influence another person; a relationship of asymmetric dependence.

**influence**
The process of affecting the thoughts, behaviour, and feelings of another person.

**authority**
The right to influence another person.

**zone of indifference**
The range in which attempts to influence a person will be perceived as legitimate and will be acted on without a great deal of thought.

**reward power**
Power based on an agent's ability to control rewards that a target wants.

**legitimate power**
Power that is based on position and mutual agreement; agent and target agree that the agent has the right to influence the target.

**referent power**
An elusive power that is based on interpersonal attraction.

**expert power**
The power that exists when an agent has specialized knowledge or skills that the target needs.

**coercive power**
Power that is based on an agent's ability to cause an unpleasant experience for a target.

**strategic contingencies**
Activities that other groups depend on in order to complete their tasks.

**information power**
Access to and control over important information.

**personal power**
Power used for personal gain.

## Power and Political Behaviour

**1** Describe the concept of power.

Power is the ability to influence others. Influence is the process of affecting the thoughts, behaviours, and feelings of others. Authority is the right to influence others. Power is an exchange relationship.

**2** Identify forms and sources of power in organizations.

Power in organizations can be categorized simply as interpersonal or intergroup. French and Raven's five forms of interpersonal power are reward, coercive, legitimate, referent, and expert power. Information power is another form of interpersonal power. Bullying is one type of coercive power that is quite prevalent in organizations. Intergroup power derives from control of critical resources and of strategic contingencies. To have control over contingencies, a group must be able to cope with uncertainty, have a high degree of centrality, and perform a function indispensable to the organization.

**3** Describe the role of ethics in using power.

The key to using all of these types of power well is to use them ethically. McClelland believes personal power is negative and social power is positive. That is, when power is used for the good of the group rather than for individual gain, the power is positive.

**4** Identify symbols of power and powerlessness in organizations.

Two theorists examine symbols of power. Rosabeth Moss Kanter's list of symbols is grounded in doing things for others: for people in trouble, for employees, for bosses. There is an active, other-directed element in her symbols. Michael Korda's list focuses on status and whether there are more people for whom you would inconvenience yourself than people who would inconvenience themselves for you.

**5** Define organizational politics and understand the role of political skill and major influence tactics.

Organizational politics is an inevitable feature of work life. Political behaviour consists of actions not officially sanctioned that are taken to influence others in order to meet personal goals. Managers should take a proactive role in managing politics. Political skill is the ability to get things done through favourable interpersonal relationships outside formally prescribed organizational mechanisms.

**6** Identify ways to manage political behaviour in organizations.

To manage political behaviour in their employees, managers can use open communication; clarify expectations regarding employee performance; use participative management techniques; encourage cooperation among work groups; manage scarce resources well; and provide a supportive organizational climate. Individuals must also manage up, that is, manage the boss. The biggest trump to political behaviour is empowerment.

## social power
Power used to create motivation or to accomplish group goals.

## powerlessness
A lack of power.

## organizational politics
The use of power and influence in organizations.

## political behaviour
Actions not officially sanctioned by an organization that are taken to influence others in order to meet personal goals.

## political skill
The ability to get things done through favourable interpersonal relationships outside formally prescribed organizational mechanisms.

## empowerment
Sharing power within an organization.

## What about You? How Politically Skilled Are You?

Using the following 7-point scale, please place the number on the blank before each item that best describes how much you agree with each statement about yourself.

1 = *strongly disagree*
2 = *disagree*
3 = *slightly disagree*
4 = *neutral*
5 = *slightly agree*
6 = *agree*
7 = *strongly agree*

1. _____ I spend a lot of time and effort at work networking with others.
2. _____ I am able to make most people feel comfortable and at ease around me.
3. _____ I am able to communicate easily and effectively with others.
4. _____ It is easy for me to develop good rapport with most people.
5. _____ I understand people very well.
6. _____ I am good at building relationships with influential people at work.
7. _____ I am particularly good at sensing the motivations and hidden agendas of others.
8. _____ When communicating with others, I try to be genuine in what I say and do.
9. _____ I have developed a large network of colleagues and associates at work whom I can call on for support when I really need to get things done.
10. _____ At work, I know a lot of important people and am well connected.
11. _____ I spend a lot of time at work developing connections with others.
12. _____ I am good at getting people to like me.
13. _____ It is important that people believe I am sincere in what I say and do.
14. _____ I try to show a genuine interest in other people.
15. _____ I am good at using my connections and network to make things happen at work.
16. _____ I have good intuition or savvy about how to present myself to others.
17. _____ I always seem to instinctively know the right things to say or do to influence others.
18. _____ I pay close attention to people's facial expressions.

A higher score indicates better political skill than a lower score.

# Key Terms

**leadership**
The process of guiding and directing the behaviour of people in the work environment.

**formal leadership**
Officially sanctioned leadership based on the authority of a formal position.

**informal leadership**
Unofficial leadership accorded to a person by other members of the organization.

**leader**
An advocate for change and new approaches to problems.

**manager**
An advocate for stability and the status quo.

**autocratic style**
A style of leadership in which the leader uses strong, directive, controlling actions to enforce the rules, regulations, activities, and relationships in the work environment.

**democratic style**
A style of leadership in which the leader takes collaborative, responsive, interactive actions with followers concerning the work and work environment.

**laissez-faire style**
A style of leadership in which the leader fails to accept the responsibilities of the position.

**initiating structure**
Leader behaviour aimed at defining and organizing work relationships and roles, as well as establishing clear patterns of organization, communication, and ways of getting things done.

**consideration**
Leader behaviour aimed at nurturing friendly, warm working relationships, as well as encouraging mutual trust and interpersonal respect within the work unit.

# Leadership and Followership

**1** Discuss the differences between leadership and management and between leaders and managers.

Leadership is the process of guiding and directing behaviour of people in the work environment. The management process reduces uncertainty and stabilizes an organization. *Leaders* agitate for change and new approaches; in contrast, *managers* advocate stability and the status quo. They differ along four separate dimensions of personality: attitudes toward goals, conceptions of work, relationships with other people, and sense of self.

**2** Explain the role of trait theory in describing leaders.

The first studies of leadership attempted to identify what physical attributes, personality characteristics, and abilities distinguished leaders from other members of a group. The trait theories have had very limited success in being able to identify the universal, distinguishing attributes of leaders.

**3** Describe the role of foundational behavioural research in the development of leadership theories.

Behavioural theories address how leaders behave. The Lewin, Lippitt, and White studies identified three basic leadership styles: autocratic, democratic, and laissez-faire. Ohio State University measured specific leader behaviours—initiating structure and consideration. University of Michigan studies suggest two styles of leadership: employee oriented and production oriented.

**4** Describe and compare the three contingency theories of leadership.

Fiedler's contingency theory proposes that the fit between the leader's need structure and the favourableness of the leader's situation determine the team's effectiveness in work accomplishment. The role of the leader in path–goal theory is to clear the follower's path to the goal. Situational leadership theory suggests that the leader's behaviour should be adjusted to the maturity level of the followers.

**5** Discuss the recent developments in leadership theory of leader–member exchange and inspirational leadership.

With leader–member exchange theory (LMX), leaders form *in-groups* whose members work within the leader's inner circle and *out-groups* whose members are outside the circle. In-group members receive greater responsibilities, more rewards, and more attention. Inspirational leadership theories, *transformational leadership, charismatic leadership*, and *authentic leadership* can result in positive, productive member behaviour because followers are inspired by the leader to perform well.

**6** Discuss how issues of emotional intelligence, trust, gender, and servant leadership are informing today's leadership models.

Emerging issues regarding leadership traits leaders must be aware of focus on emotional intelligence, trust, women leaders, and servant leadership. These trait studies can affect leaders' decision-making skills, strategy implementation, and ability to build organizational citizenship behaviours. For women as leaders, the focus is shifting to behaviours and style rather than on gender stereotypes.

**7** Define *followership* and identify different types of followers.

The follower role has alternatively been cast as one of self-leadership in which the follower assumes responsibility for influencing his or her own performance. Five types of followers are *effective, alienated, sheep, yes people,* and *survivors.* They are identified based on two dimensions: (1) activity versus passivity and (2) independent, critical thinking versus dependent, uncritical thinking.

## Leadership Grid
An approach to understanding a leader's or manager's concern for results (production) and concern for people.

**organization man manager (5,5)**
A middle-of-the-road leader.

**authority-compliance manager (9,1)**
A leader who emphasizes efficient production.

**country club manager (1,9)**
A leader who creates a happy, comfortable work environment.

**team manager (9,9)**
A leader who builds a highly productive team of committed people.

**impoverished manager (1,1)**
A leader who exerts just enough effort to get by.

**paternalistic "father knows best" manager (9+9)**
A leader who promises reward and threatens punishment.

**opportunistic "what's in it for me" manager (Opp)**
A leader whose style aims to maximize self-benefit.

**least preferred coworker (LPC)**
The person with whom a leader can work the least well over his or her career.

**task structure**
The degree of clarity, or ambiguity, in the work activities assigned to the group.

**position power**
The authority associated with the leader's formal position in the organization.

**leader–member relations**
The quality of interpersonal relationships among a leader and the group members.

**charismatic leadership**
A leader's use of personal abilities and talents in order to have profound and extraordinary effects on followers.

**followership**
The process of being guided and directed by a leader in the work environment.

---

**8** Synthesize historical leadership research into key guidelines for leaders.

Leaders and organizations appreciate the unique attributes, predispositions, and talents of each leader. Leaders challenge the organizational culture, when necessary, without destroying it. Participative, considerate leader behaviours demonstrate a concern for people. Different leadership situations call for different leadership talents and behaviours. Good leaders are likely to be good followers.

---

**9** Learn about servant leadership in action.

The Free the Children account highlights the concept of service to the vulnerable, as Craig Kielburger, his brother Marc, and their friends acted to empower others to be free from harm and to have educational opportunities they would not otherwise have.

---

**What about You?** How Does Your Supervisor Lead?

Answer the following 16 questions concerning your supervisor's (or professor's) leadership behaviours using the seven-point Likert scale below. Then complete the summary to examine your supervisor's (or professor's) behaviours.

**Not at All**                                                                    **Very Much**
1 ---------- 2 ---------- 3 ---------- 4 ---------- 5 ---------- 6 ---------- 7

1. Is your superior strict about observing regulations? 1  2  3  4  5  6  7
2. To what extent does your superior give you instructions and orders?
   1  2  3  4  5  6  7
3. Is your superior strict about the amount of work you do? 1  2  3  4  5  6  7
4. Does your superior urge you to complete your work by the time he or she has specified?
   1  2  3  4  5  6  7
5. Does your superior try to make you work to your maximum capacity?
   1  2  3  4  5  6  7
6. When you do an inadequate job, does your superior focus on the inadequate way the job was done instead of on your personality? 1  2  3  4  5  6  7
7. Does your superior ask you for reports about the progress of your work?
   1  2  3  4  5  6  7
8. Does your superior work out precise plans for goal achievement each month?
   1  2  3  4  5  6  7
9. Can you talk freely with your superior about your work? 1  2  3  4  5  6  7
10. Generally, does your superior support you? 1  2  3  4  5  6  7
11. Is your superior concerned about your personal problems? 1  2  3  4  5  6  7
12. Do you think your superior trusts you? 1  2  3  4  5  6  7
13. Does your superior give you recognition when you do your job well?
    1  2  3  4  5  6  7
14. When a problem arises in your workplace, does your superior ask your opinion about how to solve it? 1  2  3  4  5  6  7
15. Is your superior concerned about your future benefits like promotions and pay raises?
    1  2  3  4  5  6  7
16. Does your superior treat you fairly? 1  2  3  4  5  6  7

Add up your answers to Questions 1 through 8. This total indicates your supervisor's (or professor's) performance orientation:

Task orientation = _____

Add up your answers to Questions 9 through 16. This total indicates your supervisor's (or professor's) maintenance orientation:

People orientation = _____

A score above 40 is high, and a score below 20 is low.

SOURCE: Reprinted from "The Performance-Maintenance Theory of Leadership: Review of a Japanese Research Program" by J. Misumi and M. F. Peterson, published in *Administrative Science Quarterly* 30 (1985): 207. By permission of *Administrative Science Quarterly* © 1985.

# Chapter 13

# >> In Review

## Conflict and Negotiation

**1** Describe the nature of conflicts in organizations.

*Conflict* is defined as any situation in which incompatible goals, attitudes, emotions, or behaviours lead to disagreement or opposition between two or more parties. *Functional conflict* is a healthy, constructive disagreement between two or more people. *Dysfunctional conflict* is an unhealthy, destructive disagreement between two or more people.

**2** Explain the role structural and personal factors play in causing conflict in organizations.

Conflict can be classified into categories: *structural factors* and *personal factors.* Structural factors include specialization, interdependence, common resources, goal differences, authority relationships, status inconsistencies, and jurisdictional ambiguities. The causes of conflict that arise from individual differences include skills and abilities, personalities, perceptions, values and ethics, emotions, communication barriers, and cultural differences.

**3** Discuss the nature of group conflict in organizations.

*Interorganizational conflict* occurs between two or more organizations. Conflict occurring between groups or teams is known as *intergroup conflict.* Positive effects can be increased group cohesiveness, task focus, and group loyalty. Negative consequences can be extreme competition, hostility, and decreased communication between groups. *Intragroup conflict* is within groups or teams and can serve to avoid groupthink.

|  | **GROUP** | **INDIVIDUAL** |
|---|---|---|
| INTER | interorganizational | interpersonal<br>> power networks<br>> defence mechanisms<br>> compromise mechanisms |
| INTRA | intragroup | intrapersonal<br>> interrole<br>> intrarole<br>> person–role conflict |

**4** Describe the factors that influence conflict between individuals in organizations.

*Intrapersonal conflict* occurs within an individual. Tips for managing intrapersonal conflict are to analyze and match your values with the organization's, understand expectations, and develop political skills. Conflict between two or more people, or *interpersonal conflict,* can arise from individual differences. To manage interpersonal conflict, it is helpful to understand power networks in organizations, defence mechanisms exhibited by individuals, and ways to cope with difficult people.

**5** Describe effective and ineffective techniques for managing conflict.

Effective conflict management techniques include appealing to superordinate goals, expanding resources, changing personnel, changing structure, confronting, negotiating, mediation, and arbitration. Ineffective techniques include nonaction, secrecy, administrative orbiting, due process nonaction, and character assassination.

## Key Terms

**functional conflict**
A healthy, constructive disagreement between two or more people.

**dysfunctional conflict**
An unhealthy, destructive disagreement between two or more people.

**jurisdictional ambiguity**
The presence of unclear lines of responsibility within an organization.

**interorganizational conflict**
Conflict that occurs between two or more organizations.

**intergroup conflict**
Conflict that occurs between groups or teams in an organization.

**intragroup conflict**
Conflict that occurs within groups or teams.

**intrapersonal conflict**
Conflict that occurs within an individual.

**interrole conflict**
A person's experience of conflict among the multiple roles in his or her life.

**intrarole conflict**
Conflict that occurs within a single role, such as when a person receives conflicting messages from role senders about how to perform a certain role.

**person–role conflict**
Conflict that occurs when an individual is expected to perform behaviours in a certain role that conflict with his or her personal values.

**interpersonal conflict**
Conflict that occurs between two or more individuals.

**fixation**
An aggressive mechanism in which an individual keeps up a dysfunctional behaviour that obviously will not solve the conflict.

>>

**displacement**
An aggressive mechanism in which an individual directs his or her anger toward someone who is not the source of the conflict.

**negativism**
An aggressive mechanism in which a person responds with pessimism to any attempt at solving a problem.

**compensation**
A compromise mechanism in which an individual attempts to make up for a negative situation by devoting himself or herself to another pursuit with increased vigour.

**identification**
A compromise mechanism whereby an individual patterns his or her behaviour after another's.

**rationalization**
A compromise mechanism characterized by an individual trying to justify his or her behaviour by constructing bogus reasons for it.

**flight/withdrawal**
A withdrawal mechanism that entails physically escaping a conflict (flight) or psychologically escaping (withdrawal).

**conversion**
A withdrawal mechanism in which emotional conflicts are expressed in physical symptoms.

**fantasy**
A withdrawal mechanism that provides an escape from a conflict through daydreaming.

**nonaction**
Doing nothing in hopes that a conflict will disappear.

**secrecy**
Attempting to hide a conflict or an issue that has the potential to create conflict.

**administrative orbiting**
Delaying action on a conflict by buying time.

**due process nonaction**
A procedure set up to address conflicts that is so costly, time consuming, or personally risky that no one will use it.

**character assassination**
An attempt to label or discredit an opponent.

**superordinate goal**
An organizational goal that is more important to both parties in a conflict than their individual or group goals.

**distributive bargaining**
A negotiation approach in which the goals of the parties are in conflict, and each party seeks to maximize its resources.

**integrative negotiation**
A negotiation approach that focuses on the merits of the issues and seeks a win–win solution.

---

**6** Identify five styles of conflict management.

Managers have at their disposal a variety of conflict management styles: avoiding, accommodating, competing, compromising, and collaborating. One way of classifying styles of conflict management is to examine the styles' assertiveness (the extent to which you want your goals met) and cooperativeness (the extent to which you want to see the other party's concerns met).

---

## What about You? What Is Your Conflict-Handling Style?

**Instructions:**

For each of the fifteen items, indicate how often you rely on that tactic by selecting the appropriate number.

```
Rarely                                                              Always
   1 ------------------ 2 ------------------ 3 ------------------ 4 ------------------ 5
```

1. I argue my case with my coworkers to show the merits of my position.
2. I negotiate with my coworkers so that a compromise can be reached.
3. I try to satisfy the expectations of my coworkers.
4. I try to investigate an issue with my coworkers to find a solution acceptable to us.
5. I am firm in pursuing my side of the issue.
6. I attempt to avoid being "put on the spot" and try to keep my conflict with my coworkers to myself.
7. I hold on to my solution to a problem.
8. I use "give and take" so that a compromise can be made.
9. I exchange accurate information with my coworkers to solve a problem together.
10. I avoid open discussion of my differences with my coworkers.
11. I accommodate the wishes of my coworkers.
12. I try to bring all our concerns out in the open so that the issues can be resolved in the best possible way.
13. I propose a middle ground for breaking deadlocks.
14. I go along with the suggestions of my coworkers.
15. I try to keep my disagreements with my coworkers to myself in order to avoid hard feelings.

**Scoring Key:**

| Collaborating Item Score | Accommodating Item Score | Competing Item Score | Avoiding Item Score | Compromising Item Score |
|---|---|---|---|---|
| 4. ____ | 3. ____ | 1. ____ | 6. ____ | 2. ____ |
| 9. ____ | 11. ____ | 5. ____ | 10. ____ | 8. ____ |
| 12. ____ | 14. ____ | 7. ____ | 15. ____ | 13. ____ |
| Total = ____ | Total = ____ | Total = ____ | Total = ____ | Total = ____ |

Your primary conflict-handling style is: _____
(The category with the highest total.)

Your backup conflict-handling style is: _____
(The category with the second highest total.)

SOURCE: Reprinted with permission of Academy of Management, PO Box 3020, Briarcliff Manor, NY 10510-8020. *A Measure of Styles of Handling Interpersonal Conflict* (Adaptation), M. A. Rahim, *Academy of Management Journal,* June 1983. Reproduced by permission of the publisher via Copyright Clearance Center, Inc.

## Key Terms

**work**
Mental or physical activity that has productive results.

**job**
A set of specified work and task activities that engage an individual in an organization.

**work simplification**
Standardization and the narrow, explicit specification of task activities for workers.

**job enlargement**
A method of job design that increases the number of activities in a job to overcome the boredom of overspecialized work.

**job rotation**
A variation of job enlargement in which workers are exposed to a variety of specialized jobs over time.

**cross-training**
A variation of job enlargement in which workers are trained in different specialized tasks or activities.

**job enrichment**
Designing or redesigning jobs by incorporating motivational factors into them.

**job characteristics model (JCM)**
A framework for understanding person–job fit through the interaction of core job dimensions with critical psychological states within a person.

**Job Diagnostic Survey (JDS)**
The survey instrument designed to measure the elements in the Job Characteristics Model.

**social information-processing (SIP) model**
A model that suggests that the important job factors depend in part on what others tell a person about the job.

## Jobs and the Design of Work

**1** Differentiate between *job* and *work*.

A *job* is an employee's specific work and task activities in an organization. *Work* is effortful, productive activity resulting in a product or a service. A job is composed of a set of specific tasks, each of which is an assigned piece of work to be done in a specific time period. Work is an especially important human endeavour because it has a powerful effect in binding a person to reality.

**2** Explain how job enlargement and job enrichment counter Taylor's scientific management concepts.

Scientific management focuses on work simplification. The other approaches move away from work simplification. Job enlargement adds tasks to a job in order to overcome the limitations of specialized work, such as boredom. Job enrichment incorporates motivating factors into job design, such as responsibility and opportunities to achieve.

**3** Explain the job characteristics model, and how it has been expanded by subsequent research.

The JCM suggests that five core job characteristics (skill variety, task identity, task significance, autonomy, feedback from the job) create the critical psychological states of experienced meaningfulness of work, experienced responsibility for work, and knowledge of outcomes. These motivate the employee to work hard and enjoy the job. Further research refined the core characteristics (e.g., types of autonomy) and added many broad categories: social, knowledge, work context.

**4** Describe the concepts of social information processing (SIP) and job crafting.

SIP indicates that employees are more influenced by their subjective perception of the job than the objective facts of job design, and the perception is heavily influenced by social cues about the tasks from those around them. Job crafting suggests people are active architects in shaping their own jobs.

**5** Identify and describe contemporary issues facing organizations in the design of work.

Contemporary job design issues include telecommuting, alternative work patterns, technology at work, and skill development. Work is relationally designed to provide opportunities and increase flexibility for employees. Companies use these and other approaches to the design of work as ways to manage a growing business while contributing to a better balance of work and family life for employees.

>>

**job crafting**
Employees take the initiative to redefine their jobs.

**i-deals**
Customized employment terms negotiated between employees and their supervisors.

**technocentric**
Placing technology and engineering at the centre of job design decisions.

**anthropocentric**
Placing human considerations at the centre of job design decisions.

**telecommuting**
Employees work away from the company (typically at home) through the use of technology.

**job sharing**
A permanent work arrangement where two or more employees voluntarily share or split one full-time position.

**compressed work week**
Employees work longer shifts in exchange for a reduction in the number of working days.

**flextime**
An alternative work pattern that enables employees to set their own daily work schedules outside of core operational hours.

**virtual office**
A mobile platform of computer, telecommunication, and information technology and services.

**technostress**
The stress caused by new and advancing technologies in the workplace.

---

## What about You? Is Your Work Environment a Healthy One?

To determine whether your work environment is a healthy one, complete the following four steps. Answer each question in the five steps "yes" or "no."

**Step 1.** Control and Influence
_____ Do you have influence over the pace of your work?
_____ Are system response times neither too fast nor too slow?
_____ Do you have a say in your work assignments and goals?
_____ Is there an opportunity for you to comment on your performance appraisal?

**Step 2.** Information and Uncertainty
_____ Do you receive timely information to complete your work?
_____ Do you receive complete information for your work assignments?
_____ Is there adequate planning for changes that affect you at work?
_____ Do you have access to all the information you need at work?

**Step 3.** Conflict at Work
_____ Does the company apply policies clearly and consistently?
_____ Are job descriptions and task assignments clear and unambiguous?
_____ Are there adequate policies and procedures for the resolution of conflicts?
_____ Is your work environment an open, participative one?

**Step 4.** Job Scope and Task Design
_____ Is there adequate variety in your work activities and/or assignments?
_____ Do you receive timely, constructive feedback on your work?
_____ Is your work important to the overall mission of the company?
_____ Do you work on more than one small piece of a big project?

### Scoring:

Count the number of "yes" answers in Steps 1 through 4: _____

If you have 10 to 16 "yes" answers, this suggests that your work environment is a psychologically healthy one.

If you have 7 or fewer "yes" answers, this may suggest that your work environment is not as psychologically healthy as it could be.

# Chapter 15

## Key Terms

**organizational design**
The process of constructing and adjusting an organization's structure to achieve its goals.

**organizational structure**
The linking of departments and jobs within an organization.

**differentiation**
The process of deciding how to divide the work in an organization.

**integration**
The process of coordinating the different parts of an organization.

**formalization**
The degree to which the organization has official rules, regulations, and procedures.

**centralization**
The degree to which decisions are made at the top of the organization.

**specialization**
The degree to which jobs are narrowly defined and depend on unique expertise.

**standardization**
The degree to which work activities are accomplished in a routine fashion.

**complexity**
The degree to which many different types of activities occur in the organization.

**hierarchy of authority**
The degree of vertical differentiation across levels of management.

**span of control**
The number of employees reporting to a supervisor.

**mechanistic structure**
An organizational design that emphasizes structured activities, specialized tasks and centralized decision making.

**organic structure**
An organizational design that emphasizes teamwork, open communication, and decentralized decision making.

## >> In Review

### Organizational Design and Structure

**1** Explain what aspects of organizational structure are represented on an organizational chart.

An organizational chart shows the formal lines of authority and responsibility, the basis on which people are grouped for reporting purposes, and the formal systems of communication and coordination.

**2** Discuss the basic design dimensions managers must consider in structuring an organization.

Basic design dimensions combine to yield various structural configurations. Structural dimensions include the following: formalization, centralization, specialization, standardization, complexity, and hierarchy of authority. Henry Mintzberg's alternative approach is to describe what is and is not important to the success of the organization and design structures that fit each organization's unique set of circumstances

| BASIC DESIGN DIMENSIONS | SMALL ORGANIZATIONS | LARGE ORGANIZATIONS |
|---|---|---|
| FORMALIZATION | Less | More |
| CENTRALIZATION | High | Low |
| SPECIALIZATION | Low | High |
| STANDARDIZATION | Low | High |
| COMPLEXITY | Low | High |
| HIERARCHY OF AUTHORITY | Flat | Tall |

**3** Describe the basic organizational structures: simple, functional, divisional, matrix.

Simple structures are a centralized form of organization typical of a small company, emphasizing direct supervision and low formalization. Functional structures group people according to functional role (e.g., finance, marketing, production) whereas divisional structures group employees according to product, service, client, or geography. The matrix structure combines functional and divisional forms, typically through the use of project teams whose members report both to the project manager and their functional supervisors.

**4** Describe four contextual variables that influence organizational structure.

Four variables influence the success of an organization's design: size, technology, environment, and strategy and goals. These variables provide a manager with key considerations for the right organizational design. The relationship to size is evident in the table in answer #2 above. Regarding technology, the less routine an organization's technology is, the greater the need for an organic structure whereas companies with routine activities are best supported by a mechanistic structure. The more uncertain and dynamic the environment, the more an organic structure offers the needed flexibility and responsiveness. Strategy also links to structural fit, e.g., an organization that strategically focuses on cost leadership will likely use a mechanistic structure.

**simple structure**
A centralized form of organization that emphasizes direct supervision and low formalization.

**functional structure**
A form of organization that groups people according to the function they perform.

**divisionalized structure**
A form of organization that groups employees according to product, service, client, or geography.

**matrix structure**
A dual-authority form of structure that combines functional and divisional structures, typically through project teams.

**contextual variables**
A set of characteristics that influence the organization's design processes.

**technological interdependence**
The degree of interrelatedness of the organization's various technological elements.

**environment**
Anything outside the boundaries of an organization.

**environmental uncertainty**
The amount and rate of change in the organization's environment.

**organizational life cycle**
The differing stages of an organization's life from birth to death.

**5** Explain the forces reshaping organizations.

Several forces reshaping organizations are causing managers to go beyond the traditional frameworks and to examine ways to make organizations more responsive to customer needs. Some of these forces include shorter organizational life cycles, globalization, and rapid changes in information technology. These forces together increase the demands on process capabilities within the organization and emerging organizational structures. To successfully retain their health and vitality, organizations must function as open systems that are responsive to their task environment.

**6** Identify and describe emerging organizational structures.

Network organizations are weblike structures that contract some or all of their operating functions to other organizations and then coordinate their activities through managers and other employees at their headquarters. Virtual organizations are temporary network organizations consisting of independent enterprises.

**7** Identify the consequences of an inappropriate structure.

If organizational structure is out of alignment with its contextual variables, one or more of the following symptoms appears: delayed decision making, low-quality decision making, non-response to changing environment, and interdepartment conflict.

## What about You? Managers of Today and the Future

Are the roles for managers in your organization more oriented toward today or toward the future? (If you do not work, think of an organization where you have worked or talk with a friend about managerial roles in his or her organization.)

**Step 1.** Reread Table 15.2 at the end of the chapter and check which orientation (today or future) predominates in your organization for each of the following seven characteristics:

|   | **Today** | **Future** |
|---|---|---|
| **1.** Boss–employee relationships. | _____ | _____ |
| **2.** Getting work accomplished. | _____ | _____ |
| **3.** Messenger versus problem solver. | _____ | _____ |
| **4.** Basis for task accomplishment. | _____ | _____ |
| **5.** Narrow versus broad functional focus. | _____ | _____ |
| **6.** Adherence to channels of authority. | _____ | _____ |
| **7.** Controlling versus coaching subordinates. | _____ | _____ |

**Step 2.** Examine the degree of consistency across all seven characteristics. Could the organization make one or two structural changes to achieve a better alignment of the manager's role with today or with the future?

**Step 3.** Identify one manager in your organization who fits very well into the organization's ideal manager's role. What does this manager do that creates a good person–role fit?

**Step 4.** Identify one manager in your organization who does not fit very well into the organization's ideal manager's role. What does this manager do that creates a poor person–role fit?

## Organizational Culture

**Key Terms**

**organizational (corporate) culture**
A pattern of basic assumptions that are considered valid and that are taught to new members as the way to perceive, think, and feel in the organization.

**artifacts**
Symbols of culture in the physical and social work environments.

**espoused values**
What members of an organization say they value.

**enacted values**
Values reflected in the way individuals actually behave.

**assumptions**
Deeply held beliefs that guide behaviour and tell members of an organization how to perceive and think about things.

**strong culture**
An organizational culture with a consensus on the values that drive the company and with an intensity that is recognizable even to outsiders.

**adaptive culture**
An organizational culture that encourages confidence and risk taking among employees, has leadership that produces change, and focuses on the changing needs of customers.

**subculture**
A subculture is the culture created within a subset of employees within the organization.

**organizational socialization**
The process by which newcomers are transformed from outsiders to participating, effective members of the organization.

**anticipatory socialization**
The first socialization stage, which encompasses all of the learning that takes place prior to the newcomer's first day on the job.

**1** Identify the three levels of culture and evaluate the roles they play in an organization.

*Organizational culture* is a pattern of basic assumptions considered valid and taught to new members as the way to perceive, think, and feel in the organization. *Artifacts* are cultural symbols in the physical and social work environments such as personal enactment, ceremonies and rites, stories, rituals, and symbols. Deeper level *values* reflect inherent beliefs, and *assumptions* guide behaviour and tell members of an organization how to perceive situations and people.

**2** Describe the four functions of culture within an organization.

Organizational culture serves four basic functions. First, culture provides a sense of identity to members and increases commitment to the organization. Second, culture provides a way for employees to interpret the meaning of organizational events. Third, culture reinforces the values in the organization. Finally, culture serves as a control mechanism for shaping behaviour.

**3** Explain the relationship between organizational culture and corporate performance.

A *strong culture* organization acts with a consensus on the values that drive the company and with an intensity that is recognizable even to outsiders. The "fit" perspective argues that a culture is good only if it fits the industry or the firm's strategy. Three particular industry characteristics may affect culture: the competitive environment, customer requirements, and societal expectations. An *adaptive culture* is a culture that encourages confidence and risk taking among employees, has leadership that produces change, and focuses on the changing needs of customers.

**4** Describe five ways leaders reinforce organizational culture.

Leaders play a critical role in shaping and reinforcing organizational culture. Managers need to create a positive culture through what they pay attention to, how they react to crises, how they behave, the way they allocate rewards, and how they hire and fire employees. Transformational leaders create a more adaptive culture, which in turn increases business unit performance.

**5** Describe the three stages of organizational socialization and the ways culture is communicated in each step.

Newcomers are transformed from outsiders to participating, effective members of the organization through *organizational socialization*. Three stages in the socialization process are *anticipatory socialization, encounter,* and *change and acquisition.* Through positive effective socialization, newcomers understand and adopt values and norms ensuring the company's culture and central values survive. Results can be good performance, high job satisfaction, and the intention to stay with the organization.

**6** Discuss how managers assess their organization's culture.

Both qualitative and quantitative methods can be used to assess organizational culture. The Organizational Culture Inventory (OCI) and the Kilmann-Saxton Culture-Gap Survey are quantitative tools. In the hopes of generating a more accurate assessment of organizational culture, managers combine multiple instruments, a practice called *triangulation.*

**7** Explain actions managers can take to change organizational culture.

Managers can use two approaches to change organizational culture: help current members buy into a new set of values, or add newcomers and socialize them into the organization and remove current members appropriately. Managers must send consistent messages about the new values and beliefs, provide credible communication, and live the new values. Cultural change can be assumed to be successful if new behaviour is intrinsically motivated.

**8** Identify the challenges organizations face developing positive, cohesive, cultures.

Positive, cohesive corporate culture may be difficult in mergers, acquisitions, and globalization due to possible conflicts between organizations and cultural diversity on a geographic level. Developing an ethical culture requires management modelling, promoting ethical norms, and trust. Developing a culture of empowerment and quality involves including employees in decision making, removing obstacles to their performance, and reinforcing the value of product and service.

## What about You? Organizational Culture and Ethics

Think about the organization you currently work for or one you know something about and complete the following Ethical Climate Questionnaire.

Use the scale below and write the number that best represents your answer in the space next to each item.

To what extent are the following statements true about your company?

| Completely false | Mostly false | Somewhat false | Somewhat true | Mostly true | Completely true |
|---|---|---|---|---|---|
| 0 | 1 | 2 | 3 | 4 | 5 |

_____ **1.** In this company, people are expected to follow their own personal and moral beliefs.

_____ **2.** People are expected to do anything to further the company's interests.

_____ **3.** In this company, people look out for each other's good.

_____ **4.** It is very important here to follow the company's rules and procedures strictly.

_____ **5.** In this company, people protect their own interests above other considerations.

_____ **6.** The first consideration is whether a decision violates any law.

_____ **7.** Everyone is expected to stick by company rules and procedures.

_____ **8.** The most efficient way is always the right way in this company.

_____ **9.** Our major consideration is what is best for everyone in the company.

_____ **10.** In this company, the law or ethical code of the profession is the major consideration.

_____ **11.** It is expected at this company that employees will always do what is right for the customer and the public.

To score the questionnaire, first add up your responses to questions 1, 3, 6, 9, 10, and 11. This is subtotal number 1. Next, reverse the scores on questions 2, 4, 5, 7, and 8 (5 = 0, 4 = 1, 3 = 2, 2 = 3, 1 = 4, 0 = 5). Add the reverse scores to form subtotal number 2. Add subtotal number 1 to subtotal number 2 for an overall score.

Subtotal 1 _____ + Subtotal 2 _____ = Overall Score _____.

Overall scores can range from 0 to 55. The higher the score, the more the organization's culture encourages ethical behaviour.

SOURCE: Reprinted from *Organizational Dynamics*, Autumn 1989, " An Ethical Weather Report: Assessing the Organization's Ethical Climate" by John B. Cullen et al. Copyright © 1989, with permission from Elsevier Science.

## Key Terms

**planned change**
Change resulting from a deliberate decision to alter the organization.

**unplanned change**
Change that is imposed on the organization and is often unforeseen.

**incremental change**
Change of a relatively small scope, such as making small improvements.

**strategic change**
Change of a larger scale, such as organizational restructuring.

**transformational change**
Change in which the organization moves to a radically different, and sometimes unknown, future state.

**change agent**
The individual or group that undertakes the task of introducing and managing a change in an organization.

**unfreezing**
The first step in Lewin's change model, in which individuals are encouraged to discard old behaviours by shaking up the equilibrium state that maintains the status quo.

**moving**
The second step in Lewin's change model, in which new attitudes, values, and behaviours are substituted for old ones.

**refreezing**
The final step in Lewin's change model, in which new attitudes, values, and behaviours are established as the new status quo.

**organization development (OD)**
A systematic approach to organizational improvement that applies behavioural science theory and research in order to increase individual and organizational well-being and effectiveness.

## Managing Change

**1** Identify the major external and internal forces for change in organizations.

*External* forces that demand change are globalization, workforce diversity, technological change, and managing ethical behaviour. *Internal* pressures for change are generally recognizable: declining effectiveness, crisis, changes in employee expectations, and work climate. Adaptiveness, flexibility, and responsiveness are characteristics of the organizations that will succeed in meeting the challenges of change.

**2** Describe how different types of change vary in scope.

Change can be of a relatively small scope, such as a modification in a work procedure (an *incremental change*) or of a larger scale, such as the restructuring of an organization (a *strategic change*). The most massive scope of change is *transformational change,* in which the organization moves to a radically different, and sometimes unknown, future state. One of the toughest decisions faced by leaders is the "pace" of change. Researchers agree that pace is important; however, they can't agree on which pace of change is most beneficial.

**3** Discuss methods organizations can use to manage resistance to change.

The contemporary view holds that resistance is simply a form of feedback and that this feedback can be used very productively to manage the change process. Three key strategies for managing resistance to change are communication, participation, and empathy and support.

**4** Explain Lewin's organizational change model.

Lewin's model, the idea of force field analysis, contends that a person's behaviour is the product of two opposing forces; one force pushes toward preserving the status quo and the other force pushes for change. Lewin's change model is a three-step process: *unfreezing*—encouraging individuals to discard old behaviours, *moving*—new attitudes, values, and behaviours are substituted for old ones, and *refreezing*—new attitudes, values, and behaviours are established as the new status quo.

**5** Explain how companies determine the need to conduct an organizational development intervention.

*Organization development (OD)* is a systematic approach to organizational improvement. The first step, the diagnosis, should pinpoint specific problems and areas in need of improvement. Six areas to examine carefully are the organization's purpose, structure, reward system, support systems, relationships, and leadership. A needs analysis then determines the skills and competencies that employees must have to achieve the goals of the change.

**6** Discuss the major group-focused techniques for organization development intervention.

Some OD intervention methods emphasize changing the organization itself or changing the work groups within the organization. Intervention methods in this category include survey feedback, management by objectives, product and service quality programs, team building, and process consultation. All the preceding OD methods focus on changing the organization or the work group.

**survey feedback**
A widely used method of intervention whereby employee attitudes are solicited using a questionnaire.

**management by objectives (MBO)**
An organization-wide intervention technique that involves joint goal setting between employees and managers.

**quality program**
A program that embeds product and service quality excellence in the organizational culture.

**team building**
An intervention designed to improve the effectiveness of a work group.

**process consultation**
An OD method that helps managers and employees improve the processes that are used in organizations.

**skills training**
Increasing the job knowledge, skills, and abilities that are necessary to do a job effectively.

**leadership training and development**
A variety of techniques that are designed to enhance individuals' leadership skills.

**executive coaching**
A technique in which managers or executives are paired with a coach in a partnership to help the executive perform more efficiently.

**job redesign**
An OD intervention method that alters jobs to improve the fit between individual skills and the demands of the job.

**7** Discuss the major individual-focused techniques for organization development intervention.

Managers have a host of organization development techniques to facilitate organizational change. Development efforts include skills training, leadership training and development, executive coaching, job redesign, health promotion programs, and career planning. Success depends on techniques used, competence of the change agent, the organization's readiness for change, and top management commitment. Programs do not drive change; business needs do.

## What about You? Applying Force Field Analysis

Think of a problem you are currently facing. An example would be trying to increase the amount of study time you devote to a particular class.

**1.** Describe the problem, as specifically as possible.

_____

_____

_____

_____

**2.** List the forces driving change on the arrows at the left side of the diagram.
**3.** List the forces restraining change on the arrows at the right side of the diagram.

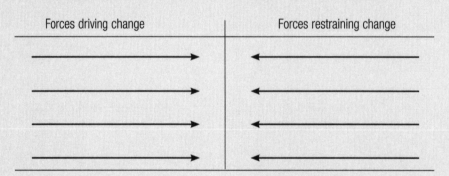

| Forces driving change | Forces restraining change |
|---|---|

**4.** What can you do, specifically, to remove the obstacles to change?

_____

_____

_____

**5.** What can you do to increase the forces driving change?

_____

_____

_____

**6.** What benefits can be derived from breaking a problem down into forces driving change and forces restraining change?

_____

_____

_____

## Career Management

**1** Explain occupational and organizational choice decisions.

Today a majority of workers no longer work in one organization for the length of their working life. The new career model is characterized by discrete exchange, occupational excellence, organizational empowerment, and project allegiance. When building a career, individuals first select an occupation that meets their needs, values, abilities, and preferences.

**2** Identify foundations for a successful career.

Two foundations for a successful career are becoming your own career coach and developing your emotional intelligence. To become your own career coach, you must acquire multiple skills, develop self-reliance, and cultivate a flexible, team-oriented attitude. Emotional competencies are of equal or greater importance than technical skills.

**3** Explain the career model.

The career stage model shows that individuals pass through four stages in their careers: establishment, advancement, maintenance, and withdrawal. Timing of career transitions varies greatly among individuals.

**4** Explain the major tasks facing individuals in the establishment stage of the career model.

*Establishment* is the first stage of a person's career. The activities that occur in this stage centre around learning the job and fitting into the organization and occupation. Individuals in this stage begin to work out their psychological contract with the organization and form attachment relationships with coworkers.

**5** Identify the issues confronting individuals in the advancement stage of the career model.

*Advancement* is a high achievement-oriented stage in which people focus on increasing their competence. A hallmark of this stage is the exploration of career paths, or sequences of job experiences along which employees move during their careers. Some companies use career lattices that move employees laterally through the organization in an attempt to build diverse skills. A mentor provides numerous sponsorship, facilitating, and psychosocial functions for the protégé. Dual-career partnerships are common now and can lead to work–home conflicts.

**6** Describe how individuals can navigate the challenges of the maintenance stage of the career model.

The *maintenance* stage finds the individual trying to maintain productivity while evaluating progress toward career goals. Individuals sustain their performance and continue to grow, although at a slower rate. Individuals in this stage may also become mentors.

**7** Explain how individuals withdraw from the workforce.

The *withdrawal* stage involves contemplation of retirement or possible career change. Increasingly, individuals in this stage are opting for phased retirement, which is a gradual cessation of work. To help workers at this stage of their careers, organizations should provide opportunities for continued involvement with the organization, such as mentoring to other employees making career transitions.

**8** Explain how career anchors help form a career identity.

Career anchors are self-perceived talents, motives, and values that guide an individual's career decisions. Five main anchors are technical/functional competence, managerial competence, autonomy and independence, creativity, and security/stability.

## Key Terms

**career**
The pattern of work-related experiences that span the course of a person's life.

**career management**
A lifelong process of learning about self, jobs, and organizations; setting personal career goals; developing strategies for achieving the goals, and revising the goals based on work and life experiences.

**realistic job preview (RJP)**
Both positive and negative information given to potential employees about the job they are applying for, thereby giving them a realistic picture of the job.

**establishment**
The first stage of a person's career in which the person learns the job and begins to fit into the organization and occupation.

**advancement**
The second, high achievement-oriented career stage in which people focus on increasing their competence.

**maintenance**
The third stage in an individual's career in which the individual tries to maintain productivity while evaluating progress toward career goals.

**withdrawal**
The final stage in an individual's career in which the individual contemplates retirement or possible career changes.

**psychological contract**
An implicit agreement between an individual and an organization that specifies what each is expected to give and receive in the relationship.

**career path**
A sequence of job experiences that an employee moves along during his or her career.

**career ladder**
A structured series of job positions through which an individual progresses in an organization.

**mentor**
An individual who provides guidance, coaching, counselling, and friendship to a protégé.

**dual-career partnership**
A relationship in which both people have important career roles.

**flexible work schedule**
A work schedule that allows employees discretion in order to accommodate personal concerns.

**eldercare**
Assistance in caring for elderly parents and/or other elderly relatives.

**career plateau**
A point in an individual's career in which the probability of moving further up the hierarchy is low.

**phased retirement**
An arrangement that allows employees to reduce their hours and/or responsibilities in order to ease into retirement.

**bridge employment**
Employment that takes place after a person retires from a full-time position but before the person's permanent withdrawal from the workforce.

**career anchors**
A network of self-perceived talents, motives, and values that guide an individual's career decisions.

**FIGURE A**  Flexible Behaviours Questionnaire (FBQ) Scoring

| Skill Area | Items | Score |
|---|---|---|
| Working with new, changing, and ambiguous situations | 1, 2, 3, 4 | |
| Working under pressure | 5, 6, 7, 8 | |
| Dealing with different personal styles | 9, 10, 11, 12 | |
| Handling feedback | 13, 14, 15, 16 | |
| Resolving conflicts | 17, 18, 19, 20 | |
| TOTAL SCORE | | |

## FBQ Scoring
The scoring sheet in Figure A summarizes your responses for the FBQ. It will help you identify your existing strengths and pinpoint areas that need improvement.

## FBQ Evaluation
Figure B shows score lines for your total score and for each category measured on the FBQ. Each line shows a continuum from the lowest score to the highest.

The score lines in Figure B show graphically where you stand with regard to the five flexible behaviours. If you have been honest

**9** Become familiar with some current tools and practices that will help you develop your own career.

The material in Part 2 of the book provides the theory behind understanding who you are, your skills and your weaknesses. The chapters on teams and decision-making provide guidance about the nature of teams and how to make effective decisions in teams. The material on organizational culture is particularly important so you know how to read organizations. Chapter 18 highlights the tools that you can use to shape your career journey.

## What about You?  Assess Your Flexibility Skills

Use the following scale to rate the frequency with which you perform the behaviours described in each question. Place the corresponding number (1–7) in the blank preceding the statement.

| Rarely | Irregularly | Occasionally | Usually | Frequently | Almost Always | Consistently |
|---|---|---|---|---|---|---|
| 1 | 2 | 3 | 4 | 5 | 6 | 7 |

_____ **1.** I manage a variety of assignments with varying demands and complexities.

_____ **2.** I adjust work plans to account for new circumstances.

_____ **3.** I modify rules and procedures in order to meet operational needs and goals.

_____ **4.** I work with ambiguous assignments when necessary and use these when possible to further my goals and objectives.

_____ **5.** I rearrange work or personal schedules to meet deadlines.

_____ **6.** In emergencies, I respond to the most pressing needs first.

_____ **7.** I change my priorities to accommodate unexpected events.

_____ **8.** I manage my personal work overload by seeking assistance or by delegating responsibility to others.

_____ **9.** I vary the way I deal with others according to their needs and personalities.

_____ **10.** I help others improve their job performance, or I assign tasks that will further their development.

_____ **11.** I accept the authority of my manager but continue to demonstrate my initiative and assertiveness.

_____ **12.** I work well with all types of personalities.

_____ **13.** I measure my performance on the job against the feedback I receive.

_____ **14.** I correct performance deficits that have been brought to my attention.

_____ **15.** When I disagree with my manager's appraisal of my work, I discuss our differences.

_____ **16.** I seek training and assignments that can help me improve my job-related skills.

_____ **17.** In disagreements concerning work-related issues, I look at matters impersonally and concentrate on the facts.

_____ **18.** I make compromises to get problems moving toward resolution.

_____ **19.** I look for new and better ways to accomplish my duties and responsibilities.

_____ **20.** I offer to negotiate all areas of disagreement.

**FIGURE B**  Flexible Behaviours Questionnaire (FBQ) Evaluation

**Total Score**

| Lowest score | | | | | Highest score |
|---|---|---|---|---|---|
| | 20 | 50 | 80 | 110 | 140 |

**Category Scores**

Working with new, changing, and ambiguous situations

| 4 | 10 | 16 | 22 | 28 |
|---|---|---|---|---|

Working under pressure

| 4 | 10 | 16 | 22 | 28 |
|---|---|---|---|---|

Dealing with different personality styles

| 4 | 10 | 16 | 22 | 28 |
|---|---|---|---|---|

Handling feedback

| 4 | 10 | 16 | 22 | 28 |
|---|---|---|---|---|

Resolving conflicts

| 4 | 10 | 16 | 22 | 28 |
|---|---|---|---|---|

with yourself, you now have a better idea of your relative strengths and weaknesses in the categories that make up the skills of flexibility.

SOURCE: From FANDT. Management Skills, 1E. © 1994 Custom Solutions, a part of Cengage Learning, Inc. Reproduced by permission. www.cengage.com/permissions.